THE ROUGH GUIDE

KT-140-104

Brittany & Normandy

There are more than two hundred Rough Guide titles
covering destinations from Alaska to Zimbabwe
and subjects from Acoustic Guitar to Travel Health

Forthcoming travel guides include
Chicago • Corfu • First-Time Round the World
Grand Canyon • Philippines • Skiing & Snowboarding in North America
South America • The Gambia • Walks Around London

Forthcoming reference guides include
Chronicles series: China, England,
France, India • Night Sky

Rough Guides Online
www.roughguides.com

ROUGH GUIDE CREDITS

Text editor: Sam Thorne
Series editor: Mark Ellingham
Editorial: Martin Dunford, Jonathan Buckley, Jo Mead, Kate Berens, Ann-Marie Shaw, Paul Gray, Helena Smith, Judith Bamber, Orla Duane, Olivia Eccleshall, Ruth Blackmore, Geoff Howard, Claire Saunders, Gavin Thomas, Alexander Mark Rogers, Polly Thomas, Joe Staines, Richard Lim, Duncan Clark, Peter Buckley, Sam Thorne, Lucy Ratcliffe, Clifton Wilkinson, David Glen, Alison Murchie, Matthew Teller (UK); Andrew Rosenberg, Stephen Timblin, Yuki Takagaki, Richard Koss (US)
Production: Susanne Hillen, Andy Hilliard, Link Hall, Helen Prior, Julia Bovis, Michelle Draycott, Katie Pringle,

Mike Hancock, Zoë Nobes, Rachel Holmes, Andy Turner
Cartography: Melissa Baker, Maxine Repath, Ed Wright, Katie Lloyd-Jones
Picture research: Louise Boulton, Sharon Martins
Online: Kelly Cross, Anja Mutić-Blessing, Jennifer Gold, Audra Epstein, Suzanne Welles (US)
Finance: John Fisher, Gary Singh, Edward Downey, Mark Hall, Tim Bill
Marketing & Publicity: Richard Trillo, Niki Smith, David Wearn, Chloë Roberts, Birgit Hartmann, Claire Southern (UK); Simon Carloss, David Wechsler, Kathleen Rushforth (US)
Administration: Tania Hummel, Demelza Dallow, Julie Sanderson

ACKNOWLEDGEMENTS

Thanks and love, as ever, to Samantha Cook, for all the many adventures in France and elsewhere. Thanks too to Robert Jones, and to Deborah Jones, whose illustrations graced the previous six editions of this book. In the Rough Guides office, thanks especially to

Sam Thorne, for his extensive input and work towards improving this latest edition. For the production of this edition, thanks to Rachel Holmes for typesetting, Ed Wright for maps, Sharon Martins for picture research and Russell Walton for proofreading.

PUBLISHING INFORMATION

This seventh edition published July 2001 by Rough Guides Ltd, 62–70 Shorts Gardens, London WC2H 9AH. Reprinted June 2002
Distributed by the Penguin Group:
Penguin Books Ltd, 80 Strand, London, WC2R ORL
Penguin Putnam, Inc., 375 Hudson Street, NY 10014, USA
Penguin Books Australia Ltd, 487 Maroondah Highway, PO Box 257, Ringwood, Victoria 3134, Australia
Penguin Books Canada Ltd, 10 Alcorn Avenue, Toronto, Ontario, Canada M4V 1E4
Penguin Books (NZ) Ltd, 182–190 Wairau Road, Auckland 10, New Zealand
Typeset in Linotron Univers and Century Old Style to an original design by Andrew Oliver.
Printed in England by Clays, St Ives PLC.
Illustrations in Part One and Part Three by Edward Briant.

Illustrations on p.1 & p.385 by Katie Pringle
© Greg Ward 2001
No part of this book may be reproduced in any form without permission from the publisher except for the quotation of brief passages in reviews.
448pp – Includes index
A catalogue record for this book is available from the British Library
ISBN 1-85828-711-1

The publishers and authors have done their best to ensure the accuracy and currency of all the information in *The Rough Guide to Brittany and Normandy*, however, they can accept no responsibility for any loss, injury, or inconvenience sustained by any traveller as a result of information or advice contained in the guide.

THE ROUGH GUIDE TO

Brittany & Normandy

written and researched by

Greg Ward

ROUGH
GUIDES

THE ROUGH GUIDES

TRAVEL GUIDES • PHRASEBOOKS • MUSIC AND REFERENCE GUIDES

 We set out to do something different when the first Rough Guide was published in 1982. Mark Ellingham, just out of university, was travelling in Greece. He brought along the popular guides of the day, but found they were all lacking in some way. They were either strong on ruins and museums but went on for pages without mentioning a beach or taverna. Or they were so conscious of the need to save money that they lost sight of Greece's cultural and historical significance. Also, none of the books told him anything about Greece's contemporary life – its politics, its culture, its people, and how they lived.

So with no job in prospect, Mark decided to write his own guidebook, one which aimed to provide practical information that was second to none, detailing the best beaches and the hottest clubs and restaurants, while also giving hard-hitting accounts of every sight, both famous and obscure, and providing up-to-the-minute information on contemporary culture. It was a guide that encouraged independent travellers to find the best of Greece, and was a great success, getting shortlisted for the Thomas Cook travel guide award,

and encouraging Mark, along with three friends, to expand the series.

The Rough Guide list grew rapidly and the letters flooded in, indicating a much broader readership than had been anticipated, but one which uniformly appreciated the Rough Guide mix of practical detail and humour, irreverence and enthusiasm. Things haven't changed. The same four friends who began the series are still the caretakers of the Rough Guide mission today: to provide the most reliable, up-to-date and entertaining information to independent-minded travellers of all ages, on all budgets.

We now publish more than 200 titles and have offices in London and New York. The travel guides are written and researched by a dedicated team of more than 100 authors, based in Britain, Europe, the USA and Australia. We have also created a unique series of phrasebooks to accompany the travel series, along with an acclaimed series of music guides, and a best-selling pocket guide to the Internet and World Wide Web. We also publish comprehensive travel information on our Web site:

www.roughguides.com

HELP US UPDATE

We've gone to a lot of effort to ensure that the seventh edition of *The Rough Guide to Brittany & Normandy* is accurate and up-to-date. However, things change — places get "discovered", opening hours are notoriously fickle, restaurants and rooms raise prices or lower standards. If you feel we've got it wrong or left something out, we'd like to know, and if you can remember the address, the price, the time, the phone number, so much the better.

We'll credit all contributions, and send a copy of the next edition (or any other Rough Guide if you prefer) for the best letters. Please mark letters: "Rough Guide Brittany & Normandy Update" and send to:
Rough Guides, 62–70 Shorts Gardens, London WC2H 9AH, or Rough Guides, 4th Floor, 345 Hudson St, New York, NY 10014.
Or send email to: mail@roughguides.co.uk
Online updates about this book can be found on Rough Guides' Web site at **www.roughguides.com**

THE AUTHOR

Greg Ward was first commissioned to write the *Rough Guide to Brittany & Normandy* in 1986, and has revisited the region regularly ever since. In that time he has also written Rough Guides to Southwest USA, Las Vegas, Hawaii, Honolulu, Maui, the Big Island, Essential Blues CDs and Online Travel, edited and co-written *The Rough Guide to the USA*, contributed to books on China, Mexico, California, France, Spain and Portugal, and edited several others. He has also written travel guides for several other publishers.

READERS' LETTERS

Thanks to all the readers who took the trouble to write in with their comments on the sixth edition (apologies for any omissions or mis-spellings):

Sian Aspden; Alexandra Baker; Pamela Brankin; Pauline Ferguson; Ken and Audrey Fogelman; Martin Garvey; Lynda Grange; A. S. Griggs; Simon Hope; Marc and Nancy Jackson; Geraint Jennings; Jane Davis Kelly; Stephen Larkin; Chris Leavy; I. W. and D. Martin; Anthony May; Jenny Morris; M. Munsey; Charlotte Newell; Johanna Nilsson; Ian Payne; Andrew Reid; Tony Stoddant; Charles Stuart; John and Judith Thorpe; John Trevitt; Julie Warner; Janet Yair.

CONTENTS

Introduction x

PART THREE BRITTANY   201

PART FOUR CONTEXTS   385

LIST OF MAPS

MAP SYMBOLS

▬▬▬	Motorway	◆	Point of interest
═══	Road	⚠	Campsite
───	Minor road	◓	Cave
▬▬▬	Pedestrianized street	▲	Peak
⊞⊞⊞	Steps	⌶	Lighthouse
- - - -	Path	⸰⸰	Marshland
───	Wall	⍟	Menhir (standing stone)
━◆━	Railway	ⓘ	Tourist office
– – –	Ferry route	⊠	Post office
───	Waterway	🅿	Parking
▬ ▬ ▬	Chapter division boundary	■	Building
▬■▬■	Regional border	✚	Church (town maps)
⊠–⊠	Gate	✝	Church (regional maps)
✕	Airport	✝✝✝	Cemetery (town maps)
⛫	Abbey	✟	Cemetery (regional map)
♜	Castle	▨	Park
▥	Château	⸰⸰⸰	Beach

INTRODUCTION

O f the many strongly individual components that make up the French nation, **Brittany** and **Normandy** rank among the most distinct. That sense of a separate identity – in cultures and peoples, landscapes and histories – is undoubtedly a major aspect of their appeal to visitors. A journey through the two regions enables you to experience much of the best that France has to offer: wild coast and sheltered white-sand beaches; sparse heathland and dense forests; medieval ports and evidence of the prehistoric past; and, every bit as important, abundant seafood and (especially in Normandy) a compelling and exuberant cuisine.

Brittany

Brittany is the more popular of the two regions, with both French and foreign tourists. Its attractions lie most obviously along the **coast**, which, speckled with offshore islands and islets, makes up over a third of the seaboard of France. In parts of the north, and in the western region of Finistère, the shoreline can be nothing but rocks and cliffs, its exposed headlands buffeted by the full force of the Atlantic and swept by dangerous currents. But elsewhere, especially in the sheltered southern resorts around the Morbihan and La Baule, it is caressed by the gentlest of seas, the sands rambling for kilometres or nestled into coves between steep cliffs.

Thanks to the sheer extent of the Breton coastline, it's always possible to find a spot where you can walk alone with the elements. Although in high season it can be hard to find solitude on the sandy beaches or in the small bays with their sun-struck swimmers, there could never be enough visitors to cover all the twists of the Finistère coast. As well as exploring the mainland resorts and seaside villages – each of which, from ports the size of **St-Malo** or **Vannes** down to little-known harbour communities such as Erquy, Le Pouldu, L'Aber-W'rach or Piriac-sur-mer, can be relied upon to offer at least one welcoming, characterful little hotel or restaurant – it's worth making the time to take in at least one of **the islands**. Boat trips out to these sea-encircled microcosms can be among the most enjoyable highlights of a trip to Brittany. The magical Île de Bréhat is just a ten-minute crossing from the north coast near Paimpol, while historic Belle-Île, to the south, is under an hour from Quiberon. Certain other islands are set aside as bird sanctuaries, while, off Finistère, the Îles d'Ouessant and Molène in the north, and Sein to the south, are as remote and strange as Orkney or the Shetland Isles.

The **Celtic** elements in Brittany are inextricably linked with its seafaring past. Anciently the land was known as *Armorica* (from the Breton for "the land of the sea", *ar-mor*), and it was from fishing and shipbuilding, along with occasional bouts of piracy and smuggling, that its people made their living. The harshness of the Breton coast and the poor communications with its interior and with "mainland" France enforced isolation. Christianity took time to establish itself, strongly but idiosyncratically, in a region where Druids survived on the Île de Sein until Roman times. Only in 1532 did the territory lose its independence and become a province of France. Even then it was a reluctant partner, treated virtually as a colony by the national government, which until well into the twentieth century felt it necessary to suppress the Breton language and traditions. In recent years there has been something of a reversal, with the **language** and **culture** being rediscovered and reasserted. If you are a Celt – Welsh, Scots or Irish – you will find shared vocabulary, and great appreciation in their use. For everyone, though, the traditions are active, accessible and enjoyable at the various Inter-Celtic **festivals**, the largest of which takes place at Lorient in early August.

Times even before the Celts are evoked by the vast wealth of **megalithic remains** scattered across Brittany. The single most famous site is **Carnac**, whose spectacular alignments of menhirs may have been erected as part of a prehistoric observatory. Lesser-known but equally compelling remains include the extraordinary burial tumuli on the island of Gavrinis, in the gulf of Morbihan, and at Barnenez outside Morlaix in the north. Not all such relics are found near the sea; the moors and woodlands of **inland Brittany**, too, conceal unexpected ancient treasures. This is the realm of legend, with the **forests** of Huelgoat and Paimpont in particular – left-overs from Brittany's mythic dark ages – identified with the tales of Merlin, the Fisher King and the Holy Grail. In the Little Britain of King Arthur's domain, an otherworldly element still seems entrenched in the land and people.

Normandy

Normandy has a less harsh appearance and a more mainstream – and more prosperous – history than its neighbour. It too is a seaboard province, colonized by Norsemen from Scandinavia, and colonizing in turn; the ruthless Norman formula for success was exported first of all, in the eleventh and twelfth centuries, to England, Sicily and parts of the Near East, and later on to Canada. Normandy has always boasted large-scale **ports**: Rouen, on the Seine, is as near as ships can get to Paris, while Dieppe, Cherbourg and Le Havre have important transatlantic trade. **Inland**, it is overwhelmingly agricultural – a wonderfully fertile belt of tranquil pastureland, where most visitors head straight for the restaurants of towns such as Vire and Conches.

The pleasures of Normandy are perhaps less intense and unique than those of Brittany. Many of the region's better-known stretches of **seaside** are a little overdeveloped. Towards the end of the nineteenth century, the last of the Napoleons created a "Norman Riviera" around Trouville and Deauville, and a somewhat pretentious air still hangs about their elegant promenades. However, the ancient ports – **Honfleur** and **Barfleur** especially – are visual delights, and numerous coastal villages remain unspoilt by crowds or affectations. Even if you just plan to visit for a weekend break from England, lovely little towns are tucked away within 20km of each of the major Channel ports – the Cotentin peninsula around Cherbourg is one of the best, and least explored, areas – while the banks of the Seine, too, hold several idyllic resorts.

Normandy also boasts extraordinary **architectural** treasures, although only its much-restored traditional capital, **Rouen**, has preserved a complete medieval centre. The attractions are more often single buildings than entire towns. Most famous of all is the spectacular *merveille* on the island of **Mont-St-Michel**, but there are also the monasteries at Jumièges and Caen; the cathedrals of Bayeux and Coutances; and Richard the Lionheart's castle above the Seine at Les Andelys. Bayeux can in addition boast its vivid and astonishing **Tapestry**. Many other great Norman buildings survived into the twentieth century, only to be destroyed during the Allied landings in 1944 and the subsequent **Battle of Normandy**, which has its own legacy in a series of war museums, memorials and cemeteries. These are hardly conventional sights, though as part of the fabric of the province they are moving and enlightening.

Routes

Individual **highlights** in each region are detailed in the chapter introductions throughout this book. Although hard-and-fast itineraries aren't given – much of the fun in both provinces consists in rambling off on side roads – the text is structured as logically as possible in continuous routes or definable areas.

Ways to get around are set out on p.27 onwards. If you read this before you decide how to travel, consider **cycling**; both provinces are ideal, with short distances between each town and the next. Otherwise, a car is probably the best alternative. Unless you plan to stay within a limited area, public transport can be frustrating.

Climate and time of year

Every French town or district eagerly promotes its own *"micro-climat"*, maintaining that some meteorological freak makes it milder or drier or balmier than its neighbours. On the whole, however, the bulk of Normandy and Brittany follows a fairly set pattern. A genuine **summer**, more reliable than in Britain, begins around mid-June and lasts, in a good year, through to mid-October. **Spring** and **autumn** are mild but sporadically wet. If you come for a week in April or November, it could be spoilt by rain; the rainy spells seldom last more than a couple of days, however, so a fortnight should yield better luck. **Winter** is not too severe, though in western Brittany especially it can be damp and very misty on the coast.

Sea temperatures are not Mediterranean, and any greater warmth felt in the Channel waters off the Norman coast as opposed to the south of England is probably more psychological than real. The south coast of Brittany is a different matter – consistently warm through the summer months, with no need for you to brace yourself before going into the sea.

The other factor that may affect planning is the **tourist season**. On the coast, this gets going properly around July, reaches a peak during the first two weeks of August and then fades quite swiftly – but try to avoid the great *rentrée* at the end of the month, when the roads are jammed with cars returning to Paris. Inland, the season is less defined; highlights such as Monet's gardens at Giverny and parts of the Nantes–Brest canal can be crowded out in midsummer but, in August at any rate, some smaller hotels close to enable their owners to take their own holidays by the sea. Conversely, those seaside resorts that have grown up without really being attached to a genuine town take on a distinctly ghostlike appearance during the winter months, when they can often be entirely devoid of facilities.

DAYTIME TEMPERATURES (°C) AND AVERAGE MONTHLY RAINFALL (MM)												
	Jan	Feb	March	April	May	June	July	Aug	Sept	Oct	Nov	Dec
BRITTANY												
Brest												
Av Temp (°C)	6.2	6.0	7.4	8.8	11.5	14.0	15.8	15.9	14.6	12.1	8.8	7.4
Rainfall (mm)	131.8	105.6	101.4	72.7	72.1	57.9	49.1	68.3	85.2	110.0	127.1	147.9
Nantes												
Av Temp (°C)	5	6	8	10	13	17	19	19	16	12	8	6
Rainfall (mm)	78	60	60	53	60	53	50	53	68	88	91	86
NORMANDY												
Cherbourg												
Av Temp (°C)	5.3	4.9	6.3	7.5	10.7	13.3	15.5	15.7	14.2	11.7	8.2	6.3
Rainfall (mm)	89.6	78.9	78.4	55.7	65.2	48.4	44.0	46.8	80.0	98.2	109.7	103.4
Rouen												
Av Temp (°C)	3.0	3.1	6.3	8.3	11.9	14.7	17.4	17.0	14.6	11.3	6.5	4.5
Rainfall (mm)	58.8	46.7	46.0	47.3	51.7	54.3	58.2	60.8	57.1	65.5	65.8	64.3

BASICS

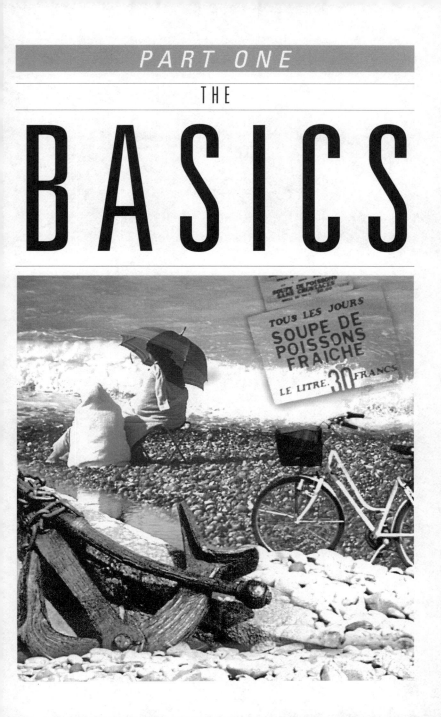

GETTING THERE FROM BRITAIN

It has never been easier for British holiday-makers to visit Brittany and Normandy. The completion of the Channel Tunnel, the advent of extra-fast new vessels on the long-established ferry routes, and even a handful of cut-rate airlines have made northern France more accessible than ever before.

However, fares have risen considerably in the last few years, as the tunnel has drawn back from its previous policy of all-out price competition with the ferries, and the abolition of Duty Free has cut deeply into the ferry companies' profits. Off-season, there are still bargains to be had, but finding a reasonable fare to cross the Channel in summer now requires a good deal of both planning and luck.

FERRIES

The most direct route to Normandy or Brittany, for motorists, cyclists and pedestrians, is still to take the cross-Channel **ferry** to any of four Norman and two Breton ports; it is, however, slightly cheaper to travel via Calais, Boulogne or Dunkerque. All these services are detailed in the box on p.5.

Ferry **fares** these days vary so enormously with the season – most operators divide the year into five or more distinct payment periods – that it's all but impossible to predict what you will actually be asked to pay. Each individual sailing has its own price code, but broadly speaking return fares for a **car** and two adults on Brittany Ferries sailings to Caen, Cherbourg, Roscoff or St-Malo range from £180 for five days in low season

up to £330 for a month-long trip in midsummer, while equivalent trips with P&O European Ferries vary between £153 and £350. The return fare for a **foot passenger** with either company varies from £38 in winter up to £75 in summer; **bicycles** are typically carried free in low season or for around £5 in summer. **Children** under 4 travel free, while those aged up to 13 are charged half the adult fare. Note, in addition, that **cabin accommodation** on overnight crossings tends to cost £20 or more per person, and may be obligatory in high season.

Currently the best deals of all are the **high-speed catamaran** services between Portsmouth and Cherbourg (on P&O's Superstar Express), Poole and Cherbourg (with Brittany Ferries), and Newhaven and Dieppe (with Hoverspeed), all of which cross the Channel in less than three hours, while charging the same fare as the much slower traditional boats. In addition, Brittany Ferries are due to introduce a new "**superferry**" on their Portsmouth–Caen route. Built to carry two thousand passengers and six hundred cars, it will feature a lounge where each seat has its own video screen, and even a cybercafé.

Booking ahead is strongly recommended for motorists, certainly in high season; foot passengers and cyclists can normally just turn up and board, at any time of year. Any **travel agent** will have a variety of fares and brochures on offer, so it's well worth shopping around for the most competitive deals. AA members who buy ferry tickets through a High-Street AA shop can get extra discounts on brochure prices.

THE CHANNEL TUNNEL

The **Channel Tunnel**, which burrows beneath the English Channel at its narrowest point – the Pas de Calais, well to the east of Normandy – plays host to two distinct services. **Eurostar** trains carry foot passengers only, with its principal routes being from London to Paris or Brussels, while **Eurotunnel** simply conveys cars and other vehicles between Folkestone and Calais, in more explicit competition with the ferries.

EUROSTAR

The **Eurostar** rail service takes a mere three hours to get from London Waterloo International

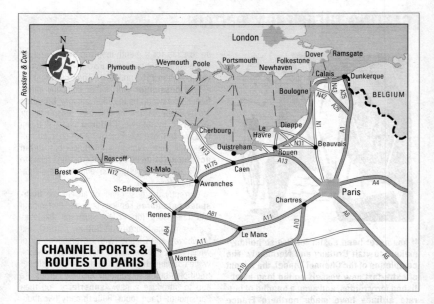

CHANNEL PORTS & ROUTES TO PARIS

to Paris Gare du Nord. More than twenty trains make the journey each day. By catching either the 8.53am (Mon–Sat) or the 12.27pm (daily) departure from London, and changing at Lille, two hours out, travellers heading for Brittany and Normandy can use connecting TGV services to bring the total journey time to **Rennes** or **Nantes** down to around six or seven hours. Standard-class return **fares** from London to Lille range from £60 with the "Leisure Apex 14", which must be bought up to fourteen days before departure and must include a Saturday night, with fixed outward and return dates and no refunds. There are other cheap deals – such as the "Leisure Flexi", which can be purchased up to thirty minutes before departure for £110 – but for a high-season ticket with changeable departure and return times, bought close to your departure date, you're looking at £220. Youth-fare **concessions** are available on all the routes (student discounted tickets are only available from STA and Usit Campus Travel, not directly from Eurostar). Further concessions apply for over-60s, and for holders of an international rail pass.

Tickets can be bought directly from Eurostar (☎020/7478 8200, *www.eurostar.co.uk*), from most travel agents or from all main train stations in Britain, including Waterloo International. You can get through-ticketing – including the tube journey to Waterloo International – if you travel on GNER or Virgin train services from Manchester and Edinburgh, or on the Alphaline Rail Service from South Wales, Avon and West Wiltshire for an extra £10–30. There is still no sign of the promised direct high-speed Eurostar services from the north of England, Scotland and the Midlands.

EUROTUNNEL

The Channel Tunnel also provides the fastest and most convenient way to take your **car** to France. For motorists, the tunnel entrance is less than two hours' drive from London, off the M20 at Junction 11A, just outside Folkestone. Once there, you drive your car onto a two-tier railway carriage; you're then free to get out and stretch your legs during the 35 minutes before you emerge from the darkness at Coquelles, just outside Calais. The sole operator, **Eurotunnel**, offers a continuous service with up to four departures per hour (only 1 per hour midnight–6am; 24hr recorded departure info ☎0891/555566, 50p per min). Because of the frequency of the service, you don't have to buy a ticket in advance, though it's highly advisable in midsummer or during school holidays. You must arrive at least thirty minutes before departure; the target loading time is just ten minutes.

SEA CROSSINGS AND PRICES FROM BRITAIN

The following services are ferry crossings, unless otherwise stated.

Route	Operator	Crossing Time	Frequency	One-way Fares Small car + 2 adults	Foot passenger
BRITTANY					
Portsmouth–St-Malo	Brittany Ferries	8hr 45min–11hr	7 weekly	£97–203	£24–47
Poole–St-Malo (via Jersey and Guernsey)	Condor Ferries	5hr 25min	1 daily	£95–187	£26
Plymouth–Roscoff	Brittany Ferries	6hr–7hr 30min	2–12 weekly	£110–189	£27–48
Weymouth–St-Malo (via Jersey and Guernsey)	Condor Ferries	5hr	May–Oct 1 daily	£95–187	£27
NORMANDY					
Newhaven–Dieppe (catamaran)	Hoverspeed	2hr	1–3 daily	£139–195	£28
Portsmouth–Cherbourg	P&O Portsmouth	2hr 45min–7hr 30min	1–7 daily	£95–178	£20–41
Poole–Cherbourg	Brittany Ferries	2hr 15min–5hr 45min	2–3 daily	£100–195	£21–42
Portsmouth–Le Havre	P&O Portsmouth	5hr 30min–7hr 30min	2–3 daily	£95–178	£20–41
Portsmouth–Caen (Ouistreham)	Brittany Ferries	6hr	2–3 daily	£80–185	£19–43
PAS-DE-CALAIS					
Folkestone–Boulogne (catamaran)	Hoverspeed	55min	4 daily	£115–155	£24
Dover–Calais	P&O Stena	1hr 15min	30–35 daily	£105–123	£24
Dover–Calais	Sea France	1hr 30min	15 daily	£118–163	£15
Dover–Calais (hovercraft)	Hoverspeed	35min	9–16 daily	£125–169	£24

FERRY COMPANIES IN BRITAIN

Brittany Ferries	☎0870/901 2400	*www.brittany-ferries.co.uk*
Condor Ferries	☎01305/761551	*www.condorferries.co.uk*
Hoverspeed	☎0870/524 0241	*www.hoverspeed.co.uk*
P&O North Sea Ferries	☎01482/377177	*www.ponsf.com*
P&O Portsmouth	☎0870/242 4999	*www.poportsmouth.com*
P&O Stena	☎0870/600 0600	*www.posl.com*
Sea France	☎0870/571 1711	*www.seafrance.com*

Tickets are available through Eurotunnel's Customer Service Centre (information and bookings ☎0870/535 3535, *www.eurotunnel.com*) or from your local travel agent. Fares are calculated per car, regardless of the number of passengers. Rates depend on the time of year, time of day and length of stay (the cheapest ticket is for a day-trip, followed by a five-day return); it's cheaper to travel between 10pm and 6am, while the highest fares are reserved for weekend departures and returns in July and August. By way of example, a five-day trip at an off-peak time starts at £99 (passengers included) in the low season and goes up to £177 in the peak period.

While the speed and efficiency of the tunnel journey itself is superb, however, drivers heading for Brittany or Normandy should not underestimate the length of time it takes to drive across northern France from the tunnel exit. Just to reach le Tréport, the eastern extremity of Normandy, takes a good two hours, while western Brittany would take more like eight. If you live any further west than London, therefore, there's not much point driving right across to the tunnel and back.

COMBINED TRAIN/FERRY ROUTES

You can buy **connecting tickets** from any British station to any French station, via any of the ferry routes. Details and prices (again with various special and seasonal offers) are obtainable from any British Rail **travel centre**. In London, the main international booking office is at Victoria Station (☎020/7834 2345). Students and anyone under 26 can buy heavily **discounted tickets** from Eurotrain outlets such as Campus Travel (see box opposite) and most student travel agents.

Rail travellers catching ferries from **Portsmouth** should be warned that "Portsmouth Harbour" station is nowhere near the cross-Channel ferry terminals; there is a connecting bus service, but allow plenty of time.

BY AIR

The only good-value **flights** to Brittany or Normandy from Britain are the twice-daily services from London Stansted to the Breton town of **Dinard** operated by **Ryanair** (☎0870/156 9569, www.ryanair.com). Return fares of as little as £5 are occasionally advertised, but it's more realistic to think in terms of around £40 return in low season, £90–100 in summer. If you're booking online, keep trying alternative dates; fares change day by day, and are only quoted for each specific day you request.

In addition, **Brit Air**, which is effectively a subsidiary division of Air France, operates a number of flights to regional airports. Return fares, if booked

---

TRAIN PASSES

If you plan to use the rail network to travel more widely than just in Brittany and Normandy, there are several **train passes** you might consider buying before you leave.

The **Euro Domino Pass**, available from Rail Europe (SNCF), Wasteels and Usit Campus offers unlimited rail travel through France for any three (£99), four (£119), five (£139), six (£159), seven (£178) or eight (£198) days within a calendar month; passengers under 25 pay £79, £95, £111, £127, £143 and £159 respectively. Children under 4 travel free, and those aged between 4 and 11 are charged half the adult price.

InterRail passes cover eight European "zones" and are available for either 22-day or one-month periods; you must have been resident in Europe for at least six months before you can buy the pass. The passes for those over 26 have been extended to cover the same territory as for those under 26 and the only difference now is the price. France is in the zone including Belgium, Netherlands and Luxembourg. A 22-day pass to travel this area is £159/229, a two-zone pass valid for a month is £209/279, a three-zone £229/309 and an all-zones pass £259/349. The pass is available from the same outlets as the Euro Domino (see above) and from STA Travel.

Note that InterRail passes do not include travel between Britain and the continent, but both the Euro Domino and InterRail passes entitle you to a discount on the Eurostar service, and on rail–ferry links to France.

USEFUL TRAIN CONTACTS

Campus Travel see box opposite.

Eurolines www.gobycoach.com. 52 Grosvenor Gardens, London SW1W 0AU; bookings and enquiries ☎020/7730 8235 or 01582/404511. Tickets can also be purchased from any National Express agent (☎0870/580 8080)

Eurostar www.eurostar.com. Eurostar House, Waterloo Station, London SE1 8SE, ☎0870/518 6186

Eurotunnel www.eurotunnel.com. Customer Services Centre, PO Box 300, Dept 302, Folkestone, Kent CT19 4QD; information and bookings ☎0870/535 3535.

Rail Europe www.raileurope.co.uk. 179 Piccadilly, London W1V 0BA ☎0870/848 848

well in advance, range from around £125 up to £175. Routes and schedules have changed greatly in recent years, and tend in any case to be seasonal. At the time of going to press, their only direct flights from Britain to either Brittany or Normandy were from London City Airport to **Le Havre** (Mon–Fri only, 2 daily) and from London Gatwick to **Nantes** (2–3 daily) and to **Deauville** (3 weekly). If money is no object, however, you could fly via Paris or Lyon and connect with Air France's full range of internal flights, making it possible to reach other airports such as Brest, Caen, Quimper, Rennes and Rouen. For current fares and schedules, contact Air France (☎0845/084 5111, *www.airfrance.fr*).

BY COACH

Eurolines coach services, marketed by National Express (☎0870/514 3219, *www.eurolines.co.uk*), connect London with all the main cross-Channel ferry routes, and thus to any destination in France. Thanks to the recent increases in the actual ferry fares, coach travel is no longer such a bargain, though it still works out cheaper than the train. Typical adult single fares from London to Caen, Cherbourg and St-Malo are in the region of £50. Schedules, tickets and further information are available from National Express offices at regional coach terminals.

PACKAGE TOURS

Any travel agent will be able to provide details of the many operators running **package tours** to Brittany and Normandy (see box overleaf), which can be a competitively priced way of travelling. Some deals are straightforward travel-plus-hotel affairs, while others offer tandem touring, air-and-rail packages and stays in country cottages. If your trip is geared around specific interests – like cycling or self-catering in the countryside – packages can work out much cheaper than the same arrangements made on arrival. Packages can also be a good idea if you are on a tight schedule, as these deals often include free transfers to your hotel and guided tours as well as flights and accommodation, leaving you more time to enjoy your holiday.

In addition to the addresses in the box overleaf, bear in mind that most of the ferry companies (see box, p.5) also offer their own travel and accommodation deals. The **French Holiday Service** at 178 Piccadilly, London W1V 0AL (☎020/7355 4747), can book an especially large range. A complete list of package operators is available from the **French Government Tourist Office**, also at 178 Piccadilly, London W1V 0AL (☎0906/824 4123).

TRAVEL AGENTS IN BRITAIN

Campus Travel *www.campustravel.co.uk*. 52 Grosvenor Gardens, London, ☎0870/240 1010; 541 Bristol Rd, Birmingham, ☎0121/414 1848; 61 Ditchling Rd, Brighton, ☎01273/570226; 39 Queens Rd, Clifton, Bristol, ☎0117/929 2494; 5 Emmanuel St, Cambridge, ☎01223/324283; 53 Forrest Rd, Edinburgh, ☎0131/668 3303; 105–106 Aldates Rd, Oxford, ☎01865/242067; Branches at YHA shops and university campuses.

Flightbookers *www.ebookers.com*. 177–178 Tottenham Court Rd, ☎020/7757 2000; London Gatwick Airport, South Terminal ☎01293/568300. Low fares on a wide selection of scheduled flights.

North South Travel. Moulsham Mill Centre, Parkway, Chelmsford, Essex, ☎01245/608 291. Friendly, competitive travel agency; profits are used to support projects in the developing world.

STA Travel *www.statravel.co.uk*. 86 Old Brompton Rd, London, ☎020/7361 6161; 117

Euston Rd, London, ☎020/7361 6161; 25 Queens Rd, Bristol, ☎0117/929 4399; 38 Sidney St, Cambridge, ☎01223/366966; 88 Vicar Lane, Leeds, ☎0113/244 9212; 75 Deansgate, Manchester, ☎0161/834 0668; 36 George St, Oxford, ☎01865/792800. Worldwide specialists in low-cost flights and tours for students and under-26s. Additional offices on university campuses.

Thomas Cook *www.tch.thomascook.com*. 45 Berkeley St, London, ☎0870/566 6222. Flights Direct ☎0870/510 1520. Long-established travel agency for package holidays and scheduled flights, with offices nationwide.

Trailfinders *www.trailfinders.com*. 1 Threadneedle St, London, ☎020/7628 7628; 215 Kensington High St, London, ☎020/7937 5400; 22–24 The Priory, Birmingham, ☎0121/236 1234; 48 Corn St, Bristol, ☎0117/929 9000; 58 Deansgate, Manchester, ☎0161/839 6969; 254–285 Sauchiehall St, Glasgow, ☎0141/353 2224.

TOUR OPERATORS IN BRITAIN

Blakes Holidays, Wroxham, Norwich NR12 8DH, ☎01603/784131, *www.blakes.co.uk*. Self-catering canal trips in Brittany, starting from either Dinan or Guipry, south of Rennes. High-season rental rates range from around £700 per week for a two-berth boat to around £2000 for a twelve-berth vessel.

Brittany Direct Holidays, 362–364 Sutton Common Rd, Sutton, Surrey SM3 9PL, ☎020/8641 6060, *www.brittany-direct.co.uk* Holidays throughout Brittany and Normandy. Self-catering accommodation, mostly in large houses, costs from £200 up to £500 each for two weeks in a group of four adults; or short city breaks, staying in hotels. They also operate less-expensive summer-only mobile-home sites at five different locations.

French Country Cruises, 54 High St East, Uppingham, Rutland LE15 9PZ, ☎01572/821330, *abrock3560@aol.com*. Self-drive canal-boat rental from Redon (mid-March to mid-Nov only). In summer the weekly cost for the boat alone ranges from £742 for two people up to almost £2000 for eight.

Gîtes de France, The UK operation of the French Government letting service is now run by Brittany Ferries (☎0870/536 0360, *www.brittanyferries. co.uk*) although you can still deal directly with Gîtes de France (see p.35). Comprehensive list of houses, cottages and chalets throughout France.

Holt's Battlefield Tours, 15 Market St, Sandwich, Kent CT13 9DA, ☎01304/612248, *www.battletours.co.uk*. Definitive guided tours to famous battlefields, including five-day tours to Normandy covering either the D-Day landings themselves or other aspects of the invasion, for between £400 and £600.

Martin Randall Travel, 10 Barley Mow Passage, London W4 4PH, ☎020/8742 3355, *www.martinrandall.com*. Art-history tours from around £700 for a five-day Monet tour, including flights to Paris and accommodation.

Morbihan Travel, 10 Little Acres, Ware, Herts SG12 9JW, ☎01920/412013, *www.brittany.co.uk*. Self-catering holidays throughout southern Brittany; weekly rental rates for four-person *gîtes* during peak periods range from £320 to £810.

Normandie Vacances, 113 Sutton Rd, Walsall, West Midlands WS5 3AG, ☎01922/721901, *normvac@btclick.com*. Self-catering accommodation in rural *gîtes* all over Normandy, costing up to £500 per adult for two weeks in high season, including ferry. Children free.

VFB Holidays, Normandy House, High St, Cheltenham, Glos GL50 3FB ☎01242/240330, *www.vfbholidays.co.uk*. Cottages all over Brittany and Normandy, especially southern Finistère, and also self-drive hotel holidays. Prices, including ferry travel, for a two-week cottage stay for four range from at least £250 per person in the low season up to as much as £600 in summer.

CAMPING OPERATORS

Allez France	☎01903/748137	**Motours**	☎01892/677777
Eurocamp	☎01606/787737	**Sandpiper**	☎01746/785100
	www.eurocamp.co.uk	**Welcome**	☎01695/574578
Keycamp	☎0845/145 7000		
	www.keycamp.co.uk		

GETTING THERE FROM IRELAND

The only direct way to get to Brittany or Normandy from Ireland is by ferry from Cork or Rosslare (outside Wexford) to either Roscoff in Brittany – though unfortunately not available between October and March – or Cherbourg in Normandy.

Ferry routes and operators are detailed in the box below. Exact **prices** vary according to the season and, for motorists, the size of car. Brittany Ferries is generally somewhat cheaper, with one-way fares for foot passengers costing IR£40–75/€51–95, and for a small car with two adults IR£140–330/€178–419; the corresponding rates for Irish Ferries are IR£45–85/€57–108 and IR£149–358/€189–455.

Both companies offer reduced rates on fixed-period return tickets, as well as all-in **packages**, with a choice of accommodation in hotels, campsites or self-catering *gîtes*. Irish Ferries sell combined **rail-and-ferry** tickets to French destinations from any station in Ireland.

You can either contact the companies direct to reserve space in advance (essential at peak season if you're driving), or any competent travel agent at home or in France can do it for you. Among those worth trying are Joe Walsh Tours (Dublin ☎01/872 2555 or 676 3053, Cork ☎021/277959), Thomas Cook (Dublin ☎01/677 0469, Belfast ☎028/9055 0232), Trailfinders (Dublin ☎01/677 7888, *www.trailfinders.ie*), and Usit (Dublin ☎01/602 1777, Belfast ☎028/9032 4073, *www.usitnow.ie*).

FERRIES ROUTES AND PRICES FROM IRELAND

Route	Operator	Crossing Time	Frequency	One-way Fares Small car + 2 adults	Foot passenger
Cork–Roscoff	Brittany Ferries	14hr	April–Sept 1 weekly	IR£140–330/ €178–419	IR£40–75/ €51–95
Rosslare–Cherbourg	Irish Ferries	16hr	March–Oct 2–3 weekly	IR£149–358/ €189–455	IR£45–85/ €57–108
Rosslare–Cherbourg	P&O Irish Sea	18hr	3 weekly	IR£110–260/ €140–330	not allowed
Rosslare–Roscoff	Irish Ferries	15hr	April–Sept 1–3 weekly	IR£149–358/ €189–455	IR£45–85/ €57–108

FERRY COMPANIES IN IRELAND

Brittany Ferries *www.brittany-ferries.com*
Republic: ☎021/277801
Northern Ireland: ☎0870/536 0360

Irish Ferries *www.irishferries.ie*
24hr information ☎1890/313131

P&O Irish Sea *www.poirishsea.com*
Republic: ☎1800/409049
Northern Ireland: ☎ 0870/598 0777

BY AIR

Only a very limited number of airlines **fly** direct between Ireland and France, and none to Brittany or Normandy. Currently the best deal available is with Ryanair (Dublin ☎01/609 7800, Belfast ☎0870/156 9569, *www.ryanair.com*), who have two flights daily from Dublin to Beauvais Tillé airport outside Paris for IR£97.50. Aer Lingus (Dublin ☎01/705 3333, Belfast ☎0845/973 7747, *www.aerlingus.ie*) fly direct from Dublin and most other regional airports, to Paris CDG for around IR£199/€253.

In **Northern Ireland**, British Airways fly directly from Belfast City Airport to Paris CDG, but prices are generally much higher than taking a routing through London or Amsterdam – for example, Ryanair fly out of Derry Airport to London Stansted for around £60, from where you can pick up their onward flight to Dinard.

GETTING THERE FROM NORTH AMERICA

Getting to France from the US or Canada is straightforward; there are direct flights from over thirty major North American cities to Paris, with connections from all over the continent. From there, it's simple to continue to Brittany or Normandy by rail – Rouen is just over an hour away, while super-fast TGV trains get to either Rennes or Nantes in around two hours – or by air. A connecting flight on Air Inter, Air France's domestic arm, to Brest, the remotest Breton city, costs approximately US$150 extra.

Although **flying to London** is usually the cheapest way to reach Europe, price differences are so minimal that there's no point travelling to France via London unless you've specifically chosen to visit the UK as well.

ROUTES AND FARES

The least expensive way to take a scheduled flight is with a nonrefundable **Apex** fare, which normally entails booking 21 days in advance of

flying, travelling midweek, and staying for at least seven days up to a maximum of three months. On transatlantic routes in winter, there are also slightly cheaper **Super Apex** tickets, sometimes known as "Eurosavers", which limit your stay to between 7 and 21 days. Some airlines also issue **Special Apex** tickets to people younger than 24, often extending the maximum stay to a year. Most cheap return fares involve spending at least one Saturday night away, and many will only give a percentage refund if you need to cancel or alter your journey, so check restrictions carefully before buying a ticket.

You can normally cut costs further by going through a specialist flight agent – either a **consolidator**, who buys up blocks of tickets from the airlines and sells them at a discount, or a **discount agent**, who deals in blocks of tickets offloaded by the airlines, and often offers special student and youth fares and a range of other travel-related services. Bear in mind, though, that penalties for changing your plans can be stiff, and that these companies make their money by dealing in bulk – don't expect them to answer lots of questions. Some agents specialize in **charter flights**, which may be cheaper than anything available on a scheduled flight, but again departure dates are fixed and withdrawal penalties are high (check the refund policy). If you travel a lot, **discount travel clubs** are another option – the annual membership fee may be worth it for benefits such as cut-price air tickets and car rental. It's also worth checking out **Web sites** such as *www.travelocity.com* for the latest worldwide discounted airfares.

If you're prepared to travel light at short notice and for a short duration, it might be worth

AIRLINES IN NORTH AMERICA

Air Canada *www.aircanada.ca*
US ☎1-800/776-3000
Canada ☎1-800/555-1212

Air France *www.airfrance.fr*
US ☎1-800/237-2747
Canada ☎1-800/667-2747

American Airlines *www.aa.com*
US/Canada ☎1-800/433-7300

AOM French Airlines *www.aom.com*
US/Canada ☎1-800/892-9136

Continental Airlines *www.flycontinental.com*
US/Canada ☎1-800/231-0856

Delta Air Lines *www.delta-air.com*
US/Canada ☎1-800/241-4141

Iceland Air *www.icelandair.com*
US/Canada ☎1-800/223-5500

Northwest Airlines *www.nwa.com*
US/Canada ☎1-800/225-2525

TWA *www.twa.com*
US/Canada ☎1-800/892-4141

United Airlines *www.ual.com*
US/Canada ☎1-800/538-2929

US Air *www.usairways.com*
US/Canada ☎1-800/622-1015

TRAVEL AGENTS

Air Brokers International, 150 Post St, #620, San Francisco, CA 94108, ☎1-800/883-3273, *www.airbrokers.com*. Consolidator.

Air Courier Association, 15000 W 6th Ave, #203, Golden, CO 80401, ☎1-800/282-1202, *www.aircourier.com*. Courier-flight broker.

Airhitch, 2641 Broadway, New York, NY 10025. ☎1-800/326-2009, *www.airhitch.org*. Stand-by-seat broker: for a set price, they guarantee to get you on a flight as close to your preferred destination as possible, within a week.

Airtreks.com, 442 Post St, #400, San Francisco, CA 94102, ☎1-800/428-8735, *www.airtreks.com*. Travel company with a highly recommended interactive Web site.

Council Travel, 205 E 42nd St, New York, NY 10017, ☎1-800/226-8624, *www.counciltravel.com*. Student-travel organization with branches in forty US cities.

Flight Centre, 3030 Granville St, Vancouver, BC V6H 3J9, ☎1-604/739-9539, *www.flightcentre.com*. Discount airfares from Canadian cities.

Last Minute Travel Club, 100 Sylvan Rd, Suite 600, Woburn, MA 01801, ☎1-800/LAST-MIN. Travel club specializing in stand-by deals.

New Frontiers, 12 E 33rd St, New York, NY 10016, ☎1-800/366-6387, *www.newfrontiers.com*. French discount-travel firm, which also markets charters to Paris and Lyon. Other branches in Montréal, LA, San Francisco and Québec City.

STA Travel, 10 Downing St, New York, NY 10014, ☎1-800/777-0112, *www.sta-travel.com*. Worldwide specialist in independent travel, with branches in LA, San Francisco and Boston.

Travac Tours, 989 6th Ave, New York, NY 10018, ☎1-800/872-8800, *www.thetravelsite.com*. Consolidator and charter broker.

Travel Avenue, 10 S Riverside Plaza, #1404, Chicago, IL 60606, ☎1-800/333-3335, *www.travelavenue.com*. Discount-travel agent.

Travel Cuts, 187 College St, Toronto, ON M5T 1P7, ☎1-800/667-2887, *www.travelcuts.com*. Canadian student-travel organization with branches all over the country.

Travelers Advantage, 3033 S Parker Rd, #1000, Aurora, CO 80014, ☎1-800/548-1116, *www.travelersadvantage.com*. Discount-travel club.

Worldtek Travel, 111 Water St, New Haven, CT 06511, ☎1-800/243-1723, *www.worldtek.com*. Discount-travel agency.

getting a **courier flight**. In return for shepherding a parcel through customs and possibly giving up your baggage allowance, you can expect to get a deeply discounted ticket. Return journeys to Paris are available for around $350, with last-minute specials (booked within three days of departure) as low as $150. Tickets are issued on a first-come, first-served basis, and there's no guarantee that the Paris route will be available at the specific time you want. For more information, get hold of *Courier Bargains: How to Travel Worldwide for Next to Nothing* by Kelly

TOUR OPERATORS IN NORTH AMERICA

Abercrombie & Kent, 1520 Kensington Rd, Oak Brook, IL ☎1-800/323-7308, *www.abercrombie-andkent.com*. Deluxe hiking, biking, rail and canal journeys, including an 8-day "Paris, The Loire Valley, and Normandy" tour, including first-class train travel, accommodation and most meals, for $4145, excluding airfare.

American Airlines Fly AAway Vacations, ☎1-800/321-2121, *www.aavacations.com*. Nine-night coach "Treasures of France" package, with stops at Mont-St-Michel, D-Day beaches and Bayeux, for $1352, including airfare and accommodation.

Back Door Travel, 130 4th Ave N, Edmonds, WA 98020, ☎425/771-8303, *www.ricksteves.com*. Off-the-beaten path, small-group travel with budget-travel guru Rick Steves and his enthusiastic guides. Their fourteen-day "Best of Western France" tour goes from Rouen to Arles and costs $2300, excluding airfare.

Backroads, 1516 Fifth St, Suite L101, Berkeley, CA 94710, ☎1-800/462-2848, *www.backroads.com*. Upmarket bike tours; an 8-night bike tour of Brittany and Normandy, staying in château accommodation, costs $3498 excluding airfare.

Discover France, 8630 E Via de Ventura, #220, Scottsdale, AZ 85258, ☎1-800/960-2221, *www.discoverfrance.com*. A week's partially guided bike tour of Normandy, staying in two-star hotels, for $1645 excluding airfare.

EC Tours, 12500 Riverside Drive, #210, Valley Village, CA 91607, ☎1-800/388-0877, *www.ectours.com*. City and regional tours including a 6-night "Normandy Landing and Loire Castles" tour, starting at $1695.

Euro-Bike Tours, PO Box 990, DeKalb, IL 60115. ☎1-800/321-6060, *www.eurobike.com*. Fourteen-day bike tours of Brittany, Normandy and the Loire Valley, overnighting in luxury hotels, for $3295 excluding airfare.

France Vacations, 9841 Airport Blvd, #1120, Los Angeles, CA 90045, ☎1-800/332-5332, *www.francevacations.net*. Air, car, train and accommodation services throughout France.

The French Experience, 370 Lexington Ave, #812, New York, NY 10017, ☎1-800/28-FRANCE, *www.frenchexperience.com*. Four-day, three-night self-drive tours of Normandy ($353) or Brittany ($405), including good hotels and rental-car pick-up anywhere in France.

Globus and CosmosTourama, 5301 S Federal Circle, Littleton, CO 80123-2980, ☎1-800/221-0090, *www.globusandcosmos.com*. Tours in the region and throughout France.

Interhome, 1990 NE 163rd St, N Miami Beach, FL 33162, ☎305/940-2299, *www.interhome.com*. Short-term house and villa rentals in Normandy, with a helpful Web site that allows online bookings.

International Study Tours, 225 W 34th St, New York, NY 10122, ☎1-800/833-2111, *www.isttours.com*. Culture/art tours, including barge trips with stops in Normandy starting at $2400, including airfare.

New Frontiers, 6 E 46th St, New York, NY 10017, ☎1-800/366-6387, *www.newfrontiers.com*. Offices also in LA and San Francisco. French discount-travel firm offering a 7-night package to Brittany and Normandy, starting at $1159 with airfare included.

Saga International Holidays, 222 Berkeley St, Boston, MA 02116, ☎1-800/343-0273, *www.sagaholidays.com*. Specialist in group travel for 50s plus.

Vacances en Campagne, PO Box 299, Elkton, VA 22827, ☎1-800/327-6097, *www.britishtravel.com*. Châteaux and country houses for rent.

Monaghan ($17.50 postpaid from the Intrepid Traveler, PO Box 438, New York, NY 10034).

Estimating the cost of **fares** to Paris is tricky, especially as routes, carriers and the state of the market are in a constant state of flux. Fares are dependent on **season**, and are highest between early June and the end of August, when everyone wants to travel; they drop during the "shoulder" seasons (April–May & Sept–Oct), while you'll get

the best deals of all during the low season (Nov–March, excluding Christmas). Travelling on Friday, Saturday or Sunday tends to carry a premium, while one-way fares are generally slightly more than half the round-trip.

Broadly speaking, however, the lowest discounted scheduled fares you're likely to get in low and high season flying midweek to Paris are US$448/966 from Chicago, US$468/876 from

Houston, US$498/1116 from Los Angeles, US$368/866 from New York, US$408/635 from Washington DC, CDN$976/1316 from Montréal, CDN$976/1316 from Toronto and CDN$1360/1728 from Vancouver.

PACKAGE TOURS

Dozens of tour operators specialize in travel to France. Many can put together very **flexible deals**, sometimes amounting to no more than a flight and accommodation. If you're planning to travel in moderate or luxury style, or if your trip is geared around special interests, such packages can work out cheaper than the same arrangements made on arrival. In addition, while a tour is almost certainly more confining than independent travel, it can help you make the most of your time if you're on a tight schedule.

The box opposite mentions a few of the possibilities, and a travel agent will be able to point out others (remember, bookings made through a travel agent cost no more than going through the tour operator).

EUROPEAN TRAIN PASSES FOR AMERICANS, AUSTRALIANS AND NEW ZEALANDERS

Before investing in any of the various European **train passes** that can only be purchased before leaving home, consider carefully how much you plan to travel: these all-encompassing passes only begin to pay for themselves if you intend to travel widely outside Brittany and Normandy.

The best-known and most flexible, the **Eurail Youthpass** (for under-26s), costs US$388/A$733 for fifteen days, with additional one-month and two-month versions. If you're 26 or over you'll have to buy a first-class **Eurail** pass, at US$554/A$1046 for the fifteen-day option. You stand a better chance of getting your money's worth out of a **Eurail Flexipass**, which is good for a certain number of travel days in a two-month period. This, too, comes in under-26/first-class versions: ten days for under-26s costs US$458/A$865, for over-26s US$654/A$1234, while fifteen days costs US$599/A$1131 and US$862/A$1627.

A scaled-down version of the Flexipass, the **Europass** allows travel in France, Germany, Italy, Switzerland and Spain for US$233/A$440 and US$348/A$657 for five days in two months, up to US$513/A$968 and US$728/A$1374 for fifteen days in two months. There are also cheaper three- and four-country combinations, as well as the option of adding adjacent "associate" countries.

You can also buy a **more specific pass** valid for travel in France only. The **France Railpass** provides three-days' unlimited travel in a one-month period for US$180/A$340, or, for those travelling in groups of two or more, US$146/A$276 per person. Up to six additional days of travel may be purchased for US$30/A$57 per day. For under-26s, the **France Youthpass** provides four days of unlimited travel in a two-month period for US$164/A$310; up to six additional days may be purchased for US$20/A$38 per day. All passes must be purchased before departure and are available through travel agents (see p.11) or with rail specialists.

In addition, the SNCF has a range of other reductions and passes, which can be purchased once in France: details of these can be found in "Getting around", p.30.

RAIL CONTACTS IN NORTH AMERICA

CIT Rail, 15 W 44th St, 10th Floor, New York, NY 10036, ☎1-800/223-7987, *www.fs-online.com*. Eurail passes only.

Rail Europe, 226 Westchester Ave, White Plains, NY 10604, ☎1-800/438-7245, *www.raileurope.com*. Official Eurail pass agent in North America; also a wide range of European regional and individual country passes.

ScanTours, 3439 Wade St, 7226, Los Angeles, CA 90066, ☎1-800/223-7226, *www.scantours.com*. Eurail, and many other European country passes.

RAIL CONTACTS IN AUSTRALIA AND NEW ZEALAND

CIT, see p.16

Rail Plus, Level 3, 459 Little Collins St, Melbourne, ☎03/9642-8644,

www.railplus.com.au, Level 2, 60 Parnell Rd, Auckland. ☎09/303-2484.

Thomas Cook, see p.15

GETTING THERE FROM AUSTRALIA AND NEW ZEALAND

Many people travelling to France from Australia and New Zealand will choose to travel via London although there are scheduled flights to Paris from Sydney, Melbourne, Brisbane, Cairns, Perth and Auckland. Most airlines can add on a Paris leg to any Australia/New Zealand–Europe ticket. Travelling time is around 22 hours via Asia and 30 hours via the USA – not counting time spent on stopovers.

Fares to France vary according to the **season** and the carrier. In general, low season lasts from mid-January to the end of February, and from the beginning of October to mid-November; high season is from mid-May to the end of August, and from the beginning of December to mid-January.

Tickets purchased direct from the airlines tend to be expensive; the **discount agents** listed in the box opposite offer much better deals, and have the latest information on limited special offers. Some of the best discounts are offered by companies such as Flight Centre, STA and Trailfinders (see box opposite); they can also help with visas, travel insurance and tours. You might also want to have a look on the **Internet**: *www.travel.com.au* and *www.sydneytravel.com* offer discounted fares online.

If you're planning to travel in style, and especially if your visit is going to be geared around special interests, such as walking, cycling, architecture or art, you may also want to consider one of the **package tours** offered by the operators in the box on p.16. Though these tours are inevitably more restrictive than independent travel, they may work out cheaper than making the same arrangements on arrival in France and can help you make the most of time if you're on a tight schedule.

AIRLINES IN AUSTRALIA AND NEW ZEALAND

		Australia	New Zealand
Air France	www.airfrance.fr	☎02/9244 2100	☎09/308 3352
British Airways	www.british-airways.com	☎02/8904 8800	☎09/356 8690
Cathay Pacific	www.cathaypacific.com	☎02/9931 5500	☎09/379 0861
Garuda		☎1300/365 330	☎09/366 1855
JAL	www.japanair.com	☎02/9272 1111	☎09/379 9906
KLM	www.klm.com	☎1300/303 747	☎09/302 1452
Lauda Air	www.lauda-air.com	☎02/9251 6155	
Lufthansa	www.lufthansa.com	☎02/9367 3887	☎09/303 1529
Malaysian Airlines	www.malaysiaair.com	☎13/2627	☎09/373 2741
Olympic Airways	www.olympic-airways.com	☎02/9251 2044	
Qantas	www.qantas.com	☎13/1313	☎09/357 8900
Singapore Airlines	www.singaporeair.com	☎02/9350 0262	☎09/303 2129
Sri Lankan Airlines		☎02/9244 2234	☎09/308 3353
Thai Airways	www.thaiair.com	☎1300/651 960	☎09/377 3886
United Airlines	www.ual.com	☎13/1777	☎09/379 3800

FROM AUSTRALIA

The only direct flights to France from **Australia** are to Paris, but add-on flights within France are common rated to the same price. Similarly, air-fares **from east-coast gateways** in Australia are common rated, with Ansett and Qantas pro-viding a shuttle service to the point of interna-tional departure. **From Perth and Darwin** fares are around A$100–300 less via Asia, and A$400 more via the US.

Flights **via Southeast Asia**, with either a trans-fer or overnight stop in the airlines' home ports, are generally the cheapest option. The lowest fares are with Sri Lankan Airways and Garuda, at A$1400 in the low season rising to A$2400 in the high season, while Alitalia/Qantas, Olympic Airways and JAL cost A$1500 low season to A$2600 high season.

Mid-range fares with KLM, Malaysian Airlines, Lauda Air, Thai International, Air France (on to 87 destinations within France), Cathay Pacific and Lufthansa, all cost A$1600–2600. Qantas/Air France, British Airways and Singapore Airlines are higher still at A$1900–2800.

Generally flights **via the US** to Paris are prici-er, with the best deals offered by United Airlines (via LA, Miami and Washington), from A$2100 to A$3000; Canadian Airlines (via Toronto or Vancouver) are more expensive at A$2200 low season and A$3000 high season.

FROM NEW ZEALAND

From New Zealand, there are also a good range of airlines flying to Paris either direct or with a transfer or overnight stop in their home ports. The best discounted deals to Paris from

---

TRAVEL AGENTS IN AUSTRALIA AND NEW ZEALAND

All the agents listed below offer competitive discounts on airfares as well as a good selection of packaged holidays and tours, and can also arrange car rental.

Anywhere Travel, 345 Anzac Parade, Kingsford, Sydney, ☎02/9663 0411, *anywhere @ozemail.com.au*

Budget Travel, 16 Fort St, Auckland, ☎09/366 0061, *www.budgettravel.co.nz*. Other branches around the city.

Destinations Unlimited, 220 Queen St, Auckland, ☎09/373 4033.

Flight Centre, 82 Elizabeth St, Sydney, ☎02/9235 3522, *www.flightcentre.com*. Other branches nationwide; call ☎13/1600. 350 Queen St, Auckland, ☎09/358 4310. Other branches nationwide.

Northern Gateway, 22 Cavenagh St, Darwin, ☎08/8941 1394, *www.flightcentre.com*. Discount flights to France from Darwin.

STA Travel, 855 George St, Ultimo, Sydney, ☎02/9212 1255. 256 Flinders St, Melbourne, ☎03/9654 7266. Other offices nationwide; call ☎13/1776. 10 High St, Auckland, ☎09/309 0458. Other offices nationwide; call ☎0800/874 773, *www.statravel.com*. Fare discounts for students and those under 26, as well as visas, student cards and travel insurance.

Student Uni Travel, 92 Pitt St, Sydney, ☎02/9232 8444, *www.sut.com.au*. Branches in other state capitals. Student/youth discounts and travel advice.

Thomas Cook, 175 Pitt St, Sydney, ☎02/ 9231 2877; 257 Collins St, Melbourne, ☎03/ 9282 0222, *www.thomascook.com.au*. Branches in other state capitals; call ☎13/1771. 191 Queen St, Auckland, ☎09/379 3920, *www.thomascook.co.nz*. Bus and rail passes and reasonable rates on currency exchange.

Trailfinders, 8 Spring St, Sydney, ☎02/9247 7666; 91 Elizabeth St, Brisbane, ☎07/3229 0887; Hides Corner, Shield St, Cairns, ☎07/4041 1199, *www.travel.com.au*.

usit Beyond, Shortland St, Auckland, ☎09/ 379 4224, *www.usitbeyond.co.nz*. Other branches in major cities. Student/youth travel specialists.

TOUR OPERATORS IN AUSTRALIA AND NEW ZEALAND

Adventure Specialists, 69 Liverpool St, Sydney, ☎02/9261 2927. A good selection of adventure holidays in the region.

The Adventure Travel Company, 164 Parnell Rd, Parnell, Auckland, ☎09/379 9755, *www.usitbeyond.co.nz*. Outdoor active tours in Normandy, Brittany and the rest of France.

Adventure World, 73 Walker St, North Sydney, ☎02/9956 7766, *www.adventureworld.com.au*. Branches in Adelaide, Brisbane, Melbourne and Perth. 101 Great South Rd, Auckland, ☎09/524 5118, *www.adventureworld.co.nz*. Small-group tours in France.

CIT, Level 2, 263 Clarence St, Sydney, ☎02/9267 1255, *www.cittravel.com.au*. Offices in Melbourne, Brisbane, Adelaide and Perth. City tours and accommodation packages, plus bus and rail passes and car rental.

European Travel Office, 122 Rosslyn St, West Melbourne ☎03/9329 8844; 368 Sussex St, #410, Sydney, ☎02/9267 7727; 407 Great South Rd, Auckland, ☎09/525 3074. Wide selection of tours and accommodation.

France Unlimited, 16 Goldsmith St, Melbourne, ☎03/9531 8787. All French travel arrangements, including walking and cycling holidays.

French Cottages and Travel, 674 High St, East Kew, Melbourne, ☎03/9859 4944. International and domestic travel, independent tours and cottage rental.

French Travel Connection, Level 6, 33 Chandos St, Sydney, ☎02/9966 8600. Good selection of country cottages in the region.

Travel Notions, 136 Bridge Rd, Glebe, Sydney, ☎02/9552 2852. Agents for the leisurely "Cycling for Softies" tours.

Yalla Tours, 661 Glen Huntley Rd, Caulfield, Melbourne, ☎1300/362 844, *www.yallatours.com.au*. Self-skippered canal and river cruises in Brittany.

Auckland are **via Southeast Asia** with Garuda at NZ$1800 low season to NZ$2400 high season. Mid-range fares are with Japanese Airlines, Thai International, Malaysia Airlines, Cathay Pacific and Singapore Airlines, all costing NZ$2000–2400. Most of these airlines also include a **side-trip** within Europe in their fare.

As with Australia, flights **via the US** are more expensive, the best deals being with United Airlines (via LA, Miami and Washington) for NZ$2200 and NZ$3000. Fares with British Airways (via LA and London) and Canadian Airlines (via Vancouver or Toronto) cost NZ$2399 to NZ$3000.

RED TAPE AND VISAS

Citizens of EU (European Union) countries can travel freely in France; citizens of Australia, Canada, the United States and New Zealand, among other countries, do not need any sort of visa to enter France, and can stay for up to ninety days. However, the situation can change and it is advisable to check with your embassy or consulate before departure. Note that the British Visitor's Passport is no longer available.

EU citizens (or other non-visa citizens) who **stay longer than three months** are officially supposed

FRENCH EMBASSIES AND CONSULATES ABROAD

AUSTRALIA
Consulates:

492 St Kilda Rd, Melbourne, VIC 300, ☎03/9820 0921.

Market St, Sydney, NSW 2000, ☎02/9261 5779, *www.france.net.au*.

CANADA
Embassy: 42 Promenade, Sussex, Ottawa, ON K1M 2C9, ☎613/789-1795, *www.amba-ottawa.fr*.

Consulates:

777 Main St, Suite 800, Moncton, NB E1C 1E9 ☎506/857-4191, *www.moncton.consulfrance.org*.

1 place Ville Marie Bureau 2601, Montréal, PQ H3B 4S3, ☎514/878-4385, *www.montreal .consulatfrance.org*.

25 rue St-Louis, Québec, QC G1R 3Y8, ☎418/694-2294, *www.quebec.consulatfrance.org*.

130 Bloor St W, Suite 400, Toronto, ON M5S 1N5, ☎416/925-8044, *www.toronto.consulat-france.org*.

1100–1130 W Pender St, Vancouver, BC V6E 4A4, ☎604/681-4345, *www.vancouver .consulatfrance.org*.

IRELAND
Embassy: 36 Ailesbury Rd, Ballsbridge, Dublin 4, ☎01/260 1666.

NEW ZEALAND
Embassy: 34–42 Manners St, PO Box 11-343, Wellington, ☎04/384 2555, *www.ambafrance .net.nz*.

UK
Embassy: 58 Knightsbridge, London SW1X 7J,. ☎020/7201 1004.

US
Embassy: 4101 Reservoir Rd NW, Washington, DC 20007, ☎202/944-6195, *www.info-france-usa.org*.

Consulates:
Prominence in Buckhead, Suite 1840, 3475 Piedmont Rd NE, Atlanta, GA 30305, ☎404/495-1660, *www.consulatfranceatlanta.org*.

31 St James Ave, Park Square Building, Suite 750, Boston, MA 02116, ☎617/542-7374, *www .franceboston.com*.

737 N Michigan Ave, Suite 2020, Chicago, IL 60611, ☎312/787-5360, *www.franceconsulat .org/chicago*

777 Post Oak Blvd, Suite 600, Houston, TX 77056 ☎713/572-2799, *www.consulatfrancehouston.org*.

10990 Wilshire Blvd, Suite 300, Los Angeles, CA 90024, ☎310/235-3200, *www.etats-unis.com /consulat-la*.

One Biscayne Tower, 17th Floor, S Biscayne Blvd, Miami, FL 33131, ☎305/372-9799, *www .info-france-usa.org/miami*.

1340 Poydras St, Amoco Building, Suite 1710, New Orleans, LA 70112, ☎504/523-5772, *www.info-france-usa.org/nouvelle-orleans*.

934 5th Ave, New York, NY 10021, ☎212/606-3689, *www.franceconsulatny.org*.

540 Bush St, San Francisco, CA 94108, ☎415/397-4330, *www.accueil-sfo.org*.

to apply for a **Carte de Séjour**, for which you'll have to show proof of income at least equal to the minimum wage (at least 6700F/€1025 per month). However, EU passports are rarely stamped, so there is no evidence of how long you've been in the country. If your passport does get stamped, you can cross the border – to Spain, for example – and re-enter for another ninety days legitimately.

COSTS, MONEY AND BANKS

Until the euro currency is introduced in 2002 (see box, below), the French unit of money is the the franc (abbreviated as F or sometimes FF), divided into 100 centimes. Francs come in notes of 500, 100, 50 and 20F, and there are coins of 20, 10, 5, 2 and 1F, and 50, 20, 10 and 5 centimes. During most of 2000, the exchange rate hovered around 11.10F to the pound, 7.60 to the US dollar, 5.10F to the Canadian dollar, 4.10F to the Australian dollar, and 3.40F to the New Zealand dollar. For the most up-to-date exchange rates, consult the useful Currency Converter Web site *www.oanda.com*.

COSTS

Brittany and Normandy are not, on the whole, expensive places to visit. Distances (and transport costs) are relatively small; the price of food and accommodation is consistently lower than in Britain and much of northern Europe; and access, at least just across the Channel, is straightforward.

On a **shoestring level**, camping and eating at least one picnic meal a day, taking buses or cycling, two people travelling together could get by easily enough on 250F/€38 (£25/US\$35) per person per day. Moving slightly **more upmarket**, staying in modest hotels, spending a bit on restaurants and driving, you should reckon on around 450F/€69 (£45/US\$65) per person per day.

Accommodation is likely to represent the bulk of your expenditure. Hotels average around 220F/€33 for a double room in the simpler places (note that in this book all hotel prices are coded

THE EURO

France is one of twelve European Union countries who have changed over to a single currency, the **euro** (€). The transition period, which began on January 1, 1999, is, however, lengthy: euro notes and coins are not scheduled to be issued until January 1, 2002, with francs remaining in place for **cash transactions**, at a **fixed rate** of 6.55957 francs to 1 euro, until they are scrapped entirely at the end of February, 2002.

Even before euro cash appears in 2002, you can opt to pay in euros by **credit card** and you can get **travellers' cheques** in euros – you should not be charged commission for changing them in any of the twelve countries in the euro zone (also known as "Euroland"), nor for changing from any of the old Euroland currencies to any other (Italian lira to francs, for example).

All **prices** in this book are given in francs and the exact equivalent in euros. When the new currency takes over completely, prices are likely to be rounded off – and if decimalization in the UK is anything to go by, rounded up.

Euro notes will be issued in denominations of 5, 10, 20, 50, 100, 200 and 500 euros, and coins in denominations of 1, 2, 5, 10, 20 and 50 cents and 1 and 2 euros.

with symbols, which are explained, in the box on p.33). If you're sharing, that works out at little more per person than the 60–120F/€9–18 per person charged by hostels. Camping, of course, can cut costs dramatically, so long as you avoid the plusher private sites; the local *Camping municipal* rarely asks for more than 30F/€4.50 a head.

Eating out is the real bargain. You should always be able to find a good three-course meal for around 100F/€15, or a takeaway for a lot less (though crêperies seldom work out as cheap as they might appear). Fresh food from shops and markets is surprisingly expensive in relation to low restaurant prices, but it's always possible to save money with a basic picnic of bread, cheese and fruit. More sophisticated meals – takeaway salads and ready-to-heat dishes – can be put together for reasonable prices if you shop at charcuteries (delis) and the equivalent counters of many supermarkets. On the other hand, **drinks** in cafés and bars can make a severe hole in your pocket. Nowhere in the region matches Paris prices, but a cup of coffee can easily cost 25F/€4, and a cognac double that; you have to accept that you're paying for somewhere to sit.

Transport costs obviously depend entirely on how (and how much) you travel. Bikes cost nothing if you bring them, and around 100F/€15.24 per day (more like 125F/€19.06 for a mountain bike) if you rent from the network of bike shops and SNCF station outlets (see p.31). Trains and buses normally operate on a fixed tariff of 50 centimes (half a franc)/€0.08 per kilometre. If you're driving, petrol prices are among the highest in Europe, at something in the region of 8F/€1.22 per litre (that's about 36F/€5.49 per imperial gallon, 30F/€4.57 per US gallon), and most motorways have tolls, which mount up at about 25 centimes/€0.04 per kilometre.

As for **sites and museums**, you may find that regular charges make you quite selective about what you visit – even with a student card to soften the blow (many museums have reduced admission for all under-26s, and not just students). But this is no special hardship: the region's attractions lie as much in its towns and landscapes as in anything fenced off or put in a showcase.

CHANGING MONEY

Standard **banking hours** are Monday to Friday 9am to 4pm or 5pm. Some close at lunchtime (noon/12.30pm–2/2.30pm); some are open on Saturday 9am to noon. All are closed on Sunday

and public holidays. They will have a notice on the door if they do currency exchange. **Rates and commission** vary from bank to bank, so it's worth shopping around; the usual procedure is a 1–2 percent commission on travellers' cheques and a flat-rate charge on cash (a 30F/€4.58 charge for changing 200F/€30.50 is not uncommon). Be wary of banks claiming to charge no commission at all; often they are merely adjusting the exchange rate to their own advantage.

There are **money-exchange counters** (*bureaux de change*) at the airports and at the train stations of all the larger towns, with usually one or two in town centres as well, often keeping much longer hours than the high-street banks.

DEBIT AND CREDIT CARDS, TRAVELLERS' CHEQUES AND VISA TRAVELMONEY

Much the easiest way to handle your money while visiting France is to use plastic. Assuming that you use an **ATM card** to obtain cash at home, that same card – especially if it bears the symbol of the Cirrus, Plus or Link networks – is likely to work in French cash-dispensing machines, which are every bit as ubiquitous as in Britain or North America. Check with your bank before you leave home if you're in any doubt.

Similarly, all major **credit cards** are widely accepted. MasterCard, American Express, Carte Bleue (Visa/Barclaycard), and Diner's Card are almost universally accepted in hotels, restaurants and shops, for a minimum purchase of around 80F/€12.20, though small-scale local businesses such as B&Bs or snack bars may well prefer cash.

It's worth noting, however, that many French credit cards incorporate a microchip (*puce*) that contains security information. British, American, Australasian and other cards with no such strip are sometimes rejected by card-reading machines in French shops and restaurants. French tourist authorities recommend that travellers who experience difficulties should say (or show) the following words to the retailer: "*les cartes anglaises ne sont pas des cartes à puce, mais à bande magnétique. Ma carte est valable et je vous serais reconnaissant d'en demander la confirmation auprès de votre banque ou de votre centre de traitement.*"

Though convenient, it's obviously not a wise idea to rely on a single ATM or credit card as your sole source of money on a long trip far from home – a lost, stolen or malfunctioning card leaves you with nothing. For that reason, it's always worth carrying some form of back up. Obtaining some

---

LOST OR STOLEN CREDIT CARDS

Before leaving home, check with your bank or credit-card company as to what number to call if your credit card is **lost or stolen**; you may have to call your home country. Otherwise, contact these numbers in France; they'll tell you the British or US numbers if necessary.

American Express cards	☎01.47.77.72.00	Diners Club	☎01.49.06.17.50
American Express cheques	☎08.00.90.86.00	MasterCard/Eurocard	☎01.45.67.53.53
Barclaycard	☎01.47.62.75.00	Visa/Carte Bleue	☎01.42.77.11.90

French cash in advance, whether from your local bank or simply at the air or ferry port as you travel, is always worthwhile, and you may also prefer to bring some **travellers' cheques**, which are available from almost any major bank. French-franc travellers' cheques are useful: they can often be used as cash, and French banks are obliged by law to give you the face value of the cheques when you change them, so commission is only paid on purchase.

Another option is to carry a **Visa TravelMoney Card**, a sort of electronic travellers' cheque. The temporary disposable debit card is "loaded up" with an amount between £100 and £5000 and can then be used (in conjunction with a PIN number) in any ATM carrying the Visa sign in France (and 112 other countries). When your funds are depleted, you simply throw the card away. It's recommended you buy at least a second card as back up in case your first is lost or stolen, though like travellers' cheques the cards can be replaced if such mishaps occur. Up to nine cards can be bought to access the same funds – useful for couples/families travelling together. Charges are 2 percent commission with a minimum charge of £3. The card is available from, among other places, Colombus Bank in the US and Thomas Cook in the UK. For further information, call Visa's 24hr toll-free customer services line on ☎1-410/581-9091 or check out their Web site at *www.visa.com*.

HEALTH AND INSURANCE

No visitor to France requires vaccinations of any kind, and general health care in the country is of the highest standard. Citizens of all EU and Scandinavian countries are entitled to take advantage of French health services under the same terms as residents, providing that they are carrying the correct documenta-tion. **British citizens need form E111, which is available in Britain from post offices, or in France, from offices of the health authorities, the Caisse Primaire d'Assurance Maladie (CPAM). North American and other non-EU citizens have to pay for most medical attention and are strongly advised to take out some form of travel insurance.**

MEDICAL TREATMENT

Under the French Social Security system, every hospital visit, doctor's consultation and prescribed medicine is charged for (though not upfront in an emergency). To find a **doctor**, stop at any **pharmacie**, and ask for an address. *Pharmacies* are signalled by an illuminated green cross; when they're closed, a notice on the door always directs you to the nearest open one, day or night. Police stations also have lists of doctors, or you can look under "Médecins qualifiés" in the Yellow Pages of the phone directory. An average consultation fee

The national number for **medical emergencies** is ☎15; for more details of what to do in a medical or other emergency, see pp.52–53.

would be between 150F/€22.87 and 180F/ €27.44. You will be given a *Feuille de Soins* (Statement of Treatment) for later documentation of insurance claims. **Prescriptions** should be taken to a *pharmacie*, where they must be paid for; the medicines will have little stickers (*vignettes*) attached to them, which you must remove and stick to your *Feuille de Soins*, together with the prescription itself. A refund of between forty and eighty percent, depending on the kind of medicines, is payable in due course, whereas ordinary **travel insurance** generally allows full reimbursement, less the first few pounds of every claim. Note that in addition to dispensing medicine, all pharmacies are equipped, and obliged, to give first-aid on request – though they will make a charge.

In serious **emergencies** you will always be admitted to the nearest **hospital** (*hôpital*), whether you arrive under your own power or by ambulance.

TRAVEL INSURANCE

A typical **travel insurance** policy usually provides cover for the loss of baggage, tickets and – up to a certain limit – cash or cheques, as well as cancellation or curtailment of your journey. Most of them exclude so-called **dangerous sports** unless an extra premium is paid. Read the small print and benefits tables of prospective policies carefully; coverage can vary wildly for roughly similar premiums. Many policies can be chopped and changed to exclude coverage you don't need

– for example, sickness and accident benefits can often be excluded or included at will. If you do take **medical coverage**, ascertain whether benefits will be paid as treatment proceeds or only after return home, and whether there is a 24-hour medical emergency number. When securing baggage cover, make sure that the per-article limit – typically under £500 equivalent – will cover your most valuable possession. If you need to make a claim, you should keep receipts for medicines and medical treatment, and in the event you have anything stolen, you must obtain an official statement from the police.

British bank and credit cards often have certain levels of medical or other insurance included and you may automatically get travel insurance if you use a major credit card to pay for your trip. If you have a good all-risks home insurance policy it may cover your possessions against loss or theft even when overseas. Many private medical schemes such as BUPA or PPP also offer coverage plans for abroad, including baggage loss, cancellation or curtailment and cash replacement as well as sickness or accident.

Americans and **Canadians** should also check that they're not already covered. Canadian provincial health plans usually provide partial cover for medical mishaps overseas. Holders of official student/teacher/youth cards are entitled to meagre accident coverage and hospital inpatient benefits. Students will often find that their student health coverage extends during the vacations and for one term beyond the date of last enrolment. Homeowners' or renters' insurance often covers theft or loss of documents, money and valuables while overseas, though conditions and maximum amounts vary from company to company.

ROUGH GUIDES TRAVEL INSURANCE

Rough Guides now offer their own **travel insurance**, customized for our readers by a leading UK broker and backed by a Lloyds underwriter. It's available for anyone of any nationality travelling anywhere in the world. There are two main plans: **Essential**, for effective, no-frills cover, starting at £10 for two weeks; and **Premier** – more expensive but with more generous and extensive benefits. Each offer European or Worldwide cover, and can be supplemented with a "Hazardous Activities Premium" if you plan to indulge in sports considered dangerous, such as skiing, scuba-diving or trekking. Unlike many policies, the Rough Guides schemes are calculated by the day, so if you're travelling for 27 days rather than a month, that's all you pay for. You can alternatively take out annual **multitrip insurance**, which covers you for all your travel throughout the year (with a maximum of sixty days for any one trip).

For a **policy quote**, call the Rough Guides Insurance Line on UK freefone ☎0800/015 0906, or, if you're calling from outside Britain, on ☎(+44) 1243/621 046. Alternatively, get an online quote or buy an insurance policy at *www.roughguides.com/insurance*.

TRAVELLERS WITH DISABILITIES

France has no exceptional record for providing facilities for disabled travellers. For people in wheelchairs, the haphazard parking habits and stepped village streets are serious obstacles, and public toilets with disabled access are rare. In the major cities and coastal resorts, however, ramps or other forms of access are gradually being added to hotels, museums and some theatres and concert halls. APF, the French paraplegic organization (see box, below), which has an office in each *département*, will be the most reliable source of information on accommodation with disabled access and other facilities.

Public transport is certainly not wheelchair-friendly, and although many train stations now have ramps to enable wheelchair users to board and descend from carriages, at others it is still up to the guards to carry the chair. The high-speed TGVs (including Eurostar) all have places for wheelchairs in the First Class saloon coach for which you must book in advance, though no higher fee is charged; on other trains, a wheelchair symbol within the timetable denotes whether that service offers special features, and you and your companion are again upgraded to First Class with no extra charge. The *Guide du Voyageur à Mobilité Réduite*, available free at main train stations, details all facilities. Taxis are obliged by law to carry you and to help you into the vehicle, also to carry your guide dog if you are blind. Specialist taxi services are available in some towns: these are detailed in the Ministry of Transport and Tourism's pamphlet *Guide des Transports à l'Usage des Personnes à Mobilité Réduite*, available at airports, main train stations and some tourist offices. The guide also gives some indication of the accessibility of urban public transport systems, and the availability of cars for rent with hand controls.

Most of the cross-Channel **ferry companies** offer good facilities, though up-to-date information about access is difficult to get hold of. **Eurostar**, having been established in the 1990s, offers an excellent deal for wheelchair users. There are two special spaces in the First Class carriages for wheelchairs, with an accompanying seat for a companion. No advance bookings are necessary, though the limited spaces might make it wise to reserve ahead of time and also to arrange the special assistance which Eurostar offers at either end. As far as **airlines** go, British Airways has a better-than-average record for treatment of disabled passengers; while, from North America, Virgin and Air Canada come out tops in terms of disability awareness (and seating arrangements) and might be worth contacting first for any information they can provide.

Up-to-date information is best obtained from organizations at home before you leave or from the French disability organizations. The publication *Touristes Quand Même!*, produced by the CNRH (see box, below), lists facilities throughout France but is not updated regularly. Some tourist offices have information but, again, it is not always very reliable. The Holiday Care Service has an information sheet on accessible **accommodation** in France.

Read your travel **insurance** small print carefully to make sure that people with pre-existing medical conditions are not excluded. And use your travel agent to make your journey simpler: airline or bus companies can cope better if they are expecting you, with a wheelchair provided at airports and staff primed to help. A **medical certificate** of your fitness to travel, provided by your doctor, is also extremely useful; some airlines or insurance companies may insist on it. Make sure that you have extra supplies of drugs – carried with you if you fly – and a prescription including the generic name in case of emergency. Carry spares of any clothing or equipment that might be hard to find; if there's an association representing people with your disability, contact them early in the planning process.

NORTH AMERICA

Access First Travel, 239 Commercial St, Malden, MA 02148, ☎1-800/557-2047. Up-to-date information for disabled travellers.

Directions Unlimited, 123 Green Lane, Bedford Hills, NY 10507, ☎1-800/533-5343. Tour operator specializing in customized tours for people with disabilities.

Mobility International USA, PO Box 10767, Eugene, OR 97440, ☎541/343-1284, *www.miusa .com*. Information, access guides, tours and exchanges. Annual membership $25 (includes quarterly newsletter).

Society for the Advancement of Travel for the Handicapped (SATH), 347 5th Ave, #610, New York, NY 10016, ☎212/447-7284, *www.sath.org*. Nonprofit travel-industry referral service.

Travel Information Service, ☎215/456-9600. Telephone-only information and referral service for disabled travellers.

Twin Peaks Press, Box 129, Vancouver, WA 98666, ☎360/694-2462 or 1-800/637-2256, *www.pacifier.com/twinpeak*. Publisher of the *Directory of Travel Agencies for the Disabled* ($19.95), listing more than 370 agencies worldwide; *Travel for the Disabled* ($19.95); the *Directory of Accessible Van Rentals* ($9.95); and *Wheelchair Vagabond* ($14.95), which is loaded with personal tips.

Wheels Up!, PO Box 5197, Plant City, FL 33564. ☎1-888/389 4335, *www.wheelsup.com*. Discounted airfare, tour and cruise prices for disabled travellers, plus a free monthly newsletter and comprehensive Web site.

AUSTRALIA AND NEW ZEALAND

AUSTRALIA
ACROD, PO Box 60, Curtin, ACT 2605, ☎02/6282 4333. Lists of agencies and tour operators.

Barrier Free Travel, 36 Wheatley St, North Bellingen, NSW 2454, ☎02/6655 1733. Independent consultant who draws up individual itineraries for people with disabilities.

NEW ZEALAND
Disabled Persons Assembly, PO Box 10, 138 The Terrace, Wellington, ☎04/472 2626, *www.dpa.org.nz*. Details of tour operators and travel agencies for people with disabilities.

INFORMATION AND MAPS

French Government Tourist Offices in various major cities of the world give away large quantities of maps and glossy brochures covering Brittany and Normandy, including lists of hotels and campsites. Some of these, such as the maps of the inland waterways, and lists of festivals and campsites, can be quite useful; others use a lot of space to say very little.

In France itself you'll find a **tourist office** – known as the Syndicat d'Initiative (SI), or sometimes Office du Tourisme (OT) – in practically every town or even village (addresses and opening hours are detailed throughout this book). These supply free town plans, and local information such as listings of hotels, restaurants, leisure activities, bike rental and laundries. Many

MAP AND GUIDE SUPPLIERS

BRITAIN

Blackwell's Map and Travel Shop, 53 Broad St, Oxford OX1 3B, ☎01865/792792, *bookshop.blackwell.co.uk.*

Daunt Books, 83 Marylebone High St, London W1M 3DE, ☎020/7224 2295; 193 Haverstock Hill, London NW3 4QL, ☎020/7794 4006.

Heffers Map and Travel, 20 Trinity St, Cambridge CB2 1TJ, ☎01223/586586, *www.heffers.co.uk.*

John Smith and Sons, 26 Colquhoun Ave, Glasgow G52 4PJ, ☎0141/221 7472, *www.johnsmith.co.uk.*

National Map Centre, 22–24 Caxton St, London SW1H 0QU, ☎020/7222 2466, *www.mapsnmc.co.uk.*

Newcastle Map Centre, 55 Grey St, Newcastle NE1 6EF, ☎0191/261 5622, *www.newtraveller.com.*

Stanfords, 29 Corn St, Bristol BS1 1HT, ☎0117/929 9966; 12–14 Long Acre, London WC2E 9LP, ☎020/7836 1321; 156 Regent St, London W1R 5TA, ☎020/7434 4744, *www.stanfords.co.uk.*

The Travel Bookshop, 13–15 Blenheim Crescent, London W11 2EE, ☎020/7229 5260, *www.thetravelbookshop.co.uk.*

IRELAND

Easons Bookshop, 40 O'Connell St, Dublin 1, ☎01/873 3811.

Fred Hanna's Bookshop, 27–29 Nassau St, Dublin 2, ☎01/677 1255.

Hodges Figgis Bookshop, 56–58 Dawson St, Dublin 2, ☎01/677 4754.

Waterstone's, Queens Bldg, 8 Royal Ave, Belfast BT1 1DA, ☎028/9024 7355; 69 Patrick St, Cork, ☎021/276522; 7 Dawson St, Dublin 2, ☎01/679 1415, *www.waterstonesbooks.co.uk.*

USA

The Complete Traveler Bookstore, 199 Madison Ave, New York, NY 10016, ☎212/685-9007; 3207 Fillmore St, San Francisco, CA 94123, ☎415/923-1511, *www.complete.traveler.com.*

Elliott Bay Book Company, 101 S Main St, Seattle, WA 98104, ☎206/624-6600, *www.elliottbaybook.com.*

SIs also publish car and walking itineraries for their areas, while some conduct free town tours, and in addition many have their own **Web sites**, again listed wherever applicable throughout this book.

A further list of useful Web sites for Brittany and Normandy appears on p.49.

MAPS

Though their town maps are often very good, the SI handouts very rarely contain usable regional maps. To supplement them – and the maps in this guide – you will probably want a reasonable **road map**. For most purposes, certainly for driving, the **Michelin** 1:200,000 area maps of Brittany (230) and Normandy (231) are more than adequate. Virtually every road they show is passable by any car, and those that are tinged in green are usually reliable as "scenic routes". Full lists of Michelin maps are available at *www.michelin-travel.com*.

A useful free map for car drivers, obtainable from petrol stations and traffic-information kiosks in France, is the *Bison Futé*, showing alternative back routes to avoid the congested main roads, which are clearly signposted on the ground by special green *Bison Futé* road signs.

If you're planning to **walk or cycle**, check the IGN maps – either the green (1:100,000 and 1:50,000) or the more detailed purple (1:25,000) series. The IGN 1:100,000 is the smallest scale available with contours marked, though the bizarre colour scheme makes it hard to read. Michelin maps have little arrows to indicate steep slopes, which is all the information most cyclists will need.

Anyone planning to visit the **battlefields of northern France** will find Major and Mrs Holt's *Battle Map Series* invaluable (mail order from T. & V. Holt, Oak House, Woodnesborough, Sandwich CT13 0NJ, UK; ☎ & fax 01304/614123).

Map Link Inc., 30 S La Patera Lane, #5, Santa Barbara, CA 93117, ☎805/692-6777, *www.maplink.com*.

Phileas Fogg's Books & Maps, #87 Stanford Shopping Center, Palo Alto, CA 94304, ☎1-800/533-FOGG, *www.foggs.com*.

Rand McNally, 444 N Michigan Ave, Chicago, IL 60611, ☎312/321-1751; 150 E 52nd St, New York, NY 10022, ☎212/758-7488; 595 Market St, San Francisco, CA 94105, ☎415/777-3131, *www.randmcnally.com*.

Travel Books & Language Center, 4437 Wisconsin Ave, Washington, DC 20016, ☎1-800/220-2665.

Traveler's Choice Bookstore, 2 Wooster St, New York, NY 10013. ☎212/941-1535, *tvlchoice@aol.com*.

CANADA

International Travel Maps and Books, 552 Seymour St, Vancouver, BC V6B 3J5, ☎604/687-3320, *www.itmb.com*.

Open Air Books and Maps, 25 Toronto St, Toronto, ON M5R 2C1, ☎416/363-0719.

Ulysses Travel Bookshop, 4176 St. Denis, Montréal, PQ H2W 2M5, ☎514/843-9447, *www.ulyssesguidess.com*.

AUSTRALIA AND NEW ZEALAND

Map Land, 372 Little Burke St, Melbourne, ☎03/9670-4383.

The Map Shop, 16a Peel St, Adelaide. ☎08/8231 2033.

Mapworld, 173 Gloucester St, Christchurch, ☎03/374 5399, *www.mapworld.co.nz*.

Perth Map Centre, 884 Hay St, Perth, ☎08/9322 5733.

Specialty Maps, 58 Albert St, Auckland, ☎09/307 2217.

Travel Bookshop, Shop 3, 175 Liverpool St, Sydney, ☎02/9261 8200.

Worldwide Maps and Guides, 187 George St, Brisbane, ☎07/3221 4330.

FRENCH GOVERNMENT TOURIST OFFICES

The official French Government Tourist Office, La Maison de France,
is on the Web at *www.franceguide.com.*

Australia, 25 Bligh St, Level 22, Sydney, NSW 2000, ☎02/9231 5244.

Canada, 1981 av McGill College, #490. Montréal, PQ H3A 2W9, ☎514/288-4264.

Ireland, 10 Suffolk St, Dublin 2, ☎01/679 0813.

UK, 178 Piccadilly, London W1V 0AL, ☎0891/ 244123 (premium rate line).

US, 444 Madison Ave, 16th Floor, New York, NY 10022, ☎212/838-7800; 676 N Michigan Ave #3360, Chicago, IL 60611-2819, ☎312/751-7800; 9454 Wilshire Blvd, #715, Los Angeles, CA 90212-2967, ☎310/272-2661.

Note that **New Zealand** does not have a French Government Tourist Office.

REGIONAL TOURIST BOARDS

BRITTANY *www.brittanytourism.com* or *www.region-bretagne.fr.*

Bretagne Info, 1 rue Raoul Ponchon, 35069 Rennes, ☎02.99.36.15.15.

La Maison de la Bretagne, 203 bd St-Germain, 75007 Paris, ☎01.53.63.11.50.

NORMANDY *www.normandy-tourism.org.*

Comité Régional du Tourisme de Normandie Le Doyenné, 14 rue Charles Courbeau, 27000 Évreux, ☎02.32.33.79.00.

Normandy Tourist Board, 44 Bath Hill, Keynsham, Bristol BS31 1HG, ☎0117/986 0036.

DEPARTMENTAL TOURIST OFFICES

Each individual *département* in Brittany and Normandy has its own **Comité Départemental du Tourisme**, which can provide detailed information on its own region. Not all have their own Web sites.

BRITTANY

Côtes d'Armor, 29 rue des Promenades, BP 4620, St Brieuc 22046, ☎02.96.62.72.00, *www.cotesdarmor.com.*

Finistère, BP 1419, Quimper 29104, ☎02.98.76.20.70.

Ille-et-Vilaine, BP 6046, Rennes 35060, ☎02.99.78.47.47, *www.bretagne35.com.*

Morbihan, Allée Nicolas Leblanc, Vannes 56010, ☎02.97.54.06.56, *www.morbihan.com.*

NORMANDY

Calvados, place du Canada, Caen 1400, ☎02.31.27.90.30, *calvatour@mail.cpod.fr.*

Eure, bd Georges Chauvin, BP 367, Évreux 27003, ☎02.32.62.04.27.

Manche, Maison du Département, St Lô 50008, ☎02.33.05.98.70.

Orne, 88 rue St Blaise, Alençon 61002, ☎02.33.28.88.71, *orne.tourisme@wanadoo.fr.*

Seine Maritime, 6 rue Couronné, BP 60, Bihorel les Rouen 76420, ☎02.35.12.10.10, *seine.maritime.tourisme@wanadoo.fr.*

GETTING AROUND

The best way to travel around Brittany and Normandy is with a car or a bike. Public transport is not very impressive. SNCF trains are efficient, as ever in France, and the Atlantique TGV has reduced the Paris–Rennes journey to a mere two hours, but the rail network circles the coast and, especially in Brittany, barely serves the inland areas.

Approximate journey times and frequencies for trains, buses and boats can be found in the "Travel details" at the end of each chapter in this book, and local peculiarities are also pointed out in the text.

Buses do complement the trains to some extent – SNCF buses often pick up routes that the trains no longer follow – but on the whole their timetables are geared much more to market, school or working hours than to meeting the needs of tourists, and it can take a very long time indeed to get where you want to go. If you come without your own transport, the ideal solution is to make longer journeys by train or bus, then to rent a bike (never a problem) to explore a particular locality.

DRIVING

Travelling by car has its disadvantages: the expense, most obviously, but also the strong likelihood of reducing your contact with people.

CAR RENTAL AGENCIES

Auto Europe	
US	☎1-800/223-5555
Autos Abroad	*www.autosabroad.co.uk*
UK	☎020/7287 6000
Avis	*www.avis.com*
Britain	☎0870/606 0100
Northern Ireland	☎0870/590 0500
Irish Republic	☎01/874 5844
US & Canada	☎1-800/331-1084
Australia	☎13/633
New Zealand	☎0800/655 111
Budget	*www.budgetrentacar.com*
UK	☎0800/181181
US & Canada	☎1-800/527-0700
Australia	☎1300/362 848
New Zealand	☎0800/652 227
Europcar	*www.europcar.com*
UK	☎0845/722 2525
Irish Republic	☎01/874 5844
Europe by Car	*www.europebycar.com*
US & Canada	☎1-800/223-1516

Fly and Drive Holidays	
New Zealand	☎09/529 3709
Hertz	*www.hertz.com*
Britain	☎0870/844 8844
Northern Ireland	☎0870/599 6699
Irish Republic	☎01/676 7476
US	☎1-800/654-300
Canada	☎1-800/263-0600
Australia	☎1800/550 067
New Zealand	☎0800/655 955
Holiday Autos	*www.kemwel.com*
Britain	☎0870/400 0011
Northern Ireland	☎0870/530040
Irish Republic	☎01/872 9366
US & Canada	☎1-800/422-7737
National Car Rental	*www.nationalcar.com*
UK	☎01895/233300
US & Canada	☎1-800/CAR-RENT
Thrifty	*www.thrifty.com*
UK	☎01494/442110
US & Canada	☎1-800/367-2277

A MOTORING VOCABULARY

car	*voiture*	oil	*huile*
garage	*garage*	airline	*ligne à air*
service	*service*	inflate the tyres	*gonfler les pneus*
to park the car	*garer la voiture*	battery	*batterie*
car park/parking lot	*un parking*	the battery is dead	*la batterie est morte*
free parking	*parking gratuit*	plugs	*bougies*
paid parking	*parking payant*	to break down	*tomber en panne*
no parking	*défense de stationner/ stationnement interdit*	insurance	*assurance*
		green card	*carte verte*
		traffic lights	*feux*
petrol/gas	*essence*	red light	*feu rouge*
(unleaded)	*(sans plomb)*	green light	*feu vert*
petrol/gas station	*poste d'essence*	slow down	*ralentir*
diesel fuel	*gasoil*	give way	*cédez le passage*
petrol/gas can	*bidon*	give way to	
fill the tank	*faire le plein*	pedestrians	*priorité aux piétons*

However, you do gain freedom of movement and, especially if you're camping, can be a lot more self-sufficient.

Few British travellers consider **car rental** in France, which costs upwards of 2000F/€305 per week (from around 300F/€46 a day), to be an economic alternative to bringing their own car across the Channel. However, the major international rental chains are represented throughout the region. North Americans and Australians in particular should be forewarned that it is very difficult to rent a car with **automatic transmission**; if you can't drive a stickshift, you should try to book an automatic well in advance, possibly before you leave home, and be prepared to pay a much higher price for it. Most rental companies will only rent cars to customers aged under 25 on payment of an extra insurance premium of around 130–150F/€20–23 per day; you still must be over 21 and have driven for at least one year. OTU Voyage (Paris office ☎01.40.29.12.12), the student-travel agency, can arrange car rental for young drivers, with prices beginning at 459F/€70 for three days, plus insurance.

Petrol/gas (*essence*) or diesel fuel (*gasoil*) is least expensive at out-of-town superstores, and most expensive on the *autoroutes*; typical prices as this book went to press were around 7.70F/€1.17 a litre for unleaded (*sans plomb*), 7.80F/€1.19 for four-star (*Super*) and 5.50F/€0.84 for diesel.

Autoroute driving, if fast, is boring when it's not hair-raising, and the tolls in Normandy are expensive. The helpful *Bison Futé* map, free from service stations, details lesser-known routes to

steer clear of the crowds – invaluable if you're trying to avoid the endless traffic jams over the weekends between July 15 and August 15. For full French driving regulations, see the *AA Traveller's Guide to Europe* (AA Publications, £6.95).

If you run into **mechanical difficulties**, all the major car manufacturers have garages and service stations in France. You can find them in the Yellow Pages (*Pages Jaunes*) of the phone book under "Garages d'automobiles". For breakdowns, look under "Dépannages". If you have an accident or break-in, you should make a report to the local police (and keep a copy) in order to make an insurance claim.

LEGAL REQUIREMENTS

British, Irish, Australian, Canadian, New Zealand, American and EU **driving licences** are all valid in France, though an International Driver's Licence makes life easier if you get a police officer unwilling to peruse a document in English. The minimum driving age is 18, and provisional licences are not valid.

The vehicle registration document and the **insurance** papers must be carried; only the originals are acceptable. It's no longer essential for motorists from other EU countries to buy a **green card** to extend their usual insurance. If you have insurance at home then you have the minimal legal coverage in France; whether you have any more than that, and (if not) whether you want to buy more, is something to discuss with your own insur-

ROAD INFORMATION

For information on traffic and road conditions on *autoroutes* throughout France, ring the multilingual service, Autoroutel (☎08.36.68.10.77) or consult their Web site *www.autoroutes.fr*. Traffic information for non-motorway routes can be obtained 24 hours per day at ☎01.56.96.33.33.

ance company, so check to see what they recommend. Breakdown insurance costs around £40 for eight days; look into the RAC's European Motoring Assistance (☎0800/550055, *www.rac.co.uk*), or the AA's Five-Star Europe cover (☎0800/444500, *www.theaa.co.uk*).

If your car is right-hand drive, you must have your **headlight dip** adjusted to the right before you go and as a courtesy change or paint them to yellow or stick on black glare deflectors. Shops at the ferry terminals sell special headlight deflectors which achieve both aims – you basically pay £6 for two small pieces of sticky yellow plastic, but they do the job.

Similarly, you must also affix **GB plates** if you're driving a British car, and carry a red **warning triangle** and a spare set of **headlight bulbs** in your vehicle.

Seat belts are compulsory for the driver and all passengers, and children under 10 can only sit in the front seat if they're in approved rear-facing child seats.

RULES OF THE ROAD

The main **rule of the road** to remember in France is that the French drive on the right. Most drivers used to driving on the left find it easy to adjust. The biggest problem tends to be visibility when you want to overtake; it's possible to buy special forward-view mirrors that may help.

The law of **priorité à droite** – which says you have to give way to traffic coming from your right, even when it is coming from a minor road – is being phased out, having long been a major cause of accidents. It still applies in built-up areas, however, so you still have to be vigilant in towns, keeping a lookout along the roadside for the yellow diamond on a white background that gives you right of way – until you see the same sign with an oblique black slash, which indicates vehicles emerging from the right have right of way. *Stop* signs mean stop completely; *Cédez le passage* means "Give way". Other signs warning of

potential dangers are *déviation* (diversion), *gravillons* (loose chippings), *nids de poules* (potholes) and *chaussée déformée* (uneven surface).

The main French national **speed limits**, which apply unless otherwise posted, are 130kph (80mph) on the tolled *autoroutes*; 110kph (68mph) on dual carriageways; and 90kph (56mph) on other roads. In wet weather, and for drivers with less than two-years' experience, these limits are 110kph (68mph), 100kph (62mph), and 80kph (50mph) respectively. There's also a ceiling of 50kph (31mph) in towns. Fines for driving violations are exacted on the spot, and only cash or a French bank account cheque are accepted. Exceeding the speed limit by 1 to 30kph can cost as much as 5000F/€762.

Random **breath tests** are common, and the legal blood alcohol limit (0.05 percent alcohol) is lower than in the UK and North America; fines range from 900F/€137 to 30,000F/€4575.

MOPED AND MOTORBIKE RENTAL

Mopeds and **scooters** are relatively easy to find: everyone in France, from young kids to grandmas, seems to ride one, and, although they're not built for any kind of long-distance travel, they're ideal for shooting around town and nearby. Places which rent out bicycles will often also rent out mopeds; you can expect to pay around 200F/€30 a day for a 50cc Suzuki, for example. No licence is needed for 50cc and under bikes, but for anything larger you'll need a valid **motorbike** licence. Rental prices are around 230F/€35 a day for an 80cc motorbike, 300F/€46 for a 125cc; also expect to leave a hefty deposit by cash or credit card – 6000F/€900 is not unusual. **Crash helmets** are compulsory on all machines.

The Comité Régional du Tourisme en Bretagne publishes a leaflet *La Bretagne à Bécane* ("Motorbiking in Brittany"), which lists all the motorbike shops in the region, while motorbiking holidays are arranged by West Euro Bikes, 4 rue Duguay-Trouin, St-Herblain 44800 (☎02.28.03 .00.68, *www.westeurobikes.com*).

TRAINS

French **trains**, operated by the nationally owned SNCF (Société National des Chemins de Fer), are by and large clean, fast and frequent, and their staff both courteous and helpful. For national train **information**, you can either phone

☎08.36.35.35.35 (2.23F/€0.34 per minute) or check on the Internet at *www.sncf.fr*. All but the smallest stations (*gares SNCF*) have an information desk, while many in larger towns operate some form of left-luggage service, or provide lockers (*consignes automatiques*). Often they also rent out bicycles.

Fares are reasonable, at an average – off peak – of a little over 50 centimes/€0.08 per kilometre. Children under 12 travel half-price, and under-4s go free. The ultrafast TGVs (Trains à Grande Vitesse) require a supplement at peak times and compulsory reservation costing around 20F/€3.05. The slowest trains are those marked "*Autotrain*" in the timetable, stopping at all stations.

Try to use the counter service for buying tickets, rather than the complicated computerized system; the latter changes the price of TGV tickets depending on the demand, and you may find you've bought an expensive ticket without realizing that a later train is cheaper.

All **tickets** – but not passes – must be date-stamped in the orange machines at station platform entrances. It is an offence not to follow the instruction to *Compostez votre billet* ("Validate your ticket"). Rail journeys may be broken any time, anywhere, for as long as the ticket is valid (usually two months), but after a break of 24 hours you must "*composte*" your ticket again when you resume your journey. On night trains an extra 100F/€15 or so will buy you a **couchette** – well worth it if you're making a long haul and don't want to waste a day recovering from a sleepless night.

Regional **rail maps** and complete **timetables** are on sale at tobacconist shops (*tabacs*). Leaflet timetables for individual lines are available free at stations. "*Autocar*" at the top of a column means it's an SNCF bus service, on which train tickets and passes are valid.

For details on taking your bicycle by train – or renting one at an SNCF station – see opposite.

DISCOUNTS AND RAIL PASSES

Anyone intending simply to visit Brittany and Normandy – or even to explore all of France – is very unlikely to make enough train journeys for it to be worth purchasing a Europe-wide **rail pass**; if you do intend to travel throughout Europe, see the boxes on pp.6 and 13 for details of the passes available, all of which must be purchased before leaving home.

Within France, there is a range of other train passes, which can be purchased through most travel agents in France or from main *gares SNCF* and are valid for one year. Over-60s can get the **Carte Senior**, which costs 285F/€43.46 for unlimited travel. It offers up to 50 percent off tickets on TGVs, subject to availability, or other journeys starting in blue periods, a 25 percent reduction on white-period journeys, as well as a 30 percent reduction on through international journeys involving most countries in western and central Europe. The same percentage reductions are available for under-26s with a **Carte 12–25** pass, which costs 270F/€41.18. Under-12s can obtain the same advantages for themselves and up to four travelling companions of any age by purchasing the **Enfant Plus Carte** (350F/€53.38).

In addition, the SNCF offers a whole range of **discounted fares** within France on standard rail prices on *période bleue* (blue period) and *période blanche* (white period) days, depending on exactly when you want to travel. A leaflet showing the blue, white (smaller discount) and red (peak) periods is given out at *gares SNCF*.

There is also a range of other **reductions** for which no pass is required. Any two people travelling together (*à deux*), or a small group of up to five people – whether a married couple, friends, family, whatever – are entitled to a 25 percent discount on return tickets on TGVs, subject to availability, or on other trains if they start their journey on a blue-period day; the same reduction applies to a group of up to four people travelling with a child under 12, to under 26-year-olds, over-60s and for anyone who books a return journey of at least 200km in distance, including a Saturday night away (this latter is called the *séjour*).

BUSES

Buses cover far more Breton and Norman routes than the trains – and even when towns do have a rail link buses are often quicker, cheaper and more direct. They are almost always short distance, however, requiring you to change if you're going further than from one town to the next. And, as stressed, **timetables** tend to be constructed to suit working, market and school hours – often dauntingly early when they do run, and prone to stop just when tourists need them most.

Larger towns usually have a central *gare routière* (bus station), most often found next to the *gare SNCF*. However, the private bus companies (who provide most of the Breton services) don't always work together and you'll frequently find them leaving from an array of different points. The most convenient lines are those run as an exten-sion of rail links by SNCF; these always run to/from the SNCF station (assuming there is one).

CYCLING

Bicycles have high status in France. The car fer-ries and SNCF trains carry them for a minimal charge, and the French (Parisians excepted) respect cyclists – both as traffic, and, when you stop off at a restaurant or hotel, as customers. French drivers normally go out of their way to make room for you; it's the great British caravan you might have to watch out for.

Most importantly, however, **distances** in Brittany and Normandy are not great, the hills are sporadic and not too steep, cities like Rennes and Nantes have useful networks of cycle lanes, and the scenery is nearly always a delight. Even if you're quite unused to it, cycling sixty kilometres per day soon becomes very easy – and it's a good way of keeping yourself fit enough to enjoy the rich regional food.

These days most cyclists seem to use **moun-tain bikes**, which the French call VTTs (Vélos Touts Terrains), for touring holidays, although if you've ever made a direct comparison you'll know it's much less effort, and much quicker, to cycle long distances and carry luggage on a traditional touring or racing bike. Whichever you prefer, do use cycle

panniers; a backpack in the sun is unbearable.

One word of warning: most cyclists have a habit of lifting their bicycles by gripping the sad-dle. If you keep on doing that when you're using panniers, even just to get over kerbs, the entire saddle will eventually snap off when you least expect it, to leave you to ride off in search of a bike shop, sitting on a long, sharp spike.

Restaurants and hotels along the way are nearly always obliging about looking after your bike, even to the point of allowing it into your room. Most large towns have well-stocked retail and **repair shops**, where parts are normally cheaper than in Britain or the US. However, if you're using a foreign-made bike, it's a good idea to carry spare tyres, as French sizes are different. Neither is it easy to find parts for mountain bikes, the French enthusiasm being directed towards racers instead. Inner tubes are not a problem, as they adapt to either size, though you should always be sure that you get the right valves. The best places to find foreign parts are in Raleigh stockists – at Rouen, Rennes and scattered around both provinces.

SNCF run various schemes for cyclists, all of them covered in the free leaflet *Guide du Train et du Vélo*, available from most stations. Trains marked with a bicycle in the timetable allow you to take a bike as free accompanied luggage.

A CYCLING VOCABULARY

to adjust	*régler*	loose	*déserré*
axle	*l'axe*	to lower	*baisser*
ball bearing	*le roulement à billes*	mudguard	*le garde-boue*
battery	*la pile*	pannier	*le pannier*
bent	*tordu*	pedal	*le pédale*
bicycle	*le vélo*	pump	*la pompe*
bottom bracket	*le logement du pédalier*	puncture	*la crevaison*
brake cable	*le cable*	rack	*le porte-bagages*
brakes	*les freins*	to raise	*remonter*
broken	*cassé*	to repair	*réparer*
bulb	*l'ampoule*	saddle	*la selle*
chain	*la chaîne*	to screw	*visser/serrer*
cotter pin	*la clavette*	spanner	*la clef (mécanique)*
to deflate	*dégonfler*	spoke	*le rayon*
dérailleur	*le dérailleur*	to straighten	*rédresser*
frame	*le cadre*	stuck	*coincé*
gears	*les vitesses*	tight	*serré*
grease	*la graisse*	toe clips	*les cale-pieds*
handlebars	*le guidon*	tyre	*le pneu*
to inflate	*gonfler*	wheel	*la roue*
inner tube	*la chambre à air*		

Otherwise, you have to send your bike parcelled up as registered luggage for a fee of 150F/€22.88. Although it may well arrive in less time, the SNCF won't guarantee delivery in under five days; and you do hear stories of bicycles disappearing altogether.

You can normally load your bike straight onto the train at the **ferry** port – as on the boat train at Dieppe – but remember that you must first go to the ticket office of the station to register it. Don't just try to climb on the train with it, as both you and your bike will end up left behind. **Eurostar** allow you to take your bicycle as part of your baggage allowance provided it is dismantled and stored in a special bike bag, and the dimensions don't exceed 120cm by 90cm. Otherwise it needs to be sent on unaccompanied, with a guaranteed arrival of 24 hours (you can register it up to ten days in advance; book through Esprit Europe ☎0800/186186); the fee is £20 one way. In addition, both British Airways and Air France take bikes free. You may have to box them, though, and you should contact the airlines first.

Bikes are available for **rental** at most SNCF stations for upwards of 80F/€12.20 per day, depending on the type of bike. You can also rent bikes from some tourist offices and a fair number of bike shops (which are much more likely to offer you a mountain bike), and, on islands such as Belle-Île and Ouessant, from seasonal **stalls**. The bikes are often not insured, however, and you will be presented with the bill for its replacement if it's stolen or damaged. Check whether your travel-insurance policy covers you for this if you intend to rent a bike.

For advice on which **maps** to take, see the "Maps" section on p.25. In the UK, the Cyclists' Touring Club, Cotterell House, 68 Meadrow, Godalming, Surrey GU7 3HS (☎01483/417217, fax 01483/426994, *cycling@ctc.org.uk*), will suggest routes and supply advice for members (£25 p.a. or £12.50 for unemployed). They run a particularly good insurance scheme. Companies running specialist bike touring holidays are listed on pp.12 and 16.

BOAT TRIPS AND INLAND WATERWAYS

Boat trips on many of Brittany and Normandy's rivers, as well as out to the islands, are detailed throughout this book. More excitingly, you can **rent a canoe**, **boat** or even **houseboat** and make your own way along sections of the

Cruises on the **River Seine** are detailed on p.86.

Nantes–Brest canal. The route along the canal is the core of Chapter Six, "Inland Brittany"; the various towns where you can rent vessels are detailed on p.344, and some British operators are listed on p.8.

French Government Tourist Offices can also provide lists of French and foreign operators who arrange boat rental, or for a full list write to the Syndicat National des Loueurs de Bateaux de Plaisance, Port de la Bourdonnais, 75007 Paris (☎45.55.10.49). Specifically for Brittany, contact **Formules Bretagnes**, 203 bd St-Germain, 75007 Paris (☎01.53.63.11.53). The Comité Tourisme d'Ille-et-Vilaine (see p.26) issues a brochure and map detailing a north–south barge route from the Channel to the Atlantic.

If you are adventurous enough to take your own boat, there is no charge for use of the waterways in Brittany or Normandy, and you can travel without a permit for up to six months in a year. For information on maximum dimensions, documentation, regulations and so forth, ask at a French Government Tourist Office for the free booklet *Boating on the Waterways*.

WALKING

Neither Brittany nor Normandy is serious hiking country. There are no mountains – or extensive areas of wilderness – and casual rambling along the clifftops and beside the waterways is the limit of most people's aims. However, if you're into **long-distance walking**, 21 of the French **GR trails** – the *sentiers de grande randonnée* – run through the area. The GRs are fully signposted and equipped with campsites and rest huts along the way. The most interesting are the GR2 (Sentier de la Seine), which runs from Le Havre to Les Andelys; the GR341 (*Sentier de Bretagne*) along the Granit-Rose coast between Lannion and St-Brieuc; and the GR347 (Val d'Oust au pays Gallo) between Josselin and Redon.

Each GR path is described in a **Topoguide**, which gives a detailed account of the route (in French), including maps, campsites, sources of provisions and so on. These are produced by the principal French walkers' organization, the Fédération Française de la Randonnée Pédestre, 14 rue Riquet, 75019 Paris (☎01.44.89.93.93, fax 01.40.35.85.67, *asp.ffrp.asso.fr/accueil.asp*), and can be ordered through good map shops overseas, such as those listed on p.24.

In addition, many tourist offices provide guides to their local footpaths.

ACCOMMODATION

Most of the year, accommodation is plentiful in both Brittany and Normandy, and visitors can just turn up at a town and find a room or a place on a campsite. Booking a couple of nights in advance can, however, be reassuring; it spares you the risk of having to trudge around to find a place and ensures that you know what you'll be paying.

Hotels, hostels and campsites are recommended throughout this book, and their phone numbers provided. The "Language" section in Contexts should help you make the necessary phone call if you're uncertain of your French, though many hoteliers and campsite managers, and almost all hostel managers, speak some English.

Problems arise mainly **between July 15 and the end of August**, when the French take their own holidays en masse. The first weekend of August is the busiest time of all. During this period, hotel and hostel accommodation can be hard

to come by – particularly in the coastal resorts – and you may find yourself falling back on local tourist offices for help and ideas. With campsites, you can be more relaxed, unless you're touring with a caravan or camper van.

The **tourist season** in Brittany and Normandy runs roughly from Easter until the end of September; while hotels in the cities remain open all year, those in smaller towns and, especially, seaside resorts often close for several months during the winter. It's quite possible to turn up somewhere in January or February to find that every hotel is closed; in addition, many family-run places close each year for two or three weeks sometime between May and September, and some hotels in smaller towns and villages close for one or two nights a week, usually Sunday or Monday. Closing dates for each establishment are indicated throughout the book, but it's worth checking ahead if you're in any doubt.

HOTELS

French **hotels** tend to be consistently better value than they are in Britain and much of northern Europe. Recommendations are given in the *Guide* for almost every town or village mentioned, with their prices indicated by the symbols ①, ②, ③, etc, as explained in the box below. In most towns, you'll be able to get a double room for around 180–240F/€27.44–36.59 (£18–24/US$26–35), or a single for around 150–180F/€22.87–27.44 (£15–18/US$21–26), though often if you're prepared to pay a little extra you can get something really special.

ACCOMMODATION PRICE CODES

All **hotel prices** in this book have been coded using the symbols below. The price shown is for the **cheapest double room in high season**, which, for categories ① and ② especially, often means a room without private bath, shower or toilet, though there's usually a washbasin. Most hotels in those categories also have a number of rooms with en-suite facilities, which typically cost around 40–60F/€6.10–9.15 extra. In the ③ category and above, all rooms tend to be equipped with private facilities.

Although many hotels offer rooms at differing prices, ranges (such as ②–⑦) are only indicated when the spectrum is especially broad, or where there are relatively few rooms in the lowest category.

① Under 160F/€24
② 160–220F/€24–34
③ 220–300F/€34–46

④ 300–400F/€46–61
⑤ 400–500F/€61–76
⑥ 500–600F/€76–91

⑦ 600–700F/€91–107
⑧ 700–800F/€107–122
⑨ Over 800F/€122

All French hotels are **graded** from zero to five stars. The price more or less corresponds to the number of stars, though the system is a little haphazard, having more to do with ratios of bathrooms per guest than genuine quality; ungraded and single-star hotels are often very good.

At the cheapest level, what makes a difference in **cost** is whether a room contains a shower: if it does, the bill will be around 35–60F/€5–9 higher. **Breakfast**, too, can add 25–45F/€4–7 per person, though there is no obligation to take it. The cost of eating **dinner** in a hotel's restaurant can be a more important factor to bear in mind when picking a place to stay. Officially, hotels are not supposed to insist that you take meals, but they often do, and in busy resorts you may not find a room unless you agree to *démi-pension* (half board). If you are unsure, ask to see the menu before checking in; cheap rooms aren't so cheap if you have to eat a 100F/€15 meal.

Genuine **single rooms** are rare; lone travellers normally end up in an ordinary double let at a slightly reduced rate. On the other hand most hotels willingly equip rooms with **extra beds**, for three or more people, at a good discount.

Especially if you're travelling in peak season, try to pick up the full **accommodation lists** available from any French Government Tourist Office (see p.26) or local SI. Look out too for the **Logis et Auberges de France**, which are independent hotels, promoted together for their consistently good food and reasonably priced rooms; they're recognizable on the spot by a green-and-yellow logo of a hearth. They have a central reservation number (☎01.45.84.83.84, fax 01.45.83.59.66) and Web site (*www.logis-de-france.fr*), which you can contact to obtain their free yearly guide (or write to 88 av d'Italie, 75013 Paris).

One of the great pleasures of travelling in the region is the sheer quality of **village hotels**. The fixtures and fittings may not always date from the twentieth century, let alone the twenty-first – at the bottom of the range, you'll find corduroy carpets creeping up the walls, blotchy linoleum curling from buckled wooden floors, and clanking great brass keys that won't quite turn in the ill-fitting doors – but the standards of service are consistently high, and it's rare indeed to stay in a hotel that doesn't take pride in maintaining a well-appointed and good-value restaurant serving traditional local food.

In recent years, outlets of several French **motel chains** have begun to proliferate, usually located alongside major through-routes on the outskirts of larger towns. Other than close to the ferry ports, there are fewer of these in Brittany and Normandy than elsewhere in the country, but those that do exist make a good alternative option for motorists, especially late at night. Among the cheapest is the one-star **Formule 1** chain, which tends to be characterless, but provides rooms for up to three people from 140F/€21.34. With a Visa, MasterCard, Eurocard or American Express credit card, you can let yourself into a room at any hour of the day or night. Other inexpensive chains include 1er Classe, Étap Hôtel and Balladins; more comfortable but still affordable chain hotels are **Campanile** (*www.campanile.fr*), **Ibis** (*www.ibis.fr*) and **Clarine** (*www.clarine.fr*), which all have en-suite rooms with cable TV and direct dial phones from 270–320F/€41–49. All three of these hotel chains can be reached by Internet and will accept reservations by email. They will also send a complete list of their locations in France by email request within a few days.

Several cities in Brittany and Normandy participate in the "**Bonne Weekend en Ville**" programme, whereby you book through the local tourist office and get two nights for the price of one (Oct–May only) at participating hotels, as well as an array of discount coupons and special deals. Participating towns include Rouen, Rennes and Dinan, but the list is growing, so it is worth enquiring about when you are making arrangements to stay in larger towns.

BED AND BREAKFAST, RENTED ACCOMMODATION AND GÎTES

In country areas, in addition to standard hotels, you will come across **chambres d'hôte**, bed-and-breakfast accommodation in someone's house or farm. These vary in standard, but are rarely an especially cheap option; they usually cost the equivalent of a two-star hotel. However, if you strike lucky, they can be good sources of traditional home cooking. Brown leaflets available in SIs list most of them.

If you are planning to stay a week or more in any one place it's worth considering **renting a house**. British travellers can check the adverts from private and foreign owners in Sunday newspapers (the *Observer* and *Sunday Times*, mainly); the boxes on pp.8, 12 and 16 of this book list holiday firms across the world that market accommodation/travel packages.

Alternatively you could contact **Gîtes de France**, 59 rue St-Lazare, Paris 75009 (Mon–Sat 10am–6.30pm; ☎01.49.70.75.75, *www.gites-de-france.fr*), a government-funded agency which promotes and manages bed-and-breakfast and self-catering accommodation in France, the latter usually consisting of a self-contained country cottage, known as a **gîte rural** or **gîte de séjour**. Further details can be found in their two very useful national guides – *Chambres et Tables d'Hôtes* and *Chambres d'Hôtes de Prestige et Gîtes de Charme*, both costing 120F/€18.30 – which are also sometimes on sale in bookstores and tourist offices.

HOSTELS, FOYERS AND GÎTES D'ÉTAPE

At anything from 60F/€9.15 up to 120F/€18.30 per night for a dormitory bed, **Auberges de Jeunesse** – youth hostels – are invaluable for single budget travellers. For couples, however, and certainly for groups of three or more people, they'll not necessarily work out less than the cheaper hotels – particularly if you've had to pay a bus fare out to the edge of town to reach them. However, many of the hostels in Normandy and Brittany are beautifully sited, and they do allow you to cut costs by preparing your own food in their kitchens, or eating in cheap canteens.

Slightly confusingly, there are three rival French hostelling associations (see box, below). The main two are the Fédération Unie des Auberges de Jeunesse (FUAJ; 180 hostels), whose hostels are detailed in the *International Handbook*, and the Ligue Française pour les Auberges de Jeunesse (LFAJ; 100 hostels). To stay at hostels run by either of these organizations, you must be a member of Hostelling International (HI) or the International Youth Hostel Federation (IYHF). Head offices are listed in the box below. If you don't join up before you leave

HOSTELLING ASSOCIATIONS

FRANCE

Fédération Unie des Auberges de Jeunesse (FUAJ), 27 rue Pajol, 75018 Paris, ☎01.44.89.87.27, *www.fuaj.org*.

Ligue Française pour les Auberges de Jeunesse (LFAJ), 38 bd Raspail, 75007 Paris, ☎01.45.48.69.84.

Union des Centres de Rencontres Internationales de France (UCRIF), 27 rue Turbigo, 75002 Paris, ☎01.40.26.57.64, *ucrif@aol.com*.

AUSTRALIA

Youth Hostel Association, 422 Kent St, Sydney, NSW 2000, ☎02/9261 1111, *www.yha.com.au*.

CANADA

Hostelling International/Canadian Hostelling Association, Suite 400, 205 Catherine St, Ottawa, ON K2P 1C3, ☎613/237-7884.

ENGLAND AND WALES

Youth Hostel Association (YHA), Trevelyan House, 8 St Stephen's Hill, St Alban's, Herts AL1 2DY, ☎0870/870 8808; 14 Southampton St, London WC2 7HY, ☎020/7836 8541, *www.yha.org.uk*.

IRELAND

An Oige, 61 Mountjoy St, Dublin 7, ☎01/830 4555, *www.irelandyha.org*.

Youth Hostels Association of Northern Ireland, 22 Donegal Rd, Belfast BT12 5JN, ☎028/9031 5435, *www.hini.org.uk*.

NEW ZEALAND

Youth Hostels Association of New Zealand, 173 Gloucester St, Christchurch, ☎03/379 9970, *www.yha.co.nz*.

SCOTLAND

Scottish Youth Hostel Association, 7 Glebe Crescent, Stirling FK8 2JA, ☎01786/451181, *www.syha.org.uk*.

US

Hostelling International, 733 15th St NW, #840, PO Box 37613, Washington DC 20005, ☎202/783 6161, *www.hiayh.org*.

home, a membership card can be purchased in relevant French hostels for 100F/€15.24. The third organization is the Union des Centres de Rencontres Internationales de France (UCRIF), with 60 hostels in France; membership is not required.

A few large towns provide a more luxurious standard of hostel accommodation in **Foyers des Jeunes Travailleurs/euses**, residential hostels for young workers and students, where you can usually get a private room for around 65F/€10. They normally have a good cafeteria or canteen.

A further hostel-type alternative exists in the countryside, especially in hiking or cycling areas, in the form of the **gîtes d'étape**. These are less formal than the hostels, often run by the local village or municipality (whose mayor may well hold the key), and provide basic hospital-style beds and simple kitchen facilities from around 40F/€6. They are marked on the large-scale IGN walkers' maps and listed in individual GR *Topoguides*. More information can be found in the guides *Gîtes d'Étapes et Sejours* (60F/€9.12), published by Gîtes de France (see overleaf), and *Gîtes d'Étape et Refuges*, published by Guides La Cadole, available in French bookshops for 110F/€16.78.

CAMPING

Practically every village and town in the country has at least one **campsite**, to cater for the thousands of French people who spend their holiday under canvas. The tourist boards for both Brittany and Normandy produce full lists of sites in their regions.

The cheapest – at around 25–35F/€4–5.50 per person per night – is usually the **Camping municipal**, run by the local municipality. In season or when they are officially open, they are always clean, with plenty of hot water, and often situated in the prime local position. Out of sea-

son, many of them don't even bother to have someone around to collect the overnight charge.

On the coast especially, there are **superior categories** of campsite, where you'll pay prices similar to those of a hotel for the facilities – bars, restaurants, sometimes swimming pools. These have a rather less transitory population than the *Camping municipals*, with people often spending a whole holiday in the one base. If you plan to do the same – particularly if you've a caravan, camper van or substantial tent – book ahead. Reckon on paying at least 35F/€5.34 per head with a tent, 40F/€6.10 with a camper van.

Inland, **camping à la ferme** – on somebody's farm – is another (generally facility-less) possibility. Lists of sites are detailed in the tourist board's free booklet *Accueil à la Campagne*.

If you're planning to do a lot of camping, an **international camping carnet** is a good investment. The carnet serves as useful identification, covers you for third-party insurance when camping, and helps you get 10 percent reductions at campsites listed in the CCI information booklet that comes with your carnet. It is available in the UK from the AA (☎0800/444500, *www.theaa.co.uk*), the RAC (☎0800/550055, *www.rac.co.uk*), or the Carefree Travel Service (☎01203/422024), who also book inspected camping sites in Europe and arrange ferry crossings; in the US from Family Campers and RVers (FCRV), 4804 Transit Rd, Building 2, Depew, NY 14043 (☎1-800/245-9755); and in Canada from FCRV, 51 W 22nd St, Hamilton, ON LC9 4N5 (also ☎1-800/245-9755).

Lastly, a **word of caution**: never camp rough (*camping sauvage*, as the French call it) on anyone's land without first asking permission. If the dogs don't get you, the guns might – farmers have been known to shoot before asking any questions. In many parts of France *camping sauvage* on public land is not tolerated – Brittany is the notable exception. On beaches it's best to camp out where there are other people doing so.

EATING AND DRINKING

The superb range of food available has to rank among the principal reasons to visit Brittany and, especially, Normandy. Restaurant quality is consistently high, prices remain reasonable and, to be honest, there are towns and villages where just about the only source of excitement is their gastronomic output.

With no wine production in Normandy (and only the Muscadet-style whites coming from the southeast of Brittany), the most interesting local **alcohol** is that derived from the region's orchards. **Cider** is made everywhere, along with its pear equivalent, **poiré**; and there is of course Norman **Calvados** (apple brandy), as well as numerous local firewaters.

BRETON FOOD

Brittany's proudest addition to world cuisine has to be the (white-flour) **crêpe** and its savoury (buckwheat) equivalent, the **galette**. Crêperies throughout the region attempt to pass them off as satisfying meals, served with every imaginable filling. However, few people seriously plan their holidays around eating pancakes, and gourmets are more likely to be enticed to Brittany by its magnificent array of **seafood**, shellfish above all – mussels, oysters, clams, scallops. Restaurants in resorts such as **St-Malo** and **Quiberon** jostle for the attention of fish fanatics, while smaller towns – such as **Cancale**, which specializes in oysters (*huîtres*), and **Erquy**, with its scallops (*Coquilles St-Jacques*) – go so far as to depend on a single specific mollusc for their livelihood.

Although they can't claim to be uniquely Breton, two appetizers feature on every self-respecting menu. These are **moules marinières**, giant bowls of succulent orange mussels steamed open in white wine, shallots and parsley (and perhaps enriched with cream or *crème fraîche* to become *moules à la crème*), and **soupe de poissons**, served with a pot of the garlicky mayonnaise known as *rouille* (coloured with pulverized sweet red pepper) and a bowl of *croutons*. Jars of *soupe de poissons* – or crab, or lobster – are always on sale in seaside poissonneries, and make an ideal way to take a taste of France home with you. Paying a little extra in a restaurant – typically on menus costing 150F/€22.87 or more – brings you into the realm of the **assiette de fruits de mer**, a mountainous heap of langoustines, crabs, oysters, mussels, clams, whelks and cockles, most of them raw and all (with certain obvious exceptions) delicious. **Main courses** tend to be plainer than in Normandy, with fresh local fish being prepared with relatively simple sauces. Skate served with capers, or salmon baked with a mustard or cheese sauce, are typical dishes, while even the **cotriade**, a stew containing such fish as sole, turbot or bass, as well as shellfish, is distinctly less rich than the Mediterranean *bouillabaisse*.

Brittany is also better than much of France in maintaining its respect for fresh green **vegetables**, thanks to the extensive local production of peas, cauliflowers, artichokes and the like. Only with the **desserts** can things get rather too heavy; **far Breton**, considered a great delicacy, is a stodgy baked concoction of sponge, custard and chopped plums, while *îles flottantes* are meringue icebergs adrift in a sea of *crème brûlée* or custard.

NORMAN FOOD

The food of **Normandy** owes its most distinctive characteristic – its gut-bursting, heart-pounding richness – to the lush orchards and dairy herds of the region's agricultural heartland, and most especially the area southeast of Caen known as the Pays d'Auge. Menus abound in meat such as veal (*veau*) cooked in *vallée d'Auge* style, which consists largely of the profligate addition of cream and butter. Many dishes also feature

WEEKLY MARKETS

The list below features the biggest and best of the **markets** of Brittany and Normandy, with a particular emphasis on those specializing in **fresh food** and local produce.

Bear in mind that in addition to the specific days listed here, most large cities – **Rennes**, **Rouen** and **Caen**, for example – tend to have markets every day (with the occasional exception of Mon).

	NORMANDY	BRITTANY
Monday	Bricquebec, Carentan, Pont-Audemer, Pont L'Éveque, St-Pierre-sur-Dives, Vimoutiers	Auray, Combourg, Concarneau, Douarnenez, Lesneven, Ploërmel, Questembert, Redon, Vitré
Tuesday	Argentan, Bagnoles, Barfleur, Brionne, Lessay, Portbail, St-Lô, Villedieu-les-Poêles	Le Conquet, Locmariaquer, Paimpol, Pont-Aven, St-Malo, St-Pol, La Trinité
Wednesday	Alençon, Carrouges, Évreux, Falaise, Orbec, Pontorson, Sées, Yvetot	Carnac, Douarnenez, Guérande, Quimper, Roscoff, St-Brieuc, Tréguier, Vannes
Thursday	Alençon, Bellême, Carteret, Cherbourg, Conches-en-Ouche, Coutances, Deauville, Étretat, Forges-les-Eaux, Ste-Mère-Église	Binic, Dinan, Hennebont, Lamballe, Lannion, Malestroit
Friday	Argentan, Domfront, Eu, Pont-Audemer, St-Valéry, Valognes, Vimoutiers, Vire	Concarneau, Douarnenez, Guingamp, Jugon-les-Lacs, Perros-Guirec, Quimper, Quimperlé, St-Malo, Le Val-André
Saturday	Avranches, Bagnoles, Barfleur, Bayeux, Caudebec, Cherbourg, Dieppe, Domfront, Falaise, Granville, Honfleur, Le Tréport, Lisieux, Mortagne-au-Perche, Orbec, Ry, St-Lô, St-Vaast	Audierne, Dinard, Douarnenez, Erquy, Fougères, Guérande, Guingamp, Josselin, Locmariaquer, Morlaix, Paramé, Quimper, St-Brieuc, Vannes
Sunday	Alençon, Argentan, Brionne, La Ferrière-sur-Risle, St-Valéry (summer only)	Auray, Cancale, Carnac, Quimper

orchard fruit, either in its natural state or in successively more alcoholic forms – either as apple or pear cider, or perhaps further distilled to produce brandies (Calvados in the case of apples, *poiré* for pears).

Normans have a great propensity for blood and guts. In addition to game such as rabbit and duck (a speciality in Rouen, where the birds are strangled to ensure that all their blood gets into the sauce), they enjoy such intestinal preparations as *andouilles*, the blood sausages known in English as chitterlings, and *tripes*, stewed for hours *à la mode de Caen*, but rendered no less palatable.

A full blowout at country restaurants in the small towns of inland Normandy – places like Conches, Vire and towns in the Suisse Normande

– will also traditionally entail one or two pauses between courses for the *trou normand* – a glass of Calvados while you catch your breath before struggling on with the feast.

Normandy's long coastline ensures that it too is a great place for **seafood**, serving up much the same range of shellfish as detailed for Brittany, overleaf. Many of the larger ports and resorts have long waterfront lines of competing restaurants, each with its "*copieuse*" *assiette de fruits de mer*. **Honfleur** is probably the most enjoyable of these, but **Dieppe**, **Cherbourg** and **Trouville** also spring to mind as offering endless eating opportunities. The menus tend to be much the same as those on offer in Brittany, if perhaps slightly more expensive.

The most famous products of Normandy's meadow-munching cows are, of course, its **cheeses**. The best-known cheeses from the area covered by this book – such as *Pont l'Evêque*, *Livarot* and, most famous of all, *Camembert* – all come from the Pays d'Auge region of Normandy, and are discussed in detail in the box on p.178.

CAFÉS AND SNACKS

The days when hotels gave you mounds of croissants or *brioches* for **breakfast** seem to be long gone; now it's virtually always bread, jam and a jug of coffee or tea for at least 30F/€4.57. It makes more sense to pick up a croissant, *pain au chocolat* (a chocolate-filled croissant) or sandwich in a bar or café, for a fraction of the price, and wash it down with hot chocolate or coffee.

For **midday meals and light snacks**, most bars and cafés – there's no real difference – advertise *les snacks*, or *un casse-croûte* (a bite), with pictures of omelettes, fried eggs, hot dogs or various sandwiches. Even when they don't, they'll usually make you a half or third of a *baguette* (French bread stick), buttered (*tartine*) and filled. Likely ingredients include *jambon* (ham), *fromage* (cheese), *thon* (tuna), *saucisson* (sausage) or *poulet* (chicken). Toasted sandwiches – most commonly *croques-monsieur* (cheese and ham) or *croques-madame* (cheese and bacon or sausage) – are also invariably on offer. Especially in rural areas, small bars may serve a moderate-priced *plat du jour* (chef's daily special) or *formule* (a limited or no-choice menu).

Many people also recommend **crêpes** for lunch. However, they may taste nice enough, but unless you buy from a market stall *crêpes* are extraordinarily poor value compared to a restaurant meal; you need to eat at least three, normally at over 25F/€3.81 each, to feel even slightly full. That they seem to excite children – presumably because they can drench them in chocolate syrup – shouldn't fool parents into thinking of a crêperie as a cheap alternative.

For **picnic and takeaway food**, nothing beats buying fresh ingredients in one of the numerous local **markets**, details of which are given in the box opposite. If there isn't a market around on the day you need it, you'll find charcuteries (delicatessens) everywhere – even in small villages. These sell cooked meats, prepared snacks such as *bouchées de la reine* (seafood vol-au-vents), ready-made dishes and assorted salads. You can buy by weight or ask for *une tranche* (a slice), *une barquette* (a carton) or *une part* (a portion). The cheapest, in towns, are the supermarkets' charcuterie counters.

Salons de thé, which open from mid-morning to late evening, serve brunches, salads, quiches, etc, as well as cake and ice cream and a wide selection of teas. They tend to be a good deal pricier than cafés or brasseries – you're paying for the ritzy surroundings.

Patisseries, of course, have impressive arrays of cakes and pastries, often using local cream to excess. In addition to standard French pastries, the Bretons specialize in heavy, pudding-like affairs, dripping with butter, such as *kouïgn-anann*, and in *gaufres*, cream-drenched waffles.

RESTAURANTS

Brittany and Normandy hold an abundance of **restaurants**, and in many towns **brasseries** add to the choice. There's no distinction between the two in terms of quality or price range, though brasseries, which resemble cafés, serve quicker meals at most hours of the day; restaurants tend to stick to the traditional meal times of noon until 2pm and 7pm to 9.30pm. After 9pm or so, restaurants often serve only *à la carte* meals – invariably more expensive than eating the set *menu fixe*. For the

VEGETARIANS

On the whole, **vegetarians** can expect a somewhat lean time in Brittany and Normandy. One or two towns have specifically vegetarian restaurants (detailed in the text), but elsewhere you'll have to hope you find a sympathetic restaurant (crêperies can be good standbys). Sometimes they're willing to replace a meat dish on the *menu fixe* with an omelette; other times you'll have to pick your way through the *carte*. Remember the phrase *je suis végétarien(ne); il y a quelques plats sans viande?* (I'm a vegetarian; are there any non-meat dishes?).

Many vegetarians swallow a few principles and start eating fish and shellfish on holiday; that of course is a matter for your conscience. If you are a vegan, however, you should probably forget about eating in French restaurants and cook your own food.

FOOD AND DISHES

BASICS

Addition	Bill/check	*À emporter*	Takeaway	*Poivre*	Pepper
Beurre	Butter	*Fourchette*	Fork	*Salé*	Salted/Spicy
Bouteille	Bottle	*Fumé*	Smoked	*Sel*	Salt
Chauffé	Heated	*Huile*	Oil	*Sucre*	Sugar
Couteau	Knife	*Lait*	Milk	*Sucré*	Sweet
Cru	Raw	*Moutarde*	Mustard	*Table*	Table
Cuillère	Spoon	*Oeuf*	Egg	*Verre*	Glass
Cuit	Cooked	*Offert*	Free	*Vinaigre*	Vinegar
Emballé	Wrapped	*Pain*	Bread		

SNACKS

Crêpe	Pancake (sweet)	*durs*	Hard-boiled eggs
au sucre	with sugar	*brouillés*	Scrambled eggs
au citron	with lemon	*Nouilles*	Noodles
au miel	with honey	*Omelette . . .*	Omelette . . .
à la confiture	with jam	*nature*	plain
aux oeufs	with eggs	*aux fines herbes*	with herbs
à la crème	with cream	*au fromage*	with cheese
de marrons	with chestnut purée	*Pâtes fraîches*	Fresh pasta
Galette	Buckwheat (savoury) pancake	*Pissaladière*	Tart of fried onions with anchovies and black olives
Un sandwich/ une baguette . . .	A sandwich		
jambon	with ham	*Salade de . . .*	Salad of . . .
romage	with cheese	*tomates*	tomatoes
saucisson	with sausage	*betteraves*	beetroot
à l'ail	with garlic	*concombres*	cucumber
au poivre	with pepper	*carottes râpées*	grated carrots
pâté	with pâté		
(de campagne)	(country-style)	**Other fillings/salads**	
Croque-monsieur	Grilled cheese and ham sandwich	*Anchois*	Anchovy
		Andouillette	Tripe sausage
Croque-madame	Grilled cheese and bacon, sausage, chicken or an egg sandwich	*Boudin*	Black pudding
		Coeurs de palmiers	Palm hearts
		Fonds d'artichauts	Artichoke hearts
		Hareng	Herring
Oeufs	Eggs	*Langue*	Tongue
au plat	Fried eggs	*Poulet*	Chicken
à la coque	Boiled eggs	*Thon*	Tuna fish

SOUPS (SOUPES) AND STARTERS (HORS D'OEUVRES)

Bisque	Shellfish soup		mayonnaise served with fish soup
Bouillabaisse	Marseillais fish soup		
		Velouté	Thick soup, usually fish or poultry
Bouillon	Broth or stock		
Bourride	Thick fish soup	**Starters**	
Consommé	Clear soup	*Assiette anglaise*	Plate of cold meats
Pistou	Parmesan, basil and garlic paste added to soup	*Crudités*	Raw vegetables with dressings
		Escargots	Snails
Potage	Thick vegetable soup	*Hors d'oeuvres*	Combination of the above
Rouille	Red pepper, garlic and saffron	*variés*	plus smoked or marinated fish

FISH (POISSON), SEAFOOD (FRUITS DE MER) AND SHELLFISH (CRUSTACES OR COQUILLAGES)

Amandes	Clams	*Homard*	Lobster
Anchois	Anchovies	*Huîtres*	Oysters
Anguilles	Eels	*Julienne*	Ling
Araigné	Spider crab	*Langouste*	Spiny lobster
Bar	Bass	*Langoustines*	Saltwater crayfish (scampi)
Barbue	Brill		
Baudroie	Monkfish or anglerfish	*Lieu*	Pollock
		Limande	Lemon sole
Bigourneau	Periwinkle	*Lotte*	Burbot
Brème	Bream	*Lotte de mer*	Monkfish
Bulots	Whelks	*Loup de mer*	Sea bass
Cabillaud	Cod	*Louvine,*	Similar to
Calmar	Squid	*loubine*	sea bass
Carrelet	Plaice	*Maquereau*	Mackerel
Claire	Type of oyster	*Merlan*	Whiting
		Morue	Cod
Colin	Hake	*Moules*	Mussels
Congre	Conger eel	*(mariniére)*	(with shallots in white-wine sauce)
Coques	Cockles		
Coquilles St-Jacques	Scallops	*Oursin*	Sea urchin
		Palourdes	Clams
Crabe	Crab	*Praires*	Small clams
Crevettes grises	Shrimp	*Raie*	Skate
Crevettes roses	Prawns	*Rouget*	Red mullet
Daurade	Sea bream	*St Pierre*	John Dory
Écrevisses	Crayfish	*Saumon*	Salmon
Éperlan	Smelt or whitebait	*Sole*	Sole
Flétan	Halibut	*Thon*	Tuna
Friture	Assorted fried fish	*Truite*	Trout
Gambas	King prawns	*Turbot*	Turbot
Hareng	Herring		

FISH: SOME TERMS

Aïoli	Garlic mayonnaise served with salt cod and other fish	*Frit*	Fried
		Friture	Deep-fried small fish
		Fumé	Smoked
Arête	Fish bone	*Fumet*	Fish stock
Assiette de fruits de mer	Assorted shellfish	*Gigot de mer*	Large fish baked whole
		Grillé	Grilled
Assiette de pêcheur	Assorted fish	*Hollandaise*	Butter and vinegar sauce
Béarnaise	Sauce made with egg yolks, white wine, shallots and vinegar	*À la meunière*	In a butter, lemon and parsley sauce
		Mousse, mousseline	Mousse
Beignets	Fritters	*Pané*	Breaded
Darne	Fillet or steak	*Quenelles*	Light dumplings
La douzaine	A dozen		**continues over**

MEAT (VIANDE) AND POULTRY (VOLAILLE)

Agneau (de pré-salé)	Lamb (grazed on salt marshes)	Langue	Tongue
Andouille, andouillette	Tripe sausage	Lapin, lapereau	Rabbit, young rabbit
Boeuf	Beef	Lard, lardons	Bacon, diced bacon
Bifteck	Steak	Lièvre	Hare
Boudin blanc	Sausage of white meats	Merguez	Spicy, red sausage
Boudin noir	Black pudding	Mouton	Mutton
Caille	Quail	Museau de veau	Calf's muzzle
Canard	Duck	Oie	Goose
Caneton	Duckling	Os	Bone
Contrefilet	Sirloin roast	Porc	Pork
Coquelet	Cockerel	Poulet	Chicken
Dinde, dindon	Turkey	Poussin	Baby chicken
Entrecôte	Ribsteak	Ris	Sweetbreads
Faux filet	Sirloin steak	Rognons	Kidneys
Foie	Liver	Rognons blancs	Testicles
Foie gras	Fattened (duck/goose) liver	Sanglier	Wild boar
Gigot (d'agneau)	Leg (of lamb)	Steak	Steak
Grillade	Grilled meat	Tête de veau	Calf's head (in jelly)
Hâchis	Chopped meat or mince hamburger	Tournedos	Thick slices of fillet
		Tripes	Tripe
		Veau	Veal
		Venaison	Venison

MEAT AND POULTRY: DISHES AND TERMS

Boeuf bourguignon	Beef stew with burgundy, onions and mushrooms	Carré	Best end of neck, chop or cutlet
Canard à l'orange	Roast duck with an orange-and-wine sauce	Civit	Game stew
		Confit	Meat preserve
Cassoulet	A casserole of beans and meat	Côte	Chop, cutlet or rib
		Cou	Neck
Coq au vin	Chicken cooked until it falls off the bone with wine, onions and mushrooms	Cuisse	Thigh or leg
		En croûte	In pastry
		Epaule	Shoulder
Steak au poivre (vert/rouge)	Steak in a black (green/red) peppercorn sauce	Farci	Stuffed
		Garni	With vegetables
Steak tartare	Raw chopped beef, topped with a raw egg yolk	Gésier	Gizzard
		Grillé	Grilled
		Magret de canard	Duck breast
Terms		Marmite	Casserole
Aile	Wing	Médaillon	Round piece
Au feu de bois	Cooked over wood fire	Mijoté	Stewed
Au four	Baked	Museau	Muzzle
Blanquette,	Type of stew	Onglet	Cut of beef
daube,	Type of stew	Pavé	Thick slice
estouffade,	Type of stew	Poitrine	Breast
hochepôt,	Type of stew	Râble	Saddle
navarin	Type of stew		
and ragoût	Type of stew		

Rôti	Roast
Sauté	Lightly cooked in butter
Viennoise	Fried in egg and bread crumbs

For steaks

A point	Medium
Bien cuit	Well done
Bleu	Almost raw
Brochette	Kebab
Saignant	Rare
Très bien cuit	Very well cooked

Garnishes and sauces

Beurre blanc	Sauce of white wine and shallots, with butter
Bonne femme	Mushroom, bacon, potato and onions
Bourgeoise	Carrots, onions and bacon.
Chasseur	White wine, mushrooms and shallots
Diable	Strong mustard seasoning
Forestière	With bacon and mushroom
Fricassée	Rich, creamy sauce
Mornay	Cheese sauce
Pays d'Auge	Cream and cider
Piquante	Gherkins or capers, vinegar and shallots
Provençale	Tomatoes, garlic, olive oil and herbs
Savoyarde	Gruyère cheese

VEGETABLES (LÉGUMES), HERBS (HERBES) AND SPICES (ÉPICES), ETC

Ail	Garlic
Algue	Seaweed
Anis	Aniseed
Artichaut	Artichoke
Asperges	Asparagus
Avocat	Avocado
Basilic	Basil
Betterave	Beetroot
Carotte	Carrot
Céleri	Celery
Champignons, cèpes, chanterelles	Mushrooms of various kinds
Chou (rouge)	(Red) cabbage
Choufleur	Cauliflower
Ciboulettes	Chives
Concombre	Cucumber
Cornichon	Gherkin
Échalotes	Shallots
Endive	Chicory
Épinards	Spinach
Estragon	Tarragon
Fenouil	Fennel
Flageolets	White beans
Gingembre	Ginger
Haricots	Beans
verts (French)	string
rouges	kidney
beurres	butter
Laurier	Bay leaf
Lentilles	Lentils
Maïs	Corn
Menthe	Mint
Moutarde	Mustard
Oignon	Onion
Pâte	Pasta, pastry
Persil	Parsley
Petits pois	Peas
Pignons	Pine nuts
Piment	Pimento
Poireau	Leek
Pois chiches	Chick peas
Pois mange-touts	Snow peas
Poivron	Sweet pepper
(vert, rouge)	(green, red)
Pommes (de terre)	Potatoes
Primeurs	Spring vegetables
Radis	Radishes
Riz	Rice
Safran	Saffron
Salade verte	Green salad
Sarrasin	Buckwheat
Tomate	Tomato
Truffes	Truffles

VEGETABLES: DISHES AND TERMS

Beignet	Fritter
Farci	Stuffed
Gratiné	Browned with cheese or butter
Jardinière	With mixed, diced vegetables
À la parisienne	Sautéed in butter (potatoes); with white-wine sauce and shallots
Parmentier	With potatoes
Sauté	Lightly fried in butter
À la vapeur	Steamed
Je suis végétarien(ne).	I'm a vegetarian.
Il y a quelques plats sans viande?	Are there any non-meat dishes?

continues over

FRUITS (FRUITS) AND NUTS (NOIX)

Abricot	Apricot	*Melon*	Melon
Amandes	Almonds	*Myrtilles*	Bilberries
Ananas	Pineapple	*Noisette*	Hazelnut
Banane	Banana	*Noix*	Nuts
Brugnon,		*Orange*	Orange
nectarine	Nectarine	*Pamplemousse*	Grapefruit
Cacahouète	Peanut	*Pêche (blanche)*	(White) peach
Cassis	Blackcurrants	*Pistache*	Pistachio
Cérises	Cherries	*Poire*	Pear
Citron	Lemon	*Pomme*	Apple
Citron vert	Lime	*Prune*	Plum
Figues	Figs	*Pruneau*	Prune
Fraises	Strawberries	*Raisins*	Grapes
(de bois)	(wild)		
Framboises	Raspberries	**Terms**	
Fruit de		*Beignets*	Fritter
la passion	Passion fruit	*Compôte de . . .*	Stewed . . .
Groseilles	Redcurrants	*Coulis*	Sauce
	and goose-	*Flambé*	Set aflame in
	berries		alcohol
Mangue	Mango		
Marrons	Chestnuts	*Frappé*	Iced

DESSERTS (DESSERTS OR ENTREMETS) AND PASTRIES (PÂTISSERIE)

Bombe	A moulded ice-cream dessert	*Palmiers*	Caramelized puff pastries
Brioche	Sweet, high-yeast breakfast roll	*Parfait*	Frozen mousse, sometimes ice cream
Charlotte	Custard and fruit in lining of almond fingers	*Petit Suisse*	A smooth mixture of cream and curds
Crème Chantilly	Vanilla-flavoured and sweetened whipped cream	*Petits fours*	Bite-sized cakes, pastries
Crème fraîche	Sour cream	*Poires Belle Hélène*	Pears and ice cream in chocolate sauce
Crème pâtissière	Thick, eggy pastry-filling	*Yaourt, yogourt*	Yogurt
Crêpes Suzettes	Thin pancakes with orange juice and liqueur		
		Terms	
Fromage blanc	Cream cheese	*Barquette*	Small boat-shaped flan
Glace	Ice cream	*Bavarois*	Refers to the mould, could be a mousse or custard
Île flottante/ oeufs à la neie	Soft meringues floating on custard	*Coupe*	A serving of ice cream
Macarons	Macaroons	*Crêpes*	Pancakes
Madeleine	Small sponge cake	*Galettes*	Buckwheat pancakes
Marrons Mont Blanc	Chestnut purée and cream on a rum-soaked sponge cake	*Gênoise*	Rich sponge cake
		Sablé	Shortbread biscuit
		Savarin	A filled, ring-shaped cake
Mousse au chocolat	Chocolate mousse	*Tarte*	Tart
		Tartelette	Small tart

more upmarket places it's wise to make reservations – easily done on the same day. In small towns it may be impossible to get anything other than a bar sandwich after 10pm; in major cities, central brasseries will serve until 11pm or midnight and one or two may stay open all night. Don't forget that hotel restaurants are open to nonresidents, and are often very good value; the green-and-yellow logis de France symbol is always worth looking out for. On the road, keep an eye open too for the red-and-blue sign of the Relais Routiers – always reasonably priced and gastronomically sound.

Prices and what you get for them are posted outside. Normally there is a choice between one or more **menus fixes** (set menus), where the number of courses has already been determined, the choice is limited, and service is included, and the **carte**, the full menu.

At the bottom price range, say below 75F/€11.43, *menus fixes* revolve around standard dishes, such as steak and chips (*steak frites*), chicken and chips (*poulet frites*) or various offal concoctions, though it's always worth looking out for the *plat du jour*, which may be more appealing. For 85F/€13 to 150F/€23, virtually any of the restaurants recommended in this guide will serve you a good three-course meal, while four-course blowouts, including a starter as well as separate meat and fish courses, cost from 150F/€23 to 300F/€46. Most expensive of the lot are the special seafood menus, offering giant platters of assorted crustaceans; away from the big centres such as Cancale and St-Malo, it pays to be wary of these, as the stuff may have been waiting around for several days for someone foolhardy enough to order it.

Going **à la carte** offers greater flexibility and, in the better restaurants, access to the chef's specialities, but you can expect to pay heavily for the privilege. A simple and perfectly legitimate ploy is to have just one course instead of the expected three or four. You can share dishes or just have several starters – a useful strategy for vegetarians. There's no minimum charge.

North American visitors should bear in mind that in France, an *entrée* is an appetizer or starter; the main course of the meal is the *plat principal*. In the French sequence of courses, any salad (sometimes vegetables, too) comes separate from the main dish, and cheese precedes a dessert. You will be offered coffee, which always costs extra, to finish off the meal.

Service compris (*s.c.*) means the **service charge** is included, which is usually the case on all set menus; *service non compris* (*s.n.c.*), or *service en sus*, means that it isn't, and you need to calculate an additional fifteen percent. **Wine** (*vin*) or a **drink** (*boisson*) is unlikely to be included, although a glass is occasionally thrown in with cheaper menus. When ordering wine, ask for *un quart* (quarter-litre), *un demi-litre* (half-litre) or *une carafe* (a litre). You'll be given the house wine if you don't specify otherwise; if you're worried about the cost, ask for *vin ordinaire*.

The French follow the North American rather than the British line in their attitude towards **children** in restaurants, not simply by offering reduced-price children's menus but in creating an atmosphere, even in otherwise fairly snooty establishments, that positively welcomes kids. It is regarded as self-evident that large family groups should be able to eat out together. A rather murkier area is that of **dogs** in the dining room; it can be quite a shock in a provincial hotel to realize that the majority of your fellow diners are attempting to keep dogs concealed beneath their tables. One final note is that you should always call the waiter or waitress *Monsieur* or *Madame* (*Mademoiselle* if a young woman), never *garçon*, no matter what you've been taught in school.

DRINKING

Where you can eat you can invariably **drink**, and vice versa. Drinking is done at a leisurely pace, whether as a prelude to food (*apéritif*), a sequel (*digestif*) or the accompaniment.

Every **bar** or **café** is obliged to display a full **price list**, which will usually show progressively increasing prices for drinks at the bar (*au comptoir*), sitting down (*la salle*) and on the terrace (*la terrasse*).

Wine (*vin*) is the regular drink. Red is *rouge*, white is *blanc*, or there's *rosé*. Vin de table – plonk – is generally drinkable and always cheap; it may be disguised (and priced up) as the house wine, or *cuvée*. Restaurant mark-ups for quality wines can be outrageous, in a country where wine is so cheap in the shops. In bars, you normally buy by the glass, and just ask for *un rouge* or *un blanc*; *un pichet* gets you a quarter-litre jug.

Strictly speaking, no wine is produced in Brittany or Normandy. However, along the lower

Loire Valley, the *département* of Loire-Atlantique, centred on Nantes, is still generally regarded as "belonging" to Brittany – and is treated as such in this book. Vineyards here are responsible for the dry white Muscadet – which is what normally goes into *moules marinières* – and the even drier Gros-Plant. You'll find a brief account of how to visit some of the vineyards where they are made on p.343.

Cider (*cidre*) is extremely popular. In Brittany it's a standard accompaniment to a meal of *crêpes* and may be offered on restaurant *menus fixes*. Normans more often consume it in bars. Most of the many varieties are very dry and very wonderful. *Poiré*, pear cider, is also produced, but on a small scale and is not commercially distributed.

The familiar Belgian and German brands account for most of the **beer** you'll find. Draught (*à la pression*, usually Kronenbourg) is the cheapest drink you can have next to coffee and wine – ask for *un demi* (defined as 25cl). Bottled beer is exceptionally cheap in supermarkets.

British-style ales and stouts are also popular. Every town seems to have some Celtic-affiliated bar that sells Guinness, and specialist beer-drinking establishments can be found in cities like Brest, Rennes and Quimper. There's even a home-grown Breton real ale, Coreff.

Strong alcohols are drunk from 5am as pre-work fortifiers, right through the day; Bretons have a reputation for commitment to this. Brandies and dozens of *eaux de vie* (spirits) and liqueurs are always available. The most famous of these in Normandy are **Calvados**, brandy distilled from apples and left to mature for anything upwards of ten years, and **Benedictine**, distilled

at Fécamp from an obscure mix of ingredients (see p.75). Measures are generous, but they don't come cheap, especially in restaurants (where Calvados is traditionally drunk as a *trou*, or hole, between courses). The same applies to imported spirits like whisky (*Scotch*).

On the **soft drink** front, you can buy cartons of unsweetened fruit juice in supermarkets, although in cafés the bottled nectars such as apricot (*jus d'abricot*) and blackcurrant (*cassis*) still hold sway. Some cafés serve tiny glasses of fresh orange and lemon juice (*orange/citron pressé*); otherwise it's the standard fizzy cans. Bottles of **mineral water** (*eau minérale*) and spring water (*eau de source*) – either sparkling (*pétillante*) or still (*eau plate*) – abound, from the best-seller Perrier to the obscurest spa product. But there's not much wrong with the tap water (*eau du robinet*).

Coffee in Normandy is invariably espresso and very strong; in Brittany, particularly in villages, it is sometimes made in jugs, very weakly. *Un café* or *un express* is black, *un crème* is white, *un café au lait* (served at breakfast) is espresso in a large cup or bowl filled up with hot milk. Most bars will also serve *un déca*, decaffeinated coffee. Ordinary **tea** (*thé*) is Lipton's, nine times out of ten; to have milk with it, ask for *un peu de lait frais*.

After overeating, **herb teas** (*infusions*), served in every café, can be soothing. The more common ones are *verveine* (verbena), *tilleul* (lime blossom) and *tisane* (camomile). **Chocolat chaud** (hot chocolate) unlike tea, lives up to the high standards of French food and drink, and can be had in any café.

COMMUNICATIONS, THE INTERNET AND THE MEDIA

You should have no problem keeping in contact with people at home while you are in France. The country has an efficient postal system and letters and packages can be sent general delivery to any of the official branches. The Internet is widely accessible, and is gradually displacing the now-primitive Minitel telnet system that was formerly France's pride and joy. Should you need to use the phone, you can use cheap pre-paid phonecards or access home-country operators via free numbers.

MAIL

As a rule, **post offices** – *bureaux de poste* or *PTTs*; look for bright yellow La Poste signs – in Brittany and Normandy are open from 9am until noon and 2pm to 5pm on weekdays, and 9am until noon only on Saturday. However, in the larger towns you'll find a main office open through the day (8am–7pm), while lunch hours and closing times in the villages can vary enormously.

You can have letters sent to you **poste restante** at any post office in the country. For whatever town you choose, always specify the main post office (Poste Centrale) to avoid possible confusion. The addresses of the two largest in the region covered by this book are:
Poste Restante, Poste Centrale, 76000 ROUEN.
Poste Restante, Poste Centrale, 44000 NANTES.

To collect mail you'll need a passport, and should expect to pay a charge of a couple of francs. If you're expecting mail, it's worth asking the clerk to check under your surname (which ide-

ally should be written in capital letters), and all possible Christian names as well – filing systems tend to be erratic.

Sending letters, the quickest international service is by *aérogramme*, sold at all post offices. You can buy ordinary stamps (*timbres*) at any *tabac* (tobacconist). When this book went to press, the current rates for standard **letters** (*lettres*, weighing 20g or less) and **postcards** (*cartes postales*) were 3F/€0.46 for the UK and Europe, 4.40F/€0.67 for North America and 5.20F/€0.79 for Australia and New Zealand. If you're sending **parcels** abroad, remember that small *postes* don't often send foreign mail and may need reminding of, for example, the huge reductions for printed papers and books. To post your letter on the street, look for the bright-yellow **postboxes**.

PHONES AND FAXES

You can make domestic and international phone calls from any call box (or **cabine**), and can receive calls where there's a blue logo of a ringing bell. Most payphones only take **phonecards** (*télecartes*). These are sold in post offices, PTT boutiques, train stations and some *tabacs*, and come in two sizes: 40.60F/€6.19 for 50 units, and 97.50F/€14.87 for 120 units. In coin-only boxes, still common in cafés, bars and rural parts, put the money in (50 centimes, 1F, 5F, 10F pieces) after you lift the receiver and before you dial – you can add more once you are connected. Certain digital British **mobile phones** also work in France.

For **calls** within France – local or long distance – simply dial all ten digits of the number. Local calls cost 0.813F/€0.123 for three minutes (1F/€0.15 minimum); long-distance calls cost up to 2.44F/€0.37 for three minutes. **Off-peak charges** apply for all calls on weekdays between 7pm and 8am, and from noon on Saturday until 8am Monday. Numbers beginning with ☎08.00 are free numbers; those beginning with ☎08.36 are premium rate (from 2.23F/€0.34 per minute), and those beginning with ☎06 are mobile and therefore also expensive to call.

The major **international calling codes** are given in the box overleaf. From a private phone, a call to the UK (*Royaume-Unis*) will cost between 1.64F/€0.25 and 2.47F/€0.38 per minute, from a

INTERNATIONAL CALLS

To place an international call **to France**, dial the following access code followed by the last nine digits of the ten-digit French number (thus omitting the initial 0).

Britain	☎00 33	**USA & Canada**	☎011 33	**New Zealand**	☎00 44 33
Ireland	☎00 33	**Australia**	☎011 33		

To make an international call **from France**, dial ☎00, wait for a tone, and then dial the relevant country code, followed by the number you want minus its initial 0.

Britain	☎00 44	**USA & Canada**	☎00 1	**New Zealand**	☎00 64
Ireland	☎00 353	**Australia**	☎00 61		

public phone 2.17–2.57F/€0.33–0.39; to Ireland, the US (*États-Unis*) or Canada 1.95–2.97F/ €0.30–0.45 a minute or 2.85–3.52F/€0.45–0.54; to Australia and New Zealand 4.31–6.55F/ €0.66–1 a minute or 7.99–10.16F/€1.23–1.55.

By far the most convenient way to make international calls is to use a **phone card**; the standard *télecartes* make calling from public phone boxes straightforward, but most *tabacs* also sell a wide-range of cut-price cards that can be used from both call boxes and private phones. To avoid payment altogether, make a reverse charge or **collect call** (*téléphoner en PCV*). You can also do this through the operator in the UK, by dialling the Home Direct number ☎08.00.89.00.33; to get an English-speaking operator for North America, dial ☎00.00.11.

To speak to the **operator** dial ☎13; **directory enquiries**, both national and international, are on ☎12; **medical emergencies**, ☎15; the **police**, ☎17; **fire**, ☎18.

Faxes can be sent from all main post offices and many photocopy stores: the official French word is *télécopie*, but people use the word fax. A typical rate for sending a fax within France is 25F/€3.81 for the first and 6F/€0.92 for subsequent pages.

MINITEL

In theory at least, every French phone subscriber has a **Minitel**, a computer terminal that allows access through the phone lines to all kinds of directories, databases, chat lines, etc. This pioneering network originated in the 1980s, but is rapidly being supplanted by the Internet; if you're at all computer-literate you shouldn't find it hard to use, but these days there's very little point.

EMAIL AND THE INTERNET

Email is the cheapest and most hassle-free way of staying in touch with home while in France. Practically every reasonable-sized town has a **cybercafé** or connection point of some sort, and in less populated areas the need is being filled by post offices, many of which now have rather expensive public Internet terminals, which are operated with a prepaid card (50F/€7.63 for the first hour). In addition France Telecom has street-side Internet kiosks in major cities. We have given details of cybercafés and other Internet access points in the *Guide* so you can stay on line while travelling. Prices range from 15F/€2.29 to 60F/€9.15 per hour, so it can be worth shopping around. It's easy to open a free email account to use while you're away with Hotmail or Yahoo: head for *www.hotmail.com* or *www.yahoo.com* to find out how.

Information about practically every aspect of French culture and travel can now be picked up on the Internet; Web sites and/or email addresses are listed wherever available throughout this book. Government agencies are online, including many of the smallest local tourist offices; in the cultural sphere even the most obscure and esoteric associations have discovered the importance of getting their message out over the Web; and the hotel and restaurant industries have come to realize that the Net is a key to foreign markets. On the down side, many or most of French Web sites do not have English-language versions. As anywhere on the Net, persistent combing of links pages and use of search engines (among the best are *www.google.com*, *www.dogpile.com* and the French *www.enfin.com*) will almost certainly get you the information you are looking for.

BRITTANY AND NORMANDY ON THE NET

www.breizh.net
A true labour of love, embracing all matters Breton, with excellent sections on learning the language and a detailed overview of Breton music.

www.bretagne.com
French-only site specializing in Brittany, run by *Le Télégramme* newspaper, and featuring up-to-the-minute listings and news.

www.bretagnenet.com
Comprehensive information, much of it in English, on Breton culture and language.

web.culture.fr
French Ministry of Culture's page, with information on everything from monuments to exhibitions and also comprehensive lists of links to organizations related to the whole gamut of artistic media.

www.franceguide.com
The official site of the French Government Tourist Office, with a good English-language version. News, information on festivals and useful links to all regions and *départements*.

www.france-pub.com
General tourist information on France, with detailed sections on Brittany and Normandy.

www.gksoft.com/govt/en/fr
Gateway to English-language listings of all French government Web sites, including embassies, departmental and regional tourist boards, political parties, municipalities and media.

www.jobvillage.com
English-language site for those looking for work. Emphasis is on the food and hospitality industries.

www.lemonde.fr
The French-language Web version of one of France's most reputable daily newspapers. Includes national and international news, culture and sports.

www.radio-france.fr
Radio France's official page has national and international news coverage, current affairs, as well as music, culture and the latest in French sports. French language only.

NEWSPAPERS AND MAGAZINES

British and North American **newspapers** – at the very least, the *International Herald Tribune* – are intermittently available. In the larger resorts, and in cities such as Nantes and Rouen, you should find reasonable selections of foreign-language papers. Elsewhere, it's mostly down to the British *Times*, *Daily Mail* or *Sun*.

As for the **French press**, the widest circulations are enjoyed by the **regional dailies**. Throughout Normandy and Brittany, the most important and influential paper is *Ouest-France*. This is based in Rennes but has numerous local editions – worth picking up for their listings supplements, if nothing else. Of the **national dailies**, *Le Monde* is the most intellectual and respected, with no concessions to entertainment (such as pictures), but a correctly styled French that is probably the easiest to understand. *Libération* (*Libé* for short; daily except Mon), is moderately left-wing, independent and colloquial with good, if choosy, coverage.

Weeklies, on the *Newsweek/Time* model, include the wide-ranging left-leaning *Le Nouvel Observateur*, and its rightist counterweight, *L'Express*. The best, and funniest, investigative journalism is in the satirical *Canard Enchaîné*, unfortunately almost incomprehensible to non-native speakers. **Monthlies** include the young and trendy – and cheap – *Nova*, which has excellent listings of cultural events, and *Actuel*, which is good for current events.

TV AND RADIO

French TV broadcasts six channels, three of them public, along with a good many more cable and satellite channels, which include the BBC World Service. If you've got a **radio**, you can tune into English-language news on the BBC World Service on 648khz at intervals throughout the day and night. BBC Radio 4 from 5am to 11.45pm GMT, and the World Service from 11.45pm to 5am GMT on 198 kHz long wave, is usually quite clear throughout Brittany and Normandy, while the Voice of America transmits on 90.5, 98.8 and 102.4 FM. Radio Classique (101.1 FM) is a classical-music station with a minimum of chat and no commercials. For **news** in French, there's the state-run France Inter (87.8 FM), Europe 1 (104.7 FM) or round-the-clock news on France Infos (105.5 FM).

OPENING HOURS AND HOLIDAYS

The basic hours of business in France are from 8am or 9am until noon or 1pm, and from 2pm or 3pm to 6.30pm or 7.30pm. In big-city centres, shops and other businesses stay open throughout the day, while in July and August most tourist offices and museums are open without interruption. Otherwise almost everything – shops, museums, tourist offices, most banks – closes for a couple of hours at midday.

If you're looking to buy a picnic lunch, you'll need to get into the habit of buying it before you're ready to think about eating. Small food shops often don't reopen until halfway through the afternoon, closing around 7.30pm or 8pm just before the evening meal.

The standard **closing days** are Sunday and Monday. Food shops tend to close on Monday rather than Sunday, but in smaller towns you may well find everything except the odd boulangerie (bakery) – including banks – shut on both days.

Museums are not very generous with their hours, tending to open at around 10am, close for lunch at noon until 2pm (sometimes 3pm) and then run through until only 5pm or 6pm. Summer opening times, usually applicable between mid-May or early June and mid-September, but sometimes only during July and August, often differ from winter times; all variations are indicated in the listings given in this book. The closing days are usually Monday or Tuesday, sometimes both. Admission charges can be very offputting, though most state-owned museums have one or two days of the week when they're free, and you can get a big reduction at most places by showing a student card (or passport if you're under 26 or over 60).

Churches and **cathedrals** are almost always open all day, with charges only for the crypt, treasuries or cloister, and little fuss about how you're dressed. Where they are closed you may have to go during Mass to take a look, on Sunday morning, or at other times which you'll see posted up on the door. In small towns and villages, however, getting the key is not difficult – ask anyone nearby or hunt out the priest, whose house is known as the *presbytère*.

PUBLIC HOLIDAYS

There are thirteen national holidays (*jours fériés*), when most shops and businesses (though not necessarily restaurants), and some museums, are closed. May in particular is a big month for holidays: as well as May Day and Victory Day, Ascension Day normally falls then, as sometimes does Pentecost.

January 1
New Year's Day

Easter Sunday

Easter Monday

Ascension Day
(forty days after Easter)

Pentecost
or Whitsun (seventh Sun after Easter, plus the Mon)

May 1
May Day/Labour Day

May 8
Victory in Europe Day

July 14
Bastille Day

August 15
Assumption of the Virgin Mary

November 1
All Saints' Day

November 11
1918 Armistice Day

December 25
Christmas Day

FESTIVALS AND EVENTS

The most interesting Breton events are without doubt the region's cultural festivals. At the largest of these, the Lorient Festival Inter-Celtique (August), music, performance, food and drink of all seven Celtic nations are featured in a completely authentic gathering that pulls in cultural nationalists (and ethnic music fans) from Ireland to Spain. If you can't get to Lorient, there are two – smaller, and more particularly Breton – alternatives in the Nantes Quinzaine Celtique (June/July) and Quimper's Festival de Cornouaille (July).

CALENDAR OF EVENTS

Whitsun	**Honfleur**	Seamen's Festival
First fortnight in May	**St-Malo**	Étonnants Voyageurs
Third Sun in May	**Tréguier**	St Yves Pardon
Last weekend in May	**St-Brieuc**	Art Rock Festival
End May/start June	**Coutances**	Jazz Festival
June 6		D-Day Ceremonies on Invasion Beaches
Third week in June	**Balleroy**	Balloon Festival (odd-numbered years only)
Last Sun in June	**Le Faouët**	Pardon
End June/start July	**Nantes**	Quinzaine Celtique
Early July	**Lamballe**	Golden Broom Folk Festival
First ten days of July	**Rennes**	Tombées de la Nuit theatre and music festival
Second Sun in July	**Locronan**	Troménie Pardon
July 16	**La Haye du Routot**	Fête de Ste-Claire
July 26	**Ste Anne d'Auray**	Pardon
Late July	**Vannes**	Jazz Festival
Late July	**Quimper**	Festival de Cornouaille
Last Sun in July	**Locquirec**	Festival of the Sea
Last Sun in July	**Paimpol**	Fête des Terres-Neuvas
Aug 2	**Le Tréport**	Blessing of the Sea
First full week in Aug	**Lorient**	Festival InterCeltique
First fortnight in Aug	**Quimper**	Semaines Musicales
First fortnight in Aug	**Île de Fedrun**	Fête de la Brière
Early Aug	**Dives**	Puppet Festival
Second Sun in Aug	**Lizio**	Festival Artisanal
Mid-Aug	**Concarneau**	Fête des Filets Bleus
Mid-Aug	**Guingamp**	Saint Loup Breton Dance Festival
Mid-Aug	**Lamballe**	Horse Festival
Mid-Aug	**Le Roche-Jagu**	Jazz Festival
First Sun in Sept	**Le Pin**	Horse Show
First Sun in Sept	**Le Folgoet**	Pardon
Early Sept	**Douarnenez**	Film Festival of International Minorities
First week in Sept	**Deauville**	American Film Festival
Second weekend in Sept	**Lessay**	Holy Cross cattle and animal fair
Second weekend in Sept	**Dieppe**	Kite-flying festival (even-numbered years only)
Sun nearest Sept 29	**Mont St-Michel**	Archangel Michael Festival
Last Sun in Sept	**Caudebec**	Cider Festival (even-numbered years only)
Late Sept	**Bellême**	Mycology Festival
First week in Oct	**Dinard**	British Film Festival
Mid-Oct	**Le Havre**	Blues Festival
Late Oct	**Beuvron-en-Auge**	Cider Festival
Mid-Nov	**Dieppe**	Herring Festival
First week in Dec	**Rennes**	Les Transmusicales international rock festival

Look out also for local **club events** put on by individual Celtic folklore groups – *Cercles, Bagadou* or, best of the lot, *Fests-Noz*. These are most prolific in Nantes, though wherever you are in the province, listings pages of the *Ouest-France* can be worth scrutiny. The "Breton music" section in Contexts has detailed recommendations of clubs and venues to check out in the province.

The religious **pardons**, sometimes promoted as tourist attractions in Brittany, are rather different affairs. These are essentially church processions, organized by a particular community on the local saint's day. Though generally small-scale, some, like that at Ste-Anne d'Auray, have over the centuries taken on more region-wide status as pilgrimages. Rather than being carnivals or fêtes, they are primarily very serious occasions, centred on lengthy and rather gloomy church services. If you're not interested by the religious aspects, only the food and drink stalls, and low-key accompaniments, hold any great appeal.

By and large, **Normandy** lacks any specific cultural traditions to celebrate, doing its best to make up with celebrations of related **historic events** – births and deaths of William the Conqueror, Ste Thérèse, etc. The **D-Day** (June 6) landings along the Invasion Beaches are always marked in some way.

In both Normandy and Brittany, avoid the **Spectacles**, camp and overpriced outdoor shows on some mythical theme or other, held most regularly (and most tackily) at Bagnoles and Elven.

On the more mainstream **cultural side**, the larger cities – Rouen, Rennes and Nantes – have active theatre, opera and classical-music seasons, though little happens during the summer. **Cinema** is most interesting in these cities, too, and the region is host to perhaps the most accessible French film festival – Deauville's American Film Festival (Sept). Almost all foreign films will be dubbed into French; *v.o.* in the listings signifies original language.

Both **Rennes** and **Rouen** have laid recent claim to be "the capital of French **rock**"; Rennes is increasingly the one to watch, with its December Transmusicales attracting international stars to share the stage with local groups. St-Brieuc's rival Art Rock Festival caters to more specialist tastes. A few large rock concerts also take place during the holiday season, at places like Brest and Concarneau, with the usual bland multinational billing of fading "rock giants".

TROUBLE AND THE POLICE

Compared to Paris or the south of France, crime is a low-key problem in Brittany and Normandy. However, you still need to take normal precautions against petty theft – keep your wallet in your front pocket or your handbag under your elbow. If you should be attacked, hand over the money and start dialling the cancellation numbers for your credit cards and travellers' cheques (see p.20).

If you need to report a theft, go to the local *gendarmerie* (police station), and do your best to persuade them to give you the requisite piece of paper for a claim; the first thing they'll ask for is your passport. The two main types of French **police**, the Police Nationale and the Gendarmerie Nationale, are for all practical purposes indistinguishable; you can go to either.

Drivers are one of the most obviously vulnerable groups, with the ever-present risk of a break-in. Vehicles are rarely stolen, but tape decks as well as luggage left in cars make tempting targets, and foreign number plates are easy to spot. Good insurance is the only answer – see p.21 – but, whether you have it or not, make sure you don't leave your valuables in sight.

EMERGENCIES
Medical emergencies ☎15
Police ☎17
Fire Service ☎18
Rape crisis (*SOS Viol*) ☎08.00.05.95.95.
AIDS information (SIDA Info Service)
☎08.00.84.08.00.
It's common to call the fire brigade (*les sapeurs pompiers*) for medical problems; they all have paramedical training and equipment.

If you have an **accident** while driving, you have to fill in and sign a *constat à l'aimable* (jointly agreed statement); car insurers are supposed to give you this with a policy, though in practice few seem to have heard of it.

For non-criminal **driving violations** such as speeding, the police can impose on-the-spot fines. Should you be arrested on any charge, you have the right to contact your nearest consulate. Although the police are not always as co-operative as they might be, it *is* their duty to assist you – likewise in the case of losing your passport or all your money.

As for offences of your own making, treatment by the police is little different from anywhere else in Europe. **Camping** outside authorized sites can bring you into contact with the authorities, though it's more likely to be the landowner who tells you to move off. **Topless sunbathing** is universally acceptable, but **nudity** is limited to a few specifically naturist beaches.

Officially, you're supposed to carry **identification documents** at all times, and the police are entitled to stop you and demand it. In practice this doesn't happen much to tourists, at least to whites. If you're black it can be a different matter; the French police have a reputation for racism. In fact, being black can make entering the country difficult, and immigration officers can be obstructive to black holiday-makers.

Sexual harassment is generally no worse than in North America or the UK, though cultural and linguistic differences can make it difficult to judge a situation correctly. Women who need help may prefer to contact women's organizations in the larger cities – Femmes Batues, Femmes en Détresse or SOS Femmes, all reachable through the Hôtel de Ville – before trying the police, while a consulate is likely to be of most immediate assistance.

Hitching is definitely not advisable.

WORK AND STUDY

Although EU citizens are in theory free to move to France and find jobs with exactly the same pay, conditions and trade-union rights as French nationals, for anyone who isn't a specialist, casual work in Brittany or Normandy is hard to come by. Furthermore, while the French minimum wage (the SMIC) is currently around 40F/€6.10 per hour, employers are likely to pay lower wages to temporary foreign workers who don't have easy legal resources.

The region has just one wine harvest (around Nantes), almost wholly automated, and there is small chance of picking up any other kind of short-term employment. Visitors from North America or Australasia without a prearranged job offer would be foolish to imagine they have any chance of finding paid employment.

For EU citizens who arrange things in advance, however, there are work possibilities in au-pairing, teaching English as a foreign language, and in the holiday industry. And if you're just looking for an interesting way to fill the summer, assorted archeological schemes, mostly on Brittany's megalithic sites, sometimes have space for foreign volunteers.

FINDING WORK

Whatever you are looking for, it's important to plan well ahead. A few books which might be worth consulting are *Work Your Way Around the World* by Susan Griffiths and *Living and Working in France* by Victoria Pybus (both published by Vacation Work), or *A Year Between* and *Working Holidays* (both Central Bureau). **In France**, check out the "Offres d'Emploi" (Job Offers) in *Le Monde*, *Le Figaro* and the *International Herald Tribune*. The national employment agency, ANPE (Agence Nationale pour l'Emploi), with offices all over France, advertises temporary jobs in all fields and, in theory, offers a whole range of services to job-seekers who are EU citizens, but is not renowned for its helpfulness to foreigners. Non-EU citizens have to show a work permit to apply for any of their jobs. Vac-Job, 46 av Réné-Coty, 17014 Paris (☎01.43.20.70.51) publishes the annual *Emplois d'Été en France* (Summer Jobs in France).

TEACHING ENGLISH

Teaching English is one of the easiest ways to find a job in France. Such posts are frequently advertised in Britain; check the *Guardian's* "Education" section (every Tues), or the weekly *Times Educational Supplement*. Late summer is usually the best time. You don't need fluent French to get a post, but a TEFL (Teaching English as a Foreign Language) qualification may well be required.

For a thorough breakdown of available TEFL courses, see the annual *ELT Guide* (£12.95), produced by EFL Ltd, 1 Malet St, London WC1E 7JA (☎020/7255 1969, fax 7255 1972), which also publishes the monthly *ELT Gazette*, filled with job ads (subscription for 12 issues £25.50). Vacation Work, 9 Park End St, Oxford OX1 1HJ (☎01865/241978, fax 790885), publishes *Teaching English Abroad* (£10.99 plus £1.50 p&p), while the British Council's Web site (*www.britcoun.org/english/engvacs.htm*) has a list of English-teaching vacancies.

If you apply from home, most schools will fix up the necessary papers for you. It's also quite feasible to find a teaching job when you're in France, but you may have to accept semi-official status and no job security. For the addresses of schools, look under "Écoles de Langues" in the "Professions" directory of the local phonebook.

Offering **private lessons** (via university notice boards or classified ads), you'll have lots of com-petition, and it's hard to reach the people who can afford it, but it's always worth a try. The best places to live and teach are probably St-Malo, Quimper, Rennes and Rouen.

BECOMING AN AU PAIR

Au pair work is usually arranged through one of a dozen agencies, all of which are listed in Vacation Work's *Living and Working in France*. In Britain, *The Lady* is *the* magazine for classified adverts for such jobs, arranged privately. As initial contacts, try Avalon Au Pairs (☎01344/778246, *www.city2000.com/avalonaupairs/top*) in Britain, the American Institute for Foreign Study (☎203/8699090, *www.aifs.com*) in the US, or Accueil Familial des Jeunes Étrangers (☎01.42.22.50.34; 690F/€105.23 joining fee) in Paris. All offer positions for female au pairs only, and will be able to fill you in on the general terms and conditions (never very generous), and the state of the market. Don't accept less than 1650F/€252.50 a month (on top of board and lodging), and make sure you have an escape route (such as a ticket home) in case you find the conditions intolerable – many people have had bad experiences.

TRAVEL INDUSTRY JOBS

Temporary jobs in the **travel industry** revolve around courier work – supervising and working on bus tours and summer campsites. You'll need good French (and maybe even another language) and should write to as many tour operators as you can, preferably in early spring. Ads occasionally appear in the *Guardian's* "Media" section (every Mon), while travel magazines like the very reliable *Wanderlust* (every two months; £2.80) have a "Job Shop" section which often advertises job opportunities with tour companies. Working on a campsite usually involves putting up tents at the start of the season, taking them down again at the end, and general maintenance and trou-bleshooting work in the months between; experienced teachers are also in demand to provide child care. Canvas Holidays (☎01383/644018) are worth approaching.

ARCHEOLOGICAL DIGS

Volunteer work on **archeological sites** varies from year to year, according to available grants and priorities. Recently, there have been opportunities to work on a number of Breton Gallo-Roman and megalithic sites – including Locmariaquer –

and on Neolithic sites in Normandy. Food and campsite or student-hall accommodation is generally provided, though there may be a small weekly charge; travel costs are not normally paid. It's best to write a number of letters to potential authorities asking for details of any projects. Excavations are regularly organized by the following:

Laboratoire d'Anthropologie Préhistorique: write c/o Dr Jean Laurent Monnier, Charge de Recherche au CNRS, Université de Rennes I, Campus de Beaulieu, 35042 Rennes.

Ministère de la Culture, Circonscription des Antiquités Historiques et Préhistoriques de Bretagne, 6 rue du Chapitre, BP 927, 35011 Rennes Cedex.

Musée d'Histoire Naturelle: write c/o Jean Pierre Watte, Archéologue Municipal, place du Vieux Marché, 76600 Le Havre.

ORGANIC FARMING

One final offbeat possibility if you want to discover green rural life is being a **working guest** on an organic farm. The period can be anything from a week to a couple of months and the work may involve cheese-making, market gardening, beekeeping, wine producing or building. For details of the scheme and a list of French addresses, contact Willing Workers on Organic Farms (WWOOF), 19 Bradford Rd, Lewes, East Sussex BN7 1RB, in the UK; WWOOF W Tree, Buchan, VIC 3885 (*www.earthlink.com.au/wwoof*) in Australia; or WWWOOF RR2, Carlson Rd, S18 C9, Nelson, BC VIL 5P5 in Canada, enclosing a self-addressed envelope.

CLAIMING BENEFIT

Any British or EU citizen who has been signing on for **jobseeker's allowance** for a minimum period of four to six weeks at home, and intends to continue doing so in France, needs a letter of introduction from their own Social Security office, plus an E303 certificate of authorization (be sure to give them plenty of warning to prepare this). You must register within seven days with the ANPE (Agence Nationale pour l'Emploi), whose offices are listed under "Administration du Travail et de l'Emploi" in the Yellow Pages or "ANPE" in the White Pages.

It's possible to claim benefit for up to three months while you look for work, but it can often take that length of time for the paperwork to be processed.

STUDYING IN FRANCE

It's relatively easy to be a **student** in France, and many foreign students perfect their fluency in the language while studying. Foreigners pay no more than French nationals to enrol for a course, and the only problem then is to support yourself. Your *carte de séjour* and – if you're an EU citizen – social security will be assured, and you'll be eligible for subsidized accommodation, meals and all the student reductions. In general, French universities are relatively informal; strict entry requirements, including an exam in French, apply only for undergraduate degrees, not for postgraduate courses. For full **details and prospectuses**, contact the Cultural Service of any French embassy or consulate (see box, p.17). In Britain, the embassy will refer you to the French Institute, 17 Queensbury Place, London SW7 2DT (☎020/7838 2148), a cultural centre with a cinema and library that provides a list of language courses in France (library hours Tues–Fri noon–7pm & Sat noon–6pm); otherwise write with SAE to request the list.

If you're a full-time non-EU student in France, you can get a non-EU **work permit** for the following summer so long as your visa is still valid.

LANGUAGE SCHOOLS

Language schools all along the coast provide intensive French courses for foreigners. Many of these are listed in the handout *Cours de Français pour Étudiants Étrangers*, also obtainable from embassy or consular cultural sections, with the most popular being those organized each summer at St-Malo by the University of Rennes.

The École des Roches, in Verneuil-sur-Avre in Normandy (see p.171), is a well-equipped institute that runs intensive short courses in French for pupils aged 11 to 18; contact BP 710, 27137 Verneuil-sur-Avre (☎02.32.23.40.00).

DIRECTORY

BEACHES are public property within 5m of the high-tide mark, so you can walk past the private villas, and set foot on islands. Another law, however, forbids you to camp.

CAMERAS AND FILM Film is considerably cheaper in North America than in France or Britain, so stock up if you're coming by that way. If you bring a camcorder, make sure any tapes you buy in France are compatible.

CHILDREN AND BABIES are generally welcome everywhere, including most bars and restaurants. **Hotels** charge by the room, with a small supplement for an additional bed or cot, and many family-run places will babysit or offer a listening service while you eat or go out. Especially in the seaside towns, most **restaurants** have children's menus or cook simpler food on request. You'll have no difficulty finding disposable nappies (*couches à jeter*), but nearly all baby foods have added sugar and salt, and French milk powders are very rich indeed. SNCF charge nothing on **trains and buses** for under-4s, and half-fare for 4–11s (see pp.29–30 for other reductions). Most SIs have details of specific activities for children – in particular, many resorts supervise "clubs" for children on the beach. And almost every town has a **children's playground** with a good selection of activities. Something to beware of – not that you can do much about it – is the difficulty of negotiating a child's **buggy** over the large cobbles that cover many of the older streets in town centres.

ELECTRICITY is almost always 220V, using plugs with two round pins. If you haven't bought the appropriate transformer before leaving home, the best place in France to find the right one is the electrical section of a department store, where someone is also more likely to speak English; cost is around 60F/€9.15.

FISHING You get fishing rights by becoming a member of an authorized fishing club – tourist offices have details. The main areas for river fishing are in Brittany, in the Aulne around Châteaulin and in the Morbihan.

GAY AND LESBIAN TRAVELLERS France is more liberal on homosexuality than most European countries. The legal age of consent is sixteen, and gay communities thrive in Paris and many southern towns, though lesbian life is rather less upfront. Brittany and Normandy, however, have little conspicuous gay life; the best source for clubs and meeting places is the *Gai Pied Guide*, widely available in French newsagents and bookshops (or online at *www.gaipied.fr*). **ARCL** (Les Archives, Recherches et Cultures Lesbiennes; ☎01.46.28.54.94, *www.mrap.asso.fr*) publishes *L'Annuaire*, a biannual directory of lesbian, gay and feminist addresses, while **Fréquence Gaie** (FG; 98.2 FM), is a 24-hour gay and lesbian radio station.

LAUNDRY Laundries/laundromats – *laveries automatiques* – are not all that common in Breton or Norman towns, although some are listed in this guide. The alternative *blanchisserie* or *pressing* services are likely to be expensive, and hotels in particular charge very high rates. If you're staying in hotels, only wash a few items yourself as most places officially forbid doing any laundry in your room.

LEFT LUGGAGE Lockers of various sizes are available at all SNCF stations, as well as *consigne* for longer periods or larger items.

SMOKING is banned on public transport and in museums in France, while all restaurants and bars are obliged to have nonsmoking areas.

SWIMMING POOLS (*piscines*) are well signposted in most French towns, and reasonably priced. Tourist offices have addresses.

TAX-FREE SHOPPING Visitors to France from non-EU countries can claim tax refunds on any purchases in a single shop of over 2000F/€305.

Ask for the relevant forms when you buy, then present them to Customs officials as you leave the country.

TIME France is one hour ahead of Britain throughout the year, except for a short period during October, when it's the same. It is six hours ahead of Eastern Standard Time, and nine hours ahead of Pacific Standard Time. This also applies during daylight-saving seasons, observed in France (as in most of Europe) from the end of March through to the end of September.

TV AND VIDEO French TV broadcasts using a different system to the British; only black-and-white portable British TVs work in France. Make sure that any video tapes you buy in France, whether blank for use in a camcorder, or prerecorded, are compatible with your own system.

VACCINATIONS are neither required nor necessary.

WATER The tap water is always safe to drink, though bottled mineral water, always available, may taste better.

PART TWO

NORMANDY

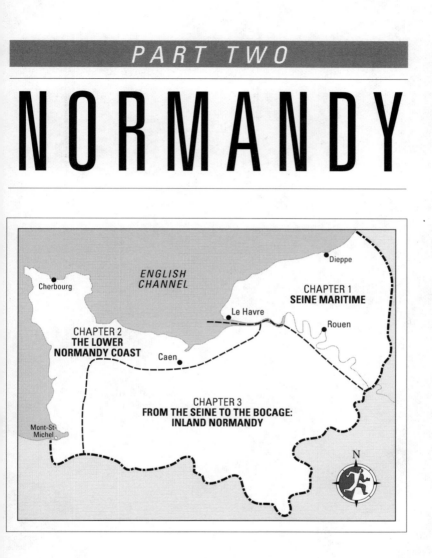

ENGLISH
CHANNEL

Cherbourg

Dieppe

CHAPTER 1
SEINE MARITIME

Le Havre

Rouen

CHAPTER 2
THE LOWER
NORMANDY COAST

Caen

CHAPTER 3
FROM THE SEINE TO THE BOCAGE:
INLAND NORMANDY

Mont-St-
Michel

N

CHAPTER ONE

SEINE MARITIME

T he *département* of **Seine Maritime** makes an uncharacteristic introduction to Normandy. Though scattered with the usual Norman half-timbered houses and small farms, the landscape is stark along the coastline and often dull in the flatlands of the chalk Caux plateau behind. Only along the sheltered ribbon of the **Seine Valley** do you find the greenery, and profusion of flowers and fruit, that you might expect of the province.

Which is not to say that this is all territory to pass through or ignore. Arriving at **Dieppe** you can take advantage of the low-key resorts along the **Côte**

d'Albâtre, which hold occasional surprises behind their windswept and tide-chased walks. At **Fécamp**, you'll find an absurd Hammer House of Horror Benedictine distillery; at **Étretat**, spectacular stacks and arches of rock, to either side of one of the nicest little coastal towns in Normandy; and at **Varengeville**, architect Edwin Lutyens' wonderful **Bois des Moutiers**. On the Seine estuary, while **Le Havre** may be less conventionally enticing, it's worth attention all the same, not only for its modern architecture and art collections but, as France's second port after Marseille, for its liveliness.

The extravagant meanders of the **River Seine**, however, determine most people's travels in this region. **Rouen**, scene of the trial and execution of Joan of Arc, is one of the major provincial capitals of France; the combination of contemporary verve with its heavily but effectively restored medieval centre makes it by far the most interesting city in Normandy. Along the valley and riverbanks there is plenty to delay your progress: tranquil villages such as **Villequier** and **La Bouille**; the evocatively ruined Romanesque abbeys of **St-Wandrille** and **Jumièges**; the English frontier-stronghold of **Château Gaillard** looming above **Les Andelys**; and, an unmissable last stop before Paris, **Monet's garden** and waterlilies at **Giverny**.

THE NORTHERN PORTS

There is no confusing the northern ports of Normandy, **Dieppe** and **Le Havre**, with their rivals to the east. Each has managed to retain a distinct individual identity in a way that Calais and Boulogne, which have to cope with ten times the number of passengers, simply have not; if you're using either port, you shouldn't feel obliged to rush on out as soon as you arrive, or dice with time to coincide to the minute with the ferries back.

Both offer the same obvious choice of **routes**: inland towards Rouen, or along the coast. If you're setting off from Dieppe with your own transport, the **coast road** is the most immediately gratifying. Until you get as far south as Rouen, there is little of interest on the plains of the Caux plateau inland, while harbour towns such as **Le Tréport** to the east, and **Étretat** and **Fécamp** to the west, make diverting overnight stops. Both are also within easy reach of Le Havre, although here you are poised at the start of the route along the Seine. As well as the river towns, places such as Honfleur (see p.113) on the lower Norman coast, covered in Chapter Two, only take a few minutes to get to via the huge Seine bridges.

Dieppe

Crowded between high cliff headlands, **DIEPPE** is an enjoyably small-scale port at which to arrive in France, very French but with a long and intimate association with England. As the closest harbour and beach to Paris, 170km southeast, it has had an eventful history. Its existence was first recorded in 1030, when the abbey of Mont Ste-Catherine-de-Rouen acquired the area for an annual rent of 5000 smoked herrings. The port was regularly used by William the Conqueror when he was King of England, and passed into French hands in 1195 when Philippe Auguste burned Richard the Lionheart's fleet in the harbour. Having changed ownership several more times during the Hundred Years War, Dieppe was finally taken for France by the future Louis XI in 1443.

Adventurers from Dieppe were in the forefront of French naval explorations. It has been claimed that Dieppois navigators reached the coast of Guinea in 1384, and Brazil in 1488; less questionably, the Italian Giovanni da Verrazano sailed from the city in 1524 to found the settlement that later became New York. Early emigrants to Canada used the port, too, and the strong links established with the French colony there were to endure long after the French lost Canada to the British in 1759.

When the edict of Nantes was revoked in 1685, Dieppe was one of the main escape routes used by fleeing Protestants; similarly, during the French Revolution, three Brighton captains of the Channel Packet Service ran a regular – and profitable – service for aristocrats on the run. In 1848, the railway from Paris reached Dieppe and, from the 1850s, the Newhaven Packet operated a daily service. The town became a fashionable seaside resort, attracting French aristocracy and British royalty. The French would promenade along the seafront, while the English colony indulged in the peculiar pastime of bathing.

Modern Dieppe has a population of just under 36,000. It's not a place many travellers go out of their way to visit, but it's one of the nicer ferry ports in northern France, and you're unlikely to regret spending an afternoon or evening here before or after a Channel crossing. With kids in tow, the aquariums of the **Cité de la Mer** are the obvious attraction; otherwise, you could settle for admiring the cliffs and the castle as you stroll the seafront lawns.

Arrival and information

Between one and three Hoverspeed SuperSeaCat **ferries** sail daily, all year round, between Newhaven in England and Dieppe's **gare maritime**, taking a little over two hours for the crossing. For information and reservations in France, call ☎08.20.00.35.55. Motorists coming off the boats are directed away from the town, and have to double back west to reach it; foot passengers can either walk the 500m to the tourist office (see p.65), or take the 15F/€2.29 **shuttle buses** that connect with each sailing.

Dieppe's **gare SNCF** (☎02.35.98.50.50) is another 500m south of the tourist office, on boulevard Clemenceau, 1km from the beach. Trains are much the quickest way to get to Rouen or Paris, but to travel along the coast you'll have to catch a bus from the **gare routière** (☎02.35.84.21.97) alongside. **Local buses** only serve three routes. All start at the *gare SNCF*, pass through the bus station and call at the tourist office. However, a **"petit train"** makes one-hour narrated

DIEPPE

ACCOMMODATION

les Arcades	6
Grand Duquesne	7
de la Jetée	2
la Plage	4
Pontoise	8
Présidence	1
Tourist	5
Windsor	3

RESTAURANTS

les Écamias	E
Festival	B
la Marmite Dieppoise	F
Newhaven	C
Sully	D
les Tourelles	A

Swimming Pool

Jardin d'Enfants

Casino

Château

St-Rémy

St-Jacques

Cité de la Mer

Ferry Terminal (Gare Maritime)

Canadian Memorial

Canadian Memorial

N-D des Grèves

Fishing Port

Bassin Duquesne

Gares SNCF & Routière

Pont Ango

0   250 m

▽ Pourville & Varengeville

▽ Paris

tours of Dieppe, starting from the tourist office and heading first to the Cité de la Mer, then back along the full length of the beach and up to the Auchan hypermarket (April to early Sept daily 8am–5pm; adults 35F/€5.34, under-10s 25F/€3.81). **Bicycles** are available for rent from Loca-Cycles, 17 rue d'Issoire (☎02.35.06.07.40).

Dieppe's **tourist office** is on the pont Ango, which separates the ferry harbour from the pleasure port (May, June & Sept Mon–Sat 9am–1pm & 2–7pm, Sun 10am–1pm & 3–6pm; July & Aug Mon–Sat 9am–1pm & 2–8pm, Sun 10am–1pm & 3–6pm; Oct–April Mon–Sat 9am–noon & 2–6pm; ☎02.32.14.40.60, *www.mairie_dieppe.fr*); you can't miss it if you're arriving by ferry. A beach annexe, at the point where quai Duquesne reaches the oceanfront, is open in summer only (mid-June to mid-Sept Mon–Thurs & Sun 10am–7.30pm, Fri & Sat 10am–8pm). The main **post office** is at 2 bd Maréchal-Joffre (Mon–Fri 8.30am–6pm, Sat 8.30am–noon; ☎02.35.04.70.14).

Accommodation

You're unlikely to experience much difficulty finding accommodation in Dieppe. There are plenty of **hotels**; on the whole, prices get progressively cheaper as you head further inland from the seafront, which is actually among the quietest areas of town, especially near the castle end, away from the car-ferry traffic. Many of the dearer hotels are at the western end of the boulevard de Verdun, facing the sea; they (and others with restaurants) are likely to insist on half board, or even full board, in the season, which can mean they work out expensive.

The town's **hostel**, which offers beds in two-, four- and six-bed dorms only, is inconveniently located atop a hill at 48 rue Louis Fromager (☎02.35.84.85.73, fax 02.35.84.89.62; 55F/€8.38; closed mid-Nov to mid-Feb). Two kilometres southwest of the *gare SNCF,* in the quartier Janval, it's served by bus #2 from the tourist office (direction "Val Druel", get off at "Château Michel"). The same bus continues to the closest **campsite** to the centre, the *Camping Vitamin*, chemin des Vertus (☎02.35.82.11.11; closed Nov–March), which is OK in itself but not in a particularly attractive, let alone convenient, location.

Hotels

Hôtel Les Arcades, 1–3 Arcades de la Bourse (☎02.35.84.14.12, fax 02.35.40.22.29, *www .les-arcades.com*). Long-established hotel, under the eponymous arcades facing the port; you couldn't ask for a more central location, nor one closer to the ferry. Restaurant with full, good-value menus from 98F/€14.94. ④.

Grand Duquesne, 15 place St-Jacques (☎02.32.14.61.10, fax 02.35.84.29.83, *www .augrandduquesne.fr*). Small, well-refurbished pension, located just off place du Puits Salé in view of the main door of the cathedral, where every room has bath and phone. The simplest menu, at 68F/€10.37, includes squid or salmon *choucroute*; 179F/€27.29 goes a long way. ②.

Hôtel de la Jetée, 5 rue de l'Asile Thomas (☎02.35.84.89.98). Simple but very welcoming place overlooking the sea, near the Cité de la Mer, with ten plain but spacious rooms. ①.

Hôtel La Plage, 20 bd de Verdun (☎02.35.84.18.28, fax 02.35.82.36.82). Slightly upmarket rooms, all with English (satellite) TV, facing the sea but set back somewhat from the street, alongside the *Windsor*. No restaurant. ③.

Hôtel-Restaurant Pontoise, 10 rue Thiers (☎02.35.84.14.57). A basic, inexpensive option, not far from the *gare SNCF* and well away from the beach. ②.

Hôtel Présidence, bd de Verdun (☎02.35.84.31.31, fax 02.35.84.86.70, *www.hotel-la -presidence.com*). This ugly, grey, modern block, below the château at the far west end of the seafront, holds 89 spacious and well-equipped rooms, while menus at the rooftop *Panoramic* restaurant start at 95F/€14.48. ④.

Tourist Hôtel, 16 rue de la Halle au Blé (☎02.35.06.10.10, fax 02.35.84.15.87). Plain rooms in a converted town house, one block from the beach behind the Casino; rooms with en-suite shower cost an additional 60F/€9.15. No restaurant. ②.

Hôtel Windsor, 18 bd de Verdun (☎02.35.84.15.23, fax 02.35.84.74.52). You pay premium rates for sea-facing rooms in this *logis*, where the glass-fronted first-floor dining room – *Le Haut Gallion* – has menus from 110F/€16.77. The rooms themselves can be quite shabby, but they do have satellite TV. ④.

The Town

Dieppe remains a busy **port**, and the sheer bustle and verve of the place cannot fail to strike any visitor. Vast quantities of **fruit** from all over the world – and forty per-cent of all **shellfish** eaten in France – are unloaded at its commercial docks, but the quayside **fish stalls** near the tourist office are what really grab the eyes. Each morning the previous night's catch is displayed with all the usual mouthwatering French flair, an appetizing profusion of sole, turbot and the local speciality, scallops.

Modern Dieppe is still laid out along the three axes dictated by its eighteenth-century town planners, though these central streets have become a little run-down, and are in any case left in continual shadow. The **boulevard de Verdun** runs for over a kilometre along the seafront, from the fifteenth-century castle in the west to the port entrance, and passes the Casino, along with the grandest and oldest hotels. A short way inland, parallel to the seafront, is the **rue de la Barre** and its pedestrianized continuation, the **Grande Rue**. Along the harbour's edge, an extension of the Grande Rue, **quai Henry IV** has a colourful backdrop of cafés, brasseries and restaurants.

The place du Puits-Salé and around

At the heart of the old town, the place du Puits-Salé is dominated by the half-tim-bered **Café des Tribunaux**, looking sprucer than ever following a lavish restora-tion. The Café was built as an inn towards the end of the seventeenth century, and briefly became Dieppe's town hall after the previous one was bombarded by the British in 1694. In the late nineteenth century, it was favoured by painters and writers such as Renoir, Monet, Sickert, Whistler and Pissarro. It's now a cav-ernous café, with sombre wooden panels and dark-brown velveteen walls, the haunt of college students and open until after midnight. For English visitors, its most evocative association is that the exiled and unhappy Oscar Wilde drank here regularly. He lived (as M. Melmouth) at Berneval, 10km east of Dieppe, which was where he wrote *The Ballad of Reading Gaol*.

From the Café, rue St-Jacques leads to the **church** of the same name, built in the twelfth century to greet English pilgrims embarking on the trail to Santiago de Compostella in Spain. The original church burned down a hundred years later, so its oldest part today is the fourteenth-century lantern tower. Inside, a chapel to the "Canadian Martyrs" neighbours the usual ones to Ste-Thérèse and the Sacred Heart. Dedicated in 1951, this has nothing to do with World War II; instead it's devoted to two Dieppe priests, shown in modern stained glass being hacked to death by "Mohawks" in 1648. Nearby, the **Mur de Trésor** bears intricate and potentially fascinating carvings of Brazilian Indians dating from the seventeenth century. Unfortunately they're too high up to see clearly, and all but indecipherable.

Northwest of the place du Puits-Salé, **rue Bouchard** heads to the sixteenth-century **church of St Rémy**, which was partly destroyed when, used as an arms dump by the Germans, it was blown up the day before the town was liberated in August 1944. Now finally restored, it is occasionally open to the public for special events.

The beach

Dieppe's wide, steeply shelving **shingle beach** was deposited by a freak tide long after the rest of the town took shape. Hence the extravagant amount of clear space between the seafront and the first buildings, taken up partly by the windswept grassy lawns that make an ideal venue for the town's biennial **kite festival** (spread across two weekends in early Sept in even-numbered years), and partly by car parks where departing ferry passengers munch last-minute picnics and twiddle their thumbs.

The château

The most obvious and conspicuous sight in Dieppe is the medieval **château** that overlooks the seafront from the west. Most of those visitors who bother to make the stiff climb up do so simply to enjoy the view, but the castle also serves as home to the **Musée de Dieppe** (June–Sept daily 10am–noon & 2–6pm; Oct–May closed Tues; 15F/€2.29). In addition to its exhibition on local history – and Dieppe's maritime past means that "local history" can stretch as far as including pre-Columbian pottery from Peru – this houses two showpiece collections. The first is a group of **Dieppe carved ivories** – virtuoso specimens of sawing, filing and chipping of the plundered riches of Africa. The ivory was shipped back to the town by early Dieppe "explorers", in such quantities that during the seventeenth century over three hundred craftsmen-carvers lived here. Earlier pieces, displayed upstairs, tend to be exquisite miniature portraits and classical scenes; by the nineteenth-century, the sculptors were concentrating instead on souvenirs, and producing an abundance of model ships.

The other permanent exhibition is made up of a hundred or so prints by the co-originator of Cubism, **Georges Braque**, who went to school in Le Havre, spent his summers in Dieppe, and is buried just west of the town at Varengeville-sur-mer (see p.72). Only perhaps a quarter tend to be displayed at any one time, but in theory you can see the rest if you ask. Other galleries upstairs hold paintings of local scenes by the likes of Pissaro, Renoir, Dufy, Sickert and Boudin, while a separate, much newer, wing of the château stages temporary exhibitions.

The square du Canada

At the foot of the steps up to the castle, the **square du Canada** originally commemorated the role played by sailors from Dieppe in that country's colonization. After World War II, however, it acquired an additional significance, for it was at Dieppe in August 1942 that the Allied **commando raid**, Operation Jubilee, took place. The first large-scale assault on the continent after Dunkerque, the operation claimed over 3000 Canadian casualties in a near-suicidal series of landings and attacks up sheer and well-fortified cliff faces. Many were cut down as soon as they left their landing craft, before they even touched dry land, while some German defenders are reputed not to have bothered with firing their weapons – simply dropping projectiles over the edge.

The Allied Command later justified the carnage as having taught valuable lessons for the 1944 invasion; the Channel ports were seen to be too heavily defended to be vulnerable to frontal attack, and the invasion plan was changed to one that required the amphibious landing armies to bring their own harbour with them (see p.135).

The Cité de la Mer-L'Estran

37 rue de l'Asile-Thomas. Daily 10am–noon & 2–6pm. Adults 28F/€4.27, under-16s 16F/€2.44.

Dieppe's latest attempt to keep tourists in town for longer than it takes to get to or from the ferry terminal is the **Cité de la Mer-L'Estran**, housed in a featureless white-concrete block in the tangle of streets just back from the harbour. Setting out simultaneously to entertain children and to serve as a centre for scientific research, it succeeds in both without being all that interesting for the casual adult visitor.

Kids are certain to enjoy learning the principles of navigation by operating radio-controlled boats (5F/€0.76 for 3min). Thereafter, the museum traces the history of seagoing vessels, leading from maps of the great Norman voyages of exploration and conquest, via a Viking *drakkar* under construction following methods depicted in the Bayeux Tapestry, right up to an oddly sketchy account of the insides of a nuclear-powered submarine. Next comes a very detailed geological exhibition covering the formation of the local cliffs, in which we learn how to go about converting shingle into sandpaper.

Visits culminate with the large **aquariums**, filled with the marine life of the Channel: flat fish with bulbous eyes and twisted faces, retiring octopuses, battling lobsters, and hermaphrodite scallops (a caption helpfully explains that the white part is male, and the orange, female). Thanks to a typical lack of sentimentality, jars of fish soup, whose exact provenance is not made explicit, are on sale at the exit.

Eating and shopping

The most promising area to look for **restaurants** in Dieppe is along the quai Henri IV, which, although it overlooks the port rather than the open sea, makes a lovely place to stroll and compare menus of a summer's evening. The beach itself holds no formal restaurants, but it does have a couple of open-air bistro-type cafés selling plates of mussels, salads, and so on, and plenty of crêpe stands. Further restaurants can be found all over town – and note that many of the hotels reviewed on p.65 also have good dining rooms. Competition for ferry passengers keeps prices relatively low, meaning that Dieppe is one of the few towns in Normandy where you can still find a good menu for under 80F/€12.20.

As well as the daily spectacle of the fish on sale in the **port de pêche**, described above, there's an all-day open-air **market** in the place Nationale and Grande Rue on Saturday. Otherwise, the main shopping streets in Dieppe are rue de la Barre and the Grande Rue. The chain store Printemps, 7 Grande Rue, incorporates a duty-free shop, and there's a Shopi supermarket at 59 rue de la Barre. L'Épicier Oliver at 18 rue St-Jacques has more specialist items. The largest of several **hypermarkets** in the area is Auchan (Mon–Sat 8.30am–10pm), out of town at the Centre Commercial du Belvédère on the route de Rouen (RN 27), and reached by free courtesy buses, as well as local bus #2, from the tourist office.

Restaurants

Les Écamias, 129 quai Henri IV (☎02.35.84.67.67). Small, friendly traditional French restaurant, at the quieter, seaward end of the main quay not far from the Cité de la Mer. Each of the two separate dining rooms (hence the plural) in neighbouring buildings serves the same menu, with a 75F/€11.43 option that includes *moules marinières* and stuffed shellfish; they also offer skate with capers. Closed Mon (except in Aug), and Sun evening in winter.

Le Festival, 11 quai Henri IV (☎02.35.40.24.29). Quick-fire brasserie at the busiest end of the quayside that delivers its fishy goods at top speed without skimping on quality. *Moules frites* is a mere 40F/€6.10, on the 110F/€16.77 menu you can get half a lobster, and there's *fruits de mer* literally by the boatload – it comes in blue-china ships.

La Marmite Dieppoise, 8 rue St-Jean (☎02.35.84.24.26). Rustic, busy little restaurant, between St-Jacques church and the arcades de la Bourse. Lunch menus from 100F/€15.24, dinners at 150F/€22.87, 175F/€26.68 or 220F/€33.54, with the latter featuring the local speciality *marmite Dieppoise* (seafood pot, with shellfish and white fish). Closed Sun evening and Mon, and also Thurs evening out of season.

Le Newhaven, 53 quai Henri IV (☎02.35.84.89.72). Reliable seafood specialist, at the slightly quieter end of the quayside, and serving good menus from 70F/€10.67. The 115F/€17.53 menu of Dieppe specialities is fine if you hanker after fish livers and squid, or 115F/€17.53 also buys you a *choucroute de la mer*. Closed Sun evening in winter.

Le Sully, 97 quai Henri IV (☎02.35.84.23.13). Some of the finest seafood on the quayside – none of it frozen – served either on bargain menus, including attractive sub-100F/€15.24 options, or in lavish platters. Closed Tues evening & Wed.

Les Tourelles, 43 rue du Commandant Fayolle (☎02.35.84.15.88). Welcoming little local restaurant, just behind the Casino, renowned for its paellas, though it also serves the standard seafood dishes. Menus from 72F/€10.98. Closed Sun evening & Mon.

The Côte d'Albâtre

The high, white cliffs that characterize the Norman coast from Picardy in the east to Le Havre in the west have earned it the name of the **Côte d'Albâtre** – the Alabaster coast. All this shoreline is eroding at a ferocious rate, and it's conceivable that the small resorts here, tucked in at the mouths of a succession of valleys, may not last more than another century or so. For the moment, however, they are quietly prospering, with casinos, sports centres and yacht marinas ensuring a modest but steady summer trade.

Although to arrive at Dieppe and promptly head **east** along the coast towards Calais and Boulogne may not be instinctive behaviour for travellers embarking on a tour of Normandy, doing so gives the opportunity to see a couple of surprising little towns: venerable **Le Tréport**, and the village of **Eu** with its thick forest surround, just inland. Head **west**, on the other hand, and the coast road dips into a series of pretty little ports, with **Étretat** as the pick of the bunch.

Le Tréport

Thirty kilometres east of Dieppe, at the mouth of the River Bresle which serves as the border with Picardy, **LE TRÉPORT** is a seaside resort that, while busy in summer, has clearly seen better days. It was already something of a bathing station when the railways arrived in 1873, and promoted this as "the prettiest beach in Europe, just three hours from Paris". It remained the capital's favoured resort until the 1950s – and is still served by around five trains daily – but it can't ever have been that pretty, and these days its charms are definitely fading.

Le Tréport divides into three distinct sections: the flat wedge-shaped seafront area, bounded on one side by the Channel, on another by the harbour at the canalized rivermouth, and on the third by imposing 100-metre-high-white chalk cliffs; the old town, higher up the slopes on safer ground; and the modern town further inland. The **seafront** itself is entirely taken up by a hideous pink and orange, concrete 1960s apartment block, with one or two snack bars but no other sign of life, facing the Casino and a drab-grey shingle beach. It's the more sheltered harbourside **quai Francois 1**er around the corner that holds most of the action, lined with restaurants, souvenir shops and cafés. A venerable little brick fish market stands across the road by the water, alongside a hundred-year-old carousel. The assorted stone jetties and wooden piers around the harbour are enjoyable to stroll around, watching the comings and goings of the fishing boats that still keep Le Tréport bustling. In its heyday it was possible to ride up the cliffs on a *téléphérique*; the tunnel through which it pierced the cliff face is still open to the air at either end, but the cables have rusted away, and the facilities are abandoned.

Climbing up from the *quai*, you come to the heavily nautical **Église St-Jacques**, built in the fifteenth century to replace an eleventh-century original that crumbled into the sea, along with the cliff on which it stood. Nearby, next to the fortified former town hall that is now the local library, successive flights of steps, 365 of them in all, climb to the top of the cliffs. As well as views to either side of the decaying mansions of Le Tréport, you can see across to the longer beach of **Mers-les-Bains**, which (being in Picardy) falls outside the scope of this book.

Practicalities

Both **trains** and **buses** arrive in Le Tréport on the far side of the harbour, a short walk from the main *quai*. Turning left as you hit the main drag will bring you to the town's **tourist office**, on quai Sadi-Carnot (Easter–Sept daily 10am–noon & 2–6pm; Oct–Easter Mon–Sat 10am–noon & 2–5pm; ☎02.35.86.05.69). That's the place to pick up a schedule of activities if you're lucky enough to be around for Le Tréport's major annual **festival**, the Blessing of the Sea on August 2.

Of the **hotels** in town, the best option is the *Riche-Lieu* at 50 quai Francois 1er (☎02.35.86.26.55; ③), with en-suite facilities in all the rooms – particularly pleasant are those with sea views – and well-priced, top-quality food served in the restaurant downstairs. The other, consistently tempting seafood **restaurants** along the *quai* are too numerous to review in detail, each boasting of its fresh *assiette de fruits de mer* and serving similar meals from around 90F/€13.72. The one with the highest gourmet reputation is the *Matelote*, 34 quai Francois 1er (☎02.35.86.01.13), where dining on the first floor gives you a panoramic overview of all the life of the port.

Eu

Queen Victoria twice visited Le Tréport with Albert. She didn't come to play on the beach, though, but to stay at the château at **EU**, a couple of kilometres inland. When she did so the first time, in the original "Entente Cordiale" in 1843, she became the first English monarch to visit France since Henry VIII arrived for the Field of the Cloth of Gold.

Today, Eu is something of a backwater, consisting of a few pedestrian streets at the top of a hill, and a straggle of newer districts reaching down the slopes. The **château** that stands at its heart was constructed in the sixteenth century, and served between 1830 and 1848 as the summer residence of the French monarch Louis Philippe. Of Eu's previous castle, deliberately burned in 1475 to forestall its capture by the English, only the tiny chapel remains, which was the site of William the Conqueror's marriage to Mathilda. At the time of writing, the castle was closed for restoration (due to finish 2002; check with tourist office for details), but its extensive formal **gardens** remain open as a free public park.

Unlikely as it may sound, Eu's Gothic church, **Notre-Dame et St-Laurent**, is dedicated to St Lawrence O'Toole, an Archbishop of Dublin who died here in 1181 while en route to visit Henry II in Rouen, to intercede on behalf of the Irish. His effigy still lies in the brightly lit and eerie crypt, along with various fourteenth-century members of the Artois family.

If you find yourself staying in Eu, you can spend an enjoyable afternoon by venturing into the **forest of Eu**, a mysterious and ancient tangled woodland dominated by tall beeches, with a lost Roman city supposedly hidden in its depths. A good way to explore it more thoroughly, though you'll need your own transport, is to follow the **River Bresle** upstream, along the border between Normandy and Picardy.

Practicalities

Eu is on the Le Tréport rail line, with its **gare SNCF** 500m down the hill from the centre, and its **tourist office** up in the pedestrianized section at 41 rue Bignon (May–Oct Mon 2–6.30pm, Tues–Sat 9.30am–12.30pm & 2–6.30pm, Sun 10am–1pm; Nov–April Tues–Sat 9.30am–noon & 2–5.30pm; ☎02.35.86.04.68). The best-value central **hotel** is the *Hôtel de la Gare* at 20 place de la Gare (☎02.35.86.16.64; ④; closed second half of Aug), in a slightly dilapidated red-brick town house next to the *gare SNCF*, offering menus from 90F/€13.72. There's also a **hostel** in the former royal kitchens, *Centre des Fontaines* (☎02.35.86.05.03; HI members 95F/€14.48), which serves meals, and acts as a general resource for local youngsters. Eu is short of places to eat, though there is a **restaurant**, *La Bragance*, in the gardens of the château, in what was once the icehouse, offering good-value alfresco lunches on its terrace.

Pourville-sur-mer

Heading **west** from Dieppe along the coastal D75, which starts from rue Faubourg de la Barre, you come after 3km to the resort of **POURVILLE-SUR-MER**, an extremely tranquil last- or first-night stop for ferry passengers. No more than a simple curving bay that briefly interrupts the line of cliffs, it lacks any form of port, but the wave conditions are enough to attract hordes of **surfers**. The beach itself was painted by Monet, a reproduction of whose *La Plage à Pourville* is displayed at the centre of the promenade.

Most of what few buildings line the road through Pourville are **hotels**, including a *logis* confusingly named *Produits de la Mer* (☎02.35.84.38.34; ③), where all eight rooms have showers or baths, and the plainest seafood menu costs 85F/€12.96 on weekdays, 120F/€18.29 at weekends. Next to it is a crazy-golf course. The two-star *Le Marqueval* **campsite** (☎02.35.82.66.46; closed Oct to mid-March) is set in the fields further back from the sea.

Varengeville-sur-mer

The straggling clifftop community of **VARENGEVILLE-SUR-MER**, 8km west of Dieppe and served by buses #311 and #312 (afternoons only), has long been popular with **artists**, including at different times Monet, Dufy, Miró and the parents of British Prime Minister Anthony Eden, who was born here. Its greatest devotee, however, was the pioneer Cubist **Georges Braque** (1882–1963), whose **grave** is situated outside a church perched spectacularly above the cliffs a couple of kilometres north of the centre, a smooth marble tomb topped by a sadly decaying mosaic of a white dove in flight. More impressive is his vivid-blue *Tree of Jesse* stained-glass window inside the church, through which the sun rises in summer.

Back along the road towards town from the church, the house at the **Bois des Moutiers**, built for Guillaume Mallet from 1898 onwards and un-French in almost every respect, was one of architect **Edwin Lutyens**' first commissions. Lutyens, then aged just 29 and heavily influenced by the "Arts and Crafts" ideas of William Morris, was at the start of a career that was to culminate during the 1920s when he laid out most of the city of New Delhi. The real reason to visit, however, is to enjoy the magnificent **gardens**, designed by Mallet in conjunction with Gertrude Jekyll, and at their most spectacular in the second half of May (mid-March to mid-Nov only: Mon–Fri & Sun 10am–noon & 2pm–sunset, Sat 2pm–sunset; admission 40F/€6.10 during May & June, otherwise 35F/€5.34). Enthusiastic guides lead you through the highly innovative engineering of the house and grounds, full of quirks and games. The colours of the Burne-Jones tapestry hanging in the stairwell were copied from Renaissance cloth in William Morris's studio; the rhododendrons were chosen from similar samples. Paths lead through vistas based on paintings by Poussin, Lorrain and other eighteenth-century artists; no modern roses, with their anachronistic colours, are allowed to spoil the effect.

Also in Varengeville, 300m south of the D75, is the **Manoir d'Ango**, the "summer palace" of sixteenth-century Dieppe's leading shipbuilder (mid-March to mid-Nov daily 10am–12.30pm & 2–6.30pm; mid-Nov to mid-March Sat 10am–12.30pm, Sun 10am–12.30pm & 2–6.30pm; 30F/€4.57). Jean Ango outfitted such major expeditions as Verrazzano's, which "discovered" the site of New York in 1524, and made himself rich from pillaging treasure ships out on the Spanish Main. His former home consists of a rectangular ensemble of fine, brick buildings arranged around a central courtyard. The intricate patterning of red bricks, shaped flint slabs, stone blocks and supporting timbers is at its finest in the remarkable central dovecote, topped by a dome that rises to an elegant point, which is aflutter with pigeons. The rooms of the various houses are all but empty except for cases of damp books, and in the absence of labelling or guidance you may find you've had enough after a few minutes' wandering.

The village of Varengeville offers little in the way of **accommodation**. Its one option, the *logis Hôtel de la Terrasse*, stands amid the pines on route de Vastérival on the cliffs west of town (☎02.35.85.12.54; ③; closed mid-Oct to Feb). Fishy menus in its panoramic dining room cost from 98F/€14.94.

On from Varengeville

The coastal road immediately beyond Varengeville is not very interesting. **QUIBERVILLE**, the main name on the map, makes a popular target for windsurfers, but in itself is little more than an overgrown caravan park; at **VEULES**, you pass a couple of ludicrous folk-sculptures, including a seashell snowman; **ANGIENS** is a pretty village but with nothing much to linger over.

St-Valéry-en-Caux

The first sizeable community west of Dieppe is **ST-VALÉRY-EN-CAUX**, a rebuilt but still attractive port where open-air stalls along the quayside of the narrow harbour sell fresh-caught fish daily. St-Valéry provides a clear reminder of the fighting – and massive destruction – of the Allied retreat of 1940. To either side of the shingle beach rise crumbling, brown-stained cliffs. A monument on the western heights pays tribute to the French division who faced Rommel's tanks on horseback, brandishing their sabres with hopeless heroism, while beside the ruins of a German artillery emplacement on the opposite cliffs a second monument commemorates a Scottish division, the 51st Highlanders, rounded up while fighting their way back to the boats home.

There's now a characterless new casino in the centre of the curve, and an even newer church in the streets a little way behind, which appears to be made almost entirely of stained glass.

Practicalities

Much the most attractive house to survive in St-Valéry is the Renaissance **Maison Henri IV** on the quai d'Aval, with its intricately carved wooden facade. It's now the **tourist office** (May to mid-Sept daily 10am–12.30pm & 3–7pm; mid-Sept to April Wed–Sat 10am–12.30pm & 3–7pm, Sun 10am–12.30pm; ☎02.35.97.00.63). Although no trains serve the town, from four to six SNCF **buses** connect each day with trains to and from Rouen at Motteville, 27km south.

The *Terrasses*, 22 rue le Perrey (☎02.35.97.11.22; ④; closed Christmas & Jan), is the only **hotel-restaurant** actually facing the sea; dinner menus start at 130F/€19.82. The other, much cheaper, *logis* in town, the seven-room *La Marine*, 113 rue St-Léger (☎02.35.97.05.09; ②; closed Fri in low season, plus Dec & Jan), is tucked away in a backstreet on the west side of the harbour, and several more small hotels surround the main market square. Otherwise try the huge *Relais Mercure*, 500m back along the pleasure port at 14 av Clémenceau (☎02.35.57.88.00; ④). Its 149 rooms are faultlessly comfortable, if also characterless, and can be a godsend in high season, when the few resources along this stretch of coast are strained to the limit.

St-Valery holds two year-round municipal **campsites**, the one-star *Falaise d'Amont* (☎02.35.97.05.07), on the eastern cliffs, and the larger four-star *d'Éten-nemare* (☎02.35.97.15.79), set back from the sea southwest of the harbour. The *Restaurant du Port*, overlooking the harbour at 18 quai d'Amont (☎02.35.97.08.93; closed Sun evening & Mon in low season), has a delicious 118F/€17.99 menu, featuring *marmite Dieppois*, and a seriously overpriced 198F/€30.18 one. **Markets** take place on Fridays and summer Sundays, and the town plays host to a **herring festival** in mid-November.

Fécamp

FÉCAMP, roughly halfway between Dieppe and Le Havre, is, like Dieppe, a serious fishing port, albeit one with a more frivolous modern sideline as a holiday resort. Its name first features in a charter of 875 AD, as Fiscannum, from the

Germanic *fisc* meaning "fish", and it has been a centre for shipbuilding ever since the Vikings set up a boatyard here in 911 AD. These days, it's a striking town, so much surrounded by high cliffs that, approaching from inland, you don't see the sea until you're right upon it. It was fortunate enough to sustain very little damage during World War II, though its reportedly magnificent Belle Époque casino was destroyed in 1945 by the Germans, who feared it could serve as a landmark for Allied invaders. The current, much uglier replacement was completed in 1958.

Fécamp still has its railway link, the tracks running right up to the small harbour, where fishing boats, yachts and *vedettes* jostle for position. The town's long promenade fronts a uniform steep beach of shingle, framed by crumbling and overhanging cliffs. As ever along this coast, windsurfing is more appealing than bathing. In the absence of any major attraction out to sea, the *vedettes* offer cruises to watch the sun set.

Arrival and information

The **gares SNCF** and **routière** lie between the port and the town centre on avenue Gambetta, on the south bank of the River Valmont, which flows westwards through the town. The main **tourist office** is in an inconvenient location, tucked away a few hundred yards from the *gare SNCF* opposite the distillery at 113 rue Alexandre-le-Grand (July & Aug Mon–Fri 10am–6pm; Sept–June Mon–Sat 9am–12.15pm & 1.45–6pm; ☎02.35.28.51.01, *www.fecamp.com*), but there's another summer-only office alongside the Musée des Terres-Neuvas (see below) on the seafront (July & Aug Mon–Fri 11am–1pm & 2.30–7.30pm, Sat 10.30am–1pm & 2.30–7.30pm, Sun 10.30am–1pm & 2.30–6.30pm; ☎02.35.29.16.34). Both can provide details of the regular programme of guided tours in and around Fécamp.

Accommodation

Fécamp's **hotels** tend to be set back away from the sea, on odd side streets. It's a popular place, so you'll need to reserve a room in summer. A lovely **campsite**, the *Camping de Reneville* (☎02.35.28.20.97; closed Jan & Feb), is a short walk out of town on the western cliffs.

Hôtel d'Angleterre, 93 rue de la Plage (☎02.35.28.01.60, fax 02.35.28.62.95). Unattractive but reasonable hotel just back from the sea, with its own restaurant (closed Sun) and "English pub" that offers weekly darts and theme nights. ③.

Hôtel du Commerce, 26–28 place Bigot (☎02.35.29.19.28, fax 02.35.28.70.50, *www .hotel-lecommerce.com*). Peaceful, appealing hotel near St-Étienne church in the old town, where some of the rooms are in individual motel-style cabins beyond the courtyard, and the restaurant downstairs (closed Sun) serves tasty menus in all price ranges. ③.

Le Martin, 18 place St-Étienne (☎02.35.28.23.82). A handful of basic rooms above one of the better restaurants in the old town (see p.76). Closed first fortnight of March and second fortnight of Sept. ①.

Hôtel de la Mer, 89 bd Albert 1er (☎02.35.28.24.64, fax 02.35.28.27.67). Simple but good-value hotel on the seafront, adjoining *La Frégate* restaurant where bd Albert 1er dead-ends just short of the casino, which is nicer inside than it looks from the outside. Closed two weeks in Feb. ③.

Hôtel de la Plage, 87 rue de la Plage (☎02.35.29.76.51, fax 02.35.28.68.30). The smartest option close to the beach; only the higher rooms have sea views, but all rooms are nicely refurbished and the location is quiet. ③.

Hôtel de l'Univers, 5 place St-Étienne (☎02.35.28.05.88, fax 02.35.27.82.58). Basic little budget hotel, facing St-Étienne church in the old town, where the most expensive menu in the lunch-only restaurant downstairs is a mere 64F/€9.76. ②.

The Town

The town proper sprawls up the slopes to the south of the River Valmont, with the venerable **Église de la Trinité** as its focus. The port lies further down the river, which at this stage disappears into a series of canalized channels and artificial harbours. The seafront is a few hundred yards further west again, along a harbour-side promenade that holds most of Fécamp's best restaurants.

THE BENEDICTINE DISTILLERY

110 rue Alexandre-le-Grand. Daily: Feb to mid-March & mid-Nov to Dec 10–11.15am & 2–5pm; mid-March to June & Sept to mid-Nov 10am–noon & 2–5.30pm; July & Aug 9.30am–6pm. Admission on guided tours only, lasting 1hr 30min. 29F/€4.42.

Fécamp owes much of its popularity to an utterly bizarre tourist attraction – the **Benedictine Distillery**, amid the narrow streets that run parallel to the port towards the town centre. This mock-Gothic monstrosity may look like a decaying mansion that has survived nightmarish aeons, but was in fact built at the end of nineteenth century for the manufacture of the sweet liqueur known as Benedictine. To see inside you have to go round on a rather dismal guided **tour**, the first part of which treks through a museum of local antiquities and oddments. Most visitors are frantic to get to the alcohol at the end, but the tour does have its moments. These include headless bishops, serpentine musical instruments, carved wood and ivory, and – a kitsch treat – a stained-glass window in which Alexandre le Grand, former owner of the Benedictine company (no relation to Alexander the Great), is being treated to a bottle of his liqueur by a passing angel.

Eventually you pass on to the distillery section (although commercial operations have moved to a new factory outside town), where boxes of exotic herbs are thrown into great copper vats and alembics. There is then a massive surge drinkwards, for the (disappointingly modest) *dégustation* across the road; it must be said it's nice stuff, especially the "B&B", Benedictine and brandy, served either neat or on crêpes. Make sure you hang onto your admission ticket to get the free drink.

ÉGLISE DE LA TRINITÉ

If your aesthetic sensibilities need soothing after the distillery, head away from the sea to the **Église de la Trinité**. This medieval abbey church is light and almost frail with age, its bare nave echoing to the sound of birds flying free beneath the high roof. The wooden carvings are tremendous, in particular the dusty, wooden bas-relief *Dormition of the Virgin*. The abbey also has a fine selection of saintly fingers and sacred hips, authenticated with wax seals, and even a drop of the Precious Blood itself, said to have floated all the way here in a fig tree dispatched by Joseph of Arimathea. Until Mont-St-Michel was built, this was the religious centre of Normandy; Edward the Confessor is more reliably known to have made extensive gifts to the abbey and may have lived here at some point before his coronation as king of England.

Opposite the main entrance, the few vestiges that remain of the palace of the early dukes of Normandy – both Richard I and Richard II are buried in the abbey – have been landscaped to create an attractive little public garden. William, bastard son of Duke Robert, was presented here at the age of 7 to the assembled lords and bishops of Normandy when his father left for the Crusades; and returned here as William the Conqueror to celebrate Easter 1067.

MUSÉE DES TERRES-NEUVAS ET DE LA PÊCHE

27 bd Albert 1er. July & Aug daily 10am–7pm; Sept–June daily except Tues 10am–noon & 2–5.30pm. Adults 20F/€3.05, under-18s free; same ticket gives admission to Musée Centre des Arts.

Just south of the rivermouth, though sealed from view of the Channel by the high sea wall, the modern **Musée des Terres-Neuvas et de la Pêche** commemorates Fécamp's association with the sea from the Viking invasions onwards. Spreading across two floors, with lots of miniature model boats and amateur paintings, it focuses in particular on the long tradition whereby the fishermen of Fécamp decamped en masse each year to catch cod in the cold, foggy waters off Newfoundland. Life on board was both brutal and lonely, and the work was hard, with the fish being cleaned and salted on deck, and then sold in Spain or Portugal rather than being carried back to France. Sailing vessels continued to make the trek from the sixteenth century right up until 1931; today, vast refrigerated container ships have taken their place.

Upstairs, there's a fascinating scale model of the port and town as it looked in 1830, shortly before Fécamp was transformed by the arrival of the first railway. At that point, it entirely lacked docks and warehouses; in fact nothing stood on the far side of the river, and the whole town was still surrounded by agricultural land.

Non-French speakers should ask at the front desk for their excellent folder of English translations of all the museum's captions.

MUSÉE CENTRE DES ARTS

21 rue Alexandre-Legros. Daily except Tues 10am–noon & 2–5.30pm. Adults 20F/€3.05, under-18s free; same ticket gives admission to Musée des Terres-Neuvas.

A splendid mansion in the small pedestrianized district at the heart of old Fécamp holds the town's fine arts museum. As usual for these parts, it's a haphazard assortment of carved ivories, painted porcelain, archeological knick-knacks and fading statues rescued from tumbledown churches. The most interesting section is up on the third floor, which holds an intriguing collection of everyday objects used in the Caux region during the eighteenth and nineteenth centuries.

Eating

In summer, Fécamp welcomes enough visitors to keep several very good **restaurants** in business – not surprisingly, the fish tends to be good – but things do get rather quieter in winter.

La Marée, 75 quai Bérigny (☎02.35.29.39.15). Very good fish restaurant, enjoying harbour views from a grand upstairs dining room above a wonderful fish shop. Menus from 98F/€14.94 to 195F/€29.73, featuring all kinds of pescatorial pleasures – the only meat anywhere is foie gras – plus a *tartellette Bénédictine* for dessert. Closed Sun evening & Mon.

La Marine, 23 quai de la Vicomté (☎02.35.28.15.94). Friendly little quayside restaurant, not far short of the beach, that's open daily for good-value 80F/€12.20 lunches and dinners from 100F/€15.24 to 170F/€25.92. The *choucroute de la mer* is recommended.

Le Martin, 18 place St-Étienne (☎02.35.28.23.82). Small old-town restaurant where the cooking is rooted in the finest Norman tradition of adding strong alcohol to just about everything, whether it's gin with your scallops or brandy on your sole; both are options on the top 150F/€22.87 menu, along with a dozen snails or oysters. Plenty of meat dishes too, and a 75F/€11.43 menu (not available on Sat nights) that's a real bargain. Also has a few budget rooms. Closed Sun evening & Mon, plus first fortnight of March & second fortnight of Sept.

Le Vicomté, 4 rue Coty (☎02.35.28.47.63). Cheery old-fashioned bistro near the distillery and port that serves just one 89F/€13.57 menu, which changes daily and includes hearty traditional meat and fish dishes. Closed Wed evening & Sun.

Yport

The tiny fishing port of **YPORT**, tucked into a narrow gap in the chalky cliffs 6km west of Fécamp, is something of a cross between Fécamp and Étretat. It's much smaller and more attractive than Fécamp, from which it's actually visible along the shoreline, without being nearly as photogenic (or crowded) as Étretat. Local legend has it that Yport was colonized over two thousand years ago by Greek fishermen from Asia Minor, who for some reason were not deterred by its complete lack of a harbour. Their descendants have remained ever since, meaning that Yport has a reputation for being an insular community. While it's not a place to spend your entire holiday, it makes an appealing and very peaceful overnight stop.

Practicalities

Yport's **tourist office**, just back from the sea in place J-P Laurens (July & Aug Mon–Sat 10am–noon & 3–7pm, Sun 10am–noon; Sept–June Mon–Fri 10am–noon & 3–5pm; ☎02.35.29.77.31), can provide details of clifftop hiking trails. Both the main **hotels** are painted to look as though they're half-timbered. The *Hôtel Normand*, also on place J-P Laurens (☎02.35.27.30.76; ③), is a *logis de France* with menus from 92F/€14.03; *La Sirène*, 7 bd Alexandre-Dumont (☎02.35.27.31.87; ②), enjoys sweeping beachfront views, and serves the usual seafood menus at 80F/€12.20 and upwards. *La Falaise*, near the *Normand* at 32 rue Émmanuel Foy (☎02.35.29.35.07), is a traditional little French **restaurant**, with pale-blue decor, which offers good-value menus from 75F/€11.43 at lunchtime.

On to Étretat

The minor road **D28** runs from Fécamp through a thickly wooded and idyllic valley to **BENARVILLE** – a good cycling route, even though it manages to lose the river somewhere along the way. The **D150** (covered by buses #261 and #311 from Fécamp) is less pastoral, but leads to the remains of the **Abbaye de Valmont** (April–Sept daily except Tues 10am–noon & 2–6pm). In its spacious grounds you can feast your eyes on a Renaissance chapel, grass-floored and open to the sky, and an intact Gothic Lady Chapel.

Étretat

The pretty little town of **ÉTRETAT**, another 20km west towards Le Havre, is a very different kettle of fish to Fécamp. Here the alabaster cliffs are at their most spectacular – their arches, tunnels and the solitary "needle" out to sea will doubtless be familiar from tourist brochures long before you arrive – and the town itself has grown up simply as a pleasure resort. There isn't even a port of any kind; the seafront consists of a sweeping unbroken curve of concrete above the shingle beach. In summer, wooden boats hauled onto the promenade serve as seasonal bars.

Arrival and information

Étretat's **tourist office** is alongside the main through-road in the centre of town, on place M. Guillard (mid-March to mid-June & mid-Sept to mid-Oct daily 10am–noon & 2–6pm; mid-June to mid-Sept daily 10am–7pm; mid-Oct to mid-March Fri 2–6pm, Sat 10am–noon & 2–6pm, Sun 10am–noon; ☎02.35.27.05.21, *www.etretat.net*). Local **buses** stop just outside, while **mountain bikes** are available for rent from an informal stand alongside (daily from 10am; ☎02.35.27.47.84; 50F/€7.62 for 2hr, 100F/€15.24 per day).

Accommodation

Though Étretat is hardly short of **hotels** – four crowd onto the corners of place Foch alone – they struggle to cope with demand during high season. It makes a lovely place to stay, however, so it's well worth booking in advance. **Campers** will find the *Camping municipal* 1km out on rue Guy-de-Maupassant (☎02.35.27.07.67; closed mid-Oct to March).

Le Corsaire, rue du Général Leclerc (☎02.35.10.38.90, fax 02.35.28.89.74). The most affordable of the seafront hotels, in the thick of things alongside the casino. The rooms are nothing special, but the beach terrace restaurant serves good menus from 75F/€11.43. ③.

Dormy House, route du Havre (☎02.35.27.07.88, fax 02.35.29.86.19, *Dormy.House@ wanadoo.fr*). Grand, modern establishment perched above town on the coastal road to the west, poised as much for the golf course as the beach. Comfortable rooms with superlative views, and a good restaurant. ④–⑧.

L'Escale, place Foch (☎02.35.27.03.69, fax 02.35.28.05.86). Simple but pleasant rooms on the main square, above a snack restaurant specializing in *moules frites* and crêpes. ③.

Hôtel des Falaises, 1 bd René-Coty (☎02.35.27.02.77). Dependable central hotel, from whose modernized rooms you get a better view of the picturesque *Résidence* across the street than if you're actually staying there. ③.

Hôtel la Résidence, 4 bd René-Coty (☎02.35.27.02.87). Dramatic, half-timbered old mansion just off place Foch, moved in its entirety from Lisieux a century ago, with beautiful wooden carvings decorating its every nook and cranny. The quality of rooms, however, is variable; some are positively luxurious, but few are anything like as elegant as the facade. The *Licorne* restaurant downstairs is run by separate management. ②–④.

The Town

Étretat centres on **place Foch** just back from the sea, where the old wooden market *halles* still stand; the ground floor is now converted into souvenir shops, but the beams of the balcony and roof are bare and ancient. **Market** day locally is Thursday, with most of the stalls spreading across the larger car park to the west.

As soon as you step onto the beach you're confronted by the cliff formations to either side. The largest arch, and the lone needle, thrust out on the west, is known as the **Falaise d'Aval**. A straightforward if precarious walk leads up the crumbing side of the cliff. On the inland side are the lush lawns and pastures of the local golf course, while on the shore side, German fortifications extend to the point where the turf abruptly stops, occasionally ripped by the latest fall. From the windswept top you can see further rock formations and possibly even glimpse Le Havre, but the views back to the town sheltered in the valley, and the **Falaise d'Amont** on its eastern side, are what stick in the memory.

Maupassant compared the profile of the smaller arch at the base of the eastern cliffs – as painted by Monet, among others – to an elephant dipping its trunk into the ocean. At any time other than high tide, it's possible to stroll along the shingles beyond the town proper to within a few metres of the arch. Alternatively, a footpath winds to the top of the cliff on this side as well, a gentler climb up the green hillside that leads to the little chapel of **Notre Dame**. Just beyond that is the futuristic white arch erected to commemorate the French aviators **Nungesser and Coli**, who set out from Paris in the *Oiseau Blanc* in May 1927, hoping to make the first transatlantic flight, and were last seen over Étretat. What happened to them is not known – there are suggestions that they crashed somewhere in deepest Maine, New England – but a mere eighteen days later Charles Lindbergh arrived coming from the opposite direction (see p.153) and went into the history books. In the turf alongside the arch, a life-size aeroplane is set in concrete relief, and there's a museum nearby.

Eating

Fierce competition keeps **restaurant** prices in Étretat appealingly low. Even the succession of oceanfront terraces offer good value for money, while away from the sea there are bargains to be had at both ends of the market.

Le Clos Lupin, 34 rue Alphonse-Kerr (☎02.35.29.67.53). Small, intimate dining room, a little way back from the seafront bustle at the western end of town, with a wide range of quality fish menus from 95F/€14.48.

La Coquille Normand, rue Général-Leclerc (☎02.35.27.02.12). A typically good example of the row of reliable seafood restaurants along the promenade, ideal for lunch especially, with an 89F/€13.57 menu that offers a basic *assiette des fruits de mer* followed by *moules frites*.

Le Galion, 4 bd René-Coty (☎02.35.29.48.74). Probably the best restaurant in Étretat, adjoining the *Résidence* hotel and with a similar antique-filled ambience. The 120F/€18.29 menu makes a definitive introduction to all that's best in Norman cuisine, while both the 198F/€30.18 and 235F/€35.83 options offer oysters poached in champagne. Closed Wed & mid-Dec to mid-Jan.

La Huitrière, place de Gaulle (☎02.35.27.02.82). Panoramic first-floor dining room, at the foot of the steps up the Falaise d'Aval, which makes the perfect setting for an absolute blowout on seafood. As well as menus from 149F/€22.71, it offers an enormous range of seafood platters, from 92F/€14.03 up to the two-person triple-decker 750F/€114.34 *Abondance*, which comes with two lobsters and a scattering of caviar.

Le Havre

Most ferry passengers head straight out of the port of **LE HAVRE**, at the mouth of the Seine, as quickly as the traffic will allow, to escape a city that guidebooks tend to dismiss as dismal, disastrous and gargantuan. While Normandy's largest town, home to a population of over 200,000, may not be the most picturesque or tranquil place in the region, neither is it the soulless urban sprawl the warnings suggest – even if the port, the second largest in France after Marseille, does take up half the Seine estuary, extending way beyond the town – and its stature is reflected in its fine contemporary array of "twin" cities, including such ports as Southampton, St Petersburg, Dalian and Tampa.

The city was originally built on the orders of François I in 1517. Its function was to replace the ancient ports of Harfleur and Honfleur, then already silting up, and its name was soon changed from Franciscopolis to Le Havre – "the Harbour". After serious flooding in 1540 it was redesigned, and rebuilt to a grid pattern, by Girolamo Bellarmato, an exiled Italian engineer who had experience of working in the unstable soil of Venice. It became the principal trading post of the northern French coast, prospering especially during the American War of Independence and thereafter, importing cotton, sugar and tobacco. In the years before the outbreak of war in 1939, it was the European home of the great luxury liners such as the *Normandie, Île de France* and *France*.

Le Havre suffered heavier damage than any other port in Europe during World War II. Following its all but total destruction, it was rebuilt to the specifications of a single architect, **Auguste Perret**, between 1946 and 1964 – which makes it a rather rare entity, and one that with its utter dependence on **reinforced concrete** is visibly circumscribed by constraints of time and money. Nonetheless, the sheer sense of space can be exhilarating, the showpiece monuments have a dramatic and winning self-confidence, and the few churches and other relics of the old city to survive have been sensitively integrated into the whole. The skyline has been kept deliberately low – there are no tower blocks, and even the new mirrored World Trade Centre only manages five storeys – but the endless mundane residential blocks, which simply had to be erected as economically and swiftly as possible after the war, do get dispiriting after a while. However, with the sea visible at the end of almost every street, and open public space and expanses of water at every turn, even those visitors who ultimately fail to agree with Perret's famous dictum that "concrete is beautiful" may enjoy a stroll around his city.

Arrival and information

Three daily P&O **ferries** sail from Portsmouth to the **Terminal de Grande Bretagne**, not far from the train and bus stations in the Bassin de la Citadelle (☎08.03.01.30.13). The terminal has a tourist information kiosk, open in summer.

The **gare SNCF** (☎02.35.98.50.50) is 1.5km west of the Hôtel de Ville, on cours de la République, right alongside the **gare routière** (☎02.35.26.67.23), across boulevard de Strasbourg. Fast **trains** (though not TGV) timed to connect with the ferries go to Rouen (1hr) and Paris (a further 1hr 15min). If you're travelling west, you have to change at Rouen – a very circuitous route. Commuter services run regularly to Harfleur in around five minutes.

Shuttle buses connect the *gare SNCF* with the ferry terminal. All the **buses** that pass the *gare SNCF* continue to the Hôtel de Ville. You can pick up timetables or make enquiries at the bus kiosk there or nearby at CGTE, 115 rue Jules Lecesne (☎02.35.41.72.22), which is where most buses park.

Express **buses** from the *gare routière*, run by Bus Verts du Calvados (☎08.01.21.42.14), take advantage of the Pont du Normandie to connect Le Havre with Honfleur eight times daily, with two services continuing as far as Caen. Les Autocars Gris (☎02.35.28.19.88) run regular services to Fécamp and Étretat, while CNA (☎02.35.52.92.00) run down to Rouen.

Le Havre's modern, helpful **tourist office** is in an inconspicuous and not very central location on the main oceanfront drag, at 186 bd Clémenceau, near its intersection with avenue Foch (May–Sept Mon–Sat 9am–7pm, Sun 10am–12.30pm & 2.30–6pm; Oct–April Mon–Sat 9am–6.30pm, Sun 10am–1pm; ☎02.35.74.04.04, *www.lehavretourism.com*), while the **post office** is at 62 rue Jules Siegfried (Mon–Fri 8am–7pm, Sat 8am–noon; ☎02.32.92.59.00).

Accommodation

It's hard to see why anyone would stay more than a single night in Le Havre. One consequence of the lack of idiosyncratic old buildings in the city is that its **hotels** tend to be faceless in the extreme, hidden away behind indistinguishable concrete facades. There are two main concentrations of hotels: one group faces the *gare SNCF*, and most of the rest lie within walking distance of the ferry terminal.

Although there's no official **hostel** in Le Havre, it is usually possible to find a dorm room in the hostel-equivalent *Union Chrétienne des Jeunes Gens*, at 153 bd de Strasbourg (☎02.35.42.47.86). The nearest **camping** is at the surprisingly attractive four-star *Forêt de Montgeon* site (☎02.35.46.52.39; closed Oct to mid-April), north of the town centre in a 700-acre forest; take bus #1 from the Hôtel de Ville or *gare SNCF*, direction "Jacques-Monod", getting off at "Ste-Cecile" or "Noisetriers".

Hotels

Hôtel de Bordeaux, 147 rue Louis-Brindeau (☎02.35.22.69.44, fax 02.35.42.09.27). Smart, comfortable hotel, affiliated to the Best Western chain, on the north side of the Espace Oscar Niemeyer, facing the Volcano. ⑤.

Hôtel Celtic, 106 rue Voltaire (☎02.35.42.39.77, fax 02.35.21.67.75). Friendly and comfortable option, in the long buildings that flank the Espace Oscar Niemeyer. ②.

Hôtel Faidherbe, 21 rue Général-Faidherbe (☎02.35.42.20.27, fax 02.35.42.57.03). Simple rooms, some with sea views, in this welcoming family hotel very near the ferry port in the old town. ①.

Hôtel Foch, 4 rue de Caligny (☎02.35.42.50.69, fax 02.35.43.40.17). Plain, cream-coloured cement building, beside the main entrance to the St-Joseph church. All rooms have TV plus bath or shower. ④.

Hôtel Jeanne d'Arc, 91 rue Émile-Zola (☎02.35.21.67.27, fax 02.35.41.26.83). Tiny little hotel, where the old-fashioned but clean rooms are given a personal touch by the owner's needlework. ①.

Hôtel Le Monaco, 16 rue de Paris (☎02.35.42.21.01, fax 02.35.42.01.01). Bright hotel on a busy corner overlooking the quay, handy for the ferries and with a good-value brasserie downstairs. Closed second fortnight in Feb, and Mon July–Oct. ②.

Grand Hôtel Parisien, 1 cours de la République (☎02.35.25.23.83, fax 02.35.25.05.06). A well-appointed place, with congenial management, facing the *gare SNCF* on a busy corner. All rooms have shower and TV. Twenty-five-percent reductions on Fri & Sat Dec–March. ②.

Hôtel Séjour Fleuri, 71 rue Émile-Zola (☎02.35.41.33.81, fax 02.35.42.26.44). On a side road off rue de Paris, close to the ferry terminal; not exactly "*fleuri*", but cheered up by some bright-red shutters and a couple of windowboxes. Two hotels knocked into one make for uneven corridors. ①.

Hôtel d'Yport, 27 cours de la République (☎02.35.25.21.08, fax 02.35.24.06.34). Another option opposite the SNCF station, this time slightly quieter, being set just back from the street, and unusually hospitable. Guests in the cheaper rooms are charged 25F/€3.81 to have a shower, so you might as well have en-suite facilities. ①–③.

The Town

One reason visitors tend to dismiss Le Havre out of hand is that it's easy, whether you're travelling by train, bus or your own vehicle, to get to and from the city without ever seeing its downtown area, and be left with an impression of an endless industrial sprawl.

The central **Hôtel de Ville**, a logical first port of call, is a low flat-roofed building, designed by Perret, that stretches for over 100m, and is topped by a seventeen-storey concrete tower. Surrounded by pergola walkways, flowerbeds and flowing water from several strata of fountains, it's an attractive, lively place with a high-tech feel, and is often the venue for imaginative civic-minded exhibitions.

Perret's other major creation is the church of **St-Joseph**, the not dissimilar steeple of which is clearly visible some way northwest of the town hall. Instead of the traditional elongated cross shape, the four arms of the cross on which this church is built are equally short. From the outside it's a very plain mass of speckled concrete, almost Egyptian in its simplicity, the main doors thrown open to the street to hint at dark interior spaces that resemble an underground car park. Once you get inside, however, it all makes sense. The altar is right in the centre, with the hundred-metre bell tower rising directly above it. Very simple patterns of stained glass, all around the church and right the way up the tower, produce a bright interplay of coloured light, all focusing on the altar to create the effect of a church "in the round".

Le Havre's boldest specimen of modern architecture is considerably more recent – the cultural centre known as the **Volcano** (or less reverentially as the "yogurt pot"), which stands at the end of the Bassin du Commerce dominating the **Espace Oscar Niemeyer**. The Brazilian architect for whom the *espace* is named designed this slightly asymmetrical, smooth, gleaming-white cone, cut off abruptly just above the level of the surrounding buildings, so that its curving planes are undisturbed by doors or windows; the entrance is concealed beneath a white walkway in the open plaza below. A large green-copper hand emerges from the Volcano just above its base, slightly cupped and pouring out water as a fountain, inscribed with the sentiment that "One day, like this water, the land, beaches and mountains will belong to all". A smaller white building alongside also forms part of the centre.

The **Bassin du Commerce**, which stretches away from the complex, is in fact of minimal commercial significance; kayaks and rowing boats can be rented to explore its regular contours, and a couple of larger boats are moored permanently to serve as clubs or restaurants. It's all disconcertingly quiet, serving mainly as an appropriate stretch of water for the graceful white footbridge of the Passarelle du Commerce to cross.

Musée Malraux

Bd J.F. Kennedy. Mon & Wed–Fri 11am–6pm, Sat & Sun 11am–7pm. 25F/€3.81, under-18s free.

Following its recent major overhaul, the modern **Musée Malraux**, overlooking the harbour entrance, ranks among the best-designed art galleries in France, using natural light to full advantage to display an enjoyable assortment of nineteenth- and twentieth-century French paintings.

The principal highlight upstairs is a collection of over two hundred canvases by **Eugène Boudin**. Two years after the painter's death, his brother Louis gave the museum the entire contents of Eugène's studio. Although many of the works were neither signed nor dated, and some are no bigger than postcards, they range throughout the artist's career. Most are arranged by theme, so one wall consists almost entirely of miniature cows, but there are also greyish landscapes produced all along the Norman and Breton coastlines, including views of Trouville, Honfleur and Étretat.

Downstairs, the focus shifts to a lovely set of works by **Raoul Dufy** (1877–1953). In his case, the artist's widow left two hundred of his paintings to be divided between three museums – the national modern art museum in Paris, the one in Nice, and this gallery in Dufy's home town. Each curator was allowed to pick a single piece in turn, with the result that Le Havre ended up with a collection of images of itself that make it seem positively radiant. Dufy depicts his native city at play, with drawings and paintings of festivals and parades, and even a panorama of the whole metropolis framed beneath an arching rainbow. Among other treasures are a Gauguin from Tahiti, several Monets – including scenes of Westminster and Varengeville, plus a few waterlilies and a snowscape sunrise – as well as works by Corot, Courbet, Pissarro (including one painted within a few metres of this spot), Sisley, Léger, Braque and Lurçat.

Musée de l'Ancien Havre

1 rue Jerome Bellarmato. Wed–Sun 10am–noon & 2–6pm. 10F/€1.52.

If you have the time, you might like to see what old Le Havre looked like in the prewar days when **Jean-Paul Sartre** wrote *La Nausée* here. He taught philosophy for five years during the 1930s in a local school, and his almost transcendent disgust with the place cannot obscure the fascination he felt in exploring the seedy dockside quarter of St François, in those spare moments when he wasn't visiting Simone de Beauvoir in Rouen. Little survives of the city Sartre knew, but pictures and bits gathered from the rubble are on display in one of the very few buildings that escaped, the **Musée de l'Ancien Havre**, somewhat incongruous amid the new concrete, just south of the Bassin du Commerce.

Harfleur

The once-great port of **Harfleur** is now no more than a suburb of Le Havre, 6km upstream from the centre. While visibly older than the modern city that engulfs it, it's no longer sufficiently distinctive to be worth visiting. It earned an undying place in history, however, as the landing place of Henry V's English army in 1415, en route to victory at Agincourt. During a month-long siege of the town, two thousand English soldiers died from eating contaminated seafood from the surrounding marshes. Harfleur surrendered in late September, following a final English onslaught spurred on – according to Shakespeare – by Henry's cry of "Once more unto the breach, dear friends . . ."

Eating and shopping

Few of the **restaurants** in Le Havre are worth making a fuss about, except perhaps for some in the suburb of **Ste-Adresse**, northwest along the coast towards Étretat, which is no longer quite as picturesque as you might imagine from Monet's depictions of it. There are, however, lots of bars, cafés and brasseries around the *gare SNCF*, and all sorts of crêperies and ethnic alternatives – couscous, South American, Caribbean – in the backstreets of the St-François quarter.

If you're **shopping** for food to take home, possibilities include the central market, just west of place Gambetta and ideal for fresh produce. The larger of the two local Auchan **hypermarkets** (both open Mon–Sat 8.30am–10pm) is at the Mont Gaillard Centre Commercial; it is reached by following cours de la République beyond the *gare SNCF*, through the tunnel, and has a good *Flunch* self-service cafeteria. The other, at Montivilliers, is signposted off the Tancarville road.

Restaurants

L'Huitrière, 12 quai Michel Féré (☎02.35.21.24.16). Seafood specialists in the historic St-François quarter, facing the rotating bridge of the port. Even the simplest 92F/€14.03 *assiette* includes clams, shrimps and langoustines; the two-person 750F/€114.34 *Abondance* has to be seen to be believed. They also have branches in Étretat and Dieppe.

L'Odyssée, 41 rue Général-Faidherbe (☎02.35.21.31.42). First-rate seafood restaurant close to the ferry terminal in the old town, serving a reliable 125F/€19.06 weekday lunch menu and a changing, more adventurous 155F/€23.63 dinner option. Closed Sat lunch, Sun evening, Mon & mid-July to mid-Aug.

Palissandre, 33 rue de Bretagne (☎02.35.21.69.00). Old-fashioned, wood-panelled bistro in the St-François quarter, where the conventional menus from 85F/€12.96 feature dishes such as fish stewed in cider, and an express menu guarantees service within 20min. Closed Wed evening, Sat lunch & Sun.

La Petite Auberge, 32 rue de Ste-Adresse (☎02.35.46.27.32). High-class traditional French cooking, aimed more at local businesspeople than at tourists, and offering few surprises but no disappointments. Menus at 120F/€18.29, 160F/€24.39 and up. Closed Mon & Sun evening.

La Petite Brocante, 75 rue Louis Brindeau (☎02.35.21.42.20). Lively central bistro, where the set menus are a little pricey at 128F/€19.51 and up, but there's always a good-value *plat du jour*, as often as not fresh fish. Closed Sun & first three weeks in Aug.

Tilbury, 39 rue Jean-de-la-Fontaine (☎02.35.21.23.50). Attractive, unusual place in the old town – individual tables are kitted out like horse-drawn carriages – where the emphasis is on baked dishes (they even bake snail *brioches*) and low-priced lunches. Closed Sat lunch, Sun evening & Mon.

Entertainment

If you're looking to pass an evening or two in Le Havre, the tourist office will be happy to provide information on **cultural events** in and around town. For all events sponsored by the municipality (a wide and impressive range), book at the

Théâtre de l'Hôtel de Ville box office (☎02.35.19.45.74). The most likely venue has to be the Volcano, in the Espace Oscar Niemeyer, described on p.82 (☎02.35.19.10.10), though you may also hear music performed in the cathedral and other churches. Among several **cinemas** in town are the Eden, in the Espace Oscar Niemeyer (also ☎02.35.19.10.10), and the Sirius, at 5 rue Duguesclin (☎02.35.26.52.15), which usually programmes *v.o.* films.

L'Audito, a FNAC-style shop selling records, CDs and videos at 104 rue Victor Hugo (☎02.35.42.13.38), is another useful source of information about local activities.

THE SEINE VALLEY

As far back as the Bronze Age, the **River Seine** was a crucial part of the "Tin Road" linking Cornwall to Paris. Fortresses and monasteries lined its banks from the time of the Romans onwards. Now, with the threat of its tidal bore and treacherous sandbanks very much a thing of the past, heavy ships make their serene way up its sinuous course from the Channel to the provincial capital of Rouen.

Travelling by car, bus or bicycle, it's worth taking this journey equally slowly, savouring such highlights as the riverside towns of **Villequier** and **Caudebec** or the abbey of **Jumiéges**. **Rouen** itself is one of the most vibrant medieval cities to be found anywhere in France, and beyond it, en route to Paris, things if anything get even better, in the shape of the dramatic castle fortress above **Les Andelys** and Monet's celebrated waterlily-filled gardens at **Giverny**.

Along the Seine to Rouen

Even though the modern metropolises of Le Havre and Rouen have become vast industrial conglomerates, long stretches of the riverbank between the two remain remarkably unspoiled and tranquil. Leaving Le Havre, however, the refineries and cement works seem to go on forever; to reach the river drivers have first to negotiate a long approach road that twists its way over the Canal du Havre. Beyond that, the huge humpback span of the **Pont de Normandie** has since 1995 spanned the mouth of the Seine to connect Le Havre with Honfleur, making access between the coasts of Upper and Lower Normandy much more direct. Crossing either that bridge – which incurs a one-way toll of 33F/€5.03, with a 50F/€7.62 day-return ticket sold on Sundays only – or the similarly immense and expensive **Tancarville** suspension bridge, 20km upriver, brings you to the **south (left) bank** of the Seine. This holds the vast majority of the **Parc Naturel Régional de Brotonne**, where peaceful rolling hillsides are evenly divided between bucolic agricultural fields and dense woodlands.

Much the quickest route up the Seine valley, however, is to follow the dramatic chalky bluffs along the **north (right) bank**. This side offers richer scenic and historic rewards, with the road sticking firmly to the riverfront and leading past such sights as the venerable towns of **Villequier** and **Caudebec**, and the magnificent ruined abbey of **Jumièges**. It's also, fortunately, the route taken by buses from Le Havre to Rouen (#191 and #192).

Only one more bridge crosses the river in the extravagant loops that lie between Tancarville and Rouen – the **Pont de Brotonne**, near Caudebec, which leads to the heart of the park. Further upstream, however, there are also intermittent *bacs*

CRUISING THE SEINE

A wide variety of vessels provide visitors with the opportunity to venture out onto the Seine. These range from simple afternoon pleasure jaunts around specific towns, priced at as little as 25F/€3.81, up to sybaritic multiday cruises with luxurious cabin accommodation, which can cost thousands of francs per night. Companies offering such trips include:

Le Cavelier de la Salle (☎02.32.08.32.40). Trips around the port of Rouen, arranged by the local tourist office.

Le Guillaume le Conquérant (☎02.35.78.31.70). Cruises between Rouen and Vernon.

Le River's King (☎02.34.78.16.32). Cruises between Paris and Honfleur.

La Salamandre (☎02.35.42.01.31). Cruises around the port of Le Havre, two-hour trips from Caudebec, and a seven-hour promenade between Rouen and Honfleur.

Le Winner (☎01.30.74.43.39, *www.fleuves-receptions.fr*). Cruises between Paris and Les Andelys.

(ferries), which charge smaller tolls, and tend to leave on the hour (and to have long lunch breaks).

Villequier

The first of the riverbank towns you come to on the **D81 along the north bank** is quite undeservedly one of the least known – **VILLEQUIER**. As a stop on the way to or from Le Havre it's ideal, having a quite exceptional **hotel**: the *Grand Sapin*, 12 rue Louis le Gaffrie (☎02.35.56.78.73; ③), is a gorgeous rambling old building, where most of the well-equipped rooms have rickety balconies overlooking the river. It's absolutely magical on a misty morning – and not bad in the evening, when the wood-panelled dining room is in full swing (menus start with a reasonable 65F/€9.91 option). Tables in the riverside garden are laid out under the shade of the eponymous *grand sapin* itself – a rather frail pine that's dwarfed by a giant blossoming lilac nearby.

There's no entertainment whatsoever in Villequier, while its principal "sight" is a mournful statue of Victor Hugo peering out into the Seine, across a helpfully marked concrete arrow, to the spot where his daughter and her husband drowned in 1843, just six months after their marriage. So weathered as to make the author appear naked, the statue stands several hundred metres upstream of the centre, reached by an attractive waterfront promenade. The couple's former home, back in town, now serves as the **Musée Victor Hugo**, probably of interest only to fluent French speakers with a passion for Hugo's writings (April–Sept Mon & Wed–Sat 10am–12.30pm & 2–6pm, Sun 2–6.30pm; Oct–March Mon & Wed–Sat 10am–12.30pm & 2–5pm, Sun 2–5.30pm; 20F/€3.05).

Caudebec-en-Caux

Just over 4km on from Villequier is the bigger and more popular **CAUDEBEC-EN-CAUX**. Few traces of this old town's past survived the firestorm devastation of World War II, but the local tourist authorities extend a rather sad invitation to visitors to join a "heritage trail" of places that used to be attractive. The damage – and previous local history – is chronicled in the museum at the thirteenth-century **Maison des Templiers**, one of the handful of buildings spared (Easter–June Sat & Sun 3–6pm; July–Sept Tues–Sun 3–6pm; 12F/€1.83). As well as enjoying "one of the most important collections of chimney plaques in France", you can take a look there at pictures of the Seine's regular tidal swell, which still threatens at this narrow point to swamp unwary promenaders. The magnificent Flamboyant **Notre Dame church** still dominates the main square, which has been the site of a **market** every Saturday since 1390.

A little way south of town, a **stone aeroplane** propels itself out of the cliff face across the water – a memorial to another curious episode of aviation history, contemporary to that commemorated at Étretat (see p.79). In 1928, a plane was being prepared here for an attempt at what would have been the first transatlantic flight. But shortly before it was due to set off, the Norwegian polar explorer Amundsen issued a worldwide appeal for help to rescue some Italian sailors who had been shipwrecked off Spitzbergen in the Arctic. The French government offered the plane, and its four crewmen left with Amundsen. Two days later they were lost.

Practicalities

Caudebec's **tourist office** is slightly south of the centre, in place Charles de Gaulle (April–Nov Mon–Sat 9.30am–1pm & 3–7pm, Sun 3–7pm; Dec–March daily 3–7pm; ☎02.32.70.46.32, *caudebec-en-caux.tourisme@wanadoo.fr*). Two absolutely indistinguishable *logis de France* stand side by side facing the river on quai Guilbaud, identical buildings with identical balconies, and all but identical prices and even phone numbers – the *Normotel La Marine* at no. 18 (☎02.35.96.20.11; ③; closed Jan), and the *Normandie* at no. 19 (☎02.35.96.25.11; ③; closed Feb); the restaurants in both are closed on Sunday evenings. Another *logis*, the slightly cheaper *Cheval Blanc*, is a little way back from the river at 4 place Réné-Coty (☎02.35.96.21.66; ②; closed mid-Jan to mid-Feb), and there's a riverside **campsite** to the north, the two-star *Barre Y Va* (☎02.35.96.26.38; closed Oct–March). You can **rent bicycles** from Cycles Velhano at 10 rue de la Vicomte (☎02.35.96.24.77).

On the last Sunday in September of every even-numbered year (2002, 2004, etc), Caudebec comes alive with a large **Cider Festival**.

The Pont de Brotonne

Slightly upstream from Caudebec, the magnificent span of the **Pont de Brotonne**, completed in 1977 as the world's highest and steepest humpback bridge (charging a 15F/€2.29 toll for motorists), climbs out above the Seine. It has an unexpectedly appealing colour scheme – the suspension cables are custard yellow, the rails pastel green, the walkway maroon, and the vast concrete columns left bare. If you don't lose both heart and hat to the sickening drop and the seaborne winds, walking across it is one of the big treats of Normandy. From a distance, its stays refract into strange optical effects, while far below small tugs flounder in the wash of mighty cargo carriers.

Parc Naturel Régional de Brotonne

Even if the **Parc Naturel Régional de Brotonne** – most but not quite all of which lies south of the Seine – is no longer entirely rural, it ranks among the most beautiful tracts of the Norman countryside. The park shelters a wide range of conservation projects and traditional industry initiatives, run by local people, as well as its more obvious abbey and château sites. Full details on all its aspects can be obtained from the very helpful Maison du Parc in **NÔTRE-DAME-DE-BLI-QUETUIT**, immediately east of the southern end of the Pont de Brotonne (March, April & Oct Mon–Fri 9am–6pm, Sun 11am–6pm; May, June & Sept Mon–Fri 9am–6pm, Sat 2–6.30pm, Sun 11am–6.30pm; July & Aug Mon–Fri 8.30am–6.30pm, Sat 2–6.30pm, Sun 11am–6.30pm; Nov–Feb Mon–Fri 9am–6pm; ☎02.35.37.23.16).

The most compelling section of the park is concentrated into a mighty meander on the southern bank of the Seine, across from Caudebec. Here the slopes are covered by the deep thick woods of the **Forêt de Brotonne**, perfect for cyclists and hikers. The pretty little village of **AIZIER** nestles beside the river at the western limit of the forest, with the edges of the Vernier marshes, grazed by Camargue horses and Scottish highland cattle, just beyond.

Hauville

The southern border of the Forêt de Brotonne marks the dividing line between the *départements* of Seine-Maritime and Eure, but still under the auspices of the park, outside the small community of **HAUVILLE** (and signposted off the road to the even tinier village of La Mare-Guérard), it's possible to look six round what's said to be the oldest still-functioning **windmill** in France. One of six owned by the monks of Jumièges, who farmed and forested all this area in the Middle Ages, its outline – based on contemporary castle towers – looks like a kid's drawing (May, June & Sept Sat & Sun 2–6.30pm; July & Aug daily 2–7pm; Oct Sun 2–6pm; 15F/€2.29).

La Haye du Routot and around

The churchyard in the neighbouring village of **LA HAYE DU ROUTOT**, 4km west of Hauville, is a real oddity, featuring a pair of 1000-year-old yew trees that are still alive but have been sufficiently hollowed out to shelter a chapel and grotto. Every year, on July 16, the feast day of St Claire, the village stages the dramatic **Fête de Ste-Claire**. Its centrepiece is a towering, conical bonfire, topped by a cross which must survive to ensure a good year. The smouldering logs are taken home to serve as protection against lightning. Should you miss the big day, a video recording of the goings-on is featured in the local crafts **museum**, which numbers among its separate sections a traditional functioning bread oven, adjacent to the church, and a clog-specialist shoemaker opposite (both April–June & Sept Sat & Sun 2–6.30pm; July & Aug daily 1.30–6.30pm; Oct to mid-Nov Sun 2–6pm; combined admission 20F/€3.05).

The closest **accommodation** to La Haye du Routot is 9km south, just across the A13 *autoroute*, in the shape of the half-timbered *chambres de hôte* offered by M. Van Tornhout in tiny **ROUGEMONTIER** (☎02.32.42.92.27; ③). For a **meal**, try the *Auberge de l'Écurie* in the main square of the slightly larger village of **ROUTOT**, 2km northeast of Rougemontier and 7km southeast of La Haye du Routot (☎02.32.57.30.30; closed Mon, Sun evening & Wed evening), a good restaurant with menus from 110F/€16.77.

Bourneville

The **Maison des Métiers** in **BOURNEVILLE**, another dozen kilometres west of La Haye du Routot and 5km south of Aziers, is a beautifully presented **museum** of traditional farming and building techniques (May–Aug daily except Wed 2–6.30pm; Sept & Oct Sun 2–6pm; 15F/€2.29). Assorted little workshops, each kitted out with the appropriate tools and inhabited by suitably costumed crafts workers, are set out in a pleasant park, with each displaying a different rural trade.

Abbaye de St-Wandrille

Just beyond the Pont de Brotonne on the north bank of the Seine, a side road climbs two kilometres up to the **Abbaye de St-Wandrille**. So legend has it, the abbey was founded by a seventh-century count who, with his wife, renounced all earthly pleasures on the day of their wedding. It remains an active monastery, home to fifty or so Benedictine monks who in addition to their spiritual duties turn their hands to money-making tasks that range from candle-making to running a modern reprographic studio. As such, it's not such an obvious tourist destination as nearby Jumièges (see below), but the abbey complex nonetheless makes an attractive if curious architectural ensemble: part ruin, part restoration and, in the case of the main buildings, part transplant – a fifteenth-century barn brought in a few years ago from another Norman village miles away.

Throughout the year, monks show visitors around the abbey on **guided tours** (Tues–Sat 3.30pm, Sun 11.30am; 20F/€3.05); in addition, in summer only, it's possible to wander through the grounds on your own for no charge (July & Aug Tues–Sun 10.45am–12.30pm & 3–5pm). You can also hear their **Gregorian chanting** in their new church at morning and evening services (Mon–Sat 9.45am & 5.30pm, Sun 10am & 5pm).

For something to **eat**, there's a crêperie opposite the abbey, while the more upmarket *Deux Coronnes* restaurant (☎02.35.96.11.44; closed Sun evening & Mon), a few doors along in the place de l'Église, is a half-timbered seventeenth-century inn, where delicious menus start at 135F/€20.58.

Abbaye de Jumièges

In the next loop of the Seine, 12km upstream from St-Wandrille, squats the more famous **Abbaye de Jumièges** (daily: mid-April to mid-Sept 9.30am–7pm; mid-Sept to mid-April 9.30am–1pm & 2.30–5.30pm; 32F/€4.88, under-18s free). A haunting ruin, it was destroyed – as a deliberate act of policy – during the Revolution. It's said to have been founded by St Philibert in 654 AD, just five years after St-Wandrille, burned by marauding Vikings in 841, and then rebuilt a century later. Its main surviving outline, however, as far as it can still be discerned, dates from the eleventh century; William the Conqueror himself attended its reconsecration in 1067. The twin towers, over 52m high, are still standing. So too is one arch of the roofless nave, while a one-sided yew tree stands in the centre of what were once the cloisters.

How evocative you find these bleached stone ruins will depend on your mood. Visits consist of an unescorted ramble across the lawns; for the most part you're obliged to keep well clear of the precarious walls themselves. Though it survived the Revolution intact, the grand château-like **abbot's residence** that commands a nearby eminence – built in the seventeenth century, by which time the abbot was appointed directly by the king rather than being elected by his fellow monks – is not open to visitors. The grounds are, however, sometimes used for temporary art exhibitions.

The *Auberge des Ruines* at no. 17 in Jumièges' place de la Mairie (☎02.35.37.24.05; ②; closed Sun evening & Mon, plus all evenings except Fri & Sat Nov–Feb), offers a handful of simple **rooms** overlooking the abbey and boasts a grand **restaurant** where dinner menus start at 130F/€19.82.

The river itself now flows roughly a kilometre west of the ruins. A tiny *bac* (ferry) crosses the Seine at this point to Heurteauville on the left bank, half-hourly in summer and hourly in winter; the riverbank *Auberge du Bac* (☎02.35.37.24.16; closed Tues evening & Wed) makes a lovely lunchtime halt, serving excellent 120F/€18.29 and 168F/€25.61 menus.

Duclair

If you want to **cycle** beside the river for any distance, the D982 tends to be forever climbing and descending, and in any event is a bit busy. However, the stretch from Le Mesnil (just beyond Jumièges) as far as Duclair is long, quiet and flat, and has a wonderful view of the lush river banks. **DUCLAIR** itself holds a nice riverside **hotel**, in the shape of the *Hôtel de la Poste* opposite the landing stage for the town's little *bac*, at 286 quai de la Libération (☎02.35.37.50.04; ②).

As you continue from here towards Rouen, you get a first panoramic prospect, from beside the church at Canteleu, of the docks, the island and the city. The road onwards coasts endlessly down into the maelstrom. (Don't attempt to cycle *out* of Rouen in this direction – the gradient, and the fumes, are unbearable.)

Rouen

ROUEN, the capital of Upper Normandy, is one of France's most ancient and historic cities. Standing on the site of Roman Rotomagus, which was the lowest point on the river then capable of being bridged, it was laid out by the Viking Rollo shortly after he became the first duke of Normandy in 911. Captured by the English in 1419, after a long siege, it became the stage in 1431 for the trial and execution of Joan of Arc, before returning to French control in 1449.

Over the centuries, Rouen has suffered repeated devastation; there were 45 major fires in the first half of the thirteenth century alone. It has had to be almost entirely rebuilt during the last sixty years, and now you could spend a whole day wandering around the city without realizing that the Seine ran through its centre. Wartime bombs, specifically during the fierce onslaught that coincided with the D-Day landings, destroyed all its bridges, the area between the cathedral and the *quais*, and much of the left bank's industrial quarter. The immediate riverside area has never been adequately restored, and what you might expect to be the most beautiful part of this venerable city is in fact something of an abomination.

Enormous sums have, however, been lavished on an upmarket restoration job on the streets a few hundred metres north of the river, which turned the centre into the closest approximation to a medieval city that modern imaginations could come up with. The project was supervised by Louis Arretche, who redesigned postwar St-Malo so successfully. The suggestion that for historical authenticity the houses should be painted in bright, clashing colours was not deemed appropriate by the city authorities, but, so far as it goes, the whole of this inner core can be very seductive, and its churches are extremely impressive by any standards.

Outside the renovated quarters, things are rather different. The city spreads deep into the loop of the Seine, with its docks and industrial infrastructure stretching endlessly away to the south, and it is increasingly expanding up into the hills to the north as well, while the riverbank itself is lined with a fume-filled, multilaned motorway. As the nearest point that large container ships can get to Paris, even in decline this remains the fourth largest port in the country.

Arrival, information and city transport

The main **gare SNCF** (☎08.36.35.35.35), high above the river at the top end of rue Jeanne-d'Arc, is Gare Rive Droite; Gare Rive Gauche on the south bank only handles goods traffic. The passenger station is not immediately conspicuous on most maps, because the train lines run underground, but on the ground you can't miss it. From the outside, its minaret makes it resemble a nineteenth-century confection, intended perhaps for Algiers or Istanbul; in fact it was completed in 1928. The main hall is decorated with garish murals. Rouen is roughly halfway between Paris and the Channel ports; both **Le Havre** and **Dieppe** are one hour away on different train routes, while the journey to **Paris** takes an hour and a quarter. You can also get trains west to **Lisieux** (1hr 15min) and **Caen** (2hr).

All **buses** except #2A from the *gare SNCF* run down rue Jeanne-d'Arc to the centre in around five minutes. From the fifth stop, the "Théâtre des Arts" by the river, the **gare routière** is one block west in rue des Charettes (☎02.35.52.92.00), tucked away behind the riverfront buildings. Out-of-town buses from here include services south to **Évreux** (1hr), to **Le Havre** along the river, to **Dieppe** via Tôtes, to **Le Tréport** and to **St-Valéry**.

Rouen's **tourist office**, opposite the cathedral at 25 place de la Cathédrale, stands in the early sixteenth-century "House of the Exchequer" (May–Sept Mon–Sat 9am–7pm, Sun 9.30am–12.30pm & 2.30–6pm; Oct–April Mon–Sat 9am–6pm, Sun 10am–1pm; ☎02.32.08.32.40, *www.mairie-rouen.fr*). It serves as the starting point for daily two-hour **walking tours** of different areas of the city, each costing 35F/€5.34. One departs at 10am to explore the area between the churches of St Romain and St Ouen; another, at 3pm heads from the cathedral to the place du Vieux-Marché. There's also a different themed tour at 12.30pm every Tuesday, and another at 2pm on Saturdays that covers the Jewish quarter. For more sedate visitors, a motorized **"petit train"** makes a forty-minute loop tour from the tourist office at regular intervals (daily 10am, 11am, 2pm, 4pm & 5pm; 30F/€4.57).

Rouen's **post office** is halfway down rue Jeanne-d'Arc, at no. 45, in the centre of town (postcode 76000; Mon–Fri 8am–7pm, Sat 8.30am–12.30pm; ☎02.35.08.73.73). For **Internet** access, head to the café-style *Cybernetics*, 59 place du Vieux-Marché (Mon & Fri 12.30pm–midnight, Tues–Thurs & Sat 12.30–7.30pm; ☎02.35.07.02.77, *www.cybernetics.fr*), or the more business-oriented *Netropole*, 113–115 rue St-Vivien (Mon–Fri 10.30am–12.30pm & 2–8pm, Sat 1–7pm; ☎02.32.76.40.90, *netropole@wanadoo.fr*).

City transport

The city centre of Rouen, north of the Seine, is small enough to stroll around with little effort, and there's also an efficient **bus** network. With an ever-expanding web of pedestrianized streets, it's not a city you can drive around with any ease; far better to park in one of the many underground car parks as soon as you arrive.

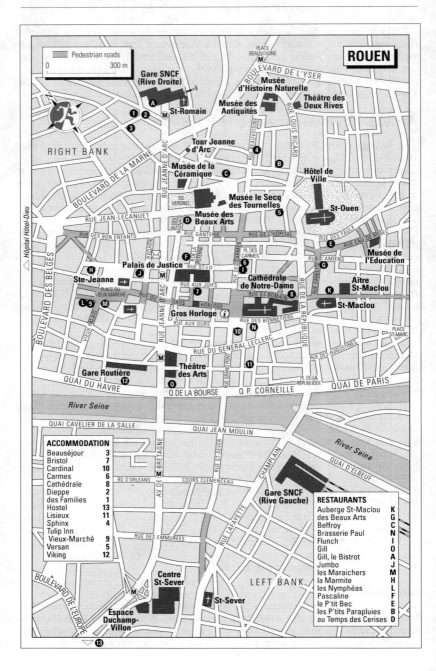

ROUEN

Pedestrian roads

0   300 m

Gare SNCF
(Rive Droite)

PLACE
BEAUVOISINE

BOULEVARD DE L'YSER

Musée
d'Histoire Naturelle

Théâtre des
Deux Rives

St-Romain

Musée des
Antiquités

RIGHT BANK

Tour Jeanne
d'Arc

Musée de la
Céramique

Hôtel de
Ville

St-Ouen

Musée le Secq
des Tournelles

Musée des
Beaux Arts

Musée de
l'Education

Palais de Justice

Ste-Jeanne

Cathédrale
de Notre-Dame

Aître
St-Maclou

Gros Horloge

St-Maclou

Gare Routière

Théâtre
des Arts

QUAI DU HAVRE

Q DE LA BOURSE

Q. P. CORNEILLE

QUAI DE PARIS

PLACE
ST-MARC

River Seine

QUAI CAVELIER DE LA SALLE

QUAI JEAN MOULIN

River Seine

QUAI D'ELBEUF

ACCOMMODATION

Beauséjour	3
Bristol	7
Cardinal	10
Carmes	6
Cathédrale	8
Dieppe	2
des Families	1
Hostel	13
Lisieux	11
Sphinx	4
Tulip Inn Vieux-Marché	9
Versan	5
Viking	12

Gare SNCF
(Rive Gauche)

RESTAURANTS

Auberge St-Maclou	K
des Beaux Arts	G
Beffroy	C
Brasserie Paul	N
Flunch	I
Gill	O
Gill, le Bistrot	A
Jumbo	J
les Maraichers	M
la Marmite	H
les Nymphéas	L
Pascaline	F
le P'tit Bec	E
les P'tits Parapluies	B
au Temps des Cerises	D

Centre
St-Sever

LEFT BANK

St-Sever

Espace
Duchamp-
Villon

Rouen's pride and joy, the multibillion-franc **métro** system unveiled in 1998, is on the whole more useful to commuters than tourists. From the Gare-Rue Verte, at the SNCF station, trains follow the line of rue Jeanne-d'Arc, making two stops before they resurface to cross the river by bridge; thereafter the tracks dip below and above ground like a roller coaster. Individual journeys cost 8F/€1.22; a book of ten tickets is 59F/€8.99.

You can rent **bicycles** from Rouen Cycles, 45 rue St-Éloi (Tues–Sat 8.30am–noon & 2–7pm; ☎02.35.71.34.30), as well as at the *gare SNCF*. Among **carrental** companies are Avis, at the *gare SNCF* (☎02.35.70.95.12), Budget, 14 rue de Lisbonne (☎02.32.81.95.00), and Hertz, 38 quai Gaston-Boulet (☎02.35.98.16.57).

Accommodation

With more than three thousand hotel rooms in town, there should be no difficulty in finding appropriate accommodation in Rouen, even at the busiest times. If you're coming for the weekend, check with the tourist office to see if any hotels are operating the "Bon Weekend En Ville" scheme, under which guests booking for a Saturday night at least eight days in advance can stay either Friday night or Sunday night free. Few of the hotels have restaurants, chiefly because there's so wide a choice of places to eat all over town, and all those listed below remain open all year. Motorists who just want to spend a day or two looking at the sights of Rouen should seriously consider the possibility of staying at one of the delightful riverside hotels in La Bouille (see p.104), or in the woods at Lyons-la-Forêt (see p.105).

The city's **hostel** is south of the river at 118 bd de l'Europe (☎02.35.72.06.45; 59F/€8.99; 11pm curfew). The easiest way to get there from the *gare SNCF* is to take the métro, direction "Hôtel de Ville" or "Technopôle", as far as the "Europe" stop.

The surprisingly small municipal **campsite**, intended more for caravanners than tent campers, is 4km northwest on rue Jules-Ferry in **Déville-lès-Rouen** (☎02.35.74.07.59; closed Jan & Feb), reached by taking bus #2 from the Théâtre des Arts, while the significantly less accessible *Camping L'Aubette* is 5km east at 23 Vert Buisson in **St-Léger du Bourg-Denis** (☎02.35.08.47.69).

Hotels

Hôtel Beauséjour, 9 rue Pouchet (☎02.35.71.93.47, fax 02.35.98.01.24, *beausejour@lerapporteur.fr*). Good-value place near the station (turn right as you come out), though once you're past the attractive orange facade with its windowboxes, and the nice garden courtyard, the rooms themselves are on the plain side, even if they do all have shower and TV. ②.

Hôtel Bristol, 45 rue aux Juifs (☎02.35.71.54.21). Clean, pretty little nine-room hotel, above its own little brasserie in a half-timbered house overlooking the Palais de Justice. All rooms are en suite, and have TV. ③.

Hôtel le Cardinal, 1 place de la Cathédrale (☎02.35.70.24.42, fax 02.35.89.75.14). Very good-value hotel in a stunning location facing the cathedral; the rooms have excellent en-suite facilities, and ample buffet breakfasts are served. ④.

Hôtel des Carmes, 33 place des Carmes (☎02.35.71.92.31, fax 02.35.71.76.96, *h.des.carmes@mcom.fr*). Twelve-room hotel in a beautifully decorated nineteenth-century house in a quiet central square, complete with blue shutters, a short walk north from the cathedral. Guests are not given keys to stay out late. Buffet breakfasts for 34F/€5.18. ③.

Hôtel de la Cathédrale, 12 rue St-Romain (☎02.35.71.57.95, fax 02.35.70.15.54, *www .hotel-de-la-cathedrale.com*). One of the most attractive and conveniently located hotels in Rouen, alongside the cathedral and archbishop's palace, though the plain rooms themselves don't live up to the appealing facade and quaint old flower-filled courtyard. Set in a quiet pedestrianized street – so parking is a problem – that's lined with fourteenth-century timber-framed houses. ④.

Hôtel de Dieppe, place Bernard Tissot (☎02.35.71.96.00, fax 02.35.89.65.21, *hotel.dieppe@wanadoo.fr*). Grand traditional hotel, immediately opposite the station, which is affiliated to the Best Western chain and is home to the top-notch *Quatre Saisons* restaurant. Prices for the well-equipped rooms are greatly discounted at weekends. ⑥.

Hôtel des Familles, 4 rue Pouchet (☎02.35.71.88.51, fax 02.35.07.54.65, *www .hoteldesfamilles.com*). Very friendly and characterful place, set back beyond a small gravel yard and a short walk to the right as you come out from the gare Rive Droite. Incorporates the old *Hôtel de la Paix* – hence the two entrances. ②.

Hôtel de Lisieux, 4 rue de la Savonnerie (☎02.35.71.87.73, fax 02.35.89.31.52, *lisieux@ hotel-rouen.com*). At the junction of rue de la Savonnerie and rue du Bec, between cathedral and river. Bishop Cauchon, who prosecuted Joan of Arc in 1431, is said to have stayed – and died – here in 1442. If so, it has been modernized since – every room now has en-suite facilities – losing much of the original character in the process. ④.

Hôtel Sphinx, 130 rue Beauvoisine (☎02.35.71.35.86). Very basic, even grim, accommodation, near the Musée des Antiquités, but this is possibly the only hotel left in Normandy where rates still start below 100F/€15.24, and that's enough to keep the budget travellers coming. None of the rooms has a shower; there's a charge of 10F/€1.52 per shower, and an extra bed in the room costs 60F/€9.15. ①.

Tulip Inn Vieux Marché, 15 rue de la Pie (☎02.35.71.00.88, fax 02.35.70.75.94, *tulip.inn@wanadoo.fr*). Very modern place, set around a venerable old courtyard, just a toss of a match from the place du Vieux-Marché. A high standard of comfort has quickly made this the most popular upmarket hotel in town. ⑥.

Hôtel Versan, 3 rue Jean Lecanuet (☎02.35.07.77.07, fax 02.35.70.04.67, *hotelversan@ wanadoo.fr*). Modern en-suite rooms at reasonable prices close to the Hôtel de Ville and the museums. Buffet breakfasts. ④.

Hôtel Viking, 21 quai du Havre (☎02.35.70.34.95, fax 02.35.89.97.12, *www.leviking.com*). Just in front of the *gare routière*, to the right at the bottom of rue Jeanne-d'Arc. Overlooking not only the river, but also the main roads, the noise of which is only partly dampened by the double glazing. ③.

The Town

Rouen has traditionally spent a higher proportion of its budget on **monuments** than any other provincial town, which maddens many a Rouennais. As a tourist, your one complaint may be the lack of time to visit them all. Certainly there are some great sights to be seen – the **Cathédrale de Notre Dame**, the **Gros Horloge**, the **Aître St-Maclou**, all the delightful twisting streets of timbered houses – and the history too is there to be relished, most notably the links with **Joan of Arc**.

Place du Vieux-Marché

One obvious place to start exploring the city is the **place du Vieux-Marché**, where a small plaque and a huge cross, 20m high, adorn the public square in which Joan of Arc was burned to death on May 30, 1431. Louis Arretche was commissioned to design a memorial **church** to the saint in 1969, and the result was dedicated in 1979 (Mon–Sat 10am–12.30pm & 2–6pm, Sun 2–6pm). A

JOAN OF ARC

Joan of Arc stands alone, and must continue to stand alone . . . There is no one to compare her with, none to measure her by . . There have been other young generals, but they were not girls; young generals, but they have been soldiers before they were generals; she began as a general; she commanded the first army she ever saw; she led it from victory to victory, and never lost a battle with it; there have been young commanders-in-chief, but none so young as she: she is the only soldier in history who has held the supreme command of a nation's armies at the age of seventeen.

Mark Twain, *Joan of Arc*

When the 17-year-old peasant girl known to history as **Joan of Arc** arrived at the French court in Chinon early in 1429, the Hundred Years War had already dragged on for over ninety years. Most of northern France was in the grip of an Anglo-Burgundian alliance, whose major strongholds were the châteaux of the Loire. Since 1425, Joan had been hearing voices in her native village of Domrémy, in Lorraine near France's eastern frontiers. Convinced that she alone could save France, she came to Chinon to present her case to the as-yet-uncrowned Dauphin. Partly through recognizing him despite a simple disguise he wore to fool her at their first meeting, she convinced him of her divine guidance; and after a remarkable three-week examination by a tribunal of the French *parlement*, she went on to secure command of the armies of France. In a whirlwind campaign, which culminated in the raising of the siege of Orléans on May 8, 1429, she broke the English hold on the Loire Valley. She then escorted the Dauphin deep into enemy territory, with town after town rallying to her standard as they advanced, so that in accordance with ancient tradition he could be crowned King Charles VII of France in the cathedral at Reims, on July 17.

Within a year of her greatest triumph, Joan was captured by the Burgundian army at Compiègne in May 1430, and held to ransom. Chivalry dictated that any offer of payment from the vacillating Charles must be accepted, but in the absence of such an offer Joan was handed over to the English for 10,000 ducats. On Christmas Day 1430, she was imprisoned in the château of Philippe-Auguste at Rouen.

Charged with heresy, on account of her "false and diabolical" visions and refusal not to wear men's clothing, Joan was put on trial for her life on February 21, 1431. For three months, a changing panel of 131 assessors – only eight of whom were English-born – heard the evidence against her. Condemned, inevitably, to death, Joan recanted on the scaffold in St-Ouen cemetery on May 24, and her sentence was commuted to life imprisonment. The presiding judge, Bishop Pierre Cauchon of Beauvais, reassured disappointed English representatives that "we will get her yet". The next Sunday, Joan was tricked into breaking her vow and putting on male clothing, and taken to the archbishop's chapel in rue St-Romain to be condemned to death for the second time. On May 30, 1431, she was burned at the stake in the place du Vieux-Marché; her ashes, together with her unburned heart, were thrown into the Seine.

Charles VII finally reconquered Rouen in 1449. Seeing the verdict against Joan as reflecting on the legitimacy of his own claim to the French throne, he instigated a *Procés en Nullité*, which took evidence from all the surviving witnesses, and resulted in a papal declaration of Joan's innocence in 1456. Joan herself passed into legend, until the discovery and publication of the full transcript of her trial in the 1840s. The forbearance and devout humility she displayed throughout her ordeal added to her status as France's greatest religious heroine. She was canonized as recently as 1920, and soon afterwards became the country's patron saint.

wacky, spiky-looking thing, said to represent either an upturned boat or the flames that consumed Joan, it's indisputably an architectural triumph, part of an ensemble of buildings that manages to incorporate in similar style a covered food market (open daily except Mon), designed more for show than practical shopping. The theme of the church's fish-shaped windows is continued in the scaly tiles that adorn its roof, which is hugely elongated to form a covered walkway across the square. Part of Arretche's brief was to incorporate some sixteenth-century stained glass, removed from the church of St-Vincent that stood on this site before it was destroyed in the war. It's now displayed beautifully, all on one facade of the new church, despite the fact that the windows that hold it are an utterly different shape. The outline of the foundations of the vanished old church is visible on the adjacent lawns, where a flowerbed marks the precise spot of Joan's martyrdom. The square itself is surrounded by fine old brown-and-white half-timbered houses; many of those on the south side now serve as restaurants.

Also on the south side of the *place*, the privately owned **Musée Jeanne d'Arc**, in an ancient cellar in the back of a gift shop, draws large crowds to its collection of tawdry waxworks and facsimile manuscripts (Tues–Sun: May to mid-Sept 9.30am–7pm; mid-Sept to April 10am–noon & 2–6.30pm; 25F/€3.81). Among the bric-a-brac is a page from the records of the Paris *parlement*, dated May 10, 1429, which refers to reports reaching Paris that, on the previous Saturday, the French had trounced the British at Orléans. A sketch in the margin, possibly by a bored clerk, depicts a young woman, with her hair tied back, a banner in one hand and a sword in the other. The only contemporary portrait of the Maid of Orléans was not drawn from life, so there's no reason to think it any more authentic than the movie stills on display in the museum, showing Ingrid Bergman as Joan in both 1948 and 1954, and Jean Seberg in the role in 1957.

Gros Horloge

From place du Vieux-Marché, rue du Gros-Horloge leads east towards the cathedral. Just across rue Jeanne-d'Arc you come to the **Gros Horloge** itself. A colourful one-handed clock, it used to be on the adjacent Gothic belfry until it was moved down by popular demand in 1529, so that people could see it better. When the restoration work that was in progress when this book went to press is completed, you should be able to pay a small fee to climb up rather too many steps to see its workings and, if the sponginess of the lead roofing agrees with your nerves, totter around the top for a marvellous view of the old city, and the startling array of towers and spires around. The bell up there, cast in 1260, still rings what's known as the "Conqueror's Curfew" at 9pm daily. A block to the north stands the former **Palais de Justice**, which was largely destroyed during World War II only to be rebuilt as good as new. Casual visitors cannot go inside, however, so you'll have to content yourself with admiring the magnificently ornate Rennaissance exterior.

Cathédrale de Notre Dame

The **Cathédrale de Notre Dame** (March–Oct Mon–Sat 9am–7pm, Sun 8am–6pm; Nov–Feb Mon–Sat 9am–6pm, Sun 8am–6pm), a couple of hundred yards east of the Gros Horloge, stands on the site of a Roman place of worship, erected some time in the third century AD at a major crossroads. Despite the addition of all sorts of different towers, spires and vertical extensions, it remains at heart the Gothic masterpiece that was built in the twelfth and thirteenth centuries. Later accretions include the Flamboyant **Tour du Beurre**, named for what was probably the erroneous belief that it was paid for by the granting of dispensations that allowed wealthy churchgoers to eat butter during Lent, and the nineteenth-century iron **spire** of the central lantern tower, known in French as the *flèche* or "arrow". Cast in the foundries of Conches, it was built to replace a tower that burned down in 1822, and was at the time, at 151m, the highest in France.

The cathedral is currently undergoing extensive restoration, an immense task which was added to when one of the spire's four greenish supports was detached by the hurricane of late December 1999, and fell, piercing the roof of the cathedral itself and destroying a section of the medieval choir stalls below. The most obvious fruits of that labour can be seen in the **west facade** of the cathedral. Intricately sculpted like the rest of the exterior, this was Monet's subject for over thirty studies of changing light, which now hang in the Musée d'Orsay in Paris. Monet might not recognize it now, however – in the last few years, it's been scrubbed a gleaming white, free from the centuries of accreted dirt he so carefully recorded. For that matter, Monet would be equally nonplussed by the melange of postmodern buskers who now congregate in the square in front, such as Andean pan-pipers playing medleys of Abba hits.

Inside, the carvings of the misericords in the choir depict fifteenth-century life, in secular scenes of work and habits, as well as the usual mythical beasts. The chapel dedicated to Joan of Arc, and paid for by an English commitee in 1956, contains a statue of Joan at the stake. The **ambulatory** and **crypt** – closed on Sundays and during services – hold the assorted tombs of various recumbent royalty, stretching back as far as **Duke Rollo**, who died "enfeebled by toil" in 933 AD. Rollo's effigy was destroyed by the bombs of 1944, and has now been replaced by a nineteenth-century copy of someone else's. Both he and **Richard the Lionheart** – whose eponymous heart reposes beneath a similar figure nearby – have detachable feet, which are occasionally removed for cleaning.

Église St-Maclou and Aître St-Maclou

A short way east of the cathedral, the intricate wooden panelling in the porch of the fifteenth-century church of **St-Maclou** is the highlight of what is often cited as the most spectacular example of Gothic Flamboyant architecture in France (April–Sept Mon–Sat 10am–noon & 2–6pm, Sun 3–5.30pm; Oct–March Mon–Sat 10am–noon & 2–5.30pm, Sun 3–5.30pm). The whole building was so badly damaged by bombs on June 4, 1944 that it could only reopen in 1980; thankfully, the ornate stone stairway up to the organ inside remains as ethereal as ever. That the interior is so light is in part because most of its stained glass was destroyed, and the windows are now clear. St Maclou himself – perhaps more familiar as St Malo – was a seventh-century missionary from Wales.

Nearby, with its entrance a little hard to find in between nos. 184 and 186 rue Martainville, is the **Aître St-Maclou** (daily 8am–8pm; free). This was built between 1526 and 1533, in an era of mass plague deaths, as a cemetery and charnel house. The ground floor was used as an open cloister and, in the rooms above, the bare bones of countless victims were exposed to view. At first sight it looks very picturesque – a tranquil garden courtyard of half-timbered houses – but look closely at the carvings on the beams of the one open lower storey of the surrounding buildings and you see traces of a macabre **Dance of Death**, while in the case to the right of the entrance is a mummified cat. The buildings are still in use, and still stimulating morbid imaginations, not as a morgue but as Rouen's Fine Arts school. In the square outside are several good antique bookshops and a few art shops.

St-Ouen

The last of Rouen's great churches is **St-Ouen**, next to the Hôtel de Ville in a large open square to the north (mid-Jan to mid-March and Nov to mid-Dec Wed, Sat & Sun 10am–12.30pm & 2–4.30pm; mid-March to Oct daily except Tues 10am–12.30pm & 2–6pm). It's larger than the cathedral and has far less decoration, with the result that its Gothic proportions and the purity of its lines have that instant impact with which nothing built since the Middle Ages can compete. Originally, it was an abbey church, founded in the seventh century before the Viking invasion. The present building was begun in 1318 and completed in the fifteenth century. Inside, it holds some stunning fourteenth-century stained glass, though much was destroyed during the Revolution – hence the 1960 Crucifixion in the choir, by Max Ingrand.

Immediately north of St-Ouen is the city's **Hôtel de Ville**, outside which parades an equestrian statue of Napoléon, weathered to an eerie green and looking like death incarnate.

Rue Eau de Robec

The **rue Eau de Robec**, which runs east from rue Damiette just south of St-Ouen, was described by one of Flaubert's characters in an earlier age as a "degraded little Venice". It's now a textbook example of how Rouen has been restored. Where once a shallow stream flowed beneath the raised doorsteps of venerable half-timbered houses, a thin trickle now makes its way along a stylized cement bed crossed by concrete walkways. It remains an attractive ensemble, if a rather ersatz one, and the houses themselves are now predominantly inhabited by antique dealers, interspersed with the odd café.

Tour Jeanne d'Arc

The pencil-thin **Tour Jeanne d'Arc** (April–Sept Mon & Wed–Sat 10am–12.30pm & 2–6pm, Sun 2–6.30pm; Oct–March Mon & Wed–Sat 10am–12.30pm & 2–5pm, Sun 2–5.30pm; 10F/€1.52), a short way southeast of the *gare SNCF* at the junction of rue du Donjon and rue du Cordier, is all that remains of the castle of Philippe-Auguste, built in 1205 and scene of the imprisonment and trial of Joan of Arc. It served as the castle's keep and entranceway, and was itself fully surrounded by a moat. It was not, however, Joan's actual prison – that was the Tour de la Pucelle, demolished in 1809 – while the trial took place first of all in the castle's St-Romain chapel, and then later in its great central hall, both of which were destroyed in 1590.

Joan came to this building only once, on May 9, 1431, to be confronted with the fearsome torture chamber in its lowest level. Threatened by Bishop Cauchon with the words "There is the rack, and there are its ministers. You will reveall all, now, or be put to the torture", she responded: "I will tell you nothing more than I have told you; no, not even if you tear the limbs from my body. And even if in my pain I did say something otherwise, I would always say afterwards that it was the torture that spoke and not I".

The tall, sharp-pointed tower was bought by public subscription in 1860, and restored to its present state. After seeing a small collection of Joan-related memorabilia, you can climb the steep spiral staircase to the very top, but you can't see out over the city, let alone step outside into the open air.

Musée des Beaux Arts

Rouen's imposing **Musée des Beaux Arts** commands the square Verdrel from just east of the central rue Jeanne-d'Arc (daily except Tues 10am–6pm; 20F/€3.05). Even this grand edifice is not quite large enough to display some of its medieval tapestries, which dangle inelegantly from the ceilings to trail along the floor, but the collection as a whole is consistently absorbing. Unexpected highlights include dazzling Russian icons from the sixteenth century onwards, and an entertaining three-dimensional eighteenth-century Nativity from Naples.

Many of the biggest names among the **painters** – Caravaggio, Velázquez, Rubens – tend to be represented by a single minor work. However, there are several Monets, including a Rouen Cathedral from 1894, Paris's rue St-Denis aflutter with flags in 1894, and a recently acquired *Vue Générale de Rouen*, as well as canvases by Blanche Hoschedé-Monet, who was both the daughter of Claude Monet's mistress Alice and the wife of his son Jean. The central sculpture court, roofed over but very light, is dominated by a wonderful three-part mural of the course of the Seine from Paris to Le Havre, prepared by Raoul Dufy in 1937 for the Palais de Chaillot in Paris.

Musée de la Céramique

Rouen's history as a centre for *faïencerie*, the manufacture of earthenware pottery, is recorded in the **Musée de la Céramique**, facing the Beaux Arts from rue Faucon to the north (daily except Tues 10am–1pm & 2–6pm; 15F/€2.29). A series of beautiful rooms, some of which incorporate sixteenth-century wood panelling rescued from the demolished nunnery of St-Amand, display specimens from the seventeenth century onwards. Until polychrome appeared in 1698, everything was blue; at that time, Rouen's main rivals and influences were the cities of Delft and Nevers, well represented in this collection. Assorted tiles and plates reflect the eighteenth-century craze for chinoiserie, although the genuine Chinese and Japanese pieces nearby possess a sophistication contemporary French craftsmen could only dream of emulating. The mood changes abruptly in the Revolutionary era, as witnessed by a fascinating collection of plates bearing slogans from both sides of the political fence.

Musée Le Secq des Tournelles

Behind the Beaux Arts, housed in the old and barely altered church of St-Laurent on rue Jacques-Villon, stands an interesting and unusual museum of ironmongery, the **Musée Le Secq des Tournelles** (daily except Tues 10am–1pm & 2–6pm; 15F/€2.29). It consists of a collection of wrought-iron objects of all dates and descriptions, among them nutcrackers and door knockers, locks and gates, nineteenth-century toys and jewellery, spiral staircases that lead nowhere and hideous implements of torture.

Musée des Antiquités

The **Musée des Antiquités** (Mon & Wed–Sat 10am–12.15pm & 1.30–5.30pm, Sun 2–6pm; 20F/€3.05), a short walk north of the town centre at the top of rue Beauvoisine, provides a dry but comprehensive run-through of ancient artefacts found in or near Rouen. Starting with an impressive pointed helmet from the

Note that the **Musée d'Histoire Naturelle, Ethnographie and Préhistoire**, next to the Musée des Antiquités, and the **Musée National de l'Éducation**, in rue Eau de Robec, were both closed for restoration as this book went to press.

Bronze Age and an assortment of early iron tools, it continues with some remarkably complete Roman mosaics from villas unearthed in Lillebonne and the Forêt de Brotonne. Then come a long gallery filled with woodcarvings rescued from long-lost Rouen houses – including a lovely bas-relief of sheep that served as the sign for a medieval draper's shop – and some fine fifteenth-century tapestries.

The Pavillon Flaubert and the Musée Flaubert et de l'Histoire de la Médicine

For an insight into the Rouen that Flaubert knew, don't go to the **Pavillon Flaubert** at Croisset-Canteleu. Like Rouen's two other literary museums – the two homes of Pierre Corneille – it only proves the pointlessness of the genre. Visit, instead, the **Musée Flaubert et de l'Histoire de la Médicine**, at the Hôtel-Dieu Hospital (Tues 10am–6pm, Wed–Sat 10am–noon & 2–6pm; 12F/€1.83). This stands on the corner of rue de Lecat and rue du Contrat-Social, walkable from the centre (or bus #2A), and it's infinitely more relevant to Flaubert's writings than the manuscript copies and personal mementos in the Pavillon museum.

Flaubert's father was chief surgeon and director of the medical school, living with his family in this house within the hospital; Gustave himself was born here in 1821. Even during the cholera epidemic when he was 11, the young Gustave and his sister were not stopped from running around the wards or climbing along the garden wall to look into the autopsy lab. Some of the medical exhibits would certainly have been familiar objects to him – a phrenology model, a childbirth demonstrator like a giant ragdoll, and the sets of encyclopedias. There's also one of his stuffed parrots, as featured in Julian Barnes' novel *Flaubert's Parrot*.

Eating

Rouen has a good reputation for **food**, with its most famous dish being *caneton* (duckling). Unlike the hotels, which sometimes have cheaper weekend rates, the city's upmarket restaurants tend to charge more over weekends, when families eat out. The greatest concentration of restaurants is in place du Vieux-Marché, an area in which, perversely, there are few hotels.

There's a daily **food market** in the square, while the area just north is full of Tunisian **takeaways**, **crêperies** and so forth. There are, too, sumptuous **patisserie** shops everywhere, and if you've had enough of all things continental the rue du Gros-Horloge holds a half-timbered *McDonald's*.

Restaurants

Auberge St-Maclou, 224–226 rue Martainville (☎02.35.71.06.67). Half-timbered building in the shadow of St-Maclou church, with tables on the street outside and an old-style ambience inside. The pedestrian street gets crowded in summer, but the menus are far from overpriced – the 83F/€12.65 set lunch includes cocktail, wine and coffee. Prices to suit all budgets, and dishes including mussels and duck, as well as excellent desserts. Closed Sun evening & Mon.

des Beaux Arts, 34 rue Damiette (☎02.35.70.17.15). Located on a pretty pedestrianized street north of St-Maclou church, this place serves very good-value Algerian cuisine: couscous from 50F/€7.62 or tajine from 68F/€10.37, with all kinds of sausages and assorted meats. Closed Mon.

Le Beffroy, 15 rue Beffroy (☎02.35.71.55.27). Intimate, very old-fashioned and very good Norman restaurant, just north of the Musée des Beaux Arts, where copper pans glow in the flames of the venerable fireplace, and they serve hearty portions of delicious food. The fish, on menus that start at 100F/€15.24, is especially good. Closed Sun evening & Tues.

Brasserie Paul, 1 place de la Cathédrale (☎02.35.71.86.07). The definitive address for Rouen's definitive bistro, an attractive Belle Époque place with seating both indoors and on a terrace in full view of the cathedral. Daily lunch specials, such as the goats' cheese and smoked-duck salad that was Simone de Beauvoir's regular favourite in the 1930s, cost around 60F/€9.15.

Flunch, 60 rue des Carmes (☎02.35.71.81.81). Large and good self-service on a street running north from the cathedral, with many fresh dishes and a 43F/€6.56 daily *formule*.

Gill, 9 quai de la Bourse (☎02.35.71.16.14). Absolutely classic French restaurant, chosen eleven years in a row as the best in the province by a local magazine on account of such Gilles Tournadre specialities as lobster grilled with asparagus and pigeon baked in puff pastry. Weekday lunches start at 185F/€28.20, while the cheapest dinner menu will set you back 220F/€33.54. Closed Sun & Mon June–Sept, otherwise Sun evening & Mon.

Gill, Le Bistrot du Chef . . . en Gare, 1st Floor, Gare Rive Droite (☎02.35.71.41.15). The name may seem convoluted to outsiders, but to Rouennais it signals a true marvel; the bistro in the main train station is now run under the auspices of the city's top chef. There's an excellent self-service cafeteria downstairs, while the more formal dining room upstairs is open for lunch only, with set menus from 89F/€13.57. Closed Mon evening, Sat lunch, Sun & all Aug.

Jumbo, 11 rue Guillaume-le-Conquerant (☎02.35.70.35.88). Another good self-service, off the northeast corner of place du Vieux-Marché. Put together your own large salad for under 25F/€3.81, or choose from a variety of cooked dishes.

Les Maraichers – Le Bistrot d'Adrien, 37 place du Vieux-Marché (☎02.35.71.57.73). Deservedly the most popular of the Vieux-Marché's many restaurants, with a streetside terrace right in front of the St-Jeanne church. Styled to resemble a *fin-de-siècle* Parisian bistro, serving varied set menus until 11pm nightly and à la carte until midnight. Menus start at 89F/€13.57, with lots of *andouillettes*, snails and tongues, but plenty of wholesome possibilities too, and great desserts.

Le Marmite, 3 rue de Florence (☎02.35.71.55.55). Romantic little place just west of the place du Vieux-Marché, offering beautiful, elegantly presented gourmet dishes on well-priced menus at 115F/€17.53, 165F/€25.15 (featuring delicious hot oysters) and 250F/€38.11. Closed Sun evening & Mon.

Les Nymphéas, 7–9 rue de la Pie (☎02.35.89.26.69). Situated beyond a half-timbered courtyard just west of place du Vieux-Marché, this is the chicest restaurant in Rouen, if a little over-the-top for most tastes. Set menus at 165F/€25.15, 200F/€30.49 and 260F/€38.11; dishes particularly worth trying are the scallop salad and the beef with truffles. Closed Sun evening & Mon, plus first fortnight of Sept.

Pascaline, 5 rue de la Poterne (☎02.35.89.67.44). Classic bistro, located to the north of Palais de Justice, near the flower market, with a green wooden enclosure attached to the front of a half-timbered house. They offer great-value buffets of salads, main courses and desserts – you can have all three for 82F/€12.50 – as well as more formal set menus from 99F/€15.09.

Le P'tit Bec, 182 rue Eau de Robec (☎02.35.07.63.33). Friendly brasserie-cum-tearoom which has become Rouen's most popular lunch spot, with a simple 75F/€11.43 menu holding such joys as salmon tagliatelle and chocolate fondants, with plenty of vegetarian options; also serves afternoon tea. There's seating both indoors and outside, on the pedestrianized street, beside the running water and in view of a fine blue half-timbered mansion next door. Closed in the evenings except for Fri & Sat; closed all day Sun.

Les P'tits Parapluies, 46 rue Bourg l'Abbé, place de la Rougemare (☎02.35.88.55.26). Elegant, secluded half-timbered restaurant not far north of the Hôtel de Ville, on the edge of an attractive little square. Counting your calories (or your pennies) is not really an option; the trio of menus, starting at 150F/€22.87, change daily, but include such delights as oxtail with foie gras and scallop flan. Closed Sat lunch, Sun evening & Mon.

Au Temps des Cerises, 4–6 rue des Basnages (☎02.35.89.98.00). If you've come to Normandy for the cheeses, this is the place to get it all out of your system. Turkey breast in Camembert, goats'-cheese crêpes, and above all fondues of every description. Lunch menus from 60F/€9.15, from 90F/€13.72 in the evening. Trendy if slightly overstyled. Closed Mon lunch, Sat lunch & Sun.

Drinking and nightlife

Some of Rouen's most agreeable **bars** lie in the maze of streets between rue Jean-Lecanuet and place du Vieux-Marché. Incoming sailors used to head straight for this area of the city, and the small bars are still there even if the sailors aren't. As one of France's most cosmopolitan cities, and one renowned for its (largely rock-oriented) music scene, Rouen enjoys a far-from-provincial **nightlife**, with new clubs springing up all the time.

Bars and clubs

Le Bateau Ivre, 17 rue des Sapins (☎02.35.70.09.05). Low-key but atmospheric hangout, with wooden tables, which puts on a mostly rock-oriented programme of music and performance, with an open-mike night on Thursdays that seems to attract lovers of traditional French *chansons*. Open Tues & Wed until 2am, Thurs–Sat until 4am. Closed Sun, Mon & all Aug.

Big Ben Pub, 95 rue du Gros-Horloge (☎02.35.88.44.50). Right under the big clock – hence the name – this always-packed bar is strictly speaking entered from a side street, at 30 rue des Vergetiers. Usually as crowded inside as is the street outside. Mon–Sat noon–2am.

Le Café Curieux, rue des Fossés Louis VIII (☎02.35.71.20.83). Incredibly loud and hectic bar, where Rouen's beautiful mingle to a techno and drum 'n' bass soundtrack, while cult and avant-garde videos flicker on all sides.

Exo 7, 13 place des Chartreux (☎02.35.03.32.30). Traditionally the centre of Rouen's heavy-rock scene, a long way south of the centre, the *Exo 7* (pronounced "Exocet") is these days becoming a bit more eclectic, with the odd techno dance night as well. Wed–Sat 10.30pm–4am.

La Luna, 26 rue St-Étienne-des-Tonneliers (☎02.35.88.77.18). Glamorous late-night club that specializes in all things South American, with steamy salsa dancing most nights. Thurs–Sat 7pm–4am.

La Taverne St-Amant, 11 rue St-Amant (☎02.35.88.51.34). Popular bar with draught Guinness and bistro meals, off rue de la République above the cathedral.

Le Traxx, 4 d Ferdinand-de-Lesseps (☎02.32.10.12.02). Rouen's top gay club offers a regular diet of house and techno to a flamboyant clientele that loves to go wild on a special occasion. Fri & Sat 11pm–4am.

XXL, 25–27 rue de la Savonnerie (☎02.35.88.84.00). Gay (male) bar that's a premier clubbing rendezvous and stays open all night Sat to serve breakfast on Sun. Closed Mon.

Entertainment

As you would expect in a conurbation of 400,000, there's always plenty going on in Rouen, from classical concerts in churches to alternative events in community and commercial centres. An annual handbook, *Le P'tit Normand*, available in all newsagents for 40F/€6.10, is helpful with addresses and telephone numbers. For current events, pick up the free *Cette Semaine à Rouen* from the tourist office. Tickets (and further information) can also be had from FNAC (see opposite).

Rouen has several **theatres**, which mainly work to winter seasons. The most highbrow and big-spectacle is the **Théâtre des Arts**, 7 rue de Dr-Rambert (☎02.35.71.41.36), which puts on opera, ballet and concerts. The more adventurous repertory company of the **Théâtre des Deux Rives** (☎02.35.70.22.82), based opposite the Antiquités museum at the top end of rue Louis-Ricard, at the junction with rue de Joyeuse, presents work by playwrights such as Beaumarchais, Shakespeare, Beckett and Gorky.

Major **concerts** often take place in the **Théâtre Duchamp-Villon** in the St-Sever complex (☎02.35.62.31.31). Also south of the river, but a long way further out, are the **Théâtre Charles Dullin**, allée des Arcades, Grand Quévilly (☎02.35.68.48.91), and the **Théâtre Maxime-Gorki**, rue François-Mitterrand, Petit Quévilly (☎02.35.72.67.55), which specializes in contemporary and traditional music from around Europe. There are two multiscreen **cinemas** just north of the river, and another in the St-Sever complex.

Shopping

Most of the classier **shops** in Rouen are in the pedestrian streets near, and slightly north of, the cathedral. If you are looking for fancy foodstuffs, patisseries, chocolates and the like, there are shops on rue Jeanne-d'Arc around and just above rue du Gros-Horloge. For **hypermarkets** and cheap clothes, however – or just for a laugh on a rainy day – go south of the river to the modern multistorey St-Sever complex. There's an open-air antiques and bric-a-brac **market** nearby in the place des Émmurées.

Much the largest **bookshop** in Rouen can be found at the all-purpose FNAC, underground in the Espace du Palais mall immediately north of the Palais de Justice (Mon–Sat 10am–7pm), which stocks a fine selection of local maps and guides, largely in French, and English-language titles, as well as a wide range of CDs, videos and computer paraphernalia. There's also an **English** specialist, the ABC Bookshop, 9–11 rue des Faulx (Tues–Sat 10am–6pm), near the St-Ouen church.

Around Rouen

Though it only takes a few minutes of travelling along the river from Rouen in either direction to reach pleasant small towns well worth an overnight stop – such as Villequier or Les Andelys, both described elsewhere in this chapter – a number of places only just outside the city proper make good day-trips while you are based in the city. Some are also worth considering as alternative bases for visits to the metropolis.

The Château du Robert-le-Diable

Perhaps the most impressively situated of all early Norman castles, the ruined **Château du Robert-le-Diable** (March–Aug daily 9am–7pm; Sept to mid-Nov Tues–Sun 10am–5pm; 45F/€6.86) towers above the left (south) bank of the Seine 15km southwest of Rouen. Robert the Devil is a legendary figure who may or may not have been William the Conqueror's father, but certainly didn't build this early Norman castle. It's now privately run, with a crazy-golf course, a slightly clumsy reconstruction of a Viking *drakkar*, and tacky waxworks of the Battle of Hastings and other such scenes. But its strengths are the very damp and spooky passages underground, and then the magnificent view from the top of the tower down to the Seine, the port of Rouen and the châteaux on the other side. The only drawback is that the château is right next to an extremely busy motorway.

Just across the motorway is the **Forêt de la Londe**. Although dissected by a number of busy train lines, it survives in the gaps – and is used by local cyclists to race the pollution of Rouen out of their systems.

No buses run to the château from the city, and neither is it a pleasant journey for cyclists or motorists. To **get there**, follow a long and very badly signposted route twelve kilometres southwest from central Rouen, past the docks and refineries of Petit and Grand Quévilly (where cyclists will be glad of the overdue appearance of cycle lanes), as far as the industrial suburb of Moulineaux. From there, you're faced with a steep three-kilometre climb up to the castle itself.

La Bouille

More or less immediately below the Château du Robert-le-Diable, 10km southwest from central Rouen along the southern riverbank, the small village of **LA BOUILLE** stands near a magnificent sweeping bend in the Seine. Little more than a couple of narrow twisting lanes lined with gnarled half-timbered houses, pressed hard against the steep hillside, it's an utter contrast to the noise and bustle of the city, and makes a perfect place to spend a couple of nights for anyone not dependent on public transport. Not far north, a little *bac* (ferry) crosses the river to the small Forêt de Roumare, which makes for a pleasant stroll.

Two expensive but exquisite **hotels**, the *Bellevue*, 13 quai Hector-Malot (☎02.35.18.05.05; ③), and the luxurious *St-Pierre*, place du Bateau (☎02.35.18.01.01; ④), overlook the main road through the village, and both have superb dining rooms.

Clères

Roughly 16km northeast of Rouen, and reachable on bus #161 from the *gare routière*, the pretty village of **CLÈRES** has a large and popular **zoo** (March–Easter, Oct & Nov Mon–Sat 9am–noon & 1.30–5pm, Sun 9am–noon & 1.30–6pm; Easter–Sept Mon–Fri 9am–6pm, Sat 9am–6.30pm, Sun 9am–7pm; 35F/€5.34), set in the grounds of an eleventh-century castle of which few traces remain. The more modern château which replaced it was in turn recently devastated by a fire, but the animals survived. One aviary is even housed in what was the château's main hall. Colette made the impenetrable but presumably complimentary remark that "At Clères, in the zoo park, it is easy to lose the melancholy feeling of inevitability".

The Forêt de Lyons

Around 25km east of Rouen, the **Forêt de Lyons** was a thousand years ago a favoured hunting ground of William the Conqueror and other dukes of Normandy. In 1135, Henry I of England died in the central village of Lyons-la-Forêt of a surfeit of lampreys consumed after a late-November hunting expedition.

Parts of the forest feel as though they can have changed little in the intervening millennium – remarkable considering its proximity not only to Rouen but also to Paris. Almost any of the little roads through these dense woods rewards exploration by cyclists or walkers; the oaks and beeches are consistently magnificent, with particularly vast specimens indicated by road signs.

Lyons-la-Forêt

At the heart of the forest, the little hill village of **LYONS-LA-FORÊT** was the site of William's now completely indiscernible castle, but has retained a superb ensemble of half-timbered Norman houses dating from around 1610. In the centre of the village stand the plain old wooden *halles*, often used as a film set, while the roads around abound in splendid rural mansions. One such, the house named *Le Fresne* on rue d'Enfer, was much used by the composer Ravel in the 1920s.

Lyons' central **tourist office**, 20 rue de l'Hôtel de Ville (June–Aug Mon 2–6pm, Tues–Sat 10am–noon & 2–6pm, Sun 10am–noon & 2–4pm; Sept–May Tues–Sat 10am–noon & 2–5pm, Sun 10am–noon & 2–4pm; ☎02.32.49.31.65), has information on the whole forest area. Of the **hotels** in the village, your best bets are the brick-fronted *Grand Cerf*, right next to the *halles* on place Bensérade (☎02.32.49.60.44; ④; closed Feb) – which has a secluded garden tucked away behind the archway and serves *moules marinières* for 50F/€7.62 and full menus from 98F/€14.94 – and the pink-painted *Licorne* nearby at 27 place Bensérade (☎02.32.49.62.02; ⑤; closed mid-Dec to mid-Jan), where the cheapest dinner menu is 195F/€29.73. There are also a couple of less expensive **restaurants** with outdoor seating in the main square.

Abbaye de Mortemer

Half a dozen kilometres south of Lyons, clearly signed off a main road, the ruins of the twelfth-century Cistercian **Abbaye de Mortemer** amount to little more than heaps of rubble scattered across gentle lawns, amid a landscape of rolling parklands (park daily 1–6pm; guided tours half-hourly Easter–Sept daily 2–6pm, Oct–Easter Sat & Sun 2–5.30pm; 20F/€3.05 admission, 35F/€5.34 with tour). Plenty of outbuildings survive, however, including a round stone *pigeonnier*, with a spider's-web tangle of wood inside, and little niches for hundreds of pigeons (reared by the monks for food); a cast-iron pigeon stands permanently on top.

The highlight of the standard visit is the **museum** in the eighteenth-century château that dominates the grounds, where you see models of the abbey as it is now, and an audiovisual show of life as it used to be, complete with plenty of tales of hauntings and bumps in the night. On several evenings each August, however, the grounds reopen at night for guided tours that lead past a series of tableaux vivants, in which costumed actors tell the story of Henry II, King of England and Duke of Normandy (call ☎02.32.49.54.34 for schedule; 70F/€10.67).

Beyond the abbey, which was quarried after the Revolution to build the nearby village of Lisors, a couple of marshy lakes are populated by geese and swans and surrounded by woods and lawns that accommodate free-roaming deer.

Charleval

In **CHARLEVAL**, on the edge of the woods 7km west of the abbey, the *Auberge de l'Écurie* at 16 Grande Rue (☎02.32.49.30.73; ②; restaurant closed Sun evening & Mon) has some of the forest's least expensive – if rather dilapidated – rooms. It also offers a very atmospheric low-ceilinged dining room, which features a

110F/€16.77 menu including salmon baked in foil, an open, wood barbecue, and flamboyantly decorated desserts.

Vascoeuil

The small but graceful **Château de Vascoeuil**, on the northwest edge of the forest 12km from Lyons, is known to have existed as early as 1050, and was home during the nineteenth century to the historian Michelet. These days, it's renowned for staging top-quality temporary **art exhibitions** (March to mid-April Sat & Sun 2.30–6.30pm; mid-April to June, Sept & Oct Mon–Sat 2.30–6.30pm, Sun 11am–7pm; July & Aug daily 11am–7pm; ☎02.35.23.62.35; prices vary).

Ry

The village of **RY**, 4km northwest of the château, is immortalized in literary history as the real-life home of Flaubert's fictionalized Madame Bovary. A monument in its churchyard commemorates Delphine Couturier, who committed suicide in Ry in 1849 having married a local doctor ten years previously, at the age of 17.

Ry consists of one main street, with green hills visible rising at either end, and a church to one side with an unusual carved wooden porch. Delphine's husband is buried in the churchyard, and Madame Bovary is immortalized throughout the village, which seems to have had little else to celebrate for a century or so. The local florist is Emma's, the video shop is Bovary, while the pharmacy was her real house.

An expensive museum of automata, of appeal largely to young children, though some of its mannequins jerkily act out the less explicit moments of Madame Bovary's career, stands next to a pretty bridge over the Crevon (Easter–June, Sept & Oct Mon, Sat & Sun 11am–noon & 2–7pm; July & Aug Mon, Sat & Sun 11am–noon & 2–7pm, Tues–Fri 3–6pm; 25F/€3.81). There are no hotels, but the *Rôtisserie Bovary* (☎02.35.23.61.46; closed Mon evening & Tues) serves reasonable lunches in the town's smartest building, near the church.

Upstream from Rouen

Upstream from Rouen towards Paris, high cliffs on the north bank of the Seine imitate the coast, looking down on waves of green and scattered river islands. By the time you reach **Les Andelys**, 25km out of Rouen, you're within 100km of the capital, meaning that accommodation and eating prices tend to be geared towards affluent weekend- and day-trippers.

Large country estates abound in this agreeable countryside, and public transport, too, is minimal – it's assumed any visitor has, if not a residence, then at least a car. However, infrequent buses run from Rouen to Les Andelys, while trains from Rouen call at **Vernon**, the closest station to **Giverny**, which is renowned as both home and inspiration to Claude Monet.

Pont St-Pierre

The first point south of Rouen at which the Seine begins to be enticing again is **PONT ST-PIERRE**, where it's joined by the River Andelle. Any surplus money you may have could be enjoyably spent on a stay at the pink-and-brown *Hostellerie la Bonne Marmite*, 10 rue Réné Raban (☎02.32.49.70.24; ⑤; closed last week of July & first two weeks in Aug), set around a little courtyard a little way south of the eponymous bridge on the main road. Duck-and-lobster-loaded menus in the restaurant start at 150F/€22.87.

At the junction of the two rivers you are confronted with the spectacularly sharp **Côte des Deux Amants**. This sheer escarpment, leading to a plateau high above the Seine, takes its name from a twelfth-century legend, in which a cruel king stipulated that the man who would marry his daughter must first run with her in his arms to the top of this hill. Noble Raoul sprinted up carrying the fair Caliste, but then dropped dead and out of sympathy, so did she. That story provides precious little incentive for anyone else to make the climb – but rumour has it that the view from the top does.

Les Andelys

The next town of any size is **LES ANDELYS**, which, as the name implies, consists in fact of two towns, overshadowed by the magnificent Château Gaillard. **Petit Andely**, which was the birthplace in 1594 of Nicolas Poussin, is a gorgeous little place. Its main street, parallel to the Seine, is lined with ancient half-timbered houses, while from the grassy riverbank behind you can see north to some imposing white bluffs as well as south to the castle. **Grand Andely**, at the end of a 1.5-kilometre-long boulevard stretching inland, is the centre for shops, bars and a **market** on Saturday.

Château Gaillard

The single most dramatic sight anywhere along the Seine short of Paris – especially awesome and magical by night – has to be **Château Gaillard**, perched high above Les Andelys. The castle was constructed in the space of a single year, 1196–97, under the auspices of Richard the Lionheart. A previous truce had expressly forbidden the construction of a castle here, but Richard went ahead and seized the rock on which it stands from Archbishop Walter of Rouen, and then bribed the pope for permission to build. His object was to deny the King of France access to Rouen by establishing total control of traffic along the Seine, by both road and river. That was successful until after Richard's death, when Philippe-Auguste managed to storm the castle in 1204 (his armies gaining access via the latrines). It might well have survived intact into the twentieth century, though, had Henry IV not ordered its destruction in 1603. Even then, it would have taken more recent devices to reduce Château Gaillard to rubble. The stout flint walls of its keep, roughly 4m thick, remain reasonably intact, and the outline of most of the rest is still clear, arranged over assorted green and chalky knolls. The castle was originally divided into two separate segments, linked by a bridge across a moat that was never intended to be filled with water – you can still explore the storage caves hidden in its depths.

Visits to the château are permitted between mid-March and mid-November only (Mon & Thurs–Sun 10am–noon & 2–6pm, Wed 2–6pm; closed Tues; 18F/€2.74). On foot, you can make the steep climb up via a path that leads off rue Richard Coeur-de-Lion in Petit Andely. The only route for motorists is extraordinarily convoluted, following a long-winded one-way system that starts opposite the church in Grand Andely.

Practicalities

The **tourist office** for Les Andelys is at 24 rue Philippe-Auguste in Petit Andely (May–Sept Mon–Fri 9.30am–12.30pm & 2.30–6pm, Sat 9.30am–12.30pm &

2.30–5pm, Sun 10am–noon & 2–5pm; Oct–April daily 2–5.30pm; ☎02.32.54.41.93). The nicest places to **stay** have to be the two attractive Seine-side hotels in Petit Andely; the eighteenth-century *Chaîne d'Or*, opposite the thirteenth-century St-Sauveur church at 27 rue Grande (☎02.32.54.00.31; ⑤; closed Jan, Sun evening, Mon, & Tues lunch), and the *Normandie* at 1 rue Grande (☎02.32.54.10.52; ②; closed Dec; restaurant closed Wed evening & Thurs). Both have high-quality expensive restaurants – even breakfast at the *Chaîne d'Or* costs 75F/€11.43, while the cheapest dinner menu is double that. If you can't get a room at either of those, the *Hôtel de Paris*, further back from the river at 10 av de la République in Grand Andely (☎02.32.54.00.33; ③; restaurant closed Sun evening), is a good alternative, with yet another top-notch dining room. There's also a lovely riverside **campsite**, far below the château, the *L'Île des Trois Rois* (☎02.32.54.23.79; closed Nov–March).

Giverny

Had it not caught the eye of Claude Monet from a passing train carriage, the little village of **GIVERNY** might by now have decayed into insignificance; instead it ranks among the most visited tourist attractions in Normandy. Standing a few hundred metres back from the right bank of the Seine, 20km south of the ancient fortifications of Les Andelys and a mere 40km from Paris, it welcomes a constant stream of traffic in summer. Between November and March, however, when Monet's house and gardens are closed to visitors, everything else seems to close down too.

The road south to Giverny from Les Andelys crosses a flat plain dotted with lovely little villages. **Port Mort** in particular, where the road is lined by an almost unbroken stone wall, is well worth a stop. The closest **trains** come to **Vernon** (see p.110), 4km north of Giverny across the river and on the Rouen–Paris-St-Lazare line. Either rent a bike at the *gare SNCF*, or catch the connecting bus to Monet's gardens.

Musée Claude Monet

Gardens and house open April–Oct Tues–Sun 10am–6pm; last ticket sold 5.30pm, no advance sales; 35F/€5.34 house and gardens, 25F/€3.81 gardens only. There's free parking opposite the house; don't be fooled by signs for private car parks elsewhere in Giverny.

If anything, art lovers who make the pilgrimage to the former home of Claude Monet are outnumbered by garden enthusiasts. None of Monet's original paintings is on display – most are in the Orangerie and Musée d'Orsay in Paris – whereas the **gardens** that many of his friends considered to be his masterpiece are still lovingly tended in all their glory.

Visits start in the huge **studio**, built in 1915, where Monet painted his last and largest canvases depicting waterlilies (in French, *nymphéas*). It now serves as a well-stocked book and gift shop, albeit disappointingly short of good-quality reproductions of the famous works. A gravel footpath leads from there to the actual **house**, a long, two-storey structure facing down to the river, and painted pastel pink with green shutters. Monet's bedroom is bedecked with family photos and paintings by friends and family, while among the washed-out reproductions in his *salon* are a depiction by Renoir of Monet at work in his earlier, less perfect garden at Argenteuil in 1875, and one by Monet himself of his dream closer to realization in the garden at Vetheuil in 1881. All the other main rooms are crammed almost floor-to-ceiling with his collection of Japanese prints, especially works by Hokusai and Hiroshige. Most of the original furnishings are gone, but you do get a real sense of how the dining room used to be, with all its walls and fittings painted a

CLAUDE MONET AT GIVERNY

Claude Monet first rented the Giverny home that now houses the Musée Claude Monet in 1883. At the age of 43, he was exactly halfway through his life. Born in Paris in 1840, he had grown up in Le Havre, and had spent the previous decade living in Argenteuil, Vétheuil and Poissy. Although his reputation as a painter was already established – the movement known as **Impressionism** had taken its name from a critic's somewhat contemptuous response to his work *Impression, Sunrise*, shown in Paris in April 1874 as part of the First Impressionist Exhibition – his personal and financial circumstances were far from settled.

The Monet ménage, whose houseboat arrived in Giverny on April 29, 1883, consisted of ten people. As well as Claude's two sons by his wife Camille, who had died in 1879, he was now also responsible for the six children of his long-term mistress **Alice Hoschedé**. Her husband, Ernest, was a former patron of the Impressionists who had fallen on hard times; she finally married Monet after Ernest's death in 1891.

Monet was to find both artistic and commercial success in Giverny. In his early years, he continued to travel to paint landscapes not only throughout Normandy but also in Brittany, on the Riviera and in England. As time went by, however, his advancing physical frailty and failing eyesight made extended trips increasingly daunting, while his growing prosperity enabled him to tailor his immediate environment to meet his needs as a painter.

Monet began to produce sequences of reworkings and renditions of the same scene, shown at different times of the day or seasons of the year, in 1890. The first such series consisted of 25 views of the **haystacks** on a neighbouring farm; all were arranged side by side in his studio, to be worked on simultaneously. Designed to be seen en masse, they went on show in Paris early in 1891, and proved hugely popular. The individual paintings sold out quickly, and from then on visiting American collectors – and would-be students – were a constant feature of life at Giverny.

In 1891, Monet painted a sequence showing the poplar trees that stood along the banks of the River Epte, about 1.5km south of his home. By now he was rich enough to buy the trees, for as long as his work was in progress, from a local timber merchant who was due to fell them. Having purchased his house outright, for 22,000F, he went on to buy a further plot of land, across the main road. With permission from the local authorities, he dammed the stream known as the Ru to feed an artificial pond, which he planted with **waterlilies** and spanned with a Japanese footbridge.

A team of gardeners worked to keep different sections of his **flower gardens** in bloom as much of the year as possible, so he would always have a suitable subject on which to work. One man had the full-time responsibility of tending the waterlilies to Monet's specifications, depending, for example, on whether he planned to use square or rectangular canvases. Monet would work outdoors for around six hours each day, avoiding the midday sun, and went on to paint over 250 versions of his waterlilies (*nymphéas*), not to mention the canvases he destroyed in disgust. One set of 48 waterlily pictures is said to have hung in his studio for six years, being constantly reworked, before it was exhibited in 1909.

Photographs of Monet in his later years show him as very much the white-bearded patrician, not only presiding over his studio and household but also playing host to leading painters and politicians. Despite a series of operations on his eyes, he continued to work almost until his death, in December 1926. The house at Giverny passed to his son, Jean Monet, who left it in turn to the Académie des Beaux Arts in 1966. After restoration, it reopened as a museum in 1980.

glorious bright yellow; Monet designed his own yellow crockery to harmonize with the surroundings. By contrast, the stairs and upstairs rooms are a pale blue.

Colourful flower gardens, with trellised walkways and shady bowers, stretch down from the house. Originally, the main footpath here led straight down to the **waterlily pond**; now, however, visitors have to reach the *jardin d'eau* by burrowing beneath the main road in a dank underpass. Once there, paths around the perimeter of the pond, as well of course as arching Japanese footbridges, offer differing views of the waterlilies themselves, cherished by gardeners in rowing boats. May and June, when the rhododendrons flower, and the wisteria that winds over the Japanese bridge is in bloom, are the best times to visit. Whenever you come, however, you'll have to contend with camera-happy crowds jostling to capture their own impressions of the waterlilies.

Musée d'Art Américain

A few minutes' walk up Giverny's village street, to the left as you leave Monet's house, stands the new **Musée d'Art Américain** (April–Oct Tues–Sun 10am–6pm; 35F/€5.34). The exterior is far from attractive, but inside you'll find a spacious and well-lit gallery devoted to American artists resident in France between 1865 and 1915, and in particular those who congregated in Giverny from 1887 onwards. Although Monet accepted no formal pupils, some, such as Theodore Robinson, joined his circle of intimates. Some took their admiration to a point that now seems embarrassing, painting many of the same scenes as Monet himself. As well as the waterlilies, for example, John Leslie Brech produced a series of twelve haystacks within a year of Monet's.

Mary Cassatt, who lived in a château at Le Mesnil-Thérebus, is represented by a far more interesting series of woodcuts, heavily influenced by *ukiyo-e* Japanese woodcuts, as well as canvases that focus on the domestic life of women while clearly belonging to the Impressionist movement. John Singer Sargent and Winslow Homer both contribute scenes of Brittany, especially Cancale, while James Henry Whistler paintings include views of Dieppe and Étretat.

Practicalities

Heading right for a hundred metres as you leave Monet's house brings you to Giverny's one **hotel**, the *Musardière*, at 123 rue Claude-Monet (☎02.32.21.03.18; ④); dinner menus in its restaurant start at 145F/€22.11, but they also serve crêpes and snacks during the day. A pleasant little tearoom and **restaurant**, *Les Nymphéas* (☎02.32.21.20.31), is located opposite the house itself; there's another restaurant inside the Musée d'Art Américain; and the *charcutier* at 60 rue Claude-Monet makes delicious sandwiches. If you've brought a picnic, eating in the grounds of the house is forbidden, and the surrounding countryside is not particularly appealing.

Vernon

VERNON straddles the Seine just before it leaves Normandy altogether, with walks laid out along either bank. Were it not for the proximity of Giverny, there'd be no reason to visit here, let alone stay; as it is the central *Hôtel d'Évreux*, 11 place d'Évreux (☎02.32.21.16.12; ③), has **rooms** at assorted prices, and a good restaurant, and you can also **eat** well at the *Restaurant de la Poste*, 26 av Gambetta (☎02.32.51.10.63; closed Tues evening & Wed), where menus start at 90F/€13.72. Elvis Presley's dad was called Vernon.

travel details

Trains

Dieppe to: Paris-St-Lazare (8 daily; 2hr 15min); Rouen (10 daily; 1hr).

Fécamp to: Rouen (6 daily; 45min).

Le Havre to: Paris (12 daily; 2hr 15min); Rouen (12 daily; 1hr).

Le Tréport to: Paris-St-Lazare (5 daily; 2hr 45min) via Eu (4min) and Beauvais (1hr 40min).

Rouen to: Caen (8 daily; 2hr 15min); Fécamp (at least hourly; 1hr 15min) via Bréauté-Brezzeville (35min); Motteville (4–6 daily; 20min) with connecting bus to St-Valéry (total 1hr 20min); Paris-St-Lazare (12 daily; 1hr 15min).

Buses

Dieppe to: Fécamp (4 daily; 2hr 20min); Le Havre (2 daily; 3hr 50min) via St-Valéry, Fécamp and Étretat; Le Tréport (3 daily; 30min); Paris (5 daily; 2hr 15min); St-Valéry (4 daily; 1hr).

Fécamp to: Étretat (8 daily; 30min); Le Havre (8 daily; 1hr 30min); Yport (8 daily; 15min).

Le Havre to: Caen (2 daily express services; 1hr 25min); Étretat (7 daily; 50min); Fécamp (7 daily; 1hr 30min); Honfleur (8 daily; 30min).

Rouen to: Clères (2 daily; 45min); Dieppe (4 daily; 1hr 45min); Fécamp (2 daily; 2hr 30min); Le Havre (hourly; 2hr 45min), #191 or #192 via Jumièges and Caudebec; Le Neubourg (2 daily; 45min); Le Tréport (2 daily; 2hr 30min); Lisieux (2 daily; 2hr 30min); Lyons-la-Forêt (3 daily; 1hr).

Ferries

Dieppe to: Newhaven (4–5 daily; 2hr 15min–4hr) with Hoverspeed (☎08.20.00.35.55).

Le Havre to: Portsmouth (3 daily; 5hr 30min) with P&O (☎08.03.01.30.13).

For more details, see p.3 onwards.

CHAPTER TWO

THE LOWER NORMANDY COAST

The **coast of Lower Normandy** progressively changes its character as you move from east to west. Along the **Côte Fleurie**, from Honfleur to Cabourg, it is moneyed and elegant, with the **Norman Riviera** styling itself as a northern counterpart to the Côte d'Azur. Then, through the much flatter **Côte de Nacre** and into the area known as the **Bessin**, around Caen and Bayeux, the shoreline is much lower key: though the coastal strip remains predominantly built up, few towns amount to more than slender ribbons sandwiched between the broad sandy **Invasion Beaches** used by the Allies in 1944, and the featureless scrubland that lies inland. West again, separated from the bulk of the mainland by a series of marshes, is the **Cotentin Peninsula**, with low-key harbour villages along its east front, cliffs across the north, and vast dunes and wild beaches to the west. And finally there is the **bay of Mont-St-Michel**, where the island abbey is swept by treacherous tides.

The most enjoyable destination along the Côte Fleurie is **Honfleur**, a real gem of a harbour town, familiar from the paintings of Eugène Boudin, Monet and other Impressionists. Elsewhere, the prevailing air tends to be one of wealthy sterility. **Trouville**, **Deauville** and **Cabourg** preoccupy themselves with such events as Rolls Royce rallies, forever harking back to a nineteenth-century past of leisured aristocrats, albeit with twenty-first-century prices.

Thanks to their lack of overdeveloped resorts, the Côte de Nacre and the Bessin are much more likeable. This region's pivotal role in the **D-Day Landings** is commemorated not only in numerous cemeteries and memorials but also in the many museums that explain aspects of its wartime history. Only a small propor-

ACCOMMODATION PRICE CODES

All **hotel prices** in this book have been coded using the symbols below. The price shown is for the least expensive double room in high season, which, for categories ① and ② especially, often means a room without shower, bath and toilet. Most such hotels have other rooms with en-suite facilities, which typically cost 40–60F/€6.10–9.15 extra.

① Under 160F/€24
② 160–220F/€24–34
③ 220–300F/€34–46
④ 300–400F/€46–61
⑤ 400–500F/€61–76
⑥ 500–600F/€76–91
⑦ 600–700F/€91–107
⑧ 700–800F/€107–122
⑨ Over 800F/€122

tion of the tourists and veterans who flock here during the day stay the night, however, so the small-scale seaside towns remain for the most part charmingly atmospheric places to spend a few days. Just inland, the venerable cathedral city of **Bayeux** would be a destination to savour even without the bonus of its world-famous **tapestry**, while its much larger neighbour, **Caen**, is less immediately captivating, but also boasts an abundance of impressive medieval architecture, and rivals Rouen as a centre for contemporary culture, too.

The main city of the Cotentin Peninsula, **Cherbourg**, may not be a port to linger over, but ferry passengers who arrive here can choose between the lovely little villages that lie to the east, and the magnificent beaches and dunes of the peninsula's western coastline (a mecca for windsurfers). Such distractions serve to delay progress towards the glorious island abbey of **Mont-St-Michel**, France's most visited and most distinctive monument (after Versailles), and visible across the bay from **Granville** onwards.

The beaches of the Baie du Mont-St-Michel, however, are no temptation – dangerous for the most part, and flanked by generally tacky resorts. Having come this far, better to head straight on to the delights of the Breton **Côte d'Émeraude** (see Chapter Four).

The Côte Fleurie and the Norman Riviera

The only section of the Norman coast to have any serious delusions of grandeur is the stretch that lies immediately east of the mouth of the Seine. The Pont de Normandie across from Le Havre has made such places as Trouville and **Deauville** altogether too hectic for comfort, but only Honfleur could really be said to have much that it would be a shame to lose, with the appealing **Côte Fleurie** just west of town. The coastline between **Trouville** and **Cabourg** has awarded itself the epithet of the **Norman Riviera**, with Trouville playing Nice to Deauville's Cannes.

There's an obvious distinction all along this stretch of the coast between old ports such as **Honfleur** and **Dives**, which have over the centuries been pushed further and further back from the sea by heavy deposits of silt from the Seine but retain their historic medieval buildings, and the new resorts that have sprung up alongside the resultant sandy beaches, most of them unimaginatively laid out during the nineteenth century and characterless in the extreme. The happiest balance is found at places such as **Houlgate**, where development has remained low-key and the rocky coastline has stood firm against the river – giving the added bonus of pleasant corniche drives.

Honfleur

HONFLEUR, the best preserved of the old ports of Normandy and the first you come to on the eastern Calvados coast, is a near-perfect seaside town which lacks only a beach. It used to have one, but with the accumulation of silt from the Seine the sea has steadily withdrawn, leaving the eighteenth-century waterfront houses of boulevard Charles V stranded and a little surreal. The ancient port, however, still functions – the channel to the beautiful Vieux Bassin is kept open by regular dredging – and though only pleasure craft now use the moorings in the harbour basin, fishing boats continue to tie up alongside the pier nearby. Fish is usually on

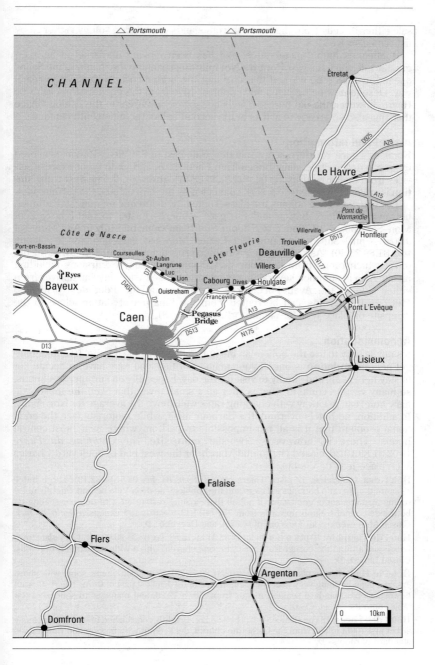

sale either directly from the boats or from stands on the pier, still by right run by fishermen's wives.

Honfleur is highly picturesque, and has been moving upmarket at an ever-greater rate since the vast **Pont de Normandie**, spanning the mouth of the Seine, opened in 1995 – be warned that crossing the bridge costs 33F/€5.03 fee each way. Despite now being just a few minutes' drive from the giant metropolis of Le Havre, however, the old port still feels not so very different to the fishing village that appealed so greatly to artists in the second half of the nineteenth century.

Arrival and information

Honfleur's **gare routière**, a few minutes' walk east of the Vieux Bassin, is served by over a dozen direct daily **buses** from Caen (#20), and up to eight express services from Le Havre (Bus Verts; ☎02.31.89.28.41). However, the nearest **train station** is at Pont l'Évêque (see p.177), connected by the Lisieux bus, #50 (20min ride).

The **tourist office** adjoins the glass-fronted Mediathèque on quai Le Paulmier, between the Vieux Bassin and the gare routière (Easter to mid-July & Sept Mon–Sat 9.30am–12.30pm & 2–6.30pm, Sun 10am–5pm; mid-July to Aug Mon–Sat 9.30am–7pm, Sun 10am–5pm; Oct–Easter Mon–Sat 9am–noon & 2–5.30pm; ☎02.31.89.23.30). Ask about their summer programme of **guided tours** of the town, which range from two-hour walkabouts to full-day excursions including meals. Also in summer, several ninety-minute **cruises** each day sail upriver from either side of the Avant-Port, for a closer look at the Pont de Normandie (40F/€6.10). **Cycles** can be rented from the Fina petrol station, close to the campsite on place Jean-de-Vienne (☎02.31.89.91.73).

Accommodation

It's not as easy to live the bohemian life in Honfleur as it used to be. If finding budget **accommodation** is one of your main priorities, you may have to decide not to stay here at all, and simply to visit for the day. Especially on summer weekends, so many visitors come to what is after all a small town, that even the most ordinary hotel can get away with charging rates well above the average for Normandy. In addition, no hotels overlook the harbour itself, while motorists face the additional problem that it is all but impossible to park anywhere near most central hotels. There is, however, a two-star **campsite**, the *Camping du Phare* (☎02.31.89.10.26; closed Oct to mid-March) at the west end of boulevard Charles V on place Jean-de-Vienne.

Hôtel des Cascades, 17 place Thiers (☎02.31.89.05.83, fax 02.31.89.32.13). Large hotel-restaurant open onto both place Thiers and the cobbled rue de la Ville behind. Slightly noisy rooms upstairs, and a good-value if not all that exciting restaurant with outdoor seating on both sides; menus climb upwards from 75F/€11.43 towards the expensive *fruits de mer*. Closed Mon evening, all Tues out of season, and Dec–Feb. ②.

Hôtel du Dauphin, 10 place Berthelot (☎02.31.89.15.53, fax 02.31.89.92.06). Grey-slate town house just around the corner from Ste-Catherine church, with a wide assortment of rooms. Closed Jan. ④–⑦.

Hôtel le Hamelin, 16 place Hamelin (☎02.31.89.16.25). Five basic rooms, some with showers, in a plain building very near the Lieutenance in the liveliest part of town. The restaurant downstairs has standard seafood menus from 80F/€12.20, and manages to squeeze a few tables onto the street. ②–④.

Hôtel des Loges, 18 rue Brûlée (☎02.31.89.38.26). Brightly refurbished hotel on a quiet side street just 100m inland from Ste-Catherine church, decked out with flowers and with a good standard of rooms. ④.

HONFLEUR

△ *The Seine*

JETÉE DE L'OUEST

Camping

PLACE DE VIENNE

Jardin Public

BOULEVARD CHARLES V

Les Maisons Satie

RUE HAUTE

Avant Port

RUE DE L'HOMME DE BOIS

△ *Côte de Grace*

RUE CHARRIERE DE GRACE

R LUCIE DE L'ARLE MANDOS

Musée Boudin

Ⓑ Ⓒ Ⓐ ❶

PL. HAMELIN

Ste-Catherine

Ⓓ ❷

Lieutenance

Ⓔ QUAI DE LA QUARANTAINE

PLACE STE-CATHERINE

❸ PLACE BERTHELOT

❹

Vieux Bassin

PLACE A BOUDIN

Ⓕ Ⓖ

QUAI DE LA JUNE

 Ⓟ

RUE DES VASES

Ⓗ St-Étienne ❺

QUAI LEPAILLEUR

QUAI STE CATHERINE

RUE BRULEE

PLACE THIERS DES FOSSES

RUE MONTPENSIERS

RUE DE LA VILLE

SAINT LEONARD

ⓘ Gare Routière

❻

RUE DE LA BAVOLE

RUE DE LA REPUBLIQUE

RUE DES PRES

PLACE ST LEONARD

St-Léonard

RUE CACHIN

✉

N

0   200 m

PLACE ALBERT-SOREL

❼

ACCOMMODATION	
Cascades	5
Dauphin	3
Hamelin	1
Loges	4
Motel Monet	6
la Salle des Fêtes	7
Tilbury	2

RESTAURANTS	
l'Absinthe	F
Auberge de la Lieutenance	D
Bistro du Port	G
au Gars Normand	E
au P'tit Mareyeur	A
Taverne de la Mer	B
la Tortue	C
le Vieux Honfleur	H

Motel Monet, Charrière du Puits (☎02.31.89.00.90, fax 02.31.89.97.16, *www.motelmonet.fr*). Not quite a motel as such, but this place is in a very quiet location ten-minutes' walk from the centre and offers modern rooms arranged around a courtyard – so parking is easy. ④.

La Salle des Fêtes, 8 place Albert-Sorel (☎02.31.89.19.69). Clean, well-priced rooms above a friendly family-run bar a short walk inland along the main road from the Vieux Bassin. ②.

Tilbury, 30 place Hamelin (☎02.31.98.83.33, fax 02.31.89.85.06). Absolutely central, a stone's throw from the Lieutenance. Well-equipped and comfortable rooms above a crêperie. ③.

The Town

Visitors to Honfleur inevitably gravitate towards the old centre, around the **Vieux Bassin**. At the *bassin*, slate-fronted houses, each of them one or two storeys higher than seems possible, harmonize despite their tottering and ill-matched forms into a backdrop that is only excelled by the **Lieutenance** at the harbour entrance. This latter was the dwelling of the king's Lieutenant, and has been the gateway to the inner town ever since Samuel Champlain sailed from Honfleur to found Québec in 1608. The church of **St-Étienne** nearby is now the **Musée de la Marine**, which combines a collection of model ships with several rooms of antique Norman furnishings (mid-Feb to March & Oct to mid-Nov Tues–Fri 2–5.30pm, Sat & Sun 10am–noon & 2–5.30pm; April–June & Sept Tues–Sun

10am–noon & 2–6pm; July & Aug daily 10am–1pm & 2–6.30pm; 15F/€2.29). Just behind it, two seventeenth-century **salt stores**, used to contain the precious commodity during the days of the much-hated *gabelle*, or salt tax, now serve as the **Musée d'Ethnographie et d'Art Populaire Normand** (same hours; 15F/€2.29, or combined with Musée de la Marine 25F/€3.81), filling ten rooms with a fascinating assortment of everyday artefacts from old Honfleur.

Honfleur's artistic past – and its present concentration of galleries and painters – owes most to Eugène Boudin, forerunner of Impressionism. He was born and worked in the town, trained the 15-year-old Monet, and was joined for various periods by Pissarro, Renoir and Cézanne. At the same time, Baudelaire paid visits to the town, which was also home to the composer Érik Satie. There's a fair selection of Boudin's works in the **Musée Eugène Boudin**, west of the port on place Érik-Satie, and his crayon seascapes in particular are quite appealing here in context, though the Dufys, Marquets, Frieszes and (above all) the Monets are the most impressive paintings on show (mid-Feb to mid-March & Oct–Dec Mon & Wed–Fri 2.30–5pm, Sat & Sun 10am–noon & 2.30–5pm; mid-March to Sept daily except Tues 10am–noon & 2–6pm; 26F/€3.96).

Honfeur's most remarkable building has to be the church of **Ste-Catherine** (daily 9am–6pm), with its distinctive detached **belfry**, which ranked among Monet's favourite subjects in his younger days. The church was built almost entirely of wood, during the Hundred Years War; all stone was at that time reserved for military use, and so the town's shipbuilders, experienced in working with wood, took responsibility for its construction. All the timbers inside are now exposed to view, having been sheathed in white plaster during the nineteenth century, when an incongruous four-columned porch (long since removed) was added to the front. The changing patterns on its tiles, both along the main body and the belfry, delineate religious symbols. It all makes a change from the great stone Norman churches, and has the added peculiarity of being divided into twin naves, with one balcony running around both. The belfry itself now holds the religious paintings of the Musée Eugène Boudin, and is open the same hours as the museum on the same ticket.

Just down the hill from the Musée Boudin, at 67 bd Charles-V, is **Les Maisons Satie** (daily except Tues: Feb to mid-June & mid-Sept to Dec 10.30am–6pm; mid-June to mid-Sept 10am–7pm; closed Jan; 30F/€4.57), the red-timbered house of Érik Satie. From the outside it looks unchanged since the composer was born there in 1866. Step inside, however, and you'll find yourself in Normandy's most unusual and enjoyable museum. As befits a close associate of the Surrealists, Satie is commemorated by means of all sorts of weird interactive surprises. It would be a shame to give too many of them away here; suffice it to say that you're immediately confronted by a giant pear, bouncing into the air on huge wings to the strains of his best-known piano piece, *Gymnopédies*, and said to represent Satie's soul leaving his body after his death in Paris on July 1, 1925. You also get to see a filmed reconstruction of *Parade*, a ballet on which Satie collaborated with Picasso, Stravinsky and Cocteau, and which created a furore in Paris in 1917.

Satie's home forms part of a row of stately shipbuilders' residences that once lined the Honfleur waterfront; now they look across reclaimed flatlands to the industrial desert of Le Havre's docks in the distance. Over the road, and beyond the public gardens by the place Augustin-Normand, you can follow the **shipping channel** out towards the mouth of the Seine and the sea. A rusty old pipeline runs alongside, inside which you can hear rats and mice scampering to and from the sea. However, it would not occur even to the most hard-nosed mud-caked sewer rat to swim in the sea once it got there – the shore is a slimy grey wasteland, the water foul and sluggish. Nonetheless, it is possible to slip and squirm your way onto the shingle and then walk along the sea coast, with the beautiful wooded hills of the Côte du Grâce tantalizingly above you. Inland, the grand old houses of ancient aesthetes, and the **Chapelle Notre Dame de Grâce**, beloved of the Impressionists, nestle dry-footed in the forests.

Eating

With its abundance of day-trippers and hotel guests, Honfleur supports an astonishing number of **restaurants**, most naturally specializing in seafood and many of them very good at it indeed. Surprisingly few restaurants actually face onto the harbour itself; the narrow buildings around the edge seem to be better suited to being snack bars, crêperies, cafés and ice-cream parlours (including a *Ben & Jerry's*). Few of the town's hotels attempt to compete with the restaurants; the *Cascades* (see p.116) is probably the best of the few that do.

One local speciality, available in October and November, is *crevettes grises* – tiny shrimp eaten with an unsalty Spanish-style bread, *pain brié*. If you're buying your own food, look out for the excellent *Panatérie*, a boulangerie selling granary and wholemeal breads, on the corner of the rue des Prés and avenue de la République.

L'Absinthe, 10 quai de la Quarantaine (☎02.31.89.39.00). This eighteenth-century mansion houses the most imaginative of the row of five restaurants that stand just around the corner from the *bassin*, with such dishes as scallop *carpaccio* or foie gras in ginger nestling on menus that range from 175F/€26.68 to a seven-course 380F/€57.93 extravaganza. Closed mid-Nov to Dec.

Auberge de la Lieutenance, 12 place Ste-Catherine (☎02.31.89.07.52). Not in fact by the Lieutenance, despite the name. Plenty of outdoor seating on the cobbled pedestrian square, facing both church and belfry and overshadowed for no obvious reason by a giant thumb. Gourmet dining with a heavy emphasis on oysters; menus start at 120F/€18.29. Closed Sun evening & mid-Nov to Dec.

Bistro du Port, 14 quai de la Quarantaine (☎02.31.89.21.84). The middle of five adjacent and substantially similar restaurants, all with outdoor seating but in a not very picturesque setting beside the main road just east of the harbour. The *Bistro* has a slight competitive edge on prices for its conventional seafood menus, with the cheapest at 75F/€11.43, and good ones at 95F/€14.48 and 135F/€20.58 (featuring a *tartare de poissons* and a *couscous de la mer*). Closed Mon evening & Tues out of season.

Au Gars Normand, 8 quai des Passagers (☎02.31.89.05.28). Right in the thick of things, two small dining rooms crammed into a little house all but next door to the Lieutenance. Menus from 85F/€12.96, with clams and mussels, but very unadventurous main courses. Closed Mon & Dec.

Au P'tit Mareyeur, 4 rue Haute (☎02.31.98.84.23). No distance from the centre, but all the seating is indoors and there are no views. Very good fish dishes – red-crab soup with garlic – plus plenty of creamy *pays d'Auge* sauces and superb desserts. The main menu, at 125F/€19.06, includes skate marinated in coriander; for a 40F/€6.10 supplement you can also enjoy warm oysters. Closed Mon & Tues.

Taverne de la Mer, 35 rue Haute (☎02.31.89.57.77). Small converted bar not far from place Hamelin, with no outdoor seating, but a magnificent selection of fresh seafood, including specialities grilled on an open wood fire. The main set menu, at 125F/€19.06, consists almost entirely of fish, with main courses such as Basque-style tuna steaks, though there is a token "*pièce de viande*"; you can also get a large *assiette de fruits de mer* for a similar price, or lesser menus at 75F/€11.43 and 95F/€14.48. Closed Mon & Tues lunch.

La Tortue, 36 rue de l'Homme de Bois (☎02.31.98.87.91). A welcoming place near the Musée Boudin, where 100F/€15.24 buys a great-value five-course meal, and there's even a 77F/€11.74 vegetarian menu, consisting of apple soup or vegetables followed by cheese or salad. Closed Tues, plus mid-Jan to mid-Feb.

Le Vieux Honfleur, 13 quai St-Étienne (☎02.31.89.15.31). The best of the restaurants around the harbour itself, with spacious alfresco dining – in shade at lunchtime – on the pedestrianized eastern side of the harbour. Very simple menus, but the seafood is very good, as befits prices starting at 175F/€26.68. Closed Jan.

Along the Côte Fleurie

For the 15km **west along the corniche** from Honfleur to Trouville, green fields and fruit trees line the land's edge, and cliffs rise from sandy beaches. The resorts, **Villerville** most conspicuously, aren't cheap, but they're relatively undeveloped, and if you want to stop by the seaside this is the place to do it.

Trouville and Deauville

The adjacent towns of Trouville and Deauville lie within a stone's throw of each other to either side of the mouth of the River Touques, sharing many of their amenities, and also their rather exclusive reputations.

    TROUVILLE retains at least some semblance of a real town, with a constant population and industries other than tourism. But it is primarily a resort, and has been ever since Napoléon III started bringing his court here for the summer in the 1860s (his empress, Eugénie, fled France from here in 1870 in the yacht of an English admirer). A long promenade marks the boundary between the sands and the succession of spectacular villas such as *L'Hôtel des Roches Noires* that line the beach, patterned with complex brickwork and topped by ornate turrets; several were painted by Monet during a visit in 1870. Slightly further back, a tangle of busy pedestrian streets are alive with restaurants and hotels.

    One of Emperor Napoléon's dukes, looking across the river, saw not marshlands but money, and lots of it, in the form of a **racecourse**. His vision materialized, and villas appeared between the racecourse and the sea to become **DEAUVILLE**. Now you can lose money on the horses, cross five streets to lose more in the casino, where Winston Churchill spent the summer of 1906 gambling every night until 5am, and finally lose yourself in the 200m of sports and "cure" facilities, and private bathing huts, that intervene before the *planches*. Beyond this 500m of duckwalk, rows of primary-coloured parasols obscure the sea.

    If you're tempted to **gamble** in Deauville's casino, formal attire is compulsory, and you have to pay a temporary membership fee of around 100F/€15.24 to be allowed anywhere near the tables. One more congenial reason to visit is the **American Film Festival** held in Deauville in the first week of September – a festival that's the antithesis of Cannes, with public admission to a wide selection of previews, but that still attracts stars on the level of, in 2000, Clint Eastwood and Harrison Ford.

Practicalities

Trouville and Deauville share their **gare SNCF** (served by trains from Paris via Lisieux) and **gare routière** (☎02.31.88.95.36), in between the two just south of the marina. Each day, seven of the hourly buses from Caen continue along the coast to Honfleur.

Visits to the **tourist office** on place de la Mairie in Deauville (Mon–Sat 9am–12.30pm & 2–6.30pm, Sun 11am–4pm; ☎02.31.14.40.00, *www.deauville.org*), or the one at 32 quai F. Moureaux in Trouville (April–June, Sept & Oct Mon–Sat 9.30am–noon & 2–6.30pm, Sun 10.30am–12.30pm; July & Aug Mon–Sat 9.30am–7pm, Sun 10am–4pm; Nov–March Mon–Sat 9.30am–noon & 2–6pm, Sun 10.30am–12.30pm; ☎02.31.14.60.70, *ot.trouville@wanadoo.fr*), are repaid with the usual lavish brochures.

As you might imagine, **hotels** tend to be either luxurious or overpriced. The *Café-Hôtel des Sports*, 27 rue Gambetta (☎02.31.88.22.67; ③; closed Sun in winter), behind Deauville's fish market, is the least expensive, while *Le Trouville*, 1 rue Thiers (☎02.31.98.45.48; ③; closed Jan), is Trouville's closest equivalent. If you do fancy staying right on the seafront, it's hard to beat the *Flaubert*, rue Gustave-Flaubert (☎02.31.88.37.23; street view ④, sea view ⑤), a grand faux-timbered mansion with a plethora of beachside balconies at the start of Trouville's board-walk, which is home to the recommended *Le Vivier* restaurant. Alternatively, Trouville does have a **campsite**, *Le Chant des Oiseaux* (☎02.31.88.06.42; closed Oct–March).

Chez Miocque at 81 rue Eugène-Colas in Deauville (☎02.31.88.09.52) is a top-quality Parisian-style **bistro** with prices that are high but not outrageous. Good **fish restaurants** in Trouville include *Les Vapeurs*, opposite the attractive old half-timbered fish market at 160 bd F-Moureaux (☎02.31.88.15.24), and *La Petite Auberge*, 7 rue Carnot (☎02.31.88.11.07; closed Tues & Wed in winter), though both get very crowded at weekends.

Villers-sur-mer

To the west of Deauville, the shoreline at first stays flat, and the main coast road passes through a succession of what are almost suburban resorts – significantly less snobbish than Trouville and Deauville, but equally crowded and equally short of inexpensive hotels. At the largest of these, **VILLERS-SUR-MER**, you're greeted by a true triumph of topiary; a giant **brontosaurus**, interrupting its browsing on the central seafront roundabout to raise its long neck skywards. Villers is also noteworthy for straddling the Greenwich Meridian, which runs right through the three-star local **campsite**, *Camping Bellevue* (☎02.31.87.05.21; closed Nov–March).

Houlgate

A hundred years ago, **HOULGATE**, 7km west of Villers-sur-mer, was every bit as glamorous and sophisticated a destination as its neighbours. What makes it different today is that it has barely changed since then. Its long straight beach remains lined by a stately procession of ornate Victorian villas, with what few commercial enterprises the town supports confined to the narrow parallel street, the **rue des Bains**, around 50m inland. As a result, Houlgate is the most relaxed of the local resorts, ideal if you're looking for a peaceful family break where the only stress is deciding whether to paddle or play mini-golf.

So long as you keep an eye on the tides, it's possible to walk between Villers and Houlgate along the foot of the **Vaches Noires** (Black Cows) cliffs, which force the main road at this point up and away from the sea. However, industrial Le Havre is a bit too visible across the water for it to be an especially picturesque stroll.

Practicalities

Houlgate's **tourist office** is by the main roundabout as you come into town from the east, on boulevard des Belges (mid-June to mid-Sept Mon–Sat 9am–7pm, Sun 9am–12.30pm & 2–7pm; mid-Sept to mid-June Mon–Sat 9am–12.30pm & 2–6.30pm; ☎02.31.24.34.79, *houlgate@wanadoo.fr*). For **accommodation**, you could try the *Hostellerie Normandie*, just off the rue des Bains at 11 rue E.Deschanel (☎02.31.28.77.77; ③; closed mid-Oct to mid-March, plus Mon evening & Tues in low season), a pretty little hotel covered with ivy and creeping flowers, with a 65F/€9.91 lunch menu on which you can follow half a dozen oysters with a plate of *moules frites*. Nearby, at 17 rue des Bains, the more formal red-brick *Le 1900* (☎02.31.28.77.77; ③; closed Mon evening & Tues in low season) holds a glassed-in Belle Époque bistro where dinner menus start at 98F/€14.94.

Above the cliffs on the corniche road east of town, *La Ferme Auberge des Aulnettes* (☎02.31.28.00.28; ③; closed Jan, plus Tues evening & Wed in low season), is a lovely country house set in pleasant gardens, with a good restaurant and room to sit outside in the evening. The best **campsite** in the area, the four-star *Les Falaises* (☎02.31.24.81.09; closed Nov–March), is not far away, though technically in the separate community of **Gonneville-sur-Mer**.

Dives

Immediately west of Houlgate, the main D513 is forced to detour away from the open sea when it reaches the mouth of the River Divette. The venerable little port of **DIVES** here was the spot from which William the Conqueror sailed for Hastings, by way of St-Valéry; contemporary chronicles tell of vast stockpiles of supplies accumulating on the beach in the days preceding the invasion. Now, like Honfleur, pushed well back from the sea, Dives has little in common with its haughty aristocratic neighbour, Cabourg, across the river, although Marcel Proust's dream vision "land's end church of Balbec" is the town's **Notre Dame** church.

A lively **Saturday market** focuses around the ancient wooden *halles*, tucked away south of the main through-road. The steep tiled roof of the *halles* must be five times the height of its walls, and its venerable weather-beaten timbers are held together by tight metal bands; on market days, it's crammed with mouthwatering delicacies and Norman specialities, while more mundane produce and imported jeans are sold in the square alongside and up and down the narrow streets. The town hosts a **puppet festival** in early August.

Dives has an inexpensive **hotel**, the *de la Gare* at 10 pace Trefouet (☎02.31.91.24.52; ②; closed Dec & Jan), and there's a year-round **campsite** on the way to Cabourg (and two more off the Cabourg–Lisieux road).

Cabourg

At **CABOURG**, you are confronted by little more than an exercise in style – a pure creation for a certain aged class, contemporary with Deauville and seemingly stuck entirely in the nineteenth century. There's an awful lot of town planning, but not really any town.

PROUST IN CABOURG

As both child and adult, between 1881 and 1914, Marcel Proust stayed repeatedly at the *Grand Hôtel* in Cabourg. The town is the "Balbec" of *Du Côté de Chez Swann*, and the hotel itself – now officially located on the boulevard Marcel-Proust – thrives on its Proustian connection. All guests are served with a *madeleine* for breakfast, and Proust's own room is available at a cost of over 1200F/€185 per night (not the most expensive in the hotel by any means). The rock star Sting stayed in that very room in 1991, and drank from the same well of inspiration. The main dining room, which has a superb sea view, is now called *Le Balbec*. For the ambivalent Proust it was "the aquarium"; each night locals would press their faces to its window in wonder at the luxurious life within, "as extraordinary to the poor as the life of strange fishes or molluscs".

At the centre of the straightest promenade in France, the **Grand Hôtel** looks out towards the sea, while behind it the crescent that defines the formal **Jardins du Casino** is the first of several concentric crescents, spreading out like ripples and lined with large, placid, undistinguished – and usually empty – houses. Cabourg makes an unlikely twin town for the raucous, downmarket gambling mecca of Atlantic City, New Jersey; notices for example request that you "avoid noise on the beach", and picnics are forbidden.

Practicalities

Trains run all the way from Paris Gare St-Lazare to the **gare SNCF** that Cabourg shares with Dives (see opposite) every day in July and August, and otherwise at weekends only. Arriving by **bus** – it's on the Caen–Honfleur route (#20) – you'll be dropped off at the gardens on avenue Pasteur; walk through them and turn right down avenue de la Mer to reach the Jardins du Casino.

The **tourist office** in the casino gardens (July & Aug daily 9.30am–7pm; Sept–June Mon–Sat 9.30am–12.30pm & 2–6.30pm, Sun 10am–12.30pm & 2.30–6pm; ☎02.31.91.20.00, *www.cabourg.net*) has full details on **hotels**. The best value, and the quietest, is the *Oie qui Fume*, at 18 av de la Brèche-Buhot (☎02.31.91.27.79; ③; closed Jan to mid-Feb, plus Mon evening, Tues & Wed in low season), 100m back from the sea on a peaceful road half a dozen streets west of the centre; its 138F/€21.04 menu features goose (*oie*) as either starter or main course. The similarly half-timbered *Hôtel de Paris*, 39 av de la Mer (☎02.31.91.31.34; ④), is more central, on Cabourg's only commercial (semi-pedestrianized) street, and offers slightly smarter rooms. It has no restaurant, but its bottom floor holds a café that serves juices and snacks. In any case, *La Crémaillère*, two doors down at no. 41 (☎02.31.91.14.40), has menus at all prices, and there are plenty of pizzerias and snack bars nearby. If money is no object, you can always stay in the seafront *Grand Hôtel Mercure*, promenade Marcel-Proust (☎02.31.91.01.79; ⑨), where both the views and the prices are tremendous; unless you go for Marcel's own room, however (see box, above), you may not find it quite as luxurious as you might expect.

Franceville

Continuing along the coast towards Caen, in **FRANCEVILLE** the main road passes a half-timbered *logis*, the *Hôtel le Vauban*, at 8 rte du Cabourg (☎02.31.24.23.37;

③); closed Tues evening & Wed), with adequate rooms and good food, and the bizarre *Le Surfer*, a disco concealed in a former German radar station. Rusty cars parked haphazardly to either side of the main coast road betray the proximity of good **surfing** beaches just beyond the dunes.

A little further on, you can turn right, across what used to be Pegasus Bridge (see p.133), for direct access to Ouistreham and the Landing Beaches.

Caen

Appropriately enough for a city that has been fought over throughout its long history, the name of **CAEN**, capital and largest city of Basse Normandie, originally came from a Celtic word meaning "battlefield". This site was first fortified in 1060 by William the Conqueror, who preferred it to Rouen because it was further from the marauding Franks, and because the navigable river Orne afforded him safe access to the Channel. During the succeeding centuries, Caen repeatedly changed hands, and was twice sacked by the English: first by Edward III in 1246, and then by Henry V in 1417. In 1432, Henry VI of England founded the university here, but Caen has been French since Charles VII took it back in 1450.

The modern city began to take shape when a canal to the sea was completed in 1850, running parallel to the heavily silted Orne. At the same time, the Bassin St-Pierre was built, creating a central marina that is now reminiscent of the "port" in Vannes (see p.368). The smaller River Odon was covered over, and the number of bridges across the Orne was doubled. **World War II**, however, devastated the city. It was the prime target of the Allied invasion in June 1944, and historians still argue as to quite why it took so long to capture. The "Battle of Caen" lasted two full months – even after the Canadians entered the city four weeks after D-Day, the southern bank of the river remained in enemy hands. Three-quarters of the town had to be destroyed before they were finally dislodged.

Caen today is not a place where you're likely to spend much time, though in parts it remains highly impressive. The central feature is a ring of ramparts that no longer has a castle to protect, and, though there are the scattered spires and buttresses of two abbeys and eight old churches, roads and roundabouts fill the wide spaces where prewar houses stood. Approaches are along thunderous dual-carriageways through industrial suburbs, now prospering once more following an influx of high-tech newcomers.

Arrival and information

Caen's **gare SNCF** (☎02.31.83.50.50) is 1km south of the town centre across the river, with the **gare routière** so close at hand that you can walk directly to it from Platform 1. **Long-distance buses** from here include those run by Bus Verts, at 11 rue des Chanoines (☎08.01.21.42.14). Line #30 goes to Bayeux; #32 to Vire; #35 to Falaise; and #20 to Dives, Deauville, Trouville and Honfleur.

The Brittany Ferries service from Portsmouth, promoted as sailing to Caen, in fact docks at **Ouistreham**, 15km north (see p.131). Buses from Caen's *gare routière* connect with each sailing, and Bus Verts' express bus #1 runs the same route.

△ Bayeux & the Caen Memorial

CAEN

0   100 m

ACCOMMODATION
Bernières	9
Central	6
Cordeliers	1
Courtonne	2
Dauphin	3
Foyer Robert-Remé	11
Ibis	4
Quatrans	5
St-Étienne	7
St-Jean	10
Univers	8

RESTAURANTS
l'Alcide	F
le Boeuf Ferré	E
le Bouchon de Vaugueux	D
le Gastronome	G
l'Insolité	A
Maître Corbeau	C
la Petite Auberge	H
les Quatre Épices	B

△ & Camping OMJ

CTAC, the extensive **local bus** service (☎02.31.15.55.50), makes a one-way circuit through town between the Tour le Roi stop just north of the pleasure port and the *gare SNCF*, travelling north up avenue du 6-Juin and south down rue St-Jean. Digital displays at the main stops show when the next bus is due, and free timetables are available from CTAC, 11 bd Maréchal-Leclerc, and the tourist office.

The **tourist office** is in the central Hôtel d'Escoville, at 14 place St-Pierre across the street from the church of St-Pierre (July & Aug Mon–Sat 10am–7pm, Sun 10am–1pm & 2–5pm; Sept–June Mon–Sat 10am–1pm & 2–6pm, Sun 10am–1pm; ☎02.31.27.14.14, *www.ville-caen.fr*); it's a beautiful sixteenth-century house, typical of the early Renaissance in Caen, with a strong Italian influence evident in its Florentine flourishes. Here you can pick up a copy of the free weekly *Caen Scope* for details of forthcoming events in the city, while with a *télécarte*, you can also use a computer terminal to access the **Internet**. The main **post office** is on place Gambetta (postcode 14000; Mon–Fri 8am–7pm, Sat 8am–noon; ☎02.31.39.35.78).

Accommodation

Caen has a great number of **hotels**, though as ever in the bomb-damaged cities of Normandy, few could be called attractive; even those that advertise their antiquity tend to have been totally rebuilt. The main concentrations are near the *gare SNCF*, around the pleasure port, and just west of the castle and tourist office – the latter being particularly convenient for motorists heading to or from the ferry. There are also a number of charmless motel-type places on the ring road around town. With plenty of dedicated restaurants in town, few hotels other than those specifically mentioned below bother to provide food.

Caen's summer-only, members-only **hostel** is at the *Foyer Robert-Remé* at 68bis rue E.-Restout, Grâce-de-Dieu (☎02.31.52.19.96; closed Oct–May), about 500m southwest of the *gare SNCF*. Though it's in an otherwise somewhat sleepy part of town, the hostel itself is lively and welcoming enough. Beds in both four-bed dorms, or two-bed private rooms, cost 62F/€9.45 per person. Take bus #17 from the town centre (stop "Tour le Roi") or *gare SNCF*, direction "Grâce-de-Dieu", getting off at stop "Lycée Fresnil". The two-star municipal **campsite** (☎02.31.73.60.92; closed Oct to mid-May) is nearby, beside the river Orne, on route de Louvigny (bus #13, direction "Louvigny", stop "Camping").

Hotels

Hôtel Bernières, 50 rue de Bernières (☎02.31.86.01.26, fax 02.31.86.51.76, *www .hotelbernieres.com*). Bright, central and very good-value hotel, halfway between the churches of St-Pierre and St-Jean. ②.

Central Hôtel, 23 place J.-Letellier (☎02.31.86.18.52, fax 02.31.86.88.11). By Caen standards a budget hotel; not as quiet as it used to be, but very central. Good views of the château from the balconies of the higher rooms (but no lift to get up to them). ②.

Hôtel des Cordeliers, 4 rue des Cordeliers (☎02.31.86.37.15, fax 02.31.39.56.51). Friendly hotel with a wide range of rooms, in small side street near the castle, and a bar. Closed Sun. ②.

Hôtel Courtonne, place Courtonne (☎02.31.93.47.83, fax 02.31.93.50.50). Very welcoming modernized hotel, overlooking the pleasure port, that's so narrow it's easy to miss. All rooms have bath or shower, phone and TV. ③.

Hôtel-Restaurant le Dauphin, 29 rue Gémare (☎02.31.86.22.26, fax 02.31.86.35.14, *dauphin.caen@wanadoo.fr*). Upmarket, central Best Western hotel, tucked away behind the tourist office. Part of it was a priory during the eighteenth century, not that you'd ever guess; the rooms are comfortable without being exciting in any way. Grand restaurant, with a 110F/€16.77 weekday menu; weekend menus 175F/€26.68 and 260F/€39.64. Closed Sat & mid-July to early Aug. ⑤–⑨.

Hôtel Ibis, place Courtonne (☎02.31.95.88.88, fax 02.31.43.80.80). Smart modern chain hotel overlooking the port de Plaisance, offering reliable creature comforts plus its own brasserie (open until 11pm nightly) and bar. ④.

Hôtel des Quatrans, 17 rue Gémare (☎02.31.86.25.57, fax 02.31.85.27.80, *www .hoteldesquatrans.com*). A little way behind the tourist office, but unmissable thanks to its garish neon sign. The pastel theme of the facade continues inside; some might find it all a bit cloying, but the service is friendly, and at least everything works. Cheaper rooms are without showers. ②.

Hôtel St-Étienne, 2 rue de l'Académie (☎02.31.86.35.82, fax 02.31.85.57.69). Friendly budget hotel in an old stone house in the characterful St-Martin district, not far from the Abbaye des Hommes. The cheapest rooms do not have showers. ②.

Hôtel St-Jean, 20 rue des Martyrs (☎02.31.86.23.35, fax 02.31.86.74.15). Simple but well-equipped rooms – all have shower or bath – facing St-Jean church near the *Petite Auberge* (see p.130). ②.

Hôtel de l'Univers, 12 quai Vendeuvre (☎02.31.85.46.14, fax 02.31.38.21.33). Small, plain but perfectly acceptable budget option near the port de Plaisance. All rooms have shower or bath. ②.

The City

A virtue has been made of the necessity of clearing away the rubble of Caen's medieval houses, which formerly pressed up against its ancient **château ramparts**. The resulting open green space means that those walls are now fully visible for the first time in centuries. In turn, walking the circuit of the ramparts gives a good overview of the city, with a particularly fine prospect of the reconstructed fourteenth-century facade of the nearby church of **St-Pierre**. Some magnificent Renaissance stonework has survived intact at the church's east end.

Within the castle walls, it's possible to visit the former **Exchequer** – which dates from shortly after the Norman Conquest of England, and was the scene of a banquet thrown by Richard the Lionheart en route to the Crusades – and inspect a garden that has been replanted with the kind of herbs and medicinal plants that would have been cultivated here during the Middle Ages. Also inside the precinct, though not in original structures, are two **museums**. Most visitors will probably prefer the **Beaux Arts**, housed in a light 1960s stone building, kept deliberately low to avoid topping the castle walls (daily except Tues 9.30am–6pm; 25F/€3.81, free on Wed). Its upstairs galleries trace a potted history of European art from Renaissance Italy through such Dutch masters as Breughel the Younger (whose *Census of Bethlehem* includes boys throwing snowballs) up to grand portraits from eighteenth-century France. Downstairs brings things up to date with some powerful twentieth-century art – though there are few big-name works – as well as paintings by Monet, Bonnard and Gustave Doré (represented by a spectacular Scottish landscape). The other museum, the **Musée de Normandie** (daily except Tues 9.30am–12.30pm & 2–6pm; 10F/€1.52, free on Wed), provides a surprisingly cursory overview of Norman history, ranging from archeological finds like stone tools from the megalithic period and glass jewellery from Gallo-Roman Rouen to artefacts from the Industrial Revolution.

Just to the north of the château lies the complex of **university** buildings, originally founded in 1432 by Henry VI of England, and now the proud home of the largest nuclear particle accelerator in Europe. The only reason for tourists to pass this way is to see the large-scale **model of Ancient Rome**, as it stood around 300 AD, which has been laid out in the Maison de la Recherche en Sciences Humaines (guided visits: July & Aug Mon, Wed & Fri 11am, 2.15pm & 4pm; Sept–June Sat 2pm; 10F/€1.52).

When William the Conqueror married Matilda in Eu (see p.70), in 1051, both incurred excommunication. Historians argue as to the precise nature of their offence – they may have been distant cousins – but Pope Nicholas II only agreed to sanction their marriage and readmit them to the church in 1059 upon the solemn vow that each would build an abbey in Caen. William's, the **Abbaye aux Hommes** to the west of the city centre, is focused on the Romanesque church known as the **Abbatiale Ste-Étienne** (daily 8.15am–noon & 2–7.30pm; free; 1hr 15min guided tours leave adjacent Hôtel de Ville daily 9.30am, 11am, 2.30pm & 4pm; 10F/€1.52). The abbey was originally designed to hold his tomb, but his burial here, in 1087, was hopelessly undignified. The funeral procession first caught fire and was then held to ransom, as various factions squabbled over his rotting corpse for any spoils they could grab. A further interruption came when a man halted the service to object that the grave had been constructed without compensation on the site of his family house, and the assembled nobles had to pay him off before William could finally be laid to rest. His tomb still occupies pride of place in front of the main altar, though the church was subsequently ransacked both by Protestants in 1562 and during the Revolution, so it now holds at most a solitary thighbone rescued from the river. Still, the building itself serves as a wonderful monument – although not enhanced by the latest desecration, "multilingual, computerized audiovisual visits" – and is also home to a fine collection of seventeenth- to nineteenth-century paintings. As you explore, look out for the huge wooden clock to the left of the altar.

The **Hôtel de Ville** alongside, which all but obscures the abbey, is housed in what used to be its convent buildings – hence the surprising harmony with which the two blend together.

William's queen, Mathilda, lies across the town in the **Abbaye aux Dames** at the end of rue des Chanoines. She had commissioned the building of the abbey church, La Trinité, well before the Conquest. It's starkly impressive, with a gloomy pillared crypt, superb stained glass behind the altar, and odd sculptural details like the fish curled up in the holy-water stoup (guided tours daily 2.30pm & 4pm; free).

The nineteenth-century **Bassin St-Pierre**, a short walk south of the Abbaye aux Dames, now serves as Caen's pleasure port, and marks the end of the canal that links the city to the sea. In summer, it's one of the liveliest areas in town, although, considering the crowds, it holds surprisingly few pavement cafés.

The Caen Memorial

Daily: mid-Jan to mid-Feb, Nov & Dec 9am–6pm, last entry 4.45pm; mid-Feb to June, Sept & Oct 9am–7pm, last entry 5.45pm; July & Aug 9am–8pm, last entry 6.45pm; closed first fortnight of Jan. ☎02.31.06.06.44 (note the significance), *www.unicaen.fr/memorial*. Adults 74F/€11.28, students, 10–19-year-olds and over-65s 65F/€9.91, under-10s and World War II veterans free. Served by buses #17 (Mon–Sat) and #S (Sun) from Tour le Roi. See p.131 for details of tours of the Landing Beaches.

The **Caen Memorial** is a war museum with a big and very welcome difference, in that it proclaims itself to be a "Museum for Peace", and for the most part succeeds admirably in that intention. Located on a plateau named after General Eisenhower, just north of Caen at the end of avenue Marshal-Montgomery, it was funded by the governments of the US, Britain, Canada, Germany, Poland, Czechoslovakia and the former USSR, as well as France, and stands immediately above the headquarters used by the German army during June and July 1944.

All visitors have to follow a prescribed route through the ultramodern building, which, with a slightly heavy-handed literalism, leads on a downwards spiral from World War I and the Treaty of Versailles towards the maelstrom of World War II. From the start you hear the voice of Hitler booming in the distance; his image recurs with increasing size and frequency on screens beside you as the events of the 1920s and 1930s are recounted.

The war itself is superbly documented, with a greater emphasis on the minutiae of everyday life in occupied France than on military technology. Nothing is glossed over in the attempt to provide a fully rounded picture of the nation under occupation and at war. The collaborationist Vichy government is set in its context without being excused, with such statements as Pierre Laval's "I wish for the victory of Germany, because without it Bolshevism will spread everywhere" on prominent display alongside a book of the "99 most touching answers of French schoolchildren to the question 'Why do you love Maréchal Petain?' ". Secret Nazi reports show how Resistance activity in Normandy grew as the war continued, and what reprisals were taken.

Visits to the upper section of the memorial culminate with three films, each in a separate auditorium. The first is a harrowing account of D-Day itself; the second traces the course of the rest of the war; and the third looks at the winners of the Nobel peace prize in arguing for the need to establish lasting peace in the world.

The former German bunkers at the foot of the hillside, reached by a short elevator ride from the memorial proper, have been refurbished as the **Nobel Peace Prizewinners' Gallery**. Portraits and short essays commemorate each recipient in turn, placing their achievements in contexts, and also point out notable omissions from the list, such as Mahatma Gandhi. Outside, various formal gardens have been laid out to honour the different Allied nations.

All in all, this museum creates something new in a genre which can occasionally seem morally suspect, and the display cannot be recommended too highly for anyone with a serious interest in the war and its lasting legacy. Allow at least two hours for a visit, as the films alone occupy a whole hour. If you feel like a break, there's a good-value self-service restaurant upstairs.

Eating

The centre of Caen offers two major areas for **eating**. The attractive pedestrianized **quartier Vaugueux** features cosmopolitan restaurants such as the *Kouba*, serving up couscous dishes, the creole *Au Pommier des Îles*, and *Tongasoa*, specializing in the fishy cuisine of the Seychelles, while the streets off **rue de Geôle**, near the western ramparts, particularly rue des Croisiers and rue Gémare, house rather more traditional French restaurants. There are also several restaurants and brasseries facing the *gare SNCF*, of which many are either in, or connected with, hotels.

Restaurants

L'Alcide, 1 place Courtonne (☎02.31.44.18.06). Very conspicuous, albeit rather anonymous-looking, bistro-style place, which turns out to be surprisingly good, serving classic French dishes cooked with great attention to detail. Menus from 82F/€12.50 up to 135F/€20.58. Closed Sat.

Le Boeuf Ferré, 10 rue des Croisiers (☎02.31.85.36.40). Gourmet restaurant, all indoors, with stone walls and timbered ceiling, serving rich and substantial meals; foie gras is the house speciality, as featured on the no-choice 135F/€20.58 menu, and there's always plenty of duck and red meat. Midday menu 75F/€11.43, dinners from 95F/€14.48. Closed Mon & Sun evening, also the first fortnight in March and the second fortnight in July.

Le Bouchon du Vaugueux, 12 rue du Graindorge (☎02.31.44.26.26). Intimate little brasserie in the Vaugueux quarter, offering a daily lunch menu at 69F/€10.52, good-value salads from around 49F/€7.47, and dinner menus from 96F/€14.64. Closed Mon evening, Sun, and first three weeks of Aug.

Le Gastronome, 43 rue St-Sauveur (☎02.31.86.57.75). Smart, modern restaurant, between the château and the Abbaye aux Hommes, offering a changing but consistently good 138F/€21.04 menu of Norman specialities, and a good-value 99F/€15.09 menu on weekdays. Closed Sat lunch, Sun evening & first fortnight of Aug.

L'Insolité, 16 rue du Vaugueux (☎02.31.43.87.87). Attractive half-timbered restaurant with terrace and indoor seating in the Vaugueux district. There's a 65F/€9.91 vegetarian menu offering a "symphonie des crudités", but the main emphasis is on seafood, with a 95F/€14.48 menu that features a trio of steamed fish, and a knockout 250F/€38.11 *Prestige* menu. Closed Sun evening, plus Mon in low season.

Maître Corbeau, 8 rue Bouquet (☎02.31.93.93.00). Fondue is the speciality in this eccentric little place, and they won't let you forget it, festooning the whole place with cheesy iconography.

A typical fondue costs around 80F/€12.20, while set menus start from 92F/€14.03. Closed Sat lunch, Sun & first three weeks of Aug.

La Petite Auberge, 17 rue des Équipes-d'Urgence (☎02.31.86.43.30). Plain and simple restaurant, with a nice view of the St-Jean church. Very-good-value Norman specialities – and a daily 68F/€10.37 menu that doesn't force you to eat tripe. Closed Sun evening, Mon & first three weeks of Aug.

Les Quatres Épices, 25 rue Porte-au-Berger (☎02.31.93.40.41). Lively West African restaurant, just off rue du Vaugueux. Everything is à la carte – prawns with sweet potato for 95F/€14.48, grilled fish with ginger for 76F/€11.59, plus plantains and meat galore – and African music plays nonstop.

Shopping

Most of the centre of Caen is taken up with busy new **shopping** developments and pedestrian precincts, where the cafés are distinguished by such names as *Fast Food Glamour Vault*. The shops are good, possibly the best in Normandy or Brittany, if Parisian style is what you're after. Outlets of the big Parisian department stores – and of the aristocrats' grocers, Hédiard, in the Cours des Halles – are here, along with good local rivals. Rue Écuyère has a fine assortment of shops full of unusual and cheap oddments, antiques, stuff for collectors and jokes.

If you're looking for books, records or tickets for local events, call in at the branch of FNAC (☎02.31.39.41.00) in the Centre Paul-Doumer, on the corner of rue Doumer and rue Bras. The main city **market** takes place on Friday, spreading along both sides of Fosse St-Julien, and there's also a Sunday market in place Courtonne.

The Invasion Beaches

Despite the best efforts of Stephen Spielberg, it is all but impossible now to picture the scene at dawn on **D-Day**, June 6, 1944, when Allied troops landed at points along the Norman coast from the mouth of the Orne to Les Dunes de Varneville on the Cotentin Peninsula.* For the most part, these are innocuous beaches backed by gentle dunes, and yet this foothold in Europe was won at the cost of 100,000 lives. That the invasion happened here, and not nearer to Germany, was partly due to the failure of the Canadian raid on Dieppe (see p.67) in 1942. The ensuing **Battle of Normandy** killed thousands of civilians and reduced nearly 600 towns and villages to rubble, but within a week of its eventual conclusion Paris was liberated.

The **beaches** are still often referred to by their wartime code names. The British and Commonwealth forces landed on **Sword**, **Juno** and **Gold** beaches between Ouistreham and Arromanches; the Americans, further west on **Omaha** and **Utah** beaches. Bits of shrapnel can still be found in the sands, six decades later, but more substantial traces of the fighting are rare. At Arromanches the remains are visible of one of the prefabricated Mulberry harbours that made such large-scale landings possible, while at Pointe du Hoc the cliff heights are still deeply pitted with German bunkers and shell-holes. Elsewhere, the reminders are **cemeteries** – British and Commonwealth, American and German, each highly distinct in character – and **war museums**, examples of which you'll find in almost every coastal town.

The "D" in "D-Day" stands simply for "day"; hence it is known as J-Jour in France.

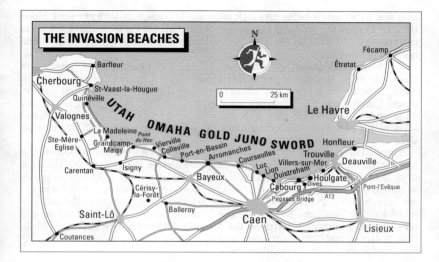

The D-Day events provide a focus for most foreign visitors to this part of the coast; travelling through, you are bound to come across veterans, and their descendants, paying their respects. Taken simply as holiday territory, however, the villages and towns offer their own rewards. They are traditional seaside resorts, without the inflated prices or flashiness of the Deauville area – old-fashioned seafront villages, with rows of boarding houses and little wooden bathing huts that must have been kept in storage somewhere during the war. And increasingly there is windsurfing on offer – better suited to these north-facing resorts than chilly bathing.

Bus Verts run all along this coast. **From Bayeux**, bus #74 goes to Arromanches and Courseulles, and bus #70 to Port-en-Bessin and Vierville. **From Caen**, bus #30 runs directly inland to Isigny via Bayeux, express bus #1 to Ouistreham, and express bus #3 to Courseulles. In July and August, Bus Verts also run a special **D-Day Line**, which for a 100F/€15.24 flat fare departs daily from Caen's *gare routière* and place Courtonne at 9.30am, calls at Courseulles, and stops for four hours at Arromanches, 45 minutes at the US cemetery, and 40 minutes at the Pointe du Hoc, before returning to Caen around 6pm.

In addition, the Caen Memorial (see p.128) organizes bilingual **guided tours** of the landing beaches all year round, which include four hours on the road plus a visit to the memorial at your own pace (April, May & Sept daily 1pm; June–Aug daily 9am & 2pm; Oct–March Sat & Sun 1pm; 380F/€57.93). Companies running tours from Bayeux include Bus Fly (☎02.31.22.00.08, *www.busfly.com*) and Normandy Tours (☎02.31.92.10.70).

Ouistreham-Riva Bella

The small community of **OUISTREHAM-RIVA BELLA**, on the coast 15km north of Caen and connected to it by a fast dual carriageway, still gives the impression that it can barely believe its luck at having become a major ferry port. Since Brittany Ferries started their regular service here from Portsmouth in 1986, the easternmost of the D-Day resorts has developed an extensive array of reasonable hotels and restaurants.

The town itself is not especially appealing, and most arriving passengers choose to press straight on out – this is one of the Channel's simpler ports to leave, as boats dock just a few hundred metres from the small central square, **place Courbonne**. Ouistreham's road system, at least in summer, is still not quite up to the task of coping with the volume of traffic, and motorists should allow plenty of time to catch their boats. All services are connected by bus with Caen.

If instead of setting off for Caen you head directly west along the coast from the ferry terminal, you come within a few hundred metres to the long straight main drag of **beach** – the **Riva Bella** itself. This is progressively shedding its somewhat run-down image; the large casino has been remodelled as a 1930s passenger liner, housing an expensive restaurant and cocktail bar, and even the old-fashioned bathing huts have had a fresh lick of paint. Nearby, the long-standing and now relatively uninspiring **Musée du Mur de l'Atlantique** (daily: mid-Feb to May & Oct to mid-Nov 10am–noon & 2–6pm; June–Sept 9am–7pm; 35F/€5.34) records the local Sword Beach landings.

Practicalities

Brittany Ferries services (☎08.03.82.88.28, *www.brittany-ferries.com*) are detailed on p.5. The **tourist office** is in place Alfred-Thomas, alongside the casino on the beach (April–June & Sept daily 10am–12.30pm & 3–6pm; July & Aug daily 10am–1pm & 2–7pm; Oct–March Mon–Sat 10.30am–12.30pm & 3–6pm, Sun 10.30am–12.30pm; ☎02.31.97.18.63, *www.ot.ouistreham.fr*). **Bikes** can be rented from Vérel, 77 av Foch (☎02.31.97.19.04), or the Cyclorama on the seafront (☎02.31.96.47.47), which also offers family-sized pedal cars for group excursions. If you're **cycling**, south from town, incidentally, the dedicated cycle path that follows the canal all the way to the centre of Caen makes a far more pleasant start to a holiday than the main road.

Several cafés and brasseries in the place Courbonne, immediately outside the *gare maritime*, are eager to liberate passengers from their spare change, while *Le Channel*, just around the corner at 79 av Michel-Cabieu (☎02.31.96.51.69; ②), is just about the best value for both **eating and sleeping**. Menus in the restaurant start with the 55F/€8.38 *menu pêcheur*, which includes mussels, while the 88F/€13.42 and 144F/€21.95 options increase in splendour; the guestrooms are in a separate building across the street. Alternatively, try the smart *Le Normandie et le Chalut*, a few doors down at 71 av Michel-Cabieu (☎02.31.97.19.57, *www.lenormandie.com*; ④; closed mid-Dec to mid-Jan, plus Sun evening & Mon Nov–March), which has pleasant, quiet rooms. Its "Normand" menu at 95F/€14.48 features a lethal triple plate of tripe, *andouille* and *boudin noir*, while the 199F/€30.34 option makes an excellent last-night blowout – even if ostrich steak isn't exactly typical of the region. Good-value hotels near the beach include the *Hôtel de la Plage* at 39–41 av Pasteur (☎02.31.96.85.16; ②; closed Nov–Feb), and the *St-Georges* at 51 av Andry (☎02.31.97.18.79; ④; closed Jan), while *Le Britania*, immediately across from the ferry terminal at 63 rue des Dunes (☎02.31.96.88.26), is a convenient top-quality restaurant.

Pegasus Bridge

Roughly 5km south of Ouistreham, the main road towards Caen passes close by the site now known as **Pegasus Bridge**. On the night before D-Day, the twin bridges here that cross the Caen canal and the River Orne were the target of a daring **glider assault** just after midnight. Possession of them intact was a crucial objective for the Allied forces because it both enabled the invaders to advance east along the coast and blocked the Germans from sending reinforcements. Three of the six Horsa gliders launched from the *Halifax*, six miles offshore, landed close enough for what was then Bénouville Bridge to be captured within half an hour, although Lieutenant Brotheridge, leading the charge, became the first British casualty of D-Day in the process.

Despite protests from veterans, the original bridge was replaced in 1994, but it has been preserved as the focus of the **Mémorial Pegasus** immediately to the east (daily: Feb–April, Oct & Nov 10am–1pm & 2–5pm; May–Sept 9.30am–6.30pm; 30F/€4.57). This vaguely glider-shaped museum, which opened in 2000, holds the expected array of helmets, goggles, medals and other memorabilia, most helpfully captioned in English, as well as various model bridges used in planning the attack. The bridge itself spans a hole in the lawns outside; you can satisfy a passing curiosity by seeing it from beyond the perimeter fence without going into the museum.

Ouistreham to Arromanches: Sword and Juno beaches

While the coast along Sword and Juno beaches is generally featureless, the towns themselves are welcoming. A long promenade curves by the sea all the way from Ouistreham to Lion – it's built up, though always in a low-key way, and makes a pleasant walk straight from the ferry.

Colleville-Montgomery, the first village after the port, is one of the few "Montgomeries" in the area really to be named after the British general rather than his Norman ancestors. It's not otherwise distinguished.

Luc-sur-mer

If you're looking for atmosphere – albeit sedate – **LUC-SUR-MER**, 11km from Ouistreham, has much to recommend it. It's a gentle resort with a small wooden pier, neon-lit crêpe-stands, and tearooms along the promenade, with the **hotel** *Beau Rivage*, right on the seafront at 1 rue Charcot (☎02.31.96.49.51; ④), as its most reasonable accommodation. Menus here start at 75F/€11.43; options on the 150F/€22.87 one include a spectacular salad of smoked fish, *langoustines* and foie gras. Further west, several rooms at the newer and much grander *Hôtel des Thermes*, at 3 rue Guynemer (☎02.31.97.32.37, *www.hotelresto-lesthermes.com*; ⑤; closed Nov–March), have large seaview balconies. There's also a huge four-star **campsite** near the beach, *La Capricieuse* (☎02.31.97.34.43; closed Oct–March).

Langrune and St-Aubin-sur-mer

Attractive individual seaside **hotels** are scattered all along the D-Day coast – typically with simple rooms upstairs above a large glass-fronted seaview dining room – so ferry passengers have a choice of several *logis* for a first- or last-night stop.

THE WAR CEMETERIES

The World War II **cemeteries** that dot the Norman countryside are filled with foreigners; most of the French dead are buried in the churchyards of their home towns. After the war, some felt that the soldiers should remain in the makeshift graves that were dug where they fell. Instead, commissions gathered the remains into purpose-built cemeteries devoted to the separate warring nations.

The **British** and **Commonwealth** cemeteries are magnificently maintained, and open in every sense. They tend not to be screened off with hedges or walls, or to be forbidding expanses of manicured lawn, but are instead intimate, punctuated with bright flowers. The family of each soldier was invited to suggest an inscription for his tomb, making each grave very personal, and yet part of a common attempt to bring meaning to the carnage. Some epitaphs are questioning – "One day we will understand"; some are accepting – "Our lad at rest"; some matter-of-fact, simply giving the home address; some patriotic, quoting the "corner of a foreign field that is forever England". And interspersed among them all is the chilling refrain of the anonymous: "A soldier . . . known unto God". Thus the cemetery at **Ryes**, 6km east of Bayeux, where so many of the graves bear the date of D-Day, and so many of the victims are under 20, remains immediate and accessible – each grave clearly contains a unique individual. Even the monumental sculpture is subdued, a very British sort of fumbling for the decent thing to say. The understatement of the memorial at **Bayeux**, with its painfully contrived Latin epigram commemorating the return as liberators of "those whom William conquered", conveys an entirely appropriate humility and deep sadness.

An even more eloquent testimony to the futility of war is afforded by the **German** cemeteries, filled with soldiers who served a cause so despicable as to render any talk of "nobility" or "sacrifice" simply obscene. What such cemeteries might have been like had the Nazis won doesn't bear contemplation. As it is, they are sombre places, inconspicuous to minimize the bitterness they still arouse. At **Orglandes**, 10km south of Valognes (see p.149) on the Cotentin peninsula, 10,000 are buried, three to each of the plain headstones set in the long flat lawn, almost hidden behind an anonymous wall. There are no noble slogans and the plain entrance is without a dedicatory monument. At the superb site of **Mont d'Huisnes**, 6km east of Mont-St-Michel, the circular mausoleum holds another 10,000, filed away in cold concrete tiers. There is no attempt to defend the indefensible, and yet one feels an overpowering sense of sorrow – that there is nothing to be said in such a place bitterly underlines the sheer waste.

The largest **American** cemetery, at **Colleville-sur-mer** near the Pointe du Hoc, may already be familiar to you from the opening sequences of *Saving Private Ryan*. Here, by contrast, neat rows of crosses cover the tranquil clifftop lawns, with no individual epitaphs, just gold lettering for a few exceptional warriors. At one end, a muscular giant dominates a huge array of battlefield plans and diagrams, covered with surging arrows and pincer movements.

The *Hôtel de la Mer*, boulevard Aristide-Briand (☎02.31.96.03.37; ②), in **LAN-GRUNE** is particularly inexpensive for what you get, while further on, facing the beach across the pedestrian-only promenade at **ST-AUBIN-SUR-MER**, *Le Clos Normand* (☎02.31.97.30.47, *closnormand@compuserve.com*; ④; closed Dec–Feb) may be large, but it's extremely peaceful. Its **restaurant** has a seafront terrace, and offers a small lunch menu at 79F/€12.04, plus a series of four-course *table d'hôte* menus, where the price depends on your choice of main course.

Courseulles

COURSEULLES, 3km west of St-Aubin, is a bit more of a town, with an enjoyable Friday market in an old square set back from the sea, and, allegedly, the best oysters in Normandy. Briefly during the invasion it served as a crucial British beachhead; within ten days of D-Day it was visited by Winston Churchill and King George VI on morale-boosting excursions.

Courseulles' main activity these days is as a yachting port, and apart from an excellent crêperie, *du Moulin*, on the outskirts, there's not much choice of hotels and restaurants. The *Crémaillère-Le-Gytan*, boulevard de la Plage (☎02.31.37.46.73; ③), is probably the best option for both **eating and sleeping**, with menus from just under 100F/€15.24.

Arromanches

At **ARROMANCHES**, 13km west of Courseulles and a total of 31km from Ouistreham, the artificial **Mulberry harbour**, "Port Winston", protected the landings of two and a half million men and half a million vehicles during the Invasion. Two of these prefab concrete constructions were built in segments in Britain, while "doodlebugs" blitzed overhead, then submerged in rivers away from the prying eyes of German aircraft, and finally towed across the Channel at 6kph as the invasion began. Meanwhile, the British 47 Royal Marine Commando were storming Arromanches itself to clear the way.

The seafront **Musée du Débarquement**, in Arromanches' main square (daily: May–Aug 9am–6.30pm; Sept–April 9am–11.30am & 2–5.30pm; closed first three weeks of Jan; 35F/€5.34), recounts the whole story by means of models, machinery and movies – and the evidence of your own eyes. A huge picture window runs the length of the museum, staring straight out to where the bulky remains of the harbour stretch away along the coast, making a strange intrusion on the beach and shallow sea bed. Its sheer scale is impossible to appreciate at this distance; for three months after D-Day, this was the largest port in the world. (The other such harbour, slightly further west on Omaha Beach, broke up within two weeks, but this one was repairable; see p.136.)

Several other war memorials are scattered throughout Arromanches, including a statue of Jesus and Mary, high up on the cliffs above the invasion site. Alongside, a steel dome contains **Arromanches 360** (daily: Feb, March, Nov & Dec 10am–5.30pm; April, May, Sept & Oct 10am–6pm; June–Aug 9.30am–7pm; 24F/€3.66), a wraparound cinema which, under the slogan of "eighteen minutes of total emotion", plunges viewers into the heart of the fighting. It's also possible to overlook the entire area on a **helicopter trip**; ask at the tourist office (see below) for details.

Practicalities

Arromanches somehow manages to be quite a cheerful place to stay, with a lively pedestrian street of bars and brasseries, and a long expanse of sand where you can rent windsurf boards. The local **tourist office** is just back from the sea at 2 rue Maréchal-Joffre (daily 9.30am–1pm & 2–6.30pm; ☎02.31.22.36.45, *www.arromanches .com*).

La Marine, at 2 quai Canada (☎02.31.22.34.19; ④; closed Nov to mid-Feb), is a slightly expensive **hotel**, with well-appointed rooms – many of which enjoy superb sea views – and an excellent restaurant serving fishy menus from 99F/€15.09

(the "Winston"); there's also a cheaper brasserie alongside. Across the main square, opposite the tourist office, the *Arromanches*, 1 rue Maréchal-Joffre (☎02.31.22.36.26; ④; closed Tues evening & Wed in winter), is less well situated but just as comfortable; here, the *Pappagall* restaurant has menus from 70F/€10.67 up to 180F/€27.44. The cheaper *Normandie* stands nearby at 5 place du 6-Juin (☎02.31.22.34.32; ②; closed Jan). The town's spacious three-star municipal **campsite** is located 200 metres back from the seafront (☎02.31.22.36.78; closed Nov–March).

West to the Cotentin: Omaha Beach

PORT-EN-BESSIN, 11km west of Arromanches, and the nearest point on the coast to Bayeux (on the #70 bus route), has a thriving fishing industry and – rare on this coast – a sheltered, enclosed site. The fish, caught off Devon and Cornwall, are auctioned three times a week. It's not, however, desperately attractive, though the *de la Marine* (☎02.31.21.70.08; ③) is a classic seaside **hotel** on quai Letourner. The squalid *La Prairie* **campsite**, on the other hand, is definitely one to avoid.

The coastline west of Port-en-Bessin becomes steadily hillier, and as **Omaha Beach** it presented a stiff challenge to the American forces on D-Day. The clifftop village of **COLLEVILLE-SUR-MER**, 10km along, marks the start of the long approach road to the larger of the two **American war cemeteries**, a sombre place, described on p.134. Unlike the British and Commonwealth forces, the Americans repatriated most of their dead. **ST-LAURENT**, 2.5km further on and the next point where road access to the sea becomes possible, holds the small **Omaha Beach Museum** (daily: mid-Feb to mid-March 10am–12.30pm & 2.30–6pm; mid-March to mid-May & Oct to mid-Nov 9.30am–6.30pm; mid-May to June & Sept 9.30am–7pm; July & Aug 9.30am–7.30pm; 29F/€4.42), a hundred metres inland, which displays a fine assortment of photos taken on D-Day itself, but few artefacts of any interest.

Just beyond St-Laurent, **VIERVILLE** was the site for the twin to Arromanches' Mulberry harbour, codenamed "Gooseberry", which lasted just thirteen days before breaking up in an unprecedented storm. A memorial to the US National Guard stands atop a ruined German pillbox at the west end of town; nearby, the weather-beaten *Hôtel du Casino* (☎02.31.22.41.02; ③), a *logis de France*, surveys the scene.

Further along, the most dramatic American landings took place along the cliff heights of the **POINTE DU HOC**, still today deeply pitted with German bunkers and shell-holes. Standing amid the scarred earth and rusty barbed wire, looking down to the rocks at the base of the cliff, it seems inconceivable that the first US sergeant was at the top five minutes after landing, and the whole complex taken within another quarter of an hour.

Grandcamp-Maisy and Isigny

GRANDCAMP-MAISY, 3km west of Pointe du Hoc, centred on a compact fishing harbour, was too severely damaged in the war to make much of a holiday des-

Note that **Utah Beach**, the westernmost of the Invasion Beaches, is on the Cotentin Peninsula, and is covered on pp.150–151.

tination now. It does, however, hold a couple of reasonably priced **hotels**, the *du Guesclin*, 4 quai Crampon (☎02.31.22.64.22; ②; closed mid-Jan to mid-Feb), which has a panoramic seaview dining room, though most of the accommodation is in the modern annexe behind, and *Au Petit Marayeur*, a long way back from the sea on place de la Mairie (☎02.31.22.65.91; ②; closed mid-Dec to mid-Jan). It also has a good **campsite**, the *Camping du Juncal* (☎02.31.22.61.44; closed Oct–Easter). **Cruises** of the landing beaches to both the north and the east, on the sixty-passenger *Colonel Rudder*, cost from 60F/€9.15 for one hour and up to 200F/€30.49 for five hours; for a full schedule, contact the Tentations shop at 11 rue A. Briand (☎02.31.21.42.93).

ISIGNY nearby is renowned for its dairy products, butter in particular. Though once again of no great beauty or interest, it does have a **hotel**, *de France*, 13 rue É. Demagny (☎02.31.22.00.33; ②; closed mid-Nov to mid-Feb), if you're stuck.

Bayeux

BAYEUX, with its perfectly preserved medieval ensemble, magnificent **cathedral** and world-famous **tapestry**, is 23km west of Caen – a mere twenty-minute train ride. It's a smaller and much more intimate city, and, despite the large crowds of summer tourists, a far more enjoyable place to visit.

A mere 10km in from the coast, Bayeux was the first French city to be liberated in 1944, the day after the D-Day landings. It was occupied so quickly – before the Germans had got over their surprise – that it managed to escape any serious damage, and briefly became capital of Free France.

Arrival and information

The **gare SNCF** (☎02.31.92.80.50) is fifteen-minutes' walk west of the town centre, just outside the "ring road", while the **gare routière** is on the other side of town on rue du Manche, alongside place St-Patrice (used as a car park, except during Saturday's market), near the fire station.

Bayeux's **tourist office** stands in the very centre of town, in what used to be the fish market on the arched pont St-Jean (June to mid-Sept Mon–Sat 9am–6pm, Sun 9.30am–noon & 2.30–6pm; mid-Sept to May Mon–Sat 9am–noon & 2–6pm; ☎02.31.51.28.28, *www.bayeux-tourisme.com*). The **post office** is just around the corner at 14 rue Larcher (Mon–Fri 8am–7pm, Sat 8am–noon; ☎02.31.51.24.90).

For information on **local buses**, call Bus Verts du Calvados (☎02.31.92.02.92), whose services stop at both the *gare SNCF* and the *gare routière*; tickets are sold at the *gare SNCF*, at Librairie 1000 Pages on place St-Patrice and on the actual buses. Travellers without cars who plan to visit the landing beaches and/or the war cemeteries are better advised to join a **minibus trip** with a local operator such as Bus Fly, 24 rue Montfiquet (☎02.31.22.00.08, *www.busfly.com*), or Normandy Tours, place de la Gare (☎02.31.92.10.70). Details of tours organized through the Caen Memorial can be found on p.131. **Bicycles** can be rented from the *Family Home* (see overleaf), Roué, boulevard Winston-Churchill (☎02.31.92.27.75), or, as usual, from the *gare SNCF*.

Accommodation

As one of Normandy's most important tourist destinations, Bayeux is well equipped with accommodation. On the whole, however, the **hotels** are more expensive than elsewhere. The **hostel** is in the municipal Centre d'Accueil at 21 rue des Marettes (☎02.31.92.08.19), 1.5km from the *gare SNCF* near the Musée de la Bataille de Normandie, and is open all year, charging 92F/€14.03 for a tiny private room. Alternatively, the *Family Home* (see below) offers hostel accommodation.

There's a large three-star **campsite** on boulevard d'Eindhoven (☎02.31.92.08.43; closed mid-Nov to mid-March), on the northern ring road (RN13) near the river – and the municipal sewage works.

Hôtel d'Argouges, 21 rue St-Patrice (☎02.31.92.88.86, fax 02.31.92.69.16, *argouges@ mail.cpod.fr*). Quiet, central and very stylish eighteenth-century building, with an imposing courtyard entered via an archway on the west side of place St-Patrice, and a well-kept garden around the back. Several rooms are very grand, with magnificent exposed wooden beams, and the rates are very reasonable for what you get. ③–⑥.

Family Home, 39 rue Général-Dais (☎02.31.92.15.22, fax 02.31.92.55.72). Central seven-teenth-century house which describes itself variously as a *maison d'hôtes* (guesthouse) and an *auberge de jeunesse* (youth hostel). Its prices are a little over the usual odds (hostel accommodation is 95F/€14.48 per person) and it's a bit self-consciously jolly – but it has its advocates, and people return again and again. Room prices include breakfast. Meals are taken communally, Madame Lefèvre presiding at the head of a long table in an old oak-beamed dining room, with dinner for 65F/€9.91 at 7.30pm. They also rent bikes and run D-Day tours. ①–③.

Hôtel de la Gare, 26 place de la Gare (☎02.31.92.10.70, fax 02.31.51.95.99). Old but perfectly adequate basic hotel, with a simple brasserie, beside the station, on the ring road fifteen-minutes' walk from the cathedral. Tours of D-Day beaches arranged. ①.

Hôtel-Restaurant Lion d'Or, 71 rue St-Jean (☎02.31.92.06.90, fax 02.31.22.15.64). Grand old coaching inn set back behind a courtyard, just beyond the pedestrianized section of the rue St-Jean, outside Les Halles des Grains (now the assembly rooms). The rooms themselves are brighter and newer than the exterior might lead you to expect. Closed mid-Dec to mid-Jan. Menus from 150F/€22.87. ⑤.

Hôtel Le Maupassant, 19 rue St-Martin (☎02.31.92.28.53, fax 02.31.92.35.40). Basic rooms not far from the river in the heart of town, with a brasserie downstairs. Can be an icebox in winter. ②.

Hôtel-Restaurant Notre Dame, 44 rue des Cuisiniers (☎02.31.92.87.24, fax 02.31.92.67.11). Friendly and very pleasant *logis*, virtually in front of the cathedral, with a magnificent view. Menus from 95F/€14.48 (with rabbit in cider), with a special Norman one at 145F/€22.11. Closed mid-Nov to mid-Dec, plus Sun evening & Mon in winter. ②–③.

Hôtel Reine Mathilde, 23 rue Larcher (☎02.31.92.08.13, fax 02.31.92.09.93). Simple but well-equipped rooms – all have showers and TV – backing onto the canal, between the tapestry and the cathedral. There's a really nice open-air brasserie downstairs that serves dinner between May and Sept, with the cheapest menu at 49F/€7.47 and a good four-course meal for 100F/€15.24. Closed Jan. ③.

Le Relais des Cèdres, 1 bd Sadi-Carnot (☎02.31.21.98.07). Pretty guesthouse, not far from the station but within sight of the cathedral. The rooms are fine, and good value, although the atmosphere is not all that welcoming. ②–③.

The Town

Within the confines of a busy ring road, the core of Bayeux is surprisingly small. It consists largely of one long street, which starts from the place St-Patrice in the west (scene of a Sat market). As the rue St-Malo and rue St-Martin this is lined with the busy little shops of a typical Norman town; it then crosses the attractive canalized River Aure, passing the tourist office and the old **watermill**, Moulin Crocquevieille, to become the pedestrianized rue St-Jean on the east side, filled with cafés, brasseries, restaurants and souvenir shops (and itself the site of a market on Wed).

Both Bayeux's principal attractions lie south of this main thoroughfare. The **Cathedral** is in an attractive tangle of old streets, best reached along rue des Cuisiniers – look out for the magnificent fourteenth-century half-timbered house that overhangs the street at 1 rue des Cuisiniers, on the corner with rue St-Malo. The **tapestry** is on the other side of the river, housed in an impressive eighteenth-century seminary, remodelled as the **Centre Guillaume le Conquérant**, and clearly signposted on rue de Nesmond.

The Bayeux Tapestry

Daily: mid-March to April & Sept to mid-Oct 9am–6.30pm; May–Aug 9am–7pm; mid-Oct to mid-March 9.30am–12.30pm & 2–6pm; last admission 45min before closing. 40F/€6.10, includes admission to the Musée Baron Gerard.

The **Bayeux Tapestry** – also known to the French as the *Tapisserie de la Reine Mathilde* – is a seventy-metre strip of linen that recounts the story of the Norman Conquest of England. Although created over nine centuries ago, the brilliance of its coloured wools has barely faded, and the tale is enlivened throughout with scenes of medieval life, popular fables and mythical beasts. Technically it's not really a tapestry at all, but an embroidery; the skill of its draughtsmanship, and the sheer vigour and detail, are stunning. The work is thought to have been carried out by nuns in England, commissioned by Bishop Oddo, William's half-brother, in time for the inauguration of Bayeux Cathedral in 1077; recent suggestions by an English historian that the tapestry is considerably newer, in view for example of the "kebabs" being grilled in one beach scene, are discounted by most authorities.

The tapestry looks – and reads – like a modern comic strip. While it's generally considered to be historically accurate, William's justification for his invasion – his contention that during a visit to Normandy Harold had sworn to accept William as King of England – remains in dispute. In the tapestry itself, Harold is every inch the villain, with his dastardly little moustache and shifty eyes. At the point when he breaks his oath and takes the throne for himself, Harold looks extremely pleased with himself; however, his comeuppance swiftly follows, as William, the noble hero, crosses the Channel and defeats the English armies at Hastings.

Visits are well planned and highly atmospheric, if somewhat exhausting. You can't actually touch or linger over the tapestry itself, which is in any case kept for its preservation under very dim light. However, the display is excellent. First comes a slide show, projected onto billowing sheets of canvas hung as sails; you then pass along a photographic replica of the tapestry, with enlargements and detailed commentaries in both French and English. These set the expedition in its historical context, as a continuation in a sense of the Viking raids that had created Normandy a century before. Dioramas and models also cover the aftermath of the conquest of England, which is absent from the tapestry itself.

If you feel you know the 1066 story well enough by now, you can skip the film that follows, which goes over much of the same ground. Beyond this, you finally approach the real thing, which has a strong three-dimensional presence you might not expect from all the flat reproductions.

Although the tapestry makes such a bullish and effective piece of propaganda that Napoléon exhibited it in Paris – to show that a successful invasion of England was indeed possible – much of the pleasure of viewing it comes from the incidental vignettes of contemporary life that parallel the main story. The preparation of William's forces is shown in sufficient detail that museums such as those in Dieppe and Douarnanez (see pp.68 & 295) have constructed boats using the same methods, while the depiction of Halley's Comet blazing in the sky helped astronomers to establish its orbit. Only the faintest smattering of Latin is required to be able to follow the captions that accompany each major scene. The saga comes to an abrupt end immediately after the turmoil, carnage and looting of the Battle of Hastings, and of course the death of Harold (who may or may not be the figure with an arrow in his eye).

Cathédrale Notre Dame

Daily: July & Aug 9am–7pm; Sept–June 9am–6pm.

The **Cathédrale Notre Dame**, the first home of the tapestry, is a short and very obvious walk away from its latest resting place. Despite such eighteenth-century vandalism as the monstrous fungoid baldachin that flanks the pulpit, Bishop Oddo's original Romanesque plan is still intact, for the most part sensitively merged with Gothic additions. The crypt, entirely original, is particularly wonderful, with its frescoes of angels playing trumpets and bagpipes, looking exhausted by their eternal performance. Along the nave is some tremendous twelfth-century sculpture, and you shouldn't miss the beautifully carved wooden choir stalls. The tiled floor of the chapterhouse features a fifteenth-century maze depicting the road to Jerusalem. To get access to both crypt and chapterhouse, you may have to seek out the sacristan.

Musée Baron Gerard

Daily: June to mid-Sept 9am–7pm; mid-Sept to May 10am–12.30pm & 2–6pm. 40F/€6.10, combined admission with Tapestry.

The courtyard that adjoins the western facade of the cathedral is dominated by the **Liberty Tree**, a 200-year-old plane tree planted with much Revolutionary rejoicing in 1797. In its shadow to the north, the former palace of the archbishops of Bayeux has over the centuries received a considerable quantity of porcelain and lace donated by local families. Named the **Musée Baron Gerard** in honour of its most generous patron, it has recently been renovated to display its collection to far better advantage, and also features an assortment of relatively minor French paintings from the sixteenth to the nineteenth centuries.

The General de Gaulle Memorial Museum

Mid-March to mid-Nov daily 9.30am–12.30pm & 2–6.30pm. 17F/€2.59.

Although the **General de Gaulle Memorial Museum** at 10 rue de Bourbesneur, near place de Gaulle, is aimed squarely at French devotees of the great man, it makes an interesting detour for foreign visitors. The sheer obsession of the displays, which focus on the five separate day-trips de Gaulle made to Bayeux during the course of his long life, somehow illuminates the extent to which he came to epitomize the very essence of a certain kind of Frenchness – which to foreigners seems scarcely removed from self-parody.

Over three floors, the life of the general is traced from his days as a dashing cadet, first seen in a magnificent plumed hat before he was united with his trademark flat-topped *képi*. He was wounded three times in World War I, including at both the Somme and Verdun. Having argued in vain that France should prepare for the new era of mechanized warfare, he became a general on the battlefield in 1940 just in time to be swept aside by the Nazi Blitzkrieg, and was in London by June 18 to launch his famous (but unrecorded) radio appeal to the "Free French"; the indecipherable manuscript is on display.

Then come his visits to Bayeux. The first and most significant was the day his exile ended; we see him addressing French sailors on the destroyer *Le Combattant*, then landing on French soil at Courseulles, with an incredible haunted look in his eyes, and finally declaiming before a delirious crowd in Bayeux, conducting them in the *Marseillaise*. De Gaulle is hailed throughout the museum as the embodiment of France, not least by the *sous-prefet* who welcomed him in 1944, narrates the closing video and who was still alive to chair the fiftieth-anniversary celebrations in 1994. The general returned in 1945 to welcome the first deportees to come home from Germany, and again on June 16, 1946, no longer in power, to proclaim his vision of a new constitution.

Place de Gaulle

A monument in **place de Gaulle**, just along from the museum, commemorates the spot where General de Gaulle made his first emotional speech after returning to French soil on June 14, 1944. That visit was a day-trip undertaken in the face of opposition from the Allied commanders; his arrival was so unexpected that the first two civilians he encountered, two policemen wheeling their bicycles, failed to recognize him.

The Musée Mémorial 1944 de la Bataille de Normandie

Daily: May to mid-Sept 9.30am–6.30pm; mid-Sept to April 10am–12.30pm & 2–6pm. 33F/€5.03.

Set behind massive guns, next to the ring road on the southwest side of town, Bayeux's **Musée Mémorial 1944 de la Bataille de Normandie** is one of the old school of war museums, with its emphasis firmly on hardware rather than humans. Much of its former heavy-handedness seems to have disappeared since the end of the Cold War, and it shows some evocative film footage of the landings, by both sea and air, but nonetheless the obsession with technical minutiae remains a little disconcerting.

By way of contrast, the understated and touching **British War Cemetery** stands immediately across the road (see box on p.134).

Eating

Several of the hotels, most notably the *Notre Dame*, have good **restaurants**, while the *Family Home* serves a filling and good-value dinner at 7.30pm each evening, for 65F/€9.91; non-guests should phone ahead to reserve a place. Otherwise, most of Bayeux's restaurants are in the rue St-Jean leading east from the river, or near the main door of the cathedral. Watch out for Sundays: virtually everywhere is shut.

La Fringale, 43 rue St-Jean (☎02.31.21.34.40). The nicest of the many pavement restaurants along the pedestrian rue St-Jean, offering good-value lunch menus and also generous salads and snacks, as well as more formal fishy dinners. Closed mid-Dec to Jan, plus Wed in low season.

Le Petit Bistrot, 2 rue Bienvenue (☎02.31.51.85.40). Bright-yellow-painted restaurant opposite the cathedral, where the menus from 98F/€14.94 upwards boast a fine assortment of scallops. Closed Sun, plus Mon in low season.

Le Petit Normand, 35 rue Larcher (☎02.31.22.88.66). Sixteenth-century house by the cathedral, offering good traditional cooking, with seafood specialities and local cider. Lunch menus from 60F/€9.15, dinner from 95F/€14.48. Closed Jan, plus Thurs Oct–April.

Le Pommier, 40 rue des Cuisiniers (☎02.31.21.52.10). Small traditional restaurant near the cathedral, with a tiny terrace. Meat- and dairy-rich Norman cuisine on menus from 76F/€11.59 to 146F/€22.26. Closed Feb, plus Sun evening, & Wed in low season.

La Table du Terroir, 42 rue St-Jean (☎02.31.92.05.53). A rendezvous for closet meat freaks, tucked away behind a butcher's shop and serving the freshest, bloodiest flesh on a well-judged quartet of menus, at 60F/€9.15, 98F/€14.94, 115F/€17.53 and 155F/€23.63 – the latter features a tureen of sweetbreads. Closed Sun evening, Mon & mid-Oct to mid-Nov.

Southwest from Bayeux

Travellers heading **southwest from Bayeux**, towards St-Lô (see p.194), pass close to two remarkable buildings: the **Abbaye de Cerisy-la-Forêt** and the

Château de Balleroy. Neither is easy to get to without transport, but if you have a bike or car they shouldn't be missed.

Cerisy-la-Forêt

The village of **CERISY-LA-FORÊT** stands at the edge of its eponymous forest 6km west of the D572 and a total of 22km southwest of Bayeux. Its eleventh-century Romanesque **abbey** (Easter to mid-Nov Tues–Sun 9am–6.30pm; free; 1hr guided tours hourly: Easter–Sept Tues–Sun 10.30am–12.30pm & 2.30–6.30pm; Oct to mid-Nov Sat & Sun 10.30am–noon & 2–6pm; 10F/€1.52) was founded by William the Conqueror's father on the site of an already venerable monastery. Set on a hill, overlooking an attractive pond just east of Cerisy itself, its triple tiers of windows and arches, lapping light onto its cream stone, make you sigh in wonder at the skills of medieval Norman masons.

Sitting in its own spacious grounds between town and abbey, the stately *Château de l'Abbaye* (☎02.33.55.71.73; closed Wed lunch in summer, all day Wed in winter; ⑤) offers luxurious country-house accommodation.

Balleroy

At **BALLEROY**, 8.5km south of Cerisy across the D572, you switch to an era when architects ruled over craftsmen. The main street of the village leads straight to the **château**, masterpiece of the celebrated seventeenth-century architect François Mansard. It stands like a faultlessly reasoned and dogmatic argument for the power of its owners and their class and, suitably enough, its most recent owner was the late American press magnate Malcolm S. Forbes, pal of presidents Nixon, Ford and Reagan, not to mention Elizabeth Taylor. You can tour the house to see its eclectic furnishings, pieces of modern sculpture and an original *salon* – with superb royal portraits by Mignard.

The focus, however, is on Forbes himself. Forbes was an acquisitor untrammelled by financial restraint – he owned the world's largest collection of Fabergé jewelled eggs (which were almost scrambled by a fire early in 1990), and his palace in Tangier, containing 100,000 lead soldiers, was the scene of a notoriously extravagant seventieth birthday party. At Balleroy, he created a museum to his principal passion, **ballooning**. It's all a bit absurd, beginning with some interesting history, but degenerating into egomania: photos of Malcolm S. Forbes in various Forbes balloons winning various Forbes prizes (as seen, of course, in his own *Forbes Magazine*). Admission is expensive at 37F/€5.64, and seems a poor substitute for indulging in the real thing, which unlike, say, running for the US Presidency – his son Steve's bid for world fame in 1996 – is more than a hobby for self-publicizing millionaires (both château and museum open mid-March to June & Sept to mid-Oct daily except Tues 9am–noon & 2–6pm; July & Aug daily 10am–6pm). Every two years, in the third week of June, Balleroy's magnificent grounds play host to Europe's largest **balloon festival**.

The Cotentin Peninsula

Hard against the frontier with Brittany, and cut off from the rest of Normandy by difficult marshy terrain, the **Cotentin Peninsula** has traditionally been seen as something of a backwater, far removed from the French mainstream. The local *patois* has a special pejorative word for "stranger", applied indiscriminately to foreigners, Parisians and southern Cotentins alike, while official disdain for the region might explain why the Cap de la Hague, the peninsula's westernmost tip, was chosen as the site for a controversial nuclear reprocessing plant. The Cotentin nonetheless makes a surprisingly rewarding goal for travellers, and one that by sea at least is very easily accessible. Regular ferries from both England and Ireland still dock at the peninsula's major port, **Cherbourg**, with a plethora of attractive little villages nestled amid the hills to both east and west.

Geographically, this is an area of transition. Little ports such as **Barfleur** and **St-Vaast** on the indented northern headland presage the rocky Breton coast, while inland the meadows resemble the farmlands of the Bocage and the Bessin. The long western flank with its flat beaches serves as a prelude to **Mont-St-Michel**, with hill towns such as **Coutances** and **Avranches** cherishing architectural and historical relics associated with the abbey. Halfway down, the approaches to the Baie du Mont-St-Michel are guarded by the walled port of **Granville**, an extremely popular destination with French holiday-makers and a sort of small-scale mirror-image of Brittany's St-Malo.

Cherbourg

If the murky metropolis of **CHERBOURG** is your port of arrival in France, the best advice is probably to head straight out and on. Despite some appealingly busy pedestrian streets and lively bars, the town itself lacks anything of substantial interest, and there are some much more appealing places within a very few kilometres to either side. Napoléon inaugurated the transformation of what had been a rather poor, but perfectly situated, natural harbour into a major transatlantic port, by means of massive artifical breakwaters. An equestrian statue commemorates his boast that in Cherbourg he would "recreate the wonders of Egypt". But there are, as yet, no pyramids nearer than the Louvre in Paris, and if you are waiting for a boat the best way to fill time is to settle into a café or restaurant or do some last-minute **shopping**, perhaps picking up some **wine** from the extensive selection at the British-run Maison du Vin, 71 av Carnot (☎02.33.43.39.79).

Cherbourg also boasts some lively **markets**, held on Tuesday and Thursday around the rue des Halles, and on Wednesday next to the church of St-Pierre. Your best bets for large-scale shopping, however, are the Auchan hypermarket at the junction of RN13 and N13, south of town, or the Carrefour, on the southeast corner of the Bassin du Commerce.

As for walking off lunch, the only area that really encourages a ramble is over by the Basilique de la Trinité and the former town beach, now grassed over to form the "Plage Vert". Over to the south, you could alternatively climb up to **Roule Fort** for a view of the whole port; the fort itself contains the **Musée de la Libération**, which with the usual dry maps and diagrams but plenty of contemporary newsreel – much of it, for once, in English – commemorates the period in 1944 when Cherbourg was briefly the busiest port in the world (May–Sept daily 10am–6pm; Oct–April Tues–Sun 9.30am–noon & 2–5.30pm; 15F/€2.29).

Arrival and information

The days of the great transatlantic liners may be over, but several cross-Channel ferry companies still sail into Cherbourg's *gare maritime*, just east of the town centre (daily 5.30am–11.30pm; ☎02.33.44.20.13). Services from **Portsmouth**, including the new Superstar Express, which takes a mere 2hr 45min for the crossing, are

CHERBOURG

Ferry Terminal

Basilique de la Trinité

Avant Port

PONT TOURNANT

Théâtre

Gare Routière

Gare SNCF

Roule Fort

RUE DE L'ABBAYE

AVENUE CESSART

RUE DE L'UNION

RUE DE LA VIEILLE

RUE TOUR CARRÉE

RUE DE LA MARINE

RUE AU BLÉ

PLACE CENTRALE

RUE MAHIEU

RUE DE LA MARINE

RUE CHRISTINE

RUE EMMANUEL LIAIS

QUAI DE CALIGNY

RUE F.LAVIEILLE

QUAI LAWTON COLLINS

QUAI DE FRANCE

QUAI DE NORMANDIE

BOULEVARD FELIX

AVENUE A. BRIAND

RUE DE TOURVILLE

RUE DU VAL DE SAIRE

RUE MAL FOCH

RUE GAMBETTA

RUE DE L'ALMA

RUE ÉMILE-ZOLA

RUE ALEXANDRE III

QUAI ALEXANDRE III

Bassin du Commerce

QUAI DE L'ENTREPÔT

AVENUE CARNOT

BD PIERRE MENDÈS-FRANCE

RUE PRÉSIDENT LOUBERT

PLACE JEAN-JAURÈS

AVENUE FRANCIS-MILLET

RUE DES BRAS

RUE SAINT-SAUVEUR

BD DE L'ATLANTIQUE

AV DE PARIS

RUE TERTRE SUD

AVENUE ÉTIENNE LECARPENTIER

▽ Valognes & Paris

0   200 m

ACCOMMODATION

La Croix de Malte	5
de la Gare	6
Hostel	1
Moderna	3
La Régence	4
Rénaissance	2

RESTAURANTS

Café de Paris	C
Café du Théâtre	D
Le Faitout	B
Le Grandgousier	A

operated by P&O (5–6 daily; ☎08.03.01.30.13, *www.poef.com*), and from **Poole** by Brittany Ferries (1–2 daily; 4hr 15min; ☎08.03.82.88.28, *www.brittany-ferries.com*) – Cherbourg is twinned with Poole, hence the British red telephone kiosk on quai de Caligny. Irish Ferries also sail to Cherbourg, from Rosslare (2–4 weekly; ☎02.33.23.44.44).

The **gare SNCF** (☎02.33.57.50.50), on avenue François-Miller/place Jean-Jaurès, is served by regular trains to Paris, Bayeux and Caen. Buses to Coutances (☎02.33.98.13.38) and St-Lô, Valognes and Barfleur (☎02.33.44.32.22) run from the **gare routière** opposite, which is hidden from view by a building on avenue François-Miller.

Cherbourg's **tourist office** is at 2 quai Alexandre III (June–Aug Mon–Sat 9am–6.30pm; Sept–May Mon 1.30–6pm, Tues–Fri 9am–noon & 1.30–6pm, Sat

9am–noon; ☎02.33.93.52.02, *www.cherbourg-channel.tm.fr*). In summer there's also a tourist-information kiosk at the ferry terminal, open to coincide with sailings (Mon–Fri 5–8.30am & 1.30–8.30pm, Sat 5–8.30am & 1.30–6.30pm, Sun 5–10am & 1.30–6pm; ☎02.33.44.39.92). The **post office** is on rue d'Ancien Quai (Mon–Fri 8am–7pm, Sat 8am–noon; ☎02.33. 08.87.01), while the Forum Espace Culture, on place Centrale, is a large book and record shop that also offers **Internet** access.

Cycles can be rented from Cycles Peugeot-Kerhir, 31 bd Schumann (☎02.33.53.04.38), and the hostel (see below), while Europcar, 4 rue des Tanneries (☎02.33.44.53.85), offer weekend rates on **car rental**.

Accommodation

By the standards of the rest of Normandy, **room** rates in Cherbourg are very reasonable. There's no great reason for ferry passengers to avoid spending a night here – it's a lively enough place to pass an evening – though the crowds and traffic can get a bit much, and for motorists the lack of parking space during the day is a real problem. Few of the hotels, however, bother to maintain their own restaurants.

The town's newly refurbished and well-equipped red-brick **hostel**, fifteen-minutes' walk west of the centre at 55 rue de l'Abbaye (☎02.33.78.15.15), offers dorm beds for 51F/€7.77 per night, serves lunch or dinner for 50F/€7.62, and also rents out bicycles. Two of its bedrooms are designed for visitors with limited mobility.

The closest **campsite** to the ferry terminal is the three-star *Camping de Collignon*, 3km east towards Barfleur at Tourlaville (☎02.33.20.16.88; closed Oct–May).

Hôtel Croix de Malte, 7 rue des Halles (☎02.33.43.19.16, fax 02.33.43.65.66). Simple hotel on three upstairs floors, one block back from the harbour and around the corner from the theatre. Clean and recently renovated rooms – all 24 have TV and at least a shower – with the cheapest rates being for the perfectly acceptable ones in the attic. ②.

Hôtel de la Gare, 10 place Jean-Jaurès (☎02.33.43.06.81, fax 02.33.43.12.20). Very convenient for the *gares SNCF* and *routière*, if not exactly stunning in itself. The cheapest rooms have a shower but no toilet. ②.

Hôtel Moderna, 28 rue de la Marine (☎02.33.43.05.30, fax 02.33.43.97.37, *www.moderna-hotel .com*). Rooms ranging from basic to lavish, slightly back from the harbour and tourist office; most have phones, showers and British TV. ①–③.

Hôtel La Régence, 42 quai de Caligny (☎02.33.43.05.16, fax 02.33.43.98.37). Small neat rooms with balconies overlooking the harbour, just around the corner from the tourist office. The restaurant downstairs kicks off with a reasonable 70F/€10.67 menu, and ranges up to 185F/€28.20; it's not the best along the *quai*, but there's something to be said for eating where you sleep. ③.

Hôtel de la Renaissance, 4 rue de l'Église (☎02.33.43.23.90, fax 02.33.43.96.10, *renaissance@cherbourg-channel.tm.fr*). Rooms of all kinds, some with sea views, in a friendly hotel, facing the port in the most appealing quarter of town – the *Église* of the address is the attractive Trinité. ①–③.

Eating

Restaurant options in Cherbourg divide readily into the glass-fronted seafood places along the quai de Caligny, each with its copious *assiette de fruits de mer*, and the more varied, more adventurous and less expensive little places tucked away in the pedestrianized streets and alleyways of the old town.

THE KEARSARGE AND THE ALABAMA

In June 1864, Cherbourg played host to one of the most extraordinary incidents of the **US Civil War** – a pitched **naval battle** between two rival warships, the Union *Kearsarge* and the Confederate *Alabama*.

The **Alabama** had been cruising the Atlantic for the previous year, harassing ships carrying supplies to the northern USA. By the time it docked at Cherbourg, to allow its crew a spell of shore leave and the boat itself a refit, it had captured, destroyed or held to ransom over eighty US merchant vessels. The **Kearsarge**, meanwhile, had been prowling the coasts of Europe in pursuit; **Captain John A. Winslow** heard of the *Alabama*'s arrival while in Amsterdam, and was anchored off Cherbourg within two days.

Both vessels then spent several days preparing for the inevitable duel. **Captain Raphael Semmes** of the *Alabama* – known as "Old Beeswax" on account of his huge pointed moustache – noted in his diary that "the combat will no doubt be contested and obstinate, but the two ships are so evenly matched that I do not feel at liberty to decline it". Cherbourg buzzed with excitement: its hotels filled with eager spectators brought by special trains from Paris, and hundreds more camped along the quaysides.

Sunday being Semmes' lucky day, he ordered the *Alabama* out of the harbour on the morning of Sunday June 12. At first, the *Kearsarge* seemed to retreat; then it turned, and charged the *Alabama* at full steam. The *Alabama* was the first to fire its guns. One shell lodged in the sternpost of the *Kearsarge*, but it failed to explode. Soon, however, a slow but steady barrage from the *Kearsarge* began to pound the *Alabama* to pieces.

To Captain Semmes' bewilderment, the *Alabama*'s shells kept bouncing off the *Kearsarge*. When it later transpired that the *Kearsarge* was lined below the water level with iron chains, he furiously expostulated that "It was the same thing as if two men were to go out and fight a duel, and one of them, unknown to the other, were to put on a suit of mail under his own garment."

Eventually, the doomed *Alabama* attempted to flee. Its escape was cut off, but Semmes himself managed to get away. As his ship went down, he whirled his sword above his head and flung it into the Channel, then leaped into the sea. Together with several members of his crew, he was picked up by a British holidaymaker who had watched the battle from his yacht, and taken to Southampton. Hailed by *The Times* as a "set of first-rate fellows", the defeated Confederates in due course managed to return home.

Captain Winslow – whose ship had suffered just three casualties, as opposed to the *Alabama*'s 43 – brought the *Kearsarge* into Cherbourg harbour after the battle. Their previous Confederate sympathies conveniently forgotten, the local citizens hailed him as a hero, before he made his way to a celebration banquet arranged by the American community in Paris.

Café de Paris, 40 quai de Caligny (☎02.33.43.12.36). Work your way up through the ranks of *assiettes de fruits de mer*, from the 85F/€12.96 *Matelot* to the *Amiral* at 520F/€79.27 for two; there's also a quick 105F/€16.01 menu if you're in a hurry. Here it's the live lobsters in the fish tanks set into the windows that get the sea views, not you – but the food is excellent. Closed Sun evening, plus Mon in low season.

Café du Théâtre, 8 place de Gaulle (☎02.33.43.01.49). Attractive setup adjoining the theatre, with a café behind plate-glass windows on the ground floor and a full-scale brasserie upstairs, arranged on three sides of the central opening. The whole ensemble offers a great sense of participating in the life of the town. The varied menus, from 79F/€12.04, hold more than just seafood; the 115F/€17.53 one features frogs' legs, for example.

Le Faitout, 25 rue Tour-Carrée (☎02.33.04.25.04). Basement restaurant in the shopping district that offers traditional French cuisine at very reasonable prices; a bowl of mussels can be had for under 40F/€6.10, and there's a daily special for 55F/€8.38. Closed Sun, & Mon lunchtime.

Le Grandgousier, 21 rue de l'Abbaye (☎02.33.53.19.43). The definitive French fish restaurant, well worth the walk to its unprepossessing location at the west end of town; the rosy glow starts, but does not end, with the decor. Menus start at 75F/€11.43, but this is a place to expect to spend a lot and dine well. Imagine any combination of fish, throw in a bit of caviar, a few crab claws, and a leavening of foie gras, and you'll find it somewhere on the menu. Closed Fri & Mon lunchtimes, plus Sun evening.

East from Cherbourg

East from Cherbourg, the **D901**, which switchbacks through a series of pretty valleys, is the most direct route to the old ports of **Barfleur** and **St-Vaast**. Following the D116 along the coast, however – signposted throughout as the **Route du Val de Saire** – takes you past a succession of stunning viewpoints, and some really lovely quasifortified villages, shielded from the sea winds by stout stone walls.

Barfleur

The pleasant little harbour village of **BARFLEUR**, 25km east of Cherbourg, was the biggest port in Normandy seven centuries ago. The population has since dwindled from 9000 to 600, and fortunes have diminished alongside – most recently through the invasion of a strain of plankton which poisoned all the mussels. It's now a surprisingly low-key place, whose grey-granite quayside and formal main street retain an appealing elegance. Although the sweeping crescent of the main harbour sees little tourist activity, clusters of tiny fishing vessels tie up alongside, and fresh fish is often for sale.

Barfleur's small **tourist office** (Tues–Sun 10am–12.30pm & 3–6pm; ☎02.33.54.02.48) is located near the church at the far left-hand end of the harbour. A lichen-covered rock on the shoreline nearby commemorates the fact that, when William the Conqueror embarked for southern England in 1066, it was in a ship constructed at Barfleur – the *Mora* – and piloted by a Barfleurais, Étienne. On November 25, 1120, his descendant, also called William, set out from here to return home after a visit to France. He was travelling in a separate vessel to his father, Henry I of England: according to a contemporary account, "she flew swifter than the winged arrow, sweeping the rippling surface of the deep; but the carelessness of the intoxicated crew drove her onto a rock, which rose above the waves not far from the shore". William (recently "outed" by historians as being gay) reached the safety of a small lifeboat, but turned back to sea upon hearing the cries of his sister, and was drowned together with 300 of his nobles.

Since 1834, the rock upon which William came to grief, north of Barfleur, has been guarded by the **Gatteville lighthouse**. A pleasant footpath leads there in thirty minutes from town, starting beside what was in 1865 the first lifeboat station to be built in France. At 75 metres, the lighthouse is the second tallest in France, with a beam that, in reaching fifty kilometres, overlaps with that of its opposite number on the Isle of Wight. Energetic visitors can climb the 365 steps to the top (daily: April–Sept 10am–noon & 2–7pm; Oct–March 10am–noon & 2–4pm; 10F/€1.52).

Barfleur has a fine selection of **hotels**. Much the best is *Le Conquérant*, a short distance back from the sea at 16–18 rue St-Thomas-à Becket (☎02.33.54.00.82; ②; closed mid-Nov to mid-March); its nicest rooms face onto a lovely garden courtyard, and there's a summer-only crêperie. Accommodation at *Le Moderne*, tucked away south of the main road at 1 place de Gaulle (☎02.33.23.12.44; ②; closed mid-Sept to mid-March), is not quite as appealing, but it's significantly cheaper, and the restaurant is quite superb, with the 144F/€21.95 menu including such treats as a fish-shaped *feuilleton* (pastry) of seafood. The house speciality is oysters, stuffed or raw.

St-Vaast

ST-VAAST-LA-HOUGUE, 11km south of Barfleur, is more of a resort, with lots of tiny Channel-crossing yachts moored in the bay where Edward III landed on his way to Crécy. The narrow spit of sand called **La Hougue**, south of the centre, holds various sporting facilities, such as tennis courts and a diving club, although the tip itself is a sealed-off military installation; the fortifications are graceful, courtesy (as ever) of Vauban. The whole area is at its best at high tide; low tide reveals, especially on the sheltered inland side, bleak, muddy flats dotted with some of the country's best-loved **oyster beds**.

In 1692 a French and Irish army gathered at St-Vaast and set sail for Britain in an attempt to restore the deposed Stuart King James II to the English throne. The fleet was, however, destroyed by a combined Anglo-Dutch force, before it could get any further than La Hougue.

That battle took place just off the sandy flat island of **Tatihou**, very close to the mainland, which now doubles as a bird sanctuary and the location of an ecologically minded Musée Maritime. A limited number of visitors each day are carried across by amphibious mud-wallowing **"ferries"** from St-Vaast; the exact schedule is determined by the state of the tides (mid-April to Sept daily 10am–12.30pm & 2–5pm; Oct to mid-April Sat & Sun 10am–noon & 1.30–5pm; ☎02.33.23.19.92, *www.saint-vaast-reville.com/tatihou*; 30F/€4.57 return, or 50F/€7.62 including admission).

The **hotel** *de France et des Fuchsias*, just back from the sea in St-Vaast at 18 rue du Maréchal Foch (☎02.33.54.42.26; ②–⑤; closed Mon in winter, & Jan to mid-Feb), with its splendid gardens, is an ideal stopover for ferry passengers – in fact both it and the annexe at the end of the garden are packed throughout the season with British visitors. The restaurant, too, is excellent, with an 85F/€12.96 weekday menu that changes daily, and gourmet four-course dinners of local produce from 130F/€19.82. If you can't get a room there, *La Granitière*, down the road at 74 rue du Maréchal Foch (☎02.33.54.58.99; ②–⑧; closed mid-Dec to mid-March), is a very acceptable alternative, and there are more rooms at the harbourside *Hôtel du Port*, 5 quai Vauban (☎02.33.23.42.42; ③; closed mid-Nov to mid-Dec). It's also possible to stay overnight in some very comfortable rooms on Tatihou island; contact *Accueil Tatihou* (☎02.33.23.19.92; ③).

Valognes

VALOGNES, around 18km through the woods from St-Vaast on the main road south from Cherbourg, is described in tourist handouts, with a dose perhaps of wishful thinking, as "the Versailles of Normandy". The description might have had some meaning before the war, when the region was full of aristocratic mansions, but now only a scattering of fine old houses remain, along with the very scant ruins of a Gallo-Roman settlement called Alauna.

All Valognes has to show for itself are a **cider museum** housed in an old water-mill (April–Sept Mon & Wed–Sat 10am–noon & 2–6pm, Sun 2–6pm; Oct–March groups by appointment; ☎02.33.40.22.73; 25F/€3.81), crammed with bizarre old wooden implements and ancient warped barrels – including a particularly obscene example upstairs – a little public garden and a big empty square, activated only for the Friday **market**. But it's a quiet, convenient alternative to waiting around in Cherbourg, and the country lanes around are enjoyable.

The rambling ivy-coated *Hôtel du Agriculture* at 16 rue L-Delisle (☎02.33.95.02.02; ①; closed Jan & Feb) is the best of several inexpensive **hotels**, and serves top-quality food on menus that start at 75F/€11.43 (restaurant closed Sun evening & Mon).

Utah Beach

The westernmost of the main Invasion Beaches, **Utah Beach**, stretches for approximately 30km south from St-Vaast. Operations here on D-Day started at 4.30am, with the capture of the uninhabited **Îles St-Marcouf**, clearly visible 6km offshore, while from 6.30am onwards 23,000 men and 1700 vehicles landed on the beach itself. A minor coast road, the D241, traces the edge of the dunes and enables visitors to follow the course of the fighting, though in truth there's precious little to see these days. Ships that were deliberately sunk to create artificial breakwaters are still visible at low tide, while markers along the seafront commemorate individual fallen heroes.

Quinéville

At the point where the D421 commences its coastal run, in **QUINÉVILLE**, the **Musée de la Liberté** (daily: mid-March to May & Oct to mid-Nov 10am–6pm; June–Sept 9.30am–7.30pm; 20F/€3.05) focuses on the everyday life of the people of Normandy under Nazi occupation. Its central reconstruction of a village street is adorned with German posters announcing the strict nightly curfew, or offering a 30,000F reward for anyone turning in a saboteur. Displays covering their American liberators include some fine shots of aircrews sporting Mohican haircuts.

A short way back from the beach, the *Hôtel de la Plage*, at 7 av de la Plage (☎02.33.21.43.54; ③; closed Mon in winter), offers six pleasant guest **rooms** and serves well-priced **meals**.

St-Martin-de-Varreville and Ste-Marie-du-Mont

Another 12km south of Quinéville, a monument at **ST-MARTIN-DE-VARRE-VILLE** salutes the French General Leclerc, who landed here with his 2nd Armoured Division on August 1, 1944; see also p.187.

The single best opportunity to learn about the Utah Beach landings comes at the southern end of the D421, however, in **STE-MARIE-DU-MONT**. Housed in a former German stronghold, the **Musée du Débarquement d'Utah-Beach** (April, May & Oct daily 10am–12.30pm & 2–5.30pm; June–Sept daily 9.30am–6.30pm; Nov–March Sat, Sun & hols 10am–12.30pm & 2–5pm; 27F/€4.12) explains operations in exhaustive detail, with huge seaview windows to lend immediacy to its copious models, maps, films and diagrams.

Ste-Mère-Église

The church of the market town of **STE-MÈRE-ÉGLISE**, a short way inland from Utah Beach on the main road between Valognes and Carentan, was immortalized in the film *The Longest Day*, thanks to scenes of an unfortunate US paratrooper dangling from its steeple during the heavy fighting. That incident was based on fact, and the man in question, John Steele, used to return occasionally to re-enact and commemorate his ordeal. He's now dead, but a uniformed mannequin is permanently entangled on the roof in his stead. The new stained glass above the main door of the church also depicts American parachutists, surrounding the Virgin with Child.

Just behind and to the right of the church, Ste-Mère's approximately parachute-shaped **Musée des Troupes Aéroportées** (Airborne Troops Museum) tells the story of the landings, complete with tanks, jeeps and even a troop-carrying plane (Feb, March & Oct to mid-Nov daily 10am–noon & 2–6pm; April daily 9am–noon & 2–6.45pm; May–Sept daily 9am–6.45pm; last fortnight of Nov Sat & Sun 10am–noon & 2–6pm; closed Dec & Jan; 25F/€3.81).

The only **hotel** in Ste-Mère-Église is the ugly modern *logis Le Ste-Mère*, south of the centre at the intersection of the main street with N13 (☎02.33.21.00.30; ③), which offers 75F/€11.43 buffet dinners and set menus from 90F/€13.72. The small *Café Au Domino* is just outside the museum entrance, facing the church; its outdoor seating makes it a good spot for lunch.

West from Cherbourg

The stretch of coast immediately west of Cherbourg is similar to that to the east, although it holds no harbour town to compare with Barfleur or St-Vaast. The old villages of **Omonville-la-Petite** and **Omonville-la-Rogue**, 20km out of Cherbourg, are lovely places to stroll around, while all the way along you'll find wild and isolated countryside where you can lean against the wind, watch waves smashing against rocks or sunbathe in a spring profusion of wild flowers.

Cap de la Hague and Goury

The real drawback of the area around **Cap de la Hague** is that the discharges of "low-level" radioactive wastes from the **nuclear reprocessing plant** may discourage you from swimming. In 1980, the Greenpeace vessel *Rainbow Warrior* chased a ship bringing spent Japanese fuel into Cherbourg harbour. The *Rainbow Warrior's* crew were arrested, but all charges were dropped when 3000 Cherbourg dockers threatened to strike in their support. In the spring of 1985 the French secret service finally took their revenge on the *Rainbow Warrior* by sinking it in Auckland harbour, and killing a member of the crew in the process. The reprocessing plant would be delighted to welcome you to inspect their facilities (3hr tours, minimum age 15: April–Sept Mon–Sat 9am–6pm, Sun 2–6pm; ☎02.33.02.73.04 for reservations; free). For a full update on the continuing controversies surrounding the plant, see p.399.

The main road, the D901, continues a couple of kilometres beyond the plant to **GOURY**, where the fields finally roll down to a craggy pebble coastline. Almost the only building amid the windswept splendour, the *Auberge de Goury* (☎02.33.52.77.01; closed Sun & Mon evenings), is a really excellent **restaurant**, facing the octagonal lifeboat station and looking out towards a slate-grey lighthouse. It specializes in charcoal-grilled fish and meat, with a wide-ranging cheeseboard that includes the extraordinary *voluptueuse*, and is (not surprisingly) very popular at lunchtimes.

From the cape of **La Hague** itself, the northern tip of the peninsula, bracken-covered hills and narrow valleys run south to the cliffs of the Nez de Jobourg, claimed in wild local optimism to be the highest in Europe. **South of La Hague**, a great curve of sand – some of it military training ground – takes the land's edge to **FLAMANVILLE** and another nuclear installation.

On the other side, facing north, **PORT RACINE** declares itself rather ludicrously to be the smallest port in France – it consists of one little jetty, some way down a hillside from a tiny and extremely tranquil pension-only hotel, *L'Erguillère* (☎02.33.52.75.31; ④).

Barneville-Carteret

The next two sweeps of beach down to Carteret, with sand dunes like miniature mountain ranges, are among the best **beaches** in Normandy if you have transport and want solitude.

CARTERET itself, sheltered by a rocky headland, is the nearest harbour to **Jersey**, just 25km away across seas made somewhat treacherous by the fast Alderney current. The old port area is not especially attractive, but does have several seafront hotels, including a couple of *logis de France*, the *Hôtel de la Marine* at 11 rue de Paris in the little shopping street (☎02.33.53.83.31; ④–⑦; closed Nov to mid-Feb, plus Sun evening & Mon in Feb, March & Oct), and the *Hôtel du Cap* on the quayside route de la Plage further out (☎02.33.53.85.89; ②; closed Jan & Feb).

Visitors who prefer to be beside a beach should head instead for the twin community of **BARNEVILLE**, directly across the mouth of the bay but a few kilometres away by road. Here an endless (and quite exposed) stretch of clean, firm sand is backed by a long row of weather-beaten villas and the odd hotel, including the *Hôtel les Isles* near the northern end at 9 bd Maritime (☎02.33.04.90.76; ②; closed mid-Nov to mid-Feb), which has a superb restaurant that offers views clear to the Channel Islands on fine evenings. Dinner prices start at 72F/€10.98, with a 138F/€21.04 *menu du terroir* that includes oysters stewed in *pommeau*.

There are two **campsites** in the dunes north of town, the two-star *Le Ranch* at Le Rozel (☎02.33.52.40.09; closed Nov–March) and the three-star *Les Mielles* at Surtainville (☎02.33.04.31.04).

Portbail

Five kilometres further down the coast from Barneville, the dunes are interrupted once again by the broad estuary of the Ollonde River. Set slightly back from the sea, **PORTBAIL** is a delightful village with a sweet little Romanesque church. Its streets are thronged on summer Tuesdays with a bustling **market**, where as well as buying spit-roasted chickens and fresh oysters you can pick up a dining table or have your chairs reupholstered. Access to two fine beaches is by way of an old stone bridge, beneath which crowds of fishermen wade thigh-deep in the river.

Portbail has a small year-round **hotel** in the main square – *La Galiche*, place E-Laquaine (☎02.33.04.84.18; ①), and a couple of good **restaurants**. Both *Aux XIII Arches*, near the start of the bridge (☎02.33.04.87.90), where you can get nine oysters and a glass of wine for 45F/€6.86, and *Au Rendezvous des Pêcheurs*, almost opposite but slightly closer to the square (☎02.33.04.81.37), specialize in seafood.

Bricquebec

Fifteen kilometres inland from Carteret, halfway to Valognes, the old market town of **BRICQUEBEC** is dominated by the well-preserved twelfth-century castle at its heart. Part of this attractive edifice, centred around a peaceful courtyard, is run as the upmarket *Hôtel-Restaurant du Vieux Château* (☎02.33.52.24.49; ④). Queen Victoria once stayed here, but unfortunately while the tacky furnishings and slapdash service make it feel at first like a treasurable piece of kitsch, the restaurant is so bad that there's not much point in coming; they also impose hefty parking fees for cars and even bicycles. Across the main square in front of the castle – scene of a busy Monday **market** – the unassuming *Donjon*, 2–4 place Ste-Anne (☎02.33.52.23.15; ②), is by contrast a very welcoming little hotel, with a good bistro restaurant.

Lessay

Heading south from Carteret, the road around the headland joins the main D900 at **LESSAY**, where an important Romanesque **monastery** stands right in the heart of town. Until the war it was one of the few early Norman churches still intact. When it had to be restored from scratch afterwards, guided by photographs, the job was done using not only the original stone but also the original tools and methods.

The square central tower of Lessay is similar to that which collapsed centuries ago on Mont-St-Michel (see p.162). Monks at the abbey sing Gregorian chants each Sunday, and are very much in evidence at the **Holy Cross Fair** in the first half of September, which also celebrates cattle and other animals (more information from the tourist office on ☎02.33.46.46.18). The town is served by **buses** en route between Cherbourg and Coutances.

Lessay's tiny aerodrome, south of town, was where **Charles Lindbergh** landed on completing the first transatlantic flight in 1927; the first beach he crossed is now called plage Lindbergh.

Château de Pirou

Off the main coastal road, the D650, roughly 2km south of the junction for Lessay, turns inland a few hundred metres to reach the **Château de Pirou** (Easter–June & Sept–Oct daily except Tues 10am–noon & 2–6.30pm; July & Aug daily 10am–noon & 2–6.30pm; Nov–Easter daily except Tues 10am–noon & 2–5.30pm; 25F/€3.81). Although you see nothing from the road, once you've passed through its three successive fortified gateways you are confronted by a ravishing little castle. Some historians have suggested that this is the oldest castle in Normandy, dating back to the earliest Viking raids; it's thought to have taken its current form around the twelfth century.

Considering that it was converted into a farm, and then for centuries forgotten and all but submerged in ivy, it remains remarkably complete. Originally built of wood, on the coast, it was later remodelled in stone and now stands encircled by a broad moat, its towers rising sheer from the water. At your own risk, you can pick your way up to the top of the keep and look out over the surrounding fields. In summer, a tapestry depicting the Norman invasion of Sicily is on display in a barn opposite the drawbridge.

Pirou-Plage

Heading towards the sea instead of inland at the turn-off for the Château de Pirou brings you to a dead-end in a couple of hundred metres at the tiny community of **PIROU-PLAGE**. When the tide is low, you can see the "*buchôts*", poles used in the cultivation of shellfish, poking up from the six-kilometre strand of sand that stretches away to either side. To sample the local produce, call in at the seafront **restaurant** *de la Mer* (☎02.33.46.43.36).

Feugères and Le Mesnilbus

If you have time, it's worth straying east of the main roads towards Coutances, to spend a while on the **D57**, and to enjoy the magnificent countryside, with undulating meadows filled with rich flowers and sleek animals placidly waiting to be eaten. The village square of **FEUGÈRES** is completely taken up by an amazing tangle of warped wood, once some sort of cider press and mill. From there on to tiny **LE MESNILBUS**, where the delightfully rural *Auberge des Bonnes Gens* (☎02.33.07.66.85; ②; closed Sun evening & Mon in low season) offers menus to suit every palate and pocket, as well as arranging **horse-riding** expeditions.

Coutances

The old hill town of **COUTANCES**, 65km south of Cherbourg and confined by its site to just one main street, has on its summit a landmark for all the surrounding countryside – the **Cathédrale de Notre Dame**, whose twin towers stand in magnificent silhouette against the sky. Essentially Gothic, it is very Norman in its unconventional blending of architectural traditions; Louis XIV's master architect Vauban said the lantern tower must be "the work of a madman". The *sons et lumières*, on Sunday evenings and throughout the summer, are for once a true complement to the light-stone building. Also illuminated on summer nights (and left open) are the fountained **Jardins Publiques**, highly formal gardens with smooth rolling lawns, a well of flowers, a fountain of obelisks and an odd ziggurat of hedges. They enclose a small **Musée Municipal** (July to mid-Sept daily except Tues 10am–noon & 2–6pm; mid-Sept to June daily except Wed 10am–noon & 2–5pm; 10F/€1.52), which has a rather dull collection of paintings but a nice line in pretentious art exhibitions.

Practicalities

Coutances's **gare SNCF** (☎02.33.07.50.77) is about 1.5km southeast of the town centre (at the bottom of the hill), and also serves as the stop for buses heading both north and south. The **tourist office** is housed in a new wing behind the Hôtel de Ville in place Georges-Léclerc (July & Aug Mon–Sat 10am–1pm & 2–7pm, Sun 3–7pm; Sept–June Mon–Fri 10am–12.30pm & 2–6pm, Sat 10am–12.30pm & 2–5pm; ☎02.33.19.08.10).

The cream-coloured *Hôtel de Normandie*, behind and below the cathedral at 2 place du Gaulle (☎02.33.45.01.40; ②; closed Sun evening, & Fri between Sept and mid-May), has **rooms** of varying quality, and menus that range from the good-value 55F/€8.38 option (not Sun) to an excellent 98F/€14.94 spread. A better alternative for motorists is the *Relais du Viaduc*, at 25 av de Verdun (☎02.33.45.02.68; ②; closed Fri evening, plus Sat in low season, and second fortnight of Feb) – the junction of the D7 and D971, south of town – which can be a little noisy but serves some fine food, with menus starting at 58F/€8.84 on weekdays. The excellent year-round municipal **campsite**, *Les Vignettes* (☎02.33.45.43.13), halfway up the hill west of town that's climbed by the D44 towards Agon, stands next to a large, comfortable chain hotel, the *Cositel* (☎02.33.07.51.64; ④).

The Manoir de Saussey

Roughly five steep kilometres south of Coutances, up the D7, the **Manoir de Saussey** is a slightly creepy old manor house containing a glass museum and an assortment of venerable furnishings (Easter–Sept daily 2–6.30pm; 20F/€3.05). Some of the fragile glassworks on show date back as far as the first century AD, when they were manufactured in the Near East; there are also pieces from six-teenth-century Venice. Outbuildings serve as antique shops, though not all of their bizarre bric-a-brac is for sale, and that which is tends to be very expensive. Visitors are welcome to walk around the lovely gardens without paying the admission fee.

Coutainville

COUTAINVILLE, the nearest resort to Coutances, is crammed in summer with bronzed and glamorous posers and their turbocharged status symbols. This is an utterly nondescript stretch of coast, where the open sea batters against an end-less, featureless beach. Huge tides expose massive sandflats, while behind the line of dunes dull holiday homes are punctuated by the occasional snack bar, campsite or motel.

A long walk south from town, fighting against the wind, brings you to the **Pointe d'Agon** after 3km or 4km, where a lighthouse commands a view of the dune envi-ronment at its most ecologically unspoiled.

Coutainville's tiny little centre, out of all proportion to the long strip of coast that comes under its sway, holds the *Hôtel Hardy*, 23 av Tourville (☎02.33.47.04.11; ③; closed mid-Jan to mid-Feb, plus Sun evening & Mon in low season), a pleasant little *logis* with high-priced but very good food. Rooms at the *Hôtel Neptune*, right on the seafront (☎02.33.47.07.66; ③; closed Oct–March), are a bit more expensive, but several enjoy magnificent sea views. Otherwise, there are several shorefront **campsites**, including *Le Martinet* (☎02.33.47.05.20; closed Nov–March) and *Le Sémaphore* (☎02.33.47.29.27; July & Aug only), both of which are two-star.

Abbaye de Hambye

What's left of the **Abbaye de Hambye** stands in a very sylvan setting 20km southeast of Coutances and 10km northwest of Villedieu (see p.197), with little lawns laid out in front, an orchard alongside, and cows grazing in the adjacent meadows (March Sun 1–6pm; April–Oct daily 10am–noon & 2–6pm; 25F/€3.81). The abbey, which is very reminiscent of such Yorkshire abbeys as Rievaulx, was constructed as a Cistercian monastery in the second half of the twelfth century, at a time when builders were trembling on the brink of abandoning the Romanesque tradition in favour of the new Gothic style. Much of the structure was quarried for stone and left in ruins after the Revolution; nineteenth-century prints show the walls drowning in rampant ivy. However, the central tower still stands foursquare above the high narrow walls of the nave, and a few delicate but-tresses remain in place, the whole ensemble crammed in tight against a wooded hillside and inhabited mostly by crows. Beyond the little exhibition in the entrance room above the ancient gateway, visitors are guided around and among the ruins, with an optional pause to examine the rather dull displays of vestments in what was once the lay-brothers' dormitory.

A luxurious rural **hotel**, the *Auberge de l'Abbaye*, is located 100m from the abbey at the turning off the D51 (☎02.33.61.42.19; ④; closed Mon, plus mid-Feb to mid-March & mid-Sept to mid-Oct). There being few alternative ways to pass an evening here, its restaurant serves up extravagant gourmet dinners.

Granville

From Coutances, the D971 runs down to the coast at **GRANVILLE**, the Norman equivalent to Brittany's St-Malo, with a similar history of piracy and a severe citadel, the **haute ville**, guarding the approaches to the bay of Mont-St-Michel across from Cancale. Thanks in part to the long beach that stretches away north of town, which disappears almost completely at low tide, it's the most lively town and most popular resort in the area. However, it simply doesn't match the appeal of its Breton rival, with its nightmarish traffic and hordes of tourists milling around in summer in the vain hope of finding some way of amusing themselves.

The great difference between Granville and St-Malo is that here the fortified **citadel**, reached by steep stairs from alongside the beach and casino, or circuitous-climbing roads from the port, contains virtually nothing of interest. Three or four long narrow parallel streets of forbidding grey-granite eighteenth-century houses lead up the church of Notre-Dame, while the gardens above the port hold a statue of the city's best-known pirate, Georges Pléville le Pellay, splendidly complete with peg leg and cutlass. The views up and down the coast, across to Mont-St-Michel and out to the Îles Chausey, are dramatic, but no more so than in many other towns along the Cotentin coast.

Granville had an unexpected brush with destiny on March 9, 1945, when it was overrun for an hour and a half by German commandos from Jersey, long after the invading Allied forces had swept on to Germany.

Arrival and information

Trains between Paris and Cherbourg arrive well to the east of the town centre at the **gare SNCF** (☎02.33.50.05.45) on avenue Maréchal-Leclerc, which doubles as the **gare routière** (☎02.33.50.77.89). Several **ferry** operators – listed on p.165 – sail to Jersey, Guernsey and Sark (all around 300F/€45.73 return), or to the Îles Chausey, while in summer Alizes Émeraude also run day-trips to St-Malo in Brittany (3–4 weekly in July & Aug only; ☎02.33.50.16.36; 100F/€15.24 return). The **tourist office** is down below the citadel at 4 cours Jonville (July & Aug Mon–Sat 9am–7.30pm, Sun 10.30am–12.30pm & 4–6pm; Sept–June Mon–Sat 9am–12.30pm & 2–6.30pm; ☎02.33.91.30.03, *www.ville-granville.fr*).

Bikes can be rented from the station or Le Coulant on avenue de la Libération, and there's a covered **market** opposite the Mairie on Saturday mornings.

Accommodation

With so many visitors in summer, Granville is a place where it's well worth booking **accommodation** in advance. There are no hotels in the *haute ville*; most of the possibilities are concentrated in the new town, either beneath the walls near the casino on the seaward side, or near the station. The modern, oceanfront *Centre Regional de Nautisme* (☎02.33.91.22.60; closed Sun in low season), 1km south of the station just south of the town centre, serves as Granville's **hostel**. Dorm beds cost 79F/€12.04, while a private double is 125F/€19.06; sailing lessons are easy to arrange.

Hôtel des Bains, 19 rue G-Clémenceau (☎02.33.50.17.31, fax 02.33.50.89.22). Very central upmarket hotel, facing the casino just below the old town, with four good-quality, mostly seaview rooms. ③.

Hotel de la Mer, 74 rue du Port (☎02.33.50.01.86, fax 02.33.50.67.56). Simple hotel in front of the piles of rusting ironmongery of the commercial port, a short walk from the town centre. The restaurant has a dull 89F/€13.57 menu but gets interesting at 115F/€17.53; there's a small streetside terrace, but you have to sit upstairs to get a view. Closed mid-Nov to mid-Dec, plus Mon & Tues in low season. ③.

Hôtel Michelet, 5 rue Jules-Michelet (☎02.33.50.06.55, fax 02.33.50.12.25). White-fronted hotel, very near the sea and facing towards the high crags of the old town, which offers reasonably well-equipped but rather characterless rooms, and has no restaurant. ①.

Hôtel Normandy Chaumière, 20 rue Paul-Poirier (☎02.33.50.01.71, fax 02.33.50.15.34). Cheerful, very central hotel, set slightly back from (and, oddly, a bit below) a narrow little street in the thick of the new town, not far from the tourist office. Nice menus in the restaurant downstairs start at 99F/€15.09, though you'll have to spend more than that if you don't fancy "crusty winkles". Closed Tues evening & Wed out of season. ③.

Hôtel Terminus, 5 place de la Gare (☎02.33.50.02.05). Simple, inexpensive hotel, immediately across from the station. ②.

Eating

Several of Granville's hotels have their own good dining rooms, as described above, but the town also has a fine selection of waterfront **restaurants**, hard below the citadel walls. Be warned that the views here are of a gritty commercial port rather than a delightful harbour.

La Citadelle, 34 rue du Port (☎02.33.50.34.10). The closest to the town centre of the port's top-notch seafood places. The 85F/€12.96 menu comes with the usual sea snails, while the superb 190F/€28.97 option features a dozen oysters grilled with Camembert. Closed Tues evening & Wed in winter.

L'Échauguette, 24 rue St-Jean (☎02.33.50.51.87). Cosy, stone-walled old-town crêperie, which serves good simple meals, grilled over an open fire. *Galettes* cost under 40F/€6.10, meat main courses more like 65F/€9.91. Closed Tues.

Le Phare, 11 rue du Port (☎02.33.50.12.94). Seafront fish restaurant, facing the small-boat harbour towards the end of the peninsula, which has the standard mussels and *soupe de poissons* on its 89F/€13.57 menu, and an extraordinarily copious *assiette des fruits de mer* on the 148F/€22.56 one. Closed Jan, Tues evening & Wed Sept–June.

Restaurant du Port, 19 rue du Port (☎02.33.50.00.55). Top-quality seafood place, just along from the *Phare* at the small-boat harbour, with a mouthwatering assortment of very fishy menus, and an unbelievably garlicky fish soup as its speciality. Menus range from 69F/€10.52 ("except weekends and off days") up to 190F/€28.97; 85F/€12.96 gets you six oysters and a plate of paella, while the good-value 139F/€21.19 menu features stuffed oysters and a delicious parcel of duck in Camembert sauce.

The Îles Chausey

Now an uninviting and virtually uninhabited wasteland – though equipped with long beaches of fine sand – the **Îles Chausey** were the site of the quarries which provided the granite that built Mont-St-Michel. They originally formed part of the ancient Forest of Scissy, until exceptional tides at the spring equinox of 709 AD, combined with strong north winds, flooded the entire region. There is just one (summer-only) **hotel**, the lonely *Hôtel du Fort et Îles* (☎02.33.50.25.02; ④; closed Oct–April, restaurant closed Mon), which insists on a minimum stay of three nights.

Two **ferry** companies operate up to three services each per day out to the islands from Granville's *gare maritime*: Jolie France II (March–Dec; ☎02.33.50.31.81) and Alizes Emeraude (April–Sept; ☎02.33.50.16.36). Precise timings and frequencies depend on the tides, the trip takes just under an hour each way, and day-returns cost around 94F/€14.33.

Around Granville

If you prefer to be out of town, the coastal countryside is best to the **north**, although the villages tend to be non-events. As well as the ubiquitous windsurfers, the huge flat sands attract hordes of sand-yachters. Among **accommodation** possibilities, **BRÉVILLE** has the small *Auberge des Quatre Routes*, 2 rue de l'Église (☎02.33.91.91.83; ②; closed first fortnight of Oct), while **COUDEVILLE** has a good campsite on its long beach, the two-star *Dunes* (☎02.33.61.60.01; closed Oct–Easter), and a large (and highly unrecommended) hotel in a converted sanatorium, the *Relais des Îles*.

To the south, **JULLOUVILLE** is younger, more upbeat and very tacky, with an endless drag of amusements, fast-food joints and soda bars, while **CAROLLES** has a good beach, but little more; its one hotel is uninviting. However, in the clifftop community of **CHAMPEAUX**, a short steep climb further on from Carolles, the *Hôtel les Hermelles* (☎02.33.61.85.94; ④; closed Tues evening, Wed & all Jan), enjoys a truly spectacular view out across the bay, and has a superb restaurant.

At **ST-JEAN-LE-THOMAS** – which promotes itself as "le Petit Nice de la Manche" but is remarkably *unlike* Nice in that it consists of a single street leading up to a beach – the bay becomes so narrow that at low tide it is possible to walk across to Mont-St-Michel. However, this is not a walk to take on a drunken, or any other, impulse; as the notices advise, "It's dangerous to risk you in the bay during the rising tide. This can surprise you at each time." A special telephone line provides details of the times of the tides, on ☎02.33.50.02.67.

Avranches

AVRANCHES, perched high above the bay on an abrupt granite outcrop, is the nearest large town to Mont-St-Michel. It has always had close connections with the abbey. The Mont's original church was founded by an eighth-century bishop of Avranches, spurred on by the Archangel Michael, who supposedly became so impatient with the lack of progress that he prodded a hole in the bishop's skull (later gold-plated, it now forms part of the *trésor* of Avranches's St-Gervais basilica). Robert of Torigny, a subsequent abbot of St-Michel, played host in the town on several occasions to Henry II of England, the most memorable being when Henry was obliged, bare-footed and bare-headed, to escape excommunication by doing public penance for the murder of Thomas à Becket, on May 22, 1172.

The arena for Henry's act of contrition was **Avranches Cathedral**. Designed by Robert himself, though without expertise, it eventually "crumbled and fell for want of proper support"; all that now marks the site of Henry's humbling is a fenced-off platform.

A more vivid evocation of the area's medieval splendours comes from the illuminated manuscripts, mostly created on the Mont, on display in the town **museum** (April & May daily except Tues 9.30am–noon & 2–6pm; June–Sept daily 9.30am–noon & 2–6pm; 15F/€2.29).

The ruins of the old **castle** stand high above the tourist office; the highest point of all is the former keep, which, together with the vestiges of a small section of ramparts, has been landscaped into a small garden. From the very top you get long views over Avranches itself, and the Mont away to the west. The terrace of Avranches' large formal public gardens, the **Jardin des Plantes** across town, is another good vantage point for the Mont.

A monument to General George Patton, southeast of the town centre, commemorates the spot where he stayed the night before his crucial Avranches breakthrough, at the end of July 1944. This small plot of land was ceded to the USA, so technically the statue stands on US soil – and literally it does, too, earth having been brought across the Atlantic to create a memorial garden.

Practicalities

Avranches' **gare SNCF** is a long way below the town centre; the walk up is enough to discourage most rail travellers from stopping here at all. The **tourist office** is located in the central square – scene of a lively market on Thursdays – at 2 place Général-de-Gaulle (July & Aug daily 9am–8pm; Sept–June Mon–Fri 10am–12.30pm & 2–7pm; ☎02.33.58.00.22). In high summer, one **bus** per day runs to Mont-St-Michel from right outside.

The nicest **hotel** has to be the gloriously old-fashioned *Croix d'Or*, near the Patton monument at 83 rue de la Constitution (☎02.33.58.04.88; ③; closed Jan), which boasts beautiful hydrangea-filled gardens and absolutely the best **restaurant** in town. Reasonable alternatives include *Le Jardin des Plantes*, 10 place Carnot (☎02.33.58.03.68; ②), where the restaurant is more basic but very good value, while for a quick meal, the *Commerce*, a busy lunch spot opposite the tourist office at 5 rue du Général-de-Gaulle (☎02.33.58.07.66), serves a tasty *choucroute*.

If you're **camping**, a better base for the Mont than Avranches would be the two-star, English-owned *Vallée de la Sélune* site (☎02.33.60.39.00; closed mid-Oct to March) at **PONTAUBAULT**, 7km to the south.

Mont-St-Michel

The island at the very frontier of Normandy and Brittany, which for over a millennium has housed – indeed, all but consisted of – the stupendous abbey of **MONT-ST-MICHEL**, was once known as "the Mount in Peril from the Sea". Many were the pilgrims in medieval times who were drowned or sucked under by quicksand while trying to cross the bay to this eighty-metre-high rocky outcrop. The Archangel Michael was its vigorous protector, the most militant spirit of the Church Militant, with a marked tendency to leap from rock to rock in titanic struggles against Paganism and Evil.

The abbey dates back to the eighth century, when the Archangel appeared to a bishop of Avranches, Aubert, who duly founded a monastery on the island poking out of the Baie du Mont-St-Michel. Since the eleventh century – when work on the sturdy church at the peak commenced – new buildings have been grafted onto the island to produce a fortified hotchpotch of Romanesque and Gothic buildings, piled one on top of the other and clambering to the pinnacle of the graceful church, to form probably the most recognizable silhouette in France after the Eiffel Tower.

Over the course of its long history, the island has many times been besieged. However, unlike all the rest of northern France, it was never captured, not even during the 27 years, from 1423 to 1450, when the English had a permanent fort on nearby Tombelaine. It took the Revolution to close the monastery down, rename the island "Free Mount", and convert it into a prison. Although the abbey was home to a large community – a fortress town – even at its twelfth-century peak it never housed more than sixty monks, who said Mass for pilgrims and ran their own school of art. On its thousandth anniversary, in 1966, the Benedictines were invited to return; today, a dozen nuns and monks from the Monastic Fraternity of Jerusalem maintain a presence.

For many years now, the Mont has no longer, strictly speaking, been an island – the causeway (*digue*) that leads to it is never submerged, and is continuing to silt up to either side. Current plans envisage that the causeway will be cut away from 2003 onwards, and replaced by a bridge, which should not only make tourist numbers easier to control but also enable the sea to wash away much of the accumulated silt.

Arrival and information

In addition to the regular **bus** service from the nearest *gare SNCF* at Pontorson (see p.163), Les Courriers Bretons (☎02.99.19.70.70, *www.lescourriersbreton.fr*) run scheduled services to Mont-St-Michel from the *gare SNCF* in **Rennes** (see p.227), and from **St-Malo** (see p.208). Mont-St-Michel has its own **tourist office**, in the lowest gateway (mid-June to mid-Sept Mon–Sat 9am–7pm, Sun 9am–noon & 2–6pm; mid-Sept to mid-June Mon, Tues & Thurs–Sat 9am–noon & 2–6pm; ☎02.33.60.14.30), and **post office**.

Tours

Walking tours across the bay to Mont-St-Michel set off from **Genêts** on a schedule that varies according to the tides. Quite how far you go, and how much time you spend once you get there, changes daily; by way of example, a half-day tour as far as Tombelaine costs 50F/€7.62, while an eleven-hour trip, with a full day on the Mont, is 115F/€17.53. Call La Maison de la Baie (☎02.33.89.64.00) for a full programme.

It's also possible to see the Mont by **helicopter**. Flash Helicoptère (☎02.33.48.51.62) takes off from the village of **Brée**, just west of Pontorson, charging 100F/€15.24 for virtually no time at all, 250F/€38.11 for five minutes, and 550F/€83.85 for a quarter of an hour.

The Island

The base of Mont-St-Michel rests on a primeval slime of sand and mud. Just above that, you pass through the heavily fortified **Porte du Roi** onto the narrow **Grande Rue**, climbing steadily around the base of the rock, and lined with medieval gabled houses and a jumble of overpriced postcard and souvenir shops, maintaining the ancient tradition of prising money out of pilgrims. A plaque near the main staircase records that Jacques Cartier was presented to King François I here on May 8, 1532 and charged with exploring the shores of Canada.

The rather dry **Musée Maritime** offers an insight into the island's ties with the sea, while the Archangel Michael manages in just fifteen minutes to lead visitors on a voyage through space and time in the **Archéoscope**, with the full majestic

---

VISITING MONT ST-MICHEL

Access to the **island** of Mont-St-Michel is free and unrestricted, although there's a 15F/€2.29 fee to **park** on either the causeway or the sands below it (which are submerged by the tides). If you're visiting by car in summer, you might prefer to park on the mainland well short of the Mont, both to enjoy the walk across the causeway and to avoid the dense traffic jams. It also pays to **get there early**, before the tour parties arrive.

Between May and September, the **abbey** is open daily from 9am to 5.30pm; from October to April, it's open daily from 9.30am until 4.30pm, except during school holidays, when the hours are 9.30am until 5pm. It's **closed** on Jan 1, May 1, Nov 1, Nov 11 and Dec 25. Paying the standard 40F/€6.10 **admission fee** – ages 12–25 25F/€3.81, under-12s free – entitles you to wander the generally accessible areas, and to join an expert-led **guided tour** in the language of your choice. Tours last 45min between mid-June and mid-Sept, and a full hour the rest of the year; the daily schedule for each language is displayed at the entrance. There are also a number of more detailed **two-hour tours**, in French only, which take you both higher and deeper and cost 65F/€9.91 (ages 12–25; 45F/€6.86). **Mass** is said at 12.15pm every day, with a nursery provided below for children under eight years old.

For several years, the Mont also reopened to visitors at night, but that experiment has now been discontinued.

panoply of multimedia trickery. Further along the Grande Rue and up the steps towards the abbey church, next door to the eleventh-century **church of St-Pierre**, the absurd **Musée Grévin** contains such edifying specimens as a wax model of a woman drowning in a sea of mud (all open Feb to mid-Nov daily 9am–6pm; 75F/€11.43 for all, or 45F/€6.86 each one).

Large crowds gather each day at the **North Tower** to watch the tide sweep in across the bay. During the high tides of the equinoxes (March & Sept), the waters are alleged to rush in like a foaming galloping horse. Seagulls wheel away in alarm, and those foolish enough to be wandering too late on the sands toward Tombelaine have to sprint to safety.

Amazingly enough, less than a third of the three million visitors who come to Mont-St-Michel each year climb up to visit the abbey itself, so the higher you go the more the crowds thin out. If you're impatient to escape all the jostling, you can duck through St-Pierre church to reach the **gardens**. From the various footpaths here, popular with picnickers, you can see the giant ramp up the side of the hill, up which prisoners used to haul supplies for the abbey by walking around a tread-mill at the top.

The Abbey

The abbey, an architectural ensemble which incorporates the high-spired archangel-topped church and the magnificent Gothic buildings known since 1228 as the **Merveille** ("The Marvel") – incorporating the entire north face, with the cloister, Knights' Hall, Refectory, Guest Hall and cellars – is visible from all around the bay, but it becomes if anything more awe-inspiring the closer you approach. In Maupassant's words:

> *I reached the huge pile of rocks which bears the little city dominated by the great church. Climbing the steep narrow street, I entered the most wonderful Gothic building ever made for God on this earth, a building as vast as a town, full of low rooms under oppressive ceilings and lofty galleries supported by frail pillars. I entered that gigantic granite jewel, which is as delicate as a piece of lacework, thronged with towers and slender belfries which thrust into the blue sky of day and the black sky of night their strange heads bristling with chimeras, devils, fantastic beasts and monstrous flowers, and which are linked together by carved arches of intricate design.*

The Mont's rock comes to a sharp point just below what is now the transept of the **church**, a building where the transition from Romanesque to Gothic is only too evident in the vaulting of the nave. In order to lay out the church's ground plan in the traditional shape of the cross, supporting crypts had to be built up from the surrounding hillside, and in all construction work the Chausey granite has had to be sculpted to match the exact contours of the hill. Space was always limited, and yet the building has grown through the centuries, with an architectural ingenuity that constantly surprises in its geometry – witness the shock of emerging into the light of the **cloisters** from the sombre Great Hall. The statue of St Francis of Assisi here commemorates the fact that 1228, when the cloisters were completed, was the same year that Francis was canonized.

Not surprisingly, the building of the monastery was no smooth progression; the original church, choir, nave and tower all had to be replaced after collapsing. The style of decoration has varied, too, along with the architecture. That you now walk through halls of plain, grey stones is a reflection of modern taste, specifically that of the director of the French Department of Antiquities. In the Middle Ages, the walls of public areas such as the refectory would have been festooned with tapestries and frescoes, while the original coloured tiles of the cloisters have long since been stripped away to reveal bare walls.

All visitors exit the monastery on its north side; as you follow the circling footpath back to the mayhem below, you pass beneath what Victor Hugo described as "the most beautiful wall in Europe".

To get a clearer sense of the abbey's historical development, be sure to take a look at the intriguing scale models in the reception area, which depict it during four different epochs.

Accommodation and eating

The island holds a surprising number of **hotels** and **restaurants**, if nothing like enough to cope with the sheer number of visitors. Most are predictably expensive, though virtually all the hotels seem to keep a few cheaper rooms (presumably there just isn't the space to refit and expand them in order to put the prices up); all charge extra if you want to enjoy a view of the sea.

The most famous **hotel**, *La Mère Poulard* (☎02.33.60.14.01; ④–⑨), uses the time-honoured legend of its fluffy omelettes, as enjoyed by Leon Trotsky and Margaret Thatcher (not simultaneously), to justify extortionate charges. Higher up the Mont, however, prices fall to more realistic levels. The cheapest option is the *Du Guesclin* (☎02.33.60.14.10; ④; closed mid-Nov to mid-March), where all the rooms have TV, but the restaurant, without outdoor seating, is almost unique in Normandy in deserving to be called bad. Both the *Hôtel La Croix Blanche* (☎02.33.60.14.04; ⑤; closed mid-Nov to mid-Dec) and the *Mouton Blanc* (☎02.33.60.14.08; ④; closed Jan) serve much better food, in both cases with basic menus for around 80F/€12.20 and more attractive options for 110F/€16.77 and upwards. Every restaurant on the island seems to serve its own version of the *Mère Poulard* omelette as a budget alternative.

In addition, the main approach road to the island, the D976, is lined shortly before the causeway by around a dozen large and virtually indistinguishable hotels and motels, each with its own brasserie or restaurant. Typical among these are the *Motel Vert* (☎02.33.60.09.33; ③; closed mid-Nov to mid-Feb); the *Hôtel Formule Verte* (☎02.33.60.14.13; ③; closed mid-Nov to mid-Feb); and the *Hôtel de la Digue* (☎02.33.60.14.02; ④; closed mid-Nov to mid-March). The three-star, 350-pitch *Camping du Mont-St-Michel* (☎02.33.60.09.33; closed mid-Nov to mid-Feb) is also on the mainland just short of the causeway.

Pontorson

Many visitors to Mont-St-Michel find themselves lodging either at Avranches or **PONTORSON**, 6km inland. The latter has the nearest **gare SNCF**, connected to the Mont by an overpriced bus service (40F/€6.10 day-return), but also (as ever) renting out cycles. Nothing much about Pontorson itself is worth staying for, although the café attached to the station isn't bad.

The **hotels** are not especially interesting, but both the *Montgomery*, in a fine old ivy-covered mansion at 13 rue du Couesnon (☎02.33.60.00.09; ③; closed Nov–March), and the *Bretagne*, just along the main road at 59 rue du Couesnon

(☎02.33.60.10.55; ③; closed Mon & Jan), have very distinguished restaurants. At the western end of the central drag, the *Tour Brette*, 8 rue de Couesnon (☎02.33.60.10.69; ②), is a friendly and inexpensive *logis* with good lunch menus from 59F/€8.99. The principal budget option is the *Hôtel de France et Vauban*, 50 bd Clemenceau (☎02.33.60.03.84; ②), which oddly consists of two formerly separate hotels on either side of the level crossing beside the station; across from the *Vauban*, the *Relax* (☎02.33.68.32.10; ①), is a late-opening, youthful bar, with a pool table and a handful of even cheaper rooms. The recently renovated IYHF **hostel** stands near the cathedral, a kilometre west of the station, in the *Centre Duguesclin* at 21 rue du Général-Patton (☎02.33.60.18.65, *aj@ville-pontorson.fr*; closed Oct–April); dorm beds cost 49F/€7.47 per night for members, 56F/€8.54 for nonmembers.

Along the bay

The most direct **route from Pontorson to the Mont** runs alongside the River Couesnon, which marks the Normandy–Brittany border. The sands at the mouth of the Couesnon are those from which Harold can be seen rescuing two floundering soldiers in the Bayeux Tapestry, in the days when he and William were still getting on with each other. The sheep that graze on the scrubby pastures of the marshes at the sea's edge provide meat for the local delicacy, *mouton pré-salé*.

A more roundabout road to the abbey can take you to the **German war cemetery** at **MONT D'HUISNES**, a grim and unforgettable concrete mausoleum on a tiny hill (see p.134).

travel details

Trains

Caen to: Cherbourg (10 daily; 1hr 15min), via Bayeux (20min) and Valognes (1hr); Le Mans (7 daily; 2hr), via Argentan (45min) and Alençon (1hr 15min); Lisieux (hourly; 30min); Paris-St-Lazare (at least hourly; 2hr); Rennes (4 daily; 3hr), via Bayeux (20min), St-Lô (50min), Coutances (1hr 15min) and Pontorson (2hr); Rouen (6 daily; 2hr); Tours (2 daily; 3hr).

Cherbourg to: Paris (10 daily; 3hr) via Valognes (15min) and Caen (1hr 15min).

Coutances to: Caen (4 daily; 1hr 15min) with connections to Paris; Lison (7 daily; 45min) via St-Lô (15min), with connections for Cherbourg.

Dives-Cabourg to: Trouville-Deauville (July & Aug 6 daily, rest of year 2 daily Sun & hols; 30min) via Houlgate (6min) and Villers (20min).

Granville to: Coutances (8 daily; 30min).

Trouville-Deauville to: Lisieux (6 daily in winter, much more frequently in summer; 20min); Paris (6 daily in winter, much more frequently in summer; 2hr).

Buses

Much the most useful network in Lower Normandy is **Bus Verts**, *11 rue des Chanoines, Caen (☎08.01.21.42.14). Contact them for details of the Carte Plus discount pass for regular passengers.*

Arromanches to: Pointe du Hoc (1 daily; 1hr).

Bayeux to: Arromanches (4 daily; 25min); Courseulles (4 daily; 50min); Grandcamp-Maisy (3–5 daily; 1hr); Ouistreham (4 daily; 1hr 15min); Port-en-Bessin (3–5 daily; 20min).

Caen to: Bayeux (4 daily; 50min); Clécy (3–5 daily; 50min); Falaise (5–6 daily; 50min); Honfleur (14 daily bus #20 coastal services; 1hr 30min) via Cabourg (40min), Houlgate (55min) and Deauville (1hr 5min), of which 4 continue to Le Havre (2hr 30min); Le Havre (2 daily bus #80 express services; 1hr 25min) via Honfleur (1hr); Luc-sur-mer (12 daily; 1hr); Ouistreham (12 daily; 20min); Pont L'Évêque (1–3 daily; 45min); Thury-Harcourt (3–5 daily; 40min); Vire (connections for Brittany; 2–3 daily; 1hr 30min).

Cherbourg to: St-Lô (2–3 daily; 1hr 30min) via Valognes (30min) and Carentan (1hr); St-Vaast (2 daily; 1hr) via Barfleur (45min).

Mont-St-Michel to: Rennes (4 daily; 1hr 20min); St-Malo (4 daily; 1hr 30min).

Ferries

Caen (Ouistreham) to: Portsmouth (2–3 daily; 6hr), with Brittany Ferries (☎08.03.82.88.28, *www.brittany-ferries.com*). See details on p.5.

Cherbourg to: Poole (1–2 daily; 4hr 15min), with Brittany Ferries (see above); Portsmouth (5–6 daily; 2hr 45min–4hr 45min), with P&O (☎08.03.01.30.13, *www.poef.com*); Rosslare (2–3 weekly, summer only; 17hr), with Irish Continental (☎02.33.23.44.44). Further details on all these services can be found on p.3 onwards.

Granville to: Jersey, Guernsey and the Îles Chausey, with Jolie France (☎02.33.50.31.81) or Alizes Émeraude (☎02.33.50.16.36).

Flights

Cherbourg to: Jersey, Guernsey and Aurigny, with Aurigny-Air-Service; Bournemouth, Bristol and Exeter, with Air Camelot. Both from Maupertus Airport (☎02.33.22.91.32).

CHAPTER THREE

FROM THE SEINE TO THE BOCAGE: INLAND NORMANDY

Specific highlights are hard to pin down in **inland Normandy**. The pleasures lie not so much in show-stopping sights, or individual towns, as in the feel of the landscapes – the lush meadows, orchards and forests of the Norman countryside. On top of that, of course, there's the **food**, always a major motivation in these rich dairy regions. To the French, the **Pays d'Auge**, **Calvados** and the **Suisse Normande** are synonymous with cheeses, creams, apple and pear brandies, and ciders.

However, the territory is not exactly devoid of other sensory pursuits. There are spas, forests, rivers and lakes for lazing or stretching the muscles in, and, everywhere, classic half-timbered houses and farm buildings. If you are staying on the Norman coast, trips inland – even just ten to twenty kilometres – will pay dividends, while if you arrive at a Norman port intending to head straight for Brittany or southern France you may find yourself tempted to linger, or at least to take a circuitous route.

Travelling from **east to west**, you pass through a succession of distinct regions. **South of the Seine**, a natural target from Le Havre, Dieppe or Rouen, lie the **river valleys** of the **Eure**, **Risle** and **Charentonne**. While certain areas – especially along the Charentonne – have been disfigured by industrial develop-

---

ACCOMMODATION PRICE CODES

All **hotel prices** in this book have been coded using the symbols below. The price shown is for the least expensive double room in high season, which, for categories ① and ② especially, often means a room without shower, bath and toilet. Most such hotels have other rooms with en-suite facilities, which typically cost 40–60F/€6.10–9.15 extra.

① Under 160F/€24　　④ 300–400F/€46–61　　⑦ 600–700F/€91–107
② 160–220F/€24–34　　⑤ 400–500F/€61–76　　⑧ 700–800F/€107–122
③ 220–300F/€34–46　　⑥ 500–600F/€76–91　　⑨ Over 800F/€122

ment, the valleys remain for the most part rural and verdant. The occasional château, castle ruin or abbey provides a focus, most memorably at **Bec-Hellouin**, near Brionne, and at the country town of **Conches**. Further south lie the wooded hills and valleys of **the Perche**, home of the mighty Percheron horse and also of the original Trappists.

Following the rivers northwest, on the other hand, as they flow towards the sea near Honfleur or Cabourg, brings you into the classic cheese and cider country of the **Pays d'Auge**, all rolling pastoral hills, grazing meadows and orchards. **Livarot**, **Pont l'Évêque** and **Camembert** here are renowned throughout the world for their cheeses, while **Lisieux**, as the home barely a century ago of Ste Thérèse, has become one of the major pilgrimage towns of France. To the **south** of the Pays d'Auge extend the forests of the **Parc Naturel Régional de Normandie-Maine**, with the sedate and famous spa at **Bagnoles** and the national stud at **Le Pin**.

Further west, on the routes inland from either Caen or Cherbourg and the Cotentin, there is something of a shift. Around Thury-Harcourt and stretching south to Pont d'Ouilly and Putanges is the area dubbed the **Suisse Normande**, for its "alpine" valleys and thick woods; fine walking country, if not genuinely mountainous. To its west, the **Bocage** begins with grim memories of war around St-Lô – this was the main 1944 invasion route – but subsides into a pastoral scene once more as you hit the gastronomic centres of the **Vire**.

South from the Seine

South across the Seine from Rouen is the long and featureless **Neubourg plain** – intensive agricultural land where the crumbling barns, Tudor-style houses and occasional grazing horses look oddly out of place. It's not an area where you can expect to find hidden charms, and the first sizeable town you come to, war-ravaged **Évreux**, provides little incentive to stop. Most visitors choose instead to press on as far as the attractive medieval towns of **Conches**, with its snug surrounding of forest, and **Verneuil**.

Le Neubourg

The only town of any size on the Neubourg plain is **LE NEUBOURG** itself, which blows any possibility of being charming by festooning its streets with deafening loudspeakers. It holds little of interest to the traveller, but, 4km northwest on the D83, the seventeenth-century **Château du Champ-de-Bataille**, with its dramatic entrance arch, is worth a look (March, April & mid-Sept to Dec Sat & Sun 2–6pm; May to mid-Sept daily 2–6pm).

If you do need to spend the night here, Le Neubourg does at least hold a good **hotel-restaurant**, the central *Au Grand St-Martin*, at 68 rue de la République (☎02.32.35.04.80; ②; closed Sun evening & Mon).

Évreux

Twenty kilometres south of Le Neubourg you come to **ÉVREUX**, which is capital of the Eure *département* despite not being on the Eure River itself. It's an extremely venerable place that throughout history has suffered violent reversals of for-

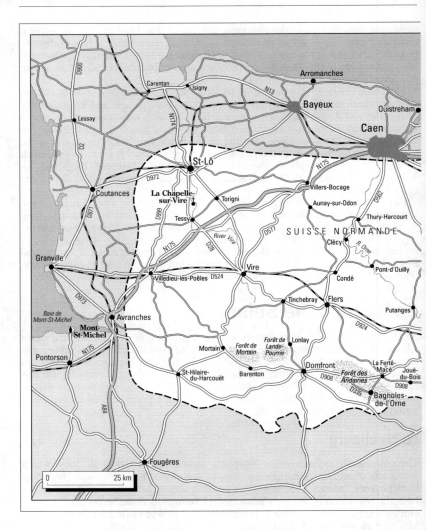

tune – as early as the fifth century its affluent Gaulish community made an inviting target for rampaging Vandals.

Bombing raids by both sides during World War II reduced much of the city to
rubble, however, and Évreux today is almost disconcertingly lifeless. Even so, an
afternoon's wander in the vicinity of the **cathedral** – a minor classic with its flamboyant exterior decoration and original fourteenth-century windows – and along
the ramparts by the Iton riverbank is pleasant enough. In January 1995, Évreux's
bishop, Jacques Gaillot, was dismissed by the pope for his advocacy of the use of
condoms to prevent AIDS, and his statement that "homosexuals will precede us

into the kingdom of heaven". Demonstrations on his behalf took place around the world, and he subsequently set himself up on the Internet as the world's first virtual bishop.

Practicalities

Évreux's **gares SNCF** and **routière** are side by side 400m south of the cathedral. The **tourist office** is right in the heart of town, 300m north of the cathedral at 3 place de Gaulle (Mon–Sat 9.30am–12.30pm & 1.30–6.15pm; ☎02.32.24.04.43, *www.evreux-tourisme.org*). Many of the cheaper **hotels** are shut during August, and in any case there is no great reason to stay. The old *Biche*, at 9 rue St-Joséphine on place St-Taurin at the edge of town (☎02.32.38.66.00; ①; closed Sun in July & Aug, Sun evening Sept–June), is, however, a strange but splendid Belle Époque structure that remains open all summer, with a lurid-pink interior, a triangular dining room and even some triangular bedrooms. In its restaurant, 135F/€20.58 buys you a magnificent meal of oysters braised in cider and a garlicky seafood *pot au feu*, to the musical accompaniment of an unlikely assortment of funk and disco classics. In the heart of town, the *Français* on place Clémenceau (☎02.32.33.53.60) is a fine traditional **brasserie**.

Perhaps a more enticing prospect than a night in Évreux, however, would be to continue as far as the riverside village of **PACY-SUR-EURE**, 13km east, where the traditional and very good-value *Hôtel de l'Étape*, 1 rue Isambard (☎02.32.36.12.77; ③), nestles at the water's edge.

Conches-en-Ouche

Everybody you meet in Normandy seems to recommend **CONCHES-EN-OUCHE** – both for the town and for the forest around. The town stands above the River Rouloir on a spur so narrow and abrupt that the railway line is forced to tunnel right beneath its centre. Arriving by train, you're barely aware that the place exists at all; all you see is the cutting, deep into the hill.

On the highest point of the spur, in the middle of a row of medieval houses on the main rue Ste-Foy, is the **church of Ste-Foy**, its windows a sequence of Renaissance stained glass. Almost opposite the church is a fascinating **ironmongery shop**, Le St-Jacques (closed Mon); Conches was once renowned for its metal foundries, which cast the iron spire of Rouen Cathedral in 1876, but the shop is the only vestige of that heritage you're likely to encounter. It's a building with an unlikely secret; descend the stone spiral staircase in the back room, and you'll find yourself in a labyrinth of eleventh-century cellars that extends under most of its neighbours.

Behind the church, in the gardens of the **Hôtel de Ville**, a robust, if anatomically odd, stone boar gazes proudly out over a spectacular view, raising its eyes to the horizon far beyond the sewage works. Next to the Hôtel de Ville, you can scramble up the slippery steps of the ruined twelfth-century **castle**, one of the many haunts of the ubiquitous Bertrand du Guesclin and twice captured by the English during the Hundred Years War. Such sights ensure that Conches remains firmly rooted in the past, but the town is given an added contemporary flavour, too, by the pieces of modern sculpture that you come upon round seemingly every corner.

On the other side of the main road from the castle, you'll find a long and subtly formal **park**, with parallel avenues of trees, a large ornamental lake and fountain.

Practicalities

Conches' **tourist office** is close to the castle, 200m south of the church in place Aristide-Briand (July & Aug Tues–Sat 10am–12.30pm & 2–6pm, Sun 10am–noon; ☎02.32.30.76.42), and rents out mountain **bikes**. The inexpensive **hotel** *Grand'Mare*, in a green and quiet location beside the park at 13 av Croix de Fer (☎02.32.30.23.30; ①), has fairly basic rooms but serves up enjoyable dinners in its restaurant, including a good 98F/€14.94 menu with oxtail braised in sherry and some fruit desserts; the *Bistro* in the same building is a less formal place to have lunch. Other accommodation options include the half-timbered *Donjon*, bulging out of the main street on the castle side, not far from the church (☎02.32.30.04.75; ②; closed Tues evening & Wed), and *Le Cygne*, at the north end of town at 2 rue Paul Guilbaud (☎02.32.30.20.60; ④; closed Sun evening & Mon), which in addition to its standard doubles holds some much cheaper single rooms. There's also a two-star **municipal campsite**, *La Forêt* (☎02.32.30.22.49; closed Oct–March), while on Thursday the whole town is taken up by a **market**.

The Forêt de Conches

The wild and open woodland of the **Forêt de Conches**, which stretches southwest of Conches, is very popular with hikers and **horse riders**. A centre for young riders up to the age of eighteen, the Village Equestre de Conches, is based in the hamlet of Le Fresne, 1km east of town (☎02.32.30.22.56, *www.pageszoom.com/village-equestre-conches*).

If you feel the need for a direction in your wanderings, head for the village of **LA FERRIÈRE-SUR-RISLE**, where there's an especially beautiful **church**, with a garish altar but some fine wooden statues, and a restored fourteenth-century covered **market hall**. Paddocks and meadows lead down to the river, while on the single, very quiet, street you'll find a small and inviting **hotel**, the *Vieux-Marché* (☎02.32.30.25.93; ②; closed mid-Sept to mid-Oct), with a daily set menu at 59F/€8.99.

Verneuil-sur-Avre

Southwest of Conches, the towns of Rugles and L'Aigle are both industrial and uninteresting. However, 25km due south on the D840 you come to the pretty little hilltop town of **VERNEUIL-SUR-AVRE**. This now marks nothing more significant than the transition from the Ouche to the Perche, but during the Hundred Years War it was a crucial fortified outpost between (English-held) Normandy and France proper. Traces of its former ramparts and deep moat can still be seen along boulevard Casati on the west side of town, while the three main streets and numerous alleyways are lined with venerable half-timbered houses.

As you approach along the arrow-straight D840 from the north, the solid bell tower of **La Madeleine** is perfectly framed for several kilometres' distance by the avenue of trees. The actual church of La Madeleine, to which it is somewhat inelegantly attached, stands in the main square, completely dwarfed by the belfry. Owing to damage incurred during the major storm of December 1999, it's not currently possible to go up the tower.

Following the pedestrian lanes that lead away from the square will bring you out at the **Notre Dame** church in the southeast, built of crude red agglomerate stone in the twelfth century, or to the sixteenth-century **Tour St-Jean** to the southwest, a former church spire separated by wartime bombing from its Gothic porch.

Practicalities

Verneuil's **gare SNCF**, five-minutes' walk north of the centre, is served by four daily trains from Paris. The local **tourist office** is at no. 129 on the main place de la Madeleine (Mon 2–6pm, Tues–Fri 10am–noon & 2–6pm, Sat 10am–noon; ☎02.32.32.17.17).

Virtually next door to the tourist office, the cream-coloured **hotel** *Le Saumon*, 89 place de la Madeleine (☎02.32.32.02.36; ②), which glows an inviting pink at sunset, offers well-equipped and comfortable rooms at very reasonable rates. A tankful of live lobsters nervously await patrons of the more expensive menus; in midweek especially, the lower-priced menus are very good value, with a 65F/€9.91 option that consists of a buffet of *hors d'oeuvres*. The *Hôtel Le Clo*s, at 98 rue de la Ferté-Vidame (☎02.32.32.21.81; ③; closed mid-Dec to mid-Jan), a bizarre little château near the Notre Dame church, has an even better restaurant and phenomenally expensive rooms. The best stand-alone **restaurant** in town is the half-timbered *Grand Sultan*, tucked in behind La Madeleine at 30 rue de la Poissonerie (☎02.32.32.13.14; closed Mon), where the traditional menus start at 90F/€13.72.

Nine kilometres southwest of Verneuil is the glass-covered dome of a family holiday complex, the *Hôtel-Residence du Lac*, run by **Center Parcs** (☎08.03.80.28.04), which can only be booked by the week.

The Perche

All roads south of Verneuil start to undulate alarmingly as you enter the region known as the **Perche**. This holds some of Normandy's most bucolically appealing countryside, with green valleys nestled between heavily forested hills. Despite its apparent fertility, however, it has never been a particularly rich area: in the seventeenth century, times were hard enough for a large proportion of the

---

THE TRAPPISTS

The **Abbaye de la Trappe** is set in open rolling fields on the fringes of the Forêt de la Trappe – a minor western appendage of the Forêt du Perche – just beyond a popular fishing lake and 10km north of Mortagne. This was the original home of one of the world's most famous – yet deliberately self-effacing, and consistently misunderstood – Christian monastic orders. Although the abbey was founded in the thirteenth century, and suffered the vicissitudes of the Hundred Years War, it was not until the reforms instigated by the **Abbé Rancé** in 1664 that its monks began to follow the principles for which the Trappists are known today. The Abbé reacted against the excesses of his time by setting out to re-create the lives of the "**Desert Fathers**" of the first few centuries after Christ, who lived in contemplative isolation in the Sinai, and to follow St Benedict's precept that true monks should live by the labour of their own hands.

The monks were driven out by the Revolution, successively to Switzerland, Poland, Russia and as far as the United States, but succeeded in returning to their utterly devastated abbey in 1815, still under the leadership of Dom Augustin l'Estrange – which made them the only order of monks in France not to be wiped out.

The abbey as it exists today is entirely a nineteenth-century creation. The monks live communally – they don't have individual cells – and not literally in the absolute silence of popular myth, but speaking only for the necessities of work and community life and spending the rest of their time in quiet reflection. Not surprisingly, tourists are not encouraged to disturb them, but anyone with a genuine interest can watch a video in a reception room beside the main entrance. There's also an unusual **shop** (Mon–Sat 10am–noon & 2.30–6pm, Sun after 10am Mass until noon & 2.30–6.30pm) which sells all things monk-made: herbal teas, muesli, metal polish, shampoo, furniture wax – even local *boudin* and coffee grown in Cameroon.

population to emigrate to Canada. It is, however, well known for the mighty **Percheron horses**, the strongest work horses in the world, while its remoteness and seclusion made it an ideal home for the first **Trappist** monks, who took their name from the Forêt de la Trappe.

Mortagne-au-Perche

The largest town of the Perche region stands on a hill set in the heart of the forests. **MORTAGNE-AU-PERCHE** has lost virtually all of its fortifications, but it remains an appealing country town, with a pleasant ensemble of stone town houses. The one part of the ramparts to survive is the **Porte St-Denis**, a fifteenth-century arch topped in the sixteenth century by two ordinary storeys of rooms that now contain an exhibition about Percheron horses.

Mortagne's liveliest square is the **place de Gaulle**, where the nineteenth-century market hall has been imaginatively converted into a cinema, with some postmodern spiral staircases attached to either side, and also holds the local tourist office. Nearby stands an unusual modern fountain, looking like an open mummy case made of copper. If you cross from here through the main gates of the Hôtel de Ville to reach the flower-filled gardens around the back, which are filled with sculpture old and new, you can enjoy fine views over the Perche hills.

Practicalities

Mortagne's former market hall, described above, is also the site of the local **tourist office** (mid-May to mid-June & last fortnight of Sept Tues–Sat 9.30am–12.30pm & 2.30–6pm; mid-June to mid-Sept Mon 10am–12.30pm & 2.30–6pm, Tues–Sat 9.30am–12.30pm & 2.30–6pm, Sun 10am–12.30pm; Oct to mid-May Tues–Sat 10am–12.30pm & 3–6pm; ☎02.33.85.11.18). The nicest **hotel** in town has to be the *Hôtel du Tribunal*, a *logis* on the sleepy little tree-lined place du Palais (☎02.33.25.04.77; ④), which consists of two or three old stone buildings with a few exposed timbers, crammed together on the corner of an alleyway leading to Porte St-Denis. This is where Yves Montand chose to stay when filming locally; the comfortable bedrooms are in an annexe at the back, while the restaurant at the front has a reasonable 90F/€13.72 menu and gets exotic if you pay more, with such dishes as scallops in orange butter.

The *Genty-Home*, just off place de la République at 4 rue Notre-Dame (☎02.33.25.11.53; ③; closed Sun evening & Mon), has a handful of very plush rooms upstairs and a couple of restaurants; the less formal *Grillade* downstairs, and another serving traditional menus from 100F/€15.24 upstairs. Both offer Mortagne's speciality – the black *boudin noir*, a crumbly black pudding or blood sausage with a healthy dose of fat and tripe thrown in.

Bellême

Tiny **BELLÊME**, 17km due south of Mortagne on the switchback D938, is actually the capital of the Perche despite being very much smaller. In many ways it's more attractive, too, crammed so tightly onto the top of a sharp hill that the views are consistently superb. Here, too, hardly anything survives of the fortifications that once ringed the very crest of the hill. The one exception is the forbiddingly thick **Porche** – now the home of the local library, but still equipped to take a portcullis if things turn bad – reached by an alleyway leading off from a corner of the place de la République near the St-Sauveur church.

Practicalities

The grand white facade of Bellême's best **hotel**, the *Relais St-Louis*, 1 bd Bansard-des-Bois (☎02.33.73.12.21; ④; closed Sun evening & Mon in low season), may be in a slight state of disrepair, but it's elegant enough inside, with its light dining room looking out on one side to a flowery garden, and across the town's diminutive ring road on the other to a small vestige of moat overlooked by an imposing eighteenth-century mansion. Its 140F/€21.34 menu includes a seafood *pot au feu*, with a more basic option at 95F/€14.48. There's also a tiny two-star municipal **campsite** on the edge of town (☎02.33.73.69.52; closed mid-Oct to mid-April).

The local **tourist office** (Sun & Mon 2–7pm, Tues–Sat 10am–12.30pm & 2–7pm; ☎02.33.73.09.69), all but next door to the *Relais St-Louis*, doubles appealingly as the headquarters of the adjoining miniature golf course. It can also provide details of Bellême's annual five-day Mycology Festival, held at the end of each September to celebrate the obscurer mushrooms of the surrounding forests.

The Charentonne and the Risle

The **River Risle** drains down from the Ouche region, north of the Perche, and passes initially through traditional and now very faded ironworking towns such as L'Aigle. Roughly 30km northwest of Conches, it's joined by a fast-flowing tributary, the **Charentonne**. In the area to either side of the confluence, and from then on northwards as the newly strengthened Risle heads towards the sea near Honfleur, several small riverside towns are worth visiting.

Broglie

The southernmost town of any size along the Charentonne is **BROGLIE**, 12km west of Orbec (see p.181). The impressive private **château** that stands on the brow of the hill above Broglie is the ancestral home of the de Broglie family. Its last but one owner, Prince Louis, won the Nobel Physics Prize for demonstrating that matter, like light, has wavelike properties. His work – to "seek the last hiding places of reality", as he put it – subsequently formed the foundation of the whole discipline of quantum mechanics. Originally a medieval historian, Louis was supposed to have been attracted to his great theory "purely on the grounds of intellectual beauty".

Downstream from Broglie

Immediately **downstream from Broglie**, the Charentonne sprawls between its banks on a wide flood plain. It is classic inland Normandy, uneventful and totally scenic; the one flaw in the whole thing is the unseemly preponderance of porcelain donkeys in people's front gardens.

At **ST-QUENTIN-DES-ISLES**, halfway along the valley, old houses are overshadowed by a derelict sawmill, which looms like a primordial swamp monster from among the riverside willows, in a dripping bulk of red ivy. A couple of kilometres north of St-Quentin on the D33, the sixteenth-century riverside windmill *Moulin Fouret* (☎02.32.43.19.95; ③; closed Sun evening & Mon), is primarily a **restaurant**, with menus from around 100F/€15.24 on weekdays and 160F/€24.39 at weekends, but also has a few **rooms**, making it the nicest place to stay in the vicinity.

Bernay

As you approach **BERNAY**, 11km northeast of Broglie, more and more factories and warehouses line both sides of the river. The town itself, however, has a few humpback footbridges and picturesque half-timbered old streets interspersed between the more serious traffic routes, and one of those churches typical of the region with a spire that looks like a stack of inverted octagonal ice-cream cones. Work has been in progress to restore the ancient **abbey church** for years – it should look good when it is finished.

Bernay has few other claims to renown, though one of its bakers has found fame for *running* each stage of the Tour de France during the night before the cyclists race over it. The *Lion d'Or*, at 48 rue Général-de-Gaulle (☎02.32.43.12.06; ③; dining room closed Mon lunchtime, plus Sun evening in winter), is a conventional, good-quality **hotel-restaurant** in the heart of town.

Beaumont-le-Roger and Serquigny

BEAUMONT-LE-ROGER is set beside the Risle 25km northwest of Conches and 17km east of Bernay, shortly before the Risle meets the Charentonne. Its ruined thirteenth-century priory **church** is gradually crumbling to the ground, the slow restoration of one or two arches unable to keep pace. Little happens in the village beyond the hourly hammering of the church bell – next door to the abbey – by a nodding musketeer; and with each passing hour, the ruins crumble a little more. Just across the Risle from here, on the D25 near Le Val-St-Martin, huge **stables** are spread across an absurdly sylvan setting, and horses are available for hire.

Beaumont-le-Roger is not exactly an exciting place to stay, but it is home to a sixteenth-century **coaching inn** with some quiet courtyard rooms – the *Lion d'Or*, 91 rue St-Nicolas (☎02.32.45.48.08; ③) – and also a top-quality and very friendly **restaurant**, *La Calèche*, nearby at 54 rue St-Nicolas (☎02.32.45.25.99; closed Wed), which offers menus from 90F/€13.72.

At **SERQUIGNY**, not only the two rivers but also several roads and rail lines converge, and the banks are once again briefly industrial, clogged with factories and fumes.

Brionne

The small town of **BRIONNE**, 10km north of Serquigny and the first stop on the rail line to Rouen, plays host to large regional **markets** on Tuesday and Sunday. The fish hall is on the left bank; the rest, by the church on the right bank. Above them both, with panoramic views, is a **donjon**, or old castle keep, spotlit by the setting sun. Should you decide to climb up the hill to reach it, you'll find a *table d'orientation* with arrows pointing out local landmarks.

Brionne holds two good but pretty-expensive **hotels** which also contain excellent restaurants: the lovely old half-timbered *Auberge du Vieux Donjon*, facing the marketplace at 19 rue Soie (☎02.32.44.80.62; ③; closed Mon, Sun evening in low season, & last fortnight in Oct), where the food is significantly better than the accommodation, and the much more modern *Logis de Brionne*, close to the *gare SNCF* but a long way west of the centre at 1 place St-Denis (☎02.32.44.81.73; ③; closed Sun evening & Mon Oct–Easter).

The Abbaye de Bec-Hellouin

Following the Risle on towards Honfleur and the sea, the **D39** is lined with perfect timbered farmhouses. Four kilometres from Brionne, the size and tranquil setting of the **ABBAYE DE BEC-HELLOUIN** give a monastic feel to the whole valley. Bells echo between the hills and white-robed monks go soberly about their business. From the eleventh century onwards, the abbey was one of the most important centres of intellectual learning in the Christian world; an intimate association with the court of William the Conqueror meant that three of its early abbots – Lanfranc, the philosopher Anselm and Theobald – became archbishops of Canterbury. Recent archbishops of Canterbury have maintained tradition by coming here on retreat.

Owing to the Revolution, most of the monastery buildings are relatively new – the monks only returned in 1948 – but there are some survivals and appealing clusters of stone ruins, and fragments of medieval lettering are still visible on the solitary tower, topped by a beehive spire. Visitors are welcome to wander through the grounds for no charge, though if you want to understand what you're seeing it's best to join one of the regular **guided tours** (June–Sept Mon & Wed–Fri 10.30am, 3pm, 4pm & 5pm, Sat 10.30am, 3pm & 4pm, Sun & hols noon, 3pm & 4pm; Oct–May Mon & Wed–Sat 11am, 3pm & 4pm, Sun & hols noon, 3pm & 4pm; 25F/€3.81).

The rather twee adjacent village of **Bec-Hellouin** holds a **vintage car museum** (mid-June to mid-Sept daily 9am–noon & 2–7pm; mid-Sept to mid-June Mon, Tues & Fri–Sun 9am–noon & 2–7pm; 25F/€3.81), and a **museum of mechanical music** (April, May & Sept daily 3pm, 4pm & 5pm; June–Aug daily 3pm, 4pm, 5pm & 6pm; 30F/€4.57). There are also a couple of distinctly unascetic gourmet **restaurants**: as well as offering dinner menus from 200F/€30.49, the wonderful *Auberge de l'Abbaye* (☎02.32.44.86.02; ⑤; closed Mon evening, all day Tues in winter, & all Jan), also has half a dozen expensive rooms, while the ivy-covered *Canterbury* (☎02.32.44.14.59; closed Tues evening, Wed, & all Feb) is a similarly lavish alternative, serving regional specialties on menus from 85F/€12.96 up to 190F/€28.97. The *Restaurant de la Tour* on place Guillaume-le-Conquérant nearby (☎02.32.44.86.15; closed Dec, plus Tues evening & Wed in low season) is more affordable, and has some outdoor tables.

Pont-Audemer

Continuing north, the last major crossing point over the Risle is at **PONT-AUDEMER**, where medieval houses lean out at alarming angles over the criss-crossing roads, rivers and canals. It's an attractive little place, the scene of busy markets on Mondays and Fridays, and boasts a gorgeous **hotel-restaurant** in the half-timbered shape of the *Auberge du Vieux Puits*, 6 rue Notre-Dame-du-Pré (☎02.32.41.01.48; ④; closed Jan, plus Mon & Tues lunchtime). Centred on a courtyard that contains a magnificent old willow, this former coaching inn is stranded on a dull, albeit quiet, side street; their pride in their kitchens is indicated by the fact that even their *Express* dinner menu is a gourmet affair costing 170F/€25.92. Rooms at the more basic riverside *Hôtel de l'Agriculture*, much more in the thick of the things at 84 av de la République (☎02.32.41.01.23; ①; closed Sun evening in winter), are half the price. Across the river from there, the *Erawan*, 4 rue de la Seule (☎02.32.41.12.03; closed Wed), must be Normandy's only traditional half-timbered Thai **restaurant**, with a 125F/€19.06 set menu.

From Pont-Audemer you have the choice of making for the sea at Honfleur (see p.113), passing some tottering Giacometti-style barns on the way to St-Georges along the thickly wooded valleys of the D38, or going on towards the Seine. If you plan to cycle across the Forêt de Brotonne towards Caudebec (see p.86), be warned that, to discourage motorists from spoiling the nicest part of the forest, the road signs direct you the long way round via La Mailleraye.

Pont l'Évêque

There was little left after the war of the old **PONT L'ÉVÊQUE**, 35km west of Pont-Audemer and technically the northernmost town of the Pays d'Auge (see below). One or two ancient houses remain, most notably along rue St-Michel, but the town as a whole has become such a turmoil of major roads as to be a rather eccentric place to choose to stay. If you do end up here, you'll find reasonable **rooms** and excellent seafood dinners at the *Lion d'Or*, at the eastern end of town at 8 place du Calvaire (☎02.31.65.01.55; ②).

A couple of kilometres south of town on the D48, an impressive medieval barn at the twelfth-century Château de Betteville is home to a **vintage car museum**, while there's a karting circuit laid out in the grounds (daily: April–June & Sept 10am–12.30pm & 1.30–7pm; July & Aug 10am–7pm; Oct to mid-Nov 2–6pm; 35F/€5.34). Immediately opposite, the *Hôtel-Restaurant Eden Park* (☎02.31.64.64.00; ③), is a large, new *logis de France*, housed in a sprawling complex of buildings beside its own lake, that makes an ideal overnight stop for restless families.

Cormeilles

The village of **CORMEILLES**, 17km southeast of Pont l'Évêque, makes a more appealing destination for a day out, having been left relatively unscathed by fighting. Each Friday sees a **market** in its tiny centre, and there are several half-timbered restaurants scattered around.

On the southern edge of town, the *Auberge du President*, 70 rue de l'Abbaye (☎02.32.57.80.37; ③; closed Wed evening in low season), is an efficient hybrid, featuring motel-style rooms around the back and a very traditional, formal and good plush-velvet restaurant in the old building facing the street, with menus from 80F/€12.20.

The Pays d'Auge

The pastures of the **Pays d'Auge**, the region that extends south from the ancient cathedral city of **Lisieux**, are the lushest in all of Normandy, renowned for producing the world-famous cheeses of Camembert, Livarot and Pont l'Évêque. Its rolling hills and green twisting valleys are scattered with magnificent half-timbered manor houses. Each sprawling farm is liable to consist of a succession of such "Tudor" (in fact the Norman tradition predates the English) treasures, each family house, as it becomes too dilapidated to live in, being converted for use as a barn, and replaced by a new one built alongside. In addition to grazing land, the area holds acres of orchards, which yield the best of Norman ciders, both apple and pear (*poiré*), as well as Calvados apple brandy.

The tourist authorities promote two main Pays d'Auge itineraries, the **Route de Fromage** and the **Route du Cidre**. It's not difficult to join either of these well-signposted routes, each of which serves as a welcome opportunity to get off the main highways. For the former, the best starting points are at St-Pierre-sur-Dives

---

THE CHEESE OF THE PAYS D'AUGE

The tradition of cheesemaking in the Pays d'Auge is thought to have been started in the monasteries during the Dark Ages; the characteristics of the standard local product seem to have become fairly constant by the eleventh century. At first it was variously known as either *Augelot* or *Angelot*; the *Roman de la Rose* in 1236 referred to *Angelot* cheese, which was identified with a small coin depicting a young angel killing a dragon.

This cheese was the forerunner of the principal modern varieties, which began to emerge in the seventeenth century – **Pont l'Évêque**, which is square, with a washed crust, and is soft but not runny, and **Livarot**, which is round, thick and firm, with a stronger flavour.

Although Marie Herel is generally credited with having invented **Camembert** in the 1790s, a smaller and stodgier version of that cheese had already existed for some time. What seems to have happened is that a priest fleeing the Revolutionary Terror at Meaux (a certain Abbé Gobert) stayed in Mme Herel's farmhouse at Camembert and watched the methods she used for making cheese. He suggested modifications in line with the techniques he'd seen employed to manufacture Brie de Meaux – a slower process, gentler on the curd and with more thorough drainage. The rich full cheese thus created was an instant success in the market at Vimoutiers, and the development of the railways (and the invention of the chipboard cheesebox in 1880) helped to give it a worldwide popularity.

More details on all such matters are to be had from the exhaustive *French Cheese Book*, by Patrick Rance (Macmillan, o/p).

---

and Livarot; for the latter, head for Cambremer, just north of the N13 between Caen and Lisieux. In any event, it doesn't matter much if you stray off the routes – much of the appeal of this area lies in the scope just to wander, rather than to look for any specific sights, and to fill the days sampling the different ciders and cheeses. That said, the manor houses of **Beuvron-en-Auge** on the Cider Route, and **Montpinçon** and **Lisores** on the Cheese Route, are well worth finding, and at Lisores there's also the **Ferme-Musée Fernand Léger** (April–Oct daily except Wed 10am–12.30pm & 2–6pm; Nov–March Sat & Sun 2–5.30pm; 25F/€3.81), with its unlikely mosaics. **Cambremer** has a special crafts market on Sunday morning in July and August.

For fans of really good, solid Norman cooking, this is the perfect area to look out for **Fermes Auberges**, working farms which welcome (paying) visitors to share their meals; lists are available from local tourist offices and from Calvados Tourisme (place du Canada, Caen; ☎02.31.86.53.30). The cider farms are signposted with the words "*Cru de Cambremer*" in green on white.

Lisieux

LISIEUX, the main town of the Pays d'Auge, was a regional capital successively under the Gauls, the Romans and the Franks. However, it was obliterated by barbarians in 275 AD, and again by the Allies in 1944, with the result that what had been a beautiful market town is now for the most part nondescript. Although it still boasts a Norman Gothic cathedral built in 1170, which holds a chapel erected by the judge who sentenced Joan of Arc to death, these days Lisieux's identity

Mont-St-Michel

Étretat

Rouen cathedral

Napoleon statue, Cherbourg

Monet's garden, Giverny

Caen

US cemetery, Omaha Beach

Villers-sur-mer

Mussel stall, Portbail

Beuvron-en-Auge

Norman farm

Mulberry harbour, Arromanches

is thoroughly wrapped up in the life and death of **Ste Thérèse** (see box below) – the most influential French spiritual figure of the last hundred years.

Pilgrims come to Lisieux in considerable numbers, and even a casual visitor will find the Thérèse cult inescapable. The garish and gigantic **Basilique de Ste-Thérèse**, on a slope to the southwest of the town centre, was modelled on the Sacré-Coeur in Paris. Completed in 1954, it was the last major religious building in France to be erected solely by public subscription. Thérèse is in fact buried in the chapel of the Carmelite convent, though her presence in the Basilica is ensured by selected bones from her right arm (in a reliquary given by Pope Pius XI) and by countless photographs, Thérèse being one of the very few saints to have lived since the invention of the camera. The huge modern mosaics that decorate the nave are undeniably impressive, but the overall impression is of a quasi-medieval hagiography.

In summer, a white, flag-bedecked funfair "train" runs fifty-minute tours around the holiest sites, chugging through the open, wide streets and squares, and past the delightful flower-filled park, raised above street level behind the restrained and sober Cathédrale St-Pierre (departures from the Basilica: July & Aug daily 11am, 2pm, 3pm, 4pm, 5pm & 6pm; Sept Sat & Sun 11am, 2pm, 3pm, 4pm, 5pm & 6pm; 30F/€4.57).

For an idea of Lisieux's former glories, take a look at the fading photos in the **Musée du Vieux-Lisieux**, 38 bd Pasteur (daily except Tues 2–6pm; 15F/€2.29).

Practicalities

Lisieux is 35 minutes by train from Caen, en route to Paris or Rouen; the **gare SNCF** is on the south side of town, below the Basilica. Turn left out of the station, then right, to reach the **tourist office**, at 11 rue d'Alençon (June–Sept Mon–Sat

---

STE THÉRÈSE

Born at Alençon in 1873, **Thérèse Martin** lived for the last nine years of her short life in the Carmelite convent in Lisieux, until she died of TB at 24. She had felt the call to take holy orders when only 9, but it took a pilgrimage to Rome and a special dispensation from the pope before she was allowed into the convent at the age of 15. The prioress said then that "a soul of such quality should not be treated as a child".

Thérèse owes her fame to her book *Story of a Soul*, in which she describes the approach to life she called her "Little Way" – a belief that all personal suffering, all thankless work and quiet faith, is made holy, and made worthwhile, as an offering to God. What to modern sensibilities might appear a meekness and lack of worldliness verging on the selfish proved astonishingly popular after her death, particularly in trying to make sense of the vast suffering of World War I, and Thérèse was rapidly beatified. In 1945, she joined her heroine Joan of Arc – she wrote several poems to Joan, and there are even photographs of her dressed as the imprisoned Joan (see p.95), chained to a wall – by being declared France's second patron saint. Her continuing contemporary relevance to Catholics has been celebrated by Pope John Paul II, who not only made his own pilgrimage to Lisieux but also declared Thérèse in 1997 to be the thirty-third "Doctor of the Church". This highest of theological honours had only previously been conferred on two women, Catherine of Sienna and Theresa of Avila.

8.30am–6.30pm, Sun 9am–12.30pm & 2–5pm; Oct–May Mon–Sat 8.30am–noon & 1.30–6pm; ☎02.31.48.18.10, *www.ville-lisieux.fr*), which can help with finding accommodation in Lisieux itself, and provides information on the rural areas further inland.

The quantity of pilgrims means that Lisieux is full of good-value places to stay – among its **hotels** are *de la Terrasse*, up on the hill near the Basilica at 25 av Ste-Thérèse (☎02.31.62.17.65; ②; closed Jan, & Mon in winter), which serves good meals on its pleasant terrace, the *Lourdes*, 4 rue au Char near the cathedral (☎02.31.31.19.48; ②), and the exceptionally cheap *Hôtel des Arts*, backing onto the Bishop's Gardens at 26 rue Condorcet (☎02.31.62.00.02; ①). There is also a large two-star **campsite**, *de la Vallée* (☎02.31.62.00.40; closed Oct–March), but campers would probably be better off somewhere more rural, such as Livarot or Orbec.

Most of the hotels are equipped with tempting **restaurants**, and you can also get a reasonable 60F/€9.15 lunch at *Au Vieux Normand*, in one of Lisieux's few surviving half-timbered houses at 14 rue H-Chéron (☎02.31.62.03.35; closed Mon). If Thérèse isn't your prime motivation, Saturday is the best day to visit, for the large **street market** – stacked with Pays d'Auge cheeses.

Beuvron-en-Auge

No village has any right to be as pretty as **BEUVRON-EN-AUGE**, 7km north of the N13 halfway between Lisieux and Caen, which consists of an oval central *place*, ringed by a glorious ensemble of multicoloured half-timbered houses. The largest of these, the yellow-and-brown sixteenth-century **Vieux Manoir** at the south end of the village, backs onto a stream and open fields. The beams around its first storey bear weather-beaten carvings, including one of a Norman soldier. A map in the main square details suggested **walking routes** through the countryside nearby, while if you step off the square into the alleyway known as **rue de la Catouillette**, opposite the Vieux Manoir, you'll find another set of lovely half-timbered structures clustered around a tiny courtyard.

Beuvron-en-Auge stages its own **Cider Festival**, with a huge local market in the square, on about October 24 each year.

Practicalities

Immediately beside the Vieux Manoir stands an eighteenth-century **hotel**, the *Auberge de la Boule d'Or* (☎02.31.79.78.78; ③; closed Jan, plus Tues evening & Wed Oct–June), where you'd be lucky to find one of the three attractive bedrooms available; a former farmhouse opposite holds a *chambre d'hôte* (Mme Hamelin: ☎02.31.39.00.62; ③; closed Nov–Easter). The very centre of the *place* is taken up by the *Pavé d'Auge* **restaurant** (☎02.31.79.26.71; closed Mon May–Aug), where menus featuring chicken and *andouille* in cider or salmon start at 145F/€22.11.

St-Germain-de-Livet

Around 7km south of Lisieux, and clearly signposted off the D579, the **château** of **ST-GERMAIN-DE-LIVET** (Feb, March & mid-Oct to Nov daily except Tues 10–11.30am & 2–5pm; April to mid Oct daily except Tues 10–11.30am & 2–7pm; 35F/€5.34) is an appealing blend of fifteenth- and sixteenth-century architectural elements. From the main gate, its half-timbered older wing – home to some stirring military frescoes – is largely concealed by the more imposing later addition, with its cheerful checked facade of coloured stones and brick. The whole edifice is topped by classic, pointed, grey-slate turrets, circled by a moat, and surrounded by scrupulously maintained lawns. In summer, **carriage rides** leave from alongside the entrance to tour the grounds (June Sun 11am–6pm; July–Sept Mon, Wed–Fri & Sun 11am–6pm; 35F/€5.34, under-13s 20F/€3.05); when not in use, the carriage is housed in an amazing tumbledown barn next door.

Orbec

The most attractive of the larger Pays d'Auge towns, **ORBEC**, lies just a few kilometres along a valley from the source of its river, the Orbiquet, 19km southeast of Lisieux. Consisting of little more than its main road, the Rue Grande, with the huge tower of Notre Dame church at its southern end, it epitomizes the simple pleasures of the region.

Along the Rue Grande, you'll see several houses in which the gaps between the timbers are filled with intricate patterns of coloured tiles and bricks. Debussy composed *Jardin sous la Pluie* in one of these, and the oldest and prettiest of the lot – a tanner's house dating back to 1568, and once again called the **Vieux Manoir** – holds a museum of local history. On the whole, though, it's more fun just to walk down behind the church to the river, and its watermill and paddocks.

Practicalities

There's a good, slightly upmarket **hotel** at the top end of Rue Grande: *de France*, at no. 152 (☎02.31.32.74.02; ②; restaurant closed Mon). You can get a good meal there for 90F/€13.72 and upwards, or stroll down the street to its narrowest point, where *Le Caneton* in the half-timbered house at no. 32 serves gourmet menus at similar prices. Orbec also has a two-star municipal **campsite**, *Les Capucins* (☎02.31.32.76.22; closed Oct–May).

Livarot

The centre of the cheese country is the old town of **LIVAROT**, 18km south of Lisieux. Set in a grand house near the Vie River on its western outskirts, the **Musée du Fromage** illustrates the history and manufacture of Livarot's eponymous cheese, and doles out free samples (March Tues–Sat 2–5pm; April, Sept & Oct Mon–Sat 10am–noon & 2–6pm, Sun 2–6pm; May & June daily 10am–noon & 2–6pm; July & Aug daily 10am–6.30pm; 17F/€2.59). For the best views of the valley, climb up to the thirteenth-century church of **St-Michel de Livet**, just above the town; to visit you contact a M Jean Fromage.

Practicalities

Livarot's **tourist office**, 1 place Georges-Bisson (Feb–June & Sept Mon–Sat 9.30am–noon & 2–6pm; July & Aug Mon–Sat 9.30am–noon & 2–6pm, Sun 10am–noon; Oct–Dec Mon–Sat 10am–noon & 2–5pm; ☎02.31.63.47.39), is almost next door to the (rather rundown and shabby) **hotel** and restaurant *du Vivier* (☎02.31.32.04.10; ③). The enjoyable *Café de la Paix* is further east, up from the central traffic lights, and there's also a tiny one-star municipal **campsite** (☎02.31.63.53.19; closed mid-Sept to mid-May). The local **cheese fair** falls on the first weekend of each August.

St-Pierre-sur-Dives

The medieval wooden *halles* at **ST-PIERRE-SUR-DIVES**, 16km west of Livarot, burned to the ground in 1944, had been rebuilt by 1949. Only traditional techniques were used: there's not a single nail or screw in the place, whose timber frame rests on low stone walls and is held together by chestnut pegs alone. The buildings of the adjacent convent now house a slightly academic annexe to the Livarot cheese museum (April–Oct Mon–Fri 9.30am–12.30pm & 1.30–6.30pm, Sat 9.30am–12.30pm & 2.30–5.30pm; Nov–March Mon–Fri 9.30am–12.30pm & 1.30–6.30pm, Sat 10am–noon & 2–5pm; 15F/€2.29), as well as the local **tourist office** (same hours; ☎02.31.20.97.90, *www.mairie-saint-pierre-sur-dives.fr*).

The town's other focus of interest is its Gothic-Romanesque **church**, whose windows depict the history of the town. A large **market** still takes place every Monday in the open space next to the *halles*.

Practicalities

St-Pierre's best bet for **accommodation** is *L'Agriculture*, a *logis de France* at 118 rue de Falaise (☎02.31.20.72.78; ②), which has a better restaurant than the slightly cheaper *Renaissance*, 57 rue de Lisieux (☎02.31.20.81.23; ②; closed Sun lunchtime). Its two-star, summer-only **campsite** (☎02.31.20.97.90; closed Oct–April) is 1km south of town.

Falaise

William the Conqueror, or William the Bastard as he is more familiarly known to Normans, was born in **FALAISE**, 40km southwest of Lisieux. His mother, Arlette, a laundress, was spotted by his father, Duke Robert of Normandy, at the washing place below the château. She was a shrewd woman, who scorned secrecy in her eventual assignation by riding publicly through the main entrance to meet him. During her pregnancy, she is said to have dreamed of bearing a mighty tree that cast its shade over Normandy and England.

From a distance, the sheer wall of the **castle keep**, firmly planted on the massive rocks of the cliff (*falaise*) that gave the town its name, and towering over the **Fontaine d'Arlette** down by the river, looks all but impregnable. Nonetheless, it was so heavily damaged during the war that it took over fifty years to reopen the castle for regular visits (daily 9.30am–6pm; English-language tours daily 11am & 3pm; 30F/€4.57). Huge resources have been lavished on restoring the central *donjon* – reminiscent of the Tower of London with its cream-coloured Caen stone – in accordance with cutting-edge contemporary concepts. A guiding principle was to avoid any possible confusion as to what is original and authentic, and what is new. Rest assured you'll be in no doubt whatever. Steel slabs, concrete blocks, glass floors and tent-like canvas awnings have been slapped down atop the bare ruins, and metal staircases even squeezed into the wall cavities. The raw structure of the keep, down to its very foundations, lies exposed to view, while the newly created rooms are used for changing exhibitions that focus on the castle's fascinating past. Add the superb views of the town and surroundings from the battlements, and you have one of Normandy's most rewarding historical sites.

The whole of Falaise was devastated in the course of the struggle to close the "Falaise Gap" in August 1944 – the climax of the Battle of Normandy, as the Allied armies sought to encircle the Germans and cut off their retreat. By the time the

Canadians entered the town on August 17, they could no longer tell where the roads had been and had to bulldoze a new four-metre strip straight through the middle. Set in almost derelict wilderness right next to the town centre is an isolated survivor, the **Château de la Fresnaye**, housing a rather earnest local museum which is only open during the summer.

Opposite the tourist office (see below), the **Musée des Automates**, also known as "Automates Avenue", preserves mechanical window displays that graced the department stores of Paris between the 1920s and 1950s (daily 10am–12.30pm & 1.30–6pm; 30F/€4.57). The highlight is a mock-up of a real-life collision that took place in a tiny village between the cyclists of the Tour de France and a herd of little pigs.

Practicalities

Falaise's modern, well-stocked **tourist office** is located in the Forum, on the boulevard de la Liberation (May & first half of Sept Mon 10am–12.30pm & 1.30–6.30pm, Tues–Sat 9.30am–12.30pm & 1.30–6.30pm, Sun 10.30am–12.30pm; June Mon–Sat 9.30am–12.30pm & 1.30–6.30pm, Sun 10.30am–12.30pm & 3–5.30pm; July & Aug Mon–Sat 9.30am–6.30pm, Sun 10.30am–12.30pm & 3–5.30pm; mid-Sept to April Mon 1.30–6.30pm, Tues–Sat 9.30am–12.30pm & 1.30–6.30pm; ☎02.31.90.17.26, *falaise-tourisme@mail.cpod.fr*).

Most of Falaise's few **hotels** stand along the main Caen–Argentan road, which can make them rather noisy. The *Poste*, not far from the tourist office at 38 rue Georges-Clémenceau (☎02.31.90.13.14; ③; restaurant closed Sun evening & Mon) serves good food on menus from 87F/€13.26, while rooms and meals at the *Hôtel de la Place*, next to the church at 1 place St-Gervais (☎02.31.40.19.00; ②; closed Sun evening & Wed), are significantly cheaper. The three-star **campsite**, *Camping du Château* (☎02.31.90.16.55; closed Oct–Easter), next to Arlette's fountain and the municipal swimming pool, is in a much better location.

Vimoutiers and Camembert

The war-ravaged and consequently rather ugly town of **VIMOUTIERS**, 10km south of Livarot, contains yet another **cheese museum**, at 10 av Général-de-Gaulle (March, April, Nov & Dec Mon 2–6pm, Tues–Fri 9am–noon & 2–6pm, Sat 9am–noon; May–Oct Mon 2–6pm, Tues–Sat 9am–noon & 2–6pm, Sun 10am–noon & 2.30–6pm; 25F/€3.81). This one features a glorious collection not to be missed by tyrosemiophiles – cheese-label collectors (they do exist) – who will find Camembert stickers ranging from remote Chilean dairies to Marks & Spencer. Most of the cheese on display, however, turns out to be polystyrene.

A statue in the main square honours Marie Harel, who, at the nearby village of **CAMEMBERT**, developed the original cheese early in the nineteenth century, promoting it with a skilful campaign that included sending free samples to Napoléon. There's a photo in the museum of the statue with its head blown off after a US air raid in June 1944; its replacement was donated by the cheesemakers of Ohio. Marie is confronted across the main street by what might be called the statue of the Unknown Cow.

Camembert itself, 3km southeast of Vimoutiers, is tiny, hilly and very rural, home to far more cows than humans. It has recently acquired its own **cheese museum** (April to mid-Nov daily 10am–7pm; 15F/€2.29), where the displays add little to those in Vimoutiers.

Practicalities

Vimoutiers is the venue of a **market** on Monday afternoons and Fridays. Its **tourist office**, in the cheese museum (same hours as museum; ☎02.33.39.30.29), has piles of information on local cheese-related attractions. Of its **hotels**, the very central but far from welcoming *Soleil d'Or*, 15 place Mackau (☎02.33.39.07.15; ②; closed mid-Feb to mid-March), has a good 75F/€11.43 menu and an even better 110F/€16.77 one.

A short way south of Vimoutiers, en route to Camembert, the beautifully sited lake known as the **Escale du Vitou** offers everything you need for windsurfing, swimming and horse-riding, as well as its own new, comfortable, rural hotel, *L' Escale du Vitou* (☎02.33.39.12.04; ②). There's also a clean and very cheap year-round **campsite** nearby, the two-star *La Campière*, 9 rue du 8-Mai (☎02.33.39.18.86).

Ste-Foy de Montgommery

A couple of kilometres north of Vimoutiers, towards Livarot, the D579 passes through the village of **STE-FOY DE MONTGOMMERY**. Outside the *Café La Gosselinais* here, on the night of July 17, 1944, **Field-Marshal Rommel** was seriously injured when RAF Typhoons attacked his Mercedes. Rommel never returned to the battlefield, and committed suicide three months later. That his nemesis should overtake him in a place called "Holy Faith of Montgommery" became part of the legend surrounding the British field marshal.

South to Gacé

The **D26** runs along the **valley of the Vie** south of Vimoutiers – a route that is something of a microcosm of Norman vernacular architecture, lined along the way with ramshackle old barns, outhouses and farm buildings. Faded orange clay crumbles from between the weathered wooden beams of these flower-covered beauties.

GACÉ itself, 18km from Vimoutiers, is not wildly exciting, but it does have a handful of reasonable hotels. The *Normandie* on its main street (☎02.33.35.52.13; closed Jan, plus Sun evening & Mon; ①) has several well-priced menus.

Nonant-le-Pin, 12km south of Gacé, was the birthplace in 1824 of Alphonsine Plessis, a celebrated courtesan who served as the inspiration for Dumas' *La Dame aux Camélias* and Verdi's *La Traviata*.

Argentan and around

ARGENTAN centres on a **ruined castle** – the site where Henry II of England received the news on New Year's Day 1171 that his knights had taken him at his word and murdered Thomas-à-Becket. In fact, the entire town was very comprehensively ruined during General Patton's bid to close the "Falaise pocket" in August 1944, and there's virtually nothing to see; the **church of St-Germain** which dominates all approaches has been under continuing restoration ever since, and remains closed to visitors. Even the castle ruin takes a bit of finding, atop the hill nearby. Although Argentan makes an enjoyable enough halt when the central market square, place du Marché, is in full swing on Tuesdays, or for boat trips on the River Orne, the main reason anyone comes here is not monuments but **horses**. Outside the town are numerous equestrian centres, with riding schools, stables, racetracks and studs.

Practicalities

Trains to Argentan pull in at the **gare SNCF**, across the Orne a short way southwest of the centre. Full information on the area is available from the **tourist office** in the old chapel at 6 place du Marché (July & Aug Mon 9am–noon & 2–7pm, Tues–Sat 9am–7pm, Sun 9am–1pm; Sept–June Tues–Sat 10am–noon & 2–6pm, Sun 10am–12.30pm & 1.30–5.30pm; ☎02.33.67.12.48). Of the **hotels** in town, the best budget option is the *Donjon*, right by the castle keep and above a brasserie at 1 rue de l'Hôtel-de-Ville (☎02.33.67.03.76; ①; closed Sun evening), while the *France*, 8 bd Carnot (☎02.33.67.03.65; ②; closed Sun evening), has an excellent restaurant, with menus from 75F/€11.43. Its 140F/€21.34 menu offers a rare chance to eat frogs' legs – not nearly as common a dish as you might imagine.

Le Pin-au-Haras

LE PIN-AU-HARAS, 15km east of Argentan on the N26, is an essential stop for horse lovers: it's the home of the **National Stud** (*Haras National*). The plan for the stud was originally conceived by Louis XIV's minister, Colbert, and the ground subsequently laid out by Le Nôtre from 1715 to 1730. It can be approached via a number of woodland avenues, but the most impressive is the D304, which climbs slowly from the hippodrome and is lined with jumps and hedges.

While the buildings are magnificent, they're nowhere near as sumptuous as the residents – around eighty of them – incalculable investments that include champions of Epsom and Longchamp, as well as prize specimens of the indigenous Norman Percheron.

Tours of the stud leave every thirty minutes from the main entrance (daily: April to mid-Oct 9.30am–6pm; mid-Oct to March 10am–noon & 2–5pm; 25F/€3.81; arrive one hour before closing for the last tour). You are escorted by a groom through stables full of stomping, snorting, glistening stallions, rooms of polished harnesses and fine carriages, and great doorways labelled in stone, until eventually you come out to a pastoral vision of the horses grazing in endless sequences of gardens and paddocks. Each tour lasts for around an hour; if you find it hard to follow the rapid French-only commentary, you can amuse yourself by watching the way everybody scrupulously affects not to notice the rampant sexuality – which, of course, is the *raison d'être* of the whole place.

Between June and September, displays of horsemanship are held on Thursdays at 3pm, while there are also special events on every Sunday between September and mid-October, as well as a few other summer weekends. Between February 15 and July 15, most of the horses are away; and the château itself is never open.

The Château d'O

Just outside Mortrée, 15km southeast of Argentan on the N158, and 6.5km northwest of Sées (see overleaf), is the privately owned and postcard-perfect **Château d'O** (daily except Tues: April–Sept 2.30–6pm; Oct–March 2.30–5.30pm; 15F/€2.29 gardens, 25F/€3.81 house). This turreted château, whose grey-slate roof rises to a pencil-case-full of sharp points, is in perfect condition, with a full moat that widens out into a lake. The house dates from the end of the fifteenth century and, unusually, was designed purely as a domestic residence, with no military pretensions, while the lawns of the grounds hold a pitch-and-putt golf course.

Within the grounds, but with its own separate entrance, the *Ferme du Château d'O* (☎02.33.35.35.27; closed Sun evening & Mon) is a restaurant that boasts quite a gastronomic reputation. Lunch menus start at 100F/€15.24, including ham cooked in cider, while on the 275F/€41.92 menu you get to sample crayfish *profiteroles*.

Sées

SÉES, midway between Argentan and Alençon, has long had an air of being lost in its own history. A succession of dusty and derelict squares, all with medieval buildings intact, surround the great Gothic, white-ceilinged **cathedral**, which is the fifth to stand on the site and is magnificently illuminated every summer evening. One of its predecessors was burned down by its own bishop, attempting to smoke out a gang of thieves – much to the scorn of the pope.

However, Sées does hold several tasteful, long-established **hotels**. The *Cheval Blanc* overlooks the pretty little place St-Pierre on the main road south (☎02.33.27.80.48; ②; closed Nov, plus Thurs evening & Fri in season, Fri & Sat out of season), and offers menus from 69F/€10.52, with a good 89F/€13.57 menu of regional specialities. The *Dauphin* is hidden away a little further west, in a quiet location at 31 place des Halles next to the old covered marketplace (☎02.33.27.80.07; ④; closed Sun evening all year, & Mon evening in winter), and has an equally good (if more expensive) restaurant, while the *Garden Hôtel* at 12 rue des Ardrillers (☎02.33.27.98.27; ②) is a peaceful, elegant refuge reached via an ivy-covered gatehouse in the northwest corner of another sleepy square, nearer the cathedral.

Le Mêle-sur-Sarthe

LE MÊLE-SUR-SARTHE, 20km southeast of Sées on the minor D42, holds another *logis* worth stopping at. The *Hotel de la Poste,* 27 place de Gaulle (☎02.33.81.18.00; ②–④; closed Sun evening all year, & Mon evening in winter), has an acceptable 89F/€13.57 menu for guests who happen not to like eating, and a very good 120F/€18.29 one for those who do. They also serve some good-value menus where the price includes drinks and coffee.

Alençon and around

ALENÇON, a fair-sized and busy town, is best known for its traditional – and now pretty much defunct – **lacemaking** industry. The **Musée des Beaux Arts et de la Dentelle**, housed in a former Jesuit school (mid-June to mid-Sept daily 10am–noon & 2–6pm; mid-Sept to mid-June closed Mon; 20F/€3.05), has all the best trappings of a modern museum. However, the highly informative history of lacemaking upstairs, with examples of numerous different techniques, can be rather deadly for anyone not already fascinated by the subject; if it does capture your imagination, time your visit to coincide with a guided tour and demonstration (July & Aug daily 2.30pm & 4.30pm; 10F/€1.52 extra). The temptation to leave without a visit to the "Minor Lace Exhibition Room" is almost overwhelming; but the room beyond it holds a collection of gruesome Cambodian artefacts, spears and lances, tiger skulls and elephants' feet, gathered by a "militant socialist" French governor at the turn of the twentieth century. The paintings in the Beaux Arts section downstairs are fairly nondescript, except for a touching Nativity by the Norman artist, Latouche, and a few works by Courbet and Géricault.

Stained glass in the **Notre Dame** church shows the medieval guilds of crafts-men who paid for each specific window, and the baptism of **Ste Thérèse** is com-memorated in the chapel in which it took place. If you haven't already had a sur-feit of the saint at Lisieux, you can also wander over to her **birthplace**, on rue St-Blaise, just in front of the *gare routière* (daily except Tues: Feb–May, Nov & Dec 9.30am–noon & 2.30–5pm; June–Oct 9am–noon & 2–6pm; free).

The **Château des Ducs**, the old town castle, looks impressive but doesn't encourage visitors – it's a prison. People in Alençon have nightmare memories of its use during the war by the Gestapo.

Thanks to wartime bombardment, little is left of the buildings that once stood on the banks of the River Sarthe. Alençon was the first town in France to be lib-erated by French forces alone, and a monument right next to the Pont-Neuf hon-ours their leader, the aristocratic **Général Leclerc** (whose headmaster at school was General de Gaulle's father). The movements of his army are chronicled through the deserts of North Africa, via Utah Beach, to Alençon, on August 12, 1944. Within two weeks he was in Paris; within a year, in Berlin; and by March 1946 he was in Hanoi – he died in a plane crash in North Africa in 1947.

Another **lace museum**, with a shop selling samples, stands opposite the mon-ument (Mon–Sat 10am–noon & 2–6pm; 15F/€2.29).

Practicalities

Alençon's **gare routière** and **gare SNCF** are both northeast of the centre, with the train station slightly the further out of the two. The **tourist office** is housed in the dramatic fifteenth-century Maison d'Ozé on the central place La Magdelaine (July & Aug Mon & Sat 9.30am–noon & 2–6.30pm, Tues–Fri 9.30am–6.30pm, Sun 10.30am–12.30pm & 2.30–5.30pm; Sept–June Mon–Sat 9.30am–noon & 2–6.30pm; ☎02.33.80.66.33, *www.ville-alencon.fr*). They also orga-nize **guided tours** of town (July & Aug daily 2.30pm & 4.30pm, plus Fri 8.30pm; 25F/€3.81).

Alençon's prime concentration of **hotels** lies in the immediate environs of the *gare SNCF*. The two *logis*, *l'Industrie*, 20 place Général-de-Gaulle (☎02.33.27.19.30; ③; closed Sun evening & Mon), and the *Grand Hôtel de la Gare*, 50 av Wilson (☎02.33.29.03.93; ②), offer decent rooms and have fixed-price menus for around 70F/€10.67. There are some good shops and cafés in a few well-pedestrianized streets at the heart of its abysmal one-way traffic system. Here you'll also find a romantic little **restaurant**, the *Jardin Gourmand* at 14 rue de Sarthe (☎02.33.32.22.56; closed Sun & Mon), with menus from 98F/€14.94. Good places to sample the thriving local **bar** scene include *La Caves Aux Boeufs*, spreading across the pedestrian rue de la Caves Aux Boeufs, and the half-timbered *Café des Sept Colonnes* at 2 rue du Château.

If you're interested in **horse riding** – along the banks of the Orne – the Association Départmentale de Tourisme Équestre et d'Équitation de Loisir de l'Orne has its headquarters in Alençon at 60 Grand-Rue. They can also tell you about the various local stud farms open to the public.

The Forêt d'Écouves

The **Forêt d'Écouves**, easily reached (under your own steam) from either Alençon or Sées (see opposite), is the centrepiece of the Parc Régional Normandie-Maine, an amorphous area stretching from Mortain in the west to within a few kilometres of Mortagne-au-Perche in the east. A dense mixture of old spruce, pine, oak and beech, set on high hills a few kilometres north of Alençon, the Écouves forest is one of the most attractive in Normandy. These commanding heights were bitterly fought over during the war, and a Free French tank still guards the **Croix-de-Médavy** at their very apex.

Unfortunately, the forest is now a favoured spot of the military – and, in autumn, of deerhunters too. To avoid risking life and limb, check with the park's offices. You can usually ramble along the cool paths, happening on wild mushrooms and even the odd wild boar. The *Camping d'Ecouves* (☎02.33.28.10.64; closed Oct–April) on the edge of the forest in **RADON**, 6km north of Alençon and 1km east of the D26, is an ideal spot from which to explore the woodlands. As well as tent sites, it also offers chalets (②) and its own inexpensive restaurant (closed Sun evening & Mon).

Carrouges

One alternative base at the western end of the Forêt d'Écouves is the appealing little hilltop town of **CARROUGES**, 28km northwest of Alençon. Down below the centre, at the foot of the hill, a fine fourteenth-century **château** commands spacious landscaped grounds (daily: April to mid-June & Sept 10am–noon & 2–6pm; mid-June to Aug 9.30am–noon & 2–6.30pm; Oct–March 10am–noon & 2–5pm; 32F/€4.88). Its two highlights are a superb restored brick staircase, and a room in which hang portraits of fourteen successive generations of the Le Veneur family, an extraordinary illustration of the processes of heredity. In the **Maison de Métiers**, the former castle chapel, local craftsmen sell their produce.

On the narrow rue Ste-Marguerite that runs through the heart of Carrouges, the *Hôtel du Nord* (☎02.33.27.20.14; ①; closed mid-Dec to mid-Jan, plus Fri Sept–June) offers a handful of small, old-fashioned bedrooms and delicious local cuisine on menus that start at 60F/€9.15. All but next door, the even smaller, but otherwise virtually identical *St-Pierre* (☎02.33.27.20.02; ②) offers five en-suite rooms, and menus from 47F/€7.17.

Heading onwards on the D908 towards Bagnoles, you come after a few kilometres to the delightful village of **JOUÉ-DU-BOIS**, home to a diminutive château, lake and a cheap but delicious restaurant, the *Pomme d'Or* (☎02.33.37.08.97; closed Sun), where you can still get a four-course meal for under 75F/€11.43.

Bagnoles de l'Orne

The spa town of **BAGNOLES DE L'ORNE**, 17km west of Carrouges, lies at the heart of a long, narrow wood, the Forêt des Andaines. Broad avenues radiate into the forest from the centre of the town. As you approach, you begin to encounter pale figures shuffling slowly outwards, blinking as if unused to the light of day, as though silently fleeing some nameless evil. In fact, the forbidding nineteenth-century building from which they emerge contains nothing more fearsome than **thermal baths**. Bagnoles is a mecca for the sick from all over France; its springs are such big business that they maintain a booking office next to the Pompidou Centre in Paris.

Although life in the town is conducted at a phenomenally slow pace, it is all surprisingly jolly – redolent with aged flirtations and gallantry. The lakeside gardens

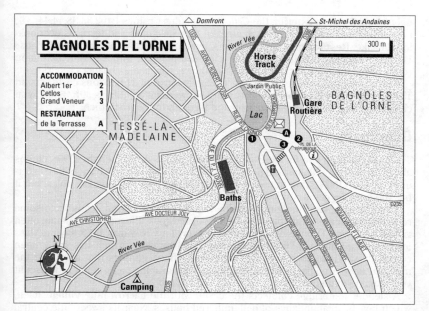

are the big scene, with pedalos, horse-drawn calèches and an enormous casino. And with so many visitors to keep entertained, and spending money, there are innumerable cultural **events**, concerts and stage shows throughout the summer; the ostensible high spot, the annual Spectacle in July, is one of the less enthralling.

Away from its main roads, the **Forêt des Andaines** is pleasant, with scattered and unspoilt villages, such as Juvigny and St-Michel, and the secluded, private **Château de Couterne**, a visual delight even from the gates, with its lake and long grass-floored avenue approach.

Practicalities

Whether you'd actually want to spend time in Bagnoles depends on your disposable income as well as your health. Furthermore, the town as a whole operates to a season that lasts roughly from early April to the end of October; arrive in winter, and you may find everything shut. The numerous **hotels** are expensive and sedate places, in which it's possible to be too late for dinner at 7pm and locked out altogether at 9pm, while the three-star **campsite**, *de la Vée* (☎02.33.37.87.45; closed Nov–March), south of town, is forlorn.

The **tourist office** on place de la République (April–Oct Mon–Sat 9am–1pm & 2–6.30pm, Sun 10am–noon & 3–6.30pm; Nov–March Mon–Fri 10am–noon & 2–6pm; ☎02.33.37.85.66, *www.bagnoles-de-lorne.com*) will provide details on accommodation in Bagnoles and its less exclusive sister town of **TESSE-MADELEINE**. Among the cheaper options in Bagnoles proper – all very near the central roundabout – are the *Albert 1er* at 7 av Dr-Poulain (☎02.33.37.80.97; ②; closed Nov–Jan), which has excellent menus from 85F/€12.96, and the *Grand Veneur* at 6 place République (☎02.33.37.86.79; ③; closed Nov–March). Despite its ugly would-be-Deco exterior, the *Cetlos*, on rue des Casinos (☎02.33.38.44.44; ④), is probably the best of the crop, bedecked with balconies and terraces overlooking the lake. **Restaurants**, in both towns, tend to be good value: the *de la Terrasse* (☎02.33.30.80.96) in Bagnoles is well tried and popular, with a traditional dining room offering six menus from 75F/€11.43 upwards, and a cheaper crêperie.

If you fancy **taking the waters**, a "complete cure" of 21 sessions costs around 1500F/€228.67, with individual baths and showers for as little as 30F/€4.57; you can also arrange an all-inclusive package through the tourist office.

Domfront

The road **through the forest** from Bagnoles, the D335 and then the D908, climbs above the lush woodlands and progressively narrows to a hog's back before entering **DOMFRONT**, 22km to the west. Less happens here than at Bagnoles, but it has the edge on countryside.

A public park, near the long-abandoned former train station, leads up to some redoubtable **castle ruins** perched on an isolated rock. Eleanor of Aquitaine often visited here, and Thomas-à-Becket came to stay for Christmas 1166, saying Mass in the Notre-Dame-sur-l'Eau church down by the river, which has sadly been ruined by vandals. The views from the flower-filled gardens that surround the mangled keep are spectacular, including a very graphic panorama of the ascent you've made to get up.

A slender footbridge connects the castle with the narrow little **village** itself, which boasts an abundance of half-timbered houses. Near its sweet little central square, the modern **St-Julien** church, constructed out of concrete segments during the 1920s, is bursting with exciting mosaics. It's an odd-looking building, especially when its belfry is swathed in green netting, which it seems to be for much of the time.

Practicalities

The **tourist office** is at 12 place de la Roirie (Mon–Sat 10am–noon & 2.30–6.30pm; ☎02.33.38.53.97); on summer afternoons (July & Aug Mon–Sat 3pm), they run free **guided tours** of old Domfront.

Domfront's **hotels**, clustered together at the foot of the hill below the old town, make useful and very pleasant stopovers. Two *logis de France* stand side by side: the *Relais St-Michel* (☎02.33.38.64.99; ②) has widely varied menus at under 100F/€15.24, while the *Hôtel de France* (☎02.33.38.51.44; ②) is a little cheaper, and has a nice little bar and garden. Campers should take note that the two-star local **campsite**, *du Champs Passais* (☎02.33.37.37.66; closed mid-Oct to mid-April), is exceptionally small.

The Suisse Normande

The area known as the **Suisse Normande** lies roughly 25km south of Caen, along the gorge of the River Orne, between Thury-Harcourt and Putanges. The name is a little far-fetched – there are certainly no mountains – but it is quite distinctive, with cliffs and crags and wooded hills at every turn. The energetic race along the Orne in canoes and kayaks, their lazier counterparts contenting themselves with pedalos or a bizarre species of inflatable rubber tractor, while high above them climbers dangle from thin ropes and claw desperately at the sheer rock face. For mere walkers, the Orne can be frustrating: footpaths along the river are few and far between, whatever maps may say, and often entirely overgrown with brambles. At least one road sign in the area warns of unexploded mines, so tread carefully.

The Suisse Normande is most usually approached from Caen or Falaise, and contrasts dramatically with the prairie-like expanse of wheatfields en route. Bus Verts #34 can take you to Thury-Harcourt or Clécy on its way from Caen to Flers, and SNCF run occasional special summer train excursions from Caen. If you're **cycling**, the least stressful approach is to follow the D212 from Caen, cruising across the flatlands to Thury-Harcourt; although swooping down the D23 from Bretteville, with thick woods to either side of you, is pretty exhilarating. Taking the D235 from Caen, follow signs for Falaise, and head straight on through Ifs. Touring the Suisse Normande on a bike, however, is an exhausting business: the minor roads do not follow the gorge floor, but undulate endlessly over the surrounding slopes.

Thury-Harcourt
THURY-HARCOURT is really two separate towns: a little village around a bridge across the Orne, and a larger market town on the hill that overlooks it.

Between May and September, the grounds of the local manor house are open (for a 25F/€3.81 fee) between 2.30pm and 6.30pm every day, giving access to the immediate riverside.

The **tourist office**, 2 place St-Sauveur (mid-June to mid-Sept Tues–Sat 9.30am–noon & 2.30–6.30pm, Sun 10.30am–noon; mid-Sept to mid-June Tues & Thurs 9.30am–noon & 2.30–5pm, Fri 9.30am–noon; ☎02.31.79.70.45), can suggest walks, rides and *gîtes d'étape* throughout the Suisse Normande; SIVOM at 15 rue de Condé rent out canoes. **Hotels** in Thury-Harcourt are for the most part quite expensive, though the flowery *Hôtel du Val d'Orne*, 9 rte d'Aunay (☎02.31.79.70.81; ②; closed Sat lunch in summer, Fri evening & all Sat in low season), keeps its room rates down, and has a decent **restaurant**. There's also an attractive four-star **campsite**, the *Vallée du Traspy* (☎02.31.79.61.80; closed mid-Sept to mid-April).

Aunay-sur-Odon

AUNAY-SUR-ODON, 14km west of Thury-Harcourt and the river, is no one's idea of a holiday destination; all but obliterated during the war, it was rebuilt from scratch in functional concrete. In summer, however, when all the **accommodation** possibilities in the Suisse Normande proper tend to be wildly over-subscribed, you may well be glad of finding a room in either the *Hôtel de la Place*, 10 rue du 12-Juin-1944 (☎02.31.77.60.73; ②), where the excellent 125F/€19.06 menu includes crayfish and sea bass, or the *Hôtel St-Michel*, 6–8 rue de Caen (☎02.31.77.63.16; ②).

Clécy

The small village of **CLÉCY**, 10km south of Thury-Harcourt, is perched on a hill about 1km up from the point where the D133A crosses the River Orne by means of the Pont du Vey. On the way up, in the Parc des Loisirs, is a **Musée du Chemin de Fer Miniature** (March–Easter Sun 2–5.30pm; Easter–June & Sept daily 10am–noon & 2–6pm; July & Aug daily 10am–noon & 2–6.30pm; Oct & Nov Sun 2–5pm; 25F/€3.81), featuring a gigantic model railway layout certain to appeal to children.

For advice on accommodation and the wide variety of holiday activities available, head for the **tourist office** (Mon–Fri 9am–12.30pm & 2.30–5pm, Sat 9am–noon; ☎02.31.69.79.95), which is tucked in behind the church. Clécy is a slightly better bet than Thury-Harcourt for finding a **room**, although its visitors outnumber residents in high season and the whole area can get much too crowded for comfort. The *logis* facing the church, *Au Site Normand*, 1 rue des Châtelets (☎02.31.69.71.05; ③; closed mid-Nov to Easter, plus Tues evening & Wed out of season), consists of an old-fashioned and good-value dining room in the main timber-framed building, and a cluster of newer units opening onto a courtyard around the back.

Down the hill, the *Moulin du Vey* (☎02.31.69.71.08, *www.oda.fr/aa/moulin .duvey*; ⑤; closed Dec & Jan), set in spacious grounds on the far bank of the river, is a luxury hotel that takes its name from the restored water mill right by the bridge, which is itself, confusingly, now a restaurant. The western riverbank continues in a brief splurge of restaurants, takeaways and snack bars as far as the two-star **campsite** (☎02.31.69.70.36; closed Oct–March).

The Pain de Sucre

Across from Clécy, the **east bank** of the Orne is dominated by the exposed rock face of the giant **Pain de Sucre**, or Sugarloaf, looming above the river. Small footpaths, and the tortuous Route des Crêtes, wind up to its flat top, making for some of the most enjoyable walks in Normandy. Picnic sites and parking places along the crest hold orientation maps so weather-beaten as to be almost abstract, but the views down to the flat fields of the Orne valley are stupendous. This is a prime site for **hang-gliders**; disconcertingly, at two points paved concrete ramps lead right to the edge of the precipice, built to facilitate launches.

Pont d'Ouilly

If you're planning on walking, or cycling, one good central spot in which to base yourself is **PONT D'OUILLY**, a dozen or so kilometres upriver from Clécy, at the point where the main road from Vire to Falaise crosses the river. It's a small town, with a few basic shops, an old covered market hall and a promenade (with bar) slightly upstream alongside the weir; a pleasant walk leads for 3.5km south along the riverside to the pretty little village of **LE MESNIL VILLEMENT**. A Grand Pardon du Ste-Roche takes place along the river on the third Sunday in August.

As well as its **campsite**, overlooking the river (☎02.31.69.46.12; closed Oct–Easter), Pont d'Ouilly can offer an attractive **hotel**, the *du Commerce* (☎02.31.69.80.16; ②; closed Sun evening & Mon Oct–May). This is the quintes-sential French village hotel, with a friendly welcome and attentive service. Its **restaurant** is very popular with local families, serving superb, definitive Norman cooking, with plenty of creamy *pays d'Auge* sauces, on menus that start at 65F/€9.91. Be sure to try the flaming *Bourdelot* for dessert, a sort of incandes-cent apple turnover. Appropriately enough, the dining room is filled with stuffed animals.

About 1km north of Pont d'Ouilly, the more upmarket *Auberge St-Christophe* stands, covered with ivy and geraniums, in a beautiful setting on the right bank of the Orne (☎02.31.69.81.23; ③; closed Sun evening, Mon & mid-Feb to mid-March). The cheapest of its imaginative menus costs 103F/€15.70.

The Roche d'Oëtre

A short distance south of Pont d'Ouilly is the **Roche d'Oëtre**, a high rock afford-ing a tremendous view, not over the Orne but into the deep and totally wooded gorge of the Rouvre. The rock itself is private property, though you're under no obligation to visit the café there.

The river widens soon afterwards into the **Lac du Rabodanges**, formed by the many-arched Rabodanges Dam. It's a popular spot, with a multifacility **campsite**, *Les Retours*, perfectly situated between the dam and the bridge on the D121. There's a play area for kids, and grassy picnic slopes lead down to the water's edge, where the occasional bather risks a swim among the waterskiers, speed-boats, windsurfers, canoes and kayaks. The imposing Rabodanges château, high-er up the hillside, is now a stud farm.

Putanges

Further climbing roads bring you to **PUTANGES**, another possible place to stay, with a well-priced **hotel**, the *Lion Verd* (☎02.33.35.01.86; ②; closed Jan), very near the river, and a small **campsite**, *le Val d'Orne* (☎02.33.35.00.25; closed Oct–Easter). The town lies a bit beyond the main attractions of the region, but nevertheless it's a pleasant stop, with a few bars and pavement cafés and, just upstream from the bridge, the weirs over which the Orne appears from its source a short way south.

The Bocage

The region centring on **St-Lô**, west of Caen and just south of the Cotentin, is known as the **Bocage Normande**. The word *bocage* refers to a type of cultivated countryside common in the west of France, in which fields are cut by tight hedgerows rooted into walls of earth well over 1m high.

An effective form of smallhold farming, at least in pre-industrial days, it also proved to be a perfect system of anti-tank barricades. When the Allied troops tried to advance through the region in 1944, it was almost impenetrable – certainly bearing no resemblance to the East Anglian plains where they had trained. The war here was hand-to-hand, inch-by-inch slaughter; the destruction of villages often wholesale.

St-Lô

The city of **ST-LÔ**, a transport junction 60km south of Cherbourg and 36km southwest of Bayeux, was crucial in the war to the Allied breakout of the Cotentin, and is still known as the "Capital of the Ruins". Black-and-white postcards of the wartime devastation are on sale everywhere and you keep coming across memorial sites as you wander about. In the main square, the gate of the old prison commemorates Resistance members executed by the Nazis, people deported east to the concentration camps and soldiers killed in action. When the bombardment of St-Lô was at its fiercest, the Germans refused to take any measures to protect the prisoners; the gate was all that survived. In similar vein, behind the cathedral, a monument to the dead of World War I is pitted with shrapnel from World War II. Less depressingly, at the foot of the rock under the castle you can see the entrance to caves where citizens sheltered from the onslaught, while somewhere far below are great vaults used by the German command. In Studs Terkel's book, *The Good War*, a GI reminisces about the huge party thrown there after the Americans found vast stockpiles of champagne; Thomas Pynchon's *Gravity's Rainbow* has a crazed drinking scene based on the tale. Samuel Beckett was here during the battle and after, working for the Irish Red Cross as interpreter, driver and provision-seeker – for such things as rat poison for the maternity hospitals. He said he took away with him a "time-honoured conception of humanity in ruins".

The newness of so much in St-Lô reveals the scale of fighting. Between the *gare SNCF* and the castle rock, for example, a walk leads along the canalized channel of the Vire – an attractive course, but unmistakably an attempt to patch over the ravages of war. All the trees in the city are the same height, too, all planted to replace the battle's mutilated stumps. But the most visible – and brilliant – reconstruction is the **Cathédrale de Notre Dame**. The main body of this, with its strange southward-veering nave, has been conventionally repaired and rebuilt. Between the shattered west front and base of the collapsed north tower, however, a startling sheer wall of icy-green stone makes no attempt to mask the destruction.

By way of contrast to such memories, a lighthouse-like 1950s folly spirals to nowhere on the main square, place Général-de-Gaulle. Should you feel the urge to climb its staircase, make your way into the brand-new and even more pointless labyrinth of glass at its feet, which now houses St-Lô's tourist office (for hours, see opposite), and pay the 10F/€1.52 admission fee. More compelling, around behind the Mairie, is a **Musée des Beaux Arts** (daily except Tues 10am–noon

& 2–6pm; 10F/€1.52). This is full of treasures: a Boudin sunset; a Lurçat tapestry of his dog Nadir and the Pirates; works by Corot, van Loo, Moreau; a Léger watercolour; a fine series of unfaded sixteenth-century Flemish tapestries on the lives of two peasants; and sad bombardment relics of the town.

Practicalities

St-Lô makes an interesting pause, but it's virtually abandoned at night. Full information on what it has to offer can be obtained from the **tourist office** in place Général-de-Gaulle, described opposite (mid-June to mid-Sept Mon–Sat 9am–6pm; mid-Sept to mid-June Mon 2–6pm, Tues–Fri 9am–noon & 2–6pm, Sat 9am–6pm; ☎02.33.77.60.35, *www.mairie-saint-lo.fr*). The **gare routière** is on the rue des 80e and 136e, a short way south.

Most of the **hotels**, restaurants and bars, however, are just across the river, near the **gare SNCF**. Overlooking the river from the brow of a ridge beside the station, the upmarket *logis Hôtel des Voyageurs*, 5–7 av Briovère (☎02.33.05.08.63; ③), is home to the *Tocqueville* **restaurant**, which serves a delicious trout soufflé on its 100F/€15.24 menu. If you'd rather be up in town, try *La Cremaillère*, 27 rue Belle (☎02.33.57.14.68; ②; closed Sat lunch & Sun).

The Vire Valley

Once St-Lô was taken in the Battle of Normandy, the armies moved speedily on to their next confrontation. The **Vire Valley**, trailing south from St-Lô, saw little action – and indeed its towns and villages have rarely been touched by any historic or cultural mainstream. The motivation in coming to this landscape of rolling hills and occasional gorges is essentially to consume the region's cider, Calvados, and butter-rich fruit pastries.

Although the countryside is filled with orchards of apples and pears, the land is less fertile than elsewhere in Normandy – and has suffered heavily from the recent depression in the fruit market. A booming trade, however, has grown up around illicit Calvados, bolstering the faltering economy of many Vire farmers. Bootleggers smuggle hundreds of thousands of litres throughout France, using the hydraulic suspension of their Citröen cars to obscure the heavy loads they are carrying from the eyes of watching taxmen. One much-arrested smuggler has such James Bond accessories as automatically rotating licence plates, smoke screens and even oil jets for use against pursuing motorcycles.

Between St-Lô and Vire

The best section of the Vire is the valley that comes down from St-Lô through the Roches de Ham to Tessy-sur-Vire. The **Roches de Ham** are a pair of sheer rocky promontories high above the river. They are promoted as a "viewing table", though the pleasure lies as much in the walk up, through lanes lined with blackberries, hazelnuts and rich orchards.

La Chapelle-sur-Vire

Just downstream from the Roches, and a good place to stopover for a night, is **LA CHAPELLE-SUR-VIRE**. Its church, towering majestically above the river, has been an object of pilgrimage since the twelfth century. There's a weir nearby and a scattering of grassy islands. Next to the bridge on the lower road is the *Auberge de la Chapelle* (☎02.33.56.32.83; ①), a good but rather expensive **restaurant** that also offers a few cheap **rooms**. The cheapest menu on weekdays is 85F/€12.96, at weekends it's well over 100F/€15.24; whenever you come, there'll be plenty of fresh river fish.

Torigni-sur-Vire

An alternative base for the Roches, 5km northeast of La Chapelle, is **TORIGNI-SUR-VIRE**, which was the base of the Grimaldi family before they achieved quasiroyal status upon moving on to the principality of Monaco. A spacious country town, it boasts a few grand buildings and an attractive **campsite**, *Camping du Lac* (☎02.33.56.71.44; closed Nov to mid-March), which offers more luxurious facilities in midsummer. The *Auberge Orangerie* (☎02.33.56.70.64; ②; closed Feb, Sun evening & Mon out of season) is a good **restaurant**, with menus starting at 65F/€9.91, and also offers half a dozen rooms.

Tessy-sur-Vire

At **TESSY-SUR-VIRE**, 18km south of St-Lô, there's little to see other than the river itself, banked by rolling meadows that make an ideal venue for a summer's day picnic, though the town again has a luxurious **campsite**, along with a couple of **hotels**, including *La Minoterie*, a nice little *logis* on the main route du Pont Farcy (☎02.33.77.21.21; ③), and a Wednesday **market**.

Le Viaduc de la Souleuvre

At the eastern end of the sinuous Vire gorge, 10km north of Vire and 6km west of Le Bény-Bocage, stands the former railway viaduct of **Le Viaduc de la Souleuvre**, designed by Gustave Eiffel. Only the six supporting granite pillars of Eiffel's original structure remain – the railway closed down in 1970 – but in 1990 a wooden boardwalk was relaid across half the span of the bridge, on which visitors can cross to the deepest part of the gorge. Once there, 61m up, they are seriously expected to jump off – this is A.J. Hackett's **bungee-jumping** centre (Feb–May & mid-Sept to mid-Dec Sat, Sun & hols, and other times on demand; June to mid-Sept daily; closed mid-Dec to Jan; reservations essential ☎02.31.67.37.38). Jumpers have to be aged at least 13, and for one to three people to make a single jump each costs 400F/€60.98; you also have to pay 15F/€2.29 for the privilege of parking in the adjacent field. Less intrepid souls can walk down to the meadows immediately beneath the viaduct and watch the plummeting from there.

Vire

The pride and joy of the people of **VIRE** are their *andouilles*, the blood sausages known in English as chitterlings. If you can avoid these hideous parcels of pigs' intestines, and the assortment of abattoirs that produce them, it's possible to have a good time; in fact Vire is a town worth visiting specifically for its food.

The only problem is what to do when you're not eating. You can look at the collection of minerals and fossils in the **belfry** that stands alone in the town centre (Mon–Sat 2.30–6.30pm; 10F/€1.52). You can visit the **museum** of "How to Restore Old Norman Farmhouses". Or you can wander by the little scrap of **canal**, equipped with twee floating houses for the ducks, that lies just below the one stark finger that survives of the castle. The only action is at the Friday **market**, again obsessively dedicated to food.

For some exercise, head 6km south along the D76 to **Lac de la Dathée**. Set in open country, the lake is circled by footpaths; in summer it sometimes dries up completely, but when it's wet it can also be crossed by rented sailing boat or windsurf board – contact the Maison des Jeunes et de la Culture, 1 rue des Halles, Vire (☎02.31.68.08.04).

Practicalities

Vire's **tourist office** is in the square de la Résistance at the heart of town (Mon–Sat 10am–noon & 2–6pm; ☎02.31.68.00.05). When choosing a **hotel**, it makes sense to go for one with a good dining room. At the central *Hôtel de France*, 4 rue d'Aignaux (☎02.31.68.00.35; ③), the 98F/€14.94 menu is packed with local specialities, including *andouille* for both starter and main course, but no one's going to make you eat it if you don't want to – there's always *tripes à la mode de Caen* instead. *Au Vrai Normand*, 14 rue Armand-Gasté (☎02.31.67.90.99), is the best **restaurant**.

West and south from Vire

Once past Vire, the roads towards Brittany present you with the choice either of heading southwest for the frontier towns of **Fougères** and **Vitré** (see pp.233 & 235), or directly to the coast and making the magnificent **Mont-St-Michel** (see p.159) your last port of call in Normandy.

West from Vire, the road to Villedieu passes through **ST-SEVER**, not in itself much to write home about but backed by a dark and magical **forest** in which there's a dolmen, an abbey and a scattering of pukka picnic spots marked by signs showing a champagne bottle in a hamper.

Villedieu-les-Poêles

VILLEDIEU-LES-POÊLES – literally "City of God the Frying Pans" – is a lively though touristy place, 28km west of Vire. Much of this ancient town still retains significant elements of its medieval appearance, especially in its backstreets where perfectly preserved old courtyards are tucked away behind unprepossessing wooden gateways. Ever since the twelfth century, Villedieu has been a centre for metalworking, despite the fact that with no mines in Normandy the only source of copper came from melting down unwanted artefacts. To this day, copper souvenirs and kitchen utensils gleam from its rows of shops, and the tourist office can provide lists of dozens of local *ateliers* for more direct purchases. You can see examples illustrating the historical development of Villedieu's copperware in the **museum** at 54 rue Général-Huard (Easter–Oct daily 9am–noon & 2–6pm; Nov–Easter Mon–Sat 9am–noon & 2–6pm; 25F/€3.81).

All of this can seem a bit obsessive, though there is more authentic interest at the **Fonderie de Cloches** at 13 rue du Pont-Chignon, one of the twelve remaining bell foundries in Europe. Work here is only part time due to limited demand, but it's open to visits all year round, and you may find the forge lit (June & Sept Mon–Sat 8am–noon & 2–5.30pm, Sun 9.30am–noon & 2–5.30pm; July & Aug daily 8am–6pm; Oct–May Tues–Sat 8am–noon & 2–5.30pm; 22F/€3.35). Expert craftsmen will show you the moulds, composed of an unpleasant-looking combination of clay, goats' hair and horse shit.

Practicalities

Villedieu's **tourist office** is located in a hexagonal glass kiosk on place des Costils (June–Sept Tues–Sat 10am–noon & 2–6pm; ☎02.33.61.05.69 – for the rest of the year, contact the Mairie, ☎02.33.61.00.16). If you're charmed into **staying**, the comfortable *Fruitier* on place Gostils (☎02.33.90.51.00; ③; closed Sat in winter) has a dining room with plate-glass windows allowing you to watch the goings-on in the square, and offers a reasonable 68F/€10.37 menu and a 128F/€19.51 menu packed with regional delights. In the heart of the main street, the very welcoming *logis Hôtel St-Pierre et St-Michel*, 12 place de la République (☎02.33.61.00.11; ③; closed Jan, plus Fri in low season), houses the stylishly refurbished *Le Sourdin* restaurant, where the 115F/€17.53 menu features fine local ham, and things get seriously gastronomic for 195F/€29.73. There's also a three-star **campsite** by the river, *La Sienne* (☎02.33.61.02.44; closed Oct–Easter).

Much the nicest **bar** in Villedieu – complete with tables in the cobbled square, Guinness, Rolling Rock and local cider, a good selection of music from around the world (especially the Celtic bits), and a youngish clientele – is *Le Pussoir Fidèle*, 2 place du Pussoir Fidèle (☎02.33.51.94.58).

The Forêt de Lande-Pourrie

South from Vire, if you are heading for Fougères (see p.233) or Domfront (see p.190), you pass through the **Forêt de Mortain** and its continuation, the **Forêt de Lande-Pourrie**. The **Fosse d'Arthur**, a remote spot in the forest to the east of Mortain, is one of the many unlikely claimants to King Arthur's death scene. A couple of waterfalls disappear into deep limestone caverns, but there's really very little to see.

Mortain

The war-ravaged town of **MORTAIN** perches high above the very deep gorge of the Cance, 24km south of Vire. It's not a place to linger very long, but the views, especially from the south end of the main street, are spectacular. A short walk west out of town leads into some lovely countryside, with two **waterfalls** – known as the Grande Cascade and the Petite Cascade – interrupting the river itself. Head up the high rocky bluff to the east, on the other hand, and from the tiny chapel at the top the neighbouring province of Maine spreads before you. On a clear day you can even see Mont-St-Michel.

If you want to **spend a night** in Mortain, the *Hôtel de la Poste*, 1 place des Arcades (☎02.33.59.00.05, *dgdesmonts@aol.com*; ③; closed Fri evening, Sat & Sun evening), is the best option, with a restaurant serving good menus from 99F/€15.09.

Lonlay l'Abbaye and Barenton

On the far side of the Forêt de Lande-Pourrie – and just 9km out of Domfront (see p.190) on the D22 towards Tinchebray – **LONLAY L'ABBAYE** has a biscuit factory along with various vestiges of its eleventh-century Benedictine past.

At nearby **BARENTON** – an entirely rebuilt and unmemorable town – *Le Relais du Parc*, place Général-de-Gaulle, is a good cheap place for lunch that also has a couple of rooms (☎02.33.59.51.38; ①; closed Mon), while the **Maison de la Pomme et de la Poire** is a mildly diverting cider museum (April–Sept daily 9.30am–12.30pm & 2–7pm; 15F/€2.29).

St-Hilaire-du-Harcoët

The thriving (Wed) market town of **ST-HILAIRE-DU-HARCOËT**, 28km north of Fougères, amounts to little more than a crossroads near the big market square. It does, however, hold a few restaurants and **hotels**, such as *Le Cygne*, 67 rue Waldeck-Rousseau (☎02.33.49.11.84; ③; closed Fri evening in winter), a comfortable, newly modernized *logis* with an appealing set of somewhat pricey menus, and the cheaper *L'Agriculture*, nearby at 79 rue Waldeck-Rousseau (☎02.33.49.10.60; ①), where the 68F/€10.37 menu includes fresh oysters in season.

travel details

Trains

Alençon to: Caen (6 daily; 1hr 15min) via Sées (13min) and Argentan (30min); Tours (5 daily; 2hr) via Le Mans (1hr).

Bagnoles to: Briouze (5 daily; 30min) for connections to Argentan and Paris.

Évreux to: Bernay (5 daily; 45min); Caen (5 daily; 1hr 30min); Conches (5 daily; 15min); Lisieux (5 daily; 1hr); Paris St-Lazare (12 daily; 1hr); Serquigny (5 daily; 30min).

Lisieux to: Cherbourg (10 daily; 2hr 40min) via Caen (30min) and Bayeux (50min); Paris (22 daily; 2hr) via Bernay (15min) and Évreux (1hr); Rouen (6 daily; 1hr 30min) via Bernay (15min) and Serquigny (30min).

St-Lô to: Caen (4 daily; 1hr) via Bayeux (30min); Rennes (4 daily; 2hr) via Coutances (20min) and Pontorson (1hr 10min).

Vire to: Paris (3–5 daily; 3hr) via Argentan (1hr) and L'Aigle (1hr 30min); Villedieu (6 daily; 20min) with connecting buses to Granville (1hr).

Buses

*The main inland bus networks are operated by **Bus Verts**, who cover Calvados in particular from their base at 11 rue des Chanoines in Caen (☎08.01.21.42.14), and **STAO**, whose routes extend across most of the Orne region further*

south (Alençon ☎02.33.29.11.11; Argentan ☎02.33.67.04.66; Mortagne ☎02.33.25.19.11).

Alençon to: Bagnoles (3 daily; 1hr); Bellême (1–2 daily; 1hr); Évreux (1 daily; 2hr), via L'Aigle (1hr 40min); Mortagne (1–3 daily; 1hr); Vimoutiers (1–3 daily; 1hr 30min) via Sées (30min).

Argentan to: Alençon (1–2 daily; 1hr 15min) via Sées (40min); Carrouges (1–3 daily; 45min); Domfront (1–3 daily; 1hr 50min) via Bagnoles (1hr).

Caen to: Falaise (4 daily; 45min); Flers (5 daily, 2 on Sun; 1hr 20min) via Thury-Harcourt (35min) and Clécy (50min); Lisieux (3–5 daily; 45min); Vire (1–3 daily; 1hr 30min) via Aunay-sur-Odon (1hr).

L'Aigle to: Évreux (2–3 daily; 1hr 20min) via Conches (45min); Gacé (1–2 daily; 1hr); Mortagne (3 daily; 1hr); Vimoutiers (1–2 daily; 1hr 10min).

Lisieux to: Le Havre (2 daily; 1hr 30min); Orbec (6 daily; 45min); Pont l'Evêque (4 daily; 25min) and on to Honfleur (50min) or Deauville (45min); St-Pierre-sur-Dives (1–3 daily; 50min); Vimoutiers (4 daily; 40min) via Livarot (30min);.

Mortagne to: Bellême (1–4 daily; 20min).

St-Lô to: Bayeux (8 daily; 30min); Cherbourg (6 daily; 1hr 30min); Coutances (5 daily; 30min).

Vire to: Avranches (5 daily; 45min); Condé-sur-Noireau (2 daily; 30min); Fougères (4 daily; 1hr 30min).

BRITTANY

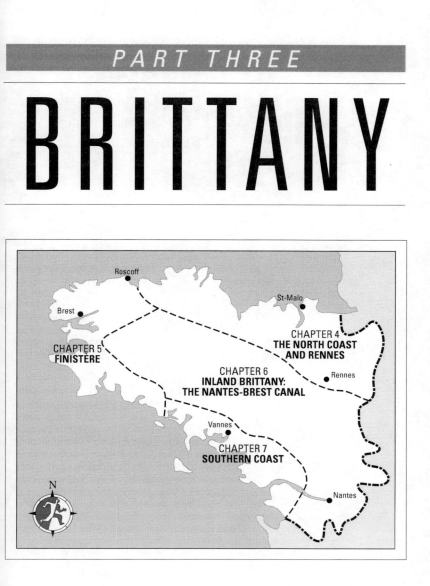

CHAPTER 4
**THE NORTH COAST
AND RENNES**

CHAPTER 5
FINISTÈRE

CHAPTER 6
**INLAND BRITTANY:
THE NANTES-BREST CANAL**

CHAPTER 7
SOUTHERN COAST

Roscoff

Brest

St-Malo

Rennes

Vannes

Nantes

N

CHAPTER FOUR

THE NORTH COAST AND RENNES

The **northern coast** of Brittany is varied in the extreme. Long sections, open to the full force of the Atlantic, are spectacular but much too dangerous for swimming; others shelter superb natural harbours and peaceful resorts. The old *citadelle* port of **St-Malo** makes an attractive point of arrival, from which you are well positioned for exploration, even if your main goals lie elsewhere, in the south or in Finistère.

The best of the **resorts** are concentrated along two separate stretches of coastline, the Côte d'Émeraude and the Côte de Granit Rose. As green as its name suggests, the **Côte d'Émeraude** remains largely unspoiled, at its wildest on the heather-covered headlands of Cap Fréhel. Thanks to gorgeous beaches, seaside towns such as **Le Val-André** and **Erquy** tend to be dominated by English visitors, but it's always possible to find a secluded campsite for a night or two's stopover.

Further west, beyond the placid **Baie de St-Brieuc** (the town of St-Brieuc itself is, for most holiday-makers, a nuisance to be avoided), the coastline erupts into a garish tangle of pink-granite boulders, the famed **Côte de Granit Rose**. This harsher territory was once, at **Paimpol** and elsewhere, the home of cod and whaling fleets that ranged right across the Atlantic. Today it's reliant on tourism, especially at the twin resorts of **Perros-Guirec** and **Ploumanac'h**. These are attractive nonetheless, and there are plenty of smaller places where you can avoid the crowds, such as **Loguivy** on the mainland, and, just offshore, the **Île de Bréhat** – among the most beautiful of all northern French islands.

The first 20km of the route **inland** from St-Malo takes you alongside the delightful **Rance estuary**. Frequent boats connect both St-Malo and Dinard with **Dinan**, a

---

ACCOMMODATION PRICE CODES

All **hotel prices** in this book have been coded using the symbols below. The price shown is for the least expensive double room in high season, which, for categories ① and ② especially, often means a room without shower, bath and toilet. Most such hotels have other rooms with en-suite facilities, which typically cost 40–60F/€6.10–9.15 extra.

① Under 160F/€24	④ 300–400F/€46–61	⑦ 600–700F/€91–107
② 160–220F/€24–34	⑤ 400–500F/€61–76	⑧ 700–800F/€107–122
③ 220–300F/€34–46	⑥ 500–600F/€76–91	⑨ Over 800F/€122

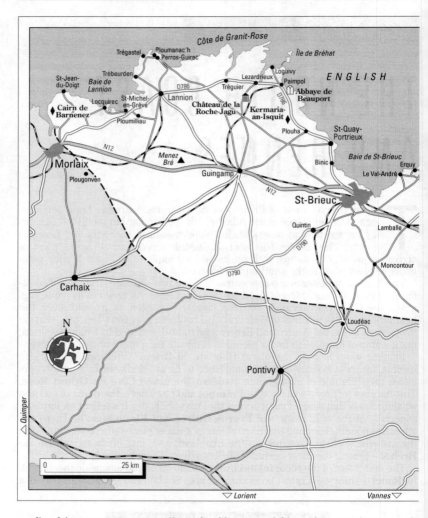

medieval fortress town *par excellence* that like most of this region owes its prosperity to an epic saga of trading and piracy on the high seas. Beyond it, to the south of the far more ancient community of **Dol** – site of several fascinating prehistoric relics – lies a patchwork of waterways and woodlands, where rivers and canals cut through characteristic Breton **forests** like **Ville-Cartier**. Further **east**, the redoubtable **citadelles** of **Fougères** and **Vitré** still guard the frontier with Normandy.

At the heart of the *département* of Ille-et-Vilaine, just over 60km southeast of St-Malo, the city of **Rennes** has after centuries of rivalry with Nantes finally established itself as the indisputable capital of Brittany. Rennes may not be the prettiest town in the province, but it is without doubt the liveliest, hosting a

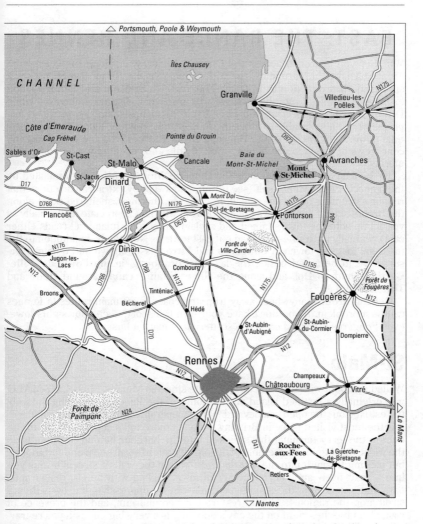

considerable university and most of the major Breton political and cultural organizations. It's also renowned for its **festivals**, devoting itself to ten days of theatre
and music each July during the **Tombées de la Nuit**, and celebrating **Les
Transmusicales**, one of the most important events in the calendar of French
rock, in December.

Among numerous other annual events in northern Brittany, the biggest and
most compelling is the **Breton Music** festival, held each July at **St-Brieuc**.
That's also the venue of the ominous-sounding **Art Rock** festival in late May,
while the region's largest traditional festival is the *pardon* of St Yves in **Tréguier**,
on the third Sunday in May.

EAST: THE RANCE AND RENNES

Whether you approach across the Channel by ferry, or along the coast from Mont-St-Michel in Normandy, the wide estuary of the **River Rance** makes a spectacular introduction to Brittany. The towns of **St-Malo** and **Dinard** stand to either side of its mouth, each with its own very distinct ambience, while **Dinan** guards the head of the river itself 20km upstream. From those few places where it's possible to cross the Rance (most notably, along the top of the tidal power dam known as the **Barrage de la Rance**), you can enjoy magnificent views of its sheltered banks – rich, fertile and repeatedly pierced by tributaries.

To the east of the river spreads the **Baie du Mont-St-Michel**, dominated by the pinnacle of the Mont itself (see p.159), and swept by extraordinary tides that render swimming out of the question. **Cancale**, the most sheltered point along the Breton side of the bay, is a good spot from which to appreciate it all, ideally as you fill up with the town's famed and acclaimed oysters. Inland, all roads either curl eventually to **Rennes**, or head out east towards Normandy. In addition to the medieval fortress towns of **Fougères** and **Vitré**, lesser-known and quieter pleasures are to be found beside the lake in **Combourg**, in the **Forêt de Ville-Cartier**, south of Dol, and along the **Ille-et-Vilaine canal**, around **Hédé** and **Tinténiac**.

Getting around anywhere away from the coast or off main routes to Rennes can be a problem. If you don't have your own transport, keep your sights low – even Fougères is served only by a scattering of market buses.

St-Malo

Walled and built with the same grey-granite stone as Mont-St-Michel, **ST-MALO** was originally a fortified island at the mouth of the Rance, controlling not only the estuary but the open sea beyond. Now inseparably attached to the mainland, it is the most visited place in Brittany – thanks more to its superb **old citadelle** than to the ferry terminal that's tucked into the harbour behind. From outside the walls, the dignified ensemble of the old city might seem stern and forbidding, but passing through into the *intra-muros* ("within the walls") streets brings you into a busy, lively and very characterful town, packed with hotels, restaurants, bars and shops. Yes, the summer crowds can be oppressive, but even then a stroll atop the ramparts should restore your equilibrium, and the presence of vast, clean beaches right on the city's doorstep is a very big bonus if you're travelling with kids in tow. Having to spend a night here before or after a ferry crossing is a positive pleasure – so long as you take the trouble to reserve accommodation in advance.

The promontory fort of Alet, south of the modern centre in what's now the **St-Servan district**, commanded approaches to the Rance even before the arrival of the Romans, but modern St-Malo traces its origins to a monastic settlement founded by saints Aaron and Brendan early in the sixth century. From 550 AD onwards the settlement was identified with the Celtic St Maclou (or possibly MacLow), and in later centuries became notorious as the home of a fierce breed of **pirate-mariners**. These adventurers were never quite under anybody's control but their own; for four years from 1590, St-Malo even declared itself to be an independent republic, under the motto "*Ni Français, Ni Bretons, Malouins Suis*". Over a period of centuries, the *corsaires* of St-Malo not only forced English ships passing up the Channel to pay tribute, but also brought wealth from further afield. Jacques Cartier, who colonized Canada, lived in and sailed from St-Malo, as did the first colonists to settle the Falklands – hence the islands' Argentinian name, Las Malvinas. Even when the duke of Marlborough landed 15,000 men just up the coast near Cancale in 1758, and attempted to take the city by land, St-Malo's defences proved too formidable.

Arrival and city transport

St-Malo presents its best face to the sea, and if you don't arrive by ferry, you may well want to consider the ten-minute shuttle across the River Rance to Dinard as an alternative. If you come in by bus or train, the old city is concealed by modern suburbs and dockside industry almost until you're in it.

St-Malo is always busy with **boats**. From the **Terminal Ferry du Naye** (☎02.99.40.64.41), Brittany Ferries sails to Portsmouth (mid-March to mid-Nov daily at 10.45am; rest of year less frequently; 8hr 45min; *www.brittany-ferries.com*) and Plymouth (mid-Nov to mid-March Fri at noon; 8hr), while Condor Ferries (☎02.99.20.03.00, *www.condorferries.co.uk*) connect in summer with both Poole and Weymouth (May–Oct one sailing daily on each route; 5hr).

Between mid-April and early Oct, regular passenger **ferries to Dinard** operate from the **quai Dinan**, just outside the westernmost point of the ramparts in front of the port (Émeraude Lines; ☎02.23.18.15.15, *www.emeraudelines.com*; 20F/€3.05 single, 30F/€4.57 return, bikes 15F/€2.29 each way); the trip across the estuary takes an all-too-short ten minutes. Émeraude Lines also conduct excursions up the river to Dinan (see p.218), day-trips to and from Granville in Normandy (see p.156), and cruises along the Brittany coast to Cap Fréhel and the Île Cézembre, to the Pointe du Grouin near Cancale, and out to the Îles Chausey (see p.157). In addition, they connect St-Malo with the **Channel Islands**; you'll find details of their services, along with those of Condor Ferries, in the "Travel details" on p.260.

For a touch of luxury, in summer Le Chateaubriand (☎02.99.46.44.44, *www.chateaubriand.com*) puts on **gastronomic cruises** in the Baie du Mont-St-Michel and up the Rance, costing around 250F/€38.11, from the Gare Maritime de la Richardais, at the Dinard end of the Barrage de la Rance.

St-Malo's **gare SNCF** (☎08.36.35.35.35) is 2km out from the *citadelle* on square Jean Coquelin, and convenient neither for the old town nor the ferry (take care if you're planning a tight connection). All trains to and from St-Malo pass through Dol. Most continue through to Rennes, so if you're heading west towards Dinan and St-Brieuc, or northeast into Normandy, you'll probably have to change at Dol.

Though almost all St-Malo buses – whether local or long-distance – also call at the *gare SNCF*, the **gare routière** – not a building, just an expanse of concrete – is officially located on the esplanade St-Vincent right next to the tourist office (see opposite). The two main local bus companies both have ticket offices here. Tourisme Verney (☎02.99.82.26.26) act as agents for the Compagnie de Transport d'Ille et Vilaine (TIV; ☎02.99.40.82.67), which run services to Dinard, Dinan, Cancale, Combourg and Rennes. Les Courriers Bretons (☎02.99.19.70.70, *www.lescourriersbreton.fr*), go to Cancale, Mont-St-Michel, Dol, Rennes and Fougères, and also run day-trips to Mont-St-Michel, starting from the hostel but calling also at the *gare routière* (Tues–Fri 1.35pm; 115F/€17.53). Dinan buses are also operated by CAT (☎02.96.39.21.05).

Approaching central St-Malo or the ferry terminal by **road** can be somewhat dismal; the signposts seem designed to confuse, and all the roads seem to end on tramlined docksides. Lost and bewildered cars circle the port like seagulls. Driving in to catch a ferry, keep well clear of the old town; the **Chaussée des Corsaires**, which links the *citadelle* with the ferry terminal, can be closed for long periods while its movable bridge is opened to let boats out of the Bassin Jacques-Cartier.

Most of the major **car-rental** companies are represented in town, including Avis at the ferry terminal and *gare SNCF* (☎02.99.40.58.68), and Budget, beside the *gare SNCF* at 46 bd de la République (☎02.99.40.15.10).

If you prefer to enjoy more active pursuits, you can rent **bicycles** from Cycles Diazo, 47 quai Duguay-Trouin (☎02.99.40.31.63), Espace Nicole Deux Roues, 11 rue Robert-Schumann in Paramé (☎02.99.56.11.06), or, as usual, from the *gare SNCF*.

Information

St-Malo's helpful **tourist office** (April–June & Sept Mon–Sat 9am–7pm, Sun 10am–noon & 2–6pm; July & Aug Mon–Sat 8.30am–8pm, Sun 10am–7pm; Oct–March Mon–Sat 9am–12.30pm & 1.30–6pm; ☎02.99.56.64.48, *www.ville-saint-malo.fr* or *www.bretagne-4villes.com*) is housed in a single-storey building, right in front of the city walls, beside the Bassin Duguay-Trouin in the **Port des Yachts**. As well as good detailed city maps, it can provide information on annual festivals such as the **Étonnants Voyageurs** ("Amazing Travellers"), dedicated to the film and literature of travel and adventure, which takes place for three days in late May.

The most convenient **post office** for visitors is within the walls at 4 place des Frères Lamennais (July to mid-Sept Mon–Fri 8.30am–6.30pm, Sat 8.30am–12.30pm; mid-Sept to June Mon–Fri 8.30am–12.30pm & 1.30–5.30pm, Sat 8.30am–noon; ☎02.99.40.89.90). If you want to receive poste restante letters, make sure the address specifies *35402 St-Malo intra-muros*. For **Internet access**, head to *Cop' Imprim*, just west of the *gare SNCF* at 39 bd des Talards (Mon–Fri 9am–7pm, Sat 9am–noon; ☎02.23.18.08.18, *copimprim@wanadoo.fr*; 50F/€7.62 per hr).

Several shops and kiosks within the *citadelle* advertise that they handle **foreign-exchange** transactions without charging commission; the rates they offer are so abysmal that they don't need to.

Accommodation

St-Malo boasts of having over a hundred **hotels**, including the traditional seaside boarding houses located just off the beach, as well as several **campsites** and a **hostel**. In high season it needs every one of them: the demand is phenomenal. Motorists intending to stay the night before catching a summer ferry sailing should make reservations well in advance; if you don't have a reservation, don't demoralize yourself hunting around, and settle for spending the night somewhere else along the coast or nearby. Apart from the obvious alternatives of Dinard and Dinan, it's worth considering peaceful smaller towns such as Combourg, Cancale, Jugon-les-Lacs, St-Jacut or Erquy.

Hotels in the citadelle

The thirty or so of St-Malo's **hotels** that stand **within the city walls** are able to charge their guests premium rates for the privilege of staying; it's inside the walls that most of the nightlife takes place, and getting there from any of the surrounding suburbs requires a fair walk in through the docks. Those *intra-muros* hotels that have their own restaurants tend to take advantage of high summer demand by insisting that all guests eat in.

Hôtel Bristol-Union, 4 place de la Poissonnerie (☎02.99.40.83.36, fax 02.99.40.35.51, *www .st-malo.com*). Very correct rooms, some of them very small too, in a nice little square facing the former fish market, just off the Grande Rue. Closed mid-Nov to Jan. ③.

Hôtel du Commerce, 11 rue St-Thomas (☎02.99.56.18.00, fax 02.99.56.04.68). Very cheap and very plain hotel, but if you're on a tight budget you can't do better within the walls. Meals in the restaurant are similarly unexciting but inexpensive. Closed Jan to mid-Feb. ②.

Hôtel Le Croiseur, 2 place de la Poissonnerie (☎02.99.40.80.40, fax 02.99.56.83.76, *www .st-malo.com*). Clean and relatively modern place, near the Grande Porte. All rooms have TV plus bath or shower. Open all year. ③.

Hôtel du Louvre, 2 rue des Marins (☎02.99.40.86.62, fax 02.99.40.86.93, *lelouvre@aol.com*). Pleasant family-run place just off Grande Rue, between the Grande Porte and Cathédrale St-Vincent, serving good buffet breakfasts. Closed Dec to mid-Feb, except Christmas and New Year. ③.

Hôtel-Restaurant Pomme d'Or, 4 place du Poids-du-Roi (☎02.99.40.90.24, fax 02.99.40.58.31). Seventeen modernized rooms in a venerable building, just inside the *citadelle* near the ramparts – take a sharp left after entering through the Grande Porte. Conventional menus start at 86F/€13.11, while the breakfast buffet spread is 40F/€6.10. The *patronne* has an eccentric predilection for animals. Closed Jan to mid-Feb. ④.

Hôtel Port-Malo, 15 rue Ste-Barbe (☎02.99.20.52.99, fax 02.99.40.29.53). Small but clean and comfortable en-suite rooms – above a bar, so go for the higher floors – with friendly and helpful management. ②.

Hôtel-Restaurant Porte St-Pierre, 2 place du Guet (☎02.99.40.91.27, fax 02.99.56.09.94, *www.st-malo.com*). Comfortable *logis de France*, peeping out to sea over the walls of the *citadelle*, near the small Porte St-Pierre and very handy for the plage de Bon Secours. Dinner menus from 140F/€21.34 upwards. Closed Dec & Jan. ④.

Hôtel Quic en Groigne, 8 rue d'Estrées (☎02.99.20.22.20, fax 02.99.20.22.30, *www.st-malo.com*). Friendly little hotel at the far end of the *citadelle*, with nicely styled en-suite rooms. ④.

Hôtel San Pédro, 1 rue Ste-Anne (☎02.99.40.88.57, fax 02.99.40.46.25, *www.st-malo.com*). Small, twelve-room refurbished hotel in a nice quiet setting, just inside the walls in the north of the *citadelle*, near the Porte des Bés. Rooms on the higher floors (reached using the world's smallest lift) enjoy sea views. ④.

Hôtel-Restaurant de l'Univers, 10 place Chateaubriand (☎02.99.40.89.52, fax 02.99.40.07.27, *www.st-malo.com*). One of the grand hotels that face you immediately upon entering the Porte St-Vincent. Some good-value rooms, and an excellent 75F/€11.43 menu in the restaurant downstairs, with tables out on the square opposite the château. Restaurant closed Wed off season. ④.

Hôtel-Restaurant aux Vieilles Pierres, 9 rue Thévenard (☎02.99.56.46.80). Six-room hotel, near place aux Herbes, which remains one of the better bargains within the walls, even if a room with a shower costs 100F/€15.24 extra. Menus at 92F/€14.03 with fish soup and steak, or 145F/€22.11 for the full spread, which in theory totals six courses – though half of those are just intended to keep you ticking over until the next one arrives. Open all year. ②.

Hotels outside the walls

If cheaper rates are a high priority, a number of lower-priced places can be found near the *gare SNCF*, or in suburban Paramé, but there's not all that much pleasure in staying outside the *citadelle* for the sake of saving a few francs.

Hôtel de l'Arrivée, 52 bd de la République (☎02.99.56.30.78, fax 02.99.56.16.05). A good budget option, on a corner very near the *gare SNCF*. Open all year. ②.

Hôtel le Beaufort, 25 chaussée du Sillon, Paramé (☎02.99.40.99.99, fax 02.99.40.99.62, *www.emeraude.net*). Grand seaview hotel, 30min walk from the *citadelle*, with modernized rooms – some with lovely balconies – and a good restaurant. ④.

Hôtel les Charmettes, 64 bd Hébert, Paramé (☎02.99.56.07.31, fax 02.99.56.85.96). One of Paramé's cheaper options, not on the front itself (though a few rooms have sea views), but very near the beach and the imposing *Grand Hôtel*. Closed mid-Nov to early March. ②.

Hôtel de l'Europe, 44 bd de la République (☎02.99.56.13.42). Year-round cheap but clean rooms in a genuinely friendly (if noisy) hotel, near the *gare SNCF*. ③.

Hôtel la Rance, 15 quai Sébastopol, St-Servan (☎02.99.81.78.63, fax 02.99.81.44.80). Small, tasteful option in sight of the Tour Solidor, with eleven spacious rooms. ④.

Hôtel-Restaurant Terminus Gare, 8 bd des Talards (☎02.99.56.14.38, fax 02.99.56.65.46). Reasonable *logis de France* across from the station (and not to be confused with the other *Hôtel Terminus*, in distant Rothéneuf), with double glazing and an inexpensive restaurant where menus start at 60F/€9.15. Open all year. ③.

Hostel

Centre Patrick Varangot, 37 av du Père-Umbricht, Paramé (☎02.99.40.29.80, fax 02.99.40.29.02). Dominated as a rule by lively young travellers, St-Malo's hostel, also known as the *Centre des Rencontres Internationales*, is one of the busiest in France, although not formally part of the national network. It's located a couple of kilometres northeast of the *gare SNCF*, out in the suburb of Paramé and far from the walled city, but it's only a short way back from the beach, and makes a nice place to stay in its own right. To get there from the *gare SNCF*, take bus #1, #2 or #5. It does not operate a curfew. Open all year. Dorm bed 72F/€10.98, private doubles 168F/€25.61; rates include breakfast.

Camping

St-Malo's four municipal **campsites** tend to be full in July and August, and you may have to travel inland to find space; there are several private sites in the locality. If in difficulties, you could try ringing the Camping Department of the Mairie (☎02.99.40.71.11) for the up-to-date position.

La Cité d'Aleth, St-Servan (☎02.99.81.60.91). Much the nearest campsite to the *citadelle*, on the headland southwest of St-Malo. Reachable in summer on bus #1. Open all year.

Les Ilôts, av de la Guimorais, Rothéneuf (☎02.99.56.98.72). Inland, to the northeast. Closed Oct–March.

Le Nicet, av de la Varde, Rothéneuf (☎02.99.40.26.32). Right on the coast, by the Pointe de Nicet. Reservations essential. Closed mid-Sept to May.

Les Nielles, av John Kennedy, Paramé (☎02.99.40.26.35). On the beach at the plage du Minhic. Closed mid-Sept to mid-June.

The Town

The **citadelle** of St-Malo, very much the prime destination for visitors, was for many years joined to the mainland only by a long causeway, before the original line of the coast was hidden forever by the construction of the harbour basin. Although its cobbled streets of restored seventeenth- and eighteenth-century houses can be packed to the point of absurdity in summer (and the cobbles present quite a challenge to parents pushing buggies), away from the more popular thoroughfares random exploration is fun.

Thanks to the limitations on space on this tiny peninsula, the buildings tend to be a little more high-rise than you might expect. Ancient as they may look, they are almost entirely reconstructed – photographs of the damage suffered in 1944, when General Patton bombarded the city for two weeks before the Germans surrendered, show barely a stone left in place. Eighty percent of the city had to be lovingly and precisely rebuilt, stone by stone.

Beneath grey skies, the narrow lanes can appear sombre, even grim, but in high summer or at sunset they become light and almost unreal. In any case, you can always surface to the sunlight on the **ramparts** – first erected in the fourteenth century, and redesigned by the master builder Vauban (see also p.356) four hundred years later – to enjoy wonderful views all round, especially to the west as the sun sets over the sea.

The main gate of the *citadelle* as you approach by road is the **Porte St-Vincent**. Until 1770, the whole town was sealed off by a 10pm curfew, and as you walk through the gateway, you pass the small room where latecomers were obliged to spend the night. To the right, as you walk though the gate, you'll see the forbidding stone walls of the **castle**, which now houses the **Musée de la Ville** (April–Sept daily 10am–noon & 2–6pm; Oct–March Tues–Sun same hours; 27F/€4.12), something of a paean to the "prodigious prosperity" enjoyed by St-Malo during its days of piracy, colonialism and slave-trading. Climbing the 169 steps of the castle keep – whose walls are up to 7m thick – you pass a fascinating mixture of maps, diagrams and exhibits. Among them are chilling handbills from the Nazi Occupation, accounts of the "infernal machine" used by the English to blow up the port in 1693, and savage four-pronged *chaussetrappes*, thrown by pirates onto the decks of ships being boarded to immobilize their crews. At the top a gull's-eye prospect takes in the whole *citadelle*.

It is possible to pass **through the ramparts** at a couple of points on the western side of the peninsula. On the open shore beyond, a huge beach stretches away beyond the rather featureless resort-suburb of **Paramé**. Out to sea stand a procession of rocky islets, many of which still hold traces of medieval fortifications.

When the tide is low, an easy short walk across the sands of the Plage du Bons Secours, past a seawater swimming pool refreshed by each high tide leads to the small island of **Grand-Bé**. It's such a popular stroll that you may even need to queue to get onto the short causeway. Solemn warnings are posted of the dangers of attempting to return from the island when the tide has risen too far – timetables are displayed by the Porte Ste-Pierre and elsewhere. If you're caught on the island, there you have to stay. Its one "sight" is the **tomb** of the nineteenth-century writer-politician Chateaubriand (who was born in St-Malo on Sept 4, 1768, and died in 1848). Marx described him as "the most classic incarnation of French *vanité* . . . the false profundity, Byzantine exaggeration, emotional coquetry . . . a never-before-seen mishmash of lies". Suitably enough he features heavily on all the tourist brochures, which – with no apparent irony – extol his "modesty" in choosing so "isolated" a burial spot.

The coast along here is safer for paddlers than for swimmers, but it is very popular for **windsurfing**. Boards are available for rental from Surf School, 2 av de la Hoguette (☎02.99.40.07.47), or the Société Nautique de la Baie de St-Malo, quai du Bajoyer (☎02.99.20.22.95); most surfers make for the beaches further along the coast towards Cancale, the **plage du Verger** and the larger **Anse du Guesclin**.

St-Servan

The district of **St-Servan**, within walking distance along the corniche to the south of the *citadelle*, is actually older than St-Malo itself. It was on the site of the Gallo-Roman city of Alet that St Maclou established his church, and the seat of the bishopric only moved onto the impregnable island fortress when danger threatened in 1142.

St-Servan curves round several small inlets and beaches to face the tidal-power dam across the river. It's dominated by the distinctive **Tour Solidor**, which consists of three linked towers built in 1382, and in cross-section looks just like the

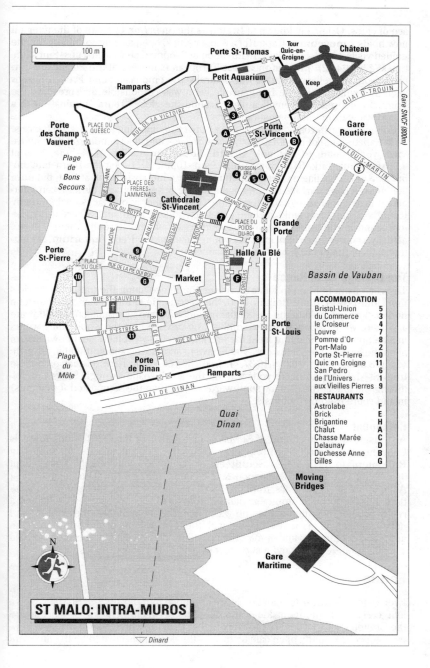

ST MALO: INTRA-MUROS

ACCOMMODATION

Bristol-Union	5
du Commerce	3
le Croiseur	4
Louvre	7
Pomme d'Or	8
Port-Malo	2
Porte St-Pierre	10
Quic en Groigne	11
San Pedro	6
de l'Univers	1
aux Vieilles Pierres	9

RESTAURANTS

Astrolabe	F
Brick	E
Brigantine	H
Chalut	A
Chasse Marée	C
Delaunay	D
Duchesse Anne	B
Gilles	G

ace of clubs. Originally known in Breton as the *Steir Dor*, or "gate of the river", it now holds a **museum** of Cape Horn clipper ships, open all year for ninety-minute guided visits (April–Sept daily 10am–noon & 2–6pm; Oct–March Tues–Sun same times; 27F/€4.12). Most of the great European explorers of the Pacific are covered, from Magellan onwards, but naturally the emphasis is on French heroes such as Louis Antoine de Bougainville, who was responsible for spreading the brightly coloured bougainvillea plant around the globe. Tours culminate with a superb view from the topmost ramparts.

Follow the main road due south from St-Servan, ignoring signs for the Barrage de la Rance – or take bus #5 from the *gare SNCF* – and at a roundabout high above town you'll come to the new **Grand Aquarium** (daily: April–June & Sept 9.30am–7pm; July 9am–8pm; Aug 9am–10pm; Oct–March 10am–6.30pm; 56F/€8.54). This postmodern structure can be a bit bewildering at first, but once you get the hang of it it's an entertaining place, where you can either learn interesting facts about slimy monsters of the deep or simply pull faces back at them. Its eight distinct fish tanks include one shaped like a Polo mint, where dizzy visitors stand in the hole in the middle as myriad fish whirl around them. There's actually another aquarium, logically enough named the **Petit Aquarium**, set into the walls of the old city, but this is far superior.

The Barrage de la Rance

The road from St-Malo to Dinard crosses the Rance along the top of the world's first **tidal-power dam**. Built in 1966, the Barrage de la Rance alas failed to set a non-nuclear example to the rest of the province, where less than a hundred years ago there were 5000 working windmills. You can see how the whole thing works in a half-hour visit, starting from the entrance on the west bank, just downstream from the lock, but unfortunately you'll have to arrange an appointment in advance (daily 8.30am–8pm; ☎02.99.16.37.14; free). If you come here on foot or bicycle from St-Malo, try to make your way on the small roads through St-Servan, following the line of the estuary southwards rather than the signposted (circuitous) inland route used by motorists.

Rothéneuf

Just inside the eastern end of St-Malo's city limits, as the D201 winds towards Cancale, signs direct visitors away from the central streets of suburban **Rothéneuf** to the **Roches Sculptées**, or "sculpted rocks" (daily: Easter–Sept 9am–9pm; Oct–Easter 10am–noon & 2–5.30pm; 15F/€2.29). The hermit priest Abbé Fouré spent 25 years, from the 1870s onwards, carving these jumbled boulders into the forms of dragons, giants and assorted sea monsters. Perched on a rocky promontory high above the water line, they're quite weathered now, and not all compelling in themselves, but with the town well out of sight this makes an appealing spot to stop and admire the coastline. The gardens of the site also hold a small, sheltered café, and a shop that sells Breton pottery.

Eating

Even more **restaurants** than hotels are crammed into *intra-muros* St-Malo, with a long crescent lining the inside of the ramparts between the Porte St-Vincent and the Grande Porte. Prices are probably higher than anywhere else in Brittany, however, especially on the open café terraces – the demand is inflated by the numbers of day-trippers, from as far afield as the Channel Islands, and ferry passengers having last-night blowouts. Bear in mind that most of the crêperies also serve *moules* and similar quasisnacks. If you just fancy an **ice cream**, call in at *Sanchez Glacier*, 9 rue de la Vieille-Boucherie. All the restaurants listed below are in the *citadelle*.

Astrolabe, 8 rue des Cordiers (☎02.99.40.36.82). Quality cuisine, down a few steps not far south of the Grande Porte. A full lunch costs 85F/E12.96, while in the evening you can compose your own menu from the extensive *carte* – 160F/E24.39 buys a superb spread, with, for example, some sensational grilled langoustines and a *gratin du Granny-Smith* from the wide range of lush desserts. Serves until late. Open all year, but closed all day Mon & Tues lunchtime.

Le Brick, 5 rue Jacques-Cartier (☎02.99.40.18.88). Perhaps the best of the many seafood restaurants set into the walls near the Grande Porte, with a 75F/E11.43 menu that offers fish soup or "big size winkles" followed by skate, and more lavish options up to 185F/E28.20. Closed Mon off season.

Crêperie la Brigantine, 13 rue de Dinan (☎02.99.56.82.82). Sweet and savoury pancakes at very reasonable prices – the seafood fillings are exceptional. An individual crêpe can cost under 10F/E1.52, and there's a 58F/E8.84 full menu. Closed Tues evening & Wed in low season.

Le Chalut, 8 rue de la Corne du Cerf (☎02.99.56.71.58). Quite an exclusive dining room, in a stylish blue-painted bistro a short way in from the Porte St-Vincent. All the menus offer a limited choice, with perhaps one or two exclusively fishy main courses, and the odd meaty appetizer. The 115F/E17.53 menu centres on the catch of the day; otherwise you pay 190F/E28.97 or 270F/E41.16 for a gourmet fish dinner, designed to be not quite as rich as the traditional norm. Reservations preferred. Closed Mon, plus Tues lunch.

Le Chasse Marée, 4 rue Grout de St-Georges (☎02.99.40.85.10). Nautical decor and *haute cuisine*, just round the corner from the post office, with a few tables out on the quiet street and more upstairs. The 87F/E13.26 menu, served until 9pm, has oysters followed by red mullet or coley; the 145F/E22.11 features scallop or duck salad to start, and a mixed fish grill or fish couscous. Closed Sun in low season, plus all Feb.

Delaunay, 6 rue Ste-Barbe (%02.99.40.92.46). Located between Porte St-Vincent and Cathédrale St-Vincent, this place – formerly owned by Jean-Paul Delaunay – has changed hands (albeit within the family) to Brigitte and Didier Delaunay, but the traditional French cooking remains at the same high standard. The cheapest lunch menu is 110F/E16.77; evening meals start at 140F/E21.34. Closed Sun.

Duchesse Anne, 5–7 place Guy-la-Chambre (☎02.99.40.85.33). Situated right next to the Porte St-Vincent, the best known of St-Malo's upmarket restaurants continues to work hard to keep up its reputation – and its prices. There are no set menus; you might manage to get a lunch for under 100F/€15.24, but dinner will be well over 200F/€30.49. Whole baked fish is the main speciality. Closed Wed, plus Sun evening in low season, and all Jan & Dec.

Gilles, 2 rue de la Pie-qui-Boit (☎02.99.40.97.25). Bright, modern, good-value restaurant, just off the central pedestrian axis. The basic 92F/€14.03 menu is fine, though as it consists of the "*suggestion du jour*" followed by the "*idée du moment*" you'll have to trust that the chef has your interests at heart; alternatively 132F/€20.12 brings you a duck-and-pistachio sausage and a rabbit crêpe with cider. Closed Wed lunch July & Aug, all day Wed Sept–June.

Shopping

For last-minute **shopping** in St-Malo before you catch the ferry home, the *citadelle* contains a few specialists. Au Poids du Roy, for example, in the place du Poids-du-Roi, is a superb, if somewhat upmarket, *épicerie*. However, buying in any quantity is best done in Le Continent **hypermarket** on the southwest outskirts of the town (follow the signs to the Barrage de la Rance if you're driving; because of the one-way systems it's a circuitous route, but you do get there). There are **markets** in

St-Malo (*intra-muros*) on Tuesdays and Fridays, in St-Servan on Mondays and Fridays, and in Paramé on Wednesdays and Saturdays.

Dinard

The former fishing village of **DINARD** sprawls around the western approaches to the Rance estuary, just across from St-Malo but a good twenty-minutes' drive away. It's a town that might not feel out of place on the Côte d'Azur, with its casino, spacious shaded villas and social calendar of regattas and ballet. Here in Brittany it's a little incongruous, though pleasant enough – and quite amusing in its uncanny resemblance to an enlarged mini-golf course.

The nineteenth-century metamorphosis of Dinard was largely thanks to the tastes of affluent English and Americans, though these days age rather than nationality seems to be the common factor uniting most of its summer influx of tourists. Although Dinard is a hilly town, undulating over a succession of pretty little coastal inlets, it attracts great numbers of older visitors; as a result, prices tend to be high, and pleasures sedate (literally so, with benches scattered in abundance where weary legs can rest while their indefatigable owners admire the views).

Arrival and information

Dinard has a small **airport**, which is served by Ryanair flights from London Stansted (see p.6), and is also connected with the Channel Islands by Aurigny Air Services (☎02.99.46.70.28). It lies 4km southeast of the town centre, off the D168 near Pleurtuit; TIV bus #56, timed to connect with the Ryanair flights, runs via Dinard proper to St-Malo's *gare SNCF* and Porte St-Vincent for a 20F/€3.05 flat fare. Avis have a **rental car** outlet in the terminal (☎02.99.46.25.20).

Many visitors to Dinard simply come over for the day on one of the regular Émeraude Lines **boats** from St-Malo; tickets can be bought in Dinard a couple of hundred metres east of the tourist office at 27 av Georges-V, directly above the pleasure port where the ferries actually come in (mid-April to early Oct only; ☎02.99.46.10.45; 20F/€3.05 one-way, 30F/€4.57 round-trip, plus 15F/€2.29 each way for bicycles). If the ten-minute crossing only serves to whet your appetite, you can also take a trip down the Rance to Dinan.

Local **buses** run regularly between Dinard and St-Malo, across the dam, while long-distance buses go from the former *gare SNCF* and "Le Gallic" stop (near the tourist office) to Dinan and Rennes (run by both TIV, ☎02.99.46.13.13, and TAE, ☎02.99.50.64.17), as well as to St-Jacut, Cancale, Dol and Mont-St-Michel (in summer, TIV only). Dinan buses are also operated by CAT (☎02.96.39.21.05).

Full information on Dinard's hotels, restaurants, local tours and transport facilities can be picked up from the **tourist office**, close to the seafront in the heart of town at 2 bd Féart (Easter–June & Sept Mon–Sat 9am–12.15pm & 2–7pm; July & Aug daily 9.30am–7.30pm; Oct–Easter Mon–Sat 9am–12.15pm & 2–6pm; ☎02.99.46.94.12, *dinard.office.de.tourisme@wanadoo.fr*).

Cycles are available for rental from Cycles Duval, 53 rue Gardiner (☎02.99.46.19.63; closed Oct).

Accommodation and eating

On the whole, Dinard is an expensive place to stay, but it does at least have a wide selection of **hotels** to choose from, many of which can be found on the **Web** at *www.dinard-hotel-plus.com*. **Campsites** include the municipal *Port Blanc*, over 1km west of the centre near the plage du Port-Blanc on rue du Sergent-Boulanger (☎02.99.46.10.74, fax 02.99.16.90.91; closed Oct–March), and the grander *Ville Mauny* (☎02.99.46.94.73, fax 02.99.88.14.68; closed mid-Sept to mid-April), 2km back from the beach in the woods southwest of the centre.

All the hotels listed below have reasonable **restaurants**. Good alternatives in town include the busy *Brasserie Le Cancaven*, whose outdoor tables take up most of place de la République (☎02.99.46.15.45); their basic 68F/€10.37 menu is not all that interesting, but for 112F/€17.07 they offer a real cornucopia of fish and shellfish, from spider crab to squid.

Hôtel-Restaurant Altair, 18 bd Féart (☎02.99.46.13.58, fax 02.99.88.20.49). Central and very English option, a little way inland from the tourist office, and boasting a nice garden. Menus range up to 200F/€30.49, but even the cheapest, at 95F/€14.48, offers *moules marinières* or *soupe de poissons*. Closed Sun evening, plus Mon in low season. ②.

Hôtel de la Gare, 28 rue de la Corbinais (☎02.99.46.10.84). Dinard doesn't have a *gare SNCF* these days, but that doesn't worry the *Hôtel de la Gare*, a basic inexpensive place 500m back from the beach in a rather dull part of town. Entrance is via the simple brasserie downstairs, *L'Épicurien*. ①.

Hôtel-Restaurant du Parc, 20 av Édouard-VII (☎02.99.46.11.39, fax 02.99.88.10.58). Friendly little hotel on a busy street a short way west of the place de la République. Simple restaurant offering menus from 65F/€9.91. Closed Nov–March. ②.

Hôtel-Restaurant Printania, 5 av Georges-V (☎02.99.46.13.07, fax 02.99.46.26.32). Good-value place around 250m east of the centre, on a relatively quiet seafront street near the Port de Plaisance. Menus in the magnificent terrace restaurant, looking over to St-Malo, start at 110F/€16.77, featuring stuffed clams and grilled salmon. Closed mid-Nov to mid-March. ④.

Hôtel-Restaurant la Vallée, 6 av Georges-V (☎02.99.46.94.00, fax 02.99.88.22.47). Attractive *logis de France*, down at sea level in the pleasure port, but unfortunately facing the wrong way for views of St-Malo. The most basic rooms look straight onto a bare cliff face, but in principle this is a nice spot. Menus from 99F/€15.09, featuring grilled sardines and skate. Closed mid-Nov to mid-March. ③–⑥.

The Town

Central Dinard faces north to the open sea, across the curving bay that holds the attractive **plage de l'Écluse**. As so often in Breton resorts, the buildings that line the waterfront are, with the exception of the casino in the middle, venerable Victorian villas rather than hotels or shops, and so the beach itself has a relatively low-key atmosphere, despite the summer crowds. An unexpected statue of Alfred Hitchcock, standing on a giant egg, with a ferocious-looking bird perched on each shoulder, dominates its main access point – he was placed here to commemorate the town's annual festival of English-language films, held in early October – while rows of delightful, blue-and-white-striped, tent-like sunshelters, which cost around 40F/€6.10 to hire for the afternoon, add colour to the sands below.

Enjoyable **coastal footpaths** lead off in either direction from the principal beach, enlivened by notice boards holding reproductions of various paintings produced at points along the way. It may well come as a surprise to see that Pablo Picasso's *Deux Femmes Courants sur la Plage* and *Baigneuses sur la Plage*, both of which look quintessentially Mediterranean with their blue skies and golden sands, were in fact painted here in Dinard, during his annual summer visits throughout the 1920s.

The path heading east leads up to the Pointe du Moulinet for views over to St-Malo, and then (as the **Promenade du Clair du Lune**) continues past the tiny and now exclusive port, and down to the estuary beach, the plage du Prieuré. Between mid-June and mid-September, the path is floodlit each evening. Setting off west, on the other hand, takes you around more rocky outcrops to the secluded strand at neighbouring **St-Enogat**, where windsurfing equipment and kayaks are available for rent in summer (☎02.99.46.83.99).

Dinan

The wonderful citadel of **DINAN** has preserved almost intact its three-kilometre encirclement of protective masonry, along with street upon colourful street of late -medieval houses. However, for all its slightly unreal perfection (it would make the ideal film set for *The Three Musketeers*), it's seldom excessively overrun with tourists. There are no very vital museums, the most memorable architecture is vernacular rather than monumental, and time is most easily spent wandering from crêperie to café, admiring the overhanging half-timbered houses along the way.

Arrival and information
Both the Art Deco **gare SNCF** (☎02.96.39.22.39) and the **gare routière** (☎02.96.39.21.05) are in Dinan's modern quarter (a rather gloomy exile from the *enclos*), on place du 11-Novembre, ten-minutes' walk west of the main entrance of the walled town on Grande Rue. Armor Express **buses** (☎02.99.50.64.17) go direct to Dinard and to Rennes, which saves changing trains at Dol.

Between mid-April and late September, **boats** along the Rance sail between the port downstream and Dinard and St-Malo. The trip takes two and a half hours, with the exact schedule varying according to the tides (adults 95F/€14.48, under-13s 60F/€9.15). It's only possible to do a day-return by boat (adults 135F/€20.58, under-13s 80F/€12.20) if you start from St-Malo or Dinard; starting from Dinan, you'd have to come back by bus or train. For details, contact Émeraude Lines in Dinan, on the quai de la Rance (☎02.96.39.18.04), in Dinard (☎02.99.46.10.45) or in St-Malo (☎02.23.18.15.15).

Dinan's **tourist office** is very central, almost opposite the Tour de l'Horloge, in the sixteenth-century Hôtel Kératry at 6 rue de l'Horloge (mid-June to Sept Mon–Sat 9am–7.30pm, Sun 10am–12.30pm & 2.30–6pm; Oct to mid-June Mon–Sat 8.30am–12.30pm & 2–6pm; ☎02.96.87.69.76, *www.dinan-tourisme.com*), where the ground floor is built of stone with pillars, the first floor is lath and plaster, and the extensive garden is complete with a weeping willow. A **petit train** sets off from outside on regular town tours (Mon–Wed, Fri & Sat 10am–6pm, Sun 10am–noon; 25F/€3.81). The **post office** is on place Duclos (☎02.96.39.25.07).

Accommodation
Dinan has a surprising shortage of the kind of welcoming mid-range hotel-restaurant that characterizes so many a Breton town; to get an en-suite room in a **hotel** with its own dining room, you have to be prepared to pay upwards of 400F/€60.98. It's also not a very nice place to try to drive around, or to find a parking space in summer, so motorists might do best to visit only as a day-trip. If you're on foot, and don't mind climbing steep hills with heavy bags, there are, however, plenty of budget options around.

In addition, there is also an attractive **hostel**, set amid green fields and trees far below the walls in the Moulin de Méen, Vallée de la Fontaine-des-Eaux

ACCOMMODATION
Arvor	4
Bed & Breakfast	6
Duchesse Anne	5
Logis de Jerzual	1
du Théâtre	3
du Vieux St-Sauveur	2

DINAN

RESTAURANTS
le Cantorbery	E
Chez la Mère Pourcel	D
Crêperie Connetable	C
la Courtine	B
le Relais des Corsaires	A
le St-Louis	F

(☎02.96.39.10.83, *dinan@fuaj.org*; dorm bed 50F/€7.62; closed Jan), 2km from the *gare SNCF*. Unfortunately it's not on any bus route; to walk there, follow the quay downstream from the port on the town side, and after a few hundred metres you'll see a small sign to the left – from there it's another 500m. **Camping** is permitted in the hostel grounds, and there's also a *Camping municipal* at 103 rue Chateaubriand (☎02.96.39.11.96, fax 02.96.87.08.40; closed Oct–May), just outside the western ramparts.

Hôtel Arvor, 5 rue Pavie (☎02.96.39.21.22, fax 02.96.39.83.09, *www.destination-bretagne.com*). Renovated eighteenth-century town house, facing the tourist office, with some surviving flourishes of the convent that previously occupied the site. Smart, well-equipped rooms and free parking. ④.

Bed & Breakfast, 55 rue de Coëtquen (☎02.96.85.23.49, fax 02.96.87.51.44). Very friendly English-run B&B just southwest of the city walls, with a couple of en-suite double bedrooms. Closed Feb. ④.

Hôtel-Restaurant La Duchesse Anne, 10 place du Guesclin (☎02.96.39.09.43, fax 02.96.87.57.26). Comfortable if not luxurious rooms on the quieter side of the square, above a basic restaurant where set menus start at 62F/€9.45. Closed mid-Nov to mid-Dec. ②.

Logis de Jerzual, 25 rue du Petit Fort (☎02.96.85.46.54, fax 02.96.39.46.94). *Chambres d'hôte* on the exquisite little lane that leads from the port, halfway up to the Porte du Jerzual. Garden terrace looking down on the street. Inaccessible by car, so deathly quiet in the mornings. ④.

Hôtel de l'Océan, 9 place du 11-Novembre (☎02.96.39.21.51, fax 02.96.87.05.27). Extremely convenient and well-run (if rather basic) hotel, outside the walls opposite the *gare SNCF*. ①.

Hôtel de la Porte St-Malo, 35 rue St-Malo (☎02.96.39.19.76, fax 02.96.39.50.67). Very comfortable rooms in a tasteful small hotel just outside the walls, beyond the Porte St-Malo. ②.

Café-Hôtel du Théâtre, 2 rue Ste-Claire (☎02.96.39.06.91). Very simple rooms above a bar, right by the tourist office and Théâtre des Jacobins, and under the same efficient management as the nearby *Restaurant Cantorbery* (see opposite). ②.

Hôtel du Vieux St-Sauveur, 19 place St-Sauveur (☎02.96.85.30.20). Ancient edifice facing the St-Sauveur church, which has a slightly noisy bar downstairs, but some nicely equipped and very good-value en-suite rooms upstairs. ③.

The Town

Like St-Malo, Dinan is best seen when arriving by boat up the Rance. By the time the ferries get to the lovely **port du Dinan**, down below the thirteenth-century ramparts, the river has narrowed sufficiently to be spanned by a small but majestic old stone bridge. High above it towers the railway viaduct now used by the N176. The steep cobbled **rue du Petit-Fort** twists up from the artisans' shops and restaurants along the quay. Taking advantage of its many stone benches to catch your breath, it makes a wonderful climb, passing ancient flower-festooned edifices of wood and stone, as well as several crêperies and even a half-timbered poodle parlour, before it enters the city through the **Porte du Jerzual**.

Above that imposing gateway, **St-Sauveur** church sends the skyline even higher. It's a real hotchpotch, with a Romanesque porch and an eighteenth-century steeple. Even its nine Gothic chapels feature five different patterns of vaulting in no symmetrical order; the most complex pair, in the centre, would make any spider proud. By contrast, a very plain cenotaph on the left contains the heart of Bertrand du Guesclin, the fourteenth-century Breton warrior (and later Constable of France) who fought and won a single combat with the English knight Thomas of Canterbury, in what is now place du Guesclin, to settle the outcome of the siege of Dinan in 1364. Relics of his life and battles are scattered all over Brittany and Normandy; in death, he spread himself between four separate burial places for four different parts of his body (the French kings restricted themselves to three burial sites).

The **place du Guesclin** only comes alive on Thursdays, when together with the adjoining place du Champ Clos it's the scene of a large **market**; for the rest of the week it serves as the main central car park. The true heart of town consists of two much smaller squares, the **place des Merciers** and the **place des Cordeliers**. These hold Dinan's finest assortment of medieval wood-framed houses, painted in all sorts of lively hues, and with their upper storeys perching precariously on splintering wooden pillars that appear to buckle beneath the weight.

Unfortunately, you can only walk along one small stretch of the **ramparts**, from the Jardin Anglais behind St-Sauveur church to a point just short of Tour Sillon overlooking the river. You can, however, get a good general overview from the wooden balcony of the central **Tour de l'Horloge**, which dates from the end of the fifteenth century (April & May daily 2–6pm; June–Sept daily 10am–7pm;

For 35F/€5.34 per person, or 85F/€12.96 per family, a **ticket** called *Les Clefs pour Dinan* grants access to the Tour de l'Horloge, the Tour Coëtquen and two other minor local museums.

16F/€2.44, or *Les Clefs pour Dinan* ticket). The original mechanism of the clock here was made in Nantes and put in place in 1498; in 1507, the ubiquitous Duchesse Anne presented the monumental bell. A small and not at all interesting shopping mall has recently been created around the foot of the belfry's stout stone walls.

As you might guess from its blending of two separate towers, the fourteenth-century keep that once protected the town's southern approach was built by Estienne Le Tour, architect of St-Malo's Tour Solidor (see p.212). It's now known as the **Château de Duchesse Anne**, with a small local-history museum housed in the ancient **Tour Coëtquen** (June to mid-Oct daily 10am–6.30pm; mid-Oct to May daily except Tues 1.30–5.30pm; 22F/€3.35, or *Les Clefs pour Dinan* ticket). On the lower floor, a group of stone fifteenth-century notables looks for all the world like a medieval time capsule, about to depetrify at any moment.

At some point during each summer (most recently in late July, but the date tends to vary – check with the tourist office) the **Fête des Remparts** is celebrated with medieval-style jousting, banquets, fairs and processions, culminating in an immense fireworks display.

Eating and drinking

All sorts of specialist **restaurants**, including several ethnic alternatives, are tucked away in the old streets of Dinan. Stroll of an evening through the town and down to the port, and you'll pass at least twenty places to choose from, with the vast majority offering better value for money than Brittany's seaside resorts.

Once you've eaten, the area to head for **bars** is the series of tiny parallel alleyways between the place des Merciers and the rue de la Ferronnerie. Along rue de la Cordonnerie, the busiest of the lot, the various hangouts define themselves by their taste in music: *À la Truye qui File* at no. 14 is a contemporary folky Breton dive, while *Morgan's Tavern*, next door at no. 12, is considerably more raucous.

Le Cantorbery, 6 rue Ste-Claire (☎02.96.39.02.52). Reasonable food served in an old stone house with rafters, a spiral staircase and a real wood fire. Lunch from 65F/€9.91, while traditional dinner menus start with a good 125F/€19.06 option. Closed Sun evening & Mon, plus all Feb.

Chez La Mère Pourcel, 3 place des Merciers (☎02.96.39.03.80). Beautiful half-timbered fifteenth-century house in the central square. The lunch menu, at 97F/€14.79, is pretty minimal, but the dinners, starting at 168F/€25.61, are gourmet class, featuring for example exquisite *agneau pré-salé* from Mont-St-Michel. Closed Sun evening, plus Mon in low season, and all Feb.

Crêperie Connetable, 1 rue de l'Apport (☎02.96.39.02.52). Magnificent old house opposite the *Mère Pourcel* beside the place des Merciers. Sit if you dare at the pavement tables, where all that prevents the upper storeys from crashing down around your ears are a couple of misshapen pillars. Crêpes and snacks in the perfect spot for people-watching.

La Courtine, 6 rue de la Croix (☎02.96.39.74.41). Friendly little restaurant not far from the St-Malo church, offering a 70F/€10.67 lunch menu during the week, and dinner menus from 98F/€14.94 featuring such delights as duck cooked with cherries. Closed Wed lunchtime in summer, all Wed & Sun evening in low season.

Le Relais des Corsaires, 7 rue du Quai, port du Dinan (☎02.96.39.40.17). Large but attractive waterfront restaurant, down by the port, which in theory is split between a formal dining room and the less expensive all-hours *Petit Corsaire*, which bills itself as a "grill". Both, however, seem to serve much the same wide range of traditional French cuisine, on menus that start with an 89F/€13.57 option that offers shrimp followed by mussels or cod; the only real difference is that the pricier menus are dropped in winter. Closed Sun evening & Wed in low season.

Le St-Louis, 9–11 rue de Léhon (☎02.96.39.89.50). Very good-value restaurant just inside the Porte St-Louis, specializing in buffets; a 79F/€12.04 menu entitles you to choose at will from extensive buffets of *hors d'oeuvres* and desserts, while the 95F/€14.48 option offers the same deal plus a conventional main course. Closed Sun evening & Wed.

Around the Baie du Mont-St-Michel

The **coastal road** D201 runs east from St-Malo to Cancale, past a succession of coves and beaches, where lines of dunes attempt to hang on against the battering from the sea. At the **Pointe du Grouin** – a perilous and windy height that also overlooks the bird sanctuary of the **Îles des Landes**, to the east – the line of cliffs turns sharply back on itself, at one extremity of the **Baie du Mont-St-Michel** (see map on p.160). This is a huge flat expanse of mud and sand, over which the tide – as just about every piece of literature on this region will tell you – can race faster than a galloping horse. It is dangerous to wander out too far, quite apart from the risk of quicksands, and, in the Breton part of the bay at least, the beaches have little appeal for bathers.

The course of the **River Couesnon**, which marks the border between Brittany and Normandy, has shifted repeatedly over the centuries. So too has the shoreline of the bay, in which traces of long-drowned villages can be seen when the tide is out. Bretons like to say that it is just an accident that the river now runs west of Mont-St-Michel; be that as it may, the Mont and Pontorson, the nearest town to it, are both in Normandy (see p.159). The pinnacle of *La Merveille*, however, remains clearly visible from every vantage point along the coast.

Cancale

Just south of the Pointe du Grouin, and less than 15km east of St-Malo, **CANCALE** is not so much a one-horse as a one-mollusc town – the whole place is obsessed with the **oyster**, and with "*ostréiculture*". Its current population is, at 4600, less than it was a century ago, but the town looks much bigger than that would suggest – and the reason must be the visitors attracted by its edible hinged bivalves.

Cancale is divided into two distinct halves; the old town up on the hill, and the port area of **La Houle** down below, now very pretty and very smart. Oysters may have been a cheap working-class staple in the past, but these days they're clasped to the bosoms and slurped by the lips of elegant *bourgeois* holiday-makers. In the old church of **St-Méen**, at the top of the hill, a small **Musée des Arts et Traditions Populaires** documents this obsession with meticulous precision (June & Sept Thurs–Sun 2.30–6.30pm; July & Aug Mon 2.30–6.30pm, Tues–Sun 10am–noon & 2.30–6.30pm; plus groups by appointment at any time – call ☎02.99.89.71.26; 15F/€2.29). Cancale oysters have been found in the camps of Julius Caesar; were taken daily to Versailles for Louis XIV; and even accompanied Napoléon on the march to Moscow. The most famous symbol of the town – and its

---

CRUISING THE BAY

Sightseeing cruises around the Baie du Mont-St-Michel, aboard the *Sirène de la Baie*, depart throughout the summer from Le Vivier-sur-Mer, 8km north of Dol (May–Oct daily at 10am, 1pm, 4pm & 7.30pm; ☎02.99.48.82.30). The standard fare is 99F/€15.09 for adults, 59F/€8.99 for children, while menus costing from 130F/€19.82 upwards are served on the slightly longer 1pm and 7.30pm trips.

oyster cultivation – is the stark **Rocher du Cancale** just offshore; the museum lists all the *Rochers du Cancale* restaurants that have ever existed, including ones in Shanghai and Phnom Penh, and one in Moscow which closed in the 1830s.

From the rue des Parcs, next to the jetty of the port, you can see at low tide the **parcs** where the oysters are grown. At one time there was an annual event, *La Caravanne*, when a huge flotilla of sailing vessels dragged nets along the bottom of the sea for wild oysters; now they are farmed like any other crop. The sea bed is divided into countless segments of different sizes, each segment having an individual owner who has the right to sell what it produces. The oysters are cultivated from year-old "spat" bought in from elsewhere. Behind, the rocks of the cliff are streaked and shiny like mother-of-pearl; underfoot the beach is littered with countless generations of empty shells.

Follow the corniche road out of Cancale to the southwest, and you'll soon come to the **Ferme Marine**, a working *parc* also more grandly known as the Musée de l'Huître et du Coquillage, where the entire oyster-raising process is described on enjoyable guided tours (mid-Feb to mid-June & mid-Sept to Oct Mon–Fri at 3pm; mid-June to mid-Sept daily at 11am, 3pm & 5pm; 40F/€6.10).

Practicalities

Cancale's main **tourist office** is up the hill at 44 rue du Port (July & Aug daily 9am–8pm; Sept–June Mon–Sat 9am–12.30pm & 2–6pm, Sun 10am–1pm; ☎02.99.89.63.72), but most visitors prefer to call in at the information office on the waterfront in the heart of the harbour, across from the upmarket glass-fronted hotels and restaurants that line quai Gambetta.

Most **hotels** insist that you eat if you want to stay, but that's no great problem considering that there's nothing much else to do in town. Among the best value are *Le Phare* (☎02.99.89.60.24; ③) and the *Émeraude* (☎02.99.89.61.76; ④) – both set above their own restaurants, at nos. 6 and 7 respectively on quai Thomas – and *La Houle*, 18 quai Gambetta (☎02.99.89.62.38; ②). Budget travellers can head for the **hostel**, 2km north of town at Port Picain (☎02.99.89.62.62, *cancale@fuaj.org*; closed Jan), where a dorm bed costs 55F/€8.38 for the night. By far the best **campsite** in the vicinity is the *Camping Municipal Pointe du Grouin* (☎02.99.89.63.79; closed Nov–Feb), a little further on, where the views are quite sensational.

There's no great reason to recommend any one of Cancale's **restaurants** above the rest; all without exception serve enticing seafood spreads, and which of the twenty or so adjacent options you choose will depend on your mood and your particular favourite dish. **Oysters** can be had for as little as 15F/€2.29 per dozen from takeaway stalls, while at *Au Pied d'Cheval*, 10 quai Gambetta (☎02.99.89.76.95), they'll dish up a dozen from the huge baskets that weigh down their wooden quayside tables for just 26F/€3.96, or prepare a massive *fruits de mer* plate for two people for 200F/€30.49. Alternatively, the *Émeraude* (see above) has a 255F/€38.87 menu that centres almost exclusively on scallops.

Cancale has a **market** on Sunday in the streets behind the main church, the rue de la Marine and the rue Cocar.

Dol-de-Bretagne and around

The foundation of **DOL-DE-BRETAGNE**, 30km west of Mont-St-Michel, is attributed to St Samson, one of the many Celtic evangelists who flooded into Brittany around the sixth century. The Breton hero King Nominoë appointed its first official bishop during the ninth century, and the city remained an important bishopric throughout the Middle Ages.

Dol is no longer large enough to merit its own bishop, but Samson's name lives on in the fortified thirteenth-century **Cathédrale St-Samson**, with its strange, squat, tiled towers and ornate porches. Housed in a former school in the cathedral square, the new and highly ambitious **Cathédraloscope** (mid-Feb to April & Oct to mid-Jan daily 10am–6pm; May–Sept daily 9am–7pm; 40F/€6.10) sets out to explain the construction and significance of not only this example but medieval cathedrals in general. For all its high-tech presentation and flair, however, non-French speakers may well find it rather heavy going. Nearby, the more traditional **Musée Historique de Dol** (Easter–Sept daily 2.30–6pm; 10F/€1.52) is bloated by the usual array of posed waxworks, but holds two rooms of astonishing wooden bits and pieces rescued in assorted states of decay from churches, often equally rotten, all over Brittany. These carvings and statues, some still brightly polychromed with their crust of eggy paint, range from the thirteenth to the nineteenth centuries.

An appealing handful of Dol's older streets are still packed with venerable buildings, most notably the pretty **Grande-Rue**, where one Romanesque edifice dates back as far as the eleventh century, an assortment of 500-year-old half-timbered houses look down on the bustle of shoppers below, and a laundry claims to have been visited by Victor Hugo in 1836.

Practicalities

Dol's **tourist office** can be found at 3 Grande-Rue (Easter–June & Sept daily 10.30am–noon & 3.30–7pm; July & Aug daily 9.30am–12.30pm & 2.30–7.30pm; Oct–Easter Thurs 2–4pm; ☎02.99.48.15.37). There's not a great deal to keep casual visitors in Dol for long, but if you do decide to stay, you'll find a reasonable **hotel**, the *Bretagne*, next to the market at 17 place Chateaubriand (☎02.99.48.02.03; ③; closed Oct), east of Grande-Rue; rooms at the back look out across a small vestige of ramparts towards Mont Dol.

Among good **campsites** nearby are the *Vieux Chêne* (☎02.99.48.09.55; closed Oct–March), 3km east towards Baguer-Pican on RN176, and the phenomenally luxurious *Castel-Camping des Ormes* (☎02.99.73.53.00, *www.lesormes.com*; closed mid-Sept to mid-May), set around a lake in the grounds of a château 6km south towards Combourg on the N795, which arranges **horse riding** for its guests, and boasts not only its own golf course but even a cricket pitch.

A couple of nice **fish restaurants** can be found in the ancient houses on rue Ceinte, as it winds its way from Grande-Rue to the cathedral: *Le Porche au Pain* at no. 1, and *La Grabotais* at no. 4 (☎02.99.48.19.89; closed Mon). After you eat, the *Katédral* **bar**, between the church and museum (☎02.99.48.05.40), is worth a brief pause.

Mont Dol

All approaches to Dol from the bay are watched over by the former island of **Mont Dol** – now eight rather marshy kilometres in from the sea. This abrupt granite outcrop, looking mountainous beyond its size on such a flat plain, was the legendary site of a battle between the Archangel Michael and the Devil. Various fancifully named indentations in the rock, such as "the Devil's Claw", testify to the savagery of their encounter, which was inevitably won by the saint. The site has been occupied since prehistoric times – flint implements have been unearthed alongside the bones of mammoths, sabre-toothed tigers and even rhinoceroses.

Later on, it appears to have been used for worship by the Druids, before becoming, like Mont-St-Michel, an island monastery.

Traces of the abbey have long vanished, though the mythic battle may recall its foundation, with Christianity driving out the old religion. A plaque proclaims that visiting the small chapel on top earns a Papal Indulgence (presumably on the condition that you don't add to the copious graffiti on its walls). The climb is pleasant, too, a steep footpath winding up among the chestnuts and beeches to a solitary bar.

If you fancy an extended walk, Dol and Mont Dol are in fact located on the long-distance **GR34** trail, which leads east to Mont-St-Michel (reckoned as an 8hr stroll), and west along the coast way beyond St-Malo.

The Menhir du Champ-Dolent

A short way out of Dol to the south, a small picnic area fenced off among the fields contains the **Menhir du Champ-Dolent**. According to one legend, this 9.6-metre standing stone dropped from the sky to separate two brothers who were on the point of mutual fratricide. Another has it that the menhir is inching its way into the soil, and the world will end when it disappears altogether. It has to be said that this would not be a particularly interesting spot on which to experience the end of the world. The unadorned stone, big though it undoubtedly is in its banal setting, has little of the romance or mystery of the megalithic sites of the Morbihan and elsewhere.

The Forêt de Ville-Cartier

The *Circuit Touristique* signposted from Dol continues beyond the menhir and the village of Trans to the **Forêt de Ville-Cartier**. The pines and beech of the forest sweep thickly down to a lake in which it is possible – in fact almost irresistible – to swim. Keeping to the *circuit*, along the D155, would lead eventually to Fougères (see p.233).

Inland to Rennes

Much the most direct route inland from the north coast to Rennes is the **N137** *autoroute*, which takes barely half an hour to drive from St-Malo. The D795 south from Dol however makes an appealing alternative, passing through the castle town of **Combourg**. The twin canalside towns of **Tinténiac** and **Hédé** also repay a brief detour.

Combourg

As well as being a pleasant little town in its own right, **COMBOURG**, 17km south of Dol and 24km southeast of Dinan, has two chief attractions. The first is a **château**, perched on a hill and dominating magnificent landscaped gardens, which was the childhood home of the writer Chateaubriand, now buried at St-Malo (see p.212), and which remains in the hands of his descendants. The Tour du Chat of the castle may be haunted, by a ghost taking the form of a cat. Chateaubriand himself claimed it was haunted by the ghost of the **wooden leg** of a former lord – and that the cat was merely an acquaintance of this phantasmal limb. The entrance to the château is not where you expect it to be: turn right at the end of Combourg's main square instead of continuing straight towards the keep, and it's a short way up on the left (gardens: April–June & Sept Tues–Sun 10am–12.30pm & 2–6pm; July & Aug daily 10am–12.30pm & 1.30–6pm; Oct Tues–Sun 10am–noon & 2–4.30pm; château: April–June & Sept Tues–Sun 2–5.30pm; July & Aug daily 11am–12.30pm & 1.30–5.30pm; Oct Tues–Sun 2–4.30pm; 25F/€3.81).

Down below both château and town, the tranquil cypress-lined **lake** is, if anything, more appealing than the château itself. Misty and quiet early in the morning, busy only with anglers, it provides a welcome opportunity for leisurely countryside walks, perhaps after a night of indulgence.

Practicalities

In summer, Combourg maintains a small **tourist office** in the Maison de la Lanterne, at 23 place Albert-Parent (June to mid-Sept Mon–Sat 10am–7pm, Sun 10am–12.30pm; ☎02.99.73.13.93, *www.combourg.org*). Two superb if somewhat expensive (and not very imaginatively named) **hotels** square off against each other across place Chateaubriand, which squeezes in between château and lake. While the *Hôtel du Château* at no. 1 (☎02.99.73.00.38; ③; closed Sun evening & Mon in low season, plus Feb) is beyond reproach, the *Hôtel du Lac* at no. 2 (☎02.99.73.05.65; ③; closed Fri evening & Sun evening in low season, plus mid-Dec to mid-Jan) just has the edge, with lake views from most of the rooms. Even its cheaper menus, which start at 68F/€10.37 at lunchtime, offer such delights as a cassoulet of mussels with wild mushrooms or half a dozen fresh oysters.

Beside the canal: Hédé and Tinténiac

The D795 south from Combourg meets the N137 *autoroute* roughly 20km north of Rennes, close to the particularly pleasant stretch of the **Canal d'Ille-et-Vilaine** that connects the two old towns of **HÉDÉ** and **TINTÉNIAC**. There are tempting places to collapse in the sun between the many locks and lock-keepers' cottages, although the towpath isn't consistent enough to follow for any distance on foot, let alone bike.

Both Hédé and Tinténiac are set on hills to the west of the canal, and have excellent **hotels**. At the southern end of Tinténiac – which is dominated by a truly bizarre multiturreted church – the *Hôtel des Voyageurs* (☎02.99.68.02.21; ②) has menus from 95F/€14.48. On the main road just north of Hédé, another *logis de France*, the *Hostellerie du Vieux Moulin* (☎02.99.45.45.70; ③; closed Sun evening, Mon & Jan) stands in a lovely rural setting below the ruined ramparts of the town castle; its restaurant is more expensive, but the food is absolutely magnificent. On the other hand, the guestrooms are pretty minimal for the price.

In addition, a flower-festooned stone cottage just off the highway between Tinténiac and Hédé, a couple of hundred metres north of the *Vieux Moulin*, holds the inexpensive but high-quality *Restaurant le Genty-Home* (☎02.99.45.46.07; closed Tues evening & Wed), whose enthusiastic young chef prepares traditional meats and fishes on menus ranging from 68F/€10.37 and up; 215F/€32.78 gets you a five-course feast including dressed crab, a mixed plate of shellfish, and pigeon or lamb.

St-Aubin d'Aubigné and St-Aubin-du-Cormier (see p.234) are other possible bases. The **Forêt du Paimpont** (see p.328), too, is well within reach and allows you to bypass Rennes.

Rennes

For a city that has been the capital and power centre of Brittany ever since it was united with France in 1532, **RENNES** is – outwardly at least – uncharacteristic of the province, with its Neoclassical layout and pompous major buildings. Much of its potential to be a picturesque tourist spot was destroyed in 1720, when a drunken carpenter managed to set light to virtually the whole city. Only sections of the area known as **Les Lices**, at the junction of the canalized Ille and the River Vilaine, were left undamaged; fortunately it was even then the oldest part of Rennes, so some traces of the medieval town do survive. After the fire, the remodelling of the rest of the city was handed over to Parisian architects, not in deference to the capital but in an attempt to rival it. The result, on the north side of the river at any rate, is something of a patchwork quilt, consisting of grand eighteenth-century public squares interspersed with intimate little alleys of half-timbered houses. It's quite a pleasant city to stroll around for half a day, but not one that impresses the casual visitor with much sense of a cohesive personality.

Rennes was first laid out by the Romans, at a convenient ford in the Vilaine that was already home to the Celtic community of *Condate*; over thirty thousand Roman coins have been found in the riverbed, it being traditional for travellers to toss in an offering whenever they crossed water. The city subsequently enjoyed around a thousand years of independence before it was successfully besieged by Charles VIII of France in 1491. That defeat obliged Duchess Anne to marry Charles, and led to the union of Brittany and France, sealed in 1532 in the Cohue in Vannes (see p.370). From 1561, the Breton parliament met in Rennes and helped to preserve a measure of autonomy for Brittany in the face of growing centralization. To "celebrate" four centuries of the union in 1932, Breton separatists blew up a statue outside the Hôtel de Ville which showed Brittany swearing allegiance to Louis XV. In 1994, during demonstrations staged by fishermen protesting against a visit by Prime Minister Édouard Balladur, a stray flare caused huge damage to the buildings of the Breton parliament.

The presence of so many students – over 40,000 all told – gives Rennes a rather more visible level of political and cultural activity than most places in Brittany (the Czech author Milan Kundera wrote *The Book of Laughter and Forgetting* while based at the university, which is on a huge campus to the east).

Arrival and information

Rennes' modern **gare SNCF** (☎02.99.65.50.50) is south of the Vilaine, around twenty-minutes' walk from the tourist office and a little more from the medieval quarter. As well as direct TGV trains to and from Paris – which take only just over two hours – it also has connections east to Brest, north to Dol and south towards Nantes.

The city has a new **gare routière**, on boulevard Solferino immediately east of the *gare SNCF*, but most local buses start and finish on or near place de la République. Rennes is a busy junction, with direct services to St-Malo (TIV; ☎02.99.79.23.44), Dinan and Dinard (Armor Express; ☎02.99.50.64.17) and Nantes (Société Transports Tourisme de l'Ouest; ☎02.40.20.45.20). Les Courriers Bretons (☎02.99.19.70.70, *www.lescourriersbreton.fr*) run day-trips to **Mont-St-Michel**, timed to connect with the morning TGV from Paris (departing Rennes *gare routière* daily 11am; 128F/€19.51 return).

The **tourist office** stands in a disused medieval church, the Chapelle St-Yves, just north of the river at 11 rue St-Yves (April–Sept Mon–Sat 9am–7pm, Sun 11am–6pm; Oct–March Mon–Sat 9am–6pm, Sun 11am–6pm; ☎02.99.67.11.11, *www.tourisme-rennes.com*). There are additional information offices in the lobby of the Palais du Parlement (Mon–Fri 9.30am–noon & 1.45–5pm) and in the *gare SNCF* to the south (Mon–Fri 8am–7pm, Sat & Sun 10am–1pm & 3–6pm; ☎02.99.53.23.23). **Post offices** are located in the Palais du Commerce in the heart of town, on the place de la République (Mon–Fri 8am–7pm, Sat 8am–noon; ☎02.99.79.50.71), and at 27 bd du Colombier, just west of the *gare SNCF* (same hours; ☎02.99.31.42.72). For **Internet access**, head to *Cybernet On Line*, near the Palais du Parlement at 22 rue St-Georges (☎02.99.36.37.41).

The town council runs a **bike-rental** kiosk in the central place de la République (daily 9am–7pm; ☎02.96.79.63.72); the first hour is free, while five hours cost just 10F/€1.52. Sadly, however, you can't take advantage of the municipal system of free white bicycles, which are parked all over town and are unlocked by special identity keys available only to city residents.

Accommodation

There are surprisingly few **hotels** in the old part of Rennes – and those that there are can be very hard to find. If you've arrived by train or bus, it's easier to settle for staying near the *gares SNCF* and *routière*. All Rennes' hotels seem to stay open all year round.

The city also has a year-round **hostel**, the welcoming *Centre International de Séjour*, 10–12 Canal St-Martin (☎02.99.33.22.33, fax 02.99.59.06.21), which is attractively located beside the Canal d'Ille et Rance, 3km north from the centre. Charging between 72F/€10.98 and 135F/€20.58 per person per night for a dorm bed in a small room, or 200F/€30.49 for a private double, it has a cafeteria and a laundry, and operates a midnight curfew; membership of a recognized hostelling association is compulsory. You can get there on bus routes #20 and #22 from the *gare SNCF*, direction "St-Gregoire", stop "Coëtlogon"; neither bus runs over the weekend, when you have to catch bus #18 instead.

Campers can head for the appealingly verdant *Camping Municipal des Gayeulles*, 1km east of central Rennes at rue de Professeur-Maurice-Audin (☎02.99.36.91.22; closed Oct–March), reached by taking bus #3, direction "St-Laurent", and getting off at "Parc des Bois".

Hotels

Hôtel d'Angleterre, 19 rue du Maréchal-Joffre (☎02.99.79.38.61, fax 02.99.79.43.85). Unexceptional, but scrupulously maintained and relatively cheap hotel a short way south of the river towards the station. ②.

Garden Hôtel, 3 rue Duhamel (☎02.99.65.45.06, fax 02.99.65.02.62). Comfortable, nicely decorated and very personal hotel, north of the *gare SNCF* not far from the river, with a pleasant little garden café. ②.

Hôtel Lanjuinais, 11 rue Lanjuinais (☎02.99.79.02.03, fax 02.99.79.03.97). Standard refurbished upmarket hotel, on a quiet little street just around the corner from the tourist office, less than 50m south of the river. ③.

Hôtel de Léon, 15 rue de Léon (☎ & fax 02.99.30.55.28). Quiet little eleven-room hotel, off the beaten track northeast of the *gare SNCF*, offering old-fashioned but adequate rooms at knockdown rates. ①.

Hôtel des Lices, 7 place des Lices (☎02.99.79.14.81, fax 02.99.79.35.44, *hotel.lices@wanadoo.fr*). Forty rooms, all with TV, in a very comfortable and friendly modern hotel on the edge of the prettiest part of old Rennes, very convenient for the place des Lices car park. ③.

Hôtel Riaval, 9 rue de Riaval (☎02.99.50.65.58, fax 02.99.41.85.30). Friendly hotel with neat budget rooms, on a quiet street well away from the centre, but only a few minutes' walk east of the *gare SNCF*. ①.

Hôtel-Restaurant au Rocher de Cancale, 10 rue St-Michel (☎02.99.79.20.83). Four-room hotel on a lively pedestrian street, between place Ste-Anne and place St-Michel, in the heart of medieval Rennes and ideally positioned for the city's nightlife. Beautifully restored frontage and ground floor, but with modern facilities upstairs. The restaurant, which is closed at weekends, has menus from 58F/€8.84 at lunchtime and 85F/€12.96 in the evening; the 130F/€19.82 exclusively fish menu is excellent. ③.

Inter-Hôtel Le Sévigné, 47bis av Janvier (☎02.99.67.27.55, fax 02.99.30.66.10). Smart, upmarket option 100m north of the *gare SNCF* en route to the centre, with a large brasserie next door. All rooms are en-suite, with satellite TV. ④.

Hôtel Tour d'Auvergne, 20 bd de la Tour-d'Auvergne (☎02.99.30.84.16, fax 02.23.42.10.01). A very simple but welcoming option, above the little *Serment de Vin* brasserie, between the *gare SNCF* and the river. Some low-priced rooms have en-suite shower facilities. ①.

The City

Rennes' original **medieval core** – the "ville rouge", bordered by the canal to the west and the river to the south – is known to have been enclosed by walls well before 1422. Those walls were enlarged in 1440, when the **Porte Mordelaise** was constructed to serve as the ceremonial entrance to the city. Thanks to recent building work, that gateway is now more prominently exposed. The old quarter remains the liveliest part of town and it stays up late, particularly in the area around St-Aubin church and along rue St-Michel and rue de Penhöet.

Today, the **place des Lices** is dominated by two empty market halls, but originally it was, as its name suggests, the venue for tournaments – that is, jousting "lists". It was here, in 1337, that the hitherto unknown Bertrand du Guesclin, then aged 17, fought and defeated several older opponents. This set him on his career as a soldier, during which he was later to save Rennes when it was under siege by the English. However, after the Bretons were defeated at Auray in 1364, he fought for the French and twice invaded Brittany. Thus, while he may be a French hero, some Bretons consider him a traitor. In 1946, Breton separatists destroyed a memorial to him in the Thabor gardens.

Magnificent medieval-style town houses overlook the place des Lices, but they're not as old as they look: most were built in the late seventeenth century to house Brittany's parliamentarians. The streets immediately northeast offer a more genuine glimpse of ancient Rennes. Wander around the back of the excellent crêperie at 5 place Ste-Anne, through an archway beside no. 7 rue Motte-Fablet, and you'll find an extraordinary specimen of medieval high-rise housing.

The one central building to escape the 1720 fire was the **Palais du Parlement** on rue Hoche downtown. Ironically, however, the Palais was all but ruined by a major conflagration in 1994. The exact circumstances remain somewhat mysterious, but it's thought the blaze was sparked by a stray flare (see p.227) set off during a demonstration by Breton fishermen. Since then, the entire structure has been rebuilt and restored, and is once more topped by an impressive array of gleaming gilded statues. Inside, its lobby houses a small tourist office (see p.228), and also stages temporary exhibitions.

The **south bank** of the river is every bit as busy, if not busier, than the north: should you feel upon arriving that Rennes seems oddly empty, the chances are that everyone's in the giant **Centre Colombier**, just west of the *gare SNCF*. This vast shopping mall is Rennes at its most modern, packed with shops of all kinds, plus cafés and snack bars, and featuring a crystal model of itself in its main entrance hall. Slightly nearer the river, **rue Vasselot** has its own array of half-timbered old houses.

The **Lycée Émile Zola**, just south of the Beaux Arts museum at the corner of avenue Janvier and rue Toullier, was the scene in 1899 of the retrial of **Captain Alfred Dreyfus**. It had taken three years – and Émile Zola's famous letter "J'accuse" – to secure him the retrial following his wrongful conviction of treason in 1896. The notorious saga is commemorated by a modern steel statue, *La Dégradation de Dreyfus*, by Igael Tumurkin.

The museums

The **Vilaine** flows through the centre of Rennes, narrowly confined into a steep-sided channel, and even forced underground at one point. An imposing former university building at 20 quai Émile-Zola on its south bank houses the city's **Musée des Beaux Arts** (daily except Tues 10am–noon & 2–6pm; 20F/€3.05). Its collection reaches back several millennia, and numbers among its artefacts mummified Egyptian cats and Etruscan urns as well as Greek and Roman statues and ceramics. Many of its finest artworks – which include drawings by Leonardo da Vinci, Botticelli, Fra Lippo Lippi and Dürer – are, however, not usually on public display. Instead you'll find a number of indifferent Impressionist views of Normandy by the likes of Boudin and Sisley, interspersed with the odd treasure such as Pieter Boel's startlingly contemporary-looking seventeenth-century animal studies, Veronese's depiction of a flying *Perseus Rescuing Andromeda*, and Pierre-Paul Ruben's *Tiger Hunt*, enlivened by the occasional lion. Only a few of its many canvases by lesser-known Breton artists tend to be on show at any one time, but if you're lucky they'll include the haunting landscapes of Théodore Aligny, painted in the 1850s but suffused with a delicate Maxfield-Parrish-style glow. Picasso also makes a cameo appearance, with a nude from 1923, a simple *Baigneuse à Dinard* from 1928, and a very late and surprisingly Cubist canvas from 1970.

The same building was long home also to the **Musée de Bretagne**, a comprehensive and very high-tech introduction to the history and culture of Brittany, but that has been closed for several years while its exhibits are moved to a new, high-tech museum, due to open on a separate site in 2003.

Also worth a look is the **Ecomusée du Pays de Rennes** (Mon & Wed–Fri 9am–noon & 2–6pm, Sat 2–6pm, Sun 2–7pm; 30F/€4.57), south of the centre on the route Chatillon sur Seiche (reached on city bus #14 from the place de la République, getting off at "Le Gacet" stop, or bus #61 from the *gare routière* to "La Bintinais"), where the Ferme de la Bintinais is being preserved as a monument to the rural history of the area. State-of-the-art techniques have been used to recount the minutiae of five centuries of daily life, showing the vital role Rennes has played in the evolution of Breton agriculture; living exhibits range from dairy cattle to honey bees.

The **Musée Automobile** (daily 9am–noon & 2–7pm; 30F/€4.57), northeast of the city on the route de Fougères, holds over eighty vintage cars. If you don't have your own much-prized vehicle, take bus #3, direction "St-Laurent", and get off at the Gayeulles roundabout – where you're still left with quite a walk.

Eating and drinking

Most of Rennes' more interesting **bars**, **restaurants** and nightlife in general are to be found in the streets just south of the place Ste-Anne, towards the place des Lices. Rues St-Michel and Penhoët, each with a fine assemblage of ancient wooden buildings, are the epicentre at the moment. Interesting ethnic alternatives can be found along rue St-Malo just to the north, which has long been the more or less exclusive preserve of students but is now decaying fast.

Rue Vasselot is the nearest equivalent south of the river, though if you're just looking for a quick snack don't forget the various outlets in the Centre Colombier. There are also plenty of brasseries, restaurants and bars both in the *gare SNCF* complex and in the surrounding streets.

L'Auberge St-Sauveur, 6 rue St-Sauveur (☎02.99.79.32.56). Classy, romantic restaurant, in an attractive medieval house near the cathedral, with rich, meaty dinner menus at 109F/€16.62 and 165F/€25.15 and lighter lunches for 78F/€11.89. Closed for lunch on Sat & Mon, & all day Sun.

La Chope, 3 rue de la Chalotais (☎02.99.79.34.54). A little way below place de la République on the south side of the river. Classic, busy brasserie open until midnight every day except Sunday, serving meals from 98F/€14.94 upwards.

Le Chouin, 12 rue d'Isly (☎02.99.30.87.86). A fine fish restaurant, a little north of the Centre Colombier towards the river. Lunch costs just 59F/€8.99 or 79F/€12.04, while both the 99F/€15.09 and 129F/€19.67 dinner menus include nine oysters to start. Closed Sun evening & Mon.

Le Gange, 34 place des Lices (☎02.99.30.18.37). Quality Indian restaurant offering 52F/€7.93 lunches, plus a vegetarian menu at 85F/€12.96, and meat-based ones from 110F/€16.77. Closed Sun.

Le Khalifa, 20 haut de la place des Lices (☎02.99.30.87.30). Assorted Moroccan dishes, served outside or in an atmospheric dining room. Couscous and brochettes 59F/€8.99 and up, *tagine* 69F/€10.52, as well as various set menus. Closed Mon.

Le Navira, 39 rue St-Georges (☎02.99.38.88.90). Simple, friendly French restaurant with outdoor seating on a busy pedestrian alley east of the Palais du Parlement, offering good-value 59F/€8.99 (two-course) and 79F/€12.04 (three-course) lunch menus. Closed Sun.

Le Parc à Moules, 8 rue Georges-Dottin (☎02.99.31.44.28). On a small street leading north from the river, near the tourist office. Mussels from Mont-St-Michel Bay cooked in 34 different delicious ways for around 55F/€8.38, and a weekday lunch menu offering *moules frites* for 54F/€8.23, plus more expensive fishy dishes. Closed Sun lunch & Tues.

La Tourniole, 37 rue Vasselot (☎02.99.79.05.91). Lovely, very traditional small restaurant halfway between the *gare SNCF* and the river, offering a hearty 65F/€9.91 set lunch, and dinner menus that start at 95F/€14.48. Fish, meat and even vegetarian specialities prepared to perfection. Closed Sun & Mon.

Entertainment and culture

Rennes is seen at its best in the first ten days of July, when the **Festival des Tombées de la Nuit** takes over the whole city to celebrate Breton culture with music, theatre, film, mime and poetry in joyful rejection of the influences of both Paris and Hollywood (advance information from 8 place du Maréchal-Juin, 35000 Rennes; ☎02.99.30.38.01).

In the first week of December, the **Transmusicales** rock festival attracts big-name acts from all over France and the world at large, though still with a Breton emphasis. Over the last decade it has helped to make Rennes an important centre for French rock (information on ☎02.99.31.12.10).

The varied season of the Théâtre National de Bretagne, 1 rue St-Helier (☎02.99.31.55.33), runs from mid-October to mid-June, while all year round, in a different auditorium on the same premises, *Club Ubu* (☎02.99.30.31.68) puts on large-scale gigs. Live **jazz** gigs take place Monday to Saturday at *Déjazey Jazz Club*, 54 rue St-Malo (☎02.99.38.70.72). The *Barantic*, 4 rue St-Michel, is one of the city's favourite **bars**, putting on occasional live music for a mixed crowd of Breton nationalists and boisterous students; if you don't like the look of it, or it's too full, there are half a dozen similar alternatives within spitting distance, including the *Loch Ness* at no. 5.

The friendly **bookshop** Co-op Breizh at 17 rue Penhoët (☎02.99.79.01.87) has cassettes of Breton and Celtic music along with books and posters. L'Arvor cinema at 29 rue d'Antrain (☎02.99.38.72.40) shows *v.o.* (original language) **films**, and there's a large FNAC bookshop in the Colombier shopping centre.

Fougères

FOUGÈRES, 50km short of Rennes on the main road into Brittany from Caen, promotes itself as the *"ville au joli nom"*, *fougères* being the French for "fern". Name apart, however, it's not an especially pretty town, and it has a topography impossible to grasp from a map. Streets that look a few metres long turn out to be precipitous plunges down the escarpments of its split-levelled site, and lanes collapse into flights of steps. The only efficient way to get around, needless to say, is on foot.

Perhaps the oddest feature of the site is the positioning of the **castle**, sited in pre-artillery days well below the main part of the town, on a low spit of land that separates, and is towered over by, two mighty rock faces. Massive and stunningly strong, it was laid out in 1166 to replace a wooden fort destroyed by English invaders. Protected by great curtain-walls, and circled by a hacked-out moat full of weirs and waterfalls, it was also shielded in its heyday by the River Nançon. None of this, however, prevented its repeated capture by such medieval adventurers as, of course, du Guesclin. Today it remains a spectacular sight; the moat remains filled with water, while every crevice of the surrounding buildings seems to erupt with bright geraniums.

Within the castle keep, a romantic setting in *Les Chouans* (see box, overleaf), the focus is disappointingly prosaic. Footwear, to this day the main industry of the town, is presented in a **museum** included in the hourly **château tours** (daily: April to mid-June & second fortnight of Sept 9.30am–noon & 2–6pm; mid-June to mid-Sept 9am–7pm; Oct–March 10am–noon & 2–5pm; 30F/€4.57). Literally the high spot of the tours, in summer only, is the view from the top of its clock tower.

The best approach to the castle is from **place des Arbres** beside St-Léonard's church off the main street of the old fortified town. Footpaths, ramps and stairways drop down through successive tiers of formal public gardens, offering magnificent views of the ramparts and towers along the way, to reach the water meadows of the River Nançon. You cross the river itself beside a little cluster of medieval houses – the sculpted doorway at 6 rue de Lusignan is particularly attractive.

If, on the other hand, you take the longer route down rue Nationale, you'll pass, at no. 51, the **Musée de la Villéon** (Easter to mid-June & first fortnight of Sept Sat & Sun 11am–12.30pm & 2.30–5pm; mid-June to Aug Wed–Sun 10.30am–12.30pm & 2–6pm; free), which commemorates the Impressionist Emmanuel de la Villéon. Born in Fougères in 1858, he painted numerous memorable Breton landscapes.

Practicalities

Fougères' old *gare SNCF*, down below the modern town, has long been inactive; the **buses** to and from Vitré and Rennes that use the square beside it are the only form of public transport to pass through. The **tourist office** at 1 place Aristide-Briand provides copious information on all aspects of the town and local countryside (July & Aug Mon–Sat 9am–7pm, Sun 10am–noon & 2–4pm; Sept–June Mon–Sat 9.30am–12.30pm & 2–6pm, Sun 10am–noon & 2–4pm; ☎02.99.94.12.20, *www.ot-fougeres.fr*). It's also a stopping-point for the usual motor-driven **petit train**, which runs regular town tours for 25F/€3.81 and is most useful for sparing weary legs the climb back up from the castle.

BALZAC'S FOUGÈRES

The flavour of eighteenth-century Fougères is evoked in Balzac's *Les Chouans* – a bit of a potboiler with its absurd twists but nonetheless an essentially historical account of the events surrounding the *Chouan* rebellion in Brittany, the attempt to restore the monarchy after the Revolution. Balzac makes great play of the town's unusual layout and of the various bloodthirsty survivors of the revolt that he met while doing his research: "In 1827, an old man accompanied by his wife was selling cattle at the Fougères market unremarked and unmolested, although he was the killer of more than one hundred persons".

Just round the corner from the tourist office, on the main road, the *Hôtel des Voyageurs* at 10 place Gambetta (☎02.99.99.08.20; ②; closed second fortnight of Aug) is a particularly nice **place to stay**, with TVs in all rooms – ask for one of the quieter rooms at the back. Selecting the cheapest 95F/€14.48 menu in the excellent downstairs restaurant (run by a different management, and closed Sat) gives you the choice of poached fillet of perch, and grants you access to a well-laden *chariot des desserts*; other menus cost 135F/€20.58 and upwards. A central alternative is the *Hôtel Balzac*, in a grey-granite town house at no. 15 in the semi-pedestrianized rue Nationale (☎02.99.99.42.46; ③), with nicely refurbished rooms.

The *Buffet*, down the street from the *Balzac* at no. 53 (☎02.99.94.35.76; closed Wed evening, Sun, & first two weeks in Aug), does more economical **meals** than the *Voyageurs*: its 61F/€9.30 menu allows you to gorge yourself on full buffets of both *hors d'oeuvres* and desserts; there's no main course, but that won't be a problem.

There are no hotels in the immediate vicinity of the château, but the squares on all sides are crammed with an abundance of appealing **bars** and **crêperies**. At *Le Medieval* (☎02.99.94.92.59), which has lots of outdoor seating beside the moat, you can snack on *moules frites* or crêpes, or get a full dinner from 79F/€12.04.

The Forêt de Fougères

The **Forêt de Fougères**, stretching for roughly 8km northeast of Fougères to either side of the D177 towards Vire (see p.196), is one of the most enjoyable in the province. The beech woods are spacious and light, with various megaliths and trails of old stones scattered among the chestnut and spruce. It's quite a contrast to their normal bleak and windswept haunts to see dolmens sporting themselves in such verdant surroundings. If you have time, walk through the forest as far as **Le Chatellier**, a village set high in thick woods.

For a **horseback** tour of the Forêt de Fougères, contact the Centre d'Initiation aux Activités de Plein Air in **Chennedet** on the western edge of the forest, 5km from Fougères (☎02.99.99.18.98).

St-Aubin-du-Cormier

Halfway between Fougères and Rennes on the N12, **ST-AUBIN-DU-CORMIER** makes a peaceful overnight stop. It's a bit too peaceful perhaps – the kind of town where the only entertainment in the only bar open at ten o'clock on a Saturday night is to take it in turns to look at a pet white hamster.

There is, however, a major sight in St-Aubin – the keep of its old **castle**, which was demolished after the great battle here in 1488 in which the forces of Duke Francis were defeated by the French army. Many Breton soldiers were dressed in the English colours of a black cross on white silk, to scare the French into believing that the duke had extensive English reinforcements. The victorious French were told to spare all prisoners except the English; and so the hapless Bretons were massacred. Just one sheer wall of the castle survives, with a fireplace visible halfway up. A small **monument** in a field nearby marks the actual site of the battle.

Practicalities

St-Aubin's very cheap *Hôtel du Bretagne*, 68 rue de l'Écu (☎02.99.39.10.22; ②), has to be recommended – a rambling old building, with lumpy lino corridors stretching off in random directions upstairs, and good food downstairs. The municipal **campsite** (☎02.99.39.10.42; closed Nov–March) sprawls immediately below the castle, next to a small lake.

Half a dozen kilometres north of St-Aubin, the **Ville Olivier** on the D102 between St-Ouen and Mezières is a château that organizes riding, canoeing and kayaking, and has its own *gîte d'étape* (☎02.99.39.34.72).

Vitré

VITRÉ, just north of the Le Mans–Rennes motorway, 30km east of Rennes, is a lesser rival to Dinan as the best-preserved **medieval town** in Brittany. Occupation of the site dates right back to the Romans, when a certain Vitrius is known to have owned a villa here. While its thirteenth-century walls are no longer quite complete, their effect is enhanced by the fact that what lies outside them has changed so little. To the north are stark wooded slopes, while into the western hillside beneath the castle burrow thickets of stone cottages that must once have been Vitré's medieval slums. This little suburb is called **Rachapt**, a corruption of the French for "repurchase", in memory of the time during the Hundred Years War when the castle's defendants finally paid the English army, by whom they'd been besieged for several years, to go away. By 1589, when the castle successfully resisted a siege by the Catholic League, Vitré had become a Huguenot stronghold.

In best fairy-tale fashion, the towers of the **castle** itself, which dominates the western end of the ramparts, have pointed, slate-grey roofs that look like freshly sharpened pencils. First erected in 1060, the castle was remodelled to its present appearance two hundred years later. Unfortunately, however, the municipal offices and **museum** of shells, birds, bugs and local history inside are not exactly thrilling (April–June daily 10am–noon & 2–5.30pm; July–Sept daily 10am–6pm; Oct–March Mon, Sat & Sun 2–5.30pm, Wed–Fri 10am–noon & 2–5.30pm; 26F/€3.96).

The admission fee for the castle also includes entry to three other museums in the general vicinity, all of which are open for the same hours as the castle. The **Musée St-Nicholas**, on the western outskirts of town, occupies the huge former chapel of a fifteenth-century hospital, with a collection of medieval reliquaries and religious paraphernalia, the **Musée de la Faucillonnaie**, 3km northwest of the centre in Montreuil-sous-Pérouse, is a general mishmash of secular artefacts, mostly of more recent origin, while the **Château des Rochers Sévigné**, 10km southeast, is a place of pilgrimage for French devotees of the seventeenth-century society letter-writer Madame de Sévigné, and holds little interest for anyone not familiar with her work.

Vitré is a market town rather than an industrial centre, with its principal **market** held on Mondays in the square in front of Notre Dame church. The old city is full of twisting streets of half-timbered houses, a good proportion of which are bars. The **rue de la Baudrairie**, formerly the town's leather-working quarter, is the most picturesque, but the **rue d'en Bas**, which climbs up from Rachapt to the castle, has the best selection of bars; the *Aston*, for example, at no. 7, is a nice place to spend an evening.

An unusual visual treat, if you happen to be using the **post office**, is its modern stained-glass window behind the counter.

Practicalities

Vitré's candy-striped **gare SNCF** is on the southern edge of the centre, where the ramparts disappear and the town imperceptibly blends into its newer sectors. Just across the square from the station, you'll find the **tourist office**, on the promenade St-Yves (July & Aug daily 10am–7pm; Sept–June Mon–Fri 10am–noon & 1.30–6pm, Sat 10am–noon; ☎02.99.75.04.46, *www.ot-vitre.fr*), which runs guided tours of the town in summer (Mon, Wed & Fri at 3pm; Tues, Thurs & Sat at 10.30am; plus nightly after-dark tours at 10pm).

Most of the **hotels**, too, are near the *gare SNCF*, and Vitré makes a cheap, as well as pleasant, place to stay. The *Petit-Billot*, 5bis place du Général-Leclerc (☎02.99.75.02.10; ③), is good value, while rooms on the higher floors of the *Hôtel du Château*, 5 rue Rallon (☎02.99.74.58.59; ③; closed Sun out of season), on a quiet road just below the castle, have views of the ramparts.

Of the **restaurants**, *Le St-Yves*, immediately below the castle at 1 place St-Yves (☎02.99.74.68.76; closed Mon), serves menus from 50F/€7.62 to 175F/€26.68; the 72F/€10.98 one should suit most requirements. *La Taverne de l'Ecu*, at 12 rue de la Baudrairie (☎02.99.75.11.09; closed Tues evening & Wed), is set in a particularly attractive medieval house and serves good fishy menus from 88F/€13.42, while *La Soupe aux Choux*, a little higher up at 32 rue Notre-Dame (☎02.99.75.10.86; closed Sun off season), prepares simple but classic French food.

Around Vitré

There are several interesting smaller towns in the area. **DOMPIERRE** is attractive in its own right and claims a tiny (and disputed) place in history as the town where Roland, Charlemagne's nephew, might have died, were one to accept that the *Chanson de Roland* got the story entirely wrong.

CHAMPEAUX, 8km west of Vitré, has – is – a central paved square, surrounded by stone houses, with an ornate well in the centre. Its fifteenth-century collegiate **church** contains a superb stained-glass *Crucifixion* by Gilles de la Croix-Vallée, the ornate tombs of its founding family, and some fine carved choir stalls.

CHATEAUBOURG, halfway to Rennes, has a wonderful but expensive **hotel**, the *Ar Milin* (☎02.99.00.30.91; ⑤–⑧; restaurant closed Sun in winter), straddling the River Vilaine in huge gardens at 30 rue de Paris. Breakfast, at 50F/€7.62, consists of an enormous buffet of fresh pastries.

The Roche-aux-Fées

About 15km to the south of Chateaubourg, not far from the road just off the D341 near Retiers, the **ROCHE-AUX-FÉES** is the least visited of the major megalithic monuments of Brittany. The "fairy rock" is a twenty-metre-long covered alleyway of purplish stones, with no apparent funerary purpose or, indeed, any evidence that it was ever buried. It's set on a high and exposed spot, guarded by just a few venerable trees, and it's thought the slabs had to be dragged a good 45km to get here. There's no admission charge.

Tradition has it that engaged couples should come to the Roche-aux-Fées on the night of a full moon and separately count the stones; if they agree on the total, things are looking good.

WEST ALONG THE COAST

To the west of the Rance, beyond Dinard, stretches the green of the **Côte d'Émeraude**. While this region has its fair share of developed family resorts, such as **St-Jacut**, **Erquy** and **Le Val-André**, it also offers wonderful camping, at its best around the heather-surrounded beaches near **Cap Fréhel** – for once unencroached upon by the military.

Further west, the coast becomes wilder and harsher. Beyond **St-Brieuc** the seaside towns tend to be crammed into narrow rocky inlets or set well back in river estuaries, and only a few beaches manage to break out from the rocks. Once past **Paimpol**, the shoreline is known as the **Côte de Granit Rose** – no figure of speech, but a literal description of its primeval tangle of vast pink-granite boulders. They certainly deserve to be seen, at the very least as a quick detour before catching the ferry at Pointe de l'Arcouest (near Paimpol) for **Bréhat**.

The Côte d'Émeraude

The coast immediately **west of Dinard** is one of Brittany's most traditional family-resort areas, with old-fashioned holiday towns, safe sandy beaches and a plethora of well-organized campsites.

St-Jacut-de-la-Mer

ST-JACUT, which takes up most of the tip of a narrow peninsula roughly 16km west of St-Malo, looks today like a classic nineteenth-century bathing resort, but was in fact founded a thousand years earlier by an itinerant Irish monk. Though possibly not the most exciting of places, it has everything young children could want – good sand, rocky pools to clamber about, and woods to scramble in.

Practicalities

St-Jacut boasts one of Brittany's most distinctive **hotels**, atop the central spine of the peninsula: the *Hôtel le Vieux Moulin*, 22 rue du Moulin (☎02.96.27.71.02; ③; closed Nov–March), centres on a fifteenth-century windmill, and as a result two of its guestrooms are completely round, and offer sea views in two directions. It also serves good, if eccentric, food, with changing dinner menus priced at

100F/€15.24 and 160F/€24.39 that are apt to include (home-made) crisps as a vegetable. The summer-only *Camping municipal* is beside the plage de la Manchette (☎02.96.27.70.33; closed Oct–March).

Much the best **fish restaurant** in the area is the *Restaurant la Presqu'île*, at 164 Grande-Rue (☎02.96.27.76.47; closed Mon in low season), where the menus start at 98F/€14.94.

St-Cast-le-Guildo

The pleasant seaside community of **ST-CAST**, on the next promontory along, is a thirty-kilometre drive from St-Malo, and connected by SNCF buses with the nearest station, at Lamballe (see p.241). Most of its commercial activity takes place in the rather uninspiring Bourg, set back from the water, but the port area down below is very nice, and there are good walks along the coast to the headland.

Practicalities

Among medium-price **hotels** in St-Cast are the attractive *Hôtel des Mielles*, 3 rue du Duc d'Auguillon (☎02.96.41.80.95; ③; closed Oct–April), just a few metres from the beach, and the plainer *Chrisflo*, 19 rue du Port (☎02.96.41.88.08; ②; closed Oct to mid-April), much further back. The **tourist office** on place Charles-de-Gaulle (July & Aug Mon–Sat 9am–12.30pm & 2–7.30pm, Sun 10am–12.30pm & 3–6.30pm; Sept–June Mon–Sat 9am–noon & 2–6pm; ☎02.96.41.81.52), can provide details of local **campsites**, such as the four-star *Châtelet* beside the bay (☎02.96.41.96.33, *www.lechatelet.com*; closed mid-Sept to Easter).

Cap Fréhel

The one truly exceptional spot along the Côte d'Émeraude is **Cap Fréhel**. This high, warm expanse of heath, cliffs and heather is overvisited, but camping is prohibited for 5km around the tip. The headland itself, 400m walk from the road, remains unspoiled, with no more than a few ruins of old buildings and a small "tearoom" nearby. The rocks sixty metres down at the foot of the cliffs, busy with puffins and guillemots, officially constitute the Fauconnière **seabird sanctuary**. Offshore, the heather-covered islands are grand to look at, although too tiny to visit; the view from the cape's **lighthouse** (July & Aug daily 2–6pm; free) can extend as far as Jersey and the Île de Bréhat.

The **Fort la Latte**, to the east, is used regularly as a film set. Its tower (containing a cannonball factory) is accessible only over two drawbridges. To visit, you have to take guided tours (June–Sept daily 10am–12.30pm & 2.30–6.30pm; Oct–May Sun & hols only 2.30–5.30pm; 20F/€3.05).

Practicalities

The nearest places to stay to Cap Fréhel are the ideal, isolated **campsite** at Pléherel, the *Camping du Pont L'Étang* (☎02.96.41.40.45; closed Oct–April), and a basic summer-only **hostel** on the D16 just outside Plévenon en route towards the cape – full address: Kérivet-en-Frehel, La Ville Hardrieux (☎02.96.41.48.98; 48F/€7.32; closed mid-Sept to March) – which also rents out bicycles.

Erquy

The perfect-crescent beach at **ERQUY**, around 20km west of Cap Fréhel, curves through more than 180 degrees, and is home to schools of both **sailing** (☎02.96.72.32.62) and **diving** (☎02.96.72.49.67). At low tide, the sea disappears way beyond the harbour entrance, leaving gentle ripples of paddling sand. Adventurers equipped with suitable boots could walk right across its mouth, from the grassy wooded headland on the left side over to the picturesque little lighthouse at the end of the jetty on the right.

In July and August, Les Vedettes de Bréhat (☎02.96.55.79.50, *www.vedettesdebrehat .com*) operate boat trips every four or five days, depending on the tides, from Erquy (8am or 8.30am; 160F/€24.39) and in some cases also nearby Dahouët (8.45am or 9.15am; 160F/€24.39) out to the Île de Bréhat (see p.249).

Practicalities

Erquy's **tourist office** on the boulevard de la Mer (mid-June to mid-Sept daily 9.30am–12.30pm & 2–7pm; mid-Sept to mid-June Tues–Sun 9.30am–12.30pm & 2–5pm; ☎02.96.72.30.12) co-ordinates information for the surrounding area. The *Hôtel Beauséjour*, 21 rue de la Corniche (☎02.96.72.30.39; ③; closed Sun evening & Mon in winter), has a good view of the bay, and excellent fish dinners from 82F/€12.50, while the more upmarket **restaurant** *l'Escurial* (☎02.96.72.31.56; closed Sun evening & Mon) by the seafront serves a five-course menu (for 220F/€33.54) that consists entirely of scallops, the town's speciality.

There are several **campsites** on the promontory (dotted with tiny coves) that leads to the Cap d'Erquy north of town, including the three-star *St-Pabu* (☎02.96.72.24.65; closed mid-Oct to March), right beside the sea.

Le Val-André and around

The beach in the broader bay of **LE VAL-ANDRÉ**, another 11km down the coast, is not only on a slightly larger scale to that of Erquy, but it's composed of finer and somehow sweeter-smelling sand. The endless pedestrian promenade that stretches along the seafront feels oddly Victorian, consisting solely of huge old houses undisturbed by shops or bars. However, Le Val-André is definitely more of a town than Erquy, and rue A-Charner, running parallel to the sea one street back, is busy with holiday-makers in summer.

Practicalities

Le Val-André's helpful **tourist office** (July & Aug Mon–Sat 9am–1pm & 2–7pm, Sun 10am–12.30pm & 4–6pm; Sept–June Mon–Sat 10am–12.30pm & 4–6pm; ☎02.96.72.20.55) is located in the modern casino at the very centre of the waterfront.

Of its **hotels**, the tastefully refurbished *Hotel de la Mer*, 63 rue A-Charner (☎02.96.72.20.44; ③; closed Jan), serves food that is utterly magnificent, using a fine muscadet to transport the *moules marinières* on their 125F/€19.06 menu onto a hitherto undreamed-of plane. However, with the success of the business many guests find themselves having to sleep in the characterless *Nuit et Jour* motel, run by the same management, and one group even reported having to sleep in their car after being locked out of the hotel after an evening drink. The imposing *Hôtel Printania*, 34 rue Charles-Cotard (☎02.96.72.20.51; ②; closed mid-Oct to Easter), is a more dependable if perhaps less exciting choice, where certain rooms have attractive seaview balconies.

The *Restaurant au Biniou*, 121 rue Clémenceau (☎02.96.72.24.35; closed Wed in low season, and all Jan), is the best of several adjacent seafood specialists just back from the casino; in addition to the usual choices, its 95F/€14.48 menu features stuffed mussels and oysters.

Dahouët

A few kilometres west of Le Val-André – reachable by an enjoyable footpath around the headland – the small lagoon of **DAHOUËT** is more secluded, and has its own **campsite**. Though it's known to have been used by Viking raiders over a thousand years ago, the construction of a large yachting marina has obliterated all significant traces of its past.

St-Brieuc

The major city on the Côte d'Émeraude, **ST-BRIEUC**, is far too busy being the industrial centre of the north to concern itself with entertaining tourists. It's an odd-looking city, with two very deep, wooded valleys spanned by viaducts at its core, and it's almost impossible to bypass, however you may be travelling. The streets are hectic, with the town centre cut in two by a virtual motorway, unrelieved by any public parks, and not much distinguished either by a mega-shopping complex. Motorists and cyclists, unfortunately, have little choice but to plough straight through rather than attempting to negotiate the back roads and steep hills around.

Every July, St-Brieuc makes a concession to summer visitors by organizing a **Festival of Breton Music**, while at the end of May comes the **Art Rock Festival** (☎02.96.33.77.50); if you're interested, the tourist office (see below) can supply relevant information on both. Worth looking in on, too, is the **Comité Départmentale de Tourisme** for the Côtes-du-Nord at 29 rue des Promenades (☎02.96.62.72.00, *www.cotesdarmor.com*). Throughout the summer they organize one-day tours in the area to visit craft workshops of every variety – taxidermists, bakers, farmers, and makers of furniture and of cider.

Practicalities

Trains between Paris, Dol and Brest stop at the **gare SNCF**, around 1km south of the centre of St-Brieuc, and regular **buses** run to the nearby resorts. There's an information desk at the station in summer, though the official **tourist office** is in the town centre, right by the cathedral at 7 rue St-Gouéno (July & Aug Mon–Sat 9am–7pm, Sun 10am–1pm; Sept–June Mon–Sat 9am–noon & 2–6.30pm; ☎02.96.33.22.50, *www.mairie-saint-brieuc.fr*).

The two best-value central places to **stay** are the *Champ de Mars*, 13 rue de Général-Leclerc (☎02.96.33.60.99; ③), where the old-fashioned green-painted brasserie downstairs serves mussels or fish soup for around 50F/€7.62, and the *Duguesclin*, 2 place Duguesclin (☎02.96.33.11.58; ③). St-Brieuc also has a **hostel**, 3km northwest of the place du Champ-de-Mars, in the magnificent fifteenth-century Manoir de la Ville-Guyomard (☎02.96.78.70.70; dorm beds around 60F/€9.15 per night); served by bus #1 from the station, it offers bicycles and canoes for rent.

Some of the nicest **eating** options in town are in the old quarter, up the small hill behind the cathedral. The traditional French cooking at *Le Madure*, 14 rue Quinquaine (☎02.96.61.21.07; closed Sun & Mon), is served à la carte, with steaks around 87F/€13.26 and salads half that; the fondues at *Le Chaudron*, 19 rue Fardel (☎02.96.33.01.72; closed Sun), start at 80F/€12.20 per person.

The Inland Route: West to Morlaix

While following the coast from Dinard and Dinan is much the most scenic route westwards across Brittany, it can also be pretty slow. Travellers in a hurry to reach Morlaix and Finistère can choose instead to head **inland**, either by branching onto the D768 just south of St-Jacut, or following the N176 west out of Dinan. Both routes pass through the occasional time-forgotten little town or village; few have much in the way of tourist facilities but all make potentially pleasant opportunities to stretch your legs.

Jugon-les-Lacs

Tiny old **JUGON-LES-LACS** lies 15km southwest of the market town of **Plancoët** (home of a popular brand of mineral water, obtainable there for free). Jugon is poised at one end of its own artificial lake – the *grand étang* – which was originally created for defensive purposes during the twelfth century. Peculiarly, the central place du Martray – scene of a market each Friday – is well below the water level, and you have to climb uphill to reach the massive cobblestone dyke that shields it from inundation. At the opposite end of town, the N176 crosses high above the valley on a viaduct. Jugon, nestled cosily between the two, has no room to expand even if it wanted to – it's a subdued but atmospheric place, whose few streets are almost deserted in the evenings.

For most of the way around **the lake**, there's no approach road or footpath, only meadows and trees sweeping down to the water. However, at *Le Bocage* **campsite** (☎02.96.31.60.16; closed Oct–April), just out of town along the D52 towards Mégrit, there's a small beach from which you can go swimming. It's very much a family campsite, with a heated swimming pool as well, and there are boats and **windsurfers** for hire – and tuition available – from its École de Voile (☎02.96.31.64.58).

Practicalities
The local **tourist office** is in the Hôtel de Ville on the main square (July & Aug Mon–Sat 9.30am–12.30pm & 3–6pm; ☎02.96.31.70.75, *www.jugon-les-lacs.com*). Among the handful of moderately priced **hotels** in Jugon is *La Grande Fontaine*, 7 rue Penthièvre (☎02.96.31.61.29; ③), a couple of hundred metres east of the centre on the main road towards Dinan, which has menus from 68F/€10.37 and a lively bar.

Lamballe

The main N176 westwards from Jugon brings you after 20km to **LAMBALLE**, an old town crammed into a narrow valley beside a broad river, dominated by a church high up on battlement walls. Its most famous former citizen was the princess of Lamballe, a lady-in-waiting to Marie Antoinette, who was guillotined in 1792.

Lamballe's picturesque main square, once again called the **place du Martray**, is dominated by fourteenth-century half-timbered buildings, the grandest of which is the **Maison du Bourreau**. Formerly home to the town's public executioner – the word "Martray" means "martyr", and so the place du Martray customarily denotes the square where executions took place – it now houses not only the **tourist office** (April–June & Sept Mon–Sat 10am–12.30pm & 2–6pm; July & Aug Mon–Sat 9.30am–6.30pm, Sun 10am–noon; Oct–March Mon–Sat 10am–12.30pm & 2–5pm; ☎02.96.31.05.38), but also a couple of tiny **museums** (same hours; 10F/€1.52). One explores the town's history, and features a fascinating model of Lamballe as it looked in 1417; the other focuses on the paintings of local-born Mathurin Méheut.

A branch of the **national stud** (the *haras national*) all but adjoins the main square. Though not quite on the same scale as Le Notre's dramatic park near Argentan (see p.185), and specializing in any case more in sturdy Breton workhorses than glossy thoroughbreds, it will still delight any horse-lover (mid-June to mid-Sept daily 10am–noon & 2–5.45pm; mid-Sept to mid-June Wed, Sat & Sun 2–5.45pm; 25F/€3.81). It's the focus of a big **horse festival** on the first weekend after August 15.

Practicalities

Central **hotel-restaurants** in Lamballe include two *logis*, the *Lion d'Or*, 3 rue du Lion d'Or (☎02.96.31.20.36; ③), and the *Tour d'Argent*, at no. 2 on rue Dr-Lavagne, which becomes the D102 (☎02.96.31.01.37; ③). *La Tête Noire*, near the tourist office on place du Martray (☎02.96.50.88.74), is a glorious medieval tavern-cum-bistro.

Moncontour

The attractive little hill town of **MONCONTOUR**, 18km southeast of Lamballe and 23km southwest of St-Brieuc, was during the Middle Ages one of the more prosperous towns of the region, thanks to its hemp industry. Having been under no pressure to grow since then, it remains largely enclosed by its medieval fortifications – not that you get much impression of them once you're actually in the town, as the houses all face inwards onto the narrow streets.

Moncontour centres on the pretty, triangular **place du Penthièvre**, where the Romanesque tower of the church of St-Mathurin was blessed in 1902 by the addition of a delightfully eccentric new belfry, a confection of wooden eaves and grey-slate domes that now constitutes the highest point on the hill.

Practicalities

Moncontour's **tourist office** can be found at 4 place de la Carrière (daily: mid-June to mid-July & Sept 10am–12.30pm & 2.30–6.30pm; mid-July to Aug 10am–6.30pm; ☎02.96.73.50.50). The village lacks any hotels, but it can offer a beautifully situated **B&B**, the four-room *Chambres d'hôte à la Garde Ducale*, in a sixteenth-century house at 10 place Penthièvre (☎02.96.73.52.18; ③). Near the tourist office, the *Chaudron Magique* (☎02.96.73.40.34; closed Sun evening & Mon off-season) is a medieval theme **restaurant** where costumed waiters can serve you a decent meal for 68F/€10.37 and upwards.

On the final Sunday of August, Moncontour echoes its days of glory by playing host to a hectic and atmospheric "medieval fair".

Quintin

QUINTIN, 20km southwest of St-Brieuc, is in the official jargon "a little city of character", which prospered as a weaving community in the seventeenth and eighteenth centuries, and remains pretty much intact. Work on its grand **château** began in 1640, and was never completed, but you can tour a few of the rooms and see displays on the area (May to mid-June & final fortnight of Sept daily except Tues 2.30–5.30pm; mid-June to mid-Sept daily 10.30am–12.30pm & 1.30–6.30pm; Oct–April Sat & Sun 2.30–5.30pm; 30F/€4.57). It's at its most imposing, however, when seen from down by the River Gouët below.

A twenty-minute stroll up from the river can show you the best of what Quintin has to offer. Follow the rue du Vau-du-Gouët from the east, and climb a stone staircase up through the vestiges of the old town walls, which are overshadowed by the round **Tour des Archives**, covered with creeping wild flowers. At the top is the late nineteenth-century **Basilique Notre Dame**. Beyond that, you enter the central place 1830, with the rue Grande stretching ahead. Most of its houses are made of elegant grey stone, standing proudly to attention, but a few of their half-timbered predecessors still slouch here and there in the ranks.

Turn right at the Hôtel de Ville at the far end of the rue Grande, and you'll soon come to the walled **Parc de Roz Maria**. These attractive formal gardens were laid out in the eighteenth century, and still hold a large public washplace that's now overgrown with green algae.

Practicalities

Quintin's **tourist office** is at no. 6 on the main place 1830 (July & Aug Mon–Sat 9am–12.30pm & 2–6.30pm, Sun 10am–12.30pm & 2–5pm; Sept–June Tues–Sat 9am–noon & 2–5.30pm; ☎02.96.74.01.51). The ivy-coated *Hôtel du Commerce*, on the western fringes of the centre at 2 rue Rochenen (☎02.96.74.94.67; ②; closed mid-Dec to mid-Jan, plus Sun evening & Mon evening in low season), is a classic little village **hotel**, tasteful if far from fancy. Its solemn but attractive dining room serves good meals from 70F/€10.67 upwards.

Guingamp and around

Should you choose to skip St-Brieuc and the Côte de Granit Rose (see p.251), the most direct route towards Finistère carries across the centre of the northern peninsula. The only town of any size here is the old weaving centre of **GUINGAMP** – its name possibly the source of the striped or checked fabric "gingham". It's an attractive place of cobbled streets, but there's not much to see beyond the main square, where a fountain bedecked in griffins and gargoyles is overlooked by a splendid pair of lopsided old timber-frame houses propping each other up, and the Black Virgin in the thirteenth-century **basilica**.

Guingamp does, however, boast the remarkable distinction, for a town with fewer than ten thousand inhabitants, of having a **football** team in the First Division of the French league. They take on the likes of Nantes and Monaco at the Roudourou stadium on the edge of town. Other events include a big *pardon*, featuring a night procession to the basilica, held on the first Saturday in July, while a ten-day **Festival de la Danse Bretonne** enlivens the middle of August.

Practicalities

Guingamp is the first rail stop west of St-Brieuc; its **gare SNCF** (☎02.96.43.70.53) is southeast of the place Champ-au-Roy, where you'll find the **tourist office** (July & Aug Mon–Sat 10am–12.30pm & 1.30–6pm, Sun 10am–1pm; Sept–June Tues–Sat 10am–noon & 2–6pm; ☎02.96.43.73.89) and the **gare routière**.

Of its **hotels**, the white-painted *Hôtel d'Armor*, 44 bd Clémenceau (☎02.96.43.76.16, *hotelarmor.guingamp@wanadoo.fr*; ③; closed Sun), is probably the best value, and has a nice garden around the back. The best **restaurant** in town, however, is in the expensive hotel *Le Relais du Roy*, 42 place du Centre (☎02.96.43.76.62; ⑤), where you can eat in the magnificent dining room for a minimum of 125F/€19.06.

The Ménéz Bré

On the road out towards Morlaix is the "mountain" of the **Ménéz Bré**, a spectacular height amid these plains. In the mid-nineteenth century the local rector was often observed to climb, laden with books, to the mountain's peak on stormy nights, accompanied only by a donkey. For all his exemplary piety, his parishioners suspected him of sorcery and witchcraft; he was in fact doing early research into natural electrical forces.

The Baie de St-Brieuc

St-Brieuc itself may be more of an obstacle to be avoided than an appealing destination, but it serves as a gateway to the further series of attractive little resorts that dot its eponymous bay. It also marks the point at which visitors usually begin to become aware that Brittany really does amount to something more than just another indistinguishable corner of the French coastline, and has its own very distinct culture and traditions.

As you move northwest from St-Brieuc along the edge of the V-shaped bay towards Paimpol, the countryside becomes especially rich – it's called the **Goëlo** – while the coast itself grows wilder and harsher. The seaside towns tend to be crammed into narrow rocky inlets or set well back in river estuaries.

Binic

BINIC is probably the nicest place to stay on the Baie de St-Brieuc. The whole place is on a very small scale with a narrow port, a sandy beach, a tiny promenade around the town and to either side Devon-like meadows that roll down to the sea. In the mid-nineteenth century, Binic was said to be one of the busiest ports in all France; these days it's simply a minor but appealing tourist resort, with a lucrative sideline of selling mud from the River Ic for fertilizer.

Six kilometres west of Binic, just off the D47, the **Jardin Zoologique de Bretagne**, also known as the Zoo de Trégomeur, is a leafy park that holds the likes of llamas, ostriches and zebras in deceptively natural surroundings, and fiercer creatures such as lions firmly behind bars (Easter–Sept daily 10am–7pm; Oct–Easter Wed & Sun 2–5pm; 50F/€7.62).

Les Vedettes de Bréhat (☎02.96.55.79.50, *www.vedettesdebrehat.com*) run occasional day-trips between July and mid-September from Binic to the Île de Bréhat (see p.249), costing 170F/€25.92 and setting off at 8am.

Practicalities

The good if relatively pricey *Hôtel Benhuyc*, 1 quai Jean-Bart (☎02.96.73.39.00; ④; closed Jan), offers the only waterfront **accommodation** in town, but there are several nearby **campsites**, the best of them the secluded three-star *Les Madières* to the south (☎02.96.79.02.48; closed Oct–April), back from the sea off the main road near the village of **PORDIC**.

St-Quay-Portrieux

ST-QUAY, a little to the north, is considerably more upmarket and a bit soulless, though there's certainly a lot of activity going on in its sister town of **POR-TRIEUX**, where a new yachting marina has encouraged what used to be a slightly seedy waterfront – dating back to the days of the Newfoundland fishing fleets (see p.247) – to smarten itself up.

Between mid-June and mid-September, Les Vedettes de Bréhat (☎02.96.55.79.50, *www.vedettesdebrehat.com*) run a few sailings each week, according to an erratic schedule, from Portrieux to the Île de Bréhat (see p.249), for a return fare of 170F/€25.92 (departures 8.30am).

Practicalities

The **tourist office** for St-Quay-Portrieux is at 17bis rue Jeanne d'Arc (July & Aug Mon–Sat 9am–12.30pm & 1.30–7.30pm, Sun 10am–12.30pm & 3–6pm; Sept–June Mon–Sat 9am–12.30pm & 2–6.30pm; ☎02.96.70.40.64, *saintquayportrieux@ wanadoo.fr*).

In St-Quay itself, the *Gerbot d'Avoine*, 2 bd de Littoral (☎02.96.70.40.09; ③; closed Jan, restaurant closed Sun evening & Mon evening in low season) beside the beach, is an entertaining *logis*, where the food is good, with menus from 90F/€13.72 upwards, but the decor upstairs is truly astonishing. Crimson carpets creeping up the corridor walls make it look hideously like the hotel in *The Shining*, while in the rooms themselves washbasins and even showers are discreetly hidden away in cupboards. The *Hôtel le Commerce*, 4 rue Georges-Clemenceau (☎02.96.70.41.53; ③), is an alternative if you'd rather stay close to the harbour in Portrieux.

Kermaria-an-Isquit

You may well get your first exposure to spoken Breton in smaller villages such as **KERMARIA-AN-ISQUIT**. This is not an easy place to find, especially coming from Lanloup to the north; the best signposted of its approaches is along the D21 from Plouha. Nonetheless, a fairly constant trickle of visitors make their way here

---

INTO THE BRETON HEARTLAND

At **Plouha**, a short way along the D786 from St-Quay, you cross what was traditionally the boundary between French-speaking "Upper Brittany" and Breton-speaking "Lower Brittany". As a general indication, you can tell which language used to be spoken in a particular area by its place names. Thus, from here on west there is a preponderance of names beginning with the Breton "PLOU" (meaning parish), "TREZ" (sand or beach), "KER" (town) or "PENN" (head). See Contexts for a comprehensive glossary of Breton words that you are likely to come across.

throughout the summer to see the village's **chapel** and its extraordinary *Dance of Death*, one of the most striking of all French medieval images. The caretaker, Mme Hervé Droniou, usually keeps the church open (daily 9am–noon & 2–6pm; donation); when it's closed, you have to find her in the house just up the road on the left to let you in.

The **Dance of Death** is no delicate miniature. This huge series of frescoes – depicting Ankou, the skeletal death-figure, leading representatives of all social classes in a *Danse Macabre* – covers the arcades all round the chapel. Painted at the end of the plague-fearing fifteenth century, they were subsequently white-washed over, not to be rediscovered until 1856. Since then, much of the work has vanished altogether, especially on the ceiling, and even in what survives the original colours have faded, and the figures are often no more than silhouettes. However, the fresco has lost little of its power to shock; a look at the hand-drawn copies made in 1861, on show below the real thing, reveals quite how grotesquely menacing the figure of death could be.

In yellow, on a red background, the skeleton alternates with such living characters as a King, a Knight, a Bishop and a Peasant. Verses below, now mostly illegible though available in transcription, have each person pleading for life and lamenting death, while Ankou insists that all must in the end come to him. A wall to the left of the altar holds a representation of the classic medieval theme of the encounter between the *Trois Vifs*, three finely apparelled noblemen out hunting, with the *Trois Morts*, three corpses reflecting in a cemetery on the transience of all things human:

> *Nous avons bien este en chance*
> *Autrefoys, comme estes a present*
> *Mais vous viendrez a nostre dance*
> *Comme nous sommes maintenant.*

In other words, we were lucky enough once to be like you, but you'll have to come and join our dance in the end.

The chapel was originally the property of the lords of the manor of Noë Vert, and is said to be linked by a tunnel, long since flooded, to their manor house 5km away. It was known in Breton as "Itron Varia An Iskuit", meaning "Our Lady Who Helps". A small display case behind the altar contains the skull of one of the lords, and a couple of grotesque heart-shaped boxes hold the hearts of another and his wife. To the right, a unique statue shows the infant Jesus refusing milk from the Virgin's proffered breast, symbolizing the choice of celestial over terrestrial food.

Abbaye de Beauport

Mid-June to mid-Sept daily 10am–7pm, with regular 1hr 30min guided tours; mid-Sept to mid-June daily except Tues 10am–noon & 2–5pm. 25F/€3.81.

As the D786 north of Kermaria and Binic meanders back towards the shoreline, a couple of kilometres short of Paimpol, it passes the substantial ruins of the **Abbaye de Beauport**. The abbey of Bellus Portus was established in 1202 by Count Alain de Goëlo, in memory of his parents. Sited halfway between St-Brieuc and Tréguier, its primary function was as a way station for English pilgrims en route to Compostella. Much of its income was drawn from thirteen parishes in Lincolnshire, and it never really recovered after the Reformation in England threw the monks here back onto their own resources. A merchant from Paimpol bought the entire estate after the Revolution, and his family owned it until 1992, when they sold it to the State.

The abbey is currently being restored, but the main appeal for visitors is the sheer romance of its setting and semi-dilapidated condition. Its stone walls are covered with wild flowers and ivy, the central cloisters are engulfed by a huge tree, and birds fly everywhere. The Norman Gothic **chapterhouse** is the most noteworthy building to survive, but wandering through and over the roofless halls you may spot architectural relics from all periods of its history.

The monks' refectory looks out across the **salt meadows** where they raised their sheep, and planted orchards on land that they reclaimed from the sea with an intricate network of dams. Footpaths lead all the way down to the sea, offering the same superb views of the hilltop abbey that must have been appreciated by generations of arriving pilgrims.

Paimpol

Though still an attractive town, with a tangle of cobbled alleyways lined with fine grey-granite houses, **PAIMPOL** has lost something in its transition from working fishing port to pleasure harbour. It was once the centre of a cod and whaling fleet that sailed for the fisheries of Iceland each February, sent off with a ceremony marked by a famous *pardon*. From then until August or September, the town would be empty of all young men. Within a few years of the first expedition in 1852, the annual exodus consisted of as many as fifty vessels, with 25 men in each. A haunting glimpse of the way Paimpol used to look can be seen in the recently rereleased silent film of Pierre Loti's book *Pêcheur d'Islande*, made on location here by Jacques de Baroncelli in 1924. Loti, and the heroine of his book, lived in the **place du Martray** in the centre of town.

Thanks to naval shipyards and the like, the open sea is not visible from Paimpol; a maze of waterways leads to its two separate harbours. Both are usually filled with the high masts of yachts, but still also used by the fishing boats that keep a fish market and a plethora of *poissonneries* busy. This is doubtless a very pleasant place to arrive by yacht, threading through the rocks, but from close quarters the tiny port area is a little disappointing, very much rebuilt and quite plain. Even so, it is always lively in summer.

Arrival and information

Between June and September, four or five daily trains take 45 minutes to connect the **gare SNCF** in Paimpol (☎02.96.20.81.22) with **Guingamp**; there are also regular **buses** to and from St-Brieuc and Lannion. In addition, also in summer only and also from the *gare SNCF*, the restored **steam train** known as **La Vapeur de Trieux** chugs its way on regular excursions through the Trieux Valley between Paimpol and **PONTRIEUX** to the southwest, passing within view of the Château de la Roche-Jagu (June & Sept departs Paimpol Wed–Sat 11.30am; July & Aug departs Paimpol between 5 and 7 days each week at 10am & 2.45pm; ☎02.96.20.52.06; 120F/€18.29 return, ages 4–11 60F/€9.15).

Paimpol's **tourist office** is in the Hôtel de Ville on rue Pierre-Feutren, near the prominent Notre Dame church (June to mid-Sept Mon–Sat 9am–7.30pm, Sun 10am–1pm; mid-Sept to May Tues–Sat 10am–noon & 2.30–6pm; ☎02.96.20.83.16).

Accommodation

Most of Paimpol's nicest **hotels** are clustered together on the northern side of the port, either right on the waterfront or in the network of semi-pedestrianized little alleyways just behind. There's also a year-round **hostel** in the grand old *Château de Kerraoul*, 2km west (☎02.96.20.83.60), which offers dorm beds for around 65F/€9.91 and has facilities for camping.

Hôtel Berthelot, 1 rue du Port (☎02.96.20.88.66). Very hospitable place, set slightly back from the pleasure port. ②.

Le Goëlo, quai Duguay-Truin (☎02.96.20.82.74, fax 02.96.20.58.93). Bright-pink, modern hotel in the ugly new block that lines the inland side of the fishing harbour, and which houses the simple brasserie *La Chaumière*. ③.

Hôtel de la Marne, 30 rue de la Marne (☎02.96.20.82.16, fax 02.96.20.92.07). Smart, twelve-room *logis de France* a little way back from the port, with a formal restaurant offering menus from 105F/€16.01. Closed Sun evenings & Mon in low season. ④.

Hôtel Origano, 7bis rue du Quai (☎02.96.22.05.49). Somewhat plain, but very comfortable hotel, opposite the *Berthelot*. Closed Dec–Easter. ③.

Le Repaire de Kerroc'h, 29 quai Morand (☎02.96.20.50.13, fax 02.96.22.07.46). The most luxurious option, in a grand old house overlooking the small-boat harbour, and serving gourmet meals from 125F/€19.06 (145F/€22.11 on Sun) up to 350F/€53.36. Closed Tues & Wed lunchtimes in low season, plus mid-Jan to Feb. ④.

Eating and drinking

Appealing **restaurants** stand on all sides of the port, as well as in the backstreets of the town proper, near the marketplace. The *Corto Maltese* **bar**, at 11 rue du Quai very near the *Origano* hotel, serves a fine selection of British and other beers.

La Cotriade, quai Armand-Dayot (☎02.96.20.81.08). On the far side of the harbour to the town centre, but a great bet for authentic fish dishes, with a simple 95F/€14.48 menu and a 165F/€25.15 menu featuring a delicious crab mousse. They positively prefer diners to pay using credit cards. Closed Wed evening & Thurs.

Crêperie-Restaurant Morel, 11 place du Martray (☎02.96.20.86.34). Cavernous place in the heart of town, popular with locals not only for its inexpensive crêpes, but also for its good-value daily bistro specials. Closed Sun in low season, plus mid-Nov to mid-Dec.

La Vieille Tour, 13 rue de l'Église (☎02.96.20.83.18). Cosy but sophisticated upstairs dining room, tucked away from the port in the cobbled pedestrian area, and offering top-quality seafood; go for the sea trout on the 120F/€18.29 menu. Closed Sun evening, plus Wed in low season.

Loguivy-sur-mer

If Paimpol is too crowded for you, it's well worth continuing a few kilometres further across the headland to reach the little fishing hamlet of **LOGUIVY**. All of the long river inlets along this northern coast tend to conceal tiny coves – at Loguivy a working harbour manages to squeeze into one such gap in the rocks. Lenin holed up here for his summer holidays for two months in 1902, straight from three years of forced labour in Siberia.

Loguivy's one **hotel** is right on the waterfront, looking out towards Bréhat: *Le Grand Large* (☎02.96.20.90.16; ④; closed Sun evening & Mon in winter, plus all Jan) serves absolutely superb fishy dinners from 90F/€13.72 – look out for the chef's speciality, a salad of seared scallops – and has a nice little outdoor terrace. However, only four of its six guestrooms enjoy sea views; the others are dark and unpleasant. There are also *chambres d'hôte* (which work out little cheaper) at **Kéréveur** (M Chaboud; ☎02.96.55.82.76; ②) and **Kerloury** (I. Le Goaster; ☎02.96.20.85.23; ②).

The Île de Bréhat

The **ÎLE DE BRÉHAT** – in reality two islands joined by a tiny slip of a bridge – gives the appearance of spanning great latitudes. On the north side are windswept meadows of hemlock and yarrow, sloping down to chaotic erosions of rock; on the south, you're in the midst of palm trees, mimosa and eucalyptus. All around is a multitude of little islets – some accessible at low tide, others *propriété privée*, most just pink-orange rocks. All in all, this has to be one of the most beautiful places in Brittany, renowned as a sanctuary not only for rare species of **wild flowers**, but also for **birds** of all kinds. Individual private gardens are also meticulously tended, so you can always anticipate a magnificent display of colour, for example in summer from the erupting blue acanthus.

As you might expect, a high proportion of the homes on this island paradise now belong to summer-only visitors from Paris and beyond, and young Bréhatins leave in ever-increasing numbers for lack of a place of their own, let alone a job. In winter the remaining three hundred or so natives have the place to themselves, without even a *gendarme*; the summer sees two imported from the mainland, along with upwards of three thousand temporary residents and a hundred times as many day-trippers.

GETTING TO BRÉHAT

Bréhat is connected regularly by **ferry** from the Pointe de l'Arcouest, 6km north-west of Paimpol, and served by regular buses in summer from the *gare SNCF* there. Sailings, with Les Vedettes de Bréhat (☎02.96.55.79.50, *www.vedettesdebrehat .com*), are roughly half-hourly in July & Aug, hourly between April and June and in September, and every two hours for the rest of the year, with the first boat out to Bréhat at 8.30am in summer, and the last boat back at 7.45pm. The return trip costs 40F/€6.10, while bringing your own bike costs an additional 50F/€7.62; to do so in summer you have to catch a ferry before 10am, and leave the island before 4pm. The same company also operates boats in summer from Erquy, Dahouët, Binic and St-Quay-Portrieux.

In addition, between six and eight 45-minute guided **boat tours** (70F/€10.67) circle the island each day in July and August, and there's at least one per day between April and mid-October.

All boats to Bréhat arrive at the small harbour of **PORT-CLOS**, though depending on the level of the tide passengers may have to walk several hundred metres before setting foot on terra firma. No **cars** are permitted on the island – there's barely a road wide enough for its few light farm vehicles – so many visitors rent **bikes** at the ferry port, at prices ranging from 35F/€5.34 for two hours up to 70F/€10.67 for a full day. However, it's easy enough to explore the whole place on foot; walking from one end to the other takes less than an hour.

Each batch of new arrivals invariably heads first to Bréhat's village, **LE BOURG**, which stands 500m up from the port and is the centre of all activity on the island. As well as a handful of hotels, restaurants and bars, it also holds a limited array of shops, a post office, a bank and an ATM machine, and hosts a small **market** most days. In high season, the attractive central square tends to be packed fit to burst, with exasperated holiday-home owners pushing their little hand-wagons through the throngs of day-trippers.

Continue a short distance north of Le Bourg, however, and you'll soon cross over the slender **Pont ar Prat bridge** to the northern island, where the crowds thin out, and countless little coves offer opportunities to sprawl on the tough grass or clamber across the rugged boulders. Though the coastal footpath around this northern half – in theory, banned to bicycles – offers the most attractive walking on the island, the best **beaches** line the southern shores, with the **Grève de Guerzido**, facing the mainland at its southeastern corner, being the pick of the crop.

Bréhat no longer has a castle (blown up twice by the English), but it does have a couple of lighthouses and a nineteenth-century **fort**, in the woods near the campsite (see opposite).

Practicalities

Bréhat's **tourist office** is in the old Mairie in the main square in Le Bourg (April–Sept Mon–Sat 10am–1pm & 2.30–6pm; ☎02.96.20.04.15, *syndicatdinitia-tive.brehat@wanadoo.fr*). All three of the island's **hotels** tend to be permanently booked through the summer, and close for at least part of the winter. Both the *Bellevue*, right by the *embarcadère* in Port-Clos (☎02.96.20.00.05; ⑤; closed mid-Nov to mid-Feb), and the *Vieille Auberge*, on your left as you enter Le Bourg (☎02.96.20.00.24; ⑤; closed Dec–Easter), insist on *demi-pension* in high season, unlike the smaller *Aux Pêcheurs* (☎02.96.20.00.14; ③; closed Nov–March), on the main square in Le Bourg, with a nice little garden terrace. There's also a wonderful **campsite** in the woods high above the sea west of the port (☎02.96.20.00.36; closed Oct–April). When that's closed, you can pitch your tent almost anywhere.

In addition to the three hotels, all of which serve the usual array of set-price menus – the *Bellevue* being the most expensive – there are several **restaurants** and snackeries in Le Bourg. Elsewhere on the island, your choice is restricted to the well-shaded *La Potinière* by the beach at Guerzido (☎02.96.20.00.29; closed Oct–Easter), which serves inexpensive *moules frites*, oysters and the like, and *Le Paradis Rose*, just short of the Paon Lighthouse on the north island, which is in reality no more than a crêpe and hot-dog stand, but is set in such a gorgeous garden that it makes an ideal lunchtime halt for round-island walkers.

The Côte de Granit Rose

The whole of the northernmost stretch of the Breton coast, from Bréhat to Trégastel, has loosely come to be known as the **Côte de Granit Rose**. Great granite boulders are indeed scattered in the sea around the island of Bréhat, and at the various headlands to the west, but the most memorable stretch of coast lies around **Perros-Guirec**, where the pink-granite rocks are eroded into fantastic shapes.

Pink granite is an absolutely gorgeous stone, wearing smooth and soft but also glittering sharply. It's hard to tire of it – which is just as well, for everything in this area seems to be made of it: the houses are faced with granite blocks, and the streets paved with them; the breakwaters in the sea are granite, and the polished pillars of the banks are granite; the hotels even have overgrown granite mini-golfs with little pink-granite megaliths as obstacles; and the markets claim to sell *granit-smith* apples.

Tréguier

The D786 turns west from Paimpol, passing over a green *ria* on the bridge outside Lézardrieux before arriving at **TRÉGUIER**. This is one of the very few hill-towns in Brittany, set at the junction of the Jaudy and Guindy rivers. It was rebuilt on this fortified elevation in 848 AD after an earlier monastery was destroyed by Norman raiders.

The central unmissable feature of Tréguier is the **Cathédrale de St-Tugdual**, whose geometric Gothic spire, dotted with holes, contrasts sharply with its earlier Romanesque "Hastings" tower. Inside, the masonry blocks are appealingly crude, and dripping with damp that has somehow spared the intricate carved animal on the wooden stalls. The cathedral contains the tomb of St Yves, a native of the town who died in 1303 and – for his incorruptibility – became the patron saint of lawyers. Attempts to bribe him continue to this day; his tomb is surrounded by marble plaques and an inferno of candles invoking his aid, including one special plea from a group of American lawyers. A *pardon* of St Yves is held each year on the Sunday closest to his feast day, May 19.

The half-timbered houses of the square outside look down on a statue of Ernest Renan, a local writer and philosopher whose work formed part of the great nineteenth-century attempt to reinterpret traditional religious faith in the light of scientific discoveries. Worthy Catholics were so incensed at the erection of this memorial in 1903 that they soon built their own "Calvary of Reparation" on the quayside.

Practicalities

Tréguier's **tourist office** is in the Hôtel de Ville, round the back of the cathedral (mid-June to mid-Sept Mon–Sat 10am–12.30pm & 2–7pm, Sun 11am–1pm & 4–7pm; mid-Sept to mid-June Mon–Fri 10am–12.30pm & 2.30–6pm, Sat 10am–noon; ☎02.96.92.30.19). The *Hôtel-Restaurant d'Estuaire* on the waterfront (☎02.96.92.30.25; ①) is a nice **place to stay** – the sea views are great – and serves reasonable menus from 75F/€11.43. *La Poissonnerie du Trégor* up in town, above a fish shop behind the cathedral at 2 rue Renan (☎02.96.92.30.27), is an excellent fish **restaurant** that's no more expensive.

The town holds a **market** each Wednesday, with clothes and so on spread out in the square up by the cathedral, and food and fresh fish further down by the port. The cafés and delis of the main square save their best displays for that day.

Château de la Roche-Jagu

Daily: Easter–June, Sept & Oct 10.30am–noon & 2–6pm; July & Aug 10am–7pm. Park access free, château 10F/€1.52, or 35F/€5.34 during special exhibitions.

About 10km inland from Tréguier and Lézardrieux, the fifteenth-century **Château de la Roche-Jagu** stands on a heavily wooded slope above the meanders of the Trieux River, just as it starts to widen. It's a really gorgeous building, a harmonious combination of fortress and home. The central solid facade is composed of irregular red-granite boulders, cemented together, and incorporating one venerable turreted tower at the front and one at the back.

Both the château and its grounds were devastated by the hurricane of 1987, but the ensemble has since been turned into a modern landscaped park, traced through by several **hiking trails**. The château itself plays host to lavish **annual exhibitions**, usually on some sort of Celtic theme. The rooms within are bare, but it's well worth climbing right up to the top. Here you can admire the beautiful woodwork of the restored eaves, and walk the two long indoor galleries, one of wood and one of stone, to enjoy tremendous views over the river.

The *Restaurant de la Château de la Roche-Jagu*, in the castle gateway, (☎02.96.95.16.08), offers lunch menus on the lawns from 75F/€11.43.

Perros-Guirec

PERROS-GUIREC is the most popular resort along this coast, if not perhaps the most exciting. It has a reputation that seems to attract the retired – its tourist brochures list "playing Scrabble" as an attraction – and an array of shops intended to match: antiques, bric-a-brac and pottery with a big line in granite guillemots and puffins. And Perros is, too, a lot less city-like than it looks on the maps: most of its network of roads turn out to be tree-lined avenues of suburban villas.

However, the commercial streets of the centre (up the hill from the port) hold little of interest, and are often jammed solid with traffic in summer. Much more enjoyable is to take a walk around the headland to see the magnificent view from the **Table d'Orientation** at the sharp curve of the boulevard Clémenceau.

The best beach is the **Plage de Trestraou**, on the opposite side of town to the port, a long curve of sand speckled with bars, restaurants and crazy-golf courses.

Practicalities

If you don't have your own transport, the town is surprisingly hard to reach. What **buses** there are arrive at and leave from the Bassin du Lin Kin in the port, a few hundred metres down from the town centre. If you arrive this way and plan to stay, a good first move is to rent a **bike**; Perros Cycles, near the *gendarmerie* at 14 bd Aristide-Briand (☎02.96.23.13.08), can oblige.

Perros-Guirec's extremely efficient **tourist office** is at 21 place de l'Hôtel-de-Ville (July & Aug Mon–Sat 9am–7.30pm, Sun 10am–12.30pm & 4–7pm; Sept–June Mon–Sat 9am–12.30pm & 2–6.30pm; ☎02.96.23.21.15, *www.perros-guirec.com*). Ask for their schedule of **guided walks** in the vicinity.

If you'd rather stay here than in the smaller community of Ploumanac'h (see p.255), good **hotels** include the old-fashioned *les Violettes*, 19 rue du Calvaire (☎02.96.23.21.33; ②), which has a seriously cheap restaurant, and two with sea views, the *Gulf Stream*, high on the hillside at 26 rue des Sept-Îles (☎02.96.23.21.86; ②; closed mid-Nov to March), and the *Bon Accueil*, 11 rue de Landerval (☎02.96.23.25.77; ④), which has a gourmet restaurant.

The nicest place to **camp** has to be the four-star *Le Ranolien* (☎02.96.91.43.58, *leranolien@wanadoo.fr*; closed mid-Nov to mid-April), which backs onto the Sentier des Douaniers (see overleaf) near a little beach about halfway round, is also directly accessible on the other side by road, and has its own swimming pools and waterslides. However, the *Camping du Trestraou*, 89 av du Casino (☎02.96.23.08.11; closed mid-Sept to April), right beside Trestraou beach, is almost equally attractive.

Almost any of the glass-fronted seaview **restaurants** that line boulevard Thalassa is worth trying, but it's hard to imagine any being able to top the *Goelette* (☎02.96.91.17.78) for a romantic sunset seafood extravaganza.

THE SEABIRD SANCTUARY OF SEPT-ÎLES

The seven craggy islands that constitute the **bird sanctuary of Sept-Îles** were originally set aside in 1912 to protect puffins – whose population had dropped in the space of twenty years from an estimated 15,000 breeding couples to a mere four hundred couples. The new sanctuary was, however, rapidly "discovered" by other seabirds, and thirteen different species now nest here for all or part of the year. The puffins take up residence between March and July; other visitors include storm petrels (April–Sept), gannets (Jan–Sept), kittiwakes (March–July) and guillemots (Feb–July).

Between March and November each year, four separate companies operate **boat trips** out to the islands. They share use of the *gare maritime* on the Plage de Trestraou in Perros-Guirec, and also have a common phone line for reservations – ☎02.96.91.10.00. Trips vary from ninety-minute excursions to the two easternmost islands, the Île Malban and the Île Rouzic (72–80F/€10.98–12.20), by way of a two-and-a-half-hour trip that includes a brief landfall on the one island that permits human visitors, the Île aux Moines (85–95F/€12.96–14.48), to extended three-and-a-half-hour cruises (also 85–95F/€12.96–14.48). Precisely what's available on any particular day depends on the tides, and in high season there may also be additional departures from Ploumanac'h, Trégastel and Port-Blanc.

THE CÔTE DE GRANIT-ROSE
PERROS-GUIREC & PLOUMANAC'H

Ploumanac'h
Lighthouse

Sept-Îles

SENTIER DES DOUANIERS

Camping
La Ranolien

SENTIER DES DOUANIERS

Plage
St-Guirec

PLOUMANAC'H

Jardin
Public

RUE DE SAINT GUIREC

Port de
Ploumanac'h

BOULEVARD DU SEMAPHORE

RUE GABRIEL VICAIRE

RUE DE LA CLARTE

BOULEVARD DES TRAQUIEROS

RUE DE LA CHAPELLE

BOULEVARD DE

Trégastel & Trébeurden

RUE DE LA VALLEE

RUE DE TOUL

ACCOMMODATION		RESTAURANTS	
Bon Acceuil	6	St-Guirec et	Coste-Mor	**B**
Gulf Stream	4	de la Plage 1	Goelette	**C**
du Parc	2	Violettes 5	Mao	**A**
les Rochers	3			

The Sentier des Douaniers

Perros-Guirec's Trestraou beach is made of ordinary sand; the pink-granite coast proper starts just beyond its western end. The long **Sentier des Douaniers** pathway winds round the clifftops to **Ploumanac'h** past an astonishing succession of deformed and water-sculpted rocks – allow around an hour to walk its full length one-way, assuming you take the time to relish the many splendours en route. The path ranks among the finest coastal walks in Brittany. Birds wheel overhead towards the sanctuary, and battered boats shelter in the narrow inlets or bob uncontrollably out on the waves. There are patches and brief causeways of grass, clumps of purple heather and yellow gorse. Occasionally the rocks have crumbled into a sort of granite grit to make up a tiny beach; one boulder is strapped down by bands of ivy that prevent it rolling into the sea.

The rocks, in good French cataloguing fashion, have all been given "names" based on supposed resemblances in their shapes. The more banal ones – such as the great big *Foot* and the *Pancake* – are in a way the best; you can't help wondering, though, what committee it was, and when, that went along labelling the *Torpedo*, the *Armchair*, the *Tortoise* and *Napoleon's Hat*.

Ploumanac'h

PLOUMANAC'H is a more active resort than Perros-Guirec, though again with a dominant and specific clientele – this time families with youngish children. In fact few places on earth can offer quite such enchantment for energetic kids, who love to scramble around the surreal sandscape that's revealed when the long tides draw out. Glinting pink-granite boulders, fringed with green seaweed, erupt from the depths, and rock pools bursting with crabs and other mysteries just wait to be explored. The most obvious focal point is the tiny **Château du Diable**, framing the horizon on one of the countless little islands in the bay – which was where the novel *Quo Vadis* was written around the beginning of the twentieth century. When the tide is in, head instead for the pleasantly wild **municipal park** that separates Ploumanac'h's two halves, the Bourg and the Plage.

Practicalities

The road into Ploumanac'h comes to a dead end at the beach, at the spot where the unfortunately named Coste Mor restaurant enjoys magnificent views across the bay. In the formal dining room indoors, or at the stone tables on its terrace, you can order anything from a cold glass of wine up to a delicious seafood feast; a large plateau de fruits de mer costs around 200F/€30.49. The adjoining hotel, St-Guirec et de la Plage (☎02.96.91.40.89, *www.hotelsaint-guirec.com*; b; closed mid-Nov to mid-Feb, and most of March), has some lovely seaview rooms at bargain rates, and serves a simple good-value menu to all guests in a separate dining room.

Just short of the beach, the small, lively rue St-Guirec leads to the little square that serves as the main local car park. The *Mao*, at 147 rue St-Guirec (☎02.96.91.40.92; no credit cards), is a former snack bar that has expanded to take over several adjacent buildings, including a Polynesian-style thatched hut, and offers bargain menus from 57F/€8.69 (even less for crêpes); like most places in Ploumanac'h, it has special cheap menus for children. The *Hôtel du Parc*, on the square itself (☎02.96.91.40.80; ③; closed mid-Nov to mid-Dec & all Jan), has reasonably priced rooms, and serves good seafood menus from 75F/€11.43, while *Les Rochers*, slightly further back from the beach (☎02.96.91.44.49; ④; closed Oct–Easter), verges on the luxurious. Be warned that the emphasis on children does mean that Ploumanac'h goes to bed early – you can find yourself locked out of a slumbering hotel at 9.30pm.

The Traouïéro valleys

A very short distance west of Ploumanac'h, two dramatic little valleys, which bear a close resemblance to the forest at Huelgoat (see p.320), lead down to the sea. It was the devastation caused by the hurricane of 1987 that led to the **Grand Traouïéro** and the **Petit Traouïéro** becoming accessible to casual visitors – the process of clearing away ancient fallen trees, and disentangling them from centuries of ivy, resulted in the paths being sufficiently opened up so that now either valley makes a gorgeous and undemanding stroll of a few kilometres inland from the coast.

Each of the two is complete with its own gurgling creek, towered over by a huge tumble of pink-granite rocks, cascading between old oaks and chestnut trees, with the occasional stand of Monterey cypresses. The Grand Traouïéro in particular is dwarfed beneath mighty boulders, reminiscent of gargantuan Henry Moore sculptures; the Petit Traouïéro is less deep and more delicate. In spring, both are filled with bright bluebells, and the broom is in full blossom.

At the mouth of the Grand Traouïéro, you can visit a 400-year-old tidal **mill**, one of several in the area that were used to grind flour until the start of the twentieth century.

Trégastel and Trébeurden

Of the smaller villages further round the coast to the west of Ploumanac'h, **TRÉGASTEL**, which holds a handful of **campsites**, including the *Tourony* by the beach (☎02.96.23.86.61; closed Oct–Easter), and **TRÉBEURDEN**, where there's a seafront **hostel**, *Le Toëno*, 2km north of town, (☎02.96.23.52.22; 49F/€7.47; closed mid-Nov to mid-Jan), are functional stopovers. Trégastel has managed to squeeze in an **aquarium** (mid-June to mid-Sept daily 10am–8pm; rest of year school hols only, for varying shorter hours; 30F/€4.57) under a massive pile of boulders, and has a couple of huge lumps of pink granite slap in the middle of its fine beach.

The strangest sight along this coast, however, outdoing anything the erosions can manage, is just south of Trégastel on the **route de Calvaire**, where an old stone saint halfway up a high calvary raises his arm to bless or harangue the gleaming white discs and puffball dome of the **Pleumier-Bodou Telecommunications Centre**. A new pink-granite "dolmen" commemorates its opening by de Gaulle in 1962, when it was the first receiving station to pick up signals from the American Telstar satellite. Now that the centre is no longer operational, it has been remodelled as a **Museum of Telecommunications**, which is also known as **Cosmopolis** (April daily except Sat 10am–6pm; May & June daily 10am–6pm; July & Aug daily 10am–7pm; Sept Mon–Fri & Sun 10am–6pm, Sat 2–6pm; otherwise peculiar hours which include being closed Sat Oct–March, & closed Sun in most of Nov & Jan; 65F/€9.91). Inside the golf ball itself, the **Radôme**, frequent spectacular *son et lumiére* shows explain the history of the whole ensemble, and there's also a smaller **planetarium** alongside. One final incongruous note is struck by the reconstructed **Gaulish village** nearby (same hours; additional donation 15F/€2.29), which is designed to raise money for a French charity working in Africa, and thus incorporates some traditional huts from Togo.

The Bay of Lannion

Despite being located significantly back from the sea on the estuary of the River Léguer, **Lannion** gives its name to the next bay west along the Breton coast – and it's the bay rather than the town that is most likely to impress visitors. One enormous beach stretches from **St-Michel-en-Grève**, which is little more than a bend in the road, as far as **Locquirec**; at low tide you can walk hundreds of metres out on the sands.

Lannion

LANNION, set amid plummeting hills and stairways, is a historic city with streets of medieval housing, and a couple of interesting old churches – but it's also a centre for a burgeoning and extremely high-tech telecommunications industry, and as such one of modern Brittany's real success stories. Hence its rather self-satisfied nickname, *ville heureuse* or "happy town".

In addition to admiring the half-timbered houses around the place de Général-Leclerc and along rue des Chapeliers (look out for nos. 3 and 4), it's well worth climbing from the town up the 142 granite steps which lead to the twelfth-century Templar **Église de Brélévenez**. This church was remodelled three hundred years later to incorporate a granite bell tower, and the views from its terrace are quite stupendous.

Practicalities

Lannion's **gare SNCF** is across the river from town. Arriving passengers reach the centre across an attractive little bridge, from which you should spot the **tourist office**, next to the post office on the quai d'Aguillon (July & Aug Mon–Sat

9am–7pm, Sun 10am–1pm; Sept–June Mon–Sat 9.30am–12.30pm & 2–6pm; ☎02.96.46.41.00, *tourisme.lannion@wanadoo.fr*).

For **accommodation**, you could try the *Hôtel le Bretagne*, opposite the station at 32 av de Général-de-Gaulle (☎02.96.37.00.33; ③; closed Sat & Sun evening out of season), a *logis* with a good restaurant, or, for a bit more luxury, the *Porte de France*, an eighteenth-century coaching inn in the heart of town at 5 rue Jean-Savidan (☎02.96.46.54.81; ③). There's also a year-round **hostel**, *Les Korrigans*, handily near the station and the town centre at 6 rue du 73e Territorial (☎02.96.37.91.28, *lannion@fuaj.org*; 74F/€11.28 with breakfast). Its friendly management do not operate a curfew, and they arrange bird-watching and similar expeditions, and rent out bikes – not that you'll necessarily relish cycling around Lannion itself, with its ferocious hills.

Ploumilliau

Taking a four-kilometre detour inland from St-Michel-en-Grève, 11km southwest of Lannion on the D30, brings you to the trim little village of **PLOUMILLIAU**. Here the weathered-granite parish **church**, surrounded by beds of colourful flowers, contains a unique white-painted wooden representation of **Ankou**, the skeletal symbol of death. The statue, carrying a scythe to catch the living and a spade to bury them, was once carried in local processions.

Locquirec

LOCQUIREC, across the bay from Lannion and officially just within the *département* of Finistère, manages to have beaches on both sides, without ever quite being thin enough to be a real peninsula. Around the main port, smart houses stand in sloping gardens, looking very southern English with their whitewashed stone panels, grey-slate roofs and jutting turreted windows.

On the last Sunday in July, Locquirec holds a combined *pardon de St-Jacques* and Festival of the Sea.

Practicalities

Locquirec veers dangerously close to being over-twee, and none of its **hotels** is all that cheap, either – although the *Grand Hôtel des Bains*, 15 rue de l'Église (☎02.98.67.41.02; ⑦; closed Jan), has so gorgeous a setting that perhaps it doesn't matter. It became widely known in France when it was used as the location for *Hôtel de la Plage*, a coming-of-age movie about youngsters summering in Brittany. If this is outside your budget, the *Sables-Blancs*, 25 rue des Sables-Blancs (☎02.98.67.42.07; ②; closed Oct–March), offers sea views at considerably lower prices, while the municipal **campsite**, the *Toul ar Goue*, 1km south along the corniche (☎02.98.67.40.85; closed mid-Sept to mid-April), is beautifully positioned, too.

St-Jean-du-Doigt

By the direct road, Locquirec is less than 20km northeast of Morlaix (see p.269), but following the longer coastal route instead enables you to pass through **ST-JEAN-DU-DOIGT**, where the parish church contains an object held in veneration as the finger of John the Baptist. This sanctified digit is dipped into the Sacred

Fountain to produce holy water. It was brought here in 1437 and is the principal object of the *pardon* on June 23 and 24 each year. A more recent tradition of pilgrimage has made St-Jean the site of massive anti-nuclear demonstrations.

The Cairn du Barnenez

At the mouth of the Morlaix estuary, 8km southwest of St-Jean and 13km north of Morlaix, the prehistoric stone **Cairn du Barnenez** surveys the waters from the summit of a hill (April–June & Sept daily 10am–12.30pm & 2–6.30pm; July & Aug daily 10am–1pm & 2–6.30pm; Oct–March Tues–Sun 10am–noon & 2–5pm; 25F/€3.81). As on the island of Gavrinis in the Morbihan (see p.374), its ancient masonry has been laid bare by recent excavations, and provides a stunning sense of the architectural prowess of the megalith builders. Radiocarbon testing has shown the work here to date back to around 4500 BC, which makes this one of the oldest large monuments in the world. In the words of André Malraux, it represents "the Breton Parthenon". There is evidence that it remained in continuous use for around 2500 years; it was probably used repeatedly as a place of burial, then sealed off and abandoned.

The ensemble consists of two distinct stepped pyramids, the older one constructed of local dolerite stone, and the other of grey granite from the nearby Île de Sterec. Each rises in successive tiers, built of large flat stones chinked with pebbles (but no mortar); the second was added onto the side of the first, and the two are encircled by a series of terraces and ramps. The whole thing measures roughly 70m long by 15m to 25m wide; the current height of 6m is thought to be smaller than that of the original structure. Both were long ago buried under an eighty-metre-long earthen mound. While the actual cairns are completely exposed to view, most of the passages and chambers that lie within them are sealed off. The two minor corridors that are open simply cut through the edifice from one side to the other, and were exposed by quarrying activities around thirty years ago – which inadvertently provided a good insight into the construction methods. Each is covered with great slabs of rock; in fact most of the familiar dolmens seen all over Brittany and elsewhere are thought to be the vestiges of similarly complex structures. Local tradition has it that one tunnel runs right through this "home of the fairies", and continues out deep under the sea.

travel details

Trains

Lannion to: St-Brieuc (June–Sept only, 1–4 daily; 1hr) via Plouaret (10min) and Guingamp (25min).

Paimpol to: Guingamp (June–Sept only, 4–5 daily; 45min).

Rennes to: Brest (8 TGVs daily; 2hr 10min); Caen (4 daily; 3hr) via Dol (35min) and Pontorson (1hr); Morlaix (8 TGVs daily; 1hr 40min); 10 daily slower services to Morlaix (2hr 10min) also stop at Lamballe (40min), Guingamp (1hr 10min) and Plouaret (1hr 25min); Nantes (4 daily; 1hr 30min); Paris-Montparnasse (8 TGVs daily; 2hr 10min; 5 slower services; 3hr 15min); Quimper (4 daily; 2hr 30min); St-Brieuc (8 TGVs daily; 45min); Vannes (4 daily; 1hr); Vitré (5 daily; 35min).

St-Malo to: Caen (8 daily; 3hr 30min); Dinan (8 daily; 1hr); Rennes (12 daily; 1hr; connections for Paris on TGV). All trains pass through Dol (25min).

Buses

Dinan to: St-Cast (2 daily; 1hr 55min); St-Jacut (2 daily; 45min).

Dinard to: Dinan (3 daily; 50min); Mont-St-Michel (1 daily; 1hr 10min) via Dol (45min).

Fougères to: Vire in Normandy (2 daily; 1hr 30min); Vitré (2 daily; 35min).

Lannion to: Locquirec (30min) and Morlaix (4 daily; 1hr 20min); Trégastel (25min) and Perros-Guirec (6 daily; 1hr).

Rennes to: Dinan (6 daily; 1hr 20min); Dinard (8 daily; 1hr 40min); Fougères (7 daily; 1hr); Mont-St-Michel (4 daily; 1hr 20min).

St-Brieuc to: Carhaix (1 daily; 3hr); Dinan (4 daily; 1hr); Lannion (4 daily; 1hr 40min) via Guingamp (45min); Moncontour (4 daily; 1hr); Paimpol (8 daily; 1hr 30min); Rostrenen (6 daily; 2hr); St-Cast (4 daily; 1hr 50min); St-Malo (2 daily; 2hr) via Lamballe (20min), Le Val-André (35min), Erquy (55min) and Cap Fréhel (1hr 15min).

St-Malo to: Cancale (4 daily; 35min); Combourg (2 daily; 1hr); Dinan (4 daily; 45min); Dinard (8 daily; 30min); Fougères (3 daily; 2hr 15min) via Pontorson (1hr); Mont-St-Michel (4 daily; 1hr 30min); Rennes (5 daily; 1hr 30min) via Tinténiac (55min) and Hédé (1hr 5min); St-Cast (3 daily; 1hr) via St-Jacut (35min).

Ferries

St-Malo to: Portsmouth (1 daily mid-March to mid-Nov, otherwise less frequently; 9hr daytime crossing) and Plymouth (1 weekly mid-Nov to mid-March; 8hr) with Brittany Ferries (St-Malo ☎02.99. 40.64.01, Portsmouth ☎01705/827701, *www. brittanyferries.co.uk*). Regular ferries to Dinard (10min) in season, operated by Émeraude Lines (☎02.23.18.15.15, *www.emeraudelines.com*), who also sail to Dinan up the River Rance, and along the Brittany coast to Cap Fréhel and Île Cézembre (May–Sept). They also go to Jersey, to Guernsey (April–Oct) and Sark (April–Sept), and to the Îles Chausey in Normandy. Condor Ferries (☎02.99.20.03.00, *www.condorferries.co.uk*) run services to Poole (1 daily May–Oct; 5hr), Weymouth (1 daily May–Oct; 5hr), Jersey (4 daily April–Sept, 2 daily Oct, 1 daily second half of March and first half of Nov; 1hr), Guernsey (2 daily April–Oct, 1 daily second half of March and first half of Nov; 1hr 30min) and Sark (1 daily April–Oct; 1hr 30min).

Île de Bréhat: Reached using Les Vedettes de Bréhat (☎02.96.55.79.50, *www.vedettesdebrehat .com*), who run regular 10min trips from Pointe de l'Arcouest (☎02.96.55.79.50), and excursions from Erquy, Dahouët, Binic and St-Quay-Portrieux. Full details are given in each of the relevant accounts.

Barges

Boats for use on the River Rance and the Canal d'Ille-et-Vilaine can be rented from the following companies:

Argoat Nautic, BP 24, Port de Betton, 35830 Betton (☎02.99.55.70.36).

Base Nautique de Pont-Réan, M le Teinturier, Pont-Réan, 35580 Guichen (☎02.99.42.21.91).

Breiz Marine, 5 quai de la Donac, 35190 Tinténiac (☎02.99.68.10.15).

Les Chemins d'Eau, Roumoulin, 35190 La-Chapelle-aux-Filtzméens (☎02.99.45.34.16).

Chemins Nautiques Bretons, M et Mme Alan Gaze, La Vicomté-sur-Rance, 22690 Pleudihen-sur-Rance (☎02.96.83.28.71).

Crown Blue Line, Port de Plaisance, 35480 Messac (☎02.99.34.60.11).

Diffusion Nautique R.M., M René Michel, La Vicomté-sur-Rance, 22690 Pleudihen-sur-Rance (☎02.96.83.35.40).

*For **general information** contact the **Comité de Promotion Touristique des Canaux Bretons**, Office du Tourisme, place du Parlement, 35600 Redon (☎02.99.71.06.04) or **Formules Bretagne**, 203 bd St-Germain, 75007 Paris (☎01.53.63.11.53).*

CHAPTER FIVE

FINISTÈRE

Finistère – literally, "the End of the World" – has always been isolated from the French, even from the Breton, mainstream. This remote rural landscape was the last refuge of the Druids from encroaching Christianity, and its forests and elaborate parish closes testify to its role as the province's spiritual heartland. Today, although the port of Roscoff has reopened the old maritime links with England, high-speed TGV trains mean that Brest is just four hours from Paris, and the motorway now makes a complete loop around the end of the peninsula, it remains only sporadically touched by tourism and modern industry. Breton survives as a spoken language here more than anywhere else, and here too, especially in the "Bigouden country" in the south, traditional costumes are still worn for other than commercial reasons.

Memories of the days when Brittany was "Petite Bretagne", as opposed to "Grande Bretagne" across the water, linger in the names of Finistère's two main areas. Both the northern peninsula – **Léon**, once Lyonesse – and its southern neighbour – **Cornouaille**, the same word as "Cornwall" – feature prominently in Arthurian legend. The ragged **coastline**, indented with a succession of estuaries each of which shelters its own tiny harbour, is the prime attraction. Rarely are conditions as bleak as you might expect from a land exposed to the full force of the Atlantic; heading west from **Roscoff**, your most likely point of arrival, there are possible stopping places all the way to **Le Conquet**. What can be a treacherous stretch of ocean separates that from **Ouessant** and **Molène**; and yet those two islands have the mildest winter climate of all France.

In the south, Cornouaille boasts two classic resorts in **Loctudy** and **Bénodet**, either side of the Odet estuary, while if you'd rather stay in a genuine lived-in town, **Quimper** is just upriver – the liveliest place here and one of the most pleasant, and least-sung, in France. A short distance east, **Pont-Aven** was Gauguin's home before he made off to the South Seas, and still maintains its artistic traditions. There are surprises everywhere – take the perfectly preserved medieval village of **Locronan**, used as a film set for Roman Polanski's *Tess*, or the extraordinary world apart that is the tiny **Île de Sein**.

All Finistère offers the enticement of growing but not quite full-blown tourist development – facilities without the crowds. Its most popular region for holiday-makers is the **Crozon Peninsula**, jutting into the sea beneath the **Ménez-Hom** mountain as a distinct entity between the two ancient realms. **Morgat** and **Camaret** here are both ideal for long and leisurely seaside stays, and all around there are opportunities for secluded camping.

LÉON

The sequence of estuaries that score the coast in the north – the wildest and most dramatic in Brittany – are known both as *abers* (as in Welsh place names) and as *rias* (as in Spanish Galicia). In season, the vast beaches and dunes on the open Atlantic coast, for example around **Porspoder**, can be magnificent, while at any time you can stumble across tiny and deserted coves as the twisting and narrowing estuaries reach inland. One of the choicest spots is at **Trémazan**, where the ruins of an ancient castle look out across a great expanse of sand, while the working fishing village of **Le Conquet** is perhaps best of all. The one coastal place to avoid is the regional capital, and lone big city, of **Brest**, the base of the French Atlantic fleet.

Inland, the **parish closes** lie strung across the little villages that lie southwest of **Morlaix**, each ornate church and its associated ensemble still perpetuating a fierce medieval rivalry. Also deserving a detour from the coast are the Renaissance **château of Kerjean** and the **Menhir de Kerloas** (the highest stone monolith still standing).

Roscoff and around

ROSCOFF has long been a significant port – Mary Queen of Scots, for example, landed here in 1548 on her way to Paris to be engaged to the son of Henri II of France, and so too did Bonnie Prince Charlie in 1746, after his defeat at Culloden – and the opening of its deep-water harbour in 1973 had especial significance in the general revitalization of the Breton economy. The town itself, however, has remained delightfully small and unspoiled. It may not look so on the map, but almost all activity is confined to the pedestrianized medieval lanes around **rue Gambetta** and the **old port** – the rest of the roads are residential backstreets full of retirement homes and stern institutions. The preservation of its old character is helped by the fact that both the ferry port and *gare SNCF* are some way from the town centre.

Arrival and information

Boats from Plymouth (6hr) and Cork (19hr) – run by Brittany Ferries (☎08.03.82.88.28, *www.brittany-ferries.com*) – and Rosslare (21hr) – run by Irish Ferries (☎02.98.61.17.17) – dock at the Port de Bloscon, just over 1.5km to the east (and just out of sight) of Roscoff. To get into the town by foot (about a thirty-minute walk), turn right from the terminal and follow the signs across a narrow promontory and down into the crescent of Roscoff's original natural harbour.

The **gare SNCF** (☎02.98.69.70.20) lies a few hundred metres south of the town proper. From here a restricted rail service runs to Morlaix, with connections beyond. Most **buses** also go from here, including a direct service to Brest run by Les Cars du Kreisker (☎02.98.69.00.93). Another service to Morlaix leaves from the fish hall (*La Criée*) by the old harbour, with connections on Mondays, Thursdays and Saturdays to Quimper (CAT; ☎02.98.90.68.40).

The helpful **tourist office** is at 46 rue Gambetta in town (April–June & Sept Mon–Sat 9am–noon & 2–6pm; July & Aug Mon–Sat 9am–12.30pm & 1.30–7pm, Sun 10am–12.30pm; Oct–March Mon–Fri 10am–noon & 2–5pm, Sat 10am–noon; ☎02.98.61.12.13), next to a boulangerie and the **post office** at 19 rue Gambetta (☎02.98.69.72.90, *www.sb-roscoff.fr/roscoff*).

Bikes can be rented from Desbordes, 13 rue Brizeux (☎02.98.69.72.44), as well as from the *gare SNCF*.

Accommodation

For a small town, Roscoff is well equipped with **hotels**, which are accustomed to late-night arrivals from the ferries. Be warned, however, that most of them close for some or all of winter. There's also a **hostel** on the Île de Batz (see p.267), and two two-star **campsites** – the beachfront *Municipal de Perharidy*, 2km west, just off the route de Santec (☎02.98.69.70.86; closed Oct–March), and the roomier *Manoir de Kérestat*, 2km south towards St-Pol (☎02.98.69.71.92; closed Nov to mid-April).

Hôtel-Restaurant des Arcades, 15 rue Amiral-Réveillère (☎02.98.69.70.45, fax 02.98.61.12.34, *www.acdev.com*). Sixteenth-century building with superb views from some of its modernized rooms and from the restaurant; menus 59F/€8.99 and upwards, with a particularly good 139F/€21.19 option. Closed Oct–Easter. ③.

Hôtel-Restaurant le Bellevue, rue Jeanne d'Arc (☎02.98.61.23.38, fax 02.98.61.11.80). Seafront *logis de France*, on the opposite side of the pleasure harbour to the town centre and thus somewhat nearer the ferry terminal. It would be quieter, were it not for the lively downstairs bar. Pleasant rooms, and fine views from the dining room, where the 115F/€17.53 menu offers salmon baked in cheese with mustard. Closed mid-Nov to mid-March, except Christmas and New Year. ④.

Hôtel du Centre, 5 rue Gambetta (☎02.98.61.24.25). Family hotel, above the café-bar *Chez Janie*, and entered via the main street but looking out on the port. Closed Jan to mid-Feb. ③.

Hôtel les Chardons Bleus, 4 rue Amiral-Réveillère (☎02.98.69.72.03, fax 02.98.61.27.86). Very friendly and helpful hotel, in the heart of the old town, with a good restaurant (menus from 95F/€14.48; closed Thurs Sept–June, plus Sun in winter) but no sea views. Closed Feb. ④.

Hôtel le Gulf Stream, 7 rue Marquise de Kergariou (☎02.98.69.73.19, fax 02.98.61.11.89, *www.perso.wanadoo/fr/gulf.stream*). One of the more expensive options, just south of the Institute of Oceanology, with a heated swimming pool and a quite superb seafood restaurant where the cheapest menu is 160F/€24.39. Closed mid-Oct to mid-March. ⑤.

Inter-Hôtel Regina, 1 rue Ropartz-Morvan (☎02.98.61.23.55, fax 02.98.61.10.89). Very comfortable rooms, but relatively expensive considering the location, near the *gare SNCF*. Menus from 98F/€14.94, and live jazz in the bar in what might otherwise be the quieter months. Closed Nov to mid-March. ③.

Hôtel les Tamaris, 49 rue É-Corbière (☎02.98.61.22.99, fax 02.98.69.74.36, *auxtamaris@dial.oleane.com*). Renovated, comfortably furnished rooms looking out towards the Île de Batz. Closed mid-Nov to Feb. ③.

The Town

The old **harbour** is very much the liveliest part of Roscoff. Two long stone jetties enclose the fishing port – the local economy is still heavily based on the sea – while pleasure boats bob in the bay behind. Tourists gather all through the day to watch the fishermen at work, and to join the low-key pleasure trips to the **Île de Batz**. The island looks almost walkable; a narrow pier stretches over 400 metres towards it before abruptly plunging into deep rocky waters. The Pointe de Bloscon and the white fisherman's chapel, the Chapelle Ste-Barbe, make a good vantage point, particularly when the tide is in; the tide goes out a long way (and dictates the precise embarkation point for the boat trips). Below the headland are the *viviers*, where you can see trout, salmon, lobsters and crabs being reared for the pot.

In addition to the island ferries, detailed on p.267, the Compagnie Armein Maritime (☎02.98.61.77.75) operate three-hour **cruises** from here around the **Bay of Morlaix** (April–June & Sept–Oct Wed & Sat 2.15pm; July & Aug Mon–Sat 2.15pm; 60F/€9.15), and excursions to the **Cairn du Barnenez** (75F/€11.43; see p.259), depending on the demand and the state of the tides.

Until the last couple of centuries, Roscoff made most of its money from piracy, like so many other ports along the Breton coast. There are a few reminders of that wealth along rue Gambetta, which becomes rue Amiral-Réveillère. Two of its

ALEXIS GOURVENNEC AND BRITTANY FERRIES

Few British holiday-makers sailing to France with Brittany Ferries will realize the significance of ideology in the origins of that company. The ferry services from Roscoff to Plymouth and to Cork were started not simply to bring tourists, but also to revive the traditional trading links between the Celtic nations of Brittany, Ireland and southwest England – links which were suppressed for centuries as an act of French state policy after the union of Brittany with France in 1532.

Until the 1960s there were no direct ferries crossing the Channel to Brittany, and, until Brittany Ferries started up, all the cross-Channel operators were British-owned. Brittany Ferries is the creation of Alexis Gourvennec, who in 1961, at 24, was the militant leader of a Breton farmers' cooperative. Frustrated at the lack of French government support, the farmers decided to start their own shipping line to find new markets for their produce – the immediate region of Roscoff and Morlaix being particularly noted for its artichokes and cauliflowers.

The financial success of the company has been such that it has expanded to run services from Britain to the Norman ports of Cherbourg and Caen, as well as to Spain; but it has also been an important factor in a resurgence of Breton fortunes that has as much cultural as commercial significance. Meanwhile, Breton farmers have been campaigning for the expansion of Brest Airport (at Guipavas) so that it will be able to handle jumbo-jet loads of artichokes for same-day sale in New York!

See Contexts for more details.

ornate grey-granite houses, including no. 25 ("the House of Mary Stuart"), claim to be where Mary Queen of Scots spent her first night after eighteen stormy days at sea – despite the fact that both were built after she landed.

More recently, the town earned a more respectable living from the **onion** trade, which began in 1828, when Henri Ollivier first took onions to England from here. The whole story of the "Johnnies" – that classic French image of men in black berets with strings of onions hanging over the handlebars of their bicycles – is told in **La Maison des Johnnies**, across from the tourist office (daily except Tues 10am–noon & 3–6pm; 10F/€1.52). The trade flourished until the 1930s, and older people of the town remember travelling as children with their fathers as far afield as Glasgow to sell their produce.

The sculpted ships and protruding stone cannons of the Renaissance belfry which tops the sixteenth-century town church, **Notre Dame de Croas Batz**, also recall the seafaring days. From the side, rows of bells can be seen hanging in galleries, one above the other, like a tall narrow wedding cake created by the young Walt Disney.

A short way past the church, on place Georges-Teissier, the **Charles Perez Aquarium** contains a well-displayed and comprehensive collection of marine fauna of the Channel (daily: April–June, Sept & Oct 10am–noon & 1–6pm; July & Aug 10am–noon & 1–7pm; 26F/€3.96). It's an interesting enough place, if a little disappointing for anyone expecting the exotic, and forms part of the Institute of Oceanology which undertakes oceanographic, and related biological, research.

Some way beyond the grand buildings of the Institute is the **Thalassotherapy Institute** of Rock Roum. Specializing in sea-water cures, it opened in 1899 as the first such establishment in France, and is still thriving a century on. A kilometre further on, you come to Roscoff's best **beach**, at Laber, surrounded by expensive hotels and apartments.

In the opposite direction from town, a short walk south along the coast from the ferry terminal, is the **Jardin Exotique** – tropical garden – at Rock Hievec (Feb, March, Nov & Dec daily except Tues 2–5pm; April–June, Sept & Oct daily 10.30am–12.30pm & 2–6pm; July & Aug daily 10am–7pm; 26F/€3.96). In this slightly surreal enclave, cactuses, palm trees and flowers of South America and the Pacific flourish in the mild Gulf Stream climate.

Eating

Very much the obvious places to **eat** in Roscoff are the dining rooms of the hotels themselves (as detailed on p.264), but the town does hold a few specialist **restaurants** as well. If you're arriving on an evening ferry, note that, out of season, it can be difficult to find a restaurant still serving any later than 9.15pm.

Crêperie de la Poste, 12 rue Gambetta (☎02.98.69.72.81). Central crêperie, open late, where an à la carte meal of sweet and savoury pancakes can work out inexpensive, so long as you don't get carried away by the exotic seafood options. Closed Wed Sept–April.

L'Écume des Jours, quai d'Auxerre (☎02.98.61.22.83). Cosy restaurant in a grand old house, offering good-value set lunches for 60F/€9.15 on weekdays, plus dinner menus from 90F/€13.72, featuring such delights as braised oysters or scallops with local pink onions. Closed Wed, plus Sat lunchtime in winter, and all of Dec & Jan.

Le Temps de Vivre, place de l'Église (☎02.98.61.27.28). Gourmet restaurant with sea views on the main church square – below but separate from the *Hôtel Ibis* – serving rich French cuisine with a modern twist. Lunch on weekdays can cost as little as 105F/€16.01, otherwise menus range from 180F/€27.44 to 395F/€60.22. Almost the only deviations from the chef's recommendations are to accommodate oyster *refuseniks*. Closed two weeks in both March & Oct.

The Île de Batz

The long, narrow **ÎLE DE BATZ** (pronounced "Ba") forms a sort of mirror image of Roscoff across the water, separated from it by a sea channel that's barely 200m wide at low tide but perhaps five times that when the tide is high. Appearances from the mainland are somewhat deceptive, however; the island's old town, home to a thousand or so farmers and fishermen, may fill much of its southern shoreline, but those parts of Batz that aren't visible from Roscoff are much wilder and more windswept. With no cars permitted, and some great expanses of sandy beach, it makes a wonderfully quiet retreat for families in particular, whether you're camping or staying in one of its two old-fashioned little hotels.

The island's first recorded inhabitant was a "laidly worm", a dragon that infested the place in the sixth century. Such dragons normally symbolize pre-Christian religions, in this case perhaps a Druidic serpent cult. Allegorical or not, when St Pol arrived to found a monastery he wrapped a Byzantine stole around the unfortunate creature's neck and cast it into the sea. These days, there are no dragons; there are hardly even any trees, just an awful lot of seaweed, which is collected and sold for fertilizer.

Ferries from Roscoff arrive at the quayside of the old town. There's a nice small beach here along the edge of the harbour, though the sea withdraws so far at low tide that the entire port turns into an endless morass of slimy seaweed. You may well have spotted the island's best beach already from the boat – it's the white-sand **Grève Blanche** towards its eastern end, reached by turning right when you get to the town church. Walking in that same direction also brings you to the hostel (see opposite), and the 44-metre **lighthouse** that stands on the island's peak, all of 23m above sea level (June & last fortnight of Sept daily except Wed 2–5pm; July to mid-Sept daily 1.30–5.30pm; 10F/€1.52).

Practicalities

Two separate **ferry** companies compete dementedly to take foot passengers across to the Île de Batz, for a return fare of 34F/€5.18. Both Compagnie Maritime Armein (☎02.98.61.77.75) and Compagnie Finistérienne (☎02.98.61.78.87) have ticket booths at the landward end of Roscoff's long pier, sporting signs that read *Prochain départ ici en 5 minutes* ("Next boat departs here in five-minutes"). At low tide, the boats sail from the far end of the pier, a good five-minutes' walk further on. Tickets are only valid for one or other company, so there's no knowing whether you'll have to wait for the right boat once you get there. The crossing takes about ten minutes. Between late June and mid-September, the service is pretty much nonstop between 8am and 8pm daily; for the rest of the year, each company runs eight to ten trips daily between 8.30am and 7pm.

The nicer of the two **hotels** on the island is the *Grand Hôtel Morvan*, at the centre of the harbour (☎02.98.61.78.06; ③; closed Dec & Jan), which serves good meals on its large seafront terraces. Closer to the ferry landing, the *Hôtel-Restaurant Roch Ar Mor* (☎02.98.61.78.28; ②; closed Oct–March), makes a cheaper alternative, though a better bet for budget travellers would be the **hostel**, in a beautiful setting, right by the beach at the evocatively named Creach ar Bolloc'h (☎02.98.61.77.69; 67F/€10.21 with breakfast; closed Oct–March), which also runs sailing classes. A quirky little **restaurant**, *Les Couleurs du Temps*, tucked away behind *Grand Hôtel Morvan*, offers a good-value 89F/€13.57 lunch menu, and prepares the weird Breton speciality *kig ha farz*, a kind of seafood stew topped by a crêpe, every Friday evening.

St-Pol-de-Léon

The main road **south from Roscoff** passes by fields of the famous Breton artichokes before arriving after 6km at **ST-POL-DE-LÉON**. Pleasantly sited amid rich gardens, this is not an exciting place but – assuming you've your own transport – has two churches that at least merit a pause.

The **Cathedral**, in the main town square, was rebuilt towards the end of the thirteenth century along the lines of Coutances' (see p.000) – a quiet classic of unified Norman architecture. The remains of St Pol are inside, alongside a large bell, rung over the heads of pilgrims during his *pardon* on March 12 in the unlikely hope of curing headaches and ear diseases.

Just downhill, the **Kreisker Chapel** is notable for its sharp-pointed soaring granite belfry, now coated in yellow moss. It was originally modelled on the Norman spire of St-Pierre at Caen, which was destroyed in World War II (see p.000), but as an elegant improvement on its Norman counterpart was itself much copied. Similar "Kreisker" spires are dotted all over rural Brittany. The dramatic view to be seen if you climb this spire (daily 10–11.30am & 2–6pm; free), out across the **Bay of Morlaix**, should be enough to persuade you to follow the road along the shore.

Practicalities

If you're looking for **accommodation** in St-Pol, you're likely to fetch up at one of the two most central options, the *Hôtel-Restaurant le Passiflore*, near the station at 28 rue Pen-ar-Pont (☎02.98.69.00.52; ②; closed Sun evening), or the slightly more comfortable *Hôtel de France*, 29 rue des Minimes (☎02.98.29.14.14; ③). Both are open all year and have reasonable restaurants.

Carantec and around

From St-Pol, if you take the foliage-covered lane down to join the D58, you can cross the **pont de la Corde** to reach the resort and peninsula of **CARANTEC**, studded with small coves and secluded beaches. The **Île de Callot**, an enticing hour's walk away from the slightly drab town itself at low tide, is the scene of a *pardon* and blessing of the sea on the Sunday after August 15 – a rather dour occasion, as are most of the religious festivals around Finistère.

The D78 runs on from Carantec beside the sea, the estuary narrowing until at Locquenolé it is just the width of the River Morlaix. From then on it is a beautiful deep valley, with promenades and gardens along the stone-reinforced banks, and views across to isolated villages such as Dourduff on the other side.

Practicalities

This stretch of coast comes alive in summer with a scattering of seasonal **campsites**, among them the excellent four-star *Les Mouettes* (☎02.98.67.02.46, *www.les-campings.com*; closed mid-Sept to April), where you pay well over the usual odds for the benefit of having a supermarket, a swimming pool with an amazing water slide, a bar and a disco on site. For **rooms** in Carantec, the *Porspol*, 7 rue Surcouf (☎02.98.67.00.52; ③; closed Oct–March), is good value. Right on the waterfront, the twin **restaurants** *La Cambusec* (☎02.98.67.08.92) and *Le Cabestan* (☎02.98.67.01.87) provide the focus of Carantec's nightlife, with the *Cabestan* having the edge on seafood, while the *Cambuse* concentrates on live music. Both close on Tuesdays, and also on Monday evenings in low season. In addition, beside the sea not far southwest of the town centre, the *Maison de l'Huître* sells prize **oysters** from the beds at Prat-Ar-Coum in western Finistère (July & Aug Mon–Sat 10am–1pm & 3–7pm, Sun 10am–noon; Sept–June Mon–Sat 10am–noon & 3–6pm, Sun 10am–noon; ☎02.98.78.30.68).

The Château de Taureau

A short way east of Carantec, the fortified **Château de Taureau**, off Pointe de Pen-al-Lann, guards the entrance to Morlaix Bay, 12km north of Morlaix itself. It was built after a succession of skirmishes that began in 1522, when Morlaix pirates raided and looted Bristol. Henry VIII's pride was hurt and, seeking revenge, he sent a sizeable fleet to storm Morlaix. The citizens were absent at a neighbouring festival when the English arrived. When they returned, they found the English drunk in their wine cellars. Once the Bretons had routed their enemies, they built the château to forestall further attacks from the sea.

In the seventeenth century, the Château de Taureau was used as a prison; now it's a sailing school. Meanwhile, Morlaix adopted the motto which it keeps to this day – "If they bite you, bite them back."

The only way to get a close-up view of the château is from out on the water; if you don't have your own yacht, then take one of the organized boat trips round the Bay of Morlaix from Roscoff (see p.264). The best place from which to admire on the mainland is at the tip of the **Pointe de Pen-al-Lann**, 2km east of Carantec. Incidentally, a steep footpath from the car park here leads 300m down to one of the most delightful – and quiet – **beaches** in this region.

Morlaix

MORLAIX, one of the great old Breton ports, thrived off trade with England – in between wars – during the "golden period" of the late Middle Ages. Its sober stone houses were built up the slopes of the steep valley where the Queffleuth and Jarlot rivers join to flow together into Morlaix Bay, originally protected by an eleventh-century castle and a circuit of walls. Little is left of either, but the old centre remains in part medieval – cobbled streets and half-timbered houses. Later, the town grew still more prosperous on piracy and the tobacco trade (both legal and illegal), and spread north, down the valley, towards the port.

Arrival and information

The **gare SNCF** (☎08.36.35.35.35) is on rue Armand-Rousseau, high above the town at the western end of its railway viaduct. It was originally supposed to be linked to town by a funicular railway, but as that was never built you still have to reach it on foot, climbing the steep steps of the Venelle de la Roche. If you can't face the long trek up to the station to buy a ticket, you can make reservations at travel agencies down in the town proper.

All **buses** conveniently depart from place Cornic, right under the viaduct; long-distance routes include those south to Carhaix and on to Rosporden and Concarneau or Lorient (SCEATA; ☎02.98.93.06.98); and also those to Quimper and Vannes (CAT; ☎02.98.62.12.72).

The **tourist office** in Morlaix is in a solitary but central one-storey building, almost under the viaduct in place des Otages (mid-June to mid-Sept Mon & Sat 10am–noon & 2–6pm, Tues–Fri 10am–noon & 2–7pm, Sun 10.30am–12.30pm; mid-Sept to mid-June Tues–Sat 9am–noon & 2–6pm; ☎02.98.62.14.94). The **post office** is on rue de Brest (☎02.98.88.23.03).

Bicycles can be rented from Henri Le Gall, 1 rue de Callac (☎02.98.88.60.47).

Accommodation

In addition to the many (fairly uninspiring) **hotels** dotted around old Morlaix, there's a **hostel** at 3 route de Paris (☎02.98.88.13.63; 48F/€7.32; open all year), 1km from the town centre; take the Kernégues bus to either rue de Paris or place Traoulan, and then it's just off to the left. Morlaix no longer has a municipal campsite.

Hôtel de l'Europe, 1 rue d'Aiguillon (☎02.98.62.11.99, fax 02.98.88.83.38, *www.hotel-europe -com.fr*). Slightly eccentric but very central old place, near the Jacobin convent. While the rooms are modern and well equipped but not all that characterful, the public spaces, furnished in a variety of styles, are more flamboyant – and the separate restaurant downstairs (see p.271) is superb. They also offer one, much cheaper, single room. ④.

Greenwood Café Hôtel, 25 place St-Martin (☎02.98.88.03.29). Inexpensive, reasonable-value en-suite rooms above an American-themed bar, close to the *gare SNCF* at the top of the hill. ②.

Hôtel du Port, 3 quai de Léon (☎02.98.88.07.54, fax 02.98.88.43.80). Bright, modern option, overlooking the port from the left bank. It doesn't have a restaurant, but each room has its own kitchenette – presumably for yacht owners who fancy a night on shore. ②.

Hôtel le Roy d'Ys, 8 place des Jacobins (☎02.98.63.30.55). Small central hotel, across the square from the town museum. The cheapest rooms do not have their own showers; guests have to pay 15F/€2.29 extra to use shared showers. No restaurant, but a downstairs bar. Closed Nov. ②.

Hôtel-Restaurant le St-Mélaine, 75–77 rue Ange-de-Guernisac (☎02.98.88.08.79). Self-styled family hotel, not easy to find, above place Cornic and all but under the viaduct. Value for money, but dull. The restaurant serves simple menus from 60F/€9.15, with a well-stocked buffet. Closed Sun & two weeks in May. ①.

The Town

Morlaix is dominated by its pink-granite **railway viaduct**, built high above the valley in the 1860s to carry trains en route between Paris and Brest. Despite all Allied attempts during World War II to destroy it with bombs, it still looms 60m above the central **place des Otages**, and as you enter the town today by road from the north your opening view is of shiny yacht masts in the pleasure harbour paralleling its slender pillars. The first level of the viaduct is intermittently open to visitors, usually (but not always) from 11am until 7pm each day.

There are few actual sights in town, but the pleasure anyway is more in roaming the length of the steep stairways that lead up from the places des Otages and Cornic, or in walking up to the viaduct from the top of Venelle aux Prêtres, along an almost rural overgrown path lined with brambles.

On her way from Roscoff to Paris, Mary Queen of Scots passed through Morlaix in 1548, and stayed at the **Jacobin convent** which fronts place des Jacobins. She was at the time just five years old, an aspect which may have contributed to local interest in the spectacle. A contemporary account records that the crush to catch a glimpse of the infant was so great that the inner town's "gates were thrown off their hinges and the chains from all the bridges were broken down".

The **Musée des Jacobins** (entrance on rue des Vignes), in what was once the convent church, contains a reasonably entertaining assortment of Roman wine jars, bits that have fallen off medieval churches, cannons and kitchen utensils, and a few modern paintings (Easter–June, Sept & Oct Mon, Wed–Fri & Sun 10am–noon & 2–6pm, Sat 2–6pm; July & Aug Mon, Wed–Fri & Sun 10am–12.30pm & 2–6.30pm, Sat 2–6.30pm; Nov–Easter Mon, Wed–Fri & Sun 10am–noon & 2–5pm, Sat 2–5pm; 25F/€3.81).

The austere church of **St-Mathieu**, off rue de Paris, contains a sombre and curious statue of the Madonna and Child, made in Cologne around 1400 AD. Mary's breast was apparently lopped off by a prudish former priest, to leave the babe suckling at nothing. The whole statue stands open down the middle, to reveal a separate figure of God the Father, clutching a crucifix; interior panels hold painted scenes from the life of the Virgin, including the Annunciation and the Assumption. In April 1993, the figure of Christ was stolen, but the thief, who preferred to pray at home, repented in October 1994 and returned it anonymously.

Duchess Anne of Brittany, who had by then become queen of France, visited Morlaix in 1506. She is reputed to have stayed at the **Maison de la Reine Anne**, 33 rue du Mur, which, although much restored, does indeed date from the sixteenth century. Its intricate external carvings, and the lantern roof and splendid Renaissance staircase inside, make it the most beautiful of the town's ancient houses, each of its storeys overhanging the square below by a few more centimetres. The house is open to the public in summer (May & June Mon–Sat 10am–noon & 2–6pm; July & Aug Mon–Sat 10am–6.30pm, Sun 2–6pm; Sept Mon–Sat 10am–noon & 2–5pm; 10F/€1.52), and at other times by arrangement (☎02.98.88.23.26).

In the eighteenth century, Morlaix's wealth was sustained by boatbuilding, textiles and tobacco, and the **tobacco factory**, on quai de Léon by the port, remains

COREFF – REAL ALE IN BRITAIN

1985 saw the inauguration of an unlikely new product in Morlaix – the first Breton real ale. Two young Frenchmen, Christian Blanchard and Jean-François Malgorn, set up their own brewery, with the ambition of emulating the beers they had enjoyed on visits to Wales.

You should be able to find the resultant brew, Coreff – logically enough, the name is an old Breton word meaning "beer" – both locally and throughout Brittany in those bars which take pride in all things Breton. In July and August, it's also possible to visit the brewery, the Brasserie des Deux-Rivières at 1 place de la Madeleine, for a tour and a sample (45-minute tours: Mon–Fri 9.30am, 10.30am, 1.30pm, 3pm & 4.30pm; ☎02.98.63.41.92).

As for the beer itself, it's a sweet, rich brown ale – authentically "real" in that it isn't filtered or pasteurized – that can make a welcome change from the lagers everywhere on offer.

active. It employs 500 people – who produce annually 300 million cigars, 50 tonnes of chewing tobacco and 15 tonnes of snuff, and can be visited on Wednesday afternoons (☎02.98.88.15.32).

Eating

The best hunting ground for **restaurants** in Morlaix is to be found between St-Mélaine church and place des Jacobins, but there are plenty of other options tucked away on the backstreets.

Les Bains Douches, 45 allée du Poan-Ben (☎02.98.63.83.83). Small bistro that doesn't quite live up to its unusual location – set in the former public baths, and reached via a little footbridge across a canal – but makes an attractive spot for a light 65F/€9.91 lunch. Closed lunchtime on Sat & Sun.

Brasserie Le Lof, 1 rue d'Aiguillon (☎02.98.88.81.15). Characterful split-level brasserie below the central *Hôtel de l'Europe*, serving imaginative gourmet menus from 85F/€12.96. The bizarre *kig ha farz*, a combination of seafood stew and pancake, is a regular feature.

Brocéliande, 5 rue des Bouchers (☎02.98.88.73.78). Located in the southeast of town, beyond the place des Halles and St-Mathieu church, this place offers elegant evening-only dining in a *fin-de-siècle* atmosphere; the one set menu costs 125F/€19.06. Closed Tues.

La Dolce Vita, 3 rue Ange-de-Guernisac (☎02.98.63.37.67). Italian place at the foot of a pretty, central alley, with pizzas mostly priced at under 50F/€7.62, plus pasta, salads and such traditional Italian dishes as *osso buco* at 70F/€10.67. Closed Mon, plus three weeks in Feb and two weeks in Oct.

La Marée Bleue, 3 rampe Ste-Mélaine (☎02.98.63.24.21). Well-respected seafood restaurant, a minute's walk up from the tourist office. The 80F/€12.20 menu is a bit limited, but 165F/€25.15 ensures you a superb *assiette de fruits de mer*, and 235F/€35.83 buys a five-course feast. Closed Sun evening & Mon Sept–June.

Drinking and nightlife

Among **bars** to look out for while you're in Morlaix are the venerable half-timbered *Ty Coz*, at 10 Venelle au Beurre (☎02.98.88.07.65; closed Thurs & all Sept), near the hostel, which has boisterous Bretons playing darts, and draught Coreff beer, and the lively and much more salubrious – or aseptic, depending on your perspective – *Tempo Piano Bar*, facing the port on quai de Tréguier (☎02.98.63.29.11), where there are regular jazz and blues concerts.

Onward routes from Morlaix

Moving on from Morlaix, you are strategically poised. To the **west** are the **parish closes** – described in the following section – and, beyond them, access to the best of the **Finistère coast** around Le Conquet and the Crozon peninsula. **South**, via the **Forêt de Huelgoat** (see p.320), is the direct route to **Quimper**; and **east** you can take in the remarkable **Cairn du Barnenez** (p.259) en route to the **Côte de Granit Rose**.

The parish closes

A few kilometres west of Morlaix, bounded by the valleys of the Elorn and the Penzé rivers, lies an area remarkable for the wealth and distinction of its church architecture. This region holds the best-known examples of what the French call *enclos paroissiaux* – a phrase that translates into English as "**parish closes**", and describes a walled churchyard which in addition to the church itself incorporates a trinity of further elements: a cemetery, a calvary and an ossuary.

The **ossuaries** – which now tend to contain nothing more alarming than a few rows of postcards – were originally charnel houses, used to store the exhumed bones of less recent burials. They are the most striking features of the closes, making explicit a peculiarly Breton proximity and continuity between the living and the dead. Parishioners would go to pray, with the informality of making a family visit, in the ossuary chapels where the dead bones of their families were on display. The relationship may have originated with the builders of the megalithic passage graves, which were believed to serve as doorways between our world and the netherworld.

The **cemeteries** tend to be small, and in many cases have disappeared altogether, while the **calvaries** that complete the ensemble are tenuously based on the hill of Calvary. Each is therefore in theory surmounted by a Crucifixion, but the definition is loose enough to take in any cluster of religious statuary, not necessarily even limited to biblical scenes, standing on a single base.

That there are so many fine *enclos* in such a small area is thanks to a period of intense inter-village rivalry during the sixteenth and seventeenth centuries, when each parish competed to outdo the next in the complexity and ornament of its village church. It's no coincidence that most such Breton churches date from the two centuries to either side of the union with France in 1532 – Brittany's wealthiest period – and nothing is more telling of the decline in the province's fortunes than the contrast between the riches on show and the relative lack of prosperity of the present-day villages. An additional, more positive, layer is contributed, however, by the current revival of artisan traditions in the parishes. In several of the towns and villages, stonemasons are once more producing sculptures in granite.

A clearly signposted **route** leading past several of the most famous churches – St-Thégonnec, Guimiliau and Lampaul-Guimiliau – can be joined by leaving the N12 between Morlaix and Landivisiau at St-Thégonnec.

St-Thégonnec

At the **ST-THÉGONNEC** *enclos*, just off the N12 *autoroute* 10km southwest of Morlaix, the church **pulpit**, carved by two brothers in 1683, is the acknowledged masterpiece, albeit so swamped with detail – symbolic saints, sybils and arcane figures – that it is almost too ornate to appreciate. The painted-oak **entombment** in the crypt under the ossuary has more immediate effect. Complete with a stunning life-size figure of Mary Magdalene, it was sculpted by Jacques Laispagnol of Morlaix in 1702, for a fee of 1550 pounds. The entire east wall of the church is a carved and painted retable, with saints in niches and a hundred different scenes depicted.

The upmarket *Auberge de St-Thégonnec*, 6 place de la Mairie (☎02.98.79.61.18, *www.auberge.thegonnec.com*; ④; closed Sun evening, plus Mon evening in summer and all day Mon otherwise), is a surprisingly smart **hotel** for such a small village. Its main building houses a superb restaurant, where menus start at 100F/€15.24; the 250F/€38.11 gourmand option, which features lobster and spinach salad followed by scallop pancakes and roast sole, is out of this world. The *Restaurant du Commerce* at 1 rue de Paris (☎02.98.79.61.07; closed Sat, Sun & Aug), very near the church, serves more basic good-value meals, while the *Crêperie Steredden*, nearby at 6 rue de la Gare (☎02.98.79.43.34), is a friendly village crêperie that offers hundreds of speciality pancakes, on menus that range from 59F/€8.99 to 66F/€10.06. Finally, in an almost absurdly pastoral riverside setting 2km west of St-Thégonnec, the *Moulin de Kerlaviou* (☎02.98.79.60.57; ③) is a ravishing farmhouse **B&B**, offering two well-equipped en-suite rooms.

Guimiliau

The showpiece at the pretty flower-filled village of **GUIMILIAU**, 6km southwest of St-Thégonnec, is its **calvary**. This incredible ensemble holds over two hundred granite figures, depicting scenes from the life of Christ and covered with what the brochure calls "secular lichen". A uniquely Breton illustration, just above the Last Supper, depicts the unfortunate Katell Gollet being torn to shreds by demons in punishment for stealing consecrated wafers to give to her lover (who of course turned out to be the Devil).

Inside the church, years of patient restoration have turned the seventeenth-century organ, until recently a tangle of mangled wood, back into its original harmonious condition.

Lampaul-Guimiliau

The third of the major parish closes, **LAMPAUL-GUIMILIAU**, is a few kilometres further on. Here the painted-oak baptistry, the dragons on the beams and the appropriately wicked faces of the robbers on the calvary are the key components.

The *Hôtel de l'Enclos* (☎02.96.68.77.08; ③), 300m beyond the church on the left, is a modern hotel with good rooms and a very reasonable restaurant.

Landivisiau

LANDIVISIAU, just south of the N12 20km west of Morlaix, makes a good alternative to Morlaix as a base from which to tour the nearby parish closes.

There's not much to the town itself, but the **tourist office** at 12 av Foch (July & Aug Mon 10am–noon & 2–7pm, Tues–Sat 9am–noon & 2–7pm; Sept–June Mon–Thurs 9am–noon & 2–6pm, Fri 9am–noon & 2–5pm; ☎02.98.68.03.50) provides details of recommended bike routes, and coach tours operate regularly from the main square. There's also a choice of cheap **hotels**, the best value of which are *Le Terminus*, 94 av Foch (☎02.98.68.02.00; ②; closed Sun evening), a *Routier* that serves excellent meals, and *de l'Avenue*, 16 av de Coatmeur (☎02.98.68.11.67; ②; closed mid-Sept to mid-Oct).

OTHER BRETON CHURCHES

Breton Catholicism has a very distinctive character, closer to the Celtic past than to Rome. Though hundreds of its saints have never been approved by the Vatican, their brightly painted wooden figures adorn every church in the province. Their stories merge imperceptibly with the tales of moving menhirs, ghosts and sorcery. Visions and miracles are still assumed; and death's workmate, Ankou, is a familiar figure, even if no one now would dread his manifestation.

If you're inspired by the parish closes to go in search of similar village churches elsewhere in Brittany, other notable closes, chapels and calvaries include those at **Kermaria-an-Isquit**, **Ploumilliau**, **Grouannec**, **Pleyben**, **St-Fiacre** and **Guéhenno**.

La Roche-Maurice

West of Landivisiau, the N12 *autoroute* races towards Brest, but the lesser D712 and the railway follow a far more pleasant route, along the banks of the pretty Elorn River. After about 12km – not far beyond the chapel of **Pont-Christ**, beside a broad waterfall – the village of **LA ROCHE-MAURICE** occupies a steep high bluff above a curve in the river.

Only the solemn ivy-covered keep now remains of the **castle** that has occupied this site since the eleventh century, and was once supposedly home to Katell Gollett. It was abandoned at the end of the seventeenth century, and its stones used to build the houses that now surround it. Visitors are free to climb the wooden stairway that's rather clumsily attached to the outside, but not to ascend any further inside the ruin itself.

Nearby stands another large **parish close**, notable mainly for its rendition of the death-figure **Ankou** (see box above). This time he's carved above the holy-water stoup on the wall of the ossuary, facing the church, beneath the warning "I kill you all". The interior of the church is gorgeous, the nave divided in two by a lovely green-and-red rood screen, which shows the twelve apostles propped up by grotesque animals. Ringed by older carvings, the blue ceiling holds a celestial choir of angels. In summer, the ossuary houses local information, and an exhibition on the history of the town.

La Roche-Maurice has no hotels, but at least the *Auberge du Vieux Château*, in the square immediately below the castle (☎02.98.20.40.52), serves excellent **food**, with menus starting at 78F/€11.89. Alternatively, there's a lovely rural restaurant halfway between Landivisiau and La Roche-Maurice – the *Moulin de Brézal* (☎02.98.20.46.57), facing a little bridge that leads to the ruined 1533 chapel of Nôtre Dame de Bon Secours. All of its menus, priced from 98F/€14.94 upwards, include a scallop kebab. This beautiful riverside spot would also make an ideal setting for a picnic.

La Martyre

The oldest parish close of all, built in 1460, stands at the heart of **LA MARTYRE**, 7km south of La Roche-Maurice on the road to Sizun (see p.319). This is the most attractive of all the local villages, with stones of its complete parish close seamlessly integrated into the walls of its main street. Ankou clutches a severed head above the stoup in the peculiarly lopsided entrance porch, watched over not only by a carved red-ochre Virgin, giving birth, but also a nestfull of house martins.

Inside, the church is damp and somewhat faded, but it does have an attractive gilt altar.

Landerneau

If instead of detouring to La Martyre you continue west on the scenic D712 beyond La Roche-Maurice, you soon reach **LANDERNEAU**, at the mouth of the Elorn estuary. This too was once a major port; now it's more of a tourist show-piece. The **pont de Rohan** in the middle of town is said to be, along with the Ponte Vecchio in Florence, the last inhabited bridge in Europe, and is also the site of the local **tourist office** (July & Aug Mon–Sat 9am–12.30pm & 1.30–7pm, Sun 10am–1pm; Sept–June Mon–Sat 9am–noon & 2–6pm, Sun 10am–1pm; ☎02.98.85.13.09).

Landerneau offers several **accommodation** possibilities. Either *Le Clos du Pontic*, south of the river on rue du Pontic (☎02.98.21.50.91; ④; closed Fri evening & Sat lunch, plus Sun evening in low season), or *l'Amandier*, 55 rue de Brest (☎02.98.83.10.89; ③; closed Sun evening & Mon), would be a real treat, both being comfortable old-style hotels with excellent restaurants.

Plougastel-Daoulas

West of Landerneau, the Elorn broadens dramatically as it enters the Rade de Brest. The city of Brest (see p.283) sprawls along its northern banks at this point, but the southern side holds one final site associated with the parish closes. The church in the village of **PLOUGASTEL-DAOULAS** was built in 1870, and is far from interesting, but just outside it stands a **calvary** that ranks among the finest in Brittany.

This extraordinarily elaborate affair was completed in 1604, to celebrate the passing of an outbreak of the Plague – hence the bumps on the shaft of the main cross, designed to recall the sores on the bodies of the victims. Carvings on each of the four sides of the base depict scenes from the Life of Christ. Sadly, the rest of the village has not been restored so sensitively after the bombing of World War II. A weird shopping mall now overlooks the calvary, equipped with a giant Scrabble board for local senior citizens and a truly awful mural recounting the history of cinema.

Kerjean

April–June & Sept daily except Tues 2–6pm; July & Aug daily 10am–7pm; Oct daily except Tues 2–5pm; Nov–March Wed & Sun 2–5pm. 25F/€3.81, students 18F/€2.74.

If not quite the "Versailles of Brittany", as it is promoted, **KERJEAN** is a surpris-ingly classic château for this remote corner of France. Though little more than 15km from Roscoff, it's not that easy to find – you need to be on the D30, running from Plouescat to Landivisiau, and to turn right shortly after St-Vougay. Roscoff–Brest buses stop at **Lanhouarneau**, 5km west of the château.

What you're confronted by when you do arrive is a moated Renaissance **château**, set in its own park. It was built in the sixteenth century by the lords of Kerjean, with the express intention of overshadowing the mansion of their former feudal overlord, the Carman of Lanhouarneau. Under some archaic quirk of feal-ty the Kerjean lords had been obliged each year to take an egg, in a cart, and to cook it for the Carman (whatever a Carman may have been). The château must have made the memory a whole lot easier to bear. In the glorious words of Louis XIII, "as one of the nicest houses in our kingdom [Kerjean] is such a charming and magnificent structure that it is worthy of receiving us as guests".

The building, state property these days, is an odd jumble of the authentic, the restored and the imported. There is one original ceiling, one original floor and one original door; and the guide on the optional 45-minute tours (some of which are in English) has one original joke to match. Nevertheless it's an interesting place, and if you choose to wander around on your own there's a certain amusement to be derived from the bizarre placing of objects and the lack of explanations. In the scullery are two thirteenth-century choirstalls from St-Pol cathedral, each seat carved with the head of its occupant; a statue of St Sebastian "run through with arrows" has not an arrow in sight; and it is unclear quite what St Anthony is doing "with the little pig". More standard Breton furnishings are the cupboard-like, panelled box-beds which people used to climb inside to sleep – shut in tight for the night.

Kerjean is also used in summer for temporary exhibitions, and open-air theatrical performances have been scheduled in recent years for Friday nights in July and August.

Lesneven and Le Folgoët

Continuing inland, whether you are headed for southern Brittany or for Le Conquet and Ouessant island, **Le Folgoët** is another stop worth planning for. It is more easily accessible than Kerjean, though by bus you'll probably find yourself dropped a couple of kilometres out at the small town of **LESNEVEN**. The main features here are an abbey, on the main square, and some eccentric houses – slate-roofed and convex-panelled – in the narrow lanes. A visit to the **German war cemetery** a short distance southeast of the centre is a sobering experience (see p.134 for a general piece on war cemeteries).

Lesneven does not itself hold any great interest, though its ivy-coated café is an attractive place to break your journey, and the **hotel** *Le Weekend*, pont du Châtel (☎02.98.25.40.57; ③; restaurant closed Mon lunch, plus Sun evening in low season), provides good-value accommodation.

Le Folgoët

LE FOLGOËT is a couple of kilometres – about half an hour's walk – southwest of Lesneven. At first sight no more than a small village, with a well-kept and rather English-looking green, it owes both its **Notre Dame** church, and its name, which means "Fool's Wood", to a fourteenth-century simpleton called Solomon. After an unappreciated lifetime repeating the four Breton words for "O Lady Virgin Mary", he found fame in death by growing a white lily out of his mouth. The church was erected on the site of his favourite spring, and holds a *pardon* on September 8 or the preceding Sunday. (On the fourth Sunday of July there is also a *pardon* of St Christopher, which involves a blessing of cars that nonmotorists may find verging on the blasphemous.) In its quieter moments, however, it's a lovely church, colourfully garnished with orange moss and clinging verdure (a sign of the penetrating damp inside), and with a bumpy and stubbly approximation of a "Kreisker" spire. It has been restored bit by bit since the damage of the Revolution, and an unusual amount of statuary has been placed on the many low niches all around the outside. The most recent expenditure has been to put fresh white-plaster noses on the apostles guarding its entrance, who in consequence look like hastily rounded-up and not quite well-scrubbed-enough choirboys.

Immediately opposite, a fifteenth-century manor house has arranged in the lush lawns by its front path a selection of decaying sculpture from the church – gargoyles and griffins and an armless Jesus.

The abers of the northwest coast

The coast west from Roscoff holds some of the most dramatic shoreline in Brittany, a jagged series of **abers** – narrow estuaries, neither as deep nor as steep-sided as the fjords with which they are occasionally compared – in the midst of which are clustered small, isolated resorts, heavy on modern holiday homes but relatively short on hotels and other amenities. It's a little on the bracing side, especially if you're making use of the numerous **campsites**, but that just has to be counted as part of the appeal. In summer, at least, the temperatures are mild enough, and things get progressively more sheltered as you move around towards Le Conquet and Brest.

Plouescat
PLOUESCAT is the first real resort to the west of Roscoff. It is not quite on the sea itself, but there are **campsites** nearby on each of three adjacent beaches, with the nicest being *Poul Foën* (☎02.98.69.81.80; closed Sept to mid-June). In the town, you'll find a high-roofed old wooden market hall, for picnic provisions, and a statue of a sea horse with a Yin and Yang symbol in its tail. Of the **hotels**, best value is the little *Roc'h-Ar-Mor*, right on the beach at Porsmeur (☎02.98.69.63.01; ①; closed Oct–March). Roscoff to Brest **buses** stop at Plouescat before turning inland.

At the village of **KEREMMA**, inland from the sea on the way between Plouescat and Brignogan, there's another lovely little **campsite** (☎02.98.61.62.79; closed mid-Sept to mid-June), set along a green avenue lined with meadows of purple and yellow flowers.

Brignogan-Plage
BRIGNOGAN-PLAGE, on the next *aber*, has a small natural harbour, once the lair of wreckers, with beaches and weather-beaten rocks to either side, as well as its own menhir. Here, once again, the tide recedes way out towards the mouth of the bay, leaving surreal clumps of seaweed-coated stone bulging up among the stranded boats. The **plage de Ménéham**, 2km west of town, is a gem of a beach.

You'll find a **tourist office** in Brignogan's main square (July & Aug Mon–Sat 10am–7.30pm, Sun 10am–1pm; Sept–June Tues–Sat 10.30am–12.30pm & 4–6pm; ☎02.98.83.41.08), which will provide details of local sailing and horse-riding

---

The council of **Plouescat** attained a certain notoriety in 1987, when its members decided they could no longer live with the embarrassing presence of an exceptionally phallic rock on one of the local beaches and dynamited it to smithereens at dead of night. Local artists responded by creating several much more embarrassing substitutes which you might care to look out for.

schools. In addition, there are two high-season **campsites** in the vicinity, both with two stars – the central municipal site at Keravézan, the *Camping de la Côte des Legendes* (☎02.98.83.41.65; closed Nov–April), and the *du Phare*, to the east of town (☎02.98.83.45.06; closed Oct–March) – while the **hotel** *Castel Regis* (☎02.98.83.40.22; ④; closed Oct–March) is a trifle expensive but beautifully situated among the rocks, right at the headland. *Ar Reder Mor*, at 35 av de Gaulle in the centre of the little town (☎02.98.83.40.09; ②; closed Nov), is cheaper but fairly nondescript.

Plouguerneau, Lilia and Grouannec

Moving west again, along the D10, **PLOUGUERNEAU** is a village of just over 5000 inhabitants that was the unlikely recipient in 1990 of the **Prix de l'Europe**, awarded each year by the Council of Europe to the most exemplary European community. Previous winners include Istanbul, Avignon and The Hague; Plouguerneau was chosen largely on the basis of its vigorous and successful twinning with the German town of Edingen-Neckerhausen, near Heidelberg, which has so far produced more than twenty Franco-German marriages.

Five kilometres northwest of Plouguerneau, the dramatic waterfront community of **LILIA** makes a perfect setting for the **hotel** *Castel Ac'h* (☎02.98.04.70.11; ②), which has an excellent seafood **restaurant**. In summer, pleasure boats from here take a short cruise out to bob at the foot of the shaft of the **Vierge lighthouse** – at 78m, said to be the tallest in Europe (boats operate Easter–Sept; standard cruise 65F/€9.91; restricted visits to the lighthouse itself are possible in July & Aug, 80F/€12.20; for schedules call ☎02.98.04.74.94).

Plouguerneau is also near to an unexpected pleasure, the church of **Notre Dame de Grouannec**, a small but complete parish close ensemble about 4km inland. It has been extensively restored, and looks all the better for it, with its fountain, ossuary, mini-cloister and profusion of gargoyles.

L'Aber-Wrac'h

The *aber* between Plouguerneau and the yachting port of **L'ABER-WRAC'H** has a stepping-stone crossing just upstream from the bridge at Lanillis, built in Gallo-Roman times, and its long, cut stones still cross the three channels of water (access off the D28 signposted "Rascoll"), and continue past farm buildings to the right to "Pont du Diable".

L'Aber-Wrac'h itself (which you may also see referred to as Landeda) is a promising place to spend a little time. It's an attractive, modest-sized resort, within easy reach of a whole range of sandy beaches and a couple of worthwhile excursions. Beyond the tiny fishing port, which is also home to a busy sailing school, the Baie des Anges stretches away towards the Atlantic, with the only sound the cry of seagulls feasting on the oyster beds. The coastal waters nearby are prime territory for **divers**; boat trips can be arranged through Abersub (☎02.98.04.81.22, *abersub.chapon@wanadoo.fr*).

At the start of the bay, a couple of hundred metres past the town's little strip of bars and restaurants, the irresistible *Hôtel la Baie des Anges*, 350 route des Anges (☎02.98.04.90.04, *www.baie-des-anges-com*; ④; closed Jan to mid-Feb), commands stunning views out to sea from the start of its vast curve; part of the Relais de Silence organization, it's a peaceful and exceptionally comfortable place to **stay**, featuring a spacious bar with a small waterfront terrace – for the use of guests only. For campers, two **campsites**, the one-star *de Penn Enez* (☎02.98.04.99.82;

closed Oct–May), and the three-star *des Abers* (☎02.98.04.93.35; closed late Sept to mid-April), nestle amid the dunes at the very tip of the headland. The best **restaurant** in L'Aber-Wrac'h, *Le Brennig* (☎02.98.04.81.12; closed Tues, plus Oct to mid-March), is back at the other end of the main strip, and prepares fine menus from 98F/€14.94. However, with space at a premium you can be surer of getting a table at the *Cap'tain* in the port proper (☎02.98.04.82.03; closed Mon & Tues in low season), a busy but friendly crêperie that offers continuous service not only of crêpes but also any seafood speciality you care to name.

Clearly signposted 4km west of L'Aber-Wrac'h, on the right side of the next inlet along, L'Aber-Benoît, the **oyster beds** of **Prat-Ar-Coum** (☎02.98.04.00.12) are renowned for producing the best oysters in western Brittany. A quayside stall sells them year-round, and a small restaurant is open in July and August only.

Portsall

At the small harbour of **PORTSALL**, 5km along the coast from L'Aber-Benoît, the gleaming new **Espace Amoco Cadiz** commemorates a defining moment in local history (daily 9.30am–1pm & 2.30–7pm; free). On March 17, 1978, the sinking of the *Amoco Cadiz* supertanker resulted in an **oil spill** that devastated 350km of the Breton coastline, and threatened to ruin the local economy. Displays and films document not only the immense task of cleaning up the mess, but also the long legal battle to obtain compensation from the "multinational monster" responsible. The French government eventually obtained 1045 million francs in 1992, of which 100 million were passed on to local councils and communities. The ship's huge anchor now stands in the car park across from the hall, while the wreck itself, 1100 metres off shore, has become a popular dive site.

Trémazan

Once past Portsall, the coast becomes a glorious succession of dunes and open spaces, with long beaches stretching at low tide way out towards tiny islands. Each little inlet here seems to shelter a treasure of a beach, ideal for family swimming, while bracing walks lead through the heather-covered headlands that abut the open sea.

One especially romantic spot comes just 5km beyond Portsall, where the crumbling walls of the *Sleeping Beauty*-style **castle** of **TRÉMAZAN** look down on a magnificent beach. The fleeing Tristan and Iseult are said to have made their first landing in Brittany here, and the cracked ivy-covered keep still stands proud, pierced by a large heart-shaped hole. The castle is not formally open to the public; it's totally overgrown, and to reach it you have to scramble your way through the brambles that fill its former moat. Once you're there, however, it's a real haven for a summer afternoon.

In the immediate vicinity, a *logis de France* in the nondescript village of **KER-SAINT LANDUNVEZ**, the *Hostellerie du Castel* (☎02.98.48.63.35; ③; closed Oct–March), makes an ideal overnight stop, with very comfortable and inexpensive en-suite rooms and a good restaurant. If you prefer a slightly busier resort, however, continue west to Porspoder a few kilometres further on – pausing to look at the exquisite wooden seaside **chapel of St Samson** on the way.

Porspoder

PORSPODER is itself a pretty quiet place, but does serve as a centre for the many campers who set themselves up on the dunes of the **Presqu'île St-Laurent**

which faces it. Most of the houses around are empty other than in summer – it must be pretty bleak in winter – but in season it's an attractive place to be, open to the ocean. There's a cheap **hotel**, the *Pen Ar Bed* (☎02.98.89.90.38; ➀; closed Oct–March), on the long seafront rue de l'Europe.

Le Conquet

LE CONQUET, the southernmost of the *abers* resorts, at the far western tip of Brittany 24km beyond Brest, makes the best holiday base of all. A wonderful place, scarcely developed, it is flanked by a long beach of clean white sand, protected from the winds by the narrow spit of the Kermorvan peninsula, and has ferry access to the islands of Ouessant and Molène. It is very much a working fishing village, the grey-stone houses leading down to the stone jetties of a cramped harbour – which occasionally floods, to the intense amusement of the locals, the waves washing over the cars left by tourists making the trip to Ouessant.

The coast around Le Conquet is low-lying, not the rocky confrontation with a savage sea that one might expect, and Kermorvan, across the estuary, seems to glide into the sea – its shallow cliffs are topped by a strip of turf that looks as if you could peel it right off. Apart from the lighthouse at the end, the peninsula is just grassland, bare of buildings and a lovely place to walk in the evening across the footbridge from Le Conquet.

The most exciting trips out from Le Conquet are to the islands – detailed in the box opposite. As a variation, though, a good walk 5km south brings you to the lighthouse at **Pointe St-Mathieu**, looking out to the islands from its site among the ruins of the Benedictine **Abbaye de St-Mathieu**. A small exhibition (April & May Wed, Sat & Sun 2.30–6.30pm; June & Sept daily 2.30–6.30pm; July & Aug daily 11am–7pm; Oct & Nov Wed, Sat & Sun 2–6pm; 10F/€1.52) explains the abbey's history, including the legend that it holds the skull of St Matthew, brought here from Ethiopia by local seafarers.

Practicalities
The *Relais du Vieux Port*, quai Drellac (☎02.98.89.15.91; ➁; closed Jan), offers a handful of inexpensive but attractive **rooms** right by the jetty in Le Conquet, and has a simple crêperie downstairs. Nearby, the larger *Pointe Ste Barbe* (☎02.98.89.00.26; ➁–➆; closed Mon out of season & mid-Nov to mid-Dec) offers amazing sea views to guests in its more expensive rooms, and has a great restaurant, where menus start at 100F/€15.24. There are also two well-equipped two-star **campsites**, *Le Théven* (☎02.98.89.06.90; closed Oct–March) and *Quère* (☎02.98.89.11.71; closed mid-Sept to mid-June). **Market** day in Le Conquet is Tuesday.

The *Hostellerie de la Pointe St-Mathieu*, housed in a thirteenth-century stone structure opposite the abbey entrance at Pointe St-Mathieu (☎02.98.89.00.19; ➃; closed Sun evening in low season), is a top-quality restaurant that has added a modern wing of tasteful ocean-view rooms.

The islands of Ouessant and Molène

The island of **Ouessant**, Ushant in English – and first described by the geographer Pytheas as early as 325 BC, under the name of Uxisama – lies 30km northwest

GETTING TO OUESSANT AND MOLÈNE

Penn Ar Bed (☎02.98.80.80.80, *www.penn-ar-bed.fr*) sail to **Ouessant** and **Molène** all year, with up to five daily departures from **Le Conquet** (first sailing at 8am daily in summer; return fare adult 157F/€23.94, under-17s 94F/€14.33), and one daily at 8.30am from **Brest** (return fare adult 186F/€28.35, under-17s 112F/€17.07). They also depart from **Camaret** at 8.45am on Wednesday from May until mid-July, and Monday to Saturday at 8.45am from mid-July until the end of August (return fare adult 170F/€25.92, under-17s 100F/€15.24).

    Finist'Mer operate high-speed ferries to **Ouessant** in summer only, from **Camaret** (☎02.98.27.88.44; return fare adult 160F/€24.39, under-17s 95F/€14.48), **Le Conquet** (☎02.98.89.16.61; adult 148F/€22.56, under-17s 84F/€12.81) and **Lanildut**, 25km northwest of Brest (☎02.98.04.40.72; adult 155F/€23.63, under-17s 90F/€13.72). Bikes cost 65–70F/€9.91–10.67 extra. In June and September, they offer a daily departure from **Camaret** at 8.30am, calling at **Le Conquet** at 9.30am, another departure from **Le Conquet** at 5pm, and an extra departure from Le Conquet at 11am on Saturday. In July and August, they offer a morning departure from **Camaret** at 9.30am, plus up to seven ferries daily from **Le Conquet** and an additional service from **Lanildut**, departing at 9.20am daily and taking just half an hour to reach **Ouessant**. Certain summer sailings call in at **Molène** as well.

    In addition, you can **fly** to Ouessant with **Finist'Air** (☎02.98.84.64.87). The fifteen-minute flights leave **Brest** daily at 8.30am and 5pm in summer, 8.30am and 4.45pm in winter. The adult single fare is 340F/€51.84 (440F/€67.08 return), under-13s travel half-price, and groups of three or more adults go for 270F/€41.16 each.

of Le Conquet. Standing at the outermost end of a chain of smaller islands and half-submerged granite rocks its lighthouse at Creac'h (said to be the strongest in the world) is regarded as the entrance to the English Channel. Most of the archipelago is uninhabited, save perhaps, like Beniguet, for a few rabbits, but **Molène**, midway, has a village and can be visited. Both Molène and Ouessant are served by at least one ferry each day from Le Conquet and Brest; however, it is not practicable to visit more than one in a single day. Note that the ferries can be very crowded in summer, and it's well worth booking your tickets in advance if at all possible.

Ouessant

The ride to **OUESSANT** is generally a tranquil affair – though the ferry has to pick its way from buoy to buoy, through a sea which is liable suddenly to blow up and become too dangerous to navigate. There have been many wrecks among the reefs, most famously the *Drummond Castle* which foundered as the finale to a concert celebrating the end of its voyage from Cape Town to England in June 1896. For all its storms, though, the climate is mild – Ouessant even records the highest mean temperatures in France in January and February.

    You arrive on Ouessant at the modern **harbour** in the ominous-sounding Baie du Stiff. There are a scattering of houses here, and dotted about the island, but the only town (with the only hotels and restaurants) is 4km distant at **LAMPAUL**. Everybody from the boat heads there, either by the bus that meets each arriving ferry, on bicycles rented for about 60F/€9.15 per day from one of the many waiting entrepreneurs, or in a long walking procession that straggles along the one

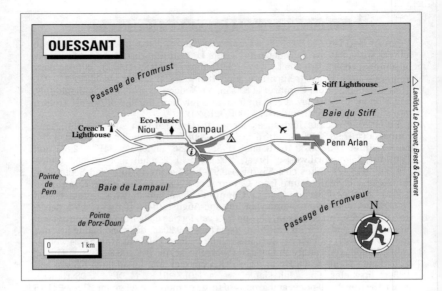

road. Bicycle rental is the most convenient option, as the island is really too big to explore on foot.

As well as its more mundane facilities, Lampaul has Ouessant's best beaches sprawled around its bay. There are few specific sights, and the whole place quickly becomes very familiar. But the town cemetery is worth visiting, with its war memorial listing all the ships in which the townsfolk were lost, and its graves of unknown sailors washed ashore. A unique Ouessant tradition is also on show in the cemetery chapel – an array of wax *proëlla* crosses, which were used during the funerals of those islanders who never returned from the sea, to symbolize their absent remains.

At **NIOU**, 1km northwest, the **Maison du Niou** is actually two houses, one of which is a museum of island history, and the other is a reconstruction of a traditional island house, complete with two massive "box-beds", one for the parents and the other for the children (April Tues–Sun 2–6.30pm; May to mid-July & Sept daily 10.30am–6.30pm; mid-July to Aug daily 10.30am–6.30pm & 9–11pm; Oct–March Tues–Sun 2–4pm; 25F/€3.81). Officially, it forms half of the **Éco-Musée d'Ouessant**, in combination with the **Creac'h lighthouse**, another kilometre northwest (same hours; same ticket). This contains a small museum about lighthouses, and makes a good point from which to set out along the barren and exposed rocks of the north coast. Particularly in September and other times of migration, it's a remarkable spot for bird-watching; puffins, storm petrels and cormorants can all be seen. The star-shaped formations of crumbling walls are not extraterrestrial relics, but built so that the sheep – peculiarly tame here – can shelter from the strong winds.

Practicalities

General information on Ouessant is available from the **tourist office** in the main square in Lampaul (April–Aug Mon–Sat 9.30am–12.30pm & 2–5pm, Sun

9.30am–12.30pm; Sept–March Mon–Sat 9.45am–noon & 2–4pm, Sun 10am–noon; ☎02.98.48.85.83).

Lampaul boasts its own brand-new little **hostel**, *La Croix Rouge* (☎02.98.48.84.53), where a dorm bed plus breakfast costs 70F/€10.67. Also in Lampaul, the adjacent **hotels** *Océan* (☎02.98.48.80.03; ②) and *Fromveur* (☎02.98.48.81.30; ②) both offer a fairly basic standard of accommodation; the *Fromveur* specializes in traditional island cooking, which consists of attempting to render seaweed and mutton as palatable as possible, while the *Océan* has a sideline in organizing musical evenings. The *Roch Ar Mor*, just down the street (☎02.98.48.80.19; ②; closed Jan–March), is a marginally more attractive alternative. There is a small official **campsite**, the *Penn ar Bed* (☎02.98.48.84.65; closed Oct–March). You could, in fact, camp almost anywhere on the island, making arrangements with the nearest farmhouse (which may well let out rooms, too).

All the hotel **restaurants** serve menus for under 100F/€15.24, but if you just come for a day it's a good idea to buy a picnic before you set out – the Lampaul shops have limited and rather pricey supplies.

Molène

MOLÈNE is quite well populated for a sparse strip of sand. The port itself is better protected than that of Ouessant, and so there are more fishermen based here. The island's inhabitants derive their income from seaweed collection and drying – and to an extent from crabbing and crayfish, which they gather on foot, canoe and even tractor at low tide. The tides are more than usually dramatic, halving or doubling the island's territory at a stroke. Hence the origin of the name Molène, which comes from the Breton for "the bald isle".

As for sights, there is even less of tangible note than on Ouessant. Walking the rocks and the coast is the basic activity. Once again, though, the island cemetery is poignant and interesting, redolent of small community life in its concentration of babies' graves from a typhoid epidemic in the nineteenth century; they are marked by silver crosses, repainted each November 1. Equally small-time is the island's main anecdote, told to anyone drinking an evening away, of the evening in 1967 when the whole population gathered to watch the oil tanker *Torrey Canyon* floundering offshore in the passage de Fromveur.

Practicalities

Few visitors do more than look around for an afternoon's excursion from Le Conquet, but it's quite possible to stay on Molène and to enjoy it. There are **rooms** – very chilly in winter – at *Kastell An Doal* (☎02.98.07.39.11; ④; closed Jan), one of the old buildings by the port, and it's also possible to arrange to stay in a private house (☎02.98.07.39.05 for details).

Brest

Set in a magnificent natural harbour, known as the Rade de Brest, the city of **BREST** is doubly sheltered from the ocean storms by both the bulk of Léon to the north, and by the Crozon peninsula to the south. The Rade (or roadstead) is entered by the narrow deep-water channel of the Goulet de Brest, 5km long and 1.5km wide, with steep banks on both sides.

As one of the finest natural harbours in Europe, Brest has always played an important role in war and in trade whenever peace allowed. All the great names in French strategic planning – including Richelieu, Colbert, Vauban and Napoléon – have been instrumental in developing the port, which is today the base of the French Atlantic Fleet. Its dry dock can accommodate ships of up to 500,000 tonnes and, as a ship-repair centre, it ranks sixth in the world.

During World War II, Brest was relentlessly bombed to prevent the Germans from using it as a submarine base. When the Americans liberated it on September 18, 1944, after a six-week siege, they found the town devastated beyond recognition. It was necessary for the city to resume normal life as soon as possible, which meant the rebuilding had to be rushed at the expense of restoration, and the architecture of the postwar town is raw and bleak. There have been attempts, as in Caen, to green the city, but despite the heaviest rainfall in France the site has proved too windswept to respond fully to these efforts.

From a distance, from across the bay, the city can look appealing. But closer in it takes a real effort of will to decide to stop longer than it takes to change buses or trains. The roads are racetracks; the suburbs, remorselessly industrial; and World War II comprehensively destroyed any historic interest that may once have existed. The most rational reason for an outsider to visit would probably be for the bagpipe festival, held here for three days in August.

Arrival and information

The **gare SNCF** (☎02.98.80.50.50) and **gare routière** (☎02.98.44.46.73) are together in place du 19ème RI at the bottom of avenue Clémenceau. Brest is very much at the end of the railway system, though connected to Paris in just four hours, thanks to the TGV (which follows the northern route, via Morlaix and Rennes; the journey via Quimper takes much longer).

Bus services include those to Plouescat and Roscoff (Les Cars du Kreisker; ☎02.98.69.00.93); to the Crozon peninsula via Landevennec (Cars Douguet; ☎02.98.27.02.02); and to Le Conquet (Sarl St Mathieu Transports; ☎02.98.89.00.94).

Brest also has an **airport**, at Guipavas, 9km northeast of the centre, which is served by flights to **London** (Brit Air; ☎02.98.62.10.22) and **Ouessant** (Finist'Air; 2 daily in season; ☎02.98.84.64.87), as well as destinations throughout France. Should you need to rent a **car** on arrival, Avis have an office at 20bis rue de Siam (☎02.98.44.63.02).

As well as the sailings to Ouessant, detailed on p.281, in summer three or four **boats** per day make the 25-minute crossing from Brest's Port de Commerce to **Le Fret** on the Crozon peninsula (Société Azenor; June–Sept; ☎02.98.41.46.23; 90F/€13.72 return). Sailings are met at the port in Le Fret by buses for Crozon (15min), Morgat (30min) and Camaret (40min). Société Azenor and other operators also do excursions around the harbour and the Rade de Brest (1hr 30min).

Brest's **tourist office** on avenue Clémenceau faces place de la Liberté (mid-June to mid-Sept Mon–Sat 9.30am–12.30pm & 2–6.30pm, Sun 10am–noon & 2–4pm; mid-Sept to mid-June Mon–Sat 10am–12.30pm & 2–6pm; ☎02.98.44.24.96, *office.de.tourisme.brest@wanadoo.fr*), while the main **post office** is on place Général-Leclerc.

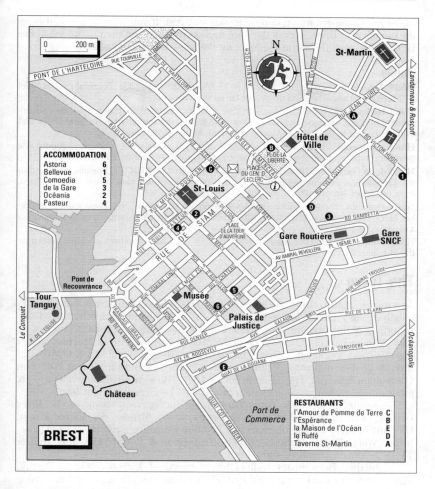

ACCOMMODATION

Astoria	6
Bellevue	1
Comoedia	5
de la Gare	3
Océania	2
Pasteur	4

RESTAURANTS

l'Amour de Pomme de Terre	C
l'Espérance	B
la Maison de l'Océan	E
le Ruffé	D
Taverne St-Martin	A

Accommodation

The vast majority of Brest's **hotels** remain open throughout the year; only a few, however, bother to maintain their own restaurants. Several lie within easy walking distance of the stations, in the vicinity of the central place de la Liberté.

The city also has a year-round **hostel**, near Océanopolis in a wooded setting on rue de Kerbriant, Port de Plaisance du Moulin-Blanc (☎02.98.41.90.41; 70F/€10.67 including breakfast). It's 3km east of the *gares SNCF* and *routière*, on bus #7.

The two-star *Camping du Goulet* (☎02.98.45.86.84) is not easy to find, and although it's close to the sea it's not in any case warmly recommended – it's hard to see why campers would choose to stay in Brest. If you need to use it, it is on the outskirts of Brest, across the Pont de Recouvrance and then to the left of the Le Conquet road (D789) in Ste-Anne du Portzic – take bus #7 or #14.

Hotels

Hôtel Astoria, 9 rue Traverse (☎02.98.80.19.10, fax 02.98.80.52.41). Peaceful central hotel with a cheerful ambience and decor, not far up from the port. ②.

Hôtel Bellevue, 53 bd Victor-Hugo (☎02.98.80.51.78, fax 02.98.46.02.84). Six-storey sound-proofed building, equipped with a lift. Not easy to find, but not far from the *gare SNCF* and well on the way to the lively St-Martin area; look for St-Michel church. ②.

Hôtel Comoedia, 21 rue d'Aguillon (☎02.98.46.54.82). Simple but very cheap rooms in a quiet street just up from the port, with an equally no-frills restaurant downstairs. ①.

Hôtel de la Gare, 4 bd Gambetta (☎02.98.44.47.01, fax 02.98.43.34.07). En-suite rooms opposite the stations; you can pay a little extra for an uninterrupted view of the Rade de Brest, from the upper storeys. ③.

Hôtel Océania, 82 rue de Siam (☎02.98.80.66.66, fax 02.98.80.65.50). Brest's finest upmarket hotel, offering large, attractively fitted rooms on the town's principal thoroughfare, plus a classy restaurant. ⑥.

Hôtel Pasteur, 29 rue Louis-Pasteur (☎02.98.46.08.73). Clean, good-value budget hotel near the St-Louis church. ②.

The Town

As a tourist centre, Brest has little to offer. Few relics of the past remain. The fif-teenth-century **castle** looks impressive on its headland, and offers a superb panorama of the city, but once inside it is not especially interesting. Three of its towers house part of the collection of the **Musée National de la Marine**, includ-ing a German "pocket submarine" based in Brest during World War II (April–Sept Mon & Wed–Sun 10am–6.30pm, Tues 2–6.30pm; Oct–March Mon & Wed–Sun 10am–noon & 2–6pm, Tues 2–6pm; 30F/€4.57). The same institution operates six other museums in France, including one at Port-Louis near Lorient (see p.348).

The fourteenth-century **Tour Tanguy** on the opposite bank of the River Penfeld, with its conical slate roof, serves as the **Musée du Vieux Brest**. Dioramas convey a vivid impression of just how attractive a city Brest used to be, before World War II (June–Sept daily 10am–noon & 2–7pm; Oct–May Wed & Thurs 2–5pm, Sat & Sun 2–6pm; free).

The **Jardins Botaniques**, a short distance north of Océanopolis in the Parc du Vallon de Strangalard beyond the football stadium, claim to be second in Europe only to Kew Gardens (gardens daily summer 9am–8pm, winter 9am–6pm, free; greenhouses July & Aug Mon–Fri 2–5pm, 20F/€3.05).

If all this fails to impress or excite you, you can always walk along the **Cours Dajot**, which displays the docklands in all their glory. It holds schools of various naval disciplines, arsenals, the marine records office and the **Pont de Recouvrance**, the largest drawbridge in Europe.

Océanopolis

Daily: June–Sept 9am–7pm; Oct–May 9am–6pm. 90F/€13.72, under-13s 70F/€10.67.

Brest's most up-to-the-minute attraction is **Océanopolis**, a couple of kilometres east of the city centre beside the Port de Plaisance du Moulin-Blanc. Year on year, this futuristic complex seems to get larger and larger (not to mention more and more expensive), and currently consists of three distinct **aquariums**. Its original white dome, now known as the **Temperate Pavilion**, focuses on the Breton littoral and Finistère's fishing industry, with its half-million gallons of water holding all kinds of fish, seals, molluscs, seaweed and sea anemones. The emphasis is very much on the edible, with displays on the life-cycle of a scallop, for example, culminating in a detailed recipe.

To that has been added a **Tropical Pavilion**, with a tankful of ferocious-looking sharks plus a myriad of rainbow-hued smaller fish that populate a highly convincing coral reef; a **Polar Pavilion**, complete with polar bears and penguins; and a **3-D cinema**. Everything's very high-tech, and perhaps a little too earnest for some visitors' tastes, but it's quite possible to spend a whole entertaining day on site – especially if you take the assorted restaurants, snack bars and gift stores into consideration.

Eating

As well as a concentration of low-priced places in the immediate area of the stations, Brest also offers a wider assortment of **restaurants**. Rue Jean-Jaurès, which climbs up east from the place de la Liberté, holds plenty of bistros and bars, while just off to the north, place Guérin is the centre of the student-dominated quartier St-Martin.

L'Amour de Pomme de Terre, 23 rue des Halles (☎02.98.43.48.51). The name says it all: this central restaurant, open daily until late, specializes not merely in potatoes, but in one single kind of potato, the "samba". Most dishes are simply baked potatoes topped with cheese or sausage, but they're better than any British equivalent, and there are also some tasty Breton stews.

L'Espérance, 6 place de la Liberté (☎02.98.44.25.29). Busy, inexpensive conventional restaurant in the lively square that faces the Hôtel de Ville, with a wide range of imaginative menus that start at 70F/€10.67 midweek. Closed Sun evening & Mon, plus last two weeks in Aug and first week of Sept.

La Maison de l'Océan, 2 quai de la Douane (☎02.98.80.44.84). Blue-hued fish restaurant down by the port, open every day and serving wonderful assortments of seafood from 85F/€12.96.

Ma Petite Folie, plage du Moulin-Blanc (☎02.98.42.44.42). Converted fishing boat, moored in the pleasure port, which serves a wonderfully fishy 110F/€16.77 set menu and also offers a wide range of à la carte dishes and daily specials. Closed Sun & two weeks in mid-Aug.

Le Ruffé, 1 rue Yves-Collet (☎02.98.46.07.70). An attractive place, open late, between the *gare SNCF* and the tourist office that prides itself on good, traditional French seafood dishes, served on menus costing 80F/€12.20 and upwards. Closed Sun.

La Taverne St-Martin, 92 rue Jean-Jaurès (☎02.98.80.48.17). Warm and friendly brasserie/restaurant, a few hundred metres east (and up) from the tourist office, behind a wooden half-timbered facade. Lunch from 60F/€9.15, dinner from 90F/€13.72, plus lots of à la carte snacks. Steak tartare is the house speciality. Open daily 8am–1am.

Drinking

Brest is unusual by Breton standards in having plenty of lively **bars.** The basic choice lies between hanging out with the sailors and fishermen down by the port, with the business community around the place de la Liberté, or with the seriously trendy student population in the St-Martin quarter, high up on and around Jean-Jaurès. In July and August, Thursday night is party night, with a free open-air festival taking place along the quai de la Douane.

Café de la Plage, 32 rue Massillon (☎02.98.43.03.30). Classic-looking open-fronted bar, on one corner of place Guérin. Heavy maroon decor and a transient population of citizens of all ages who share a common interest in talking at the tops of their voices.

Les Dubliners, 28 rue Mathieu-Donnart (☎02.98.46.04.98). Lively Irish pub in the St-Martin district, open daily from mid-afternoon until late, with Irish dancing on Mondays and live music on Thursdays and Sundays.

Les Quatres Vents, 18 quai de la Douane (☎02.98.44.42.84). Busy, friendly café-bar down by the port, which also sells simple snacks.

Around Brest

Exploring Léon from a base in Brest, Le Conquet and Ouessant are very much the places to head for – ideally by boat from the Port du Commerce (see p.281 for timetable). Otherwise, the immediate area is far from bursting with interest.

Take **ST-RÉNAN** for example, 15km northwest of the city on the D5. French towns often set up signs along approach roads to advertise their splendours – "*son château*", "*sa charme*", and so on. St-Rénan can only find "*son Syndicat d'Initiative*" to boast about – but for all that it's quite a pleasant small town and there are two noteworthy prehistoric sites in the immediate area.

Lanrivoaré

Five kilometres northwest of St-Rénan is the **church** of **LANRIVOARÉ**, which has a tiny plot in its graveyard where, alongside eight round stones, the 7777 victims of a fifth-century massacre are supposed to lie buried. Legend records that the stones were transformed from loaves of bread by St Hervé – but they're in fact most likely to be "cursing-stones", which exist in several Irish chapels and were used for calling down disease or destruction on an enemy. The person invoking the curse, after a certain number of prayers, turned the stone round seven times.

The Menhir de Kerloas

To find the **Menhir de Kerloas** (also known as Kervéatous or Plouarzel), you need to walk or drive (there's no bus) about 5km west of St-Rénan on the *old* Plouarzel road, parallel to the more modern D5. The menhir stands in a small clearing hedged in by fields, and is the highest point for miles around in these flatlands. Although the tip was knocked off by lightning 200 years ago (and was subsequently used as a cattle-trough), it is (at 11m) the tallest menhir still standing in western Europe.

The stone is probably at its best looming out of a damp and ominous Breton mist, producing, in this isolated spot, a powerful effect on the imagination. A further aid to fantasy are the circular protuberances over a metre from the ground on either side, against which newly married couples would rub their naked bodies in the hope of begetting children.

Towards the Crozon peninsula

Heading south from Brest, cyclists and pedestrians can cut straight over to the Crozon peninsula by **ferry**. A regular service will shuttle you across the bay, for a few francs, to Le Fret (see p.311). The ferry doesn't, however, carry cars, so **drivers** have a longer and more circuitous route, crossing the Elorn River over the vast spans of the **Pont Albert-Louppe** (42m high and almost 1km long) and then skirting the estuaries of the **Plougastel peninsula**.

Plougastel-Daoulas, just across the bridge, is at the edge of the main parish closes region, and described on p.275.

Daoulas

Ten kilometres beyond Plougastel-Daoulas, the **abbey** at **DAOULAS** holds Brittany's only Romanesque cloister. It now stands beautiful and isolated at the edge of cool monastery gardens, since its surrounding buildings were destroyed during the Revolution. The abbey is a short walk above the town, and a welcome oasis on a hot summer's day. It doubles as a cultural centre for Finistère, staging ambitious historical exhibitions lasting for around six months at a time (usual summer opening hours are daily 10am–7pm; information ☎02.98.25.84.39, *centre.culturel.abbaye.daoulas@infini.fr*; 35F/€5.34).

Le Faou

From Daoulas the motorway and railway cut down to Châteaulin (see p.315) and Quimper. For Crozon, you'll need to veer west at **LE FAOU**, a tiny medieval port, still with some of its sixteenth-century gabled houses and set on its own individual estuary. From beside the pretty little village church – whose porch holds some intriguing carved apostles – a sheltered corniche follows the river to the sea, where there are sailing and windsurfing facilities.

Le Faou holds two good and very similar **hotels**, each equipped with a top-class restaurant – the *Relais de la Place* (☎02.98.81.91.19; ③; closed mid-Sept to mid-Oct), and the Best Western *Hôtel de Beauvoir* (☎02.98.81.90.31, *www.hotel-beauvoir.com*; ④; closed Mon Sept–June, & mid-Nov to end Dec). The one snag is that they're not in the most attractive part of town, near the river, but a few hundred metres south in the newer and much noisier main square.

THE CROZON PENINSULA

The **Crozon peninsula** forms part of the **Parc Régional d'Armorique**, a haphazard area stretching from the forest of Huelgoat to the island of Ouessant that is, in principle at least, a protected natural-landscape area. What this means in reality is hard to fathom. Doubtless there are firm French bylaws against disturbing the wild flowers. However, for some reason these don't prevent nuclear submarines from lurking in the bay of Brest, nor low-flying helicopters from sporadically sweeping the skies above.

Nevertheless, military installations and operations notwithstanding, **Crozon**, with its wild beaches and craggy cliffs, is an attractive slice of countryside. A dramatic one, too, especially if you make the detour to climb up the **Menez-Hom** for an initial overview.

Regular summer ferries run between the port du Commerce in **Brest** and **Le Fret**, on the Crozon peninsula (see p.311). It's also possible to take a ferry direct from Le Fret to **Océanopolis** for the day (Société Azenor; June & Sept departures Mon–Sat 8.45am & 1pm, Sun 1pm; July & Aug departures Mon–Sat 8.45am, 10.30am & 1pm, Sun 10.30am & 1pm; ☎02.98.41.46.23; 160F/€24.39 return, including admission).

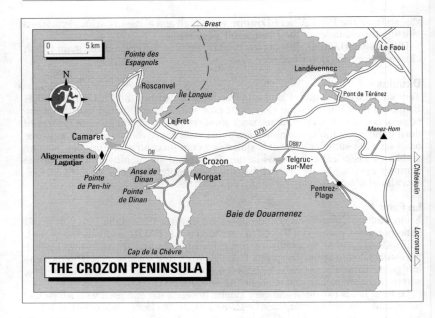

THE CROZON PENINSULA

The Menez-Hom and around

At just 330m, the **Menez-Hom** is not really a mountain. But the summit stands sufficiently alone to command tremendous views across Crozon – a chaos of water, with lakes, rivers and bridges wherever you look, and usually a scattering of hang-gliders dangling in the sky. The exposed and windswept viewing table reveals it to be 300 miles (483km) from both London and Paris.

Landévennec

Nine kilometres west of Le Faou, by way of a beautiful shoreline road, the **Pont de Térénez** spans the Aulne – outlet for the Nantes–Brest canal – to the Crozon peninsula.

Doubling back to the right as soon as you cross the bridge brings you after a further 5km to **LANDÉVENNEC**, where archeologists are uncovering the outline of what may be Brittany's oldest **abbey** (June & last two weeks of Sept daily 2–6pm; July to mid-Sept Mon–Sat 10am–7pm, Sun 2–7pm; Oct–May Sat, Sun & hols 2–6pm; 25F/€3.81). Nothing survives above ground of the original thatched hut, constructed in a forest clearing by St Gwennolé around 485 AD. After the abbey had been pillaged by raiding Normans in 913 AD, however, it was rebuilt in stone. Those foundations can now be seen, together with displays on monastic history and facsimile manuscripts.

There's a small but attractive **hotel** in the heart of Landévennec, *Le St-Patrick* (☎02.98.27.70.83; ②; closed Wed & Sun in low season).

Saint-Malo

Côte de Granit Rose

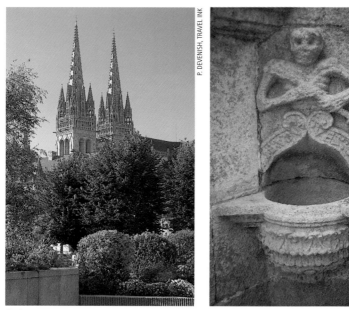
P. DEVENISH, TRAVEL INK

Quimper

Ankou, La Roche-Maurice
GREG WARD

GILES STOKOE

Beach huts, Brittany

The château at Vitré

Thatched cottage, Grande-Brière

Dance of Death, Kermaria-an-Isquit

Côte de Granit Rose

Concarneau

Carnac

Rural Breton scene

The Musée de l'École Rurale

Still inland from the peninsula, roughly 3km north of the Menez-Hom and unfortunately not on any bus routes, is the village of **TRÉGARVAN**. At a solitary crossroads outside town, where the Argol–Dineault and Trégarven–Menez-Hom roads meet, you'll find the **Musée de l'École Rurale** (April daily except Sat 2–6pm; May, June & Sept daily 2–6pm; July & Aug daily 10.30am–7pm; Oct & Nov daily except Sat 2–5pm; Dec–March Mon–Fri 2–5pm; 22F/€3.35). Housed in what used to be the local secondary school, it's one of those small, quirky French museums that sound slightly ludicrous on paper but are distinctly fascinating on the spot.

The school was closed down due to lack of numbers in 1974, then reopened a decade later as a re-creation of a Breton classroom circa 1920. At that time, all the kids would have spoken Breton at home – but they were forbidden to speak it here. The teacher gave a little wooden cow to the first child to utter a word in the mother tongue, and they could get rid of the *vache* only by squealing on the next offender. The lesson, to parents and pupils alike, was obvious enough: that Breton was backward and a handicap. Breton was suppressed, with considerable efficiency, throughout the province, and only recently have things begun to change. As well as Breton-language nursery and primary schools, there's one secondary school and a fund-raising campaign for a lycée. While a few years back SNCF had to be taken to court before it would accept a cheque made out in Breton, there is now a Breton bank.

St-Nic Pentrez and Telgruc-sur-mer

Beyond the Menez-Hom, a magnificent road sweeps down across the heather onto the Crozon peninsula. At the foot of the hill, to the south, **ST-NIC PENTREZ** has excellent beaches – this is the sandy side of the peninsula – and several **campsites**, among them the three-star *Ker-Ys* on the main beach (☎02.98.26.53.95; closed mid-Sept to April).

Another good beach, this time with a four-star campsite, *Le Panoramic* (☎02.98.27.78.41; closed mid-Sept to mid-May), is located further round towards Crozon at **TELGRUC-SUR-MER**. Some of the smaller towns inland hold **hotels**, such as the *Hôtel-Crêperie de Pors Morvan* (☎02.98.81.53.23; ④; closed Oct–April) at **PLOMODIERN**.

Morgat, Camaret and the beaches

The first town on the peninsula proper, **CROZON**, is not much more than a one-way traffic system to distribute tourists among the various resorts – though it does keep a market running most of the week.

Morgat

MORGAT, just down the hill from Crozon, makes a more realistic and enticing base than its larger neighbour. It has a long and very sandy crescent beach, much-loved by windsurfers, which ends beneath a pine slope, and a well-sheltered harbour that's filled with pleasure boats raced down from England and Ireland – and the leathery rich telling each other about their spinnakers.

The main plebeian attractions are **boat trips** around the various headlands, such as the Cap de la Chèvre (which is a good clifftop walk if you'd rather make your own way). The most popular is the 45-minute tour of the **Grottes**, multi-coloured caves in the cliffs, accessible only by sea but with steep "chimneys" up to the clifftops, where in bygone days saints would lurk to rescue the ship-wrecked. These cruises are organized by Vedettes Rosmeur on the quay (daily May–Sept; ☎02.98.27.10.71; 50F/€7.62), and run as frequently as every quarter of an hour in high season. They often leave full, however, so it's worth booking a few hours in advance.

Practicalities

The **tourist office** for the whole peninsula is in what used to be the *gare SNCF* at Crozon (mid-June to mid-Sept Mon–Sat 9am–7pm, Sun 10am–1pm; mid-Sept to mid-June Mon–Fri 10am–12.30pm & 2.30–5.30pm, Sat 10am–noon; ☎02.98.26.17.18); an information office for the Crozon–Morgat area stands at the start of Morgat's beach crescent on the boulevard du France (May, June & Sept Mon–Sat 9.15am–noon & 2–6.30pm; July & Aug Mon–Sat 9.30am–7pm, Sun 10am–1pm; ☎02.98.27.07.92).

Hotels in Morgat tend to be on the expensive side. Appealing options include the grand *Hôtel-Restaurant de la Ville d'Ys*, which enjoys fabulous views from its perch just above the port (☎02.98.27.06.49; ③; closed Oct–March), and has a good dinner-only restaurant where menus start at 95F/€14.48, and the quieter *Julia*, set 400m back from the beach at 43 rue de Tréflez (☎02.98.27.05.89; ③; closed Nov to mid-Feb). Immediately below the *Ville d'Ys* at the far end of the beach, *Les Échoppes*, 24 quai du Kador (☎02.98.26.12.63; closed Oct–Easter), is a flowery stone cottage with tiny little windows. Though there's no sign to tell you so, it's Morgat's best **restaurant**, serving good menus from 100F/€15.24.

With a total of 865 pitches available, **campers** are spoilt for choice in Morgat; best are the three-star sites at *Plage de Goulien* (☎02.98.27.17.10; closed mid-Sept to mid-June) and *Les Pins*, towards the Pointe de Dinan (☎02.98.27.21.95; closed mid-Sept to mid-June).

Camaret

CAMARET is another sheltered port, at the very tip of the peninsula. Its most dis-tinguishing feature is the pink-orange **château de Vauban**, standing foursquare at the end of the long jetty that runs back parallel to the main town waterfront. Walled, moated and accessible via a little gatehouse reached by means of a draw-bridge, it was built in 1689 to guard the approaches to Brest. These days it guards no more than a motley assortment of decaying half-submerged fishing boats, abandoned to rot beside the jetty. There are two **beaches** nearby – a small one to the north and another, larger and more attractive, in the low-lying (and rather marshy) Anse de Dinan to the south.

Camaret also boasts one moment of historical significance. It was here in 1801 that an American, Robert Fulton, tested the first **submarine**. The *Nautilus* was a stuffy, leaking, oar-powered wooden craft, whose five-man crew spent some time scuttling about beneath the waves in the hope of sinking a British frigate. Fulton was denied his glory, though, when the frigate chose to sail away, ignorant of the heavy-breathing peril that was so frantically seeking it out.

Practicalities

Camaret is not a large town, but in season it offers all the shops and supplies you could need. A little walk away from the centre, around the port towards the protective jetty, the quai du Styvel contains a row of excellent **hotels**. Both the *Vauban* (☎02.98.27.91.36; ②; closed Dec & Jan) and *du Styvel* (☎02.98.27.92.74; ②; closed Jan) are exceptionally hospitable, and the *Styvel* has a restaurant, with an 80F/€12.20 menu offering *moules à la Ouessane*, and crabs, oysters and scallops rearing their assorted heads on the 115F/€17.53 menu. Both have rooms that look right out across the bay, as does the more modern, upmarket *Thalassa* next door (☎02.98.27.86.44; ④; closed mid-Oct to March), which has a heated sea-water swimming pool. There are also various **campsites** to fall back on, such as the four-star *Le Grand Large* (☎02.98.27.91.41, *lglca@club-internet.fr*; closed Oct–March) and the two-star municipal *Lannic* (☎02.98.27.91.31; closed mid-Sept to mid-June).

Back along the quayside in the centre of town, *La Voilerie*, 7 quai Toudouze (☎02.98.27.99.55; closed Wed & Sun evening in low season), is an excellent **fish restaurant**. Lunch menus start at 65F/€9.91, featuring a flavourful *soupe de poissons*, while four-course dinners, bursting with oysters and prawns, range 85F/€12.96 to 160F/€24.39. À la carte options include poached skate, grilled sea bream, and game dishes such as roast guinea fowl.

From mid-June until September, Vedettes Sirènes (☎02.98.27.91.41) run boat trips that tour the offshore bird sanctuary of the Tas de Pois; their office is next to the **tourist office** on quai Toudouze in the port (mid-June to mid-Sept Mon–Sat 9am–7pm, Sun 10am–noon & 3–6pm; mid-Sept to mid-June Mon–Fri 9am–12.30pm & 2–6.30pm, Sat 9am–12.30pm; ☎02.98.27.93.60, *www.camaret -sur-mer.com*).

In summer, Penn Ar Bed (☎02.98.27.88.22, *www.penn-ar-bed.fr*) operate an irregular **ferry** service from Camaret to the islands of **Ouessant** (see box on p.281; 170F/€25.92 return) and **Sein** (see p.298; 170F/€25.92 return), while Finist'Mer sail to **Ouessant** only (☎02.98.27.88.44; 160F/€24.39 return).

The Pointe du Penhir

At the **Pointe du Penhir**, 3km south of Camaret, footpaths lace around the various exposed and windy headlands, frequented mainly by binocular-toting twitchers eyeing up the guillemots and other seabirds that swoop on the Tas de Pois rock stacks, scattered out in the sea. Even crazier individuals abseil their way down similar rock stacks still attached to the mainland; here and there, a few paths pick their way down the sheer cliffs, but most peter out in the little natural amphitheatre that faces the Tas de Pois. A monument to the Breton Resistance stands nearby.

To one side of the road on the way out to the *pointe*, amid the brilliant purples and yellows of the heathland, are the megalithic **Alignements de Lagatjar**. Perhaps, though, you need to imagine that this heath is still blasted and empty, and that there's no "Dolmens" housing estate next to the stones, to appreciate this forlorn, unsignposted prehistoric ruin. The stones are little more than weather-beaten stumps, and it's hard to discern a pattern on the ground; the experts responsible for their restoration say there are four distinct lines rather than a circle.

The Pointe des Espagnols

Heading north from Camaret or Morgat, on the other hand, brings you to the **Pointe des Espagnols**, where a viewing point signals the end of the peninsula. Brest is very close and very visible – without being any the more enticing. Around the cape are several forbidden military installations and abandoned wartime bunkers. You're not allowed to leave the road, and neither are you encouraged to turn the provided telescope towards Robert Fulton's modern counterparts at the nuclear submarine base on the Île Longue. Nearby **ROSCANVEL** offers a hotel, the *Kreis Ar Mor* (☎02.98.27.48.93; ②).

Locronan

LOCRONAN, a short way from the sea on the minor road that leads down to Quimper from the Crozon peninsula, is a prime example of a Breton town that has remained frozen in its ancient form by more recent economic decline.

From 1469 through to the seventeenth century, Locronan was a hugely successful centre for woven linen, supplying sails to the French, English and Spanish navies. It was first rivalled by Vitré and Rennes, before suffering the "agony and ruin" of the nineteenth century so graphically described in its small **museum** (daily 10am–7pm; 20F/€3.05), just off the main square. The consequence of that ruin has been that the rich medieval houses of the town centre have never been superseded or surrounded by modern development. Film directors love its authenticity, even if Roman Polanski, to film *Tess*, deemed it necessary to change all the porches, put new windows on the Renaissance houses, and bury the main square in mud to make it all look a bit more English.

Today Locronan is once more prosperous, with its main source of income the tourists who buy wooden statues carved by local artisans, pottery brought up from the Midi, and handbags and leather jackets of less specified provenance. This commercialization shouldn't, however, put you off making at least a passing visit, for the town itself is genuinely remarkable, centred around the focal **Église St-Ronan**. Paying a fee of 10F/€1.52 entitles you to climb to the top of the church's square tower, for a bird's-eye view of the whole ensemble. Be sure also to take the time to walk down the hill of the **rue Moal**, where there's a lovely little stone chapel, with surprising modern stained glass, and a wooden statue of a depressed-looking Jesus, sitting alone cross-legged.

Each year on the second Sunday in July the town hosts a **pardon** at St-Ronan church; the procession, known as the *petit Tromenie*, expands to a week-long festival, the *grand Tromenie*, every sixth year (the next is in 2007). The processions follow a time-hallowed route said by some to be St Ronan's favourite Sunday walk; by others, to be the outline of a long-vanished Benedictine abbey. It could even follow a pre-Christian circuit of megalithic sites.

Practicalities

Simply to **park** on the outskirts of town costs 15F/€2.29, though at least your ticket remains valid for a full year. Once in the centre, you'll find the **tourist office** next to the museum (July & Aug Mon–Sat 10am–1pm & 2–7pm; Sept–June Mon–Sat 10am–noon & 2–6pm; ☎02.98.91.70.14). The one **hotel**, *du Prieuré*, stands on the main approach street at 11 rue du Prieuré (☎02.98.91.70.89; ③);

closed mid-Nov to mid-March), and has a good restaurant with menus from 78F/€11.89 up to 200F/€30.49, but is normally reserved well in advance. In season, and probably out, you'll do a lot better heading on to the bay of Douarnenez.

The latest craze in Locronan is to follow the *Tromenie* route on a **mountain bike**, which you can rent from a garage in rue des Charettes (☎02.98.91.71.71).

CORNOUAILLE

Once past Locronan, you enter the ancient kingdom of **Cornouaille**. Its capital, **Quimper**, is a city as enticing as any in France, while thriving resorts such as **Bénodet**, **Loctudy** and **Pont-Aven** (made famous by Gauguin) line the south coast. Roads radiate from Quimper in all directions, but the **western tip** of Finistère, if you follow the line of the Bay of Douarnenez, still feels isolated. With a few exceptions – most notably its "land's end" capes – it has kept out of the tourist mainstream.

The seaside village of **Ste-Anne-la-Palud**, north of **Douarnenez**, holds one of the best-known *pardons* in Brittany on the last Sunday in August.

Douarnenez

Sufficient quantities of tuna, sardines and assorted crustaceans are still landed at the port of **DOUARNENEZ**, in the superbly sheltered Baie du Douarnenez, south of the Crozon peninsula, to keep the largest fish canneries in Europe busy. However, the catch has been declining ever since 1923, when 800 fishing boats brought in 100 million sardines during the six-month season. Over the last twenty years or so, Douarnenez has therefore set out – at phenomenal expense, the subject of considerable local controversy – to redefine itself as a living museum of all matters maritime.

Since 1993, the area of **Port-Rhû**, on the west side of town, has officially been designated as the **Port-Musée**, with its entire waterfront taken up with fishing and other vessels gathered from throughout northern Europe. Its centrepiece, the **Boat Museum** in place de l'Enfer (daily: mid-March to mid-June & Oct 10am–noon & 2–6pm; mid-June to Sept 10am–7pm; 30F/€4.57), doubles as a working boatyard, where visitors can watch or even join in the construction of seagoing vessels, using techniques from all over the world and from all different periods. It has a strong emphasis on fishing, with the craft on display including a *moliceiro* from Portugal and coracles from Wales and Ireland.

When the Port-Musée first opened, it was possible to roam in and out of all the boats in the port itself, and even down into their oily metallic-smelling engine rooms and cramped sleeping quarters. Sadly, however, although you can still admire them from the quayside all year, for no charge, financial constraints have progressively diminished both the number of boats that are open to visitors, and the length of the season. Currently only three remain accessible, and those only during four months of the year (July to mid-Sept daily 10am–7pm; mid-Sept to Oct Sat & Sun 10am–noon & 2–6pm; 40F/€6.10 including Boat Museum). Across from the museum, the far shore has been relandscaped to reproduce a nineteenth-century environment populated by oystercatchers and the like (free ferries operate when the tide is high enough; otherwise you walk over a bridge).

Of the three separate harbour areas still in operation in Douarnenez, much the most appealing is the rough-and-ready **port du Rosmeur**, on the east side, which is nominally the fishing port used by the smaller local craft. Its quayside – which is far from totally commercialized, but holds a reasonable number of cafés and restaurants – curves between a pristine wooded promontory to the right and the fish canneries to the left, which continue around the north of the headland. You can buy fresh fish at the waterfront, or go on a sea-fishing excursion yourself. The various **beaches** around town look pretty enough, but they are dangerous for swimming.

Practicalities

The **tourist office** in Douarnenez is at 2 rue du Dr-Mével (July & Aug Mon–Sat 9am–7pm, Sun 10am–12.30pm & 3–6.30pm; Sept–June Mon–Sat 9am–noon & 2–6pm; ☎02.98.92.13.35, *www.douarnenez.com*), a short walk up from the Port-Musée; they can inform you of the current status of plans to open a **hostel** in town.

Among good-value **hotels** are *de la Rade*, 31 quai du Grand-Port (☎02.98.92.01.81; ②; closed Nov–Easter), where behind the blue-and-white facade there's a bar downstairs and a restaurant on the first floor looking out on the port de Rosmeur, and the more upmarket *de France*, close to the tourist office (☎02.98.92.00.02; ③), home to the high-quality *Le Doyen* restaurant.

Close by on the bay, there's a two-star **campsite**, *Croas Men* (☎02.98.74.00.18, *croas.men@wanadoo.fr*; closed Oct–March), at Tréboul/Les Sables Blancs. Good seafood **restaurants** near the port du Rosmeur include *Le Tristan*, 25 rue du Rosmeur (☎02.98.92.20.17; closed Wed, plus Sun in winter), and *La Criée* (☎02.98.92.13.55; closed Tues in low season), which has great views and is open at lunchtimes only in winter.

Audierne and the Pointe du Raz

Though on the whole the exposed southwestern extremities of Brittany are not areas you'd immediately associate with a classic summer sun-and-sand holiday, **AUDIERNE**, 25km west of Douarnenez on the Bay of Audierne, is something of an exception. An active fishing port, specializing in prawns and crayfish, it squeezes into the narrow inlet of the Goyen estuary, a short way back from the Atlantic. From out to sea, you'd hardly know there was a town here, though a little crescent bay near the tip of the headland, 1km beyond the town centre, holds the surprisingly sheltered **beach** of Ste-Evette, which has its own crop of hotels and grand homes. Its southern end, 1km further on and close to the open ocean, is the departure point for boats to the Île de Sein (see p.298).

Practicalities

Audierne's **tourist office** is on the main square in the heart of town, at 8 rue Victor-Hugo (July & Aug Mon–Sat 9am–7pm; Sept–June Mon–Sat 9.30am–noon & 3–6pm; ☎02.98.70.12.20). One of the few buildings on the seaward side of the road to Ste-Evette beach is the **hotel** *Au Roi Gradlon*, in a superb position facing the mouth of the estuary at 3 bd Manu-Brusq (☎02.98.70.04.51; ④; closed Sun evening, Mon Oct–May, & all of Jan to mid-Feb). Its unusual design means that the street-level dining room – where the 120F/€18.29 menu includes fresh tuna steaks – is in fact on the top storey, with several further floors, concealed from the road, dropping down below it to the beach. Rooms in the newer and significantly larger *L'Horizon*, slightly nearer the town proper at 40 rue J-J-Rousseau (☎02.98.70.09.91; ③; closed mid-Nov to mid-Dec), are a little cheaper. Fish dinners start at just 80F/€12.20; the 130F/€19.82 menu is a killer, featuring a delicious skate wing cooked with red fruits.

Plogoff

Most people take in Audierne en route to the Pointe du Raz, which is connected directly to Quimper by bus. Just short of the Pointe du Raz, signalled by fading graffiti on its walls and hoardings, is the tiny village of **PLOGOFF**, where ecologists, autonomists and local people fought riot police and paratroopers for six weeks in 1980, attempting to stop the opening move in a nuclear power station project. Although they lost the fight, abandonment of the project was part of François Mitterrand's manifesto for the 1980 presidential election – and he kept his promise.

The Pointe du Raz

The **Pointe du Raz** – the Land's End of both Finistère and France – has recently been designated as a "Grande Site Nationale", and with its former military installations now thankfully cleared away it makes a dramatic spectacle. You can walk out to the plummeting fissures of the *pointe*, filling and draining with a deafening surf-roar, and beyond, high above on precarious paths. (Shoes that can grip are not a bad idea.)

The Baie des Trépassés

The **Baie des Trépassés** (Bay of the Dead), just north of the Pointe du Raz, gets its grim name from the shipwrecked bodies that are washed up there, and is a possible site of sunken Ys (see box, p.301). However, it's actually a very attractive spot: green meadows, too exposed to support trees, end abruptly on the low cliffs to either side, there's a huge expanse of flat sand (in fact little else at low tide), and out in the crashing waves surfers and windsurfers get thrashed to within an inch of their lives. Beyond them, you can usually make out the white-painted houses along the harbour on the Île de Sein, while the various uninhabited rocks in between hold a veritable forest of lighthouses.

In total, less than half a dozen scattered buildings intrude upon the emptiness. There are no facilities for casual visitors on the beach, but the car park just back from the dunes is usually filled with campervans from all over Europe, and there are also two **hotels**, both with tremendous views. Right in the middle is the pink *Hôtel de la Baie des Trépassés* (☎02.98.70.61.34; ②–④; closed mid-Nov to mid-Feb), which has menus of wonderfully fresh seafood from 102F/€15.55. The larger *Relais de la Pointe du Van*, run by the same management, is slightly higher up, to the right (☎02.98.70.62.79; ③; closed Oct–March).

The Île de Sein

Of all the Breton islands, the tiny **Île de Sein**, just 8km off the end of the Pointe du Raz, has to be the most extraordinary. Its very grip on existence seems so tenuous – nowhere does it rise more than six metres above the surrounding ocean, and for much of its 2.5-km length it's barely broader than the breakwater wall of bricks that serves as its central spine – that it's hard to believe anyone could truly survive here.

In fact, however, the island has been inhabited since prehistoric times. Roman sources tell of a shrine served by nine virgin priestesses, and it was reputed to have been the very last refuge of the Druids in Brittany, who held out there long after the rest of the country was Christianized. It also became famous during World War II, when its entire male population, a total of 140 men, answered General de Gaulle's call to join him in exile in England. During his first muster of the Free French army, de Gaulle observed that Sein appeared to constitute a quarter of France. He subsequently awarded the island the Ordre de la Libération, and came here in 1960 to unveil a monument to its bravery. Over three hundred islanders continue to make their living from the sea, gathering rainwater and seaweed and fishing for scallops, lobster and crayfish.

According to a traditional saying, "Who sees Sein, sees his death", though that's more because it happens to rhyme in French (*"qui voit Sein, voit sa fin"*) than because it holds any particular evil. Setting off to reach the island on a misty morning, however, feels as though you're sailing off the edge of the world; in fact it's so notoriously inconspicuous that it was described by the French Admiral Tourville as the most dangerous reef in the world.

Depending on tide levels, island boats pull in at one or other of the two adjoining harbours that constitute Sein's one tightknit village. There are no cars on the island, its few streets being far too narrow for them to squeeze through, and even bicycles are not permitted. A little beach appears in front of the village at low tide, and it also holds a **museum** of local history (daily 10am–noon & 2–6pm; 15F/E2.29), packed with black-and-white photos and press clippings, and displaying a long list of shipwrecks from 1476 onwards. The basic activity for visitors, however, is to take a bracing walk.

The **eastern** tip of the island, barely connected to the rest when high tides eat away at the slender natural causeway, was in days gone by laboriously cleared to create scores of tiny agricultural terraces. These have long been overgrown with sparse yellow broom and left to the rabbits, however, so if you fancy picking your way through the rock pools you'll have the place to yourself. Heading **west** from town, on the other hand, takes you past the Free French Monument and a couple of sandy little bays to the island's main **lighthouse**, the Phare de Goulenez. You'd have to look long and hard to find a tree on Sein – let alone a public toilet – so you'll probably find yourself back in town again an hour or so after setting off.

Practicalities

The principal departure point for **boats** to Sein is Ste-Evette beach, just outside **Audierne** (see p.296); the crossing takes around an hour. Services are operated by Vedette-Biniou (daily: June to early July & first half of Sept 10am; early July to Aug 10am, 1.30pm & 5pm; ☎02.98.70.21.15; adults 125F/€19.06 return, under-17s 70F/€10.67), and Penn Ar Bed (daily: July & Aug 9am, 11.30am & 4.50pm; Sept–June 9.30am; ☎02.98.70.70.70, *www.penn-ar-bed.fr*; adults 127F/€19.36 return, under-17s 77F/€11.74). On Sundays in July and August, Penn Ar Bed also run trips to Sein from **Brest** (departs 8am; adults 186F/€28.35 return, under-17s 112F/€17.07) via **Camaret** (8.45am; adults 170F/€25.92 return, under-17s 100F/€15.24).

If you come for the day in high summer, you may well be asked to specify in advance which ferry you'll return on (Penn Ar Bed sail at 3.30pm & 6.15pm,

Vedette-Biniou at 3.40pm & 6.30pm). Great day out it may be, but nonetheless you may be glad to opt for a shorter trip and return by the afternoon rather than the evening boat as you may well run out of things to do.

Sein is hardly bursting with facilities for tourists, but it does have two **hotels**. The *Trois Dauphins*, looking out over the beach from the middle of the port (☎02.98.70.92.09; ②, sea view ③; closed Mon), offers cosy and attractive rooms, completely fashioned and furnished in wood, above a bar that sells sandwiches, while the *Hôtel-Restaurant d'Armen* (☎02.98.70.90.77, *www.armen.web.com*; ③) is the very last building you come to as you walk west out of town, making it the last restaurant in Europe, which goes some way towards explaining why it refuses on principle to sell Coke, resisting Americanization by selling Breton apple juice instead. All its rooms face the sea, as there's ocean on both sides, while its restaurant – with seating outside when weather permits – serves a good 100F/€15.24 menu and an even better 140F/€21.34 one.

Of the other **restaurants** in town, *Le Men Brial*, right by the picturesque little Men Brial lighthouse (☎02.98.70.90.87), makes a good lunch spot, offering crêpes, menus from 55F/€8.38, and *moules frites* for 70F/€10.67, while *Chez Brigitte*, facing the beach (☎02.98.70.91.83; closed Oct), is a fancier option, with seafood specialities ranging up to 300F/€45.73.

The Penmarch peninsula

At one time the **Penmarch peninsula** – the southwestern corner of Finistère, which stretches south of Audierne and southwest of Quimper – was one of the richest areas of Brittany. That was before it was plundered by the pirate La Fontenelle, who led three hundred ships in raids on the local peasantry from his base on the island of La Tristan in the Bay of Douarnenez; also before the cod, staple of the fishing industry, stopped coming.

Now, in the local tourist literature, the region is known as the **Pays de Bigouden**, after the elaborate lace *coiffes* (traditional hats) you see worn in many of the villages. Often as much as a foot high, they are sometimes supported by half-tubes of cardboard; sometimes just very stiffly starched. The white of the *coiffes* swaying in the wind provides one of the memorable colours of the area, along with the red fields of poppies and verges of purple foxgloves.

Pont l'Abbé

PONT L'ABBÉ, the principal town of the peninsula, has a Bigouden museum, spread over three storeys of the keep of its fourteenth-century château (Easter–May Mon–Sat 10am–noon & 2–5pm; June–Sept daily except Thurs 10am–noon & 2–6pm; 15F/€2.29) – though you'd need to be quite inspired by the costumes to find it of great interest. More accessible pleasures lie in a stroll through the woods along the banks of its estuary.

The *Hôtel de Bretagne*, in the main square at 24 place de la République (☎02.98.87.17.22; ③; closed Mon out of season), is the prettiest hotel in town, and has a fine restaurant.

Le Guilvinec

West of Pont L'Abbé, the world **windsurfing** championships have frequently been held at **Pointe de la Torche**, and at any time there are likely to be aficionados of the sport twirling effortlessly about on the dangerous water. The coast only becomes swimmable, however, as you round the Pointe de Penmarch towards Loctudy. The first village you come to, **LE GUILVINEC**, is a not especially attractive (but surprisingly busy) fishing port, which is home to the fourth largest fish auction (*criée*) in France. The boats start to come home to the harbour, sheltered in the mouth of a little river, around 4pm most afternoons. A small but very pleasant beach faces onto the open sea.

For a place to **stay**, the excellent *Hôtel du Port*, at 53 av du Port in **LÉCHIAGAT**, on the far side of the estuary (☎02.98.58.10.10, *www.hotelrestaurantduport.com*; ③), is thoroughly recommended – especially for its fish suppers, which start at 110F/€16.77 with a tasty array of scallops, skate and all sorts of dessert, and culminate in a lobster feast for 395F/€60.22. Don't confuse the *Hôtel du Port* with the *Auberge du Port*, back in Le Guilvinec itself; if you do choose to stay in town, the very plain exterior of the *Hôtel du Centre* at 16 rue du Général-de-Gaulle conceals an attractive garden within (☎02.98.58.10.44; ③; closed Jan). The restaurant here isn't bad, so long as you ignore the cheapest menu and go for the 100F/€15.24 one instead.

Loctudy

LOCTUDY is a good target – an equally well-positioned but much less commercial version of Bénodet (see p.306) which it faces across the mouth of the Odet. There are several **campsites** along its main beach, including the two-star *Kergall* (☎02.98.87.45.93; closed Oct to late April) and the three-star *Mouettes* (☎02.98.87.43.51; closed mid-Sept to April), as well as some good-value **hotels**, such as the *de Bretagne*, 19 rue du Port (☎02.98.87.40.21; ③).

Boats from Loctudy sail up the Odet, as well as out to the Îles de Glénan (May–Sept; ☎02.98.87.45.63, *www.vedettes-odet.com*; 130F/€19.82 return). The trips to Quimper should depart daily during the summer, but you need to make sure they are running on any particular day; services are cancelled in bad weather or simply if not enough people show up.

Quimper

QUIMPER, capital of the ancient diocese, kingdom and later duchy of Cornouaille, is the oldest Breton city. According to the only source – legend – the first bishop of Quimper, St Corentin, came with the first Bretons across the channel to the place they named Little Britain some time between the fourth and seventh centuries. He lived by eating a regenerating and immortal fish all his life, and was made bishop by one King Gradlon, whose life he later saved when the seabed city of Ys was destroyed (see box, opposite).

Modern Quimper is very relaxed, though active enough to have the bars – and the atmosphere – to make it worth going out café-crawling. Still "the charming little place" known to Flaubert, it takes at most half an hour to cross it on foot. The word *kemper* denotes the junction of the two rivers, the Steir and the Odet, around which are the cobbled streets (now mainly pedestrianized) of the medieval quarter, dominated by the cathedral towering nearby. As the Odet curves from east to southwest, it is crossed by numerous low flat bridges, bedecked with geraniums, and chrysanthemums in the autumn. You can stroll along the boulevards on both banks of the river, where several ultramodern edifices blend in an oddly harmo-

THE DROWNED CITY OF YS

Legend has it that King Gradlon built Ys in the Baie de Douarnenez, protected from the water by gates and locks to which only he and his daughter had keys. She sounds like a pleasant sort, giving pet sea-dragons to all the citizens to do their errands, but St Corentin saw decadence and suspected evil. He was proved right: at the urging of the Devil, the princess used her key to open the floodgates, the city was flooded, and Gradlon escaped only by obeying St Corentin and throwing his daughter into the sea. Back on dry land, and in need of a new capital, Gradlon founded Quimper. Ys remains on the sea floor – it will rise again when Paris ("*Par-Ys*", "equal to Ys") sinks – and, according to tradition, on feast days sailors can still hear church bells and hymns under the water.

nious way with their ancient – and attractive – surroundings. Overlooking all is **Mont Frugy** (all of 87m above the river), once again green with trees after being denuded by the hurricane of 1987. There is no great pressure in Quimper to rush around monuments or museums, and the most enjoyable option may be to take a boat and drift down "the prettiest river in France" to the open sea at Bénodet.

Arrival, information and city transport

The **gare SNCF** (☎02.98.98.31.26) and **gare routière** (☎02.98.90.88.89) are next to each other on avenue de la Gare, 1km east of the town centre. Local **buses** #1 and #6 connect with both, but all pass through place de la Résistance near the tourist office.

Although Quimper is well connected with the rest of Brittany by both train and bus, if you want to use public transport to get to the coast anywhere in the immediate vicinity the **bus** is your only option. Services include those to **Bénodet**, which leave from place de la Résistance (Compagnie Amoricaine de Transport, 5 bd de Kérguelen; ☎02.98.95.02.36); to **Audierne** and Pointe du Raz, from the *gare routière* or boulevard de Kérguelen (also CAT); to **Pont l'Abbé** and St-Guenolé, from place St-Corentin (Cariou Castric Lecoeur; ☎02.98.47.04.08); and to **Concarneau** and **Pont-Aven**, also from place St-Corentin (Sarl Transports Caoudal Réné; ☎02.98.56.96.72).

Between July and September you can **sail** from Quimper down the Odet to Bénodet, which takes about 1hr 15min, on Vedettes de l'Odet (Bénodet ☎02.98.57.00.58, Quimper ☎02.98.52.98.41, *www.vedettes-odet.com*; 115F/€17.53 return). Between two and four boats each day leave from the end of quai de l'Odet; times vary with the tides so check with the tourist office (who also sell tickets). The same company also sails in July and August to the **Îles de Glénan**, for 130F/€19.82 return.

Quimper's **tourist office** is housed in a small single-storey building on the south bank of the Odet at 7 rue de la Déesse, place de la Résistance (April & last two weeks of Sept Mon–Sat 9am–12.30pm & 1.30–6.30pm; May to mid-June & first two weeks of Sept Mon–Sat 9am–12.30pm & 1.30–6.30pm, Sun 10am–1pm & 3–6pm; mid-June to Aug Mon–Sat 9am–7pm, Sun 10am–1pm & 3–6pm; Oct–March Mon–Sat 9am–noon & 1.30–6pm; ☎02.98.53.04.05, *www.bretagne-4villes.com*). They organize daily **guided tours** of the city in season (March–May Sat & Sun 3pm; June Wed, Sat & Sun 3pm; July & Aug Mon, Tues & Thurs–Sat 10.30am, plus

QUIMPER

ACCOMMODATION
le Derby 5
Dupleix 3
Gradlon 1
de l'Ouest 6
Pascal 4
la Tour d'Auvergne 2

RESTAURANTS
l'Ambroisie A
Cambuse E
Capucin Gourmand C
Folie Blanche D
Krampouzerie B

English-language tour Tues 2pm; Sept every 2nd day 3pm; 30F/€4.57). For **Internet access**, call in at *Cybercopy*, 3 bd de Kerguélen (Mon–Fri 9am–7pm, Sat 9am–6pm; ☎02.98.64.33.99), just along from the **post office** at 37 bd de Kerguélen (☎02.98.64.28.28).

Bicycles can be rented from the *gare SNCF*, or from Torch VTT, 58 rue de la Providence (☎02.98.53.84.41).

Accommodation

There are remarkably few **hotels** in the old streets in the centre of Quimper, though more can be found near the station. Rooms can be especially difficult to find in late July or early August, when reservations are advisable.

Quimper's refurbished **hostel** is 2km downstream (west) of town at 6 av des Oiseaux in Bois de Seminaire (☎02.98.64.97.97; 49F/€7.47; closed weekends mid-Oct to Feb), on bus route #1 (direction "Penhars", stop "Chaptal"). You can **camp** either at the municipal campsite alongside (☎02.98.55.61.09), which stays open year round but is reserved for caravans in winter, or at the plusher four-star *Orangerie de Lanniron* site on the route de Bénodet (☎02.98.90.62.02, *www.lanniron.com*; closed mid-Sept to mid-May).

Hotels

Hôtel le Derby, 13 av de la Gare (☎02.98.52.06.91, fax 02.98.53.39.04). Surprisingly quiet option above a bar facing the station. ②.

Hôtel le Dupleix, 34 bd Dupleix (☎02.98.90.53.35, fax 02.98.52.05.31). Quite expensive and modern hotel, overlooking the Odet with fine views across the river to the cathedral. ④.

Hôtel Gradlon, 30 rue du Brest (☎02.98.95.04.39, fax 02.98.95.61.25). Central but quiet, and exceptionally friendly. The rooms are not cheap, but they're very nicely decorated. ⑤.

Hôtel de l'Ouest, 63 rue le Déan (☎02.98.90.28.35). Small, unassuming, but very friendly hotel near the station, offering consistently the cheapest rooms in town. Closed Sun Sept–June. ③.

Hôtel-Restaurant Pascal, 19 av de la Gare (☎02.98.90.00.81, fax 02.98.53.21.81). Run-of-the-mill rooms, conveniently near the station; the unexciting restaurant has menus at 80F/€12.20 and 130F/€19.82. ②.

Hôtel-Restaurant La Tour d'Auvergne, 13 rue des Réguaires (☎02.98.95.08.70, fax 02.98.95.17.31, *www.la-tour-dauvergne.fr*). Thirty-eight very comfortable refurbished rooms, tucked away in a quiet street just east of the cathedral, with an excellent restaurant (see p.305). Closed Sun Oct–April. ⑥.

The Town

The enormous **Cathédrale St-Corentin** is said to be the most complete Gothic cathedral in Brittany, though its neo-Gothic spires date from 1856, and several years of elbow grease have now turned it a sparkling white. When the nave was being added to the old chancel in the fifteenth century, the extension would either have hit existing buildings or the swampy edge of the (then) unchannelled river. The masons eventually hit on a solution and placed the nave at a slight angle – a peculiarity which, once noticed, makes it hard to concentrate on the other Gothic splendours within.

The exterior, however, gives no hint of the deviation, with King Gradlon now mounted in perfect symmetry between the spires – though whether he would have advised a riverbed nave is another question. Before the Revolution, each St

Cecilia's Day a climber would ascend to give the king a drink, and there was a prize of 100 *écus* for whoever could catch the glass, thrown down afterwards. During the sixteenth century, 1500 refugees died of plague inside the building.

Alongside the cathedral, the quirky-looking **Bishop's Palace** nestles against one of the few remaining fragments of the old city walls. Inside you'll find a wonderful staircase, and the intriguing **Musée Départemental Breton**, displaying a remarkable assortment of Breton oddments and *objets d'art* from prehistoric golden jewellery to medieval wood carvings (June–Sept daily 9am–6pm; Oct–May Tues–Sat 9am–noon & 2–5pm, Sun 2–5pm; 25F/€3.81). Much more compelling is the **Musée des Beaux Arts**, alongside the Hôtel de Ville at 40 place St-Corentin (April–June & Sept daily except Tues 10am–noon & 2–6pm; July & Aug daily 10am–7pm; Oct–March Mon & Wed–Sat 10am–noon & 2–6pm, Sun 2–6pm; 25F/€3.81), which holds amazing collections of drawings by Cocteau, Gustave Doré and Max Jacob (who was born in Quimper), nineteenth- and twentieth-century paintings of the Pont-Aven school, and Breton scenes by the likes of Eugène Boudin. Only the dull Dutch oils upstairs let the collection down.

The heart of **old Quimper** lies in and to the west of place St-Corentin, in front of the cathedral. This is where you'll find the liveliest shops and cafés, housed in the old half-timbered buildings, such as the Breton Keltia-Musique record shop at 1 place au Beurre, and the Celtic shop, Ar Bed Keltiek, between the cathedral and the river at 2 rue du Roi-Gradlon. The old market hall was burned down in 1976, but the light and spacious new **Halles St-Francis**, rue Astor, built to replace it is quite a delight, not just for the food, but for the view past the upturned boat rafters through the roof to the cathedral's twin spires. It's open from Monday to Saturday, with an extra-large market spreading into the surrounding streets on Saturdays.

The faïenceries of Quimper

Faïence – tin-glazed earthenware – was first popularized by the city of Faenza in Italy in the sixteenth century. Its production was subsequently taken up by Delft in Holland, Majolica in Spain – and in Quimper, from 1690 onwards. The whole story is told by the city's excellent pottery museum, the **Musée de la Faïence**, not far west of the tourist office, on the south bank of the Odet at 14 rue Jean-Baptiste-Bosquet (mid-April to Oct Mon–Sat 10am–6pm; 26F/€3.96).

As well as revealing the minerals used to create different colours, such as copper (green), cobalt (blue) and antimony (yellow), the museum demonstrates that little has changed in the Breton pottery business since some unknown artisan hit on the idea of painting ceramic ware with naive "folk" designs. That was in around 1875, just as the coming of the railways brought the first influx of tourists in search of authentic souvenirs. Highlights of the collection include pieces commemorating such events as World War I, the first automobile accident and the death of Zola, but there are also some fascinating specimens produced by fine artists in the 1920s. In the age before plastics, they handled commissions like designing hood ornaments for Citroën cars.

As you walk through the town, it is impossible to ignore faïence – you are invited to look and to buy on every corner. On weekdays, it's also possible to visit the major atelier **H-B Henriot**, which under American ownership continues to produce hand-painted pottery in the allées de Locmarion just behind the museum (March to mid-July & Sept Mon–Fri 9am–11.15am & 1.30–4.15pm; mid-July to Aug Mon–Fri 9am–11.15am & 1.30–4.45pm; Oct–Feb Mon–Thurs tours 11am &

3.45pm only; ☎02.98.90.09.36, *www.hb-henriot.com*; 20F/€3.05). H-B Henriot
maintain a bright, modern **gift shop** alongside; the prices, even for the seconds,
are similar to those on offer everywhere else, but the selection is superb
(Mon–Thurs 9.30am–7pm, Fri & Sat 9.30am–6pm).

Eating and drinking

Although the pedestrian streets west of the cathedral are unexpectedly short on
places to eat, there are quite a few **restaurants** further east on the north side of the
river, en route towards the *gare SNCF*. Rue Aristide-Briand here is a particularly
promising area, and also contains a lively Celtic **bar**, the *Ceili* at no 4. For crêperies,
the place au Beurre, a short walk northwest of the cathedral, is a good bet.

Restaurants

L'Ambroisie, 49 rue Élie-Fréron (☎02.98.95.00.02). Upmarket French restaurant a short
climb north from the cathedral, with menus from 120F/€18.29. Closed Mon evening, except
in summer.

La Cambuse, 11 rue Déan (☎02.98.53.06.06). Lively place, south of the river, serving inexpensive crêpes, salads, and quiche-like savoury *tartes*. Behind the bright-orange facade
there's more orange panelling, with wooden tables and a little garden as well. Closed Sun
lunch and all day Mon.

Le Capucin Gourmand, 29 rue des Réguaires (☎02.98.95.43.12). Gourmet French cooking,
not far east of the cathedral. Menus start at 100F/€15.24 and zoom on up to 360F/€54.58;
most offer very little choice, though all feature at least some meat dishes. Closed Mon lunch
& all Sun.

La Folle Blanche, 39 bd de Kerguélen (☎02.98.95.76.76). Lovely Art Deco restaurant, facing the river close to the cathedral, which serves top-value menus at 95F/€14.48 and
145F/€22.11 and often features live jazz at weekends. Closed Sun, plus Tues evening in winter.

La Krampouzerie, 9 rue du Sallé, on the place au Beurre (☎02.98.95.13.08). One of the best
of Quimper's many crêperies, with some outdoor seating on the square. Most crêpes cost
around 20F/€3.05, though you can get a wholewheat galette with scallops for 42F/€6.40, or
with seaweed for 30F/€4.57. Closed Sun, & Mon in winter.

La Tour d'Auvergne, 13 rue des Réguaires (☎02.98.95.08.70). Formal hotel dining room
that offers high-quality menus from 125F/€19.06 at lunchtime up to 198F/€30.19 in the
evening, with an emphasis on fresh local seafood: the mussels and monkfish are recommended, the baked strawberries divine. Closed Sat evening, plus Sun Oct–April.

Entertainment

Quimper's **Festival de Cornouaille** started in 1923 and has gone from strength
to strength since. This great jamboree of Breton music, costumes, theatre and
dance is held in the week before the fourth Sunday in July, attracting guest
performers from the other Celtic countries and a scattering of other, sometimes
highly unusual, ethnic-cultural ensembles. The whole thing culminates in an
incredible Sunday parade through the town. The official programme does not
appear until July, but you can get provisional details in advance from the tourist
office; it's well worth planning a little way ahead, as accommodation is at a premium in Quimper while the festival is on.

Not so widely known are the **Semaines Musicales**, which follow in the first
three weeks of August. The music is predominantly classical, and tends to favour

French composers such as Berlioz, Debussy, Bizet and Poulenc. Founded in 1978, the event serves to bring the rather stuffy nineteenth-century theatre on boulevard Dupleix alive each year.

Bénodet

Once out of its city channel, the Odet takes on the anarchic shape of most Breton inlets, spreading out to lake proportions then turning narrow corners between gorges. The resort of **BÉNODET** at the mouth of the river (reachable by boat from Quimper – see p.301) has a long sheltered beach on the ocean side. The town is a little overdeveloped but the beach is undeniably good, especially for kids, for whom there's a lot laid on – including horse riding, windsurfing and "beach club" crèches. During its less busy periods, such as spring or autumn, Bénodet is a strong contender to be rated as the best spot for a family holiday in the whole of Brittany.

Across the rivermouth, the equally attractive **Ste-Marine** is served by regular pedestrian-only ferries. You can also drive there in a matter of minutes over the graceful **Pont de Cornouaille**, 1km upstream, which offers spectacular views of the estuary.

Practicalities

During the school holidays, three **buses** a day run each way between Quimper and Bénodet; in school time, services are more frequent, but tend to run early in the morning. For details, contact CAT in Quimper (☎02.98.95.02.36). **Boat excursions** from Bénodet or Quimper to the rather nondescript **Îles de Glénan** are less exciting than the river trips between the two towns. These services, plus sailings west along the coast to Loctudy and excursions in glass-bottomed boats, are run by Vedettes de l'Odet (see p.301).

Bénodet's **tourist office** is at 51 av de la Mer (mid-June to mid-Sept Mon–Sat 9am–7pm, Sun 10am–12.30pm & 2–7.30pm; mid-Sept to mid-June Mon–Sat 9am–noon & 2–7pm, Sun 10am–noon; ☎02.98.57.00.14, *benodet.tourisme@ wanadoo.fr*). **Bicycles** can be rented from Cycletty, 5 av de la Mer (☎02.98.57.12.49).

Among the nicest **hotels** in Bénodet are the *Hôtel-Restaurant Le Minaret*, an odd-looking building in a superb position overlooking the sea on the corniche de l'Estuaire (☎02.98.57.03.13; ③; closed mid-Oct to March), and the *Bains de Mer*, 11 rue du Kerguélen (☎02.98.57.03.41; ③; closed mid-Nov to mid-March). *Hôtel l'Hermitage*, 11 rue Laënnec (☎02.98.57.00.37; ②; closed Oct to mid-May), which is a few hundred metres up from the beach, is a reasonable low-priced alternative.

Bénodet also has several large **campsites** – if anything, too many of them – including four-star ones such as the *Camping du Port de Plaisance* (☎02.98.57.02.38; closed Oct to mid-April), which has a heated swimming pool, the enormous *du Letty*, southeast of the village next to the plage du Letty, on rue du Canvez (☎02.98.57.04.69; closed early Sept to mid-June), and the *de la Pointe St-Gilles* (☎02.98.57.05.37; closed Oct–April).

For a good **meal**, the restaurants of the *Hôtel Gwell-Kaër*, 3 av de la Plage (☎02.98.57.04.38; ④), and the *Hôtel de Ste-Marine* at 19 rue Bac across the rivermouth (☎02.98.56.34.79; ④; closed Wed in low season, & all Nov), are also recommended, though neither offers a menu for under 100F/€15.24, and in summer the *Ste-Marine* tends to be too full to feed non-guests.

Along the South Coast

The final, rocky stretch of the Finistère coast that lies east of Bénodet, cut repeatedly by deep valleys, holds some of the region's most ruggedly attractive scenery. Every little indent and inlet seems to harbour its own gorgeous pocket **beach**, and there are also a couple of more substantial communities to attract day-trippers: the walled town of **Concarneau**, and the artists' haven of **Pont-Aven**.

Fouesnant

Not so much a town as a loose conglomeration of villages, **FOUESNANT**, 9km east of Bénodet, is coming to rival its neighbour as a prime destination for family holidays. While Fouesnant itself is renowned for its cider-makers, and holds a pretty little Romanesque church, most local tourist amenities are gathered in its sister community of **LA FORÊT-FOUESNANT**, 3km further east. Clustered along the waterfront at the foot of a hill so steep that caravans are banned from even approaching, it holds an assortment of attractive **hotels** such as the *Hôtel de l'Esperance*, place de l'Église (☎02.98.56.96.58; ②; closed Oct–March) and the pricier *Aux Cerisiers*, 3 rue des Cerisiers (☎02.98.56.97.24, *www.auxcerisiers.com*; ④; closed mid-Dec to mid-Jan).

The small resort of **BEG-MEIL**, perched at the headland 3km south of Fouesnant but still under its overall aegis, barely survived the hurricane of 1987, with just a handful of trees to protect its vast expanse of dunes. However, as well as boasting the **hotel** *Thalamot*, just back from the seafront at 4–6 Le Chemin-Creux (☎02.98.94.97.38; ③; closed Oct–April), it makes an ideal spot for **campers**, with several four-star campsites, including *La Roche Percée* (☎02.98.94.94.15; closed Oct to mid-April), which has two pools and a waterslide, and the seafront *Kervastard* (☎02.98.94.91.52; closed mid-Sept to mid-June).

In July and August, Vedettes Glénn runs a ferry service between Beg-Meil and Concarneau across the bay (departs Beg-Meil Mon–Thurs 11am, 2.25pm, 5.30pm & 6.30pm; Fri 9.45am, 11am, 2.25pm, 5.30pm & 6.30pm; ☎02.98.97.10.31; 60F/€9.15 return).

Concarneau

CONCARNEAU, on the far side of Fouesnant's Baie de la Forêt and 20km east of Bénodet, ranks as the third most important fishing port in France. Nonetheless, it does a reasonable job of passing itself off as a holiday resort. Its greatest asset is its **Ville Close**, the small and very well-fortified old city located a few metres offshore on an irregular rocky island in the bay.

Arrival and information

Concarneau's **tourist office** (May & June Mon–Sat 9am–noon & 2–6.30pm, Sun 9.30am–12.30pm; July & Aug daily 9am–8pm; Sept–April Mon–Sat 9am–noon & 2–6.30pm; ☎02.98.97.01.44) is just outside the Ville Close on the quai d'Aiguillon, not far from the long-distance bus stop; there's no rail service, but SNCF buses connect with Quimper and Rosporden. It's also possible in summer to take **ferries** up the Odet to Quimper or out to the Îles de Glénan, with either Vedettes de l'Odet (☎02.98.57.00.58, *www.vedettes-odet.com*) or Vedettes Glénn (☎02.98.97.10.31), who also run ferries to Beg-Meil (July & Aug departs Concarneau Mon–Fri 10.15am, 1.30pm, 5pm & 6pm; ☎02.98.97.10.31; 60F/€9.15 return).

Accommodation

The Ville Close is almost completely devoid of **hotels**, so most of those that Concarneau has to offer skulk in the backstreets of the mainland and tend to be full most of the time. Probably the best bet of all is the **hostel** (☎02.98.97.03.47; 50F/€7.62; open all year), for once, very near the city centre and also enjoying magnificent ocean views. It's just around the tip of the headland on the quai de la Croix, with a good crêperie opposite and a windsurfing shop a little further along.

Hôtel de France et d'Europe, 9 av de la Gare (☎02.98.97.00.64, fax 02.98.50.76.66). Bright, modernized and very central hotel near the main bus stop. Closed Sat mid-Nov to mid-Feb. ④.

Hôtel des Halles, place de l'Hôtel de Ville (☎02.98.97.11.41, fax 02.98.50.58.54). Spruce pastel-orange hotel near the fish market, across from the entrance to the Ville Close, offering well-equipped rooms at reasonable rates. Closed Sun evening in low season. ④.

Hôtel-Restaurant les Océanides, 3 rue du Lin (☎02.98.97.08.61, fax 02.98.97.09.13). *Logis de France*, a couple of streets up from the sea above the fishing port, with a highly recommended and far from expensive restaurant. Some of the fancier rooms are in the nominally distinct *Petites Océanides* across the street. Closed Sun evening in May & June, all Sun Oct–April. ②/③.

Hôtel des Voyageurs, 9 place Jean-Jaurès (☎02.98.97.08.06). Cheap basic accommodation above a bar, right opposite the entrance to the Ville Close. ②.

The Town

Although in the height of summer the **Ville Close** can get too crowded for comfort, it's otherwise a real delight. You reach it by crossing a narrow bridge and then passing through two successive gateways, marked by a little clock tower and a sundial. Like those of the *citadelle* at Le Palais on Belle-Île (see p.356), the ramparts were completed by Vauban in the seventeenth century. The island itself, however, had been inhabited for at least a thousand years before that, and is first recorded as the site of a priory founded by King Gradlon of Quimper.

Concarneau boasts that it is a *ville fleurie*, and the flowers are most in evidence inside the walls, where climbing roses and clematis swarm all over the various gift shops, restaurants and crêperies. Walk the central pedestrianized street to the far end, and you can pass through a gateway to the shoreline to watch the fishing boats go by. In summer, however, the best views of all come from the promenade on top of the ramparts (daily: May, June & Sept 10am–6pm; July & Aug 10am–9pm; 5F/€0.76).

The **Musée de la Pêche**, immediately inside the Ville Close (daily: mid-June to mid-Sept 9.30am–8pm; mid-Sept to mid-June 9.30am–12.30pm & 2–6pm; 36F/€5.49), provides an insight into the traditional life Concarneau shared with so many other Breton ports. The four rooms around the central quadrangle illuminate the history and practice of four specific aspects of fishing. The whaling room contains model boats and a genuine open boat from the Azores; the tuna room shows boats dragging nets the size of central Paris; a herring room; and a model of a sardine cannery – which this building once was. And there are oddities collected by fishermen in the past: the swords of swordfish and the saws of sawfish; a Japanese giant crab; photos of old lifeboatmen with fading beards; cases full of sardine and tuna cans; and a live aquarium, where the lobsters little realize they are in no immediate danger of being eaten. In addition, you can buy diagrams and models of ships, and even order a diorama of the stuffed fish of your choice.

Eating

For an atmospheric **meal** in Concarneau, your best bet is to choose from any of the restaurants along the main street that runs through the Ville Close, or explore the little lanes that lead off it. There are, however, plenty of cheaper places back in town.

The main **market** is held in front of the Ville Close on Friday, with a smaller one on Monday; the covered market *halles* on the far side of the square are open every morning, and hold plenty of snack stalls.

L'Assiette de Pêcheur, 12 rue St-Guénolé (☎02.98.70.75.84). Smart seafood restaurant at the far end of the Ville Close, with a good 98F/€14.94 menu. Closed Oct–Easter, plus Sun evening & Mon except July & Aug.

Le Bélem, place Jean-Jaurès (☎02.98.97.02.78). Pretty little indoor restaurant, next to the market on the mainland, serving mussels for 50F/€7.62 and good seafood menus from 79F/€12.04. Closed Wed.

Chez Armande, 15 av du Dr-Nicholas (☎02.98.97.00.76). Excellent seafood not far south of the market on the mainland, on menus starting at 105F/€16.01. Closed Wed, & Tues in winter.

L'Écume, 3 place St-Guénolé (☎02.98.97.15.98). One of several good-value crêperies in the heart of the Ville Close. A great spot to watch the world go by, and menus to suit all tastes from 60F/€9.15. Closed Wed, plus Nov to mid-March.

L'Escale, 19 quai Carnot (☎02.98.97.03.31). Waterfront restaurant on the main road in town that's a favourite with local fishermen, with lunch menus for around 54F/€8.23. Closed Sun.

Pont-Aven

PONT-AVEN, 14km east of Concarneau and just inland from the tip of the Aven estuary, is a small port packed with tourists and art galleries. This was where Gauguin came to paint in the 1880s, before he left for Tahiti in search of a South Seas idyll. By all accounts Gauguin was a rude and arrogant man who lorded it over the local population (who were already well used to posing in "peasant attire" for visiting artists). As a painter and printmaker, however, he produced some of his finest work in Pont-Aven, and his influence was such that the **Pont-Aven School** of fellow artists developed here. He spent some years working closely with these – the best known of whom was Émile Bernard – and they in turn helped to revitalize his own approach.

For all the local hype, however, the town has no permanent collection of Gauguin's work. The **Musée Municipal** (daily: mid-Feb to mid-June & mid-Sept to Dec 10am–12.30pm & 2–6pm; mid-June to mid-Sept 10am–7pm; 27F/€4.12) in the Mairie holds changing exhibitions of the numerous members of the school, and other artists active in Brittany during the same period, but you can't count on paintings by the man himself.

Gauguin aside, Pont-Aven is pleasant in its own right, with countless galleries making it easy to while away an afternoon, and the small, neat pleasure port boasting a water mill and the odd leaping salmon. Just upstream of the little granite bridge at the heart of town, the **promenade Xavier-Grall** crisscrosses the tiny river itself on landscaped walkways, offering glimpses of the backs of venerable mansions, dripping with red ivy, and a little "chaos" of rocks in the stream itself. A longer walk – allow an hour – leads into the **Bois d'Amour**, wooded gardens which have long provided inspiration to visiting painters – and a fair tally, too, of poets and musicians.

If you can't afford to take a souvenir canvas home with you, the town's other speciality is more affordable, and tastes better too. Pont-Aven is the home of two manufacturers of **galettes** – which here means "butter biscuits" rather than "pancakes" – and their products are on sale everywhere.

Throughout the summer, Les Vedettes Aven-Belon (☎02.98.71.14.59) run **cruises** from the pleasure port down to the sea at Port-Manech. Some continue around to **Port-Belon** near the mouth of the next estuary, where it's also possible to board the boats. The precise schedule is determined by the state of the tides (April–June & Sept 1 departure virtually every day; July & Aug 1–2 departures daily; short cruises 58F/€8.84, long trips 79F/€12.04).

Practicalities

Pont-Aven's **tourist office**, 5 place de l'Hôtel de Ville (April–June & Sept–Oct daily 9.15am–12.30pm & 2–7pm; July & Aug daily 9.30am–7.30pm; Nov–March Mon–Sat 10am–12.30pm & 2–6pm; ☎02.98.06.04.70, *ot.pont.aven@wanadoo.fr*), sells an excellent English-language guide booklet to the town, plus route maps of local walks, for a mere 2F/€0.30.

Once the day-trippers have gone home, Pont-Aven makes a tranquil place to spend a night. Much the best of its three relatively expensive **hotels** is the central *Hôtel des Ajoncs d'Or*, 1 place de l'Hôtel de Ville (☎02.98.06.02.06; ③; closed Jan), where the gourmet menus start at 85F/€12.96. The nicest of the local **campsites** is *Le Spinnaker* (☎02.98.06.01.77; closed Oct–April), set in a large wooded park.

Riec-sur-Bélon

From the unremarkable village of **RIEC-SUR-BÉLON**, 5km southeast of Pont-Aven, backroads snake down for another 4km to reach a dead end at the **port du Bélon**, on the delightfully sinuous estuary of the Bélon River. The coastal footpath that leads away from here along the thickly wooded shoreline is clearly signposted to offer optional loop trails of 3km, 6km and 8km.

Some of the oyster beds visible at low tide in the sands off the port du Bélon belong to the private Château de Bélon, and others to *Chez Jacky* (☎02.98.06.90.32; closed Mon, plus Oct–Easter), a deservedly popular seafood **restaurant**. Once past the well-stocked vivarium at its entrance, you'll find bare wooden benches and tables inside, and beyond that a lovely seafront terrace. The ambience is informal, but both the food and the prices are to be taken seriously. Local oysters are 80F/€12.20 a dozen and a huge platter of mostly raw shellfish costs 200F/€30.49 per person, while totally fishy menus range from the 105F/€16.01 *le Matelot* up to the gourmet 450F/€68.60 *l'Amiral*, which features a grilled lobster.

Quimperlé

Another 14km east of Pont-Aven, **QUIMPERLÉ**, the final town of any size in Finistère, straddles a hill and two rivers, the Isole and the Elle, cut by a sequence of bridges. It's an atmospheric place, particularly in the medieval muddle of streets around **Ste-Croix church**. This was copied in plan from schema of the Church of the Holy Sepulchre in Jerusalem, brought back by crusaders, and is notable for its original Romanesque apse. There are some good bars nearby and, on Fridays, a market on the square higher up on the hill.

The **hotels** *Le Brizeux*, 7 quai Brizeux (☎02.98.96.19.25; ②), and *de Kervidanou*, in the village of Mellac 5km northwest (☎02.98.39.18.00; ③), both have reasonable rooms. The nicest **campsite** in the vicinity has to be the two-star, British-owned *Bois des Ecureuils* (☎02.98.71.70.98), 15km northeast in the verdant countryside at Guilligomarch, north of **ARZANO**.

Le Pouldu

At the mouth of the River Laïta, which constitutes the eastern limit of Finistère, the community of **LE POULDU** was another of Paul Gauguin's favourite haunts. It is divided into two distinct sections. The tiny **port**, on one bank of the estuary – most of which has not even a road alongside, let alone any buildings – is shielded from the open sea by a curving spit of sand. The **beach**, more developed than in Gauguin's day but still very picturesque, is a couple of kilometres away, with the headland that separates the two indented with a succession of delightful little sandy coves.

The *Hôtel des Bains* (☎02.98.39.90.11; ③; closed Sept–April) drops down to the beach from the main road, with its large glass-fronted rooms commanding superb views, and menus starting at 95F/€14.48, while the appealingly weather-beaten, white *Hôtel du Pouldu* (☎02.98.39.90.66; ③; closed Oct–March) stands next to the port. Le Pouldu would also make an ideal spot to **camp** for a few days; among sites near the beach is the *Vieux Four* (☎02.98.39.94.34; closed mid-Sept to Easter).

travel details

Trains

Brest to: Châteaulin (6 daily; 1hr), with connecting SNCF buses for Crozon, and inland to Carhaix; Landerneau (10 TGVs daily; 12min); Landivisiau (10 TGVs daily; 20min); Morlaix (10 TGVs daily; 35min); Paris-Montparnasse (10 TGVs daily; 4hr 20min; 2 cheaper, slower services daily; 6hr); Quimper (6 daily; 1hr 20min); Rennes (10 TGVs daily; 2hr 15min).

Quimper to: Lorient (7 daily; 40min); Redon (7 daily; 1hr 40min); Vannes (7 daily; 1hr 5min) plus 5 slower services to all three.

Roscoff to: Morlaix (2–3 daily; 30min).

Buses

Brest to: Le Conquet (4 daily; 30min); Quimper (6 daily; 1hr 30min); Roscoff (5 daily; 1hr 30min), via Gouesnou (20min), Lesneven (45min), Lanhouarneau (55min) and Plouescat (1hr 10min).

Châteaulin to: Camaret (5 daily; 50min); Carhaix (3 daily; 45min); Crozon (5 daily; 30min).

Landévennec to: Camaret (3 daily; 45min), via Crozon (25min) and Roscanvel (35min).

Morlaix to: Carantec (4 daily; 20min); Carhaix (3 daily; 1hr 30min); Huelgoat (3 daily; 45min); Lannion (Mon–Sat 2 daily; 1hr); Plougasnou (5 daily; 30min); Quimper (2 daily; 1hr 50min); Roscoff (2–4 daily; 50min); St-Jean-du-Doigt (5 daily; 25min); Vannes (1 daily; 3hr 30min).

Quimper to: Audierne (3 daily; 1hr); Beg-Meil (6 daily; 1hr 10min); Bénodet (8 daily; 45min); Camaret (5 daily; 1hr 30min); Concarneau (6 daily; 30min); Crozon (5 daily; 1hr 20min); Douarnenez (5 daily; 40min); Fouesnant (6 daily; 1hr); Locronan (5 daily; 20min); Lorient (5 daily; 2hr); airport at Plugaffan (9 daily; 10min); Pointe du Raz (1 daily; 1hr 15min); Quimperlé (6 daily; 1hr 30min); Telgruc (5 daily; 1hr); Vannes (5 daily; 3hr).

Roscoff to: Morlaix (3–6 daily; 50min); Vannes (1 only, Mon, Thurs & Sat; 4hr), via Quimper (3hr).

Ferries

Audierne to: the Île de Sein (see details on p.298).

Brest to: Île de Sein (see details on p.298); Le Fret on the Crozon peninsula (June–Sept 3–4 daily;

25min; ☎02.98.41.46.23; foot passengers and cyclists only, each trip is met by a minibus for Crozon and Camaret); Ouessant and Molène (ferries run by two separate operators are detailed on p.281).

Camaret to: the Île de Sein (see details on p.298); Ouessant and Molène (ferries run by two separate operators are detailed on p.281).

Lanildut to: Ouessant and Molène (ferries run by two separate operators are detailed on p.281).

Le Conquet to: Ouessant and Molène (ferries run by two separate operators are detailed on p.281).

Roscoff to: Cork (April–Sept 1 weekly; 19hr), with Brittany Ferries (Roscoff ☎08.03.82.88.28, Cork ☎215/07666; *www.brittany-ferries.com*); Plymouth (2–12 weekly; 6hr), with Brittany Ferries (Plymouth ☎0870/536 0360); Rosslare (April–Sept 1–3 weekly; 21hr), with Irish Ferries (☎02.98.61.17.17). See p.3 onwards for more details. Also trips to Île de Batz (very frequently;

15min; details of the two ferry operators are on p.267); and in July and August, tours of the Bay of Morlaix.

Trips also run from **Brest** around the Rade de Brest. From **Douarnenez** trips around Baie du Douarnenez are run by Vedettes Rosmeur (☎02.98.92.83.83). From **Morgat** you can take trips to caves and headlands (May–Sept; ☎02.98.27.10.71). From **Quimper** boats run to Bénodet, down the Odet and vice versa (July–Sept; ☎02.98.57.00.58, *www.vedettes-odet.com*). You can also tour the **Odet** from **Loctudy** (May–Sept; daily; ☎02.98.87.45.63), and from **Concarneau** (mid-June to mid-Sept ☎02.98.97.10.31). All the Odet companies also do trips (average 1hr) to the Glénan islands.

Flights

Brest airport (Guipavas) to: Ouessant, subject to good weather (2 daily; ☎02.98.84.64.87; see p.281). **Quimper** airport (Plugaffan) to: Paris (2 daily; ☎02.98.84.73.33).

CHAPTER SIX

INLAND BRITTANY: THE NANTES—BREST CANAL

The meandering chain of waterways known as the **Nantes–Brest canal**, which interweaves natural rivers with purpose-built stretches of canal, runs all the way from Finistère down to the Loire. En route it passes through medieval riverside towns, such as **Josselin** and **Malestroit**, which long predate its construction; commercial ports and junctions – **Pontivy**, most notably – that developed along its path during the nineteenth century; the old port of **Redon**, a patchwork of water, where the canal crosses the River Vilaine; and a succession of scenic splendours, including the string of lakes around the **Barrage de Guerlédan** near Mur-de-Bretagne.

As a focus for exploring **inland Brittany**, perhaps cutting in to the towpaths along the more easily accessible stretches, and then detouring out to the towns and sights around, the canal is ideal. The detours can be picked almost at will – the **sculpture park** at Kerguéhennec, near Josselin, and the village of **La Gacilly** near Malestroit, are among the least known and most enjoyable.

All this area is supposed – in myth at any rate – to have been covered in the long-distant past by one vast forest, the *Argoat*. Though vestiges of ancient woodland do remain in several areas, natural and human forces seem to be conspiring to destroy them. The **forest of Huelgoat**, which, with its boulder-strewn waterfalls, bubbling streams and grottoes, was the most dramatic natural

---

ACCOMMODATION PRICE CODES

All **hotel prices** in this book have been coded using the symbols below. The price shown is for the least expensive double room in high season, which, for categories ① and ② especially, often means a room without shower, bath and toilet. Most such hotels have other rooms with en-suite facilities, which typically cost 40–60F/ €6.10–9.15 extra.

① Under 160F/€24
② 160–220F/€24–34
③ 220–300F/€34–46
④ 300–400F/€46–61
⑤ 400–500F/€61–76
⑥ 500–600F/€76–91
⑦ 600–700F/€91–107
⑧ 700–800F/€107–122
⑨ Over 800F/€122

landscape in Brittany, is still recovering from the devastating hurricane of 1987. **Paimpont** – the legendary forest of Brocéliande, which concealed the Holy Grail – survived that storm, only to be damaged by a serious fire in the autumn of 1990.

You cannot make the whole journey described in this chapter by literally keeping next to the canal. For much of the way there is no adjacent road, and even though the **towpath** is normally clear enough for walking it's not really practicable to cycle along for any great distance. However, it is certainly worth following the canal in short sections, which you can do quite easily by car, better by bike, or best of all by renting a **boat**, **barge** or even a **houseboat** along the navigable stretches. Full listings of **rental** outlets are given in the "Travel details" at the end of this chapter.

The canal in Finistère

The westernmost section of the canal, passing through Finistère, is now one of its least-used stretches. Those travellers who do set out to follow its course are far more likely to do so from the Crozon peninsula or the Menez-Hom – both covered in the previous chapter – than from Brest itself.

However, as recently as the 1920s, steamers made their way across the Rade de Brest and down the River Aulne to Châteaulin. The contemporary *Black's Guide* reckoned the six-hour journey "tedious [in a] boat often overcrowded with cattle" – a judgement that seems a little churlish now that such pleasures are no longer available.

Châteaulin and onwards

CHÂTEAULIN is the first real town on the canal route, though in actuality no more than a brief, picturesque waterside strip, overlooked by the pretty little chapel of Notre Dame. It's a quiet place, where the main reason to stay is the River Aulne itself. Enticingly rural, it is renowned for its salmon and trout fishing; if you're interested, most bars sell permits (as do angling shops, some of which rent tackle). The only other factor that might draw you is cycling: regional championships are held each September on a circuit that races through the centre, and on occasion it's used for the French professional championship, too.

Along the **riverbank**, a statue commemorates Jean Moulin, the Resistance leader of whose murder SS man Klaus Barbie was found guilty in Lyon in 1987. Moulin was *sous-préfet* in Châteaulin from 1930 to 1933; the inscription reads "mourir sans parler".

THE CANAL

The idea of joining together the inland waterways of Brittany dates back to 1627 – though, as ever, nothing was done to implement the scheme until it was seen as a military necessity. That point came during the Napoleonic wars, when English fleets began to threaten shipping circumnavigating the Breton coast. To relieve the virtual blockade of Brest in 1810, Napoléon authorized the construction of a canal network to link it with both Nantes and Lorient.

In the event, economic disasters held up its completion, but by 1836 a navigable path was cut and the canal officially opened. It was not an immediate success. Having cost sixty million francs to construct, the first years of operation, up to 1850, raised a mere 70,000 francs in tariffs. It survived, however, helped by a navy experiment of transporting coal cross-country to its ports. By the twentieth century the canal's business was booming. In the years between 1890 and the outbreak of World War I an annual average of 35,000 tonnes of cargo were carried. In addition to coal, the cargoes were mainly slate, from the quarries near Châteaulin, and fertilizer, which helped to develop agricultural production inland.

After the war, motor transport and more effective roads brought swift decline. The canal had always been used primarily for short journeys at either end – from Brest to Carhaix and Pontivy to Nantes – and in 1928 the building of a dam at Lac Guerlédan cut it forever into two sections, with the stretch from Carhaix to Pontivy becoming navigable only by canoe. Plans for the dam were approved on the basis that either a hydraulic lift, or a side channel, would enable barges to bypass it – but neither was ever built. In 1945 the last barge arrived at Châteaulin, and these days the only industry that has much use for the canal is tourism.

Within a couple of minutes' walk upstream from the statue, and the town centre, you're on towpaths overhung by trees full of birds, with rabbits and squirrels running ahead of you on the path. For the first couple of kilometres, diagrams of corpulent yet energetic figures incite you to join them in unspeakable exercises – if you can resist that temptation, you'll soon find yourself ambling in peace past the locks and weirs that climb towards the Montagnes Noires.

Practicalities

Unless a major cycling event is taking place, you should have little difficulty finding a room in any of Châteaulin's three or four modest **hotels**. The best value of them is *Le Chrismas* at 33 Grande-Rue (☎02.98.86.01.24; ②), a *logis de France* a short walk up the road that climbs east of the town centre towards Pleyben; menus in its **restaurant** start with a good 80F/€12.20 option, while wonderful hot oysters are the stars of the 130F/€19.82 alternative.

The two-star municipal **campsite**, *Rodaven* (☎02.98.86.32.93; closed Nov–Feb), is very attractively situated beside the river.

Pont Coblant

If you set out to walk the canal seriously from Châteaulin, the small village of **PONT COBLANT** may look just 10km distant on the map, but be warned: the meanders make it a hike of several hours (pick your side of the water, too, as there are no bridges between Châteaulin and Pont Coblant; if you stay on the north side, it's easier to take a short-cut back by road if you're getting tired).

It's possible to rent both **kayaks** and **houseboats** from Pont Coblant (contact Crabing-Loisirs, M. Mercier, 20 rue de Frout, 29000 Quimper; ☎02.98.95.14.02; or call the local representative in Pont-Coblant on ☎02.98.73.34.69). The village also has a tiny **hotel**, the *Auberge du Poisson Blanc* (☎02.98.73.34.76; ③), and a two-star **campsite** (☎02.98.73.31.22; closed mid-Sept to May).

Pleyben

PLEYBEN, 4km north of Pont Coblant, is renowned for its sixteenth-century **parish close** (see p.272). On its four sides the calvary traces the life of Jesus, combining great detail with an appealing naivety. The well-scrubbed church of St-Germain itself – twin-towered, with a huge ornate spire dwarfing its domed Renaissance neighbour – features an altarpiece that's blackened and buckled by age.

A summer-only **tourist office** (mid-June to mid-Sept Mon–Sat 10am–12.30pm & 2.30–6pm; ☎02.98.26.71.05) stands in the spacious and grandiose main square, the place de Gaulle, across from the village's only **hotel**, *La Croix Blanche* (☎02.98.26.61.29; ②). On the N164 in between Châteaulin and Pleyben, the *Run Ar Puns* (☎02.98.86.27.95; closed Sun & Mon) is a lively **music club** and bar, housed in old farm buildings, serving a wide selection of beers and specializing in Breton music; rock bands from further afield also play here, but there are no concerts in summer.

Châteauneuf-du-Faou

CHÂTEAUNEUF-DU-FAOU, a little way south of the N164 25km east of Châteaulin, is in a similar sort of vein to Chateaulin and Pleyben, sloping down to the tree-lined river. It's a little more developed, though, with a **tourist complex**, the *Penn ar Pont* (☎02.98.81.81.25; closed Nov–March), which boasts a swimming pool, *gîtes* and camping, as well as cycle and boat rental.

The **canal proper** separates off from the Aulne a few kilometres to the east at Pont Triffen, making its own way past Carhaix, and out of Finistère.

Carhaix and onwards

CARHAIX, a further 25km east, is a road junction that dates back to the Romans, with cafés and shops to replenish supplies, but not much else to recommend it. The most interesting building in town is the granite Renaissance **Maison de Sénéchal** on rue Brisieux, which houses the **tourist office** (July & Aug Mon–Sat 9am–12.30pm & 1.30–7pm, Sun 10am–1pm; Sept–June Mon–Sat 10am–noon & 2–6pm; ☎02.98.93.04.42). The modern *Hôtel Gradlon* at 12 bd de la République, near the church (☎02.98.93.15.22; ③), makes a comfortable if slightly pricey place to spend the night, and serves good food, with dinner menus starting at 85F/€12.96.

Beyond Carhaix, the canal – as far as Pontivy – is navigable only by canoe. If that's not how you're travelling, it probably makes more sense to loop round to the south, through the **Montaignes Noires**, Le Faouët and Kernascléden, before rejoining the canal at **Lac Guerlédan**. Alternatively, to the north – assuming you resisted the detour from Morlaix – you could explore the **Forêt de Huelgoat** and the **Monts d'Arrée** which are covered on p.319 and p.320 respectively.

South through the Montaignes Noires

South of Châteauneuf, the **Montaignes Noires** delineate the southern borders of Finistère. Despite the name, they are really no more than escarpments, though bleak and imposing nonetheless in a harsh, exposed landscape at odds with the gentle canal path. Their highest point is the stark slate **Roc de Toullaëron**, on the road between Pont Triffen and Gourin. From its 318-metre peak, you can look west and north over kilometres of what seems like totally deserted countryside.

Le Faouët to Kernascléden

If you are driving, the D769 beyond Gourin offers access to the twin churches of St-Fiacre and Kernascléden, built simultaneously, according to legend, with the aid of an angelic bridge. En route is the secluded town of **LE FAOUËT**, served neither by buses nor trains, and distinguished mainly by its large, old market hall. Above a floor of mud and straw, still used by local traders, rises an intricate latticework of ancient wood, propped on granite pillars and topped by a little clock tower.

Practicalities

Two similar and highly recommendable **hotels** in the immediate area of Le Faouët both offer good food. The *Croix d'Or*, opposite the old market in the heart of town at 9 place Bellanger (☎02.97.23.07.33; ③; closed mid-Dec to mid-Jan, plus Sun evening & Mon in low season), has a 135F/€20.58 menu that features snail ravioli and skate's wing with thyme. The *Cheval Blanc* (☎02.97.34.61.15; ④) stands by a lake a few kilometres east in **PRIZIAC**, reached along the pleasant (but steep) D132. Le Faouët also has its own three-star riverside municipal **campsite**, the *Beg-er-Roch* (☎02.97.23.15.11; closed mid-Sept to mid-March).

St-Fiacre

The church at **ST-FIACRE**, just over 2km south, is notable for its rood screen, brightly polychromed and carved as intricately as lace. The original purpose of a rood screen was to separate the chancel from the congregation – the decorations of this 1480 masterpiece go rather further than that. They depict scenes from the Old and New Testaments as well as a dramatic series on the wages of sin. Drunkenness is demonstrated by a man somehow vomiting a fox; theft, by a peasant stealing apples; and so on.

Ste-Barbe

The fifteenth-century chapel of **Ste-Barbe** perches on a rocky outcrop a couple of kilometres east of Le Faouët. Accessible only along a very poor road that crosses a bridge over the main D769, it commands views of the deep, wooded ravine of the Ellé River. Visitors ring a large bell in the crude bell tower on the hilltop, before descending a steep stone staircase to the chapel itself.

Kernascléden

At the ornate and gargoyle-coated church at **KERNASCLÉDEN**, 15km southeast of Le Faouët along the D782, the focus turns from carving to frescoes. The themes, however, contemporary with St-Fiacre, are equally gruesome. On the damp-infested wall of a side chapel, horned devils stoke the fires beneath a vast cauldron filled with the the souls of the damned, and you may be able to discern the outlines of a Dance of Death, a faded cousin to that at Kermaria (see p.245). The ceiling above the main altar holds better-preserved but less bloodthirsty scenes.

The Monts d'Arrée

A broad swath of the more desolate regions of Finistère, stretching east from the Crozon peninsula right to the edge of Finistère, is designated as the **Parc Régional d'Armorique**. The park, in theory at least, is an area of conservation and of rural regeneration along traditional lines; in reality, lack of funding creates rather less impact. The **Monts d'Arrée**, however, which cut northeast across Finistère from the Aulne estuary, are something of a nature sanctuary; kestrels circle high above the bleak hilltops, sharing the skies with pippits, curlews and great black crows.

Over to the east, the ancient woods of the **Forêt de Huelgoat** can offer an atmospheric afternoon's walking, with the lakeside village of Huelgoat itself making an attractive base if you have the time to linger.

East across the Monts d'Arrée

The administrative centre of the Parc d'Armorique is at **MENEZ-MEUR**, off the D342 near the Forêt de Cranou – just inland from the Brest–Quimper motorway. Menez is an official **animal reserve**, with wild boar and deer roaming free, and a museum of Breton horses (Feb–April & Oct–Dec Wed, Sun & hols 10am–noon & 1–6pm; May daily except Sat 1.30–5.30pm; June–Sept daily 10am–7pm; 20F/€3.05). At the reserve gate you can pick up a wealth of detail on the park and all its various activities (☎02.98.68.81.71, *perso.wanadoo.fr/parc.regional.naturel.armorique*).

Ten kilometres north, at **SIZUN**, a research station, **aquarium** and fishing exhibition sets out to increase public awareness of the significance of Brittany's rivers and inland waterways (March–May & Oct Wed, Sun & hols 2–5pm; June & Sept daily except Sat 2–5pm; July & Aug daily 10am–6.30pm; Nov–Feb Wed 2–5pm; 25F/€3.81).

The Moulins de Kerouat
Another 3km east of Sizun, along the D764 to Commana, is the abandoned hamlet of **MOULINS DE KEROUAT** (*Milin-Kerroc'h* in Breton – and on the Michelin map), which has been restored as an **Eco-Musée** (Feb hols & Christmas hols Mon–Fri 10am–5pm; mid-March to May, Sept & Oct Mon–Fri 10am–noon & 2–6pm, Sun 2–6pm; June Mon–Fri 10am–noon & 2–6pm, Sat & Sun 2–6pm; July & Aug daily 11am–7pm; 27F/€4.12). Kerouat's last inhabitant died in 1967 and, like many a place in the Breton interior, it might have crumbled into indiscernible ruins. However, one of the hamlet's water mills has been restored to motion, and its houses repaired and refurnished as part of the museum. The largest belonged in the nineteenth century to the mayor of Commana, who also controlled the mills, and its furnishings are therefore those of a rich family.

Into the mountains
The highest point of the Monts d'Arrée is the **ridge** which curves from the **Réservoir de St-Michel** (also known as the Lac de Brennilis) to Menez Kaldor. It is visible as a stark silhouette from the underused but attractive and

well-equipped **campsite** at **NESTAVEL-BRAZ** on the eastern shore of the lake (☎02.98.99.66.57; closed mid-Sept to mid-June). From this deceptively tranquil vantage point, the army's antennae near **Roc Trévezel** to the north are obscured, as are those of the navy at Menez-Meur to the west. Right behind you, however, is the Brennilis nuclear power station. In a rare manifestation of separatist terrorism, Breton nationalists attacked this in 1975 with a rocket-launcher; it survived. In 1987, the British SAS conducted an astonishingly offensive exercise in this area, when they were invited by the French government to subdue a simulated Breton uprising, and in the process managed to run over a local inhabitant.

Perhaps appropriately, across the lake where the tree-lined fields around the villages end, is **Yeun Elez** – a hole to hell, according to legend. You can walk around the lake – gorse and brambles permitting; be very careful not to stray from the paths into the surrounding peat bogs. The ridge itself is followed most of the way by a road, but in places it still feels as if miles from any habitation.

In the village of **BOTMEUR**, a couple of kilometres northwest of Yeun Elez, you'll find an attractive and welcoming **B&B**, run by Mme Solliec, in a small cluster of converted country houses (☎02.98.99.63.02, *msol@club-internet.fr*; ③).

The Forêt de Huelgoat

The **Forêt de Huelgoat** spreads out to the north and east of the village of **HUELGOAT**, the halfway point between Morlaix and Carhaix on the minor road D769 and served by the four daily buses that connect the two towns.

While there may be doubt as to whether the *Argoat*, the great forest supposed to have stretched the length of prehistoric inland Brittany, ever existed, the antiquity of Huelgoat cannot be questioned. Until 1987, indeed, this was a staggering, almost impossible landscape, of trees, giant boulders and waterfalls tangled together in primeval chaos. Just how fragile it really was, just how miraculous had been its long survival, was demonstrated by the hurricane of that October, which smashed it to smithereens in the space of fifteen minutes.

After several years of cleaning up, the forest has now returned to a fairly close approximation of its former glories. You might be a little puzzled by some of the hyperbolic descriptions that survive from the old days in the local tourist literature and other sources, but it is (once again) possible to walk for several kilometres along the various paths that lead into the depths of the woods, and in spring and autumn in particular Huelgoat deserves a substantial detour.

Granite being less delicate than timber, the strange rock formations of Huelgoat have survived better than the trees, and a half-hour stroll in the area close to the village enables you to scramble over, among, and even under a number of inconceivably large specimens. At the **Grotte du Diable**, you can make a somewhat perilous descent, between the rocks, to a subterranean stream. The local story is that a Revolutionary soldier, fleeing from the *Chouans* (see p.395), hid in the cave, lighting a fire to keep warm; when his pursuers saw him by the red glow, brandishing a pitchfork to defend himself, they thought they'd found the Devil. In summer, a "teahouse" and crêperie (☎02.98.99.93.00) serves snacks to walkers, a few metres from the disappointingly stable **Roche Tremblante**.

Further into the forest, not far from the waterfall known as the **Mare aux Sangliers**, the **Camp d'Arthus** has been identified as a Gallo-Roman *oppidum*, or hillfort, large enough to be a settlement for a whole community rather than just a military encampment. Until the hurricane, it was also the spitting image of

Astérix the Gaul's fictional village. It's now barely recognizable, although the obliteration of the tree cover enabled archeologists to get a clearer view of its history.

Practicalities

The village of Huelgoat still makes quite a pleasant overnight stop, next to its own small **lake** (on which they hold aquatic Citroën 2CV championships each July).

The local **tourist office**, in the old Maison du Moulin, alongside the outflow from the lake where the forest footpath begins (July & Aug Mon–Sat 9.30am–12.30pm & 1.30–5.30pm, Sun 10am–12.30pm & 2.30–5pm; Sept–June Mon–Sat 10am–12.30pm & 2–5.30pm; ☎02.98.99.72.32), supplies walking maps of the forest. One or two of the village's **hotels** were too hard hit by the post-hurricane decline in tourism to survive, but the *Hôtel du Lac*, beside the lake at 12 rue du Général-de-Gaulle (☎02.98.99.71.14; ③; closed mid-Nov to mid-Dec), is still there, offering well-refurbished **rooms** and good food, ranging from pizzas and salads up to full seafood menus. Also alongside the lake, on the road towards Brest, the two-star *Camping du Lac* (☎02.98.99.78.80; closed mid-Sept to mid-June) is complete with swimming pool. **Bikes** are rented out at the garage at 1 rue du Lac.

Le Gouffre

A walk out from Huelgoat that avoids the heart of the forest takes you along the **canal** to the east. This stretch – not linked to any of the main Nantes–Brest waterways – was originally built to serve the old lead and silver mines, worked here from Roman times right up to the twentieth century. **LE GOUFFRE** is close by (at the junction where the road out from Huelgoat joins the D769 between Morlaix and Carhaix), worth the walk for its deep cave and, more so, for an exceptionally good (and cheap) *Routiers* **restaurant**.

Back to the canal

Although between Carhaix and Pontivy the **Nantes–Brest canal** is limited to canoeists, it's worth some effort to follow on land, particularly for the scenery along the middle stretch from **Gouarec** to **Mur-de-Bretagne**. At the centre trails the artificial **Lac de Guerlédan**, backed to the south by the **Forêt de Quénécan**.

Approaching by road, the canal path is easiest joined at Gouarec, covered by the five daily buses between Carhaix and Loudéac. En route, you pass the rather subdued (and unmemorable) town of **ROSTRENEN**, whose old facades are given a little life at the Tuesday **market**.

Gouarec

At **GOUAREC** the River Blavet and the canal meet in a confusing swirl of water that shoots off, edged by footpaths, in the most unlikely directions. The old schist houses of the town are barely disturbed by traffic or development, nor are there great numbers of tourists.

For a comfortable overnight stop, the *du Blavet* **hotel** (☎02.96.24.90.03, *louis.le-loir@wanadoo.fr*; ②) is in an ideal waterside position; its restaurant is principally aimed at gourmets prepared to spend several hundred francs on a single bottle of wine, but they're quite happy to serve you with the same excellent food, such as a tasty leek flan or a fish terrine, on their cheapest menu (weekdays only; 85F/€12.96) with no wine. The 175F/€26.68 menu features a *millefeuille* of *langoustines*.

There's also a well-positioned two-star municipal **campsite**, the *Tost Aven* (☎02.96.24.85.42; closed Oct–March), next to the canal and away from the main road.

Lac de Guerlédan

For the 15km between Gouarec and Mur-de-Bretagne, the **N164** skirts the edge of the **Forêt de Quénécan**, within which is the series of artificial lakes created when the Barrage of Guerlédan was completed in 1928. Though the forest itself suffered severe damage in the 1987 hurricane, this remains a beautiful stretch of river, a little overpopular with British camper-caravanners, but peaceful enough nonetheless.

The best bases to stay are just off the road, past the villages of **ST-GELVEN** and **Caurel**. At the former, the ravishing *Hôtellerie de l'Abbaye Bon-Repos* (☎02.96.24.98.38; ③; closed Tues evening & Wed in low season) is an absolutely irresistible, amazingly inexpensive **hotel-restaurant**, nestling beside the water at the end of a venerable avenue of ancient trees, and housed in the intact outbuildings of a twelfth-century Cistercian abbey destroyed during the French Revolution. Porthole-like windows pierce the thick slate walls of its six cosy guestrooms, to look out across extensive riverfront grounds to the wooded slopes beyond. Even if you don't stay, it's worth pausing for a meal in the gorgeous dining room, where menus start at 105F/€16.01 and a five-course seafood banquet costs 180F/€27.44.

The **abbey** ruins themselves are open to visitors (Easter–May & Sept Mon–Fri 10am–noon & 2–6pm, Sat 2–6pm, Sun 2–7pm; June Mon–Fri 10am–7pm, Sat & Sun 2–7pm; July & Aug daily 10am–7pm; Oct–Easter daily except Sat 2–6pm; 18F/€2.74), and also play host to occasional *son et lumière* spectacles in summer, while its grounds are taken over by an **organic farmers' market** on Sundays. A little further down the lane, a tiny stone bridge crosses the canal, and the towpath squeezes alongside meadows that are popular with picnickers. A yellow barge known as the *Constance de Bon-Repos* (☎02.96.28.52.64) runs two-hour **river cruises** from the bridge for 40F/€6.10.

From just before Caurel, the brief loop of the D111 leads to tiny sandy beaches – a bit too tiny in season – where there's a two-star **campsite**, *Les Pins* (☎02.96.28.52.22; closed Oct–March). At the spot known, justifiably, as **BEAU RIVAGE**, a lavish holiday complex contains the *Nautic International* campsite (☎02.96.28.57.94; closed Oct–April), and the *Hôtel Beau Rivage* (☎02.96.28.52.15; ③; closed Mon evening & Tues in low season), plus a restaurant, a snack bar and a 140-seat glass-topped cruise boat.

Mur-de-Bretagne and Loudéac

MUR-DE-BRETAGNE, set back from the eastern end of the lake, is a lively place with a wide and colourful pedestrianized zone around its church. It's the nearest town to the barrage – just 2km distant – and has a **campsite**, the *Rond-Point du Lac* (☎02.96.26.01.90; closed mid-Sept to mid-June), with facilities for windsurfing and horse riding. There's also a pretty little **hostel**, 3km northeast along the D65 at **ST-GUEN** (☎02.96.28.54.34; 63F/€9.60; closed Nov–March) – take the Loudéac bus and get off at the "Bourg de St-Guen" stop.

LOUDÉAC, useful for changing buses, is in itself unmemorable. Travelling on from Mur-de-Bretagne under your own steam, you'd do better to take the D767 instead and follow the River Blavet south.

The central canal

Beyond the barrage of Guerlédan, the historic town of **Pontivy** is the central junction of the Nantes–Brest canal, where the course of the canal breaks off once more from the Blavet and you can again take **barges** – all the way to the Loire.

Pontivy and on to Bréhan

PONTIVY owes much of its appearance, and its size, to the canal. When the waterway opened, the small medieval centre was expanded, redesigned and given broad avenues to fit its new role. It was even renamed Napoléonville for a time, in honour of the instigator of its new prosperity.

These days it is a bright market town, its twisting old streets contrasting with the stately riverside promenades. At the north end of the town, occupying a commanding hillside site, is the **Château de Rohan**, built by the lord of Josselin in the fifteenth century (June–Sept daily 10.30am–7pm; Oct–May Wed–Sun 10am–noon & 2–6pm; 20F/€3.05). Used in summer for low-key cultural events and temporary exhibitions, the castle still belongs to the Josselin family, who are slowly restoring it. At the moment, one impressive facade, complete with deep moat and two forbidding towers, looks out over the river – behind that, the structure rather peters out.

Practicalities

Pontivy's **gare SNCF** is close to the River Blavet, roughly ten-minutes' walk south of the helpful local **tourist office**, which is immediately below the castle in a former leprosy hospital at 61 rue du Général-de-Gaulle (June–Sept daily 10am–6pm; Oct–May Mon–Sat 10am–noon & 2–6pm; ☎02.97.25.04.10). If you're looking for a place to stop over, the town holds several **hotels**, among them the low-priced *Robic*, 2 rue Jean-Jaurès (☎02.97.25.11.80; ②; closed Sun evening in winter), which has a good restaurant with menus from 60F/€9.15, and the smarter *Porhoët*, near the tourist office at 41 rue du Général-de-Gaulle (☎02.97.25.34.88; ③). In addition, the local **hostel**, 2km from the *gare SNCF* on the Île des Récollets (☎02.97.25.58.27; 51F/€7.77), has undergone a long-overdue renovation, and is looking great; it also serves cheap meals.

Rohan and Bréhan

Immediately beyond Pontivy, the **course of the canal** veers north for a while, away from the Blavet. As it curves back, the stretch from St-Maudan to Rohan is wide and smooth-flowing, with picnic and play areas but without a road or towpath you can follow for any distance.

ROHAN looks prominent on the map but it's little more than a strip of houses by the canalside. To the northeast, the attractive village of **LA CHÈZE** has a tiny and private lake, with an equally diminutive two-star **campsite**, *La Rivière* (☎02.96.26.70.99; closed mid-Sept to mid-June). **LA TRINITÉ PORHOËT**, beyond, also has a two-star **campsite**, *St-Yves* (☎02.97.93.92.00; closed mid-Sept to mid-June), on the long wooded slopes of the valley of the Ninian – otherwise scattered with stone farms and manor houses.

Southeast from Rohan, continuing along the canal towards Josselin, is the Cistercian **Abbaie de Timadeuc**, founded as recently as 1841. You can enter only to attend Mass, but it's beautiful anyway from the outside, with its front walls and main gate covered in flowers at the end of an avenue of old pines. The abbey also provides an excuse to stay at **BRÉHAN**, a couple of kilometres away – a quiet little village whose central **hotel**, the *Cremaillère* (☎02.97.38.80.93; ①), is among the least expensive in the province, with daily set menus at 58F/€8.84 and 75F/€11.28.

West from Pontivy: along the Blavet

If you choose to follow the **River Blavet** west from Pontivy towards Lorient – rather than the canal – take the time to go by the smaller roads along the valley itself. The Blavet connects the canal with the sea, and once linked Lorient to the other two great ports of Brittany, Brest and Nantes.

Quistinic

The D159 to **QUISTINIC** passes through lush green countryside, its hedgerows full of flowers, where by June there's already been one harvest and grass is growing up around the fresh haystacks. The ivy-clad church of **St-Mathurin** in Quistinic is the scene of a *pardon* (in the second week of May) that dates from

Roman times. The devotion to the saint is strongly evident on the village's war memorial, too – his name is that of almost half the victims.

You can **camp** on the edge of Quistinic, near the river at the two-star *Île de Ménazen* (☎02.97.39.71.08; closed mid-Sept to mid-June).

Baud: the Venus de Quinipily

The main reason to go on to **BAUD**, a major road junction just to the east of the river, is to see the **Venus de Quinipily**. Signposted off the Hennebont road, 2km out of town, the Venus is a crude statue that at first glance looks Egyptian. Once known as the "Iron Lady", it is of unknown but ancient origin. It stands on, or rather nestles its ample buttocks against, a high plinth above a kind of sarcophagus, commanding the valley in the gardens of what was once a château. Behind its stiff pose and dress, the statue has an odd informality, a half-smile on the impassive face. It used to be the object of "impure rites" and was at least twice thrown into the Blavet by Christian authorities, only to be fished out by locals eager to reindulge. It may itself have been in some way "improper" before it was recarved, perhaps literally "dressed", some time in the eighteenth century.

The **gardens** around the statue, despite being next to a dry and dusty quarry, are luxuriantly fertile. To visit, you pay a small fee to a woman at the gatehouse, who matter-of-factly maintains that "pagans" still come to worship (Jan–April & Nov to mid-Dec daily except Tues 11am–5pm; May–Oct daily 10am–7pm).

There are **rooms** to suit all price ranges at the *Relais de la Forêt* (☎02.97.51.01.77; ②), opposite the town hall in Baud, while **meals** in the wood-panelled dining room start at 80F/€12.20. A pricier *logis* stands nearby, the *Auberge du Cheval Blanc*, at 16 rue de Pontivy (☎02.97.51.00.85; ②; closed Jan).

Camors and Locminé

CAMORS, just south of Baud, has a smart square-towered **church**, with a weathercock on top and a little megalith set in the wall. You can spend the night here at the *Hôtel-Restaurant Ar Brug*, at 14 rue Principale opposite the church (☎02.97.39.20.10; ②), which has an excellent restaurant (and one that doesn't scrimp on the portions). For campers, there's a two-star **campsite**, *du Petit Bois* (☎02.97.39.22.06; closed mid-Sept to mid-June), situated at one end of the series of forests that grow bleaker and harsher eastward to become the Lanvaux Moors.

Heading east from Baud, to rejoin the canal at Josselin, you pass through **LOCMINÉ**, another one of those towns reduced to piping rock music in its lifeless streets on summer afternoons in a desperate attempt to draw visitors. It, too, has a reasonable little **hotel**, the *Hôtel-Restaurant de Bretagne*, 10 rue Max-Jacob (☎02.97.60.00.44; ②), with a cheap, good-value dining room.

Josselin and onwards

The three Rapunzel towers of the **Château de Rohan** at **JOSSELIN**, embedded in a vast sheet of stone above the water, are the most impressive sight along the Nantes–Brest canal. However, they turn out on close inspection to be no more than a facade. The building behind was built in the nineteenth century, the bulk of the original castle having been demolished by Richelieu in 1629 in punishment for Henri de Rohan's leadership of the Huguenots. The Rohan family, still in possession, used to own a third of Brittany, though the present incumbent contents himself with the position of local mayor.

Tours of the pompous apartments of the ducal residence are not very compelling, even if it does contain the table on which the Edict of Nantes was signed in 1598. But the duchess's collection of **dolls**, housed in the **Musée des Poupées**, behind the castle, is something special (château and doll museum both April, May & Oct Wed, Sat, Sun & hols 2–6pm; June & Sept daily 2–6pm; July & Aug daily 10am–6pm; closed Nov–March; both 33F/€5.03, combined ticket 62F/€9.45). English-language tours of the castle start daily at 2.30pm in June and September, and daily at 11am and 2.30pm in July and August.

The **town** is full of medieval splendours, from the castle ramparts to the gargoyles of the basilica of **Notre Dame du Roncier**, as well as the half-timbered houses in between. The basilica was built on the spot where in the ninth century a peasant supposedly found a statue of the Virgin under a bramble bush. The statue was burned during the Revolution, but an important *pardon* is held each year on September 8. As ever, the religious procession and open-air services are solemn in the extreme, but there's a lot else going on to keep you entertained.

One of the most famous episodes of late chivalry, the **Battle of the Thirty**, took place nearby in 1351. Rivalry between the French garrison at Josselin and the English at Ploërmel led to a challenge being issued to settle differences in a combat of thirty unmounted knights from each side. The French won, killing the English leader Bemborough. The actual battle-site, marked by a small monument, is now isolated between the two carriageways of the N24 from Josselin to Ploërmel.

Practicalities

Josselin's **tourist office** is in a superb old house on the place de la Congrégation, up in town next to the castle entrance (April–June, Sept & Oct daily 10am–noon & 2–6pm; July & Aug daily 10am–6pm; Nov–March Mon–Fri 10am–noon & 2–6pm; ☎02.97.22.36.43, *ot.josselin@wanadoo.fr*).

A good place to **stay** is the *Hôtel de France*, just across from the basilica at 6 place Notre Dame (☎02.97.22.23.06; ②; closed Sun evening & Mon between Oct and March), an ivy-covered *logis* which is amazingly quiet considering its central location, and which offers a good-value 50F/€7.62 lunch, and a 81F/€12.35 menu on which you can choose between duck *à l'orange* and trout with almonds. The lovely *Hôtel du Chateau*, facing the castle from across the river at 1 rue du Général-de-Gaulle (☎02.97.22.20.11; ③; closed Feb), is also a treat. The nearest good **campsite** is the three-star *Bas de la Lande* (☎02.97.22.22.20; closed Oct–April), half an hour's walk from the castle, south of the river and west of town. There's also a **gîte d'étape** nearby, right below the castle walls, where you can rent canoes (☎02.97.22.21.69).

Guéhenno

At **GUÉHENNO**, 10km south of Josselin on the D123, you'll find one of the largest and best of the Breton **calvaries**. Built in 1550, the figures include the cock that crowed to expose Peter's denials, Mary Magdalene with the shroud, and a recumbent Christ in the crypt. Its appeal is enhanced by the naivety of its amateur restoration. After damage caused by Revolutionary soldiers in 1794 – who amused themselves by playing *boules* with the heads of the statues – all the sculptors approached for the work demanded exorbitant fees, so the parish priest and his assistant decided to undertake the task themselves.

Kerguéhennec Sculpture Park

Another unusual sculptural endeavour, this time contemporary, is taking place at the **Domaine de Kerguéhennec**, which is signposted a short way off the D11 near St Jean-Brévelay, 7km west of Guéhenno. This innovatory **sculpture park** (Tues–Sun: April–Oct 10am–7pm; Nov–March 10am–6pm; guided tours: mid-June to mid-Sept daily 4pm; mid-Sept to mid-June Sat & Sun 4pm; ☎02.97.60.44.44; 25F/€3.81) is progressively building up a fascinating permanent international collection, under the auspices of the *département* of Morbihan.

Among the first pieces to be installed, back in 1986, were a massive railway sleeper painstakingly stripped down by Giuseppe Penone to reveal the young sapling within; since then the park has become an increasingly compelling stop. Its setting is the lawns, woods and lake of an early eighteenth-century château; studios and indoor workshops in the outbuildings are used by visiting artists.

Lizio

Nine kilometres in the opposite direction from Guéhenno, off the D151, the little village of **LIZIO** has also set itself up as a centre for arts and crafts, with ceramic and weaving workshops as its speciality. For most of the year, you might pass along its single curving street of stone cottages without seeing a sign of life; on the second Sunday in August, however, it's the scene of a **Festival Artisanal**, featuring street theatre (and pancakes). In addition, if you do take the trouble to stop, you may spot that one venerable old cottage, from the outside looking much like the rest, houses an **Insectarium** (April–Sept daily 10am–noon & 2–6pm; 35F/€5.34). Creepy-crawlies within include all sorts of hairy spiders, giant millipedes, huge iridescent butterflies, praying mantises that look like dead leaves, and stick insects in amazing colours. It's a trifle expensive for twenty minutes on the verge of nausea, but the kids will probably love it.

Various farmers in the nearby countryside, who welcome visitors, are working to re-create traditional skills such as bee keeping and cider-making, and one is even rearing wild boars for food. For details of them all, and an overview of long-lost agricultural techniques and implements, call in at the **Eco-Musée des Vieux Métiers**, 4km out of Lizio on the D174 towards Ploërmel (daily 10am–noon & 2–7pm; 30F/€4.57).

Lizio has no hotels, but it does have a couple of restaurants. There are also several **gîtes** (information on ☎02.97.74.92.67) in the immediate area, and a two-star municipal **campsite**, *Le Val Jouin* (☎02.97.74.84.76; closed mid-Oct to mid-June).

Ploërmel

PLOËRMEL, defeated by Josselin in the fourteenth century Battle of the Thirty (see opposite), is still not quite a match for its rival. It's not on the canal, and is no longer served by trains either. Attractions are the artificial **Étang au Duc**, well stocked with fish, 2km to the north, and an interesting array of houses: James II is said to have spent a few days of his exile in one on rue Francs-Bourgeois, while the **Maison des Marmosets** on rue Beaumanoir has some elaborate carvings.

A couple of good-value **hotels** – *St-Marc* (☎02.97.74.00.01; ②), near the long-defunct train station, and the very fancy *Cobh*, 10 rue des Forges (☎02.97.74.00.49, *lecobh@wanadoo.fr*; ②) – make suitable bases for venturing further away from the canal, up into Paimpont forest.

The Forêt de Paimpont

A definite magic still lingers about the **FORÊT DE PAIMPONT**. Though now just forty square kilometres in extent, it seems to retain the secrets of a forest once much larger, and everywhere recalls legends of the vanished *Argoat*, the great primeval forest of Brittany. The one French claimant to an Arthurian past that carries any real conviction, it is just as frequently known by its Arthurian name of Brocéliande.

The Forest and its myths

Medieval Breton minstrels, like their Welsh counterparts, set the tales of King Arthur and the Holy Grail both in *Grande Bretagne* and here in *Petite Bretagne*. The particular significance of Brocéliande was as Merlin's forest – some say that he is still here, in "Merlin's stone", where he was imprisoned by the enchantress Viviane.

The stone is next to the **Fontaine de Barenton**, a lonely spot high in the woods that is far from easy to find. Turn off the main road into the forest from Concoret (a village notable for having once had the Devil as its rector) at La Saudrais, and you will come to the village of Folle Pensée. Go past the few farm-houses, rather than up the hill, and you arrive at a small car park. A footpath leads up to the right, running through pine and gorse. At a junction of forest tracks, continue straight ahead for about 200m, then veer left along an unobvious (and unmarked) path which leads into the woods, turning back to the north to the spring – walled in mossy stone in the roots of a mighty tree, and filled with the most delicious water imaginable.

FORÊT DE PAIMPONT

Chrétien de Troyes sang of the fountain in the early Middle Ages:

> *You will see the spring which bubbles*
> *Though its water is colder than marble.*
> *It is shaded by the most beautiful tree*
> *That Nature ever made,*
> *For its foliage is evergreen*
> *And a basin of iron hangs from it,*
> *By a chain long enough*
> *To reach the spring;*
> *And beside the spring you will find*
> *A slab of stone which you will recognize –*
> *I cannot describe it*
> *For I have never seen one like it.*

Legend has it that, if after drinking, you splash water on to the stone slab, you instantly summon a mighty storm, together with roaring lions and a horseman in black armour. This story dates back at least to the fifth century and is recounted, somewhat sceptically, in Robert Wace's *Romance of the Rose*, written around 1160:

> *Hunters repair (to the fountain) in sultry weather; and drawing water with their horns, they sprinkle the stone for the purposes of having rain, which is then wont to fall, they say, throughout the forest around; but why I know not. There too fairies are to be seen (if the Bretons tell truth), and many other wonders happen. I went thither on purpose to see these marvels. I saw the forest and the land, and I sought for the marvels, but I found none. I went like a fool, and so I came back. I sought after folly, and found myself a fool for my pains.*

The parish priest of Concoret and his congregation are reported nonetheless to have successfully ended a drought by this means in 1835, and a procession endorsed by the church went to the spring as recently as 1925.

Comper and the Val sans Retour

At Barenton, you are at the very spot where Merlin first set eyes on Viviane, although you are not at the Fountain of Eternal Youth, which is hidden somewhere nearby and accessible only to the pure in heart. The enchantress is supposed to have been born at the château at **COMPER**, at the northern edge of the forest near Concoret. Today it serves as the **Centre de l'Imaginaire Arthurien**, which means that each summer it's the venue of different exhibitions and entertainments on Arthurian themes; the centre also organizes tours of the actual forest. Unless you're sure the theme of this year's temporary exhibition will interest you, don't bother paying to go in – the permanent displays of pointlessly posed mannequins are boring in the extreme (March–May, Sept & Oct Mon, Wed, Thurs, Sat & Sun 10am–7pm; June–Aug daily except Tues 10am–7pm; 30F/€4.57).

Viviane's rival, Morgane le Fay, ruled over the **Val sans Retour** (Valley of No Return) on the western edge of the forest. The valley is situated just off the GR37 footpath from Tréhorenteuc to La Guette. Follow the path that leads out from the D141 south of Tréhorenteuc to a steep valley from which exits are barred by thickets of gorse and giant furze on the rocks above. At one point it skirts past an overgrown table of rock, the **Rocher des Faux Amants**, from which the seductress Morgane was wont to entice unwary and faithless youths.

Paimpont village and other forest bases

PAIMPONT village is the most obvious and enjoyable base for exploring the forest. It's right at the centre of the woods, backs onto a marshy lake whose shores are thick with wild mushrooms (*cêpes*), and has some excellent accommodation. At the **hotel** *Relais de Brocéliande* in town (☎02.99.07.81.07; ②), a real flower-bedecked delight, you can stuff yourself for 125F/€19.06 in the restaurant under the gaze of stuffed animal heads. The food is hearty in the extreme, with menus packed with veal and guinea fowl; the owners raise their own pigs and even their own lobsters.

Information on local walking opportunities – the best megalithic site in the vicinity is undoubtedly the **Site des Pierres Droites**, a stone circle not far to the south – can be picked up from the summer-only **tourist office** next to the lakeside abbey (June–Sept daily 9.30am–12.30pm & 1.30–6.30pm; ☎02.99.07.84.23). There are a couple of **campsites** in the heart of the forest, including the two-star municipal one on the edge of the village (☎02.97.07.89.16; closed Oct–April), a *gîte d'étape*-cum-*chambre d'hôte* in tiny Trudeau on the D40, 2km east (☎02.99.07.81.40; dorm beds 52F/€7.93, B&B ③), and a lovely **hostel** at Le Choucan-en-Brocéliande, a couple of kilometres out on the Concoret road (☎02.97.22.76.75; 49F/€7.47; closed early Sept to mid-June).

Alternative places in which to base yourself include **Les Forges** and **Plélan-le-Grand**, at the southern edge of the forest, **Mauron** at the north, and, further out to the east, **Montfort-sur-Meu**.

Les Forges

The forges that gave **LES FORGES** its name, and once smelted iron from the surrounding forest, have long since disappeared. Now it's just a rural hamlet, set by a calm lake and disturbed only by the dogs in the hunting kennels. Among the houses coated with red ivy is a **gîte d'étape** (keys held by Mme Farcy; ☎02.97.06.93.46).

Plélan-le-Grand

The tiny village of **PLÉLAN-LE-GRAND**, at the other end of the lake, has an oddly dramatic history. In the ninth century it was the capital of one of Brittany's early kings, Solomon; its appeal presumably lay in its inaccessibility to Norse or other raiders. Later, in the sixteenth century, it was a part of the short-lived independent republic of Thélin, awarded to the local people after they had paid the ransom of their liegelord. And finally, after the Revolution, Plélan served as the headquarters of Puisaye, the Breton *Chouan* leader.

Don't imagine from that that Plélan is in any sense an attractive place to stay. It does, however, have an affordable **hotel** in the *Bruyères* (☎02.99.06.81.38; ②), while just outside the village is the *Manoir du Tertre* (☎02.99.07.81.02; ④; closed Tues & Feb), a very grand old country house, preserved with all its furnishings and operating as a superb hotel-restaurant, with high but not outrageous prices (cheapest dinner menu 135F/€20.58).

Bellevue and Guer

If you continue south you come to **BELLEVUE-COËTQUIDAN**, dominated by a large military camp; its hotels, full of the anxious relatives of soldiers, aren't the most attractive resting places.

Another 4km or 5km beyond is **GUER**, a gentle little town containing not much more than a rusty ideas box placed in the main square and a heated covered swimming pool. From here, the D776 rolls and tumbles through further woods until it reaches the canal at Malestroit.

Mauron

At the **northern** edge of the forest, the nearest rooms are at **MAURON**. A rambling country town, this has quite a charm – and a reasonable **hotel**, the *Brambily* (☎02.97.22.61.67; ②; closed Mon), in the town centre. It also has a swimming pool; on the small side, but still more than welcome after a hot day in the forest.

Montfort-sur-Meu

If you've been seduced by the Paimpont forest, **MONTFORT-SUR-MEU**, east of the forest 25km short of Rennes, has an illuminating **Eco-Musée** which serves to provide some background information (Mon–Fri 8.30am–noon & 2–6pm, Sat 10am–noon & 2–6pm, Sun 2–6pm; 20F/€3.05). Set in the one surviving tower of what in the fourteenth century was a complete walled town, it appears at first the usual small-town museum assortment – costumed dolls and the like. But don't be put off. Upstairs there is a detailed comparison between the forests of Paimpont and Trémelin, proving the shocking fact that the former is artificially planted (and therefore a poor candidate really to be Brocéliande). Of more tangible appeal, there's a remarkable display of the area's quarries – some of which can be seen from the top of the tower – and its stone, exhibited along with modern sculptures exploring their texture or building techniques. The museum also runs workshops, where children are taught traditional crafts with materials such as cow dung, and where sculptors explain their work to casual visitors.

Montfort is on the railway, with a reasonable **hotel**, the *Relais de la Cane*, 2 rue de la Gare (☎02.99.09.00.07; ③), close by the **gare SNCF**. Being only a few minutes away from Rennes by train, it is a possible point from which to set out if you're coming to Paimpont from the north. You can rent **bikes** at the station, as ever.

Malestroit, Rochefort and La Gacilly

Should you choose to follow the course of the canal southwest from Josselin, as opposed to making the detour to the Forêt de Paimpont, the next significant town you come to is the small but appealing **Malestroit**. Beyond that, if you are not actually travelling on the canal, which at this stage is the **River Oust**, the D764 on the south bank, or the D147/149 on the north, will keep you parallel for much of its course towards Redon. Along the way there are two worthwhile detours: south of the canal to **Rochefort-en-Terre**, or north to **La Gacilly**.

Malestroit

Although not a lot happens in **MALESTROIT**, which was a thousand years old in 1987, the town is full of unexpected and enjoyable corners. As you come into the main square, the **place du Bouffay** in front of the church, the houses are covered with unlikely carvings – an anxious bagpipe-playing hare looks over its shoulder at a dragon's head on one beam, while an oblivious sow in a blue-buckled belt threads her distaff on another. The **church** itself is decorated with drunkards and acrobats outside, torturing demons and erupting towers within; a placard outside explains the various allegories, while each night the display is completed by the sullen parade of metal-festooned youth that weaves in and out of the *Vieille Auberge* bar opposite. The only ancient walls without adornment are the ruins of the **Chapelle de la Madeleine**, where one of the many temporary truces of the Hundred Years War was signed.

Beside the grey canal, the matching grey-slate tiles on the turreted rooftops bulge and dip, while on its central island overgrown houses stand next to the stern walls of an old mill.

Practicalities

If you arrive in Malestroit by barge – this being a good stretch to travel on the water – you'll moor very near the town centre. The helpful local **tourist office** stands at the edge of the main square at 17 place du Bouffay (Mon–Fri 9am–12.30pm & 2–6.30pm, Sat 9am–noon & 2–6pm; ☎02.97.75.14.57, *www .malestroit.com* or *www.morbihan-valdoust.com*); they can provide details of **boat rental**.

The nearby **gare routière** is served by buses from Vannes and Rennes, while across the river there's a two-star **campsite**, *La Daufresne* (☎02.97.75.13.33; closed Oct–May), down below the bridge in the Impasse d'Abattoir next to the swimming pool, and a **gîte d'étape** up at the canal lock (c/o M Hallier; ☎02.97.75.11.66). Sadly, however, there's no longer a hotel in town.

The Musée de la Résistance Bretonne

Two kilometres west of Malestroit (and with no bus connection), the village of **ST-MARCEL** hosts the **Musée de la Résistance Bretonne** (April to mid-June daily 10am–noon & 2–6pm; mid-June to mid-Sept daily 10am–7pm; mid-Sept to March daily except Tues 10am–noon & 2–6pm; 25F/€3.81). The museum stands on the site of a June 1944 battle in which the Breton *maquis*, joined by Free French forces parachuted in from England, successfully diverted the local German troops from the main Normandy invasion movements.

The museum's newest buildings house documents and artefacts highlighting the history of the Free French SAS. Its strongest feature, however, remains its presentation of the pressures that made so many French collaborate: the reconstructed street corner overwhelmed by the brooding presence of the occupiers; the big colourful propaganda posters offering work in Germany, announcing executions of *maquis*, equating resistance with aiding US and British big business; and, against these, the low-budget, flimsily printed Resistance pamphlets. All the labelling is in French, which non-speakers may find rather frustrating.

Rochefort-en-Terre

ROCHEFORT-EN-TERRE, overlooking the River Arz from a high eminence 17km south of Malestroit, may be a prettified and polished version of its neighbour, and something of a tourist trap with its little antique shops and expensive restaurants, but it ranks nonetheless among the most delightful villages in Brittany. Every available stone surface, from the window ledges to the picturesque wishing well, is permanently bedecked in flowers, to the extent that Rochefort has been banned since 1967 from taking part in regional and national contests for the town with the best floral decorations (*villes fleuries*).

The flowery tradition originated with the painter Alfred Klots, who was born in France to a wealthy American family in 1875, and who bought Rochefort's ruined **château** in 1907. Perched on the town's highest point, the castle is now open for guided tours (April, May & Oct Sat, Sun & hols 10.30am–noon & 2–6.30pm; June & Sept daily 10.30am–noon & 2–6.30pm; July & Aug daily 10am–7pm; 25F/€3.81), though not until you go through its dramatic gateway do you find out that in fact that gateway is all that survives of the original fifteenth-century structure. Instead, the castle as it stands today was cobbled together by Klots using assorted pieces from various other ruins in the vicinity. It contains his own relatively unremarkable paintings, along with those of his son, plus family memorabilia such as the "Cardinal Room", where a US Cardinal once stayed and appears to have left his clothes and suitcase behind when he left. The highlights are Klots' former studio, a detached building with magnificent views over the surrounding hills and gorges, and garden terraces on all sides.

At the bottom end of town, the church of **Notre Dame de Tronchaye** holds a Black Virgin that was found hidden from Norman invaders in a hollow tree in the twelfth century, and is the object of a pilgrimage on the first Sunday after August 15. More interesting, though, is the **Lac Bleu**, just to the south, where the deep galleries of some ancient **slate quarries** are the home of blind butterflies and long-eared bats.

Practicalities

Rochefort's modern **tourist office**, in the central place des Halles (June & Sept Mon–Fri 10am–12.30pm & 2.30–6pm, Sat & Sun 2–6pm; July & Aug Mon–Fri 10am–12.30pm & 2–6.30pm, Sat & Sun 2–6.30pm; Oct–May Mon–Fri 10am–noon & 2.30–5pm, Sat 2–5pm; ☎02.97.43.33.57), displays a list of rather expensive *chambres d'hôte* in the neighbourhood, and operates the three-star municipal **campsite**, *Le Moulin Neuf*, in the chemin de Bogeais (☎02.97.43.37.52; closed Oct–March). The one **hotel** in town, *Le Pélican* (☎02.97.43.38.48; ③), stands alongside the tourist office, and offers reasonable rooms and good food, with dinner menus starting at under 100F/€15.24. A short way down the main street towards the château, the *Lion d'Or* (☎02.97.43.32.80; closed Tues evening & Wed) is a grand sixteenth-century coaching house converted into an expensive gourmet **restaurant**.

At the village of **ST-VINCENT-SUR-OUST**, on the D764 halfway between Rochefort and Redon, a **hostel**, *Ty Kendalc'h* (☎02.99.91.28.55; 51F/€7.77; closed mid-Dec to Jan), serves as a centre for Breton music and dance.

The Parc de Préhistoire de Bretagne

Two kilometres southeast of Rochefort, outside the small community of **MALANSAC**, the very heavily publicized **Parc de Préhistoire de Bretagne** is a theme park aimed overwhelmingly at children (daily: April to mid-Oct 10.30am–7.30pm; mid-Oct to mid-Nov 1.30–6pm; 50F/€7.62). Separate landscaped areas contain dioramas of gigantic (if stationary) dinosaurs, and human beings at various stages in their evolution; the story ends shortly after a bunch of deformed but enthusiastic Neanderthals hit on the idea of erecting a few megaliths.

La Gacilly

Fourteen kilometres north of the canal, **LA GACILLY** makes a good base for walking trips in search of megaliths, sleepy villages and countryside. The town itself has prospered recently thanks to the creation of a beauty-products industry based on the abundantly proliferating flowers in the Aff valley. It is, too, a centre for many active craftsworkers; a walk down the old stone steps of the cobbled street that runs parallel to the main road between town centre and river is both a pleasure in itself and an opportunity to look in on their workshops. The only real disappointment is that the riverfront is not accessible to walkers, though you can enjoy views of it from a couple of restaurants, and take two-hour **cruises** on it in summer (June & Sept Sun 2.30pm & 4.30pm; July & Aug daily 2.30pm & 4.30pm; ☎02.99.08.56.36; 60F/€9.15).

Practicalities
Up in the town centre, the *Hôtel de France*, 15 rue Montauban (☎02.99.08.11.15, *hotel.france.lagacilly@wanadoo.fr*; ②; closed Sun evening in winter), is an extremely hospitable *logis*, with quiet and comfortable **rooms** in what used to be the separate *Hôtel du Square*, reached through the long gardens at the back, and a good traditional restaurant. The *patron* is happy to provide detailed information on local walks and attractions for his guests.

Alternatively, the luxurious *chambres d'hôte* (☎02.99.70.04.79; ④) in the nearby Château de Trégaret in **SIXT-SUR-AFF** provide ideal countryside accommodation.

The Megaliths of St-Just
Around 10km east of La Gacilly, in the vicinity of the village of **ST-JUST**, the small windswept **Cojoux** moor is rich in ancient megalithic remains. Only in the last decade or so have they received any great public attention, as a programme of excavations has gradually uncovered all sorts of ancient tombs and sacred sites.

During the summer, you should find posters in local villages giving the times of explanatory Saturday **walking tours** of the various sites, many of them led by the archeologists responsible for the digs; alternatively, call ☎02.99.72.61.02 for the current schedule. In any case, it's a rewarding area to ramble around yourself; the larger menhirs and so on are signposted along dirt tracks and footpaths, and you'll probably stumble upon a few lesser ones by chance.

Redon

Thirty-four kilometres east of Malestroit, at the junction of the rivers Oust and Vilaine, on the Nantes–Brest canal, linked by rail to Rennes, Vannes and Nantes, and at the intersection of six major roads, **REDON** is not a place it's easy to avoid. And you shouldn't try to, either. A wonderful mess of water and locks – the canal manages to cross the Vilaine at right angles in one of the more complex links – the town has history, charm and life. It's among the best stops along the whole course of the canal.

Arrival and information
The **gare SNCF** (☎02.99.71.74.10) is in place de la Gare, five minutes' walk west of the tourist office (see below). Long-distance **buses** – it takes less than an hour to get to Rennes, Nantes or Vannes – also operate from here (details from Redon Transports; ☎02.99.71.47.33).

Redon's **tourist office** is in the place de la République, north across the railway tracks from the town centre (July & Aug Mon–Sat 9am–7pm, Sun

10am–noon & 4–7pm; Sept–June Mon–Sat 9am–noon & 2–6pm; ☎02.99.71.06.04, *www.ville-redon.fr*); in summer they have an annexe in the port to serve the needs of what the notices in English call the "Pleasure People". There's a **post office** on rue St-Michel, north of the centre (☎02.99.71.02.30).

Bicycles can be rented from Cycles Gicquel in the place St-Sauveur (☎02.99.71.02.82), and **canoes** and **barges** from the Comptoir Nautique at 2 quai Surcouf (☎02.99.71.46.03); further details of canal-boat rental are given in "Travel details" at the end of this chapter.

Comptoir Nautique also run **boat trips** along the Vallée d'Oust on Wednesdays (11am; 90F/€13.72) and Sundays (4pm; 60F/€9.15), while on Thursday afternoons in July and August, Vedettes Jaunes (☎02.97.45.02.81; 100F/€15.24) head downstream past La Roche-Bernard to the Arzal dam, which is as close as they can get to the sea (2hr 30min); passengers then return by coach via Lantierne, Le Guerno, Beganne and Rieux (a further 2hr 30min). Tickets can also be reserved at the tourist office.

Accommodation

Redon's **hotels** are mostly concentrated in the town and near the *gare SNCF* rather than in the port area, but it's a small enough place that it makes little difference where you stay. The off-white *Hôtel le France* looks down on the canal from 30 rue Duguesclin, at the corner with the quai de Brest (☎02.99.71.06.11; ②); its recently renovated rooms, all with en-suite bathrooms and TVs, offer a considerable degree of comfort for the price, but it lacks a restaurant. Across (or rather under) the railway tracks from the tourist office, the *Hôtel Asther*, 14 rue des Douves (☎02.99.71.10.91; ②), has its own brasserie, *Le Théâtre*. A little nearer the station, the *Hôtel Chandouineau*, at 1 rue Thiers (☎02.99.71.02.04; ⑤), is a luxurious establishment with just seven bedrooms, where the restaurant serves gourmet menus from 120F/€18.29.

The Town

Redon was founded in 832 AD by St Conwoïon at the instigation of Nominoé, the first king of Brittany, and was a place of pilgrimage until the seventeenth century. Its Benedictine abbey is now the focus of the church of **St-Sauveur** – the rounded angles of the dumpy twelfth-century Romanesque lantern tower are unique in Brittany. All but obscured by later roofs and the high choir, the four-storey belfry is best seen from the adjacent cloisters. The later Gothic tower was entirely separated from the main building by a fire in 1780. Every Friday and Saturday from the end of June to the end of July, Redon puts on a large-scale *son et lumière* re-enactment of ten of the earliest years of its history, 835–845 AD.

Under the chapel of Joan of Arc, the church crypt holds the tomb of Pierre l'Hospital, the judge who condemned Gilles de Rais to be hanged in 1440 for satanism and the most infamous orgies. Gilles had fought alongside Joan, burned for heresy, witchcraft and sorcery in 1431, and in both cases the court procedures were irregular to say the least. Legends of the atrocities of Gilles de Rais served as the source for tales of the monstrous wife-murderer Bluebeard.

Until World War I Redon was the seaport for Rennes. Its industrial docks – or what remains of them – are therefore on the Vilaine, while the canal, even in the very centre of town, is almost totally rural, its towpaths shaded avenues. Shipowners' homes from the seventeenth and eighteenth centuries can be seen in the port area – walk via quai Jean Bart next to the *bassin* as far as the **Croix des**

Marins, returning along quai Duguay-Truin beside the river, where you'll also find the *Attis*, a US boat that was used in the Normandy landings, and being no longer seaworthy is now moored here permanently. A rusted wrought-iron work-bridge, equipped with a crane rolling on tracks, still crosses the river, but the main users of the port now are **cruise ships**, which head 40km downstream to the Arzal dam (see p.335 for details).

Flowers abound throughout Redon, which achieves regular success in *villes fleuries* – in 1983, it won the national first prize. As late as October, swaths of chrysanthemums in autumn tints hang from balconies and the numerous iron bridges.

Eating, drinking and entertainment

La Bogue, in a flowery mansion in place du Parlement at 3 rue des États (☎02.99.71.12.95; closed Sun evening), is a friendly and good-value **fish restaurant** where menus start with a very simple 79F/€12.04 option and range up to a sumptuous feast for 299F/€45.57, while *L'Akene*, 10 rue de Jeu-de-Paume (☎02.99.71.25.15; closed Tues evening & Wed in winter), is a crêperie in an equal-ly lovely old house in an alleyway close to the port. Also close to the port at 14 rue du Plessis is the *Pub Beer*, a dark cave of a **bar** that lives up to its splendid name. On Mondays a large **market** (at which you can buy superb crêpes) sprawls through most of town on both sides of the railway tracks. Redon also has a mod-ern **theatre**, Le Canal (☎02.99.71.09.50), near the main square – the season here runs from October to June.

Châteaubriant

Sixty kilometres east of Redon, and the same distance north of Nantes, the for-tified town of **CHÂTEAUBRIANT** guards the border of Brittany and Anjou. While it's not a place to go out of your way to see, and the flat surrounding coun-tryside holds precious little of interest, a couple of hours spent wandering in and around its venerable **château** makes a welcome interruption in a day spent trav-elling.

The castle walls still encircle the crest of a knoll just east of the town proper, although only the entrance keep (*donjon d'entrée*) remains of the original tenth-century structure. Visitors can simply stroll through that mighty gateway, to find a disparate assembly of buildings of different eras, in similarly assorted states of repair, interspersed with peaceful lawns and formal gardens. The most complete edifice is a self-contained Renaissance château, built from 1521 onwards, and equipped with a sort of secular cloisters. To see some of the apartments inside, join one of the regular **guided tours** (mid-June to mid-Sept Mon & Sun 2–7pm, Wed–Sat 10am–noon & 2–7pm; free).

Practicalities

Châteaubriant's **tourist office** is in the centre of the old town, just north of the church, at 21 rue du Couéré (Mon 2–6pm, Tues–Sat 10am–noon & 2–6pm; ☎02.40.28.20.90). Immediately opposite the château, the *Hôtel au Vieux Château* (☎02.40.81.22.27; ①) has inexpensive **rooms** and serves pizzas from 39F/€5.95.

Nantes

NANTES, the former capital of Brittany, is no longer officially part of the province: it was transferred to the Pays de la Loire in 1962 when the modern administrative regions were established. Nonetheless, such bureaucracy is not taken too seriously in a city whose history is so intimately bound up with Breton fortunes, and whose inhabitants still consider it to be an integral part of the province. A considerable medieval centre, it later achieved great wealth from colonial expeditions, and by the end of the eighteenth century had become the principal port of France. Huge fortunes were made on the "ebony" (slave) trade, which brought in as much as 200 percent profit per ship. However, the abolition of slavery coincided with an increased use of domestic French sugar beet as opposed to Caribbean sugar cane, the port began to silt up as it declined in significance, and heavy industry and wine production became more important.

Thanks to the tower blocks that mask the Loire and the motorways that tear past the city, Nantes is no longer especially attractive on first acquaintance. Although it's not a place to make a great priority on your travels, if you have the time and energy it holds plenty that is worth seeing – especially the **Château des Ducs** and the **Beaux Arts** museum – while the River Erdre, the vineyards of the Loire and the remarkable Italianate town of **Clisson** all lie within reach.

Arrival and information

The **gare SNCF** (☎02.40.08.11.00), a little way east of the château, is served by fast trains between Paris and Brittany – a dozen TGVs daily reach Paris in as little as two hours – as well as being the terminus for the local line westwards to St-Nazaire, La Baule and Croisic. The station has two exits; for most facilities (tramway, buses, hotels) use *Accès Nord*.

There are two central **bus** stations. Local buses use the Gare des Bus on cours Franklin, alongside place du Commerce, while the long-distance **gare routière** (☎02.40.47.62.70) is 400m away on allée Baco, near place Ricordeau. Modern rubber-wheeled **trams** run along the old riverfront, past the *gare SNCF* and the two bus stations. Flat-fare tickets are valid for one hour, rather than just a single journey, though one-day tickets are also available.

Nantes' **tourist office**, in the foyer of the colonnaded Palais de la Bourse, in place du Commerce (Mon–Sat 10am–7pm; ☎02.40.47.04.51, *www.reception.com/nantes*), provides free book-size guides to local hotels and restaurants, rents out bikes at 50F/€7.62 per day, and runs various guided tours of the city. They also sell the **Nantes City Card**, available in 1-day (90F/€13.72), 2-day (160F/€24.39) and 3-day (200F/€30.49) versions, which grants unrestricted use of local transport, including river cruises, and free admission to a wide range of museums. The bulk of the *palais* itself is given over to a FNAC book store. A subsidiary information office is located alongside the château at 1 rue de la Château (July & Aug daily 10am–7pm; Sept–June Mon–Sat 10am–7pm, Sun 10am–noon & 2–6pm). The main **post office** is on place Bretagne (☎02.40.12.60.60), while *Cyber City*, 14 rue de Strasbourg, offers **Internet access** (daily 12.30pm–midnight; 25F/€3.81 per hr).

NANTES

N

PLACE DU
PONT MORAND

RUE SULLY

RUE DU BOIS ALBERT

PLACE
MARECHAL
FOCH

**Musée des
Beaux Arts**

RUE JEAN JAURÈS

RUE DU POITOU

RUE DE STRASBOURG

Cathédrale
PLACE
ST-PIERRE

RUE HENRI IV

PLACE
BRETAGNE

**Château
des Ducs**

COURS DES 50 OTAGES

RUE DU MOULIN

RUE DE VERDUN

Gare SNCF & ③

RUE DE CALVAIRE

PLACE
ST-CROIX

St-Nicholas

R DE LA MARNE

Ste-Croix

RUE DE LA JUVERIE

COURS JOHN F. KENNEDY

Square Elisa Mercœur

RUE DU CHAPEAU ROUGE

PLACE
ROYALE

RUE D'ORLÉANS

R DE BOUFFAY
PLACE DU
BOUFFAY

PLACE
NEPTUNE

ALLÉE BACO

Ⓐ

④

⑤ ⑥ ⑧

Ⓒ Ⓑ

Ⓓ

RUE SCRIBE

COURS FRANKLIN-ROOSEVELT

ÎLE FEYDEAU

⑦

Théâtre

**Passage
Pommeraye**

PLACE
DU
COMMERCE

Ⓔ

RUE CREBILLON

Ⓕ

ⓘ

RUE KERVEGAN

PLACE
GRASLIN

RUE J.J. ROUSSEAU

⑥

ALLÉE TURENNE

Gare Routière ▲

⑧

RUE PIRON

⑨ ⑩

RUE M. DE LATTRE

PLACE A
RICORDEAU

COURS DE LA MADELEINE

RUE FOURCROY

QUAI DE LA FOSSE

Mediathèque

RESTAURANTS	
Brasserie Côté Rive	E
Cigale	G
Clin d'Oeil	C
Lou Pescadou	D
Mangeoire	A
Petit Bacchus	B
Sumo	F

ACCOMMODATION	
Amiral	7
Cholet	8
des Colonies	4
Duchesse Anne	2
Fourcroy	9
l'Hôtel	1
l'Océan	10
Rénova	6
St-Daniel	5
Terminus	3

0   100 m

Accommodation

Although it holds plenty of **hotels** to suit all budgets, Nantes is one of those cities where you won't necessarily stumble upon a suitable place just by walking or driving around at whim. Instead, there are two main concentrations; one, as ever, in the immediate vicinity of the *gare SNCF*, and one in the narrow streets around the place Graslin. With the exception of the *St-Daniel* (see opposite), surprisingly few are to be found in the older part of town.

Nantes' summer-only **hostel**, *La Manu*, is easy to reach, being within 100m of the *gare SNCF* and also accessible by taking tramway #1 towards "Malachère" and getting off at stop "Manufacture". It offers both dorms and individual rooms, using student accommodation in a postmodern former tobacco factory at 2 place de la Manu (☎02.40.29.29.20; 72F/€10.98 per night; closed mid-Sept to June).

The nearest **campsite** is the well-managed and tree-shaded three-star *du Petit Port*, 21 bd du Petit-Port (☎02.40.74.47.94; open all year).

Hotels

Hôtel Amiral, 26bis rue Scribe (☎02.40.69.20.21, fax 02.40.73.98.13). Well-maintained little hotel on lively pedestrianized street just north of place Graslin, and perfect for young night owls. All rooms have TV, bath and double-glazing; rates for Saturday and Sunday nights drop by up to 70F/€10.67. ④.

Hôtel Cholet, 10 rue Gresset (☎02.40.73.31.04, fax 02.40.73.78.82). Quiet, friendly option very close to place Graslin, where all the wide assortment of rooms have en-suite facilities. Rates drop at weekends. ③.

Hôtel des Colonies, 5 rue du Chapeau Rouge (☎02.40.48.79.76, fax 02.40.12.49.25). Spruce, good-value hotel a couple of blocks up from place Graslin, and in walking distance of everything. Discounts on weekends. No restaurant. ④.

Hôtel Duchesse Anne, 3–4 place de la Duchesse Anne (☎02.51.86.78.78, fax 02.40.74.60.20). Large and very grand hotel in a slightly noisy location, alongside the Château du Ducs less than 500m from the *gare SNCF*, with castle views from the most opulent of its consistently palatial rooms. Dinner menus range from 98F/€14.94 up to 248F/€37.80, parking costs 30F/€4.57 extra per night. ③–⑤.

Hôtel Fourcroy, 11 rue Fourcroy (☎02.40.44.68.00). Basic and economical rooms in a back-street just below place Graslin, near the Médiathèque. ②.

L'Hôtel, 6 rue Henri-IV (☎02.40.29.30.31, fax 02.40.29.00.95). An insouciant name for perhaps the city's finest option, a very grand new edifice facing the château that offers all mod cons. Parking costs 30F/€4.57. ⑤.

Hôtel l'Océan, 11 rue Maréchal-de-Lattre-de-Tassigny (☎02.40.69.73.51). A pleasant hotel, with helpful management, just below place Graslin near the Médiathèque. Parking space is available around the back. No restaurant, though there is a café of the same name on the quai de la Fosse a few metres away at the bottom of the street. Closed last two weeks of Dec. ②.

Hôtel Rénova, 11 rue Beauregard (☎02.40.47.57.03, fax 02.51.82.06.39). Basic central rooms; far from fancy, but the price is unbeatable. ①.

Hôtel St-Daniel, 4 rue du Bouffay (☎02.40.47.41.25, fax 02.51.72.03.99). These simple but pleasant and well-lit rooms, on a cobbled street just off the place du Bouffay in the very heart of the old city, are much in demand in summer. Paying 20F/€3.05 extra gets you a TV in your room. ①.

Hôtel Terminus, 3 allée du Commandant-Charcot (☎02.40.74.24.51, fax 02.40.74.44.11). Simple hotel, very near the *gare SNCF*, on the way towards the château. All rooms have double beds and TV. Features a reasonable restaurant, so long as you skip the very limited 55F/€8.38 menu and head for those at 90F/€13.72 and upwards. ③.

The City

The **Loire**, the source of Nantes' riches, has dwindled from the centre. As recently as the 1930s the river crossed the city in seven separate channels, but German labour as part of reparations for World War I filled in five of them. What are still called "islands" in the centre are now surrounded and isolated not by water, but by hectic dual carriageways. These thoroughfares are not easy to cross, but they do at least mean that Nantes is separated into a series of readily discernible districts, each of which can be experienced on its own terms.

The main distinction lies between the older **medieval city**, concentrated around the cathedral and with the château prominent in its southeast corner,

---

RIVER CRUISES FROM NANTES

To explore the **last section of the Nantes–Brest canal**, you can take a river cruise from the **gare fluviale**, on quai de la Motte-Rouge a little way north of central Nantes. These cruises run up the **Erdre** as far as the point where it is joined by the canal coming from Redon. They thrive mainly because the Loire is not at present navigable by this sort of boat (although there are plans to change that), but the Erdre is itself beautiful and wide, with a fine selection of châteaux along its banks, chief among them **La Gascherie**. Boats operate between April and November, on weekends only in low season but with much greater frequency in midsummer. Typically, the choice is between a simple cruise (1hr 45min) costing a little over 50F/€7.62, and setting off at around 3pm, or a three-hour trip on a floating restaurant for lunch (noon) or dinner (8pm), for something in the region of 250F/€38.11. The tourist office in town is bursting with brochures and leaflets from rival companies, the best known of which is Bateaux Nantais (☎02.40.14.51.14), who also operate similar trips southwards along the **Sèvre**.

---

and the elegant **nineteenth-century town** to the west, across the cours de 50-Ôtages (whose name commemorates a bloody incident during the Nazi Occupation in World War II). In a sense, that division has an additional political significance, for Nantes is not solely Breton. As trade along the Loire made the French influence on the city ever more significant, from the end of the eighteenth century onwards the newer area earned the nickname of "little Paris".

Place Royale, at the heart of the nineteenth-century town, was first laid out in the 1790s; damaged by bombing in 1943, it has now been restored. **Place Graslin**, 200m to the west, with its **theatre**, dates from the same period; the theatre's Corinthian portico contrasts with the 1895 Art Nouveau of *La Cigale*, opposite, embellished with mosaics and mirrors and still a popular brasserie (see p.342).

A spectacular nineteenth-century multilevel indoor shopping centre, the **Passage Pommeraye**, drops down three flights of stairs towards the river on nearby rue Crebillon. The attention to detail lavished upon it by its architects is on a scale undreamed of in modern malls; each of the gas lamps that light the central area is held by an individually crafted marble cherub. While the building itself remains impressive, however, business is not exactly booming, and the place is starting to look run-down.

Many of the streets in the two principal regions of the city have been semipedestrianized, and they abound in pavement cafés, brasseries and shops. Just south of them both is the elongated **Île Feydeau**, a typical victim of the modern "development" of Nantes. Its eighteenth-century houses, seen at their best in rue Kervegan, retain some of their Baroque charm – but the road is bisected by cours Olivier-de-Clisson and the traffic jams of today.

The Château des Ducs

Though no longer on the waterfront, and subjected to a certain amount of damage over the centuries, the **Château des Ducs** (daily: July & Aug 10am–7pm; Sept–June 10am–6pm; free; irregular guided tours in July & Aug only;

20F/€3.05) still preserves the form in which it was built by two of the last rulers of independent Brittany, François II, and his daughter Duchess Anne, born here in 1477. The list of famous people who have been guests or prisoners, defenders or belligerents of the castle is impressive. It includes Gilles de Rais (Bluebeard), publicly executed in 1440; Machiavelli, a member of a Florentine delegation in 1498; John Knox as a galley slave in 1547–49; and Bonnie Prince Charlie preparing for Culloden in 1745. The most significant act in the castle, from the point of view of European history, was the signing of the **Edict of Nantes** in 1598 by Henri IV (who is said to have exclaimed, on first sight of the castle, "God's teeth, these Dukes of Brittany were no small beer"). The edict ended the Wars of Religion by granting a certain degree of toleration to the Protestants, but had far more crucial consequences when it was revoked, by Louis XIV in 1685. To their credit the people of Nantes took no part in the subsequent general massacres of the Huguenots.

The stout ramparts of the château remain pretty much intact, and most of the encircling moat is filled with water, surrounded by well-tended lawns that make a popular spot for lunchtime picnics. Within the walls stand a rather incongruous potpourri of buildings added in differing styles over the years. Until recently, these housed a number of museums, but all are currently closed while their contents are rationalized into one much larger mega-museum, which is unlikely to open much before 2005. Until then, visits will probably continue to consist of a brief walk into the courtyard and up onto the walls.

The cathedral

In 1800 the Spaniards' Tower, the castle's arsenal, exploded, shattering the stained glass of the fifteenth-century **Cathédrale de St-Pierre-et-St-Paul** over 200m away. This was just one of many disasters that have befallen the church. It was used as a barn during the Revolution; bombed during World War II; and damaged by a fire in 1971, just when things seemed sorted out again.

Restored and finally reopened, the building is made to seem especially light and soaring by its clean, white stone. It contains the tomb of François II and his wife, Margaret, the parents of Duchess Anne – with somewhat grating symbols of Power, Strength and Justice for him and Fidelity, Prudence and Temperance for her. This imposing monument is illuminated by a superb modern stained-glass window devoted to Breton and Nantais saints.

The Mur des Cheminées

Five centuries of Nantais history can be seen written in stone, brick and mortar on the **Mur des Cheminées**, just off the place du Bouffay in the centre of the old city, where bomb damage during the war left exposed the huge wall of a venerable and much-reconstructed town house. Successive layers of masonry show the development of the building since it was erected in 1453; a fascinating diagram of this living cross-section illustrates exactly which pieces belong to which era.

The Museums

The **Musée des Beaux Arts**, east of the cathedral on rue Clémenceau, has a respectable collection of paintings displayed in excellent modern galleries, and plays host to a very high standard of temporary exhibitions (Mon, Wed, Thurs &

Sat 10am–6pm, Fri 10am–9pm, Sun 11am–6pm; 20F/€3.05). Not all its Renaissance and contemporary works are on display at any one time, but you should be able to take in canvases ranging from a gorgeous *David Triumphant* by Delaunay and Léon Comerre's distrubing *Le Déluge*, a writhing orgy of drowning flesh, to Chagall's *Le Cheval Rouge* and Monet's *Nymphéas*.

On rue Voltaire, west of place Graslin, the **Musée d'Histoire Naturelle** at no. 12 (Tues–Sat 10am–noon & 2–5pm, Sun 2–5pm; 30F/€4.57) centres on a vivarium, whose miserable animals are not for the squeamish (the soft-shelled turtle in particular tugs at the heartstrings). But don't let this put you off the eccentric assortment of oddities of its museum collection: rhinoceros toenails, a coelacanth and an aepyornis egg, and slightly tatty stuffed specimens of virtually every bird and animal imaginable. There is an Egyptian mummy, too, as well as a shrunken Maori head and a complete tanned human skin, taken in 1793 from the body of a soldier whose dying wish was to be made into a drum.

Also in rue Voltaire, at no. 18, you'll find the **Palais Dobrée** (Tues–Sun 10am–noon & 1.30–5.30pm; 20F/€3.05), a nineteenth-century mansion given over to two museums, one of which claims to feature Duchess Anne's heart in a box. The **Musée Jules-Vernes**, further northwest of the centre at 3 rue de l'Hermitage (Mon & Wed–Sat 10am–noon & 2–5pm, Sun 2–5pm; 10F/€1.52), commemorates the birthplace of the first serious writer of science fiction.

If you have time to kill, take the tram to the **Médiathèque** at 24 quai de la Fosse, where you'll find a superb modern library with bookshops and facilities to watch any of an eclectic selection of videos – *Sir Alf Ramsey* and the *Battle of Iwo Jima* side by side (Mon–Fri noon–7pm, Sat 10am–6pm). From there, you can walk along quai de la Fosse to the point where the two remaining branches of the Loire meet up, with a good view of the port.

Eating

Unlike hotels, **restaurants** fill the winding lanes of the old city in abundance. It shouldn't take you long to come up with something once you start wandering the pedestrian streets in the centre. Nantes is a big enough city to have all sorts of ethnic alternatives as well, with lots of Algerian, Italian, Chinese, Vietnamese and Indian places – especially in the rue de la Juiverie – in addition to those listed here.

Brasserie Côté Rive, 5 square Fleuriot-de-l'Angle (☎02.40.20.35.20). Bright, brisk brasserie a short walk west of the cours des 50-Ôtages and just east of place Royale. All-you-can-eat *moules frites* for 64F/€9.76, a good fishy menu for 119F/€18.14, and even kangaroo in cheese sauce. Open daily until after midnight, with outdoor seating on the pedestrianized square.

La Cigale, 4 place Graslin (☎02.51.84.94.94). Famous late nineteenth-century brasserie, offering fine meals in opulent surroundings. Fish is a speciality. Menus 75F/€11.28 and 135F/€20.58, served until midnight in keeping with the tradition of providing post-performance refreshments for patrons of the theatre opposite.

Le Clin d'Oeil, 15 rue Beauregard (☎02.40.47.72.37). Characterful and cheap little local restaurant in the heart of the old city, offering reliable French favourites plus quirky daily specials. Lunch from 54F/€8.23, dinner from 78F/€11.89 or 98F/€14.94 at weekends. Closed Sun & Mon.

Lou Pescadou, 8 allée Baco (☎02.40.35.29.50). Despite being somewhat off the beaten track, near the *gare routière*, this is Nantes' most fashionable venue for fresh fish, with menus from 119F/€18.14. Closed Sat lunch & Sun.

La Mangeoire, 16 rue des Petites-Écuries (☎02.40.48.70.83). Very good country food. The 58F/€8.84 lunch menu in particular is a real bargain, there's a solid 88F/€13.42 dinner menu, and the *Chef* for 148F/€22.56 is a delight; even if you can't stomach the dozen snails, there's a mixed fish grill to sate any appetite. Closed Sun & Mon.

Le Petit Bacchus, 5 rue Beauregard (☎02.40.47.50.46). Red-painted, half-timbered house, with the atmosphere and decor of a World War I *estaminet*, just off rue des 50-Ôtages in a little alley leading down to the cours F-Roosevelt. Lovely 89F/€13.57 menu featuring duck *à l'orange* or fish of the day. Closed Sun, plus first three weeks in Aug.

Le Sumo, 4 rue Thurot (☎02.40.48.57.20). Quite a rarity – a Japanese restaurant, just off the place du Commerce within a few metres of the tourist office. Sushi and sashimi menus at 80F/€12.20, or entire set meals with skewered chicken, beef or salmon, plus soup and salad from 65F/€9.91. Closed Sun.

Drinking and nightlife

By regional standards, Nantes by night is very lively indeed. Most of the action takes place in the alleyways of the medieval city, where students crowd out the **bars** until the small hours, though more mature visitors may prefer the fancier but less atmospheric cafés around the place Graslin to the west.

Buck Mulligan's, 12 rue du Château (☎02.40.20.02.72). Irish-themed bar with genuine Irish owners, tucked away close to the château and open until 2am nightly.

La Maison, 4 rue Lebrun (☎02.40.37.04.12). Small bar-cum-bistrot, just off rue Sully near the place Maréchal-Foch, which features regular live music and attracts a pretty youthful throng. Closed Mon.

Quai Ouest, 3 quai François-Mitterand (☎02.40.47.68.45). Large and quite garish nightclub on the south bank of the Loire, roughly opposite the Médiathèque and specializing in contemporary dance music. Closed Mon & Tues.

Around Nantes

Immediately **upstream from Nantes** you are into the Loire wine-growing country that produces the two classic dry white wines, Gros-Plant and Muscadet. Any **vineyard** should be happy to give you a *dégustation*. Most operate on a very small scale. The largest, however, the **Chasseloir vineyard** (☎02.40.54.81.15) at **ST-FIACRE-SUR-MAINE**, is perhaps the most interesting. This occupies the grounds of a former château, with fifty acres of vines – some a century old. The vineyard sells mostly within the catering trade, but anyone is welcome to visit their cellars, which are decorated with painted Rabelaisian carvings and candelabras made from vine roots. Like so many of the vineyards in this region, the grapes are now picked and pressed by machines. The old tradition of employing seasonal migrant labour on the harvest is a thing of the past.

Clisson

To the south, at the point where the Sèvre meets the Maine, and the crossroads of the three ancient duchies of Brittany, Anjou and Poitou, is the town of **CLISSON**. This was remodelled by two French architects in the nineteenth century into a close approximation of an Italian hill town. The fact that they already had the raw material of a ruined fortress (daily except Tues 9.30am–noon & 2–6pm; free), a covered market hall and a magnificent situation makes it a sight not to be missed. The best **place to stay** is the *Hôtel de la Gare*, on place de la Gare (☎02.40.36.16.55; ②).

travel details

Trains

No railway line cuts across central Brittany; however, certain towns mentioned in this chapter can be reached by train.

Carhaix to: Guingamp (4–6 daily; 1hr).

Châteaulin to: Brest (5–8 daily; 1hr); Quimper (5–8 daily; 20min).

Loudéac to: St-Brieuc (3–4 daily; 1hr–1hr 30min).

Nantes to: Paris (12 TGVs daily; 2hr 5min); Quimper (5 daily; 2hr 40min); Rennes (5 daily; 1hr 40min).

Pontivy to: St-Brieuc (3–4 daily; 1hr–1hr 30min).

Redon to: Nantes (12 daily; 50min); Quimper (10 daily; 2hr); Rennes (14 daily; 40min); Vannes (10 daily; 30min).

Buses

Carhaix to: Châteaulin (5 daily; 30min); Loudéac (5 daily; 1hr); Morlaix (hourly; 1hr); Quimper (4 daily; 1hr).

Pontivy to: Rennes (4 daily; 2hr) via Josselin (30min) and Ploërmel (45min).

Vannes to: Elven (4 daily; 25min); Malestroit (4 daily; 45min); Ploërmel (4 daily; 1hr 25min); Pontivy (3 daily; 1hr 45min); Rennes (8 daily; 2hr) via Josselin (1hr) and St-Jean Brévelay (45min); Rochefort-en-Terre (2 daily; 1hr) via Questembert (50min).

Boats

*For **general information** on barges with accommodation, which can be available with bicycles and even caravans on board, contact **Formules Bretagnes**, 203 bd St-Germain, 75007 Paris (☎01.53.63.11.53). Barges can also be rented from the following companies:*

Argoat Plaisance, BP41 Port de Plaisance, 29520 Châteauneuf-du-Faou (☎02.98.81.72.11).

Ateliers Navals de la Couronne, Port-Neuf, 56130 La Roche-Bernard (☎02.99.90.66.77, *ledoux.laroche@wanadoo.fr*).

Les Bateaux de l'Aulne, Châteaulin (☎02.98.86.37.59).

Bretagne Croisières, 71 rue de Vannes, 35600 Redon (☎02.99.71.08.05, *www.bretagne croisieres.com*).

Bretagne Plaisance, 12 Quai Jean-Bart, 35600 Redon (☎02.99.72.15.80).

Comptoir Nautique de Redon, 2 quai Surcouf, 35605 Redon (☎02.99.71.46.03).

Crabing-Loisirs, M Mercier, 20 rue de Frout, 29000 Quimper (☎02.98.95.14.02) – boats at Pont Coblant, near Pleyben.

Finistère Canal, Pleyben (☎02.98.73.35.20).

Gîtes Nautiques Bretons, La Cour, 44630 Plesse (☎02.40.51.90.77).

Le Grand Large, M Bonami, quai de Versailles, le Pont-Morand, 44000 Nantes (☎02.40.35.44.37), and 254 route de Vannes, 44000 Nantes-Orvault (☎02.40.63.37.87).

Heron Cruisers, M David Chin, La Daufresne, 56140 Malestroit (☎02.97.75.19.57).

Nicols, route de St-Gouvry, 56580 Rohan (☎02.97.38.90.17).

Plasmor, M Bourçois, Z A 56460 Serent (☎02.97.75.95.70).

Le Ray Loisirs, 14 rue Caradec, 56120 Josselin (☎02.97.75.60.98), and at 44000 Nantes (☎02.40.89.22.42).

Rohan Plaisance, Écluse de Rohan, BP19, 56580 Rohan (☎02.97.38.98.66).

CHAPTER SEVEN

THE SOUTH COAST

Brittany's **southern coast** takes in the province's most famous sites and offers its warmest swimming. Not surprisingly, therefore, it's very popular with tourists. Around the **Gulf of Morbihan**, and especially to the south at **La Baule**, you can be hard pushed to find a room in summer – or to escape the crowds.

The whole coast is a succession of wonders, of both natural and human creation. If you have any interest in prehistory, or even if you just enjoy ruins, then the concentration of **megaliths** around the **Morbihan** should prove irresistible. **Carnac**, the most important site, may well be Europe's oldest settlement; the sun has risen more than two million times over its extraordinary and intriguing alignments of menhirs. **Locmariaquer**, too, has a gigantic ancient stone, which some theories hold to be the key to a prehistoric astronomical observatory, and the most beautifully sited of all is the great tumulus on **Gavrinis**, one of the fifty or so islets scattered in chaos around the Morbihan's inland sea.

As for more hedonistic pastimes, in theory the best of the south's **beaches** are at La Baule. This, however, is also the one resort in Brittany to be conspicuously affected and overpriced, and almost entirely lacks the character of the rest of the region. Excellent, lower-key alternatives can be found all along the south coast: close by La Baule at **Le Croisic** and **Piriac-sur-mer**; at the megalith centres of Carnac and Locmariaquer; at **Quiberon**; and out on the **islands** of **Groix** and **Belle-Île**. The largest Breton island, Belle-Île is a perfect microcosm of the province – a beautiful place with grand countryside and a couple of lively towns.

The south coast is also host to Brittany's most compelling **festival**, the ten-day **Inter-Celtic** gathering at Lorient in August. The same month sees a **jazz festival** at the main Morbihan town, **Vannes**.

ACCOMMODATION PRICE CODES

All **hotel prices** in this book have been coded using the symbols below. The price shown is for the least expensive double room in high season, which, for categories ① and ② especially, often means a room without shower, bath and toilet. Most such hotels have other rooms with en-suite facilities, which typically cost 40–60F/ €6.10–9.15 extra.

① Under 160F/€24	④ 300–400F/€46–61	⑦ 600–700F/€91–107
② 160–220F/€24–34	⑤ 400–500F/€61–76	⑧ 700–800F/€107–122
③ 220–300F/€34–46	⑥ 500–600F/€76–91	⑨ Over 800F/€122

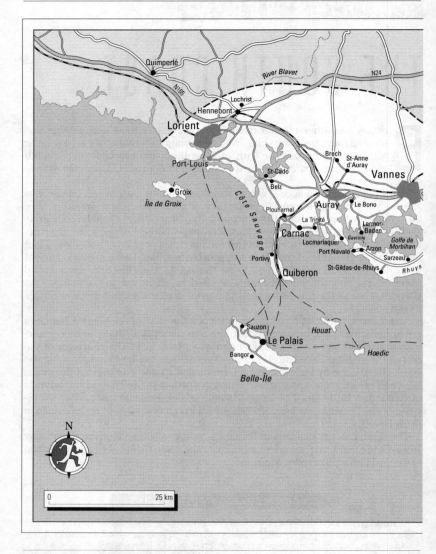

Lorient and its estuary

LORIENT, the fourth largest city in Brittany, is an immense natural harbour, sheltered from the ocean by the **Île de Groix** and strategically located at the junction of the rivers Scorff, Ter and Blavet. Though still the second most important fishing port in France, it's now far more functional than it is exciting. Once, how-

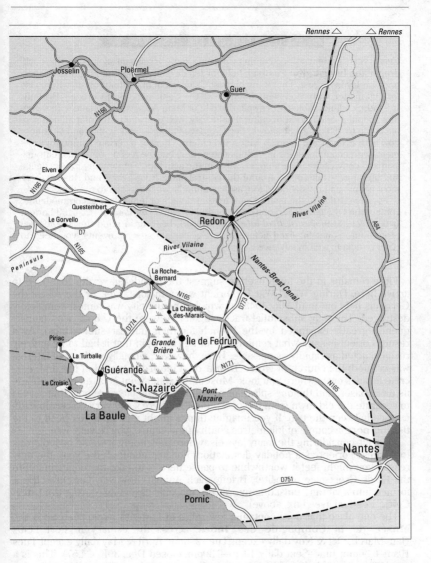

ever, it was a key base for French colonialism, founded in the mid-seventeenth century (in what its charter called a "vague, vain, and useless place") for trading operations by the Compagnie des Indes, the French equivalent of the Dutch and English East India Companies. The port's name was originally *L'Orient* ("The East"), and came from a mighty trading vessel, the *Soleil d'Orient*, which was the first ship to be built in its nascent dockyards.

Every year, Lorient's shortcomings become quite irrelevant alongside the back-drop of the **Inter-Celtic Festival**, held for ten days from the first Friday to the second Sunday in August. This is the biggest Celtic event in Brittany, or anywhere else for that matter, with representation from all the Celtic nations of Europe – Brittany, Ireland, Scotland, Wales, Cornwall, the Isle of Man, Asturias and Galicia. In a genuine, popular celebration of cultural solidarity, well over a quarter of a million people come to 150 different shows, five languages mingle, and Scotch and Guinness flow with French and Spanish wines and ciders. There is a certain competitive element, with championships in various categories, but the feeling of mutual enthusiasm and conviviality is paramount. Most of the activities – embracing music, dance and literature – take place around the central place Jules-Ferry, and this is where most people end up sleeping, too, as accommodation is pushed to the limit.

For **schedules** of the festival, and further details of temporary accommodation, contact the Office du Tourisme de Pays de Lorient, 2 rue Paul-Bert, 56100 Lorient (☎02.97.21.24.29, *www.festival-interceltique.com*), bearing in mind that the festival programme is not finalized before May. For certain specific events, you need to reserve tickets well in advance.

Little remains in the town itself to suggest the plundered wealth that used to arrive here. During World War II, Lorient was a major target for the Allies; the Germans held out until May 1945, by which time the city was almost completely destroyed. The only substantial traces to survive were the U-boat pens (subsequently greatly expanded by the French for their nuclear submarines). As a result, Lorient is somewhat reminiscent of Le Havre, in that it had to be entirely reconstructed as rapidly as possible. Here, however, virtually nothing of interest was created; the church of **Notre Dame de Victoire** is typical of the drab concrete facades everywhere you look. Most of the waterfront is taken up by off-limits naval bases, and the one splash of colour is the little pleasure port that serves to separate the old town from the new – not that there's any very discernible difference between the two. If you imagine things might pick up if you head to the **fishing port**, a couple of kilometres south of the centre, you're very wrong.

All in all, considering the many joys elsewhere in Brittany, it would be ludicrous to suggest Lorient as a holiday destination. For just about all the year, the only reason you might feel it worthwhile to pause here is to take the boat trip out to the Île de Groix (see opposite). Briefly each August, however, Lorient is transformed into a vibrant, pulsating maelstrom of Celtic cavorting, during the **Inter-Celtic Festival** (see box, above).

The one place that does contain a few relics of Lorient's exploitive past is the **Musée de la Compagnie des Indes**, across the estuary in Port Louis (Jan–March, Oct & Nov daily except Tues 2–6pm; April & May daily except Tues 10am–6.30pm; June–Sept daily 10am–6.30pm; closed Dec; 30F/€4.57). This is a good 20km by road, though you can get a ferry across from the Embarcadère des Rades, and it is in any case a somewhat dismal temple to imperialism.

Practicalities

Arriving in the main-line **gare SNCF**, you're faced with a 1km or so hike into the centre. Lorient's **tourist office**, beside the pleasure port on the quai de Rohan

(July & Aug Mon–Sat 9am–7pm, Sun 10am–6pm; Sept–June Mon–Sat 9am–12.30pm & 2–6pm; ☎02.97.21.07.84, *www.lorient.com*), can provide full details on local boat trips, and organizes some excursions itself; it also rents out **bikes** for 40F/€6.10 per day.

Unless you arrive during the festival, there's a huge choice of **hotels**. Among reasonable, fairly central options are two on rue Lazare-Carnot as it curves away south of the tourist office. All the rooms in the *Victor Hugo Hôtel* at no. 36 (☎02.97.21.16.24, *www.contacthotel.com*; ②) have TV – which, not wishing to labour the point or anything, is something to be thankful for in Lorient – and there's an action-packed 99F/€15.09 menu offering *langoustines*, wild pheasant pâté and duck *à l'orange*, while the more spartan *Hôtel d'Arvor*, further west at no. 104 (☎02.97.21.07.55; ②), also has a good-value restaurant.

If you're desperate to find somewhere at festival time, there are a few more hotels along avenue de la Perrière, the main thoroughfare in the fishing port, including the basic but inexpensive *Hôtel-Restaurant Gabriel* at no. 45 (☎02.97.37.60.76; ①; closed Sun Oct–June); assuming you're not such a cheap-skate as to get the hard-boiled egg and the intestine-packed *andouillette* on its 58F/€8.84 menu, sensible dinners here cost 68F/€10.37 and upwards. There's also an appealing (if noisy) **hostel**, next to the River Ter at 41 rue Victor-Schoelcher, 3km out on bus line C from the *gare SNCF* (☎02.97.37.11.65; 71F/€10.82; closed Jan), which has space for **camping** as well in summer. The *Oeuvres Sociales* hostel at 12 rue Colbert (☎02.97.21.42.80) was especially designed for the **physically handicapped**.

Le Pic, just south of the *gare SNCF* at 2 bd Maréchal-Franchet-d'Esperey (☎02.97.21.18.29; closed Sat lunchtime & Sun) is an imaginative little **restaurant**, with varied menus from 75F/€11.28. More central alternatives include *Yesterday's*, 1 cours de la Bôve (☎02.97.84.85.07), a brasserie near the town hall that serves an excellent 98F/€14.94 menu, and *Le Café Leffe* (☎02.97.21.21.30; closed Jan), in the same building as the tourist office, facing the port, which is particularly strong on seafood. One of the most congenial **bars** is the *Galway Inn*, near the train station, at 18 rue Belgique (☎02.97.64.50.77) – not that Jimmy the guard dog thinks of himself as particularly congenial. Plenty more bars can be found around place Aristide-Briand.

The Île de Groix

The steep-sided, eight-kilometre-long rock of the **Île de Groix**, shielding Lorient ten kilometres out to sea from the mouth of the Blavet estuary, is a sort of little sister to the better-known island of Belle-Île (see p.355). With its own crop of lovely beaches – and its own throngs of summer visitors – not to mention a similar abundance of exclusive holiday homes – it's in no way inferior to its larger neighbour, however, and taking a day-trip out from Lorient is well worth the effort.

Groix flourished during the seventeenth and eighteenth centuries in tandem with Lorient, and was even the target of invasions by both the English (in 1663) and the Dutch (in 1774). Subsequently, after the island's first proper port was constructed in 1792, it went on to become a major centre for catching and canning tuna. That industry has long since gone into decline, however, and Groix now makes its living from summer tourism, with beach-lovers joined both by bird-watchers in search of migratory species, and by geologists, who come to study its peculiar rock formations.

The boat from Lorient (see below) docks at **PORT-TUDY**, where a former tuna cannery houses the **Eco-Musée**, chronicling the island's history since the Bronze Age (mid-April to May daily 10am–12.30pm & 2–5pm; June–Sept daily 9.30am–12.30pm & 3–7pm; Oct to mid-April Tues–Sun 10am–noon & 2–5pm; 24F/€3.66). While the more general displays are interesting enough, the museum's real strong point is in its depiction of the patterns and traditions of individual life. Countless personal and family sagas are covered in exhaustive detail upstairs, from birth and the acquisition of language (which meant Breton at least until World War I), through school, apprenticeship and marriage, all the way to death.

About 500m uphill from the port is the largest of the island's 27 villages, **LE BOURG** (also known as Loctudy, or even, simply, Groix). Although it's attractive enough, with a tuna-fish weathervane topping its little church, its appeal soon palls, and the obvious way to spend a day on Groix is to tour its dramatic coastline. The easiest and cheapest way to do this is to rent a **bicycle** from one of several outlets at the port, costing around 60F/€9.15 per day. Crossing the island north to south takes barely ten minutes by bike; east to west requires more like an hour, especially as it can be hard to spot which coastal paths will prove negotiable, and which merely peter out into the sand.

At their tallest, at the **Pointe du Grognon** in the northwest, the cliffs of Groix rise fifty metres out of the sea; that may not sound all that high, but only Belle-Île in Brittany surpasses it. Much of the western tip serves as a bird sanctuary; the southeastern corner, by contrast, close to the **Pointe des Chats** and its little lighthouse, is renowned for its unusual green-tinged mineral deposits.

The best **beaches** are also at the eastern end of the island. Locals claim that the **Plage des Grandes Sables**, jutting out into the sea, is the only convex beach in Europe. Palpable nonsense that may be, but it is a beautiful little unsheltered strip of sand that offers calm swimming (supervised by lifeguards in summer), with pleasure boats bobbing at anchor just off shore. The next group of beaches to the south are even better, a succession of little sandy coves tucked between the rocks known collectively as **Les Sables Rouges**.

Practicalities

It takes 45 minutes to reach the Île de Groix by **boat** from the south quay of Lorient's new port (Societé Morbihannaise et Nantaise de Navigation; 4–9 sailings daily depending on the season; ☎02.97.64.77.64, *www.mn-les-iles.com*; adults 112F/€17.07 return, under-13s 69F/€10.52, under-26s 69F/€10.52 on certain sailings only, bicycles 52F/€7.93, cars 418F/€63.72); the first daily departure from Lorient is at 7.30am in July and August, and usually 8am otherwise. On weekends during July and August, Vedettes Transrade (☎02.97.64.77.68) run tours that include a 45-minute stop on the island, departing from Lorient (Sat 2.30pm; 107F/€16.31), Port-Louis (Sat 2.50pm; 107F/€16.31), and Hennebont (Sun 9am; 115F/€17.53).

Groix's **tourist office** is the first building you come to on quayside at **Port-Tudy** (Mon–Sat 9.30am–1.30pm & 3.30–6.30pm, Sun 9.30am–1.30pm; ☎02.97.86.53.08). Three **hotels** stand nearby: the pink-pastel *de l'Escale* (☎02.97.86.80.04; ④), which has rather characterless but perfectly adequate guestrooms inside and café seating outside; the slightly fancier *Ty Mad* (☎02.97.86.80.19; ③; closed Feb), set back behind an attractive lawn, which serves good seafood meals in the open air; and the *de la Jetée* (☎02.97.86.80.82; ③;

closed Jan), at the far right end of port, which also has a café terrace and holds the nicest rooms of the lot. For seafood lovers, the best of the **restaurants** here is *Le Pub à Port Tudy*, alongside the *Jetée*, where the simple menu is dominated by oysters of various shapes; half a dozen can be had for 45F/€6.86.

Up the hill in **Le Bourg**, the **hotel-restaurant** *de la Marine*, 7 rue Générale-de-Gaulle (☎02.97.86.80.05; ③; closed Jan, plus Sun evening, & Mon in low season), is a large, well-furnished house that offers comfortable rooms and serves delicious fish dinners in its front garden, including an 82F/€12.50 menu featuring *cotriade* (stew), while the *Moulin d'Or*, 8 rue St-Jean (☎02.97.86.82.16; ②), is a much more basic alternative in terms of both accommodation and food.

A few hundred metres east of town, close to the sea en route towards the small beach at the Pointe de la Croix, the **Fort du Méné** holds a simple but beautifully sited summer-only **hostel** (☎02.97.86.81.38; 60F/€9.15 including breakfast; closed Nov–March), with a **campsite** alongside (☎02.97.86.53.08; open July & Aug only). The nicest campsite on the island, however, is further on – the lovely three-star *Les Sables Rouges* (☎02.97.86.81.32; closed mid-Sept to May), above the beaches at the southeast corner.

Hennebont

A few kilometres upstream from Lorient, at the point where the River Blavet first starts to widen into the estuary, is the old walled town of **HENNEBONT**. The fortifications, and especially the main gate, the Porte Broerec'h, are imposing, and walking around the top of the ramparts there are wide views of the river below. What you see of the old city within, however, is entirely residential – an assortment of washing-lines, budgies and garden sheds. All its public buildings were destroyed by wartime bombing, and now not even a bar (or rented room) is to be found in the former centre.

The one time Hennebont comes alive is at the **Thursday market**, held below the ramparts and through the squares by the church. It's one of the largest in the region, with a heady mix of good fresh food, crêpes and Vietnamese delicacies, alongside livestock, flowers, carpets and clothes. On other days, the only places where you'll find any activity are along the **place Maréchal-Foch** (in front of the basilica) and the **quai du Pont-Neuf** beside the river.

Practicalities

Hennebont's **gare SNCF** is roughly 1km from the centre, on the west bank of the Blavet. Cross the river to reach the **tourist office**, at 9 place Foch (mid-June to mid-Sept Mon–Fri 9am–7pm, Sat 9am–12.30pm & 1.30–7pm, Sun 10am–12.30pm; mid-Sept to mid-June Mon–Sat 9am–12.30pm & 2–6pm; ☎02.97.36.24.52). If you decide to **stay** – and few people do – the renovated *Hôtel-Restaurant du Centre* at 44 rue du Maréchal-Joffre (☎02.97.36.21.44; ①) is good value, and as near the town centre as its name implies. The seafood-dominated menus in its restaurant (closed Sun evening & Mon) are uniformly superb, starting with a 110F/€16.77 *Menu du Terroir* featuring hot oysters. Alternatively, try the *Auberge de Toul-Douar*, on the edge of town nearest Lorient across the river (☎02.97.36.24.04; ①; closed Sun evening & Mon in low season), a *logis* that serves good meals from 70F/€10.67 in a grand dining room; it takes a bit of finding but it's closer to the *gare SNCF*.

The town's two-star **campsite**, *Camping Municipal de St-Caradec* (☎02.97.36.21.73; closed mid-Sept to May), has a prime site on the riverbank opposite the fortifications. You can rent **bicycles** at 5 av de la République and at 87 rue du Maréchal-Joffre, and take **boat trips** either up the Blavet towards the Nantes–Brest canal (see Chapter Six) or out into the estuary around Lorient, with Transrade (☎02.97.36.24.52).

Lochrist

At **LOCHRIST**, just north of Hennebont, the great chimneys of the town's **iron-works** still stand, smokeless and silent, looking down on the Blavet. Strikes and demonstrations failed to prevent the foundry's closure in 1966, and the only work since then has been to convert it into the **Musée Forges d'Hennebont** (June Mon–Fri 10am–noon & 2–6pm, Sat & Sun 2–6pm; July & Aug Mon–Fri 10am–6.30pm, Sat & Sun 2–6.30pm; Sept–May Mon–Fri 10am–noon & 2–6pm, Sun 2–6pm; 25F/€3.81), which documents its hundred-year history from the workers' point of view. Some of the men put on the dole contributed their memo-ries and tools; for others turning their workplace into a museum was adding insult to injury. It is in fact excellent, both in content and presentation, though in view of the joyful pictures of successful strikes in the 1930s its very existence seems a sad defeat.

St-Cado

Fifteen kilometres southeast of Hennebont, or 12km east of Port-Louis, a large bridge spans the broad estuary of the **Etel** River. A short detour north of the vil-lage of Belz on the eastern side of the bridge brings you to the delightful islet of **ST-CADO**, a round speck on the water dotted with perhaps twenty white-painted houses.

From the mainland, you walk across a spindly little bridge to reach the island itself. Its main feature is a **twelfth-century chapel** that stands on the site of a Romanesque predecessor built by St Cado around the sixth century. Cado, who was a prince of "Glamorgant", returned in due course to his native Wales and was martyred, but Welsh pilgrims still make their way to this pretty little spot. As Cado is a patron saint of the deaf, it's said that hearing problems can be cured by lying on his stone "bed" inside the chapel. A little fountain behind the chapel only emerges from the sea at low tide.

There's nowhere to stay on St-Cado, but a couple of **restaurants** catering for day-trippers face it from the quayside on the mainland. The better of these, *Les Asturies* (☎02.97.55.42.66), specializes in seafood of all kinds, and offers *moules marinières* for 50F/€7.62.

The Quiberon peninsula

The **Presqu'île de Quiberon** is as close to being an island as any peninsula could conceivably be; the long causeway of sand that links it to the mainland nar-rows to as little as 50m in places. In the past this was always a strategic military location. The English held the peninsula for eight bloody days in 1746; *Chouans* (see p.395) and royalists landed here in 1795 in the hope of destroying the Revolution, only to be sealed in and slaughtered; and the defoliation that threat-ens the dunes today is in part the result of German fortifications constructed during World War II. The peninsula is now, in the summer, packed with tourists. They come not so much to visit the towns, which, other than **Quiberon** itself, are generally featureless, but to use them as a base for trips out to **Belle-Île** or around the contrasting coastline.

The coast here has two quite distinct characters. The **Côte Sauvage**, facing the Atlantic to the west, is a bleak rocky heathland, lashed by heavy seas. It is the scene of innumerable drownings – the official tourist brochure contains a chilling description of just why it is absolutely impossible for *un imprudent* to swim back to land having once strayed beyond a certain distance. The sheltered eastern side, however, the **Baie de Quiberon**, contains safe sandy beaches, as well as one of the innumerable Thalassotherapy Institutes that line the Breton coast.

The route onto the peninsula

As the D768 curves around the bay outside **PLOUHARNEL**, on its way to the start of the peninsula, you can't fail to notice a reconstructed **Spanish galleon**, standing in something less than 8cm of water. This is an obsessive shell museum and shop, with dioramas, created entirely from shells, of eighteenth-century street scenes in Venice and in China, of Donald Duck and his friends, Sioux Indians and flamenco dancers (daily: Easter–May 10am–noon & 2–6pm; June–Sept 9.30am–noon & 2–7pm; 25F/€3.81). Across the road and the train line, there's a rather uninspiring **waxwork museum** (Easter to mid-Sept daily 10am–noon & 2–6pm; 25F/€3.81), which focuses on the *Chouan* rebellion of 1795.

PORTIVY, tucked into the only real shelter along the Côte Sauvage just beyond the slender neck of the *presqu'île*, is a popular rendezvous point for **surfers** and **windsurfers**. If you want to join them, you can rent boards in Port Haliguen, near Quiberon town, at 16 rue des Corlis (☎02.97.50.25.03). There is a **campsite** just outside Portivy, *Camping de Port Blanc* on the route du Port Blanc (☎02.97.30.91.30; closed Oct–May). Others nearby include the *Camping Municipal de Penthièvre* (☎02.97.52.33.86; closed Nov–March) and the *Camping Municipal de Kerhostin* (☎02.97.30.95.25; closed Nov–April).

Quiberon

The town of **QUIBERON** itself is a lively place, which centres on a miniature golf course surrounded by bars, pizzerias and some surprisingly good clothes and antique shops. The cafés by the long bathing beach are the most enjoyable, along with the old-fashioned *Café du Marché* next to the PTT.

Port-Maria, the fishing harbour and **gare maritime** for the islands of Belle-Île, Houat and Hoëdic, is the most active part of town and has the best concentration of **hotels** and **fish restaurants**. Port-Maria was once famous for its sardines, canned locally, but those days are long gone.

Port-Haliguen, the other port, is on the eastern coast. Today, it is an active marina, with a little commercial fishing. Boats from the islands occasionally shelter here, and use it for embarkation in rough weather. Captain Alfred Dreyfus disembarked here on his return from Devil's Island in 1899.

Arrival and information

In July and August, the special Tire Bouchon train links Quiberon's **gare SNCF**, which is a short way above the town proper, with Auray. (The name, which means "corkscrew", refers to the bottleneck at the mouth of the peninsula rather than any circuitousness in the route.) There are also buses right to the *gare maritime* from Vannes (#23 and #24) and Auray (#24) via Carnac.

The **tourist office** at 14 rue de Verdun (July & Aug Mon–Sat 9am–8pm, Sun 9.30am–noon & 3–7pm; Sept–June Mon–Sat 9am–12.30pm & 2–6.30pm; ☎02.97.50.07.84, *www.quiberon.com*), downhill and left from the *gare SNCF*, has an illuminated map outside which purports to monitor exactly which hotels are full, hour by hour. The **post office** is on rue Gambetta (☎02.97.50.09.16).

Bicycles can be rented from Cycl'omar, 47 place Hoche (☎02.97.50.26.00), and **horse riding** can be arranged with the Centre Équestre l'Éperon, 38 rue Jean-Pierre-Callock, in Kerne (☎02.97.50.28.32).

Accommodation

For much the greater part of the year, it's hard to get a **room** in Quiberon. In July and August, the whole peninsula is packed, while in winter it gets very quiet indeed, with virtually all its facilities closed down. The nicest area in which to stay is along the seafront in Port-Maria, where several good hotel-restaurants face the Belle-Île ferry terminal.

The local **hostel**, the spartan *Filets Bleus*, inland at 45 rue du Roc'h-Priol (☎02.97.50.15.54; 50F/€7.62; closed Oct–April), 1.5km southeast of the *gare SNCF*, also provides space for camping. **Campsites** along the sheltered east coast near Quiberon town include the three-star *Do-Mi-Si-La-Mi*, St-Julien Plage (☎02.97.50.22.52, *www.acdev.com/domisilami*; closed Nov–March), and the four-star *du Conguel*, bd de la Teignouse (☎02.97.50.19.11, *www.campingdeconguel .com*; closed Nov–March), which has a large pool with elaborate water slides. The Côte Sauvage has only one site, the *Camping Municipal* in the village of **KERNE**, 2km northwest of central Quiberon (☎02.97.50.05.07; open July & Aug only).

Hôtel-Restaurant Bellevue, rue de Tiviec (☎02.97.50.16.28, fax 02.97.30.44.34). Relatively quiet *logis de France*, set slightly back from the sea near the casino 500m east of the port, with its own pool and a good restaurant. Closed Oct–March. ④.

Hôtel-Restaurant au Bon Accueil, 6 quai de Houat (☎ & fax 02.97.50.07.92). One of the best value of Port-Maria's seafront hotels. The rooms are basic but inexpensive, and the friendly dining room downstairs, with something of the atmosphere and decor of a village bar, serves good fish soup and seafood specialities on menus that start at 85F/€12.96. Closed Jan. ②.

Hôtel de la Mer, 8 quai de Houat (☎02.97.50.09.05, fax 02.97.50.44.41). Blue-trimmed hotel at the western end of Port-Maria's seafront strip, offering a good standard of comfort and sea views from some rooms. Menus range from an 89F/€13.57 option via the 139F/€21.19 *Houat* up to the six-course 240F/€36.59 *Belle Île*. Closed mid-Nov to Jan. ④.

Le Neptune, 4 quai de Houat (☎02.97.50.09.62, fax 02.97.50.41.44). Very close to *Au Bon Accueil* in Port-Maria, and offering a bit more luxury. Some rooms enjoy seafront balconies, and there are the usual seafood menus ranging from 89F/€13.57 to 198F/€30.33. Closed Jan, & Mon in low season. ④, sea view ⑤.

L'Océan, 7 quai de l'Océan (☎02.97.50.07.58, fax 02.97.50.27.81). Attractive little hotel in the port, with multicoloured pastel shutters. It seems to have given up the unequal struggle to keep a restaurant going, but still has reasonably priced rooms. Closed Oct–March. ②.

Eating

Once again, the most appealing area in which to go browsing the menus looking for a good **meal** is along the waterfront in Port-Maria, with its line of seafood restaurants competing to attract the ferry passengers. Hotel owners are very insistent on persuading guests to pay for half-board – and at the *Bon Accueil*, for example, that's no great hardship – but there are plenty of alternatives to choose from if you do manage to escape their clutches. To stock up on provisions, try the morning **markets** at Kerhostin, at the neck of the peninsula 5km north of Quiberon, on Wednesday, St-Pierre-Quiberon, just south of Kerhostin, on Thursday and Quiberon on Saturday.

Ancienne Forge, 20 rue Verdun (☎02.97.50.18.64). Set back from the road that leads down to the port from the *gare SNCF*, with slightly unadventurous but good-value seafood-heavy menus from 85F/€12.96. Closed Jan, & Wed in low season.

Le Corsaire, 24 quai de Belle-Île (☎02.97.50.15.05). Large waterfont restaurant, facing the ferry terminal and serving fine seafood spreads on a sprawling terrace for 79F/€12.04 and upwards.

De la Criée, 11 quai de l'Océan (☎02.97.30.53.09). Changing fish specialities served every day, fresh from the morning's catch at the quayside as displayed in baskets arrayed along the front. The 89F/€13.57 menu includes stuffed mussels, for example, and fish smoked on the premises. Closed Jan, Sun evening, & Mon in low season.

Belle-Île

The island of **Belle-Île**, 15km offshore, due south of Quiberon, mirrors Brittany in its make-up. On the landward side it is rich and fertile, interrupted by deep estuaries with tiny ports; facing the ocean, along its own Côte Sauvage, sparse heather-covered cliffs trail rocky crags out into the sea.

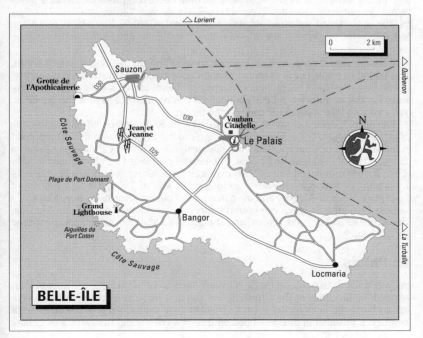

GETTING TO BELLE-ÎLE

Throughout the year, at least five **ferries** each day (up to 7 daily in high summer) sail from Port-Maria, at the southernmost tip of the Quiberon peninsula, to Belle-Île. They are operated by the Societé Morbihannaise et Nantaise de Navigation (Le Palais ☎02.97.31.80.01, Port-Maria ☎02.97.50.06.90, *www.mn-les-iles.com*; adults 112F/€17.07 return, under-13s 69F/€10.52, under-26s 69F/€10.52 on certain sailings only, small car 418F/€63.72 return, bicycles 52F/€7.93 return); the first departure each day from Quiberon is usually at 8am, and the crossing takes 45 minutes. The main port of call in Belle-Île is **Le Palais**, but in July and August the same company sends two or three boats daily direct to **Sauzon**, which takes 25 minutes, and costs 112F/€17.07 return. It also runs a limited service between Le Palais and **Lorient** (July & Aug departs Lorient daily 8am & 1.30pm; 50min; adults 158F/€24.08 return, under-13s 92F/€14.03, ages 13–24 117F/€17.84; Lorient ☎02.97.21.03.97).

In summer, Compagnie Vendéenne (☎02.40.23.34.10) sails direct to Le Palais from **La Turballe**, between Piriac and Guérande on the coast not far north of La Baule. The crossing takes an hour and twenty minutes (April–June & first ten days of Sept Wed & Sun only; July & Aug daily, departing 9am; adults 165F/€25.15 return, under-15s 105F/€16.01, bicycles 100F/€15.24). In summer, and occasionally out of season as well, day-trips to the island, organized by Navix, set out regularly from **Vannes**, **Port-Navalo** and **La Trinité** (May & June Wed–Sun; July & Aug daily; ☎02.97.46.60.00, *navix@wanadoo.fr*; 175F/€26.68).

Finally, two operators also send day-trips from **Locmariaquer** to Belle-Île, in July and August only: Vedettes l'Aiglon (Tues–Fri & Sun 8.45am; ☎02.97.57.39.15; 140F/€21.34) and Vedettes l'Angélus (Sun 8.30am; ☎02.97.57.30.29; 150F/€22.87).

With the island measuring 17km east to west and up to 10km north to south, some kind of transport is essential to appreciate these contrasts, even if you just come for a day-trip. This presents no great problem: bicycles are available in profusion at the island port of **Le Palais**, and if you're happy to pay for the privilege, you can also take a small car over on the ferries.

The island once belonged to the monks of Redon; then to the ambitious Nicholas Fouquet, Louis XIV's minister; later to the English, who in 1761 swapped it for Minorca in an unrepeatable bargain deal. Along the way Belle-Île has seen a fair number of distinguished exiles. The citadel prison at Le Palais closed only in 1961, having numbered among its inmates an astonishing succession of state enemies and revolutionary heroes – including the son of Toussaint L'Ouverture of Haiti, Ben Bella of Algeria, and even, for a brief period after 1848, Karl Marx.

Less involuntarily, such celebrated figures as the painters Monet and Matisse, the writers Flaubert and Proust, and the actress Sarah Bernhardt all spent time on the island.

Le Palais

As you dock at the pleasant little harbour town of **LE PALAIS**, the abrupt star-shaped fortifications of the **Citadelle** are the first thing you see. Built along stylish and ordered lines by the great fortress-builder Vauban early in the eighteenth century, it is startling in size – filled with doorways leading to mysterious cellars and underground passages, endless sequences of rooms and dungeons and deserted cells. Though derelict, the structure is quite sound: large signs – "DON'T BE AFRAID" – are scattered about the place, exhorting visitors to explore the abandoned shell. An informative, if over-literary **museum** (daily: April–June, Sept & Oct 9.30am–6pm; July & Aug 9am–7pm; Nov–March 9.30am–noon & 2–5pm; 20F/€3.05) documents the island's history, including its entanglement in Dumas' tales of *The Three Musketeers* (which feature an account of the death of Porthos on the island).

Practicalities

The **tourist office** for the whole island is right alongside the *gare maritime* in Le Palais (July to mid-Sept Mon–Sat 9am–7.30pm, Sun 9am–1pm; mid-Sept to June Mon–Sat 9.30am–6.30pm, Sun 10am–noon; ☎02.97.31.81.93, *www.belle-ile-en-mer .com*).

Accommodation in Le Palais includes the simple *Frégate* at the quayside (☎02.97.31.54.16; ①–③; closed mid-Nov to March) and a couple of more expensive options, the *Hôtel Vauban*, 1 rue des Remparts (☎02.97.31.45.42; ⑤; closed Nov–March), and the recently refitted *Hôtel-Restaurant de Bretagne* on quai Macé (☎02.97.31.80.14; ⑤), both of which have excellent seaview **restaurants**.

There are also three **campsites** in the immediate vicinity of the town, the best of which is the three-star *Camping de l'Océan* (☎02.97.31.83.86; closed mid-Nov–March), and a **hostel** (☎02.97.31.81.33; 52F/€7.93; closed Oct), which despite holding over a hundred beds is always wildly oversubscribed. It's located a short way out of town along the clifftops from the *citadelle*, at Haute-Boulogne.

Sauzon

SAUZON, Belle-Île's second town, is set at the mouth of a long estuary 6km to the west of Le Palais. If you're staying any length of time, and you've got your own transport, it's probably a better place to base yourself.

In addition to a good, inexpensive **hotel** in a magnificent setting, the *du Phare* (☎02.97.31.60.36; ③; closed Oct–March) – which insists that guests eat its delicious 85F/€12.96 fish dinners – Sauzon can also offer two two-star **campsites:** *Pen Prad* (☎02.97.31.64.82; closed Oct–March) and *La Source* (☎02.97.31.60.95; closed Oct–March).

Around the island

Assuming that you have a car or bicycle to aid your explorations of the island, the ideal way to get to know it is to cross to its southern side and then walk at least part of the coastal footpath that runs on bare soil for the full length of the **Côte Sauvage**. Head first for the village of **BANGOR**, 6km south of Le Palais, where you're confronted by an incongruous row of huge and very expensive hotels. President Mitterrand, a regular guest, came for a farewell visit shortly before his death to the *Castel Clara* here (☎02.97.31.84.21, *www.castel-clara.com*; ⑨; closed mid-Nov to mid-Feb).

Another 2km west of Bangor, the **Grand Lighthouse**, which dates from 1835, commands sweeping views of the entire coastline. Even if you don't have the energy to climb its 256 steps (summer daily 10.30am–noon & 2–5.30pm; free), you'll be able to see the **Aiguilles de Port-Coton** just offshore to the south, where a savage sea foams in the pinnacles of rock, and the delicate beach of **Port-Donnant** a kilometre to the west. The beach is an easy stroll from the light-house, but unfortunately swimming, despite appearances, is dangerous.

You can get to the beach by road, but the only way to follow the coastline any further north is on foot, by means of the footpath that clings to the clifftops. Five kilometres along – a walk of something over an hour – the path meets up with another road just short of the **Grotte de l'Apothicairerie**. This precarious ocean-front cave is so called because it used to be filled with the nests of cormorants, arranged like the jars on a pharmacist's shelves. It's reached by descending a slip-pery flight of steps cut into the rock: take care, as most years at least one person falls – and drowns – from these stairs.

The **D30 inland** from the cave leads along a miniature tree-lined valley shel-tered from the Atlantic winds. If you take the **D25** back towards Le Palais you pass the two **menhirs**, Jean and Jeanne, said to be lovers petrified as punishment for wanting to meet before their marriage. Another (larger) menhir used to lie near these two – it was broken up to help construct the road that separates them.

Houat and Hoëdic

Houat and **Hoëdic**, two smaller and much quieter islands to the east of Belle-Île, can also be reached by ferries from Quiberon and elsewhere. Most visitors come to the islands on day-trips, to seek out their magnificent – and usually all but empty – golden **beaches**, but both do offer facilities for extended stays if you can't tear yourself away.

The Île de Houat

The island of **Houat**, which in Breton means "duck", measures 5km from east to west, and much less than half that north to south. It's an idyllic spot, populated largely by rabbits and lizards, with hardly a tree to its name. Most of what mar-ginally higher ground it has to offer consists of open heathland, with its thin cov-ering of turf petering out at the head of pink-granite cliffs which look down on long sandy beaches and lovely little coves.

GETTING TO HOUAT AND HOËDIC

Ferries to **Houat** and **Hoëdic** from **Quiberon-Port-Maria** are operated by the Societé Morbihannaise et Nantaise de Navigation (1–7 sailings daily depending on the season; ☎02.97.50.06.90, *www.mn-les-iles.com*; adults 112F/€17.07 return, under-13s 69F/€10.52, under-26s 69F/€10.52 on certain sailings only, bicycles 52F/€7.93). The crossing to Houat takes forty minutes, to Hoëdic another 25.

In addition, Vedettes Ar'moor sail to Houat and Hoëdic from **Le Croisic** and **La Turballe**, daily in July and August and to erratic schedules between March and June and in September (☎02.97.62.94.43; 135F/€20.58 return). This crossing takes much longer; the usual summer departure times are 7.40am from Le Croisic and 8.15am from La Turballe, to arrive on Hoëdic at 9.45am and Houat at 10.25am.

Finally, Navix run day-trips to Houat only from **Vannes**, **Port-Navalo** and **La Trinité** daily in July and August (☎02.97.46.60.00, *navix@wanadoo.fr*; half-day 120F/€18.29, full day 150F/€22.87).

Boats draw in at **Port St-Gildas**, a not especially picturesque little harbour just below the island's one "town", the flowery village of **HOUAT**. A private house to the right of the road up into the village rents out poor-quality **bicycles** at 80F/€12.20 per day, but the island is small enough for walking to be a pleasure, and it's not in any case legal to cycle along the coastal footpaths. The finest **beaches** lie to the east and south, in the shape of the sheltered **Tréac'h er Gouréd** that runs the full length of the eastern shoreline, and the **Tréac'h Salus** nearby.

During the 1980s, the islanders tried to boost their economy by raising lobsters in tanks in a large shed-like building known as the *écloserie*, 1km southwest of Houat. That experiment never proved profitable, so the structure has since 1994 served instead as the **Eclosarium** (daily 10am–6pm; 22F/€3.35), a museum dedicated almost exclusively to the microscopic marine world of **phytoplankton**, the organisms responsible for producing eighty percent of the oxygen on earth. It's more interesting than it might sound, with a healthy dose of local history thrown in. Fetid-looking vials demonstrate how algae is now being cultivated locally, for use in the manufacture of products such as shower gel, sun cream, moisturizer and even pasta – if you're tempted, the gift shop sells them at discounted prices.

Practicalities

Two small **hotels** offer Houat's most comfortable accommodation. At the edge of town, overlooking the harbour, the *Hôtel-Restaurant des Îles* (☎02.97.30.68.02; ③; closed Dec & Jan) offers tasteful seaview rooms and serves good food both indoors and out on its terrace; it's a great spot for lunch, the main set menu costing 90F/€13.72. Alternatively, *L'Ezenn*, on the main road above the Tréac'h er Gouréd beach (☎02.97.30.69.73; ③), has excellent modernized rooms but no restaurant. Strictly speaking, **camping** is not legal, but in summer scores of visitors set up their tents along the slender ridge that divides the two beaches south of town.

The Île de Hoëdic

At a mere 2.5km end to end, Hoëdic – in Breton the "duckling" to Houat's "duck" – is that much tinier still. It's such a sleepy place, the story goes, that during the eighteenth century the rector of Hoëdic lost not only his sense of time but also his calendar, and ended up reducing Lent from forty days down to a more manageable three.

The island's sole settlement – **HOËDIC**, naturally – stands right in the centre, a short walk up from the ferry landing at **Port-Argol**. Other than the appealing nineteenth-century church of St-Goustan, the only activity is to walk off in search of **beaches**. Once again the best are to the south and east; take care how far you stroll out at low tide, as some patches become isolated offshore sandbanks when the sea comes in.

Practicalities

Hoëdic boasts just one **hotel**, *Les Cardinaux* (☎02.97.52.37.27; ③; closed Sun evening & Mon in winter), which offers extensive sea views and good cooking, with dinner menus from 135F/€20.58. There's also a large, well-equipped municipal **campsite** (☎02.97.30.63.32), between the harbour and the village, plus a dozen or so **gîtes**, rented by the week through the local council (☎02.97.30.68.32).

Carnac

CARNAC is the most important prehistoric site in Europe – in fact this spot is thought to have been continuously inhabited longer than anywhere else in the world. Its **alignments** of two thousand or so menhirs stretch over 4km, with great burial tumuli dotted amid them. In use since at least 5700 BC, the site long predates Knossos, the Pyramids, Stonehenge and the great Egyptian temples of the same name at Karnak.

The town of Carnac is split into two distinct halves – the popular seaside resort of Carnac-Plage and, further inland, Carnac-Ville near the alignments. It's an amalgam that can verge on the ridiculous, with rows of shops named Supermarché des Druides and the like; but, for all that, Carnac is a relaxed and attractive place, and any commercialization doesn't intrude on the megaliths themselves. Fortunately, the ancient builders had the admirable foresight to construct their monuments well back from the sea.

Arrival and information

Buses to Auray, Quiberon and Vannes stop near the tourist office on avenue des Druides, and on rue St-Cornély in Carnac-Ville. The Tire Bouchon **rail** link with Auray and Quiberon runs in July and August; the nearest station to Carnac is at Plouharnel, 4km northwest. Pick up details from the *gare SNCF* there (☎08.36.35.35.35), or the SNCF bureau, 74 av des Druides (☎02.97.52.26.70), alongside the main tourist office. In addition, a motorized **Petit Train** chugs around a circuit between the town, the beach, the Archéoscope, La Trinité, and various alignments in summer (June–Sept every 30min roughly 10am–6pm; 30F/€4.57).

The main **tourist office** for Carnac is slightly back from the main beach at 74 av des Druides (July & Aug Mon–Sat 9am–7pm, Sun 3–7pm; Sept–June Mon–Sat 9am–noon & 2–6pm; ☎02.97.52.13.52, *www.ot-carnac.fr*). An annexe in the place de l'Église in town is open between April and September (Mon–Sat 9.30am–7pm, Sun 10am–1pm). Both provide fully comprehensive maps and details. You can access the **Internet** at *Le Baobab*, 3 allée du Parc (☎02.97.52.29.96), a cybercafé in Carnac-Plage.

Bicycles are available for rent from several of the town's campsites (see p.362), or from Le Randonneur, 20 av des Druides, Carnac-Plage (☎02.97.52.02.55), or Lorcy, 6 rue de Courdiec, Carnac-Ville (☎02.97.52.09.73). The *Grande Metairie* site (see p.362) also arranges tours on **horseback**.

Accommodation and eating

Hotels in Carnac are at a premium in July and August, when you can expect higher prices and intense pressure to take half-board (*demi-pension*). Carnac-Ville is marginally cheaper than Carnac-Plage, although the distinction is blurred where the two merge.

In **Carnac-Ville** *Hôtel Chez Nous*, at 5 place de la Chapelle (☎02.97.52.07.28; ③; closed Nov to mid-April), is central and convenient, with a nice garden, but no restaurant; the old stone, ivy-clad *Hôtel le Ratelier*, at 4 chemin de Douët (☎02.97.52.05.04; ③; restaurant closed Sun evening, plus Mon Oct–March), has slightly fancier rooms and menus from 95F/€14.48.

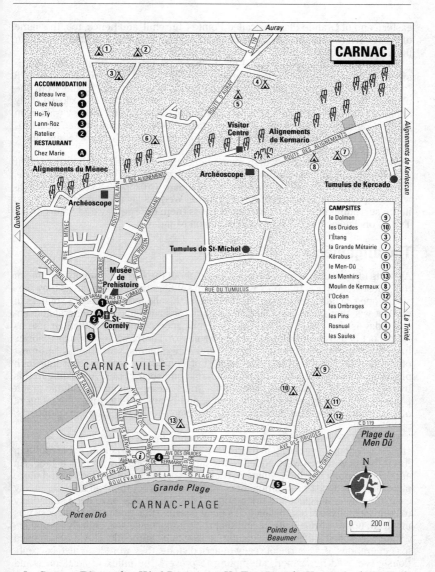

CARNAC

ACCOMMODATION
Bateau Ivre ⑤
Chez Nous ①
Ho-Ty ④
Lann-Roz ③
Ratelier ②
RESTAURANT
Chez Marie Ⓐ

CAMPSITES
le Dolmen ⑨
les Druides ⑩
l'Étang ③
la Grande Métairie ⑦
Kérabus ⑥
le Men-Dû ⑪
les Menhirs ⑬
Moulin de Kermaux ⑧
l'Océan ⑫
les Ombrages ②
les Pins ①
Rosnual ④
les Saules ⑤

In **Carnac-Plage**, the *Hôtel-Restaurant Ho-Ty*, 15 av de Kermario (☎02.97.52 .11.12; ②), is the best value, with clean, cosy little rooms in a traditional prewar seaside house. The much more luxurious and more expensive *Hôtel Le Bateau Ivre*, 71 bd de la Plage (☎02.97.52.19.55; ⑤), is set in large gardens that were formerly owned by Antoine de St-Exupèry (author of *Le Petit Prince*) and Sydney Churchill, a relative of Sir Winston Churchill. Hence the adjacent headland, at the eastern end of Grande Plage, is called Pointe Churchill, and hence, too, the name of the hotel's restaurant, *Le Churchill*, comfortably alongside a heated swimming pool.

As befits such a family-oriented place, there are as many as nineteen **camp-sites** in and around Carnac. Among the best are the two-star *Men Dû* (☎02.97.52.04.23; closed late Sept to mid-April), near the sea, inland from the plage du Men Dû; the central three-star *Dolmen* (☎02.97.52.12.35; closed early Sept to early June), immediately north of Carnac-Plage but still an easy walk from the sea; and the more expensive four-star *Grande Métairie* (☎02.97.52.24.01; closed mid-Sept to March), near the Kercado tumulus, which offers tennis, horse riding and a swimming pool.

Most of the **restaurants** worth recommending are in hotels, such as the bright and cheerful *Hôtel Lann-Roz* at 36 av de la Poste (☎02.97.52.10.48; ⑤). *Chez Marie*, facing St-Cornély church in the main town square (☎02.97.52.83.05), is a worth-while crêperie. There's a **market** in Carnac on Wednesday and Sunday mornings; in the surrounding area, Locmariaquer holds them on Tuesday and Saturday, La Trinité on Tuesday and Friday, and Auray on Monday.

The alignments

All sorts of conjectures have been advanced about the **Carnac megaliths**. One of the oldest stories was that they were Roman soldiers turned to stone as they pursued Pope Cornély; among the most recent is the alleged belief of US soldiers in the last war that they were German anti-tank obstructions. The general consensus today is that they had a religious significance connected with their use as some sort of astronomical observatory. Professor Thom, whose popular theories have made him the best-known writer on the alignments, sees them – and most of the megaliths of the Morbihan – as part of a unified system for recording such phenomena as the extreme points of the lunar and solar cycles. According to this hypothesis, the Carnac stones provided a grid system – a kind of neolithic graph paper – for plotting heavenly movements, and hence to determine the siting of other stones (see the further account, together with map, in Contexts, pp.387–390).

However, it's hard to see any real consistency in the size or the shape of the stones, or enough regularity in the lines to pinpoint their direction. Local tradition has it that new stones were added to the lines, illuminated by fire, each June. An annual ceremony in which willing participants set up one stone does sound more plausible than a vast programme of slave labour to erect them all at once. In any case, the physical aspect and orientation of the stones may have been subsidiary to their metaphysical significance. It's quite possible that no practical purpose was involved, nor a precise pattern, and that their importance was entirely symbolic.

The way you see them today cannot be said to be authentic. Having been used for generations as a source of ready quarried stone, they were later also surreptitiously removed by farmers attempting to prevent the influx of academics and tourists damaging precious crops. Not only is it impossible to say how many of the stones have disappeared, but those that remain are not necessarily in their original positions – small holes filled with pink concrete at the base of the stones denote those that have been restored or re-erected.

The **menhirs** range in size from mere stumps to five-metre-high blocks; some stand alone, others in circles known as **cromlechs**, or in approximate lines. In

Thanks to increasing numbers of visitors (and despite vehement local opposition), the principal alignments are currently fenced off – you are no longer free to wander at will among them, as was possible until just a few years ago. The long-term plan is to allow the area to revegetate at a natural pace, but there's no predicting how long that process will take, and even when it's complete the chances are that access will still be restricted.

For the moment, a temporary **visitor centre** at the Alignements de Kermario (daily: March–June, Sept & Oct 9am–6pm; July & Aug 9am–10pm; Nov–Feb 10am–5.30pm) sells books and maps of the site, and holds an interesting scale model; a much larger facility is due to be constructed in the near future. The stones themselves are clearly visible on the far side of the fence, though from this (or, indeed almost any) distance they tend to look like no more than stumps in the heather.

addition there are **dolmens**, groups of standing stones roofed with further stones laid across the top, which are generally assumed to be burial chambers. And there are tumuli – most notably the **Tumulus de St-Michel**, near the town centre, a vast artificial mound containing rudimentary graves. You can scramble through subterranean passages and tunnels beneath the mound to view little stone cairns and piles of charred bones; the tunnels are, however, again not authentic, being the recent creation of archeologists.

Taken all together, the stones make up three distinct major alignments, running roughly in the same northeast–southwest direction, but each with a slightly separate orientation. These are the **Alignements de Menec**, "the place of stones" or "place of remembrance", with 1169 stones in eleven rows; the **Alignements de Kermario**, "the place of the dead", with 1029 menhirs in ten rows; and the **Alignements de Kerlescan**, "the place of burning", with 555 menhirs in thirteen lines. All three are sited parallel to the sea alongside the *Route des Alignements*, 1km or so to the north of Carnac-Ville.

The Archéoscope

Alignements de Menec. Mid-Feb to mid-Nov daily 10am–noon & 2–6.30pm. 50F/€7.62. Call for the times of English-language performances ☎02.97.52.07.49.

The grandly named **Archéoscope** is presumably intended as some sort of substitute for a close-up inspection of the actual Alignements de Menec across the road. In fact, it's a terribly designed and uncomfortable building, containing a small theatre that puts on overpriced half-hour audiovisual presentations about the megaliths. Some of the effects are quite spectacular, but basically it takes a lot of portentous booming to inform you that no one knows very much about them. Its roof – a vantage point perhaps 4m above ground level – offers inadequate views.

The Museum of Prehistory

10 place de la Chapelle, Carnac-Ville. May–Sept Mon–Fri 10am–6.30pm, Sat & Sun 10am–noon & 2–6.30pm; Oct–April daily except Tues 10am–noon & 2–5pm. April–Sept 30F/€4.57, Oct–March 25F/€3.81.

Carnac's **Musée de Préhistoire** is a disappointingly dry museum of archeology that's likely to leave anyone whose command of French is less than perfect almost completely in the dark as to what all the fuss is about. It traces the history of the area from earliest times, starting with 450,000-year-old chipping tools and leading by way of the Neanderthals to the megalith builders and beyond. As well as authentic physical relics, such as the original "twisted dolmen" of Luffang, with a carving of an octopus-like divinity guaranteed to chill the blood of any devotee of H.P. Lovecraft, there are reproductions and casts of the carvings at Locmariaquer, a scale model of the Alignements de Menec, and diagrams of how the stones may have been moved into place. The captions are exclusively written in an impenetrable academic French, and the exhibits alone tend to be too mundane to hold the interest for long.

The town and the beaches

Carnac itself, divided between the original **Carnac-Ville** and the seaside resort of **Carnac-Plage**, is extremely popular and crowded, swarming with holiday-makers in July and August. For most of these, the alignments are, if anything, only a sideshow. But, as a holiday centre, it has its special charm, especially in late spring and early autumn, when it is less crowded – and cheaper. The town and seafront remain well wooded, and the tree-lined avenues and gardens are a delight – the climate is mild enough for the Mediterranean mimosa and evergreen oak to grow alongside the native stone pine and cypress.

Near the Museum of Prehistory (see above), in the centre of Carnac-Ville, the **church of St-Cornély** was built in the seventeenth century in honour of the patron saint of horned animals. Archeological discoveries suggest that the custom of bringing diseased cattle to Carnac to be cured, still honoured at least in theory at the saint's *pardon* on the second Sunday in September, dates back as far as the Romans. The Romans also had heated seawater baths here; today the **Thalassotherapy Centre** is an ultramodern building where, among other things, they treat *maladies de civilisation*.

Carnac's five **beaches** extend for nearly 3km in total, with the largest of them – logically enough, the Grande Plage – running for the full length of the built-up area known as Carnac-Plage. For much of the way it's hidden from view by the slightly raised line of dunes that separates it from the boulevard de la Plage, which is in turn very low-key; the parallel avenue des Druides, a couple of blocks inland, is much busier, with shops and restaurants.

Further west, nearer the yacht club, the small **plage Légenèse** is reputed to be the beach on which the ill-fated *Chouan* Royalists landed in 1795. The two most attractive beaches, usually counted together as one of the five, are **plages Men Dû** and **Beaumer**, which lie to the east towards La Trinité beyond Pointe Churchill.

La Trinité

An alternative base to Carnac proper is **LA TRINITÉ**, 3km or 4km along the coast to the east, around the sweep of Beaumer bay. The town itself is uninteresting – a modern and very upmarket yacht harbour without a proper beach – but has achieved fame as the former home of yachtsman Eric Tabarley, twice winner of the single-handed transatlantic race in 1964 (*Pen Duick I*) and 1976 (*Pen Duick VI*), who was lost at sea off Wales in 1998, and as the birthplace of Jean-Marie Le Pen, founder of the ultra-Right National Front.

Practicalities

La Trinité does at least hold some high-quality **hotel-restaurants**, among them the *Ostrea*, 34 cours des Quais (☎02.97.55.73.23; ④; closed Jan), where you dine on a seaview terrace, and a crop of four-star **campsites** nearby, including the attractive *Camping La Baie* on the plage de Kervillen (☎02.97.55.73.42, *labaie@clubinternet.fr*; closed mid-Sept to mid-May).

Locmariaquer

LOCMARIAQUER, easily accessible from Auray or Carnac, stands right at the mouth of the Gulf of Morbihan – its cape separated by only a few hundred metres from the tip of the Rhuys peninsula. On the ocean side, it has a long sandy beach, popular not only with swimmers but also with beachcombers and shellfish-scavengers; on the Gulf side, it has a small tidal port. Like Carnac, however, the main reason to go out of your way to visit Locmariaquer is for its fine crop of megaliths.

Menhirs and dolmens

The **Grand Menhir Brise** at Locmariaquer (daily: mid-Jan to March & Oct to mid-Dec 2–5pm; April & May 10am–1pm & 2–6pm; June–Sept 10am–7pm; July & Aug 32F/€4.88, Sept–June 25F/€3.81) is supposed to have been the crucial central point of the megalithic observatory of the Morbihan (see Contexts, pp.387–390). Before being floored by an earthquake in 1722, it was by far the largest known menhir – 20m high and weighing rather more than a full jumbo jet, at 347 tonnes. It now lies on the ground in four pieces (a possible fifth is missing). Archeologists have established that the stone itself was quarried at Kerdaniel, 4km north, and estimate that the job of moving it required a workforce of between two thousand and four thousand people.

Alongside the Grand Menhir, and covered by the same ticket, the **Table des Marchands** is a dolmen that was once exposed but has now been reburied for its protection under a tumulus. You can, however, go inside, along a narrow passage, and stand beneath its huge roof. Carvings overhead seem to depict ploughing, which may well have been a recent innovation at the time they were made. It has recently been discovered that this roof is part of the same stone as that on the tumulus at Gavrinis and on another local dolmen – the carvings match like a jigsaw. That constitutes a fresh puzzle for the archeologists, as it appears to imply that the builders did not revere the stones in themselves, as most theories had previously assumed. In addition, the stone at the end of the central chamber was originally erected as a stand-alone menhir, so the "table" must have been built around an earlier monument.

The rest of the megaliths of Locmariaquer are open at all times – and open to the weather as well, so watch out for muddy and waterlogged underground passages, and be sure to take a torch if you want to explore them thoroughly. The most interesting are the **Dolmen des Pierres Plates**, at the end of the town beach, with what looks like an octopus divinity deep in its long chamber, and the **Dolmen de Mané-Rethual**, a long covered tunnel leading to a burial chamber capped with a huge rock, reached along a narrow footpath that starts behind the phone boxes next to the Mairie/tourist office. At a third dolmen, the **Mané-Lud**, a horse's skull was found on top of each stone during excavations.

Practicalities

There are a couple of reasonable small **hotels** in Locmariaquer, both with good restaurants. *L'Escale* (☎02.97.57.32.51; ③; closed Oct–March) is right on the waterfront, so you get a great view from its terrace, while the *Lautram* is set slightly back from the sea, facing the church on place de l'Église (☎02.97.57.31.32; ②; closed Oct–March). While the food at the *Lautram* is superb, however, it has to be said that the cheaper rooms are pretty minimal.

Campsites include the excellent two-star *Ferme Fleurie* (☎02.97.57.34.06; closed Dec & Jan), 1km towards Kerinis, and the two-star, summer-only *Lann Brick* (☎02.97.57.32.79; closed mid-Sept to May), 1.5km further on, nearer the beach.

Boats from Locmariaquer

Boat trips set out from Locmariaquer in all directions, for which rival companies sell tickets both in the town centre and at the port further down towards the narrow straits, with precise departure points depending on the level of the tides. Two main operators, Vedettes l'Aiglon (☎02.97.57.39.15) and Vedettes l'Angélus (☎02.97.57.30.29), run gulf tours, as detailed on p.375, and day-trips to Belle-Île (see p.355). In summer, they also regularly make the three-kilometre crossing to Port Navalo on the Rhuys peninsula (see p.377), carrying bikes but not cars.

Auray and around

Though some people find **AURAY**, with its overrestored ancient quarter, slightly dull, it's a lot less crowded than Vannes, a lot cheaper than Quiberon town, and usefully placed for exploring Carnac, the Quiberon peninsula and the Gulf of Morbihan.

The natural centre of the town these days is the **place de la République**, with its eighteenth-century Hôtel de Ville. In a neighbouring square, linked to the place de la République by rue du Lait, is the seventeenth-century **church of St-Gildas**, with its fine Renaissance porch. A **covered market** adjoins the Hôtel de Ville, while on Mondays an open-air market fills the surrounding streets with colour – and stops all traffic for a considerable radius.

However, Auray's showpiece is undoubtedly the ancient quarter of **St-Goustan** down by the river, with its delightful, albeit restored, fifteenth- and sixteenth-century houses. This bend in the River Loch, an early defended site, made a natural setting for a town – and, with its easy access to the gulf, it soon became one of the busiest ports of Brittany. Today, as you look at it from the Promenade du Loch on the opposite bank, with the diminutive seventeenth-century stone bridge still spanning the river, it is not difficult to imagine it in its heyday. In 1776, Benjamin Franklin landed here on his way to seek the help of Louis XVI in the American War of Independence; Auray is also said to have been the last place Julius Caesar reached in his conquest of Gaul.

Practicalities

Auray's **gare SNCF** is twenty-minutes' walk from the centre; alternatively buses run from the station through the centre of Auray and on to La Trinité, Carnac and the *gare SNCF* at Quiberon. The **tourist office** is up in town at 20 rue du Lait, very near the Hôtel de Ville on place de la République (Mon–Sat 9.30am–noon &

2–6pm; ☎02.97.24.09.75). A small annexe is maintained in July and August at the *gare SNCF*. If you're making for the islands, you can pick up comprehensive details at the Îles du Ponant Promotional Association at 11 place du Joffre.

The most appealing place to **stay** in Auray would be right by the port in the St-Goustan quarter, but in the absence of waterfront hotels the best option is the *Hôtel Le Branhoc*, 300m short of the sea on the road down at 5 route du Bono (☎02.97.56.41.55; ④; closed mid-Dec to Jan), which offers clean, well-equipped rooms and a reasonable restaurant. Up in town, *Hôtel Le Cadoudal*, 9 place Notre-Dame (☎02.97.50.78.51; ②), is a cheaper, more basic alternative, while out near the station there are a couple of other hotels, including the *Hôtel Terminus*, place de la Gare (☎02.97.24.00.09; ①), which has a snack bar and crêperie. The *Olympic Bar*, 19 rue Clémenceau (☎02.97.24.06.69), is a friendly restaurant-cum-bar, with menus at 49F/€7.47 and 78F/€11.89.

North of Auray

A short way north of Auray's train station – and thus quite a long way out from the town, on the B768 towards Baud – the imposing and evocative **Abbaye de Chartreuse** (daily 10am–noon & 2–5.30pm; free) houses a David d'Angers mausoleum of black and white marble, commemorating the failed *Chouan* landing at Quiberon in 1795 (see p.395). For Bretons the event was something more than an attempt at a Royalist restoration, with strong undertones of a struggle for independence. Another gloomy piece of counter-Revolutionary history is recalled by the nearby **Champ des Martyrs**, where 350 of the *Chouans* were executed. It's located on the right of the D120, going out of town.

Two kilometres further along the D120, towards Brech, you come to the **Eco-Musée St-Degan** (Feb to mid-April & Oct–Dec Sat & Sun 2–5.30pm; mid-April to June & Sept daily 2–5.30pm; July & Aug daily 10am–7pm; 25F/€3.81), a group of reconstructed farm buildings, representing local peasant life at the beginning of the twentieth century. It's a bit determinedly rustic and charming, but at least it does attempt to escape the glass cases and wax models of most folk museums.

In **BRECH** itself there's a fine parish **church**, with a weather-beaten and faded calvary in its yard; a nice **café**, *des Bretons*; and a **gîte d'étape** – not a very eventful place to stay, perhaps, but a peaceful one.

Ste-Anne d'Auray

Should you be in the area of Auray around July 26, you should head for **STE-ANNE D'AURAY**, which holds one of the largest of the Breton *pardons* on that day. Some 25,000 pilgrims gather for the occasion to hear Mass in the church, mount the *scala sancta* on their knees and buy trinkets and snacks from the street stalls.

The origin of this **pardon**, typical of many, was the discovery in 1623 of a statue of St Anne (the mother of Mary) by a local peasant, one Nicolazic. He claimed that the saint directed him to the spot where the statue had been buried for over nine hundred years and instructed him to build a church. Twenty years later, on his deathbed, Nicolazic was still being interrogated by the ecclesiastical authorities as to the truth of his story, but the church had been constructed and had already become a place of pilgrimage. Nicolazic was an illiterate peasant who spoke no French; it is a testimony to his obduracy that his claims were eventually accepted against the opposition of sceptical clergy and nobility. The continuing campaign for his canonization is polarized along similar lines today. Nicolazic's supporters see him as a representative of the downtrodden classes, and as a symbol of Breton independence; the wealthy Church establishment, on the other hand, continues to oppose him.

As a major centre for pilgrimage – Pope John Paul II visited as recently as September 1996 – Ste-Anne was chosen as the site for the vast **Monument aux Morts** erected by public subscription as a memorial to the 250,000 Breton dead of World War I. One in fourteen of the population died, the highest proportion of losses of any region involved. The monument, a crypt topped by a dome with a granite altar, is surrounded by a wall that must be 200m long, covered with inscriptions to the dead; and yet even that huge and sombre wall does not contain room to list them all by name, often just cataloguing the horrific death tallies of tiny and obscure villages.

A short distance north on the D102 is a **National Necropolis**, holding dead from all wars since 1870.

Practicalities

Ste-Anne is a sad and solemn place. The town, away from the spacious promenades for the pilgrims, is small, low and drab; not really a place for a long stay, although there is no particular shortage of **hotels**. Among the best value in the centre are the *Moderne*, 8 rue de Vannes (☎02.97.57.66.55; ③; closed mid-Dec to mid-Jan), which has a good restaurant, and the *Croix Blanche*, nearby at 25 rue de Vannes (☎02.97.57.64.44; ②; closed mid-Jan to mid-Feb, plus Sun evening & Mon out of season).

Vannes

Thanks to its position at the head of the Golfe de Morbihan, **VANNES**, 20km east of Auray, is southern Brittany's major tourist town. Modern Vannes is such a large and thriving community that the small size of the old walled town at its core, **Vieux Vannes**, may well come as a surprise. Its focal point, the old gateway of the **Porte St-Vincent**, commands a busy little square at the northern end of the long canalized port that provides access to the gulf itself. Once inside the ramparts, the old centre of chaotic streets – crammed around the cathedral, and enclosed by gardens and a tiny stream – is largely pedestrianized, in refreshing contrast to the somewhat insane road system beyond.

It was from Vannes that the great Breton hero Nominoë set out to unify Brittany at the start of the ninth century; he beat the hell out of the Franks, and pushed the borders past Nantes and Rennes to where they were to remain up until the French Revolution nearly a millennium later. Here too, the Breton *États* assembled in 1532 to ratify the Act of Union with France, in the building known as La Cohue; and here, also, 22 of the Royalists captured at Quiberon (see p.395) were executed in the Jardins de la Garrène in 1795. Parisian soldiers fired the shots because local regiments refused.

Arrival and information

Vannes' **gare SNCF** (☎08.36.35.35.35) is 25-minutes' walk north of the town centre. Buses to Auray, Carnac, Quiberon and other destinations leave from the **gare routière** alongside; the one to Nantes, run by Societé Transports Tourisme de

VANNES

Gares SNCF & Routière

Steps

St-Patern

RUE DE LA BOUCHERIE

RUE DU COLONEL-MAURY

RUE HOCHE

RUE J. LE BRIX

RUE DU MÉNÉ

Porte
St-Jean

Porte-Prison

Hôtel de Ville

PLACE
M.
MARCHAIS

RUE ÉMILE BURGAULT

RUE DES CHANOINES

Cathédrale St-Pierre

RUE DE CLISSMADEU

RUE ST-SALOMON

La Cohue

Musée
Archéologique

PLACE
VALENCIA

PLACE
LAROCHE

RUE FRANCOIS DECKER

PLACE DE LA
RÉPUBLIQUE

RUE RICHEMONT

RUE THIERS

PLACE
DU POIDS
PUBLICS

PLACE
DES LICES

RUE PORTE POTERNE

RUE DE LA MONNAIE

Poissonnerie

Porte
St-Vincent

PLACE
GAMBETTA

RUE A. LE PONTOIS

RUE DU PORT

Port

ACCOMMODATION

le Bretagne	2
le Marina	3
Mascotte	1

0   200 m

RESTAURANTS

Breizh Caffe	C
Cave St-Gwenaël	A
Commodore	E
Jonquière	D
Roscanvec	B

Gare Maritime   Gulf of Morbihan

l'Ouest (☎02.97.47.29.64), avoids the rail journey via Redon, and allows a stop-over in La Roche-Bernard. **Parking** can be a problem unless you head straight for the west side of the port, south of town.

The **tourist office**, which has a well-restored seventeenth-century frontage, is close to the waterfront, near place Gambetta at 1 rue Thiers (July & Aug Mon–Sat 9am–7pm, Sun 10am–1pm & 3–7pm; Sept–June Mon–Sat 9am–noon & 2–6pm; ☎02.97.47.24.34, *www.vannes-bretagne-sud.com*). Staff can advise on availability at local hotels, though they charge 5F/€0.76 to make an actual booking for you; they also have details of an extensive summer programme of **walking tours** around the town. **Mountain bikes** are available for rent from a stand on rue du Féty, just east of place Gambetta near the port (daily 9am–7.30pm; ☎02.97.47.64.88).

Boats around the gulf are operated from the **gare maritime**, a little way south of the centre on the parc du Golfe, by Navix (☎02.97.46.60.00) and Compagnies des Îles (☎02.97.46.60.00), among others (see p.375). Pick up all the latest brochures and schedules in the tourist office.

Accommodation

In peak season Vannes can become quite claustrophobic, but it still offers a more extensive choice of **hotels** than anywhere else around the Golfe de Morbihan, though most, unfortunately, are well away from the centre. Much the nicest place to stay, if you can get a room, is **place Gambetta** overlooking the port. This is the one part of Vannes that stays busy well into the evening throughout the year, and the traffic noise is not too bad at all.

Vannes has finally acquired its own **hostel**, 4km southeast of the town centre in Séné (☎02.97.66.94.25; dorm bed 70F/€10.67), on the daytime-only bus route #4 from place de la République. The nearest **campsite** is the three-star *Camping Conleau* at the far end of avenue du Maréchal-Juin, beyond the Aquarium, and alongside the gulf (☎02.97.63.13.88; closed Oct–March).

Hôtel le Bretagne, 36 rue du Méné (☎02.97.47.20.21, fax 02.97.47.90.78, *www.bretagne-hotel.com*). Reasonable hotel situated just outside the walls, around the corner from the Porte-Prison. The rooms aren't fancy, but all have showers or bath plus TV. ②.

Hôtel Ibis Vannes, rue Emile-Jourdan (☎02.97.63.61.11, fax 02.97.63.21.33, *h0650@accor-hotels.com*). Large, comfortable, and dependable chain option, with its own restaurant, in a very unexciting setting 2km north of town, just north of the N165 motorway. ④.

Hôtel le Marina, 4 place Gambetta (☎02.97.47.22.81, fax 02.97.47.00.34). Fourteen pleasantly refurbished rooms – and a downstairs bar – right in the thick of things by the port, with sea views and bright sun in the morning. ②.

Hôtel Mascotte, av Jean-Monnet (☎02.97.47.59.60, fax 02.97.47.07.54). Functional, reasonable-value hotel a short walk northwest of the walled town, with 65 en-suite rooms and an adequate restaurant. ④.

The Town

The new town centre of Vannes is **place de la République**; the administrative headquarters were shifted outside the medieval city during the nineteenth-century craze for urbanization. The grandest of the public buildings here, guarded by a pair of sleek and dignified bronze lions, is the **Hôtel de Ville** at the top of rue Thiers.

By day, however, the cobbled streets of the old city, especially in the area around the cathedral, are the chief source of pleasure, as well as being where most of Vannes' busy commercial life takes place. With their skew-windowed and half-timbered houses – most overhanging and witch-hatted, some tumbling down, some newly propped-up and painted – they amply repay time spent wandering. **Place Henri-IV** in particular, with its charming fifteenth- and sixteenth-century gabled houses, is stunning, as are the views from it down the narrow side streets.

Here and there, it's possible to climb up onto the **ramparts** to admire the views, though much of the way you have to trace the circuit instead around the outside, from the far side of what used to be the city moat, which now consists of neat and colourful flowerbeds. Near the **Porte Poterne**, the "back gate", an old slate-roofed wash house survives.

La Cohue, which fills a block between rue des Halles and place du Cathédrale, currently houses the **Musée de Vannes** (June–Sept daily 10am–6pm; Oct–May Mon & Wed–Sat 10am–noon & 2–6pm, Sun 2–6pm; 26F/€3.96), having served at various times over the past 750 years as High Court and assembly room, prison, Revolutionary tribunal, theatre and marketplace. Upstairs it still houses the dull collection of what was the local Beaux Arts museum, heavy on worthy Breton artists such as J.-F. Boucher and Jean Frélaut, while the main gallery downstairs is the venue for different temporary exhibitions.

The **Cathédrale St-Pierre** is a rather forbidding place, with its stern main altar almost imprisoned by four solemn, grey pillars. The light, purple through the new stained glass, spears in to illuminate the finger of the Blessed Pierre Rogue, who was guillotined in the main square on March 3, 1796. Opposite this desiccated digit is the black-lidded sarcophagus that marks the current site of the tomb of fifteenth-century Spanish Dominican preacher St Vincent Ferrier (which has meandered around the cathedral for centuries). For a small fee, you can in summer examine the assorted **treasure** in the chapterhouse, which includes a twelfth-century wedding chest, brightly decorated with enigmatic scenes of romantic chivalry.

Housed in the sombre fifteenth-century Château Gaillard on rue Noé, the **Musée Archéologique** is said to have one of the world's finest collections of prehistoric artefacts (Mon–Sat: April–June & Sept–Oct 9.30am–noon & 2–6pm; July & Aug 9.30am–6pm; Nov–March 2–6pm; 20F/€3.05). But, much like the displays at Carnac, it's all pretty lifeless – some elegant stone axes, more recent Oceanic exhibits by way of context, but nothing very illuminating. Further collections of fossils, shells and stuffed birds, equally traditional in their display, are on show around the corner in the **Hôtel de Roscannec** at 19 rue des Halles (same hours as museum).

There's a bit more life about the city's excellent **fish market**, active in the covered hall on place de la Poissonnerie every morning between Tuesday and Saturday. A general market spreads slightly higher up on the streets towards the cathedral on Wednesday and Saturday.

The Parc du Golfe

Vannes' **parc du Golfe**, 500m south of place Gambetta along the west (right) bank of the port, features a modern **aquarium** (daily: June–Aug 9am–8pm; Sept–May 9am–noon & 1.30–7pm; 52F/€7.93, under-12s 32F/€4.88) that claims to have the best collection of tropical fish in Europe. Certainly it holds some pretty extraordinary specimens, including four-eyed fish from Venezuela that can see simultaneously above and below the surface of the water, and are also divided into four sexes for good measure; cave fish from Mexico that by contrast have no eyes at all; and *arowana* from Guyana, which jump two metres out of the water to catch birds. A Nile crocodile found in the Paris sewers in 1984 shares its tank with a group of piranhas, while elsewhere there's a huge tank of black- and white-tipped sharks. Most species are identified with their French and Latin names, not necessarily their English ones.

Across the car park, the **Palais des Automates** (daily: Feb–June & Sept–Nov 10am–noon & 2–6pm; July & Aug 10am–7pm; 30F/€4.57), holds a collection of antique mechanical dolls, some of which do no more than roll their eyes or heave their bosoms, while others perform acrobatics or magic tricks. Young kids will enjoy having lots of buttons to press, and seeing an entire village of manic teddy bears and window-cleaning monkeys; adults may well feel short-changed, and recoil from some offensive racial stereotyping.

Eating and nightlife

Dining out in old Vannes can be an expensive experience, whether you eat in the intimate little restaurants along the rue des Halles, or down by the port. If you're just looking for a snack, try the area outside the walls in the northeast, extending from the Porte-Prison towards the *gare SNCF*.

The leading venues for **live music** are *La Route du Rhum*, 7 place Stalingrad (☎02.97.42.26.94), which puts on local rock, blues and Breton bands, and *John R. O'Flaherty*, at 22 rue Hoche (☎02.97.42.40.11; closed Sun), which is more a jazz buffs' hangout. During the first week of August, the open-air concerts of the **Vannes Jazz Festival** take place in the Théâtre de Verdure.

Breizh Caffe, 13 rue des Halles (☎02.97.54.37.41). One of the less pricey options on this attractive cobbled street, but every bit as good as its rivals, with a strong emphasis on Breton dishes and ingredients. Weekday lunches for 68F/€10.37, traditional evening menus from 93F/€14.18. Closed Sun & Mon lunchtime in low season.

Le Commodore, 3 rue Pasteur (☎02.97.46.42.62). Unassuming marine-themed local restaurant, tucked away around the back of the post office, which offers plenty of fishy treats on menus that start at 63F/€9.60 at lunchtime, and from around 75F/€11.28 in the evening. Closed Feb, plus Sun, & Mon lunchtime.

Crêperie La Cave St-Gwenaël, 23 rue St-Gwenaël (☎02.97.47.47.94). Atmospheric, good-value crêperie in the cellar of a lovely old house, facing the cathedral. Closed Sun, Mon lunchtime & all Jan.

La Jonquière, 9 rue des Halles (☎02.97.54.08.34). Very central option, part of a popular Brest-based chain with a modern approach and efficient multilingual staff. Despite the road being very narrow, it manages to squeeze a few tables onto the cobbles. For 76F/€11.59 you can choose a main course plus a buffet of either hors d'oeuvres or desserts; for 99F/€15.09 you can take your pick of both; 117F/€17.84 buys a full *assiette de fruits de mer*.

de Roscanvec, 17 rue des Halles (☎02.97.47.15.96). Formal gourmet restaurant in a lovely half-timbered house in the heart of the old town. Lunch at 88F/€13.42 is a bargain, dinner menus go all the way up to 300F/€45.73. Closed Sun evening, plus Mon Sept–June.

East of Vannes

Though Gavrinis and the Morbihan islands are the most exciting excursions from Vannes, various sights inland, to the **east of the city**, can fill a day's round-trip. Vannes' **traffic system** will do its damnedest to prevent you leaving the city in any direction, however, so you can't be too choosy about where you end up.

The Château de Largoët

If you follow the **N166** 10km towards Elven, and then turn off to the left about 4km short, you come to the ruins of the **Château de Largoët**, perched on an eminence in the small forest (mid-March to May & Oct Sat & Sun 2–6.30pm; June–Sept daily 10.30am–6.30pm; 25F/€3.81). It's still guarded by its old gatehouse, carved all over with granite bunnies.

The castle consists mainly of two stark towers, inside which the wooden flooring has long since rotted away to leave the shafts open to the sky. The *donjon* proper is topped by a finger-like watchtower, one of the highest in the country at over 45m, where from 1474 until 1476 the Breton Duke Francis imprisoned the future English king, Henry VII. At that time simply Henry Tudor, Duke of Richmond – a title traditionally awarded to royal bastards or English nobility with Breton connections – he had fled to Brittany after the Battle of Tewkesbury, in which Lancastrian ambitions in the Wars of the Roses were defeated. François welcomed Henry as a guest, then realized his value and held him for ransom.

Le Gorvello and Questembert

There's little point going to Elven itself, though if you've always wondered where René Descartes grew up you can find the answer en route at the manor house of

Kerleau. More rewarding is to head south to the beautiful village of **LE GORVEL-LO**, 10km from the château, at a crossroads with the D7. Bedecked with potted geraniums and huge azaleas, it has at its centre a perfect roadside cross.

Beyond Le Gorvello, the D7 leads on into **QUESTEMBERT**, where the low-roofed wooden market hall from 1675 makes a classy cycle park. Purely as a **hotel**, the ivy-coated *Hôtel du Bretagne* at 13 rue St-Michel (☎02.97.26.11.12; ⑧) is very appealing, with lavish fittings to merit its sky-high room rates. As a **restaurant**, it's a strange place. Chef Georges Paineau is regarded, not least by himself, as one of the finest chefs in France, and prepares unarguably sumptuous menus starting at 210F/€32.01 for lunch and 295F/€44.97 for dinner; specialities include steamed parcels of oysters wrapped in spinach, and cabbage stuffed with lobster. However, the air of formality in the oak-panelled and often all-but-empty dining room can be very intimidating – which is especially ludicrous because M Paineau also fancies himself as a painter, and his truly dreadful pop-art acrylics adorn every spare centimetre of wall space. If you can't take that sort of pressure, head for the *Hôtel de la Gare* (☎02.97.26.11.47; ②), a *logis* with a good restaurant in rather nondescript surroundings well north of town near the *gare SNCF*.

Continue east or north from Questembert, and you come to the **Nantes–Brest canal** at Malestroit (see p.331) or Redon (see p.334).

The Golfe de Morbihan

By popular tradition, the **Golfe de Morbihan** ("little sea" in Breton) holds 365 scattered islands – one for every day of the year. For centuries, though, the waters have been rising, and the figure now is more like one per week. Of these, some thirty are owned by film stars and the like, while two – the **Île-aux-Moines** and **Île d'Arz** – have regular ferry services and permanent populations, and end up extremely crowded in summer. The rest are the best, and a **boat tour** around them, or at least a trip out to **Gavrinis**, near the mouth of the gulf, and a short ferry-trip from the port of **Larmor-Baden**, ranks among the most compelling attractions in southern Brittany.

As the boats thread their way through the baffling muddle of channels you lose track of which is island and which is mainland; and everywhere there are megalithic ruins, stone circles disappearing beneath the water and solitary menhirs on small hillocks. At the time when they were built, the sea level is thought to have been around 5m lower than it is today, and the islands may have been mounds amid the marshlands. Flaubert evocatively described Celtic mercenaries far off in Carthage pining for the Morbihan – "*Les Celtes regrettaient trois pierres brutes, sous un ciel plouvieux, dans un golfe remplie d'îlots*" – not that the Celts actually set up the stones in the first place.

Le Bono and Larmor-Baden

Making your own way to Larmor-Baden, the departure point for trips to Gavrinis, the best route is along the main road down the Auray estuary, the D17. This crosses the River Bono on a high bridge; visible way below it to the left is a beautiful iron bridge. A side turning before the river leads across that bridge into **LE BONO**, a harbour village that looks almost ludicrously idyllic seen from one of the *vedettes* out in the gulf. Simple rooms are available at the *Vieux-Pont*, a

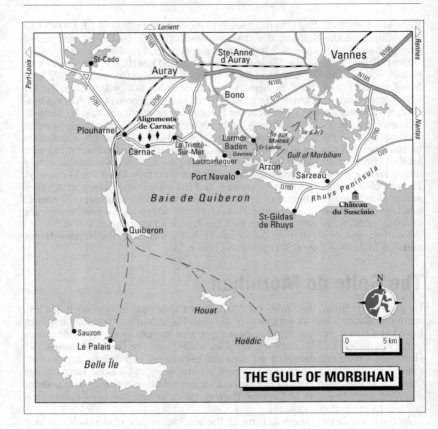

THE GULF OF MORBIHAN

crêperie in the heart of the village at 23 rue Pasteur (☎02.97.57.87.71; ①; closed Mon in low season), but for most visitors Le Bono is simply a tempting stopover for a meal or picnic. *Au Matefaim*, 9 rue du Port (☎02.97.57.84.16), is another good crêperie, known for its gorgeous flambéed crêpes.

LARMOR-BADEN itself is a subdued little town lying at the bottom of a long slope of fields of dazzling sunflowers. The port looks out on the tangle of islands in the Gulf of Morbihan, which at this point is so narrow that Arzon on the Rhuys peninsula (see p.377) appears to be on just another nearby island. It is not an inspiring place to stay – not really a resort or town – but there's a three-star beachfront **campsite**, *Les Algues* (☎02.97.84.26.26; closed mid-Sept to mid-June), and a fair number of **hotels** including the *du Centre*, 3 rte de Vannes (☎02.97.57.04.68; ③; closed Jan & Feb).

Gavrinis

The reason to visit the island of **Gavrinis** is its megalithic site. The most impressive and remarkable in Brittany, it would be memorable just for its location. But it

---

GULF TOURS

In season, dozens of boats leave for **gulf tours** each day from Vannes, Port Navalo, La Trinité, Locmariaquer, Auray and Larmor-Baden. These are among the options:

Compagnie des Îles
(☎02.97.46.18.19) run gulf tours (105–160F/€16.01–24.39) and excursions to the Île-aux-Moines (80–105F/€12.20–16.01) from **Vannes**. They also operate a more limited programme of similar cruises from **Port Navalo** (105–145F/€16.01–22.11) and Port Haliguen in **Quiberon** (125–145F/€19.06–22.11).

Izenah Croisières
(☎02.97.57.23.24 or 02.97.26.31.45, *www.izenah-croisieres.com*) run gulf tours in summer (April–Sept daily 3pm; 90F/€13.72; July & Aug additionally at 11am & 5pm, 65F/€9.91) and a year-round ferry service, with departures every half-hour, to the Île-aux-Moines (21F/€3.20 return) from **Port Blanc** at **Baden**.

Navix
(☎02.97.46.60.00, *navix@wanadoo.fr*), who are based in **Vannes**, run deluxe *vedettes* around the gulf, including half-day (105F/€16.01) and full-day (125F/€19.06) tours, excursions to the Île-aux-Moines and the Île d'Arz, and gastronomic cruises for lunch (July & Aug Tues–Sun departs 12.30pm;

140F/€21.34 plus food) and dinner (July & Aug Wed & Sat departs 8pm; 140F/€21.34 plus food). Other Navix sailings depart, to no fixed schedule, from **Port Navalo** and **Locmariaquer** (60–160F/€9.15–24.39, plus expensive dinner cruises) and from Auray, Le Bono and La Trinité. Between May and September, they also go to **Belle-Île** (up to 175F/€26.68 return) and **Houat** (150F/€22.87) from **Vannes**, **Port Navalo** and **La Trinité**.

Vedettes L'aiglon
(☎02.97.57.39.15) run an extensive itinerary of gulf tours from **Locmariaquer** (mid-June to mid-Sept daily at 9.45am, 11am, 2.15pm & 4.15pm; 60–130F/€9.15–19.82), plus summer day-trips to **Belle-Île** (July & Aug Tues–Fri & Sun 8.45am; 140F/€21.34).

Vedettes L'angelus
(☎02.97.57.30.29) also run gulf tours to no fixed schedule from **Locmariaquer** (60–130F/€9.15–19.82), as well as excursions on summer Sundays to **Belle-Île** (July & Aug Sun 8.30am; 150F/€22.87).

---

really is extraordinary as a structure, standing comparison with Newgrange in Ireland and – in shape as well as size and age – with the earliest pyramids of Egypt.

It is essentially a **tumulus**, an earth mound covering a stone cairn and "passage grave". However, in 1981 half of the mound was peeled back and, using the original stones around the entrance as a basis, the side of the cairn that faces the water was reconstructed to make a facade resembling a step-pyramid. Inside, every stone of the passageway and chamber is covered in carvings, with a restricted "alphabet" of fingerprint whorls, axe-heads and other conventional signs, including the spirals familiar in Ireland but seen only here in Brittany. The long-held view of archeologists that the stones had been brought at least the few kilometres from Locmariaquer received dramatic confirmation in 1984, when the roof was shown to be made from the self-same piece of carved stone as covers the Table des Marchands there (see p.365).

Another mystery, however, has consistently eluded explanation: the purpose of the three holes leading to a recessed niche in one of the walls of the chamber.

Some medieval monks were buried in the mound, but the cairn itself seems never to have been a grave.

Erosion since the site was opened has so rapidly damaged the tumulus that it may well soon be barred to visitors altogether; it is no longer possible to climb on the mound itself, and conceivably a replica will be built.

From Gavrinis, you can look across to the half-submerged stone circle on the tiny island of **Er Lanic**, which rests on its skirt of mud like an abandoned hovercraft. It has been identified as a major centre for the manufacture of ceremonial axes, using stone brought from Port Navalo.

Practicalities

The island of Gavrinis is a fifteen-minute **ferry** ride from Larmor-Baden, with the cost of the trips including guided tours of the cairn (departures every 30min: April & May Mon–Fri 2–6pm, Sat & Sun 10am–noon & 2–6pm; June–Sept daily 10am–noon & 2–6pm; Oct daily except Tues 10am–noon & 2–6pm; ☎02.97.57.19.38; April, May & Oct 51F/€7.77, June–Sept 56F/€8.54). Most gulf cruises sail close enough to the island to give a view of the cairn, but do not land.

Southern Morbihan: the Rhuys peninsula

Though the tip of the **Presqu'île de Rhuys** is just a few hundred metres across the mouth of the Gulf of Morbihan from Locmariaquer, it somehow seems to mark a distinctly southwards shift in climate. The Côte Sauvage is lost and in its wake appear pomegranates, fig trees, camellias, even vineyards (Rhuys produces the only Breton wine), along with cultivated oysters down below in the mud.

Due, unfortunately, to fierce currents in the gulf, it's very unsafe for swimming all the way along the north side of the peninsula. The **ocean beaches**, however, have potential. They break out intermittently to either side of **St-Gildas-de-Rhuys**, amid the glittering gold- and silver-coloured rocks. For details on the whole peninsula, call in at the **information centre** (daily: mid-June to mid-Sept 9am–8pm; mid-Sept to mid-June 9am–noon & 2–6pm; ☎02.97.26.45.26), just off the D780 as you come into **Sarzeau**.

Sarzeau and the Château de Suscinio

The D780 runs through the heart of the Rhuys peninsula, with no sea views to speak of. As it starts an extravagant curve to the south of the central town of **SARZEAU**, a short detour to the left, south along the D198, will bring you to the impressive fourteenth-century **Château de Suscinio**. This completely moated castle, once a hunting lodge of the dukes of Brittany, is set in marshland at the edge of a tiny village, and contains a sagging but vivid mosaic floor. You can take a precarious stroll around its high ramparts (April & May daily 10am–noon & 2–7pm; June–Sept daily 10am–7pm; Oct–March Mon–Wed & Fri 2–5pm, Thurs, Sat & Sun 10am–noon & 2–5pm; June–Sept 30F/€4.57, Oct–May 25F/€3.81), and you can also visit on summer evenings, when it opens for musical or theatrical performances.

The best **place to stay** in Sarzeau is the little *Hôtel Bar du Port* (☎02.97.41.93.51; ④), whose seven rooms all have balconies that look out across the port to the gulf.

St-Gildas-de-Rhuys

At **ST-GILDAS-DE-RHUYS**, 6km southwest of Sarzeau, Pierre Abélard, the theologian/lover of Héloïse, was abbot for a period from 1126, having been exiled from Paris. "I live in a wild country where every day brings new perils", he wrote to Héloïse, eventually fleeing after his brother monks – hedonists unimpressed by his stern scholasticism – attempted to poison him.

Alongside the beaches around the village are a handful of **campsites**, among them the luxurious four-star *du Menhir* (☎02.97.45.22.88; closed mid-Sept to mid-May); there's also a **hotel**, the *Giquel* (☎02.97.45.23.12; ③).

Arzon and Port Navalo

If you're spending any length of time on the peninsula, the most appealing places to stay are congregated at its far western end, around the village of **ARZON**. Immediately before the centre, however, the **Port du Crouesty** is a desperately unattractive modern marina, dominated by the hideous crab-like *Hôtel Miramar* (☎02.97.67.68.00; ⑨; closed mid-Nov to mid-Dec), where the cheapest single room costs well over 1100F/€167.69.

On first glance, **PORT NAVALO** at the very tip has little more character, but there's a cute little beach tucked into the headland, and the *Hôtel de la Plage*, 21 av de Gaulle (☎02.97.53.75.92; ②; closed Dec–March), offers some cosy little rooms above its busy bar. The *Grand Largue* (☎02.97.53.71.58; ④; closed mid-Nov to mid-Dec) is a considerably more luxurious option, with dinner menus from 140F/€21.34. Vedettes Thalassa (☎02.97.53.70.25) run **ferries** to the islands and across the gulf from the jetty nearby.

The two-star **campsite** *de Bilouris*, on the pointe de Kerners immediately north of Arzon (☎02.97.53.70.55; mid-Nov to Feb), is well poised for the less crowded beaches east of St-Gildas.

The Tumulus de Thumiac

Not far from the end of the peninsula, clearly visible to the north of the main road, the **Tumulus de Thumiac** is also known as the Butte de César, or "Caesar's Mount". From its summit, Julius Caesar is supposed to have watched the sea battle in which the Romans defeated the Veneti (see p.390) – the only naval victory they ever won away from the Mediterranean, and out on the ocean. In fact, excavations in the nineteenth century revealed a 5000-year-old burial, complete with 32 stone axes and a pearl necklace.

Today, it's easy enough to walk to the top of the tumulus, but there's nothing to see apart from the view over the gulf. A short way north, the ivy-covered twelfth-century **Moulin du Pen Castel** is no longer run as a restaurant, but still makes an attractive spot for a picnic.

East to the Vilaine: La Roche-Bernard

The southern shoreline of the Rhuys Peninsula blends imperceptibly into the northern bank of the estuary of the Vilaine, which flows into the sea roughly thirty kilometres southeast of Vannes. When the Vikings first settled this region, their longboats used the river to access the heart of Brittany. Approaches to the Vilaine were guarded by the fortified settlement of **LA ROCHE-BERNARD** on the south bank, where the harbour continued to serve as what the French call the *avant-port* for Redon and Rennes into the twentieth century. Thanks to a massive dam near **ARZAL**, 5km downstream, sea-going vessels can no longer enter the Vilaine but La Roche-Bernard remains a pretty little village that's well worth the detour down from the mighty suspension bridge that now carries the N165 *autoroute* across the Vilaine gorge towards Nantes.

Most of the village stands atop the rocky headland that gave it its name, and fine medieval buildings cluster around the lovely little central square, among them a flower-bedecked **hotel-restaurant**, *Les Deux Magots*, 3 place du Bouffay (☎02.99.90.60.75; ④; closed second fortnight in June & Oct). The harbour lies a short walk below, and holds a couple of small waterfront **bars**. In season, hour-long **river trips** depart every hour to explore the broad estuary waters as far downstream as the dam, offering close-up views of the densely wooded slopes along the north bank.

The Grande-Brière

South of the **River Vilaine** at La Roche-Bernard you leave the Morbihan – and technically you leave Brittany as well, entering the *département* of Loire Atlantique. The roads veer firmly east and west – to Nantes and La Baule respectively. Inland between them, as you approach the wide Loire estuary, are the otherworldly marshes of the **Grande-Brière**.

These 20,000 acres of peat bog have for centuries been deemed to be the common property of all who live in them. The scattered population, the *Briéroise*, continue to make their living by fishing for eels in the streams, gathering reeds, and – on the nine days permitted each year – cutting the peat. The few villages are known as *îles*, being hard granite outcrops in the boggy wastes. Most of them consist of a circular road around the inside of a ring of thatched cottages, slightly raised above the waters onto which they back. For easy access to the watery flatlands, filled with lilies and irises and browsed by Shetland ponies, each village is encircled by its own canal, or *curée*. The houses themselves typically consist of two rooms and a stable, with a door on the north side and windows on the south. A few crops are grown in the adjacent ring of fields, which always remain above high water.

This can be quite a captivating region for unhurried exploration – though, if you're simply passing through, the waterways are not very visible from the road unless you pause on one of the occasional humpback bridges. Instead, the widely touted attraction is **renting a punt**, known as a *chaland* or a *blain*. This activity seems to be promoted with the unstated intention of getting you lost for a few hours with your pole tangled in the rushes. Operators include La Chassée Neuve (☎02.40.01.24.64), based 6km northeast of La Baule at **ST-ANDRÉ-DES-EAUX**.

Much of the Grande-Brière has been designated as a **bird sanctuary**, with waterfowl the obvious main beneficiaries. The main **tourist office** for the region is on the northern fringes of the marshes, at 38 rue de la Brière in the village of **LA CHAPELLE-DES-MARAIS** (June–Sept daily 10am–12.30pm & 2.30–6.30pm; Oct–May Mon–Sat 10am–12.30pm & 2–6pm; ☎02.40.66.85.01), but the headquarters of the sanctuary itself is in the most authentic surviving village, the **ÎLE DE FEDRUN** (same hours; ☎02.40.91.68.68, *www.parc-naturel-briere.fr*). Filled with traditional dwellings, the village also has a small but pricey **hotel**, the *Auberge du Parc* (☎02.40.88.53.01; ④; closed Jan & Feb), where dinner menus start at 150F/€22.87.

The coast at the mouth of the Loire

There is something very surreal about emerging from the Brière to the coast at **La Baule**. For this is by far Brittany's most upmarket pocket – an imposing, moneyed landscape where the dunes are bonded together no longer with scrub and pines but with massive apartment blocks and luxury hotels. **St-Nazaire**, guarding the mouth of the Loire itself, is a run-down industrial port. However, in the vicinity of La Baule, **Guérande** is a superb medieval walled town, while **Piriac-sur-mer**, and to a lesser extent **Le Croisic**, are less frenetic alternatives to the giant resort.

Guérande

On the southwestern edge of the marshes of the Grande-Brière, just before you come to the sea, stands the gorgeous walled town of **GUÉRANDE**, which no visitor to the region should miss. Guérande gave its name to this peninsula, and derived its fortune from controlling the salt pans that form a chequerboard across the surrounding inlets. This "white country" is composed of bizarre-looking *oeillets*, each 70 to 80 square metres in extent, in which sea water, since Roman times, has been collected and evaporated.

Guérande today, a tiny little place, is still entirely enclosed by its stout fifteenth-century **ramparts**. Although you can't walk along them, a spacious promenade leads right the way around the outside, passing four fortified gateways; for half its length the broad old moat remains filled with water. Historically, the main entrance was the **Porte St-Michel** on the east side of town, the upper three floors of which now hold a small **museum** of local history (daily: April–Sept 10am–12.30pm & 2.30–7pm; Oct 10am–noon & 2–6pm; 20F/€3.05).

Within the walls, pedestrians throng the narrow cobbled streets during high season; the main souvenir on sale is locally produced salt, but abundant shops sell the usual trinkets from all over the world, and there are also lots of restaurants and crêperies. So long as the crowds aren't too oppressive, it makes a great day out, with the old houses bright with windowboxes. On Wednesdays and Saturdays, there's a market in full swing in the centre, next to the **church of St-Aubin**. Another, smaller church stands just to the south; this is **Notre Dame La Blanche**, where the second Treaty of Guérande was signed in 1381.

Practicalities

Guérande's **tourist office** is just outside the Porte St-Michel at 1 place du Marché au Bois (July & Aug Mon–Sat 9.30am–7pm, Sun 10am–1pm; Sept–June Mon–Sat 9.30am–12.30pm & 1.30–6pm; ☎02.40.24.96.71, *office.tourisme.guerande @wanadoo.fr*).

Near St-Aubin church, but tucked out of sight behind the market, the pretty *Roc-Maria*, 1 rue des Halles (☎02.40.24.90.51; ③; closed mid-Nov to mid-Dec, plus Wed & Thurs in low season), is a lovely little village **hotel** that offers cosy rooms above a crêperie in a fifteenth-century town house. Opposite the porte Vannetoise and the most impressive stretch of ramparts, to the north, the *Hôtel de Voyageurs*, 1 place du 8-Mai-1945 (☎02.40.24.90.13; ③; closed Sun evening & Mon in low season; restaurant closed Oct–March), is a *logis* serving good menus from 102F/€15.55. A short way further around the walls, near the tourist office, the *Remparts*, 14–15 bd du Nord (☎02.40.24.90.69; ③; closed Jan; restaurant closed Sun evening & Mon Sept–June), offers less appealing rooms but better food.

Of the many **restaurants** in the centre, the *Vieux Logis*, set within the walled garden of a grand old house facing the main church doors at 1 place de la Psalette (☎02.40.62.09.73), has something to suit every palette, with traditional menus from 105F/€16.01 at dinner, plus a separate crêperie/pizzeria.

Piriac-sur-mer

If you prefer your seaside resorts quiet and peaceful, head west from Guérande to **PIRIAC-SUR-MER**, 13km distant, instead of continuing to La Baule. Although the adjacent headland offers some fine sandy beaches within a couple of minutes' walk from the centre, the pleasant little village itself turns its back on the Atlantic, preferring to face the protective jetty that curls back into the little bay to shield its small fishing fleet.

Practicalities

Piriac's twisting narrow lanes see enough tourists in summer to keep half a dozen crêperies in business, of which the nicest is the *St-Michel*, whose courtyard tables take up most of the place de la Chope, between the old granite church and the beach.

There are also a handful of **hotels**, including the atmospheric and attractively situated, if slightly faded *Hôtel-Restaurant de la Pointe*, 1 quai de Verdun (☎02.40.23.50.04; ③; closed Nov to mid-March, plus Wed in low season), looking out over the port, and the less characterful *Hôtel de la Poste*, in a large house at 26 rue de la Plage (☎02.40.23.50.90; ④; closed Nov–March), a few streets in from the sea. The shady four-star *Parc du Guibel* (☎02.40.23.52.67; closed Oct–March), further on towards Mesquer, is among the best of several local **campsites**.

La Baule

LA BAULE certainly is a place apart from its rival Breton resorts, almost any of which can seem appealingly rustic and shambolic by comparison. Sited on the long stretch of dunes that link the former island of Le Croisic to the mainland, it owes its existence to a violent storm in 1779 that engulfed the old town of Escoublac in silt from the Loire, and thereby created a wonderful crescent of sandy beach that's sometimes claimed to be the largest in Europe. That has survived, albeit now lined for several kilometres with a Riviera-style spread of palm-tree-fronted hotels and residences.

Neither La Baule's permanence nor its affluence seems in any doubt these days. This is a resort that very firmly imagines itself in the south of France: around the crab-shaped bay, bronzed nymphettes and would-be Clint Eastwoods ride across the sands into the sunset against a backdrop of cruising lifeguards, horse-dung removers and fantastically priced cocktails. It can be fun if you feel like a break from the more subdued Breton attractions – and the beach is undeniably impressive. It's not a place to imagine you're going to enjoy strolling around in search of hidden charms, however; the backstreets have an oddly rural feel, but hold nothing of any interest.

Practicalities

La Baule has two **gares SNCF**, the barely used La-Baule-les-Pins, and the main La-Baule-Escoublac on place Rhin-et-Danube (☎08.36.35.35.35), where the

TGVs from Paris arrive. The **gare routière** is at 4 place de la Victoire (☎02.40.11.53.00).

Full details on staying in La Baule can be had from the **tourist office**, away from the seafront in a new postmodern office at 8 place de la Victoire (mid-May to mid-Sept daily 9am–7.30pm; mid-Sept to mid-May Mon–Sat 9.30am–noon & 2–6pm; ☎02.40.24.34.44), or from the local **Web site** *www.pays-blanc.com*.

Few of the **hotels** are cheap, particularly in high season, and in low season more than half of them are closed. The best-value options are near the main *gare SNCF*, less than 1km from the beach; these include *Le Clémenceau*, 42 av Clémenceau (☎02.40.60.21.33; ③; closed Dec), and the *Marini*, 22 av Clémenceau (☎02.40.60.23.29; ③). The finest of the many local **campsites** is the four-star *La Roseraie*, 2km back from the beach at 20 av Sohier (☎02.40.60.46.66, *la-roserie@post.club-internet.fr*; closed Oct–March).

Right in the centre, set back less than 50m from the sea and not far from the tourist office, is the *Lutetia* at 13 av des Evens (☎02.40.60.25.81; ⑤), where the *Rossini* restaurant (closed Sun evening & Mon) offers magnificent fish cookery on menus that start at 125F/€19.06.

Le Croisic and beyond

The small port of **LE CROISIC**, sheltering from the ocean around the corner of the headland, is probably a more realistic (and to many perceptions, more attractive) place to stay than La Baule.

These days Le Croisic is basically a pleasure port, but fishing boats do still sail from its harbour, near the very slender mouth of the bay, and there's a modern **fish market** near the long Tréhic jetty, where you can go to see the day's catch auctioned. Incidentally, the hills on either side of the harbour, Mont Lénigo and Mont Esprit, are not natural; they are formed from the ballast left by the ships of the salt trade.

Practicalities

If you are staying in Le Croisic, choose between the **hotels** *Les Nids*, 15 rue Pasteur (☎02.40.23.00.63; ④; closed mid-Nov to March), which has its own swimming pool, or the purple-and-white *Estacade*, near the end of the port at 4 quai de Lénigo (☎02.40.23.03.77; ③), where the 95F/€14.48 menu includes *soupe de poissons* and fish of the day.

Close by, all around the rocky sea coast known as the **Grande Côte**, are a whole range of **campsites**. Just outside Le Croisic itself is the *Océan* (☎02.40.23.07.69; closed Oct–March); and at Batz, another former island, is the *Govelle* (☎02.40.23.91.63; closed Oct–March).

For equally good beaches and a chance of cheaper **hotel** accommodation, you could alternatively go east from La Baule to **PORNICHET** (though preferably keeping away from the plush marina) or to the tiny **ST-MARC**, where in 1953 Jacques Tati filmed *Monsieur Hulot's Holiday*.

St-Nazaire

The best sandy coves in the region, bizarrely enough, are to be found on the outskirts of **ST-NAZAIRE**: just off to the west, they are linked by wooded paths and almost deserted. But the city itself is gloomy, distinguishable from afar by the black silhouettes of its mighty cranes and the soaring arch of the Loire bridge. Bombed to extinction in World War II, its shipyards, in more or less continuous operation since they built Julius Caesar's fleet, are closing all around it.

Practicalities

The one reason you might want to stay in St-Nazaire is the relative ease of finding inexpensive **hotel** space – so elusive in this area in summer. Modern, well-equipped options include the *Touraine*, 4 av de la République (☎02.40.22.47.56; ①), and the *Korali*, opposite the train station on place de la Gare (☎02.40.01.89.89; ③).

South of the Loire

From St-Nazaire you can cross the mouth of the Loire via an inspired piece of engineering, the **Pont St-Nazaire**. This is a great elongated S-curve of a suspension bridge, its lines only visible at an acute angle at either end. A hefty toll is demanded for the privilege of driving across its three-kilometre length, but bikes go for free.

From this high viewpoint (up to 131m), you can see that the **Loire** is a definite climatic dividing line (a point regularly confirmed by French television weather bulletins). To the north of the river, the houses have steep grey-slate roofs against the storms; to the south, in the Pays de Retz, the roofs are flat and red-tiled. Nonetheless the vast deposits of Loire silt have affected both banks of the huge estuary – they buried the ancient town of Montoise on the southern side just as they did Escoublac to the north.

As you continue **south** along the coast, Brittany begins to slip away. Dolmens stand above the ocean, and the rocky coast is interspersed with bathing beaches, but the climate, the architecture, the countryside and, most obvious of all, the vineyards make it clear that this is the start of the south.

Pornic

The **Pays de Retz** coast is developed for most of its length – an almost unbroken line of holiday flats, Pepsi, frites and crêpes stands. **PORNIC** is the nicest of the resorts, with a functional fishing port and one of "Bluebeard" Gilles de Rais' many castles. It is a small place: you can walk beyond the harbour and along the cliffs to a tiny beach where the rock walls glitter from phosphorescent sea water.

The **hotels** in town are not cheap, though they are better value than those of La Baule. The *Relais St Gilles*, 7 rue Fernand de Mun (☎02.40.82.02.25; ③; closed mid-Oct to mid-March), just down the road from the post office, is the most reasonable, with a menu to match.

Inland towards Nantes

As you head away from the coast, towards the metropolis of Nantes, the countryside is once more marshy, although richer than that of the Brière, with some scenic lakes and waterways. The largest of the lakes, the **Grand-Lieu**, contains two drowned villages, Murin and Langon. Along the Loire **estuary** itself, the towns are depressed and depressing, their traditional industries struck hard by unemployment.

For **NANTES** itself, see p.337.

travel details

Trains

Auray to: Plouharnel (July & Aug 5–8 times daily; 15min), with connecting buses to Carnac and La Trinité; Quiberon (July & Aug 5–8 times daily; 40min).

Le Croisic to: La Baule (5 daily TGVs; 10min); Nantes (5 daily TGVs; 1hr 10min; 5 slower services; 1hr 20min); Paris (5 daily TGVs; 3hr 10min); St-Nazaire (5 daily TGVs; 20min).

Vannes to: Auray (7 daily TGVs; 15min; 7 daily slower services; 30min); Lorient (7 daily TGVs; 30min; 7 daily slower services; 1hr); Quimper (7 daily TGVs; 1hr 15min; 7 daily slower services; 2hr).

Buses

Auray to: Carnac (4 daily; 30min); Quiberon (4 daily; 1hr); Vannes (4 daily; 30min). Services operated by Transports Le Bayon (☎02.97.57.31.31).

Lorient to: Carnac (2 daily; 1hr); Pontivy (4 daily; 1hr).

Vannes to: Auray (8 daily; 30min); Carnac (8 daily; 1hr 15min); Josselin (8 daily; 1hr); Larmor-Baden (8 daily; 40min); La Roche-Bernard (8 daily; 45min); Nantes (8 daily; 1hr 30min); Quiberon (8 daily; 1hr 45min); Rennes (8 daily; 2hr). All these services run by TTO (☎02.97.47.29.64). Vannes to: Arzon (4 daily; 50min); Pontivy (3 daily; 1hr); Ploërmel (4 daily; 50min) via Elven (15min) and Malestroit (30min), with CTM (☎02.97.01.22.10) from the place de la Gare. Also to: Port-Blanc (4 daily; 25min), for the Île-aux-Moines, with Transport Cautru, 26 rue Hoche (☎02.97.47.22.86).

Ferries

Belle Île: For details of ferries to Belle-Île from Quiberon, Lorient, Vannes, Locmariaquer, La Trinité, and Port-Navalo, see p.356.

Groix: For details of ferries to Groix from Lorient, see p.350.

Gulf of Morbihan: For details of gulf tours and trips to the islands, from Vannes, Locmariaquer, Auray, Port-Navalo, La Trinité and Le Bono: See p.375 or contact Navix (☎02.97.46.60.00, *navix@wanadoo.fr*) or Compagnie des Îles (☎02.97.46.18.19).

Houat and Hoëdic: For details of ferries to Houat and Hoëdic from Quiberon, Vannes, Port-Navalo, Le Croisic and La Turballe, see p.358.

Lorient: Shuttle service to Port-Louis, 20 per day (☎02.97.33.40.55).

Flights

Lorient to: Paris (Easter–Oct 2 daily; Lorient ☎02.97.82.32.93, Vannes ☎02.97.60.78.79); Belle-Île, by arrangement with Insul'Air (☎02.97.31.41.14).

Quiberon: Easter–Oct, trips around Gulf of Morbihan, over Carnac, and to Belle-Île (☎02.97.31.83.09 or 02.97.30.40.00).

PART THREE

THE

CONTEXTS

A BRIEF HISTORY OF BRITTANY AND NORMANDY

Although Brittany and Normandy have belonged to the French State for over 450 years, they have been distinct entities throughout recorded history and their traditions and interests remain separate.

Brittany, for most of the five millennia during which its past can be traced, drew its cultural links and influences not inland, from the rest of France, but from the Atlantic seaboard. Isolated both by the difficulty of its marsh and moorland terrain, and its sheer distance from the heartland of Europe, it was nonetheless at the centre of a sophisticated prehistoric culture that was intimately connected with those of Britain and Ireland. It is populated today by the descendants of the Celtic immigrants who arrived from Britain and Ireland at around the time that the Romans were leaving Gaul. The "golden age" of Brittany came in the fifteenth century, when it was ruled as an independent duchy – but it was eventually absorbed into France after centuries of military and dynastic struggles with the English.

The economic decline of the province in recent centuries is attributed by Breton nationalists wholly to the union with France. Other factors, inevitably, were also at play, but it's certainly true to say that the rulers of France often ignored or oppressed their westernmost region, and even now the current revival of Brittany's fortunes is largely due to the conscious attempt to revive the old pan-Celtic trading routes.

Normandy has no equivalent prehistoric remains, and only very briefly did it possess the identity of an independent nation. Its founders were Scandinavian, the Vikings who raided along the Seine in the ninth century. These Northmen gave the region its name, and were the warriors who brought it military glory in the great Norman age of the eleventh century, when William conquered England and his nobles controlled swaths of land as far afield as Sicily and the Near East. They were also responsible for the cathedrals, castles and monasteries that still stand as the most enduring monuments of Normandy's past.

The Normans blended into the general mass of the population, both in France and in England, and Normandy itself was formally surrendered to Louis IX by Henry III of England in 1259. After the fluctuations of the Hundred Years' War, the province was firmly integrated into France, and all but disappears from history until the Allied invasion of 1944. Supposedly, a handful of Normans still regard Queen Elizabeth II as the true duchess of Normandy – which is one of the many titles she still bears. The majority of contemporary Normans, however, put their faith in the industrial and agricultural wealth of the province, and take pride in their individualism and conservatism.

THE MEGALITHS OF BRITTANY

Megalithic sites can be found all around the Mediterranean, most notably in Malta and Sardinia, and along the Atlantic seaboard from Spain to Scandinavia. Among the most significant are Newgrange in Ireland, Stonehenge in England, and the Ring of Brodgar in the Orkneys. However, it is by no means certain that the megalith-building culture originated in the Mediterranean and spread out to the "barbarian" outposts of Europe. In fact, the tumuli, alignments and single standing stones of Brittany are of pre-eminent importance. The very words used for the megaliths are Breton: *menhir* (long stone), *dolmen* (flat stone), *cromlech* (stone circle).

Archeological evidence suggests that late Stone Age settlements had been established at various points along the Breton coast by around

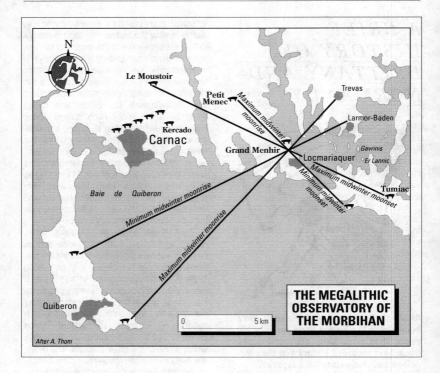

N

Le Moustoir

Petit Menec

Maximum midwinter moonrise

Trevas

Larmor-Baden

Kercado

Carnac

Grand Menhir

Gavrinis

Er Lannic

Locmariaquer

Maximum midwinter moonset

Baie de Quiberon

Minimum midwinter moonset

Tumiac

Minimum midwinter moonrise

Maximum midwinter moonrise

Quiberon

0   5 km

THE MEGALITHIC OBSERVATORY OF THE MORBIHAN

After A. Thom

6000 BC. Soon afterwards, the culture responsible either evolved to become the megalith builders, or was displaced by megalith-building newcomers. Dated at 5700 BC, the tumulus of Kercado at **Carnac**, in southern Brittany, appears to be the earliest stone construction in Europe, predating the palace of Knossos on Crete and even the Egyptian pyramids.

Each megalithic centre seems to have had its own distinct styles and traditions. Brittany has relatively few stone circles, and a greater proportion of freestanding stones; fewer burials, and more evidence of ritual fires; different styles of carving; and, uniquely, the sheer complexity of the Carnac alignments, which may be an astronomical observatory. (The fact that so many megalithic remains are on bleak seaside heathland sites may just be because these were the most likely to survive; for example those at Rétiers and Fougères do not fit the stereotype.)

Little is known of the **people** who erected the megaliths. Only rarely have skeletons been found in the graves, but what few there have been seem to indicate a short, dark, hairy race with a life expectancy of no more than the mid-30s. Legends speak of shambling subhuman giants who served as their slaves, assisting Merlin, for example, in bringing the slabs of Stonehenge from Wales, and building the Giant's Causeway on the coast of Antrim in Northern Ireland. What is certain is that the civilization was a long-lasting one; the earliest and the latest constructions at Carnac are over five thousand years apart.

As for the actual **purpose of the stones**, there are numerous theories and few definite conclusions. Flaubert commented: "those who like mythology see them as the Pillars of Hercules; those who like natural history see here a symbol of the Python . . . lovers of astronomy see a zodiac". In the eighteenth century, for example, enthusiasts managed to see snakes in everything, and declared the megalithic sites to be remnants of some Druidic serpent cult. In fact, the stones were already ancient before the Druids appeared. Innumerable theses have wandered off into considerations of "Lost Atlantis", water divining, mysterious psychic energies and extraterrestrial assistance.

The **theories** that have become most fashionable with the general public these days see the megaliths as part of a vast system of **astronomical measurement**, record-keeping, and prediction. Precise measurements of sites all over Europe suggest that they share a standard measure of length, the "megalithic yard" – equivalent to 83 modern centimetres. In Brittany, the argument goes, the now fallen Grand Menhir of Locmariaquer was erected, using this prehistoric calibration, as a "universal lunar foresight". Its alignments with eight other sites are said to correspond to the eight extreme points of the rising and setting of the moon during its 18.61-year cycle. The Golfe de Morbihan made an ideal location for such a marking stone – set on a lagoon surrounded by low peninsulas, the menhir was visible from all directions. Once the need for the Grand Menhir was decided upon, it would then have taken hundreds of years of careful observation of the moon to fix the exact spot for it. It is thought that this was done by lighting fires on the top of high poles at trial points on the crucial nights every nine years. The alignments of Carnac are thus explained as the graph paper, as it were, on which the lunar movements were plotted.

This "megalithic observatory" explanation, researched in great detail by Professor Thom – despite being hindered by occasional "encounters with irate peasants" – and most clearly expounded in his *Megalithic Remains in Britain and Brittany* (1978), is certainly appealing. However, **rival experts** have come up with damning counterevidence. To quote from Aubrey Burl's authoritative *Megalithic Brittany* (1985): "of the eight proposed backsights, three do not exist, and of the five others the Carnac mound at Tumiac is not accurately placed, the Goulvarch menhir, the stone at Kerran, the Carnac mound of Le Moustoir with its menhir, and the passage grave of Petit-Mont, are too dissimilar in architecture and date to be convincing purpose-built Neolithic viewing-stations." Controversy rages as to whether the Grand Menhir ever stood or, if it did, whether it fell or was broken up before the eight supposedly associated sites came into being, and the measurements are accused of ignoring the fact that the sea level in southern Brittany 6600 years ago was 10m lower than it is today.

In any case, the stones at Carnac have been so greatly eroded that perhaps it is little more than wishful thinking to imagine that their original size, shape and orientation can be accurately determined. They have been knocked down and pulled out by farmers seeking to cultivate the land; they have been quarried for use in making roads; they have been removed by landowners angry at the trespass of tourists and scientists; nineteenth-century pseudo-scientists have tampered with them, re-erecting some and shifting others; and what may have gone on in much earlier periods is anyone's guess.

An alternative approach, more popular with conventional archeologists, places much greater emphasis on sociological factors. This argues that the stones date from the great period of transition when humankind was changing from a predatory role to a productive one, and that they can only have been put in place by the co-ordinated efforts of a large and stable **community**. It's possible that the megaliths were erected by Neolithic settlers, who generation by generation advanced across Europe from the east bringing advances in agriculture. As they came into conflict with existing Stone Age groups, they may have set up menhirs as territorial markers. The ability to construct large monuments – which probably required the acquisition of a large agricultural surplus – would also have demonstrated that the group in question was "favoured" by the gods, and thus of "pure" or "noble" lineage.

An experiment carried out in 1979 demonstrated that 260 people, using rollers, were required to set up a 32,000-kilogramme stone, together with a large number of auxiliaries to provide food and shelter. The united physical exertion created very much a festival atmosphere, and the participants described the event as a "bonding" experience. Those who originally and perhaps unwillingly dragged the Carnac stones into place might feel that to be a trifle sentimental. Even so, it does make some sense to imagine the act of setting up a menhir as serving a valuable social purpose, both as an achievement in its own right and as a celebration of some other event. The annual or occasional setting-up of a new stone is easier to envisage than the vast effort required to erect them all at once – in which case the social significance of constructing these lines, mounds and circles could have been of greater importance than any physical characteristics of the arrangements themselves.

For all the pervasive legends, the megaliths cannot be attributed to the Celts. Even so, theological parallels have been drawn between ancient and modern **Breton beliefs**. It is argued that there is a uniquely Breton attitude to death, dating back thousands of years, in which the living are in everyday communication with the dead. The phenomenon of the "parish close" is said to mirror the design of the ancient passage graves, with the Christian ossuary serving the same function as the buried passageways of the old tombs – a link between the place of the dead and the place of the living.

True or false, the popular significance of the prehistoric sites was something about which later Christian authorities were somewhat ambivalent. They felt it necessary to place crosses on the top of many menhirs, or even to destroy them altogether. There are reports of the "Indecent Stone" at Reguiny being "cut down and made harmless" in 1825, and of steps being taken to stop naked couples sliding down the Grand Menhir on May Day as a fertility rite, or rubbing against the "protuberances" of the Kerloas menhir.

CELTS AND ROMANS

While Brittany in particular prospered during the **Bronze Age** and was a major manufacturer of bronze axes that were distributed throughout Atlantic Europe, its peoples were left behind by the technological advances of the **Iron Age**, and became increasingly peripheral from around 700 BC onwards. The economy turned instead towards supplying raw materials to the more developed cultures of Germany and southern France, and it is as traders in **tin and copper** that both the Bretons and the Normans make their first appearance in recorded history. Small trading ports emerged all along the Atlantic coast, and the routes went up the rivers Loire and Seine. The tin itself was mined in both Brittany and Cornwall, and the Seine became important as the "Tin Road", the most direct means for the metals to be transported towards the heart of Europe. Iron Age forts, traces of one of which remain in the forest of Huelgoat, show

evidence of large-scale, stable communities even far inland.

That was why the **Romans**' top priority, when they came to Gaul centuries later, was to secure control of the Seine valley and tie the province firmly into the network of empire. Brittany, less accessible to the invading armies, was able to put up a more spirited resistance, although sadly there was no such last-ditch rebel stronghold as Astérix's fictional village. The **Breton Gauls**, descendants of a first influx of Celts, were divided into five major tribes, each of which controlled an area roughly corresponding to the modern *départements*.

The most powerful of these tribes were the **Veneti**, based in the Morbihan with what is now Vannes as their capital. The decisive sea battle in which they were defeated in 56 BC took place around the Golfe de Morbihan, and was the only major naval battle the Romans ever won outside the Mediterranean. Seafaring was not one of the Romans' strong points – hence their predilection for roads and foot-slogging – but on this occasion their galleys, built somewhere near St-Nazaire, had far superior mobility to the leather-sailed ships of the Veneti. The cost of defeat for the tribes was severe; those who were not killed were sold into slavery, and their children mutilated. Julius Caesar was there to see the battle; he went no further than Auray, but the whole Breton peninsula was swiftly conquered, and incorporated with much of Normandy into the province of Armorica.

Roman Armorica experienced five hundred years of peace, though without the benefit of any great prosperity. While the Roman-built roads were the first efficient means of land communication, they served mainly to channel wealth away towards the centre of their empire. Walled cities were founded, such as Rennes, Vannes, Rouen and Caen, but little was done to change, let alone improve, the lives of the native population. During the fourth century, a couple of Bretons, Magnence and Maximus, managed to become emperors of Rome, but by then pirate incursions had made fortifications essential along the coast.

What civilizing effect the Romans had had disappeared in any case during the **barbarian invasions** as the empire disintegrated at the start of the fifth century. The one thread of continuity was provided by the **Christian** Church.

The first Christians had already arrived in Normandy during Roman rule, and at Rouen the bishopric had been established by St Mellon as early as 300 AD. They were followed in the fifth and sixth centuries by waves of Celtic immigrants crossing from Britain to Brittany. Traditional history considered these to be "Dark Ages" of terror and chaos throughout Europe, with the immigrants as no more than panic-stricken refugees. However, recent evidence of stable diplomatic and trading contact across the Channel suggests that there was a much more ordered process of movement and interchange.

The vigorous Welsh and Irish missionaries named their new lands **Little Britain**, and their Christianity supplanted the old Celtic and Roman gods. The era is characterized by great legendary confrontations of elemental forces – the Devil grappling with the Archangel Michael from Dol to Mont St-Michel, St Pol driving out the "laidley worm" from the Île de Batz – symbolizing the forcible expulsion of paganism. Often the changes were little more than superficial: crosses were erected on top of menhirs, mystical springs and wells became the sites of churches, Christian processions such as *pardons* traced circuits of megalithic sites, and ancient tales of magic and witchcraft were retold as stories of Jesus and the saints. The names of innumerable Celtic religious leaders – Malo, Brieuc, Pol – have survived in place names, even if the Church has never officially recognized them as saints.

The cultural links with Britain and Ireland meant that Brittany played an important role in many of the **Arthurian legends**. Breton minstrels, like their Welsh counterparts, did much to popularize the tales in the Middle Ages. None of the local claimants to Arthur's Camelot carry much conviction, although Tristan who loved Iseult came from Brittany (the lovers may have hidden at Trémazan castle in Finistère), as did King Ban and his son Lancelot. Sir Galahad found the Holy Grail somewhere in Brocéliande Forest, said also to be the home of such diverse residents as Merlin, Morgan le Fay and the Fisher King.

Such legends reflect the fact that, for all this time, central Brittany was an almost impenetrable wilderness, and the region as a whole was split into two separate petty monarchies, Dumnonia in the north and Cornubia (the basis of Cornouaille) in the south. Charlemagne amalgamated the two by force under **Frankish control** in 799, after they had consistently failed to pay tribute. When the Frankish Empire began to fall apart, their appointee as governor, **Nominoë**, seized the opportunity to become the first leader of an independent Brittany, by defeating Charles the Bald in the Battle of Redon (near modern La Bataille) in 845. He has taken on the status of a prototype independent leader in Breton history.

Without Celtic immigration on anything like the same scale, it took longer for **Normandy** to become fully Christianized. It was only when it too came under the control of Charlemagne's **Merovingian** dynasty that the newly founded monasteries of Jumièges and St-Wandrille became pre-eminent.

As the Franks' authority weakened over the succeeding centuries, there were repeated Viking raids along the Seine, while raids on the Breton coast drove many monks into exile across the Channel. Major Viking incursions took place in the second half of the ninth century, interspersed with attempts to conquer England. They came more often and for longer, until in 911 King Charles the Simple acknowledged the inevitable and granted their leader **Rollo** formal title to the **Duchy of Normandy**. A few years later, in 932 AD, the Breton prince known as Alain Barbetorte returned from England to re-establish control over Brittany, and many of its monasteries were subsequently rebuilt in the new Romanesque style.

THE NORMANS

In the eleventh century **the Normans** became one of the most significant forces in Europe. Not only did the Dukes of Normandy invade and conquer England, but Norman mercenaries and adventurers fought to gain lands for themselves wherever they found the opportunity. They insinuated themselves into the wars of Italy, individually acquiring control of Aversa, Apulia and Calabria, and most of Sicily, their greatest prize. They took part in the church's wars, too, fighting in campaigns in Greece against Byzantium, and in the First Crusade – which in 1098 saw the Norman leader Bohemond take Antioch.

In their adopted French homeland, the pagan Scandinavians had so rapidly acquired the culture, language and religion of their new subjects that spoken Norse had died out in Rouen by the time of Rollo's grandson, Duke Richard I. Yet they were still seen as a race apart – and not a very pleasant one at that. One authority describes them as without exception physically repellent, cruel and unscrupulous.

Duke William's **invasion of England** is portrayed by the Bayeux Tapestry as a just struggle: the result solely of William's conviction that he was the rightful heir to Edward the Confessor, a succession acknowledged under oath by Harold. Be that as it may, the sheer speed of what proved to be such a permanent conquest indicates the extent of Norman power at the time. Having crossed the Channel to defeat the usurper Harold in September 1066, the Conqueror was crowned king in Westminster Abbey on Christmas Day, and by the next Easter was secure enough to be able to return to Normandy. The Battle of Hastings was a decisive moment in the balance of Europe. Almost paradoxically, the Norsemen from France finally freed England from the threat of invasion from Scandinavia, which had persisted for centuries up until 1070. English attention was thus reorientated towards the mainland of Europe – a shift that was to have a major impact on history.

The Norman capacity for **organization** was primarily responsible not just for the military triumphs, but also for the consolidation of power and wealth that followed. The Domesday Book, which catalogued the riches of England, was paralleled by a similar undertaking in Sicily, the *Catalogus Baronum*. William's son Henry introduced trial by jury in the king's courts – justice that had to be paid for. Henry II established the Exchequer to collect royal revenue.

Intellectually, too, the Normans were dominant; the Abbey of Bec-Hellouin, for example, was a renowned centre of learning, inspired first by Lanfranc and then by the theologian Anselm, each of whom moved on to become archbishop of Canterbury. And **architecturally**, the wealth and technical expertise of the Normans made possible the construction of such lasting monuments as the cathedrals of Bayeux, Coutances and Durham, and the monasteries of Mont St-Michel, Jumièges and Caen.

The twelfth-century "**Anglo-Normans**" who invaded Ireland were recognizably descended from the army of the Conqueror, and Norman French remained the legal and administrative language of England until 1400. Elsewhere the mark of the conquerors was less distinct. The Norman kings of Sicily did not style themselves Normans, and ruled over a cosmopolitan society dependent largely on the skills of Moslem craftsmen. Their architecture barely resembles what is thought of today as "Norman", and the Norman bloodline soon vanished into the general population of Sicily.

However, for the duchy and the kingdom on either side of the Channel, the shared rulers made close connections inevitable. The Norman lords in England required luxury items to be imported. Flemish weavers were encouraged to settle in London and East Anglia, and gradually the centre of affluence and importance shifted away from Normandy. By the time Henry II, great-grandson of William the Conqueror, inherited the throne, England was a major power and the seeds of the Hundred Years' War had been sown. Fifteen years later Château Gaillard on the Seine was taken by **Philippe Auguste**, and Normandy for the first time became part of France.

THE HUNDRED YEARS' WAR

While Normandy was at the height of its power, the Bretons lived in constant fear of invasion by their belligerent neighbours. Although their own leaders had managed to prevent a parallel Viking takeover of **Brittany**, it was at the price of numerous **warlords** setting up their own private strongholds. Their emergence seriously weakened the authority of Nominoë's successors, and the resultant anarchy devastated the Breton economy. Frequent power bids by the Norman English and the kings of France – the Hundred Years War – hardly helped the situation.

Bertrand du Guesclin, born in 1321 in the unprepossessing town of Broons, south of Dinan, was the outstanding military genius of the Middle Ages. After an ignominious start, when his father disowned him because of his ugliness, he practised his novel tactics as an outlaw chief in the heart of Brittany. With little truck for chivalric conventions, he simplified the chaotic feudal map, and in a bewildering succession of French and Spanish campaigns earned the command of the French army. Eschewing prearranged battles in favour of ambush and general guerrilla tactics, he taught the French to fight dirty – in medieval terms. Nobles were forced to dismount and fight on foot, while the fact that his soldiers were paid ensured that they did not alienate the peasantry by plundering. This formidable man was also responsible for the development of the use of gunpowder, combined with new assault techniques capable of devastating the strongest fortresses.

The net result of du Guesclin's strategies was that by 1377 the English had been driven almost completely out of France. Virtually every town and castle in Brittany and Normandy seems to have some du Guesclin connection; not only did he live, besiege or fight almost everywhere, but after his death in 1380 parts of his body were buried in no fewer than four different cities. Yet, despite all his myriad intrigues and battles, Brittany benefited very little from his activities.

The **Hundred Years War** resurfaced after du Guesclin's death, with much of the fighting taking place in Normandy. Henry V of England recaptured the province step by step, until by 1420 he was in a position to demand recognition of his claim to the French throne. Eight years later, the French were defending their last significant stronghold, Orléans on the Loire. It was here that the extraordinary figure of **Joan of Arc** appeared on the scene and relieved the siege of the city. In a very different way to du Guesclin she ensured that the mass of ordinary, miserable peasants, not to mention the demoralized soldiers of the French army, made the enemy occupation untenable. Within two astonishing years, the Dauphin, not Henry, had been crowned, to become King Charles VII of France. Joan herself was captured by the Burgundian allies of the occupiers, tried by a French bishop and an English commander, and burned at the stake as a witch in Rouen – for a full account, see p.95. Nonetheless, in 1449, Charles VII was able to make a triumphal entry into the regional capital. Within twelve months this latest 32-year English occupation of Normandy was at an end.

THE DUCHY OF BRITTANY

Breton involvement in the opening stages of the second phase of the Hundred Years' War was minimal and from 1399 to 1442 **Duc Jean V** took a neutral stand, allowing the economy of the province to prosper. Fishing, shipbuilding and sail manufacture developed, accompanied by a flowering of the arts. It was in this period

that the Kreisker chapel and the church of Folgoët were built.

Although involvement in the Anglo-French conflict was inevitable, Jean's heirs for a time continued to rule over a successful and **independent duchy**. Arthur III, duke in the mid-fifteenth century, had fought alongside Joan of Arc but used his connections with the French army to protect Breton autonomy. His successor, however, Duke François II, was less astute. Brittany, the last large region of present-day France to resist agglomeration, was a very desirable prize for King Louis XI. To resist encroachment, François needed allies beyond France; and in looking for those allies he antagonized and alarmed the French. A pretext was eventually found for the royal army to invade Brittany, where the Breton army was defeated at the battle of St-Aubin-du-Cormier in 1488. Duke François was forced to concede to the French king the right to determine his own daughter's marriage, and died of shame (so the story goes) within a few weeks.

François's heiress, **Duchess Anne**, was to be the last ruler of an independent Brittany. Having once been engaged to the Prince of Wales, she then married Maximilian of Austria by proxy in December 1490, in the hope of a strong alliance against the French. Charles VIII of France (who was himself in theory married to Maximilian's daughter) demanded adherence to the treaty of 1488, captured Nantes, advanced north and west and proposed to Anne.

By and large the population preferred a royal wedding to death by starvation or massacre, and it duly took place on September 16, 1491. Anne bemoaned "Must I thus be so unfortunate and friendless as to have to enter into marriage with a man who has so ill-treated me?" – and then, to the amazement of all, the couple actually fell in love with each other. Despite the marriage, the duchy remained independent, but Anne was contractually obliged to marry Charles's successor should he die before they produced an heir. When Charles duly bumped his head and died in 1498, his successor, Louis XII, divorced his wife and married Anne. This time Anne's position was considerably stronger, and in the contract she laid down certain conditions that were to be a source of Breton pride and frustration for many centuries. The three main clauses stipulated that no taxes could be imposed without the consent of the Breton

États; conscripts were only to fight for the defence of Brittany; and Bretons could only be tried in their own courts. When Anne died, Bretons mourned – all records show that she was a genuinely loved leader.

In 1514, the still independent duchy passed to Anne's daughter Claude, whom the future François I of France married with every intention of incorporating Brittany into his kingdom. This he did, and the permanent **union of Brittany and France** was endorsed by the Breton *États* at Vannes in 1532. In theory, the act confirmed Anne's stipulations that all the rights and privileges of Brittany would be observed and safeguarded as inviolable. But it was rarely honoured and their subsequent violation by successive French kings and governments has been the source of conflict ever since.

THE ANCIEN RÉGIME

As the French Crown gradually consolidated its power and began to centralize its economy, the ports of the two western provinces developed, serving the **colonial interests** of the State. In fact as early as 1364 sailors from Dieppe had established the city of Petit Dieppe in what is now Sierra Leone. Le Havre was founded in 1517 to be France's premier Atlantic port and, between intermittent attacks and takeovers by the English, became a centre for the coffee and cotton markets. Sailors from Granville, Dieppe and Cherbourg set up colonies in Brazil, Canada, Florida and Louisiana.

In Brittany, St-Malo and Lorient were the two top trading ports, with the latter benefiting every time the English decided to harass Channel ports and shipping. **Jacques Cartier** of St-Malo sailed up the St Lawrence River and added Canada to the possession of the French Crown. Nantes too was an important base for trade with the Americas, India and the Middle East, with **slaves** one of the most profitable "commodities". Though the business of exploitation and battles with rival foreign ships was motivated by private profit, the net result was very much to the advantage of the State.

The early contact with England, and the cosmopolitan nature of its Channel ports, meant that Normandy became one of the main **Protestant** centres of France, with Caen and its university having very active Huguenot populations. The region was therefore in the front line when the **Wars of Religion** flared up in

1561–63, and again in 1574–76. When the Edict of Nantes with its Protestant privileges and immunities was revoked, large-scale Huguenot emigration took place, seriously damaging the local textile industry.

Brittany on the other hand was an area of minimal Protestant presence, and the Wars of Religion were only significant as a cover for a brief attempt to win back independence. Breton linen manufacture had taken advantage of the lack of French tolls and customs dues, and only declined much later – when England, post-Industrial Revolution, was flooding the market with mass-produced textiles.

Although the power of the French kings increased over the centuries, practical considerations meant that outlying regions were not always completely under royal control. The rural nobles were persistently lawless, and intermittent **peasant revolts** took place, such as that of the dispossessed *nu-pieds* in 1639. In 1675 came the most serious rebellion against the Crown, when Louis XIV's finance minister put a tax on tobacco, pewter and all legal documents to raise money for the war with Holland. This "Stamped Paper" revolt, which started with riots in Nantes, Rennes and Guingamp, soon spread to the country, with the peasants making demands very similar in their content to those of the revolutionaries over a hundred years later. The aristocracy took great delight in brutally crushing the uprising, pillaging several towns and stringing up insurgents and bystanders from every tree.

The reign of **Louis XIV** saw numerous infringements of Breton liberties, including the uprooting of vines throughout the province on the royal grounds that the people were all drunkards. If the Bretons could not get revenge they could at least be entertained by court scandals. In 1650 Louis's Superintendent of Finance, **Nicolas Fouquet**, bought the entire island of Belle-Île and fortified it as his own private kingdom. The alarmed king had to send D'Artagnan and the three musketeers to arrest him before his ambitious plans went any further.

While taxes on Brittany increased in the early eighteenth century, Normandy found new prosperity from the proximity of Paris for its edible produce. Lacemaking became a major regional industry, and several abbeys that had been closed during the Wars of Religion were now revitalized. However, by 1763 France had lost Canada and given up all pretensions to India. The ports declined and trade fell off as England became the workshop of the world.

THE REVOLUTION

The people of both Brittany and Normandy at first welcomed the **Revolution**. Breton representatives at the *États Généraux* in Paris seized the opportunity to air all Brittany's grievances, and the "Club Breton" they formed was the basis of the **Jacobins**. Caen, meanwhile, became the centre of the bourgeois **Girondist** faction. In August of 1789 it was a Breton *député* who proposed the abolition of privileges. However, under the Convention it became clear that the price to be paid for the elimination of the *ancien régime* was further reductions in local autonomy and the suppression of the Breton language.

Neither province was sympathetic to the execution of the king – in Rouen 30,000 people took to the streets to express their opposition. The Girondins came out worst in the factional infighting at the Convention, having opposed the abolition of the monarchy and supported the disastrous war in the Netherlands. Some Girondist deputies managed to flee the edict of June 2, 1793 which ordered their arrest, but the army they organized to march on Paris was defeated at Pacy-sur-Eure. The final major Norman contribution to Revolutionary history was provided on that same day by **Charlotte Corday** of Caen, when she stabbed Jean-Paul Marat in his bath.

The concerted attack on religion and the clergy was not happily received, particularly in Brittany where the Church was closely bound up with the region's independent identity. The attempt to conscript an army of 300,000 Bretons was deeply resented as an infringement of the Act of Union. The popular image of the Revolution in Brittany, where the riots and disturbances of 1787 had been crucial, was now further damaged by the brief **Reign of Terror** in 1793 of Carrier, the Convention's representative in Nantes. Under the slogan "all the rich, all the merchants are counter-revolutionaries", he killed perhaps 13,000 people in three months, by such methods as throwing prisoners into the Loire tied together in pairs. This was done without Tribunal sanction or approval, and Carrier was himself guillotined before the end of the year.

All this made Brittany an inevitable focal point for the Royalist **counter-revolution** known as the *Chouannerie*, which also had adherents in a few outlying areas of Normandy. A vast invasion force of exiled and foreign nobility, backed by the English, was supposed to sweep through France, rallying all dissenters to the Royalist flag. In the event only 8000 landed at Quiberon in 1795, and were not even capable of escaping from the self-imposed trap of the peninsula. They devastated what little they could before themselves being brutally massacred. Much of the local support was motivated by the age-old desire to win back independence, but the Breton *Chouans* ("screech owls") fighting elsewhere ended up being tarred with the same aristocratic brush and then abandoned to years of quixotic and doomed guerrilla warfare.

A rebel army continued to fight sporadically in the Cotentin and the Bocage until 1800, while in Brittany another **royalist revolt** in 1799 was easily crushed. In 1804, Cadoudal, "the last *Chouan*", was captured and executed in Paris, where he had gone to kidnap Napoléon – having refused the emperor's offer of a generalship if he surrendered.

The rebel movement lingered on until 1832, when the duchess of Berry failed to engage anyone's interest in the restoration of the *ancien régime*.

THE NINETEENTH CENTURY

Normandy, at the beginning of the nineteenth century, remained a wealthy region despite the crippling of its ports by the blockade imposed by the European coalition against Napoléon. It had proportionally five times as many people elegible, as property owners, to vote as the impoverished mountain areas of the south. Its agriculture accounted for eleven percent of France's produce on six percent of its land, while industry remained relatively unadvanced.

When protectionist tariffs were removed from grain in 1828, and Normandy was forced to compete with other producers, widespread **rural arson and tax riots** ensued. But, when the revolution of 1848 offered the prospect of socialism, the deeply conservative Catholic peasantry showed little enthusiasm for change. Even the re-emergence of a rural textile industry in the 1840s, relying on outworkers brutally exploited by the capitalists of Rouen, added no radical impetus.

The advent of the **railways** and the patronage of the imperial court encouraged the development of Normandy's resorts, while along the Seine water mills provided the power for the major spinning centres at Louviers, Évreux and Elbeuf. Serious decline did not come until the 1880s, when **rural depopulation** was brought on by emigration combined with a low birth rate – and a high death rate in which excessive drinking played a part.

Nineteenth-century Brittany was no longer an official entity, save as five *départements* of France. The railways were of negative benefit, submitting the province to competition from more heavily industrialized regions, while the Nantes–Brest canal did not achieve the expected success, and **emigration** increased. Culturally, the century witnessed a revival of Breton language, customs and folklore, but the initiative came from intellectuals, not the mainly illiterate masses.

Around the beginning of the **twentieth century** both provinces experienced a surge of artistic creativity, with painters such as Gauguin in Pont-Aven and Monet in Giverny, and such writers as Proust in Normandy and Pierre Loti in Brittany.

As everywhere in Europe, this idyll was shattered by the **Great War** – although removed from the actual battlefields, both Brittany and Normandy were dramatically affected. Brittany, for its size, suffered the heaviest death toll of anywhere in the world. The vast memorial at Ste-Anne-d'Auray is testimony to the extent of the loss, while a parallel spiritual grief can be seen in the dramatic growth in Normandy of the cult of the recently dead Thérèse of Lisieux. Symbols of a changing world are embodied in the two leading aristocratic families of the regions; the heir to the Rohans of Josselin was killed on the Somme, while Prince Louis de Broglie became the first physicist to question the solidity of matter.

WORLD WAR II AND THE BATTLE OF NORMANDY

That the **beaches of Normandy** were chosen as the site of the Allied invasion of Europe in June 1944 was by no means inevitable. Far from the major disputed areas and communication routes of Europe, Normandy had seen almost no military activity since the Hundred Years' War. But in that blazing summer six armies and millions of men fought bloody battles across the placid Norman countryside. A whole swath of the province was laid in ruins before Hitler's defensive line was broken and the road to Paris cleared.

France, under **Marshal Pétain**, had surrendered to the Germans in 1940. A year later, the Fascist armies turned east to invade the Soviet Union – America and Britain declaring full support for the Soviets but resisting Stalin's demand for a second front. In 1942 the two western powers promised a landing in northern France, but all that ensued was an abortive commando raid on Dieppe. By the time the second front materialized, the tide of the war had already been turned at Stalingrad.

The Germans had meanwhile fortified the whole northwest seaboard of Europe. Their **Atlantic Wall** was constructed from spring 1942 onwards by the Todt organization, previously responsible for building the German *autobahn* network, and used thirteen million cubic metres of concrete and 1.2 million tons of steel.

From the Allied point of view, any invasion site had to be within range of air support from Britain, which meant anywhere from Rotterdam to St-Malo. Nonetheless, the Nazis expected the attack to come at the Channel's narrowest point, across the Straits of Dover. The **D-Day invasion** of June 6, 1944, was presaged by months of intensive aerial bombardment across Europe, without concentrating too obviously on the chosen landing sites. In the event, the Nazis vastly overestimated Allied resources – two weeks after D-Day Rommel still thought the Normandy landings might be no more than a preliminary diversion to a larger-scale assault around Calais. After all, as a British photographic survey of the whole Norman coast – even prewar holiday snaps were requisitioned – had conclusively established, none of the Norman channel ports was susceptible to easy capture.

As a result, the landings used amphibious craft to storm the beaches of Normandy rather than its ports. On Utah Beach, the Atlantic Wall lasted for little more than five minutes; on Gold, Juno and Sword beaches, it was overrun in about an hour; and even on Omaha, where the sea turned red with blood, it took less than a day for the Allies to storm through.

Albert Speer summed up the failure of the wall by saying: "A fortnight after the first landings by the enemy, this costly effort was brought to nothing by an idea of simple genius . . the invasion forces brought their own harbours with them". These **"Mulberry" harbours**, as described on p.135, proved the key to the Allied victory. The basic plan was for the British and Commonwealth forces under Montgomery to strike for Caen, the pivot around which the Americans (whose General Eisenhower was in overall command) were to swing following their own landings further west.

Not everything went smoothly. There are appalling stories of armoured cars full of men plunging straight to the bottom of the sea as they rolled off landing craft unable to get near enough to the shore. Many of the early objectives took much longer to capture than was originally envisaged – the British took weeks rather than hours to reach Caen, while American hopes of a rapid seizure of the deep-water port at Cherbourg were thwarted. Most notorious of all, the opportunity to capture the bulk of the German army, which was all but surrounded in the "Falaise pocket", was lost.

On D-Day itself, almost five thousand of the 150,000 soldiers who landed were killed. In all, between June 6 and August 22, 1944, a total of 124,400 US soldiers and 82,300 from the UK and Canada lost their lives.

Military historians say that man for man the German army was the more effective fighting force; but with their sheer weight of resources the Allies achieved a fairly rapid victory. Crucially, the concentration of German air power on the eastern front meant that there was never a significant German air presence over Normandy. Parachutists, reconnaissance flights and air support for ground troops were all able to operate virtually unimpeded, as too were the bombing raids on Norman towns and on every bridge across the Seine west of Paris. Furthermore, the muddled enemy command, in which generals at the front were obliged to follow broad directives from Berlin, caused an American general to comment, "one's imagination boggled at what the German army might have done to us without Hitler working so effectively for our side".

Within a few days of D-Day, **de Gaulle** was able to return to Free France, making an emotional first speech at Bayeux (see p.141), while a seasick Winston Churchill sailed up to Deauville in a destroyer and "took a plug at the Hun". At the end of July, General Patton's Third Army broke out across Brittany from Avranches with the aid of 30,000 **French Resistance** fighters, and on August 25 Allied divisions entered Paris, where the German garrison had already been routed by the Resistance.

Though the war in Europe still had several bloody months to run, with Hitler coming very close to smashing the western front in December 1944, the road to Berlin was finally opening up.

POSTWAR: THE BRETON RESURGENCE

The war left most of **Normandy** in ruins: while it remained a relatively prosperous area in terms of its produce, decades of reconstruction were required. The development of private transport also meant that Normandy became ever more filled with the second homes of the rich. This has often been resented – the film actor Jean Gabin, for example, was literally besieged in his new country house by hundreds of peasants insisting that he had "too much land", and was obliged to sell some of it off.

Meanwhile, there was very little happening in **postwar Brittany** save ever-increasing migration from the countryside to the main towns, and from there, often, out of the province altogether. By the 1950s some 300,000 Bretons lived in Paris, industry was almost exclusively limited to the Loire estuary, and agriculture was dogged by archaic marketing and distribution.

However, since the late 1960s Brittany has experienced considerable economic advance, due in part to the initiatives of **Alexis Gourvennec**. He first came to prominence at the age of 24, in 1961, when he led a group of fellow farmers into Morlaix to occupy the government's regional offices in an effective (if violent) protest at exploitation by middlemen. The act set the pace for his lifetime's concern – to obtain the best possible price for Breton agricultural produce. To this end he lobbied Paris for a deep-water port at Roscoff, and once that was built his farmers' co-operative set up Brittany Ferries to carry Breton artichokes and cabbages to English markets. The company was an explicit move to re-establish the old trading links of the Atlantic seaboard, independent of Paris and central French authority.

Brittany Ferries has prospered, thanks to the British and Irish entry to the EC upon which Gourvennec had gambled. And it has proved that Brittany's future economic fortunes are more closely linked to its old Celtic connections than to the French state. Yet, despite Gourvennec's enthusiasm for his Celtic cousins, there have been several instances of ugly right-wing **protectionism** – attacking British lorries importing meat, violently breaking up strikes in Brittany, and forcibly preventing Townsend Thoresen from starting a rival ferry service to St-Malo.

In 1973 a semi-decentralized **regional administration** was set up to provide an intermediate level between the *départements* and the State. Normandy, being rich, was divided into two *régions* – Basse, with its capital in Caen, and Haute, centred on Rouen – while Brittany remained a single entity, but lost the Loire-Atlantique *département*, which included what was traditionally its principal city, **Nantes**. The new boundaries had no impact on people's perception of the provinces, though they did start to have some practical consequence when the Socialist government increased regional powers in 1981.

Today, **fishing** and **agriculture** remain the mainstays of the Breton economy, though the former has never benefited from an equivalent to Gourvennec, and both arenas have been subject to increasingly bitter inter-European disputes. The economic survival of Breton fishermen in particular has been seriously threatened by a flood of cheap imports from the factory-fishing trawlers of the former Soviet Union. In February 1994, the streets of Rennes were turned into a battlefield when five thousand fishermen rioted during a visit by Prime Minister Édouard Balladur, and a stray flare set light to the roof of the ancient Breton Parliament, which was so badly damaged that it only reopened in 2000. The following month, the GATT talks on world trade were briefly derailed by a French blockade on fish flown in from the US; American threats to retaliate by banning imports of Camembert and other French cheeses soon forced a climbdown.

Thirty percent of fish caught by British vessels are exported to Europe through French ports, and there have been repeated instances of the blockading of various Channel ports, with hypermarkets being ransacked and Scottish fish landed at Roscoff destroyed by angry mobs. In response to a threat by trawlermen wishing to fish for scallops and spider crabs to blockade the Channel Islands, the French government reduced the tax burden on self-employed fishermen, and set minimum prices for cod, haddock, coley and monkfish. The summer of 2000 saw further disputes, focusing on the cost of diesel oil to fishermen, and following the usual disruption to cross-Channel ferries, the French government once again caved in and cut the relevant taxes.

Despite the loss of its traditional industrial centres on the Loire estuary, including the shipbuilding town of St-Nazaire, Brittany has nonetheless managed to expand its industrial base – the advent of a Citroën plant at Rennes being one high profile example. The development of the ultrafast Paris–Brest TGV rail link in particular, inaugurated in 1989, has made a considerable difference. The simultaneous boom in Ireland has even led to talk of Brittany as being a "Celtic tiger". Growth in Normandy has been less spectacular, but after a recession during the the 1990s the region has entered the twenty-first century with something of a resurgence, spearheaded by the high-tech facilities of Caen.

Politically, Bretons have consistently provided an above-average proportion of the conservative vote, with the most traditional, rural areas being the most conservative of all. Perhaps for that reason the **separatist movement**, as a positive celebration of the Breton nation rather than a reactionary throwback, has never been all that powerful. In 1932 a bomb in Rennes destroyed the monument to Franco-Breton unity, and since 1966 the Front de Libération de Bretagne has intermittently attacked such targets as the nuclear power station in the Monts d'Arrée, and the Hall of Mirrors at the palace of Versailles in 1978.

They were joined in 2000 by the shadowy **Breton Liberation Army**, which carried out a succession of bombings including attacks on the town hall in La Baule and a post office in Rennes. The campaign culminated with an explosion at a *McDonald's* restaurant outside Dinan in which an employee was killed, an extreme manifestation of a nationwide surge of resentment that saw *McDonald's* as the epitome of multinational incursion into France. While Government ministers have expressed sympathy with such views, however, the official response to the perceived threat to French identity and traditions has mitigated against Breton aspirations. President Jacques Chirac has refused to ratify the European Charter on Regional and Minority Languages, which would require France to alter its constitution to recognize the rights of Breton speakers.

Meanwhile, the emphasis for most Breton activists these days is on cultural pride rather than militancy. The idea is to establish a clear and vital sense of national identity – to create, as one leader put it, "the spiritual basis for a new political thrust". Although overall use of the Breton language may be declining, great stress has been placed on its historical and artistic significance.

Perhaps the biggest ongoing story in recent years has been the catastrophic succession of **oil spills** along the coastline. Ever since the foundering of the *Torrey Canyon* off Ouessant in March 1967 (see p.283), and the devastation when the *Amoco Cadiz* sank off northern Finistère in 1978, Bretons have come to dread the coming of the ***marées noires*** or "black tides". The latest major disaster came at the end of 1999, when the Maltese super-tanker *Erika* sank off southern Brittany, releasing around 23,000 tonnes of pollutants into the Atlantic ocean. The subsequent mopping-up operation was thrown into jeopardy by reports that its cargo consisted of cancer-causing toxic waste from refineries rather than ordinary fuel oil, as its owners claimed. While the clean-up of physical traces of the wreck was ultimately deemed a success, its economic impact far outweighed any potential compensation, and included an estimated fifteen percent drop in tourism during the summer of 2000. While French authorities have been pushing for a tightening of international marine regulations – traditionally tanker owners have not even been legally accountable for oil leaks – the year ended with yet another when an Italian chemical tanker, the *Ievoli Sun*, foundered off Normandy, spilling several thousand tonnes of styrene into the Channel.

Another headline-hitting controversy has centred on Cogema's UP3 nuclear reprocessing plant at **Cap de la Hague**, near Cherbourg in Normandy. The state-owned facility "reprocesses" spent nuclear fuel from power stations all over the world, and in doing so discharges 230 million litres of nuclear waste each year into the Atlantic. Analysis of the ocean floor in the vicinity has shown it to be so contaminated that legally the stones on the sea bed should themselves be classified as controlled nuclear waste. Researchers from the environmental group **Greenpeace** have labelled the La Hague plant as being "the single largest source of radioactive contamination in the European Union", and also "the single largest source of aerial radioactivity in the world". Campaigners have focused in particular on the demonstrable contamination of the beach at the Plage des Moulinets, nearby, where a waste pipe from the plant is exposed at low tide, and also on the independently verified high incidence of leukemia in the local population. Traditionally, the French authorities have stonewalled on the issue, proud of the fact that 75 percent of the country's electricity is produced by nuclear power stations. However, with the advent of left-wing governments – not only in France itself, but also in Germany, which has long been Cogema's single largest customer – it is at least conceivable that the French espousal of nuclear power may be coming to an end.

AN HISTORICAL CHRONOLOGY

BC

c450,000 Evidence of Paleolithic activity at St Columban

c5700 Earliest megalithic site – tumulus of Kercado

c4600 Tomb containing antlers and shells, Hoëdic island

up to 1800 Megalithic age; construction of Carnac alignments

2500 on Seine becomes the "Tin Road"

6th C First wave of Celts arrive, the Gauls

56 Julius Caesar's fleet defeats Veneti

AD

up to 476 Roman occupation of Armorica

497 Franks arrive in Normandy; Clovis occupies Rouen

5th–6th C Celts fleeing from Britain rename Brittany

6th C First monasteries founded in Brittany and Normandy

St Pol kills "laidley worm" on Île de Batz

709 Mont-St-Michel consecrated by bishop of Avranches

799 Charlemagne controls all Brittany

8th–9th C Forest of Scissy drowns to form Mont-St-Michel Bay

Viking expeditions against Normandy

845 Battle of Redon; Nominoë first duke of Brittany

911 Rollo becomes first duke of Normandy, capital Rouen

9th–10th C Repeated Norman invasions of Brittany

1035 Birth of William "The Bastard" at Falaise

1064 Harold and William together at Battle of Brittany (Dol)

1066 William invades and conquers England

1067 Abbey of Jumièges consecrated

1077 Bishop Odo dedicates Bayeux cathedral, complete with Tapestry

1087 William dies, making William Rufus king of England and leaving Normandy to his eldest son Robert

11th C Golden age of Abbey of Bec – Lanfranc and Anselm

1120 William, heir to the English throne, drowns at Barfleur

1136 Pierre Abelard abbot of St Gildas

12th C Romanesque cloister of Abbey of Daoulas

1160 Robert Wace visits Brocéliande forest "like a fool"

1171 Henry II, in Argentan, hears news of Becket's murder

1172 Henry does public penance at Avranches

1195 Richard the Lionheart builds Château Gaillard

1204 Normandy reunited with French throne

1211–28 Building of *La Merveille* at Mont-St-Michel

1218 Construction of cathedral at Coutances

1303 St Yves dies, Tréguier

1351 "Battle of the Thirty" between Josselin and Ploërmel

1359 Du Guesclin fights single combat at Dinan

1375 Building of Kreisker belfry at St-Pol

1420 Henry V of England king of France, after Agincourt

1431 Joan of Arc's trial and execution (May 30) at Rouen

1437	John the Baptist's finger arrives at St-Jean-du-Doigt
1440	"Bluebeard" burned at stake in Nantes
	Normandy finally recovered by France
1450	Frescoes at Kermaria-an-Isquit
1469	Locronan starts its ascendancy in the linen trade
1474–6	Henry Tudor, England's future king, prisoner at Elven
1491	Duchess Anne of Brittany becomes queen of France
1499	Duchess Anne becomes queen of France again
1510	Monk, Vincelli, invents Benedictine liqueur
1517	Construction of Le Havre
1526	Aître de St-Maclou, charnel house, built at Rouen
1532	Vannes parliament ratifies Brittany–France union
1548	Mary Queen of Scots at Morlaix
1550–1750	Rival Breton towns build the "parish closes"
1562	Rouen sacked by Protestants
1598	Henry IV signs Edict of Nantes
1608	Champlain sails from Honfleur to found Québec
1661	Three musketeers end Fouquet's ownership of Belle-Île
1668	10,000 die of plague in Dieppe
1675	"Stamped Paper" peasant revolt in Brittany
1693	English "infernal machine" devastates St-Malo
1698	Gouin de Beauchère of St-Malo colonizes the Falklands
1722	Dec 22; Drunken carpenter burns down most of Rennes
1745	Bonnie Prince Charlie sails from Nantes
1758	Duke of Marlborough attacks St-Malo with 15,000 men
1776	Benjamin Franklin lands at Auray (by mistake)
1789	Revolution makes no concessions to Breton autonomy
1793	Carrier kills thousands in "marriages" at Nantes
1794	Soldiers play *boules* with heads from Guéhenno calvary
1795	Royalist and exile *Chouans* land at Quiberon
1801	Robert Fulton tests first submarine at Camaret
1808	Napoléon arrives by barge for his ball at Nantes
c1810	Marie Herel invents Camembert
1821	Flaubert born at Rouen
1836	Opening of the Nantes–Brest canal
1843	Victor Hugo's daughter drowns in Seine
1852	First major Icelandic fishery expedition from Paimpol
1866	Composer Érik Satie born in Honfleur
1873	Thérèse Martin born, Lisieux; died 1897, sainted 1925
1881	Young Marcel Proust pays his first visit to Combourg
1883–1926	Monet paints waterlilies in his garden at Giverny
1888	Gauguin at Pont-Aven
1896	*Drummond Castle* goes down off Ouessant
1899	Second trial of Dreyfus at Rennes
1905	France secularized, although Brittany votes against
1927	Nungesser and Coli disappear over Étretat attempting first transatlantic flight
1928	Amundsen's air-rescue flight from Caudebec disappears
1932	Bomb destroys Rennes monument to Franco-Breton unity
1930s	Nauseous Jean-Paul Sartre teaches philosophy in Le Havre
1940	All the men of Sein join de Gaulle in England

1942	March 28; British commando raid on St-Nazaire
	August; 1000 Canadians die in commando raid on Dieppe
1944	June 6; D-Day – Battle of Normandy
1954	Consecration of Basilica of St Thérèse at Lisieux
1962	First Telstar transatlantic signals at Pleumeur-Bodou
1966	Tidal power dam built across the Rance estuary
1967	*Torrey Canyon* disaster; oil slicks hit Brittany
1972	Loire-Atlantique no longer officially in Brittany
1978	*Amoco Cadiz* founders off Finistère
1980	*Rainbow Warrior* pursues nuclear-dumping vessel into Cherbourg; anti-nuclear riots at Plogoff
1987	Oct 15; hurricane causes extensive damage in Finistère
1988	Brest Charter on Brittany's economic future approved by French government
1994	World leaders attend commemorations of fiftieth anniversary of D-Day
	Burning of Breton Parliament in Rennes during protests by fishermen
1995	Opening of the Pont de Normandie
1999	Sinking of the oil tanker *Erika*

BOOKS

Where separate editions exist in the UK and US, publishers are detailed below with the British publisher first, followed by the American publisher. Where books are published in one country only, this follows the publisher's name. O/p signifies an out-of-print, but still recommended, book. University Press has been abbreviated to UP.

PREHISTORY AND MEGALITHS

Aubrey Burl *Megalithic Brittany* (Thames & Hudson, o/p). Detailed guide to the prehistoric sites of Brittany, area by area. Very precise on how to find each site, and what you see when you get there, but little historical or theoretical overview. It is not intended as a practical guidebook for anything other than ancient stones.

John Michell *Megalithomania* (Thames & Hudson; Cornell UP). General popularizing work about megaliths everywhere, with a lot of entertaining descriptions of how modern visitors have reacted to them.

Mark Patton *Statements in Stone* (Routledge). Sober, scientific account of Brittany's megalithic heritage, reappraised in the light of recent archeological discoveries.

A. Thom and A. S. Thom *Megalithic Remains in Britain and Brittany* (OUP, UK, o/p). A scientific rather than anecdotal account of the Thoms' extensive analysis. The mathematics and astronomy can be a bit overpowering without necessarily convincing you of anything.

Uderzo and Goscinny *Astérix the Gaul* (Hodder). Breton history mixed together in a magic cauldron.

HISTORY AND POLITICS

John Ardagh *France Today* (Penguin). Detailed journalistic survey of modern France, with an interesting and relevant section on "Brittany's revival".

Alfred Cobban *A History of Modern France* (Penguin, three vols). Very complete political history from Louis XIV to de Gaulle.

David C. Douglas *The Norman Achievement 1050–1100* (Fontana, o/p; University of California Press, o/p). Comprehensive and readable assessment of the Norman conquerors.

Jonathan Fenby *On The Brink* (Warner Books; Arcade). Entertaining overview of French politics and culture at the end of the twentieth century.

Patrick Galliou and Michael Jones *The Bretons* (Basil Blackwell). Accessible and illuminating hardback account of Breton history from the megaliths, through the Romans, as far as the union with France.

Kendalc'h *Breiz Hor Bro* (Éditions Breiz). Produced by a Breton youth association in French, this militant pamphlet covers history, language, literature and folklore, without ever losing an opportunity to take a swipe at the age-old oppressors of Brittany.

Morvan Lebesque *Comment Peut-on Être Breton?* (Éditions du Seuil). A classic of Breton separatism, taking a psychological and sociological approach rather than a political one. The author argues that awareness of one's cultural identity is vital for participation in the international community.

Barbara Tuchman *Distant Mirror* (Papermac; Ballantine). A history of the fourteenth century as experienced by a French nobleman. Makes sense of the human complexities of the Hundred Years' War.

Mark Twain *Joan of Arc* (Ignatius, US). Little-known fictionalized biography of Joan by America's greatest nineteenth-century writer; quite extraordinarily hagiographic considering his normal scorn for religion.

Marina Warner *Joan of Arc* (Vintage). Stimulating examination of the symbolism and mythology of the Maid of Orléans.

Theodore Zeldin *France 1845–1945* (OUP). Five thematic volumes on French history.

THE NORMANDY LANDINGS

Max Hastings *Overlord* (Papermac; Simon & Schuster). Detailed history of D-Day and its aftermath. Balanced and objective, Hastings distances himself thoroughly from propaganda and myth-making.

Donald Horne *The Great Museum: the Representation of History* (Pluto; Westview). A stimulating analysis of how history is presented to the tourist. Particularly interesting for its treatment of the D-Day landing sites.

John Keegan *Six Armies in Normandy* (Pimlico; Penguin). A fascinating military history, which combines the personal and the public to original effect. Each of the participating armies in the Battle of Normandy is followed during the most crucial phase of its involvement; some of the lesser details of the conflict are missed, but the overall sweep is compelling.

Anthony Kemp *D-Day; The Normandy Landings and the Liberation of Europe* (Thames & Hudson; Abrams). Full-colour pocketbook guide to the D-Day story, with a wealth of fascinating information. Published to mark the fiftieth anniversary of the invasion.

Studs Terkel *The Good War* (New Press, US). Excellent collection of interviews with participants of every rank and nation, including civilians, in World War II.

ART AND ARCHITECTURE

Henry Adams *Mont St-Michel and Chartres* (Princeton UP, US). Extraordinary, idiosyncratic account of the two medieval masterpieces, attempting through prayer, song and sheer imagination to understand the society and the people that created them. A tribute to Norman wisdom.

John Ardagh *Writers' France* (Hamish Hamilton, o/p). Entertaining anecdotes about most of the writers mentioned in this book, with colour photos.

Christina Björk *Linnea in Monet's Garden* (Raben & Sjogern; Farrar, Straus & Giroux). A Swedish book for children, which tells the story of a young girl achieving her unlikely lifetime's dream of visiting Monet's home in Giverny. A well-illustrated introduction to the Impressionists.

Sophie Bowness and others *The Dieppe Connection* (Herbert Press; New Amsterdam Books). Companion volume to a fascinating exhibition in Brighton, exploring Dieppe's nineteenth-century role as a meeting place for artists. Colour reproductions of Dieppe scenes by Turner, Whistler, Gauguin and Renoir, among others.

Alfonso Castelao *Les Croix de Pierre en Bretagne* (available by post for 59F/€8.99 from the Comité Bretagne-Galice, BP66A, 35031 Rennes). A real collector's item; a pocket-sized collection of sketches of Breton calvaries made by the Gallego writer and illustrator during a visit in the 1920s. Includes an obsessive series of studies of Christ's ribcage. For more on Castelao, see *The Rough Guide to Spain*.

Claire Joyes *Monet at Giverny* (Matthews Millar Dunbar). Large-format account of Monet's years at Giverny, combining biography with good reproductions of the famous waterlilies.

BRITTANY IN FICTION

Honoré de Balzac *The Chouans* (Penguin). A hectic and crazily romantic story of the royalist *Chouan* rebellion shortly after the Revolution, set mainly in Fougères.

Alexandre Dumas *The Three Musketeers* (OUP; Penguin). Brilliant swashbuckling romance with peripheral Breton scenes on Belle-Île and elsewhere.

Victor Hugo *Ninety-Three* (Carroll & Graf, US). Rather more restrained, but still compelling, *Chouan* novel.

Jack Kerouac *Satori in Paris* (Flamingo; Grove) . . . and in Brittany. Inconsequential anecdotes.

Pierre Loti *Pêcheur d'Islande* (Livre de Poche). Much-acclaimed novel (on which the film was based) which focuses on the whaling fleets that sailed from Paimpol. Not available in translation.

NORMANDY IN FICTION

Julian Barnes *Flaubert's Parrot* (Picador; Random House). A lightweight novel which rambles around the life of Flaubert, with much of the action taking place in Rouen and along the Seine.

Peter Benson *Odo's Hanging* (Sceptre, UK). Delicate but dramatic fictionalized account of the human stories behind the creation of the Bayeux Tapestry.

Gustave Flaubert *Bouvard and Pécuchet* (Viking, US). Two petits-bourgeois retire to a village between Caen and Falaise and attempt to practise every science of the time. Very funny or dead boring, according to taste.

Gustave Flaubert *Madame Bovary* (Wordsworth; Bantam Books). "The first modern novel", by the Rouennais writer. Drawn from a real-life story from Ry – see p.106 – it contains little that is specifically Norman, however.

Marcel Proust *In Remembrance of Things Past* (Penguin; Random House). Dense, dreamily disturbing autobiographical trilogy, evocative of almost everything except the places in Normandy and Brittany to which his memories take him back.

Julian Rathbone *The Last English King* (Abacus, UK). Lyrical and extremely readable fictionalized version of the Norman Conquest, as told by King Harold's one surviving bodyguard. The Normans themselves are depicted as heartless villains.

Jean-Paul Sartre *Nausea* (Norton, US). Sartre's relentlessly gloomy description of just how unpleasant it was to drag out one's existence in Le Havre (or "Bouville") in the 1930s.

BRETON MYTH AND FOLKTALES

Pierre-Jakez Hélias *The Horse of Pride* (Yale UP). A deeply reactionary and sentimental account of a Breton childhood in the Bigouden district of the early twentieth century, which has sold over two million copies in France.

Professor Anatole Le Braz *La Legende du Mort* (Éditions Jeanne Laffitte). The definitive French text on Breton myths centred on Ankou and the prescience of death.

F. M. Luzel *Celtic Folk-Tales from Armorica* (Llanerch Enterprises, Lampeter, Wales). A collection of timeless Breton fairy stories, in English, complete with commentaries.

W. Y. Evans-Wentz *The Fairy Faith in Celtic Countries* (Citadel Press; Carol Publishing). Bizarre survey of similarities and differences in folk beliefs and religion between Celtic nations, with extensive details about Brittany.

BRETON MUSIC

Breton music, which draws richly in its themes, style and instrumentation on the common Celtic heritage of the Atlantic seaboard, has remained for centuries a unifying and inspiring part of the culture of the province. Despite the intermittent efforts of a reactionary clergy to stifle its popularity, it survived the union with France and the general suppression of indigenous art and language.

However, attempting to pin even an approximate date on the origins of traditional Breton music is a haphazard business. No literature survives in the native tongue from any period prior to the fifteenth century, although we do know that wandering Breton minstrels, known as *conteurs*, had enjoyed great popularity

DISCOGRAPHY

A few Breton discs – mainly of the rock-crossover variety – find their way into international sections of music stores abroad, or onto the major English-language Internet retail sites. For the real roots stuff, however, you'll need to go to Brittany itself, and in particular to **Ar Bed Keltiek**, a record store with branches in Quimper and Brest (and a useful Web site at *www.arbedkeltiek.com*), or, best of all, to **Chant de l'Alouette** (4 rue des États, 35600 Redon, Brittany; ☎02.99.72.44.94), run by musician Jakez le Soueff – a living Breton encyclopedia on all matters musical, who will track down any recording that exists. These shops are also good for information about forthcoming gigs and events.

COMPILATIONS

Various *Celtic La Compile* (Le Cine Jaune, France). An eclectic eighteen-track compilation of Breton music of just about every style: sentimental balladeers, marching bands, loud rockers, quirky accordions and bagpipes – it's all here.

Various *Dans* (Iguane, France). Traditional dance tunes given new life with superb new arrangements and restrained electrification.

Various *Gwerziou et Chants de Haute-Voix* (Keltia Musique, France). Unaccompanied Breton songs by the region's top artists; the best example of the genre.

ARTISTS/BANDS

Afro Celt Sound System *Volume 1: Sound Magic* (Real World, UK). Groundbreaking 1996 fusion of Celtic pipes and African rhythms, by loose-structured group that's become a fixture on Brittany's live summer circuit.

Dan Ar Braz *Essential en 3CD* (Keltia Musique, France). Definitive career-spanning compilation from the ex-Stivell, Malicorne and Fairport guitarist; for single-CD releases, try *Septembre Bleu* or *Borders of Salt*.

Barzaz *An den Kozh dall* (Keltia Musique, France). A classic 1992 release of mellow, intense acoustic music, with some lovely flute-playing.

The Chieftains *Celtic Wedding* (RCA, UK). The Irish band turn their hand to traditional Breton dance tunes. A fresh, and highly accessible, perspective.

Duo Ars Celtica *Fréhel* (Keltia Musique, France). Lyrical, mystical 2000 collaboration between hippy harpist Myrzhin, and his wife and fellow-harpist Zil.

Gwerz *Live* (Gwerz, France). Electric and acoustic material from perhaps the best Breton musicians of recent years, now pursuing individual projects.

Kornog *Kornog* (Green Linnet, US). Wide-ranging 2000 studio album from this adventurous Breton (and Scots) band, formed by ex-Gwerz guitarist Soïg Siberil.

Patrick Molard, Jack Molard and Jacques Pellen *Triptyque* (Gwerz, France). An innovative release of jazzy interpretations of Breton traditions.

Gilles Servat *Touche Pas à la Blanche de Hermine* (Keltia Musique, France). Angry, abroad long before this. Many of the songs they wrote were translated into French, being otherwise unintelligible to audiences outside Brittany, but unfortunately both versions have vanished with time. Only a number of Norse and English translations, probably dating from the twelfth century, escaped destruction. These works tell of romances won and lost, acrimonious relationships between fathers and their sons, and the testing of potential lovers.

The historical record of Breton music really begins with the publication of **Barzaz-Breizh**, a major collection of traditional songs and poems, in 1839. It was compiled by a nobleman, Hersart de la Villemarqué, from his discussions with fishermen, farmers and oyster-and-pancake women, and in view of the scarcity of other literature in the native language has come to be acknowledged as a treasure of Breton folk culture. Though serious doubts have frequently been raised as to its authenticity – many sceptics believe Villemarqué doctored those parts of the material he found distasteful, and even composed portions of it himself – it is unquestionably a work of linguistic brilliance and great beauty, and its appearance triggered the serious study of popular Breton culture.

INSTRUMENTATION

As for the traditional **instruments** on which the music is played, perhaps the most important is the **bombard** – an extremely old and

---

impassioned CD by the veteran singer-songwriter, sparked by the 1998 appropriation of one of his best-loved songs by the Front National.

Les Soeurs Goadeg *Moueziou Brudez à Vreiz* (Keltia Musique, France). Alan Stivell produced this disc of old-time Breton singing in 1975. Goadeg, a trio of sisters, were into their seven-ties at the time, and the album showcases their highly traditional *gwerziou* (ballads) and *kan ha diskan* singing.

Alan Stivell *Journée à la Maison* (Rounder, US). A good compilation of Stivell's Breton Celtic harp folk-rockery – more accessible than the recent esoteric output.

LIVE MUSIC AND FESTIVALS

Visitors to Brittany get the chance to enjoy Breton music at several annual **festivals**. The most famous of these is the pan-Celtic Lorient festival (see p.348); others include Quimper's Festival de Cornouaille (mid- to late July), Rennes's Tombées de la Nuit (early July), and the intimate Printemps de Chateauneuf-du-Faou (Easter Sun).

In addition, most Breton towns and villages, even in the middle of nowhere, have pubs that offer **live music**, often of the spontaneous boot-tappin' booze-swillin' variety. Among the best of these are:

Brest: *Café de la Plage*, *Café le Triskel* and the *Bar Écossais*.

Douarnenez: *Le Pourquois Pas* promotes larger bands in the mainstream mould.

Gouarec, near Gourin: *Bar de Daoulas*.

Gwern, near Pontivy: The *Korn Ar Pont* is a highly regarded venue which promotes mostly rock music and attracts punters from kilometres around for a weekend's bopping and bevvying. Own transport essential.

Île de Bréhat: *La Mary Morgan*.

Lorient: The *Galway Inn* – run by an Irishman – puts on touring bands of an acoustic nature, and has regular Irish folk sessions too.

Plouha: The *Ti Elise*, owned by a Welshman from Merthyr, is the local of Yann Skoarnek, a venerable old character who'll sing you songs about horse-thieving in Breton.

Plouhinec, near Lorient: *Café de la Barre*.

Quimper: The *Ceili Bar* specializes in folk music. Very small, very cramped and very drunk.

Quimperlé: The superb hosts at the *OK Pub* arrange occasional summer gigs of a folksy sort – and it serves Murphy's into the bargain.

Redon: Ask at *Le Chant de l'Allouette* music shop just off the main street for info. They sometimes promote events at a nearby farm.

Rennes: *Barantic* puts on semi-regular gigs in the folk-rock vein as well as less-organized affairs at the weekend. Friendly bar staff, relaxed atmosphere.

shortened version of the oboe which, depending on the condition of your brain on any given day, sounds either like a hypnotic trance-inducing paean to the gods, or a sackful of weasels being yanked through a mincer. The **biniou**, the Breton bagpipe, dates in its current form from the nineteenth century, although several types are still in use, distinguished by the length of the chanter.

The harp, **telenn**, was also a native instrument long ago. Its influence had declined to a barely peripheral level until **Alan Stivell**'s appearance on the scene in the 1960s inspired a resurgence. His international hit *Renaissance of the Celtic Harp* introduced Breton as well as Irish, Welsh and Scottish traditional music to a worldwide audience, and subsequently stimulated interest in less accessible material.

FESTOU-NOZ

The most rewarding setting in which to witness traditional Breton music is undoubtedly a **Fest-Noz** ("Night Feast") – a night of serious eating, drinking and dancing which can sometimes verge on the orgiastic. During the summer months, such events are very common, attracting hordes of revellers from kilometres around. Though they are often held in barns and halls in the more isolated parts of the region, discovering their whereabouts shouldn't present any problems, as an avalanche of posters advertising them appears absolutely everywhere. Once the evening gets underway, the dancers, often in their hundreds, whirl around in vast dizzy circles, hour after hour, sometimes frenzied and leaping, sometimes slow and graceful with their little fingers intertwined. It can be a bizarre and exhilarating spectacle – and a very affordable one too, with admission fees rarely amounting to more than a few pounds.

Traditionally, the most common form of *fest-noz* music is that of a **couple de sonneurs**, a pair of musicians playing *bombard* and *biniou*. They play the same melody line, with a drone from the *biniou*, and keep up a fast tempo – one player covering for the other when he or she pauses for breath. This is defiantly dance music, with no vocals and no titles for the tunes, although there are countless varieties of rhythms, often highly localized and generally known by the name of the dance. There is a purely vocal counterpart to this, known as **kan ha diskan**. Once again dance music, this is per-

For up-to-the minute **listings** of forthcoming *festou-noz*, look on the Web at *www.bretagnenet.com/festnoz*, which even on a quiet winter weekend is likely to feature as many as twenty events. More general information on Breton music can be found at *www.breizh.net/icdbl*, *www.dastum.com* and *www.bretagnenet.com/celtique*.

formed by a pair of unaccompanied "call-and-response" singers. In its basic form the two singers – the *kader* and *diskader* – alternate verses, joining each other at the end of each phrase. As dances were in the past unamplified, the parts were (and are) often doubled up, creating a startling rhythmic sound. The best singers might also give the dancers the odd break with a *gwerz*, or ballad, again sung unaccompanied. Over the past couple of decades, these traditional accompaniments have been supplanted more and more by four- or five-piece **bands**, who add fiddle and accordion, and sometimes electric bass and drums, to the *bombard*, and less often the *biniou*. The tunes have been updated with more of a rock sound, while the balladeers have given way to folk-style singer-songwriters, with guitar backing. Purists might regret the changes, but they have probably ensured the survival of *festou-noz*, with the enthusiastic participation of musicians and dancers of pretty much all ages. They have also nurtured successive generations of Breton musicians who move onto the festival and concert circuit.

BARDS AND BANDS

The godfather of the modern Breton music scene, **Alan Stivell**, started the ball rolling in the mid-1960s with one of the first folk-rock bands in Europe. He played harp, bagpipes and Irish flute, alongside **Dan Ar Braz** on electric and acoustic guitar, on a repertoire that drew on wider Celtic traditions. Both artists are still performing and recording, individually. Stivell's efforts are increasingly esoteric, while Ar Braz, who played with Fairport Convention in 1976, is a fixture at that band's Cropredy reunions, and produces mellow acoustic solo albums. The other key figure from Stivell's band was **Gabriel Yucoub**, who led **Malicorne**, the best-known Breton band of the 1970s and 1980s, through a series of experiments with folk-rock and electronic music, often using archaic instruments. Latterly, he has played as an acoustic duo, with his wife Marie Matheson.

Folk-rock, however, has been just one direction for Breton music in recent years. On the concert circuit, the biggest Breton names tend to be the singers, among whom the most famous is **Andrea Ar Gouilh**. Her recent output includes a return to Breton roots with a recording of old songs taken from the *Barzaz-Breizh*, though her concert repertoire is as likely to include a rendition of Bob Dylan's *Blowin' in the Wind*, which sounds rather marvellous sung in Breton.

Youenn Gwernig, a Druid and singer, is another name to look out for at festivals. He lived for many years in New York and delivers his own ballads in a deep, booming voice, sometimes accompanied by his two daughters, who sing Brooklyn English translations.

Equally weird is **Kristen Nikolas**, a wandering poet who makes his own idiosyncratic records, in Breton, in foreign studios, while the most compelling name has to be that of the duo **Bastard Hag e Vab** (Bastard and Son), who have been stalwarts of the live circuit for years. Best known of all is the singer-songwriter **Gilles Servat**, who sings in both Breton and French, mixing his own protest songs with renderings of Breton poems, and has also written a four-part novelization of Arthurian myths.

Fest-noz singers are sometimes accompanied by harpists, among whom the best contemporary players are **Anne-Marie Jan**, **Anne Auffret**, **Job Fulup** and **Ar Breudeur Keffelean**, virtuoso twin brothers who also have a group, **Triskell**. The more mystic 1960s side of the tradition is encapsulated by the suitably bearded and misty Merlin-type, **Myrzhin**, harper of the mysterious.

If you have a more casual interest in Breton sounds, though, you're likely to find some of the bands rather more rewarding. A fine *fest-noz*

act to look out for is **Strobinell**, who have a lineup of *bombard*, *biniou*, violin, flute and guitar, and make occasional forays into a looser, jazzier groove, while the trio **Tud** (which means "the people" in Breton) have become a fixture on the festival circuit in Finistère, backing either the *bimbard* or the *biniou* with guitar and accordion.

For the electric *fest-noz* sound, complete with full rock-drum kit, the best exponents are **Bleizi Ruz** (Red Wolves) and **Sonerien Du** (Black Musicians). Bleizi Ruz, who started out some 25 years ago playing traditional songs, play less at *fest-noz* these days and more on concert stages. Perhaps the most adventurous band has been **Gwerz**, who made several records of traditional songs and ethereal instrumentals, using *bombard*, *biniou*, uilleann pipes and guitars. Their singer, **Erie Marchand**, has also collaborated with Indian musicians to interesting effect, and, as an accomplished clarinettist, he plays with the classically-oriented **Quintet Clarinettes**, known for adding a punchy new take to traditional standards.

More folk-oriented, and purely acoustic, are **Kornog**, who feature Scots singer, mandolin and bouzouki player Jamie McMenemy, alongside three Breton instrumentalists, among them Soïg Siberil, who played guitar in Gwerz. They have rearranged Breton material quite radically for guitar, fiddle and *bouzouki*, slowing down the tempo to highlight solo playing and adding the occasional Scots ballad.

Inevitably, the latest hybrid to appear has been a sort of Breton **folk-rap**, in the shape of **Manau** and **Denez Prigent**, who mix techno and dance rhythms with traditional airs and ballads, and blend contemporary messages into time-honoured lyrics.

Adapted from an original piece by **Raymond Travers**, which appears in *The Rough Guide to World Music*.

LANGUAGE

Although Breton does remain a living language, in both Brittany and Normandy every encounter you are likely to have with the local people will be conducted in French. This is of course a lot more familiar than Breton, sharing numerous words with English, but it's not a particularly easy language to pick up.

The bare essentials of **French**, though, are not difficult, and make all the difference. Even just saying "Bonjour Madame/Monsieur" when you go into a shop, and then pointing, will usually get you a smile and helpful service. People working in hotels, restaurants and tourist offices almost always speak some English, and tend to use it even if you're trying in French — be grateful, not insulted.

Breton is one of the Celtic family of languages, with an especially strong oral tradition ranging from medieval minstrels to modern singers and musicians. If you have a familiarity with Welsh or Gaelic, you should find yourself understanding, and being understood, in it.

Current estimates put the number of people who understand spoken Breton at between 400,000 and 800,000. However, only perhaps a third of those actually speak the language with any fluency or frequency, and you are only likely to find it spoken as a first, day-to-day language either among the old or in the more remote parts of Finistère. For centuries it was discouraged by the State; its use was forbidden for official and legal purposes, and even Breton-speaking parents would seek to enhance their children's prospects by bringing them up to speak French. Although it is now taught in schools once again, learning Breton is not really a viable prospect for visitors who do not already have a grounding in another Celtic language. However, as you travel through the province it's interesting to note the roots of Breton place names, many of which have a simple meaning in the language. The box below lists some of the most common.

A GLOSSARY OF PLACE NAMES

Aber	estuary	_Lann_	heath
Avel	wind	_Lech_	flat stone
Bihan	little	_Loc_	isolated, holy place
Bran	hill	_Mad_	good
Braz	big	_Mario_	dead
Breizh	Brittany	_Men_	stone
Creach	height	_Menez_	mountain
Cromlech	stone circle	_Menhir_	long stone
Dol/Taol	table	_Meur_	big
_Du_	black	_Mor_	sea
Enez	island	_Nevez_	new
Gavre	goat	_Parc_	field
Goat/Coat/Koat	forest	_Penn_	end, head
Goaz	stream	_Plou_	parish
Guen	white	_Pors_	port, farmyard
Hen	old	_Roch_	stone
Heol	sun	_Ster_	river
Hir	long	_Stivel_	fountain, spring
Kastell	castle	_Traez_	sand, beach
Ker	town, village	_Trou_	valley
Koz	old	_Ty_	house
Lan	church, holy place	_Wrach_	witch

A BRIEF GUIDE TO SPEAKING FRENCH

FRENCH PRONUNCIATION

One easy rule to remember is that **consonants** at the ends of words are usually silent. *Pas plus tard* (not later) is thus pronounced "pa-plu-tarr". But when the following word begins with a vowel, you run the two together: *pas après* (not after) becomes "pazaprey".

Vowels are the hardest sounds to get right. Roughly:

a	as in h**a**t		*i*	as in mach**i**ne
e	as in g**e**t		*o*	as in h**o**t
é	between g**e**t and g**a**te		*o, au*	as in **o**ver
è	between g**e**t and g**u**t		*ou*	as in f**oo**d
eu	like the **u** in h**u**rt		*u*	as in a pursed-lip version of **u**se

More awkward are the **combinations** *in/im, en/em, an/am, on/om, un/um* at the ends of words, or followed by consonants other than *n* or *m*. Again, roughly:

in/im	like the **an** in **an**xious	*on/om*	like the **don** in **Don**caster said
an/am, en/em	like the **don** in **Don**caster when		by someone with a heavy cold
	said with a nasal accent	*un/um*	like the **u** in **u**nderstand

Consonants are much as in English, except that: *ch* is always "sh", *c* is "s", *h* is silent, *th* is the same as "t", *ll* is like the "y" in yes, *w* is "v", and *r* is growled (or rolled).

BASIC WORDS AND PHRASES

French nouns are divided into masculine and feminine. This causes difficulties with adjectives, whose endings have to change to suit the gender of the nouns they qualify. If you know some grammar, you will know what to do. If not, stick to the masculine form, which is the simplest – it's what we have done in this glossary.

today	*aujourd'hui*	that one	*celà*
yesterday	*hier*	open	*ouvert*
tomorrow	*demain*	closed	*fermé*
in the morning	*le matin*	big	*grand*
in the afternoon	*l'après-midi*	small	*petit*
in the evening	*le soir*	more	*plus*
now	*maintenant*	less	*moins*
later	*plus tard*	a little	*un peu*
at one o'clock	*à une heure*	a lot	*beaucoup*
at three o'clock	*à trois heures*	cheap	*bon marché*
at ten-thirty	*à dix heures et demie*	expensive	*cher*
at midday	*à midi*	good	*bon*
man	*un homme*	bad	*mauvais*
woman	*une femme*	hot	*chaud*
here	*ici*	cold	*froid*
there	*là*	with	*avec*
this one	*ceci*	without	*sans*

continued

NUMBERS

1	*un*	15	*quinze*	80	*quatre-vingts*
2	*deux*	16	*seize*	90	*quatre-vingt-dix*
3	*trois*	17	*dix-sept*	95	*quatre-vingt-quinze*
4	*quatre*	18	*dix-huit*	100	*cent*
5	*cinq*	19	*dix-neuf*	101	*cent-et-un*
6	*six*	20	*vingt*	200	*deux cents*
7	*sept*	21	*vingt-et-un*	300	*trois cents*
8	*huit*	22	*vingt-deux*	500	*cinq cents*
9	*neuf*	30	*trente*	1000	*mille*
10	*dix*	40	*quarante*	2000	*deux milles*
11	*onze*	50	*cinquante*	5000	*cinq milles*
12	*douze*	60	*soixante*	1,000,000	*un million*
13	*treize*	70	*soixante-dix*		
14	*quatorze*	75	*soixante-quinze*		

DAYS AND DATES

January	*janvier*	October	*octobre*	Saturday	*samedi*
February	*février*	November	*novembre*	August 1	*le premier*
March	*mars*	December	*décembre*		*août*
April	*avril*	Sunday	*dimanche*	March 2	*le deux mars*
May	*mai*	Monday	*lundi*	July 14	*le quatorze*
June	*juin*	Tuesday	*mardi*		*juillet*
July	*juillet*	Wednesday	*mercredi*	November 23	*le vingt-trois*
August	*août*	Thursday	*jeudi*		*novembre*
September	*septembre*	Friday	*vendredi*	2002	*deux mille deux*

TALKING TO PEOPLE

When addressing people you should always use *Monsieur* for a man, *Madame* for a woman, *Mademoiselle* for a young woman or girl. Plain *bonjour* by itself is not enough. This isn't as formal as it seems, and it has its uses when you've forgotten someone's name or want to attract someone's attention.

Excuse me	*Pardon*	OK/agreed	*d'accord*
Do you speak English?	*Parlez-vous anglais?*	please	*s'il vous plaît*
How do you say it in	*Comment ça se dit en*	thank you	*merci*
French?	*français?*	hello	*bonjour*
What's your name?	*Comment vous*	goodbye	*au revoir*
	appelez-vous?	good morning/afternoon	*bonjour*
My name is . . .	*Je m'appelle . . .*	good evening	*bonsoir*
I'm English	*Je suis anglais[e]*	good night	*bonne nuit*
Irish	*irlandais[e]*	How are you?	*Comment allez-vous?/*
Scottish	*écossais[e]*		*Ça va?*
Welsh	*gallois[e]*	Fine, thanks	*Très bien, merci*
American	*américain[e]*	I don't know	*Je ne sais pas*
Australian	*australien[ne]*	Let's go	*Allons-y*
Canadian	*canadien[ne]*	See you tomorrow	*A demain*
a New Zealander	*néo-zélandais[e]*	See you soon	*A bientôt*
yes	*oui*	Sorry	*Pardon, Madame/*
no	*non*		*Je m'excuse*
I understand	*Je comprends*	Leave me alone	*Fichez-moi la paix!*
I don't understand	*Je ne comprends pas*	(aggressive)	
Can you speak slower?	*S'il vous plaît, parlez*	Please help me	*Aidez-moi, s'il vous*
	moins vite?		*plaît*

FINDING THE WAY

bus	*autobus/bus/car*	on foot	*à pied*
bus station	*gare routière*	Where are you going?	*Vous allez où?*
bus stop	*arrêt*	I'm going to . . .	*Je vais à . . .*
car	*voiture*	I want to	*Je voudrais*
train/taxi/ferry	*train/taxi/ferry*	get off at . . .	*descendre à . . .*
boat	*bâteau*	the road to . . .	*la route pour . . .*
plane	*avion*	near	*près/pas loin*
train station	*gare SNCF*	far	*loin*
platform	*quai*	left	*à gauche*
What time does it leave?	*Il part à quelle heure?*	right	*à droite*
What time does it arrive?	*Il arrive à quelle heure?*	straight on	*tout droit*
		on the other side of	*à l'autre côté de*
a ticket to . . .	*un billet pour . . .*	on the corner of	*à l'angle de*
single ticket	*aller simple*	next to	*à côté de*
return ticket	*aller retour*	behind	*derrière*
validate your ticket	*compostez votre billet*	in front of	*devant*
valid for	*valable pour*	before	*avant*
ticket office	*vente de billets*	after	*après*
how many kilometres?	*combien de kilomètres?*	under	*sous*
		to cross	*traverser*
how many hours?	*combien d'heures?*	bridge	*pont*
hitchhiking	*autostop*		

QUESTIONS AND REQUESTS

The simplest way of asking a question is to start with *s'il vous plaît* (please), then name the thing you want in an interrogative tone of voice. For example:

Where is there a bakery? *S'il vous plaît, la boulangerie?*

Which way is it to the Eiffel Tower? *S'il vous plaît, la route pour la tour Eiffel?*

Similarly with requests:

Can we have a room for two? *S'il vous plaît, une chambre pour deux?*

Can I have a kilo of oranges? *S'il vous plaît, un kilo d'oranges?*

Question words

where?	*où?*	why?	*pourquoi?*
how?	*comment?*	at what time?	*à quelle heure?*
how many/how much?	*combien?*	what is/which is?	*quel est?*
when?	*quand?*		

ACCOMMODATION

a room for	*une chambre pour*	a room over the street	*une chambre sur la rue*
one/two people	*une/deux personnes*	first floor	*premier étage*
a double bed	*un lit double*	second floor	*deuxième étage*
a room with a	*une chambre avec*	with a view	*avec vue*
shower	*douche*	key	*clef*
a room with a bath	*une chambre avec salle de bain*	to iron	*repasser*
		do laundry	*faire la lessive*
for one/two/	*pour une/deux/*	sheets	*draps*
three nights	*trois nuits*	blankets	*couvertures*
Can I see it?	*Je peux la voir?*	quiet	*calme*
a room on the courtyard	*une chambre sur la cour*	noisy	*bruyant*
		hot water	*eau chaude*

continued

cold water	*eau froide*	Can we camp here?	*On peut camper ici?*
Is breakfast included?	*Est-ce que le petit déjeuner est compris?*	campsite	*un camping/terrain de camping*
I would like breakfast	*Je voudrais prendre le petit déjeuner*	tent	*une tente*
I don't want breakfast	*Je ne veux pas de petit déjeuner*	tent space	*un emplacement*
		hostel	*auberge de jeunesse*

CARS

service station	*garage*	put air in the tyres	*gonfler les pneus*
service	*service*	battery	*batterie*
to park the car	*garer la voiture*	the battery is dead	*la batterie est morte*
car park	*un parking*	plugs	*bougies*
no parking	*défense de stationner/ stationnement interdit*	to break down	*tomber en panne*
		gas can	*bidon*
petrol station	*poste d'essence*	insurance	*assurance*
fuel	*essence*	green card	*carte verte*
(to) fill it up	*faire le plein*	traffic lights	*feux*
oil	*huile*	red light	*feu rouge*
air line	*ligne à air*	green light	*feu vert*

HEALTH MATTERS

doctor	*médecin*	stomach ache	*mal à l'estomac*
I don't feel well	*Je ne me sens pas bien*	period	*règles*
medicines	*médicaments*	pain	*douleur*
prescription	*ordonnance*	it hurts	*ça fait mal*
I feel sick	*Je suis malade*	chemist	*pharmacie*
I have a headache	*J'ai mal à la tête*	hospital	*hôpital*

OTHER NEEDS

bakery	*boulangerie*	bank	*banque*
food shop	*alimentation*	money	*argent*
supermarket	*supermarché*	toilets	*toilettes*
to eat	*manger*	police	*police*
to drink	*boire*	telephone	*téléphone*
camping gas	*camping gaz*	cinema	*cinéma*
tobacconist	*tabac*	theatre	*théâtre*
stamps	*timbres*	to reserve/book	*réserver*

LEARNING MATERIALS

Rough Guide French Phrasebook (Rough Guides). Mini dictionary-style phrasebook with both English–French and French–English sections, along with cultural tips for tricky situations and a menu reader.

Mini French Dictionary (Harrap/Prentice Hall). French–English and English–French, plus a brief grammar and pronunciation guide.

Breakthrough French (Pan; book and 2 cassettes). Excellent teach-yourself course.

French and English Slang Dictionary (Harrap/Prentice Hall); **Dictionary of Modern**

Colloquial French (Routledge). Both volumes are a bit large to carry, but they are the key to all you ever wanted to understand about the French vernacular.

Verbaid (Verbaid, Hawk House, Heath Lane, Farnham, Surrey GU9 0PR). CD-size laminated paper "verb wheel" giving you the tense endings for the regular verbs.

A Vous La France; Franc Extra; Franc-Parler (BBC Publications/EMC Publishing; each has a book and 2 cassettes). BBC radio courses, running from beginners' level to fairly advanced.

GLOSSARY OF FRENCH TERMS

ABBAYE abbey
ABER estuary
ACCUEIL reception
ARRÊT D'AUTOBUS bus stop
ASSEMBLÉE NATIONALE French Parliament
AUBERGE DE JEUNESSE (AJ) hostel
AUTOBUS city bus
BANQUE bank
BASSIN harbour basin
BEAUX ARTS Fine Arts school (and often museum)
BIBLIOTHÈQUE library
BISTRO small restaurant or bar
BOIS wood
BOULANGERIE baker
BRASSERIE café/restaurant
BUREAU DE CHANGE money exchange
CAR coach, bus
CAVE (wine) cellar
CHARCUTERIE delicatessen
CHASSE, CHASSE GARDÉE hunting grounds (beware)
CHÂTEAU castle or mansion
CIMETIÈRE cemetery
CITADELLE fortified city
CLOÎTRE cloister
CODENE French CND
CONSIGNE left luggage
COUVENT monastery
CRÊPERIE pancake restaurant
DÉGUSTATION tasting
DÉPARTEMENT county equivalent
DOLMEN megalithic stone "table"
DONJON castle keep
ÉGLISE church
ENCLOS group of church buildings
ENTRÉE entrance
FERMETURE closing time/period
FORÊT forest

FOUILLES archeological excavations
GARE ROUTIÈRE bus station
GARE SNCF train station
GÎTE D'ÉTAPE countryside hostel
GROTTE cave
HALLES covered market
HLM publicly subsidized housing
HÔPITAL hospital
HÔTEL hotel – but also used for an aristocratic town house or mansion
HÔTEL DE VILLE town hall
ÎLE island
JOURS FÉRIÉS public holidays
MAIRIE town hall
MAISON literally a house – can also be an office or base of an organization
MARCHÉ market
MENHIR single megalithic stone
OFFICE DU TOURISME (OT) tourist office
OUVERTURE opening time/period
PÂTISSERIE pastry shop
PHARMACIE chemist
PLACE square
PLAGE beach
PORTE gate
POSTE post office
PRESQU'ÎLE peninsula
PRIVÉ private
PTT post office
QUARTIER quarter of a town
RELAIS ROUTIER truck-stop restaurant
REZ-DE-CHAUSSÉE ground floor (UK), first floor (US)
RN route nationale (main road)
SALON DE THÉ tearoom
SI tourist office (see syndicat d'initiative below)
SNCF French railways
SYNDICAT D'INITIATIVE (SI) tourist office
TABAC bar or shop selling stamps, cigarettes, etc
TOUR tower
VAUBAN seventeenth-century military architect
ZONE BLEUE parking zone
ZONE PIÉTONNIÈRE pedestrian zone

INDEX

around the world

Alaska ★ Algarve ★ Amsterdam ★ Andalucía ★ Antigua & Barbuda ★ Argentina ★ Auckland Restaurants ★ Australia ★ Austria ★ Bahamas ★ Bali & Lombok ★ Bangkok ★ Barbados ★ Barcelona ★ Beijing ★ Belgium & Luxembourg ★ Belize ★ Berlin ★ Big Island of Hawaii ★ Bolivia ★ Boston ★ Brazil ★ Britain ★ Brittany & Normandy ★ Bruges & Ghent ★ Brussels ★ Budapest ★ Bulgaria ★ California ★ Cambodia ★ Canada ★ Cape Town ★ The Caribbean ★ Central America ★ Chile ★ China ★ Copenhagen ★ Corsica ★ Costa Brava ★ Costa Rica ★ Crete ★ Croatia ★ Cuba ★ Cyprus ★ Czech & Slovak Republics ★ Devon & Cornwall ★ Dodecanese & East Aegean ★ Dominican Republic ★ The Dordogne & the Lot ★ Dublin ★ Ecuador ★ Edinburgh ★ Egypt ★ England ★ Europe ★ First-time Asia ★ First-time Europe ★ Florence ★ Florida ★ France ★ French Hotels & Restaurants ★ Gay & Lesbian Australia ★ Germany ★ Goa ★ Greece ★ Greek Islands ★ Guatemala ★ Hawaii ★ Holland ★ Hong Kong & Macau ★ Honolulu ★ Hungary ★ Ibiza & Formentera ★ Iceland ★ India ★ Indonesia ★ Ionian Islands ★ Ireland ★ Israel & the Palestinian Territories ★ Italy ★ Jamaica ★ Japan ★ Jerusalem ★ Jordan ★ Kenya ★ The Lake District ★ Languedoc & Roussillon ★ Laos ★ Las Vegas ★ Lisbon ★ London ★

in twenty years

London Mini Guide ★ London Restaurants ★ Los Angeles ★ Madeira ★ Madrid ★ Malaysia, Singapore & Brunei ★ Mallorca ★ Malta & Gozo ★ Maui ★ Maya World ★ Melbourne ★ Menorca ★ Mexico ★ Miami & the Florida Keys ★ Montréal ★ Morocco ★ Moscow ★ Nepal ★ New England ★ New Orleans ★ New York City ★ New York Mini Guide ★ New York Restaurants ★ New Zealand ★ Norway ★ Pacific Northwest ★ Paris ★ Paris Mini Guide ★ Peru ★ Poland ★ Portugal ★ Prague ★ Provence & the Côte d'Azur ★ Pyrenees ★ The Rocky Mountains ★ Romania ★ Rome ★ San Francisco ★ San Francisco Restaurants ★ Sardinia ★ Scandinavia ★ Scotland ★ Scottish Highlands & Islands ★ Seattle ★ Sicily ★ Singapore ★ South Africa, Lesotho & Swaziland ★ South India ★ Southeast Asia ★ Southwest USA ★ Spain ★ St Lucia ★ St Petersburg ★ Sweden ★ Switzerland ★ Sydney ★ Syria ★ Tanzania ★ Tenerife and La Gomera ★ Thailand ★ Thailand's Beaches & Islands ★ Tokyo ★ Toronto ★ Travel Health ★ Trinidad & Tobago ★ Tunisia ★ Turkey ★ Tuscany & Umbria ★ USA ★ Vancouver ★ Venice & the Veneto ★ Vienna ★ Vietnam ★ Wales ★ Washington DC ★ West Africa ★ Women Travel ★ Yosemite ★ Zanzibar ★ Zimbabwe

also look out for our maps, phrasebooks, music guides and reference books

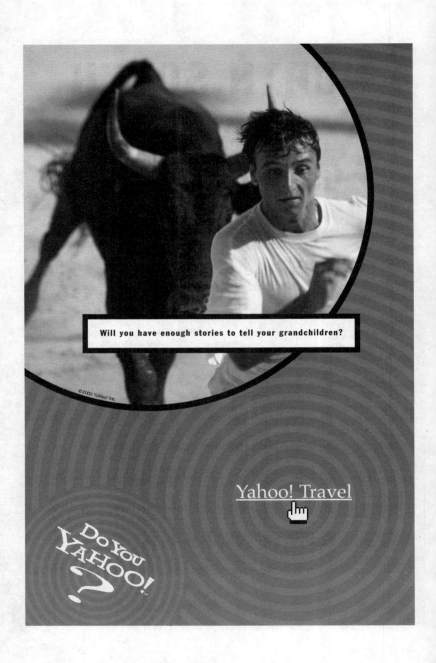